THE NEW YORK TIMES ON
EMERGING DEMOCRACIES IN EASTERN EUROPE

MARY KING

A Division of SAGE
Washington, D.C.

CQ Press
2300 N Street, NW, Suite 800
Washington, DC 20037

Phone: 202-729-1900; toll-free, 1-866-4CQ-PRESS (1-866-427-7737)

Web: www.cqpress.com

Copyright © 2010 by CQ Press, a division of SAGE. CQ Press is a registered trademark of Congressional Quarterly Inc.

All content reprinted from *The New York Times* is copyright © *The New York Times*.

All rights reserved. No part of this publication may be reproduced or transmitted in any form or by any means, electronic or mechanical, including photocopy, recording, or any information storage and retrieval system, without permission in writing from the publisher.

Cover and interior design: Matthew Simmons, Myself Included Design
Composition: C&M Digitals (P) Ltd.

♾ The paper used in this publication exceeds the requirements of the American National Standard for Information Sciences—Permanence of Paper for Printed Library Materials, ANSI Z39.48-1992.

Printed and bound in the United States of America
13 12 11 10 09   1 2 3 4 5

Library of Congress Cataloging-in-Publication Data
King, Mary.
    The New York Times on emerging democracies in Eastern Europe / Mary King.
        p. cm. — (Timesreference from CQ Press series)
    Includes bibliographical references and index.
    ISBN 978-1-60426-471-5 (alk. paper)
  1. Democratization—Europe, Eastern—History. 2. Democratization—Europe, Eastern—History—Sources. 3. Europe, Eastern—Politics and government—1989- 4. Europe, Eastern—Politics and government—1989—Sources. I. New York times. II. Title. III. Series.

    JN96.A91K56 2010
    320.947—dc22

2009041188

TITLES IN THE TIMESREFERENCE FROM CQ PRESS SERIES

2008

The New York Times on the Presidency, 1853–2008

The New York Times on the Supreme Court, 1857–2008

2009

The New York Times on Critical Elections, 1854–2008

The New York Times on Emerging Democracies in Eastern Europe

2011

The New York Times on Booms and Busts

The New York Times on Gay and Lesbian Issues

The New York Times on Immigration

CONTENTS

About TimesReference from CQ Press	ix
About the Author	xi
Map of Eastern Europe, 1977 and 2009	xii
Introduction: Strikes, Sinatra, and Nonviolent Revolution	1
Poland and the Solidarity Union	19
Hungary: Collective Memory and a Negotiated Revolution	72
East Germany and the Pastors' Movement	106
Czechoslovakia's Velvet Revolution	150
Independence of the Baltic States	212
Serbia: From Dictatorship to Democracy	285
Georgia's Rose Revolution	334
Ukraine's Orange Revolution	377
Index	421

ABOUT TIMESREFERENCE FROM CQ PRESS

The books in the TimesReference from CQ Press series present unique documentary histories on a range of topics. The lens through which the histories are viewed is the original reporting of *The New York Times* and its many generations of legendary reporters. Each book consists of documents selected from *The New York Times* newspaper accompanied by original narrative written by a scholar or content expert that provides context and analysis. The documents are primarily news articles, but also include editorials, opinion essays, letters to the editor, columns, and news analyses. Some are presented with full text; others, because of length, have been excerpted. Ellipses indicate omitted text. Using the headline and date as search criteria, readers can find the full text of all articles in *The Times'* online archive at nytimes.com, which includes all of *The Times'* articles since the newspaper began publication in 1851.

The Internet age has revolutionized the way news is delivered, which means that there is no longer only one version of a story. Today, breaking news articles that appear on *The Times'* Web site are written to provide up-to-the-minute coverage of an event and therefore may differ from the article that is published in the print edition. Content could also differ between early and late editions of the day's printed paper. As such, some discrepancies between versions may be present in these volumes.

The books are illustrated with photographs and other types of images. While many of these appeared in the print or online edition of the paper, not all were created by *The Times,* which, like many newspapers, relies on wire services for photographs.

Some editorial features in these books did not appear in *The Times*—they were created or selected by CQ Press to enhance the documentary history. For example, in *The New York Times on Emerging Democracies in Eastern Europe,* we added country Quick Facts and Key Player biographies to help readers learn more about some of the important people and events that played critical roles in the stories being told.

Readers will note that many articles are introduced by several levels of headlines—especially in pieces from the paper's early years. This was done to emphasize the importance of the article. For very important stories, banner headlines stretch across the front page's many columns; every attempt has been made to include these with the relevant articles. Over the years, *The Times* added datelines and bylines at the beginning of articles.

Typographical and punctuation errors are the bane of every publisher's existence. Because all of the documents included in this book were re-typeset, CQ Press approached these problems in several different ways. Archaic spellings from the paper's early days appear just as they did in the original documents (for example, "employe" rather than "employee"). CQ Press corrected minor typographical errors that appeared in the original articles to assist readers' comprehension. In some cases, factual or other errors have been marked [*sic*]; where the meaning would be distorted, corrections have been made in brackets where possible.

About the Author

Mary Elizabeth King is professor of peace and conflict studies at the University for Peace, an affiliate of the United Nations. A political scientist, she is also distinguished scholar at the American University Center for Global Peace, Washington, D.C., and Rothermere American Institute Fellow, University of Oxford, United Kingdom. She is a veteran of the U.S. civil rights movement and in 1988 won a Robert F. Kennedy Memorial Book Award for her memoir, *Freedom Song: A Personal Story of the 1960s Civil Rights Movement.* She has spent her career studying and writing extensively about collective nonviolent action in political conflicts. Her latest book is *A Quiet Revolution: The First Palestinian Intifada and Nonviolent Resistance.* Supported by the United States Institute of Peace, she is working on a study of a Gandhian struggle in India against untouchability during 1924–1925. In 2003 in Mumbai (Bombay), India, King was given the Jamnalal Bajaj International Award, which recognizes the promotion of Gandhian values.

Acknowledgments

The author would like to acknowledge the contributions of acquisitions editor January Layman-Wood, copy editor Robin Surratt, production editor Joan Gossett, proofreader Inge Lockwood, indexer Deborah Patton, researcher Andrew Boney, and editorial intern Katrina Overland. The author particularly wishes to thank Ross Baird for his research assistance, and expresses her appreciation to David Hartsough, Ivan Marovic, Christopher A. Miller, Jamila Raqib, and Marek Zelazkiewicz for their contributions.

INTRODUCTION: STRIKES, SINATRA, AND NONVIOLENT REVOLUTION

"Revolution" had, until the American and French Revolutions in the eighteenth century, meant a sudden change of political direction, often a restoration. In the twentieth century, violence and bloodshed developed into the stock-in-trade of revolutionary movements. Exploited peoples began to believe that violence was the only way that they could remedy their situation under severe oppression. In 1989, the citizens of Eastern Europe disproved this notion beyond a doubt. Not only did they topple regimes backed by the Soviet Union, they also caused to buckle the assumption of violence as the strongest force available. Despite the seemingly indomitable military might of the Soviet Union backing the communist-controlled regimes of the East bloc, a handful of democracies emerged—without slaughter. The nonviolent "revolutions" that accompanied the fall of the Soviet Union have made clear that armed insurrection is not the only course of action available for aggrieved groups and societies.

The New York Times on Emerging Democracies in Eastern Europe does more than explain what happened. It also tells the tales of academicians, activist intellectuals, journalists, literary figures, playwrights, and theater performers, politicians, and ordinary citizens who used nonviolent means to change their circumstances, reform their governments, assert their individual liberties, and improve their lives. Through the lens of *The New York Times,* the ideas, strategies, symbols, and tactics that shaped the nonviolent revolutions in Eastern Europe emerge in what journalists like to call the "first draft" of history.

"Eastern Europe" here refers to ten nation-states under Communist rule after World War II, some as part of the Soviet Union, some occupied by the Soviet army: Poland, Hungary, East Germany, and Czechoslovakia in central Europe; Estonia, Latvia, and Lithuania in the Baltics; Serbia, Georgia, and Ukraine in the Balkans and Caucasus. In examining how millions of people in these diverse countries were able to overthrow oppressive regimes without resort to violence, this reference work offers a unique view of history while critically analyzing the role that peaceful solutions can play in resolving problems thought to be impossible to settle absent violence or warfare.

COMMUNISTS TAKE CONTROL OF EASTERN EUROPE

The 1917 Bolshevik Revolution in Russia helped to entrench the idea that revolutions must be bloody. Over the next half-century, communist regimes in Moscow, Beijing, and their satellites established totalitarian systems of government. Bolshevik leaders, including Vladimir I. Lenin, Josef Stalin, and Leonid I. Brezhnev, promoted their worldview to other leaders; communist influence eventually dictated policy to approximately one-third of the world's population. As they proceeded to install one-party states, the communists offered utopian solutions for age-old problems that had perturbed saints and seers for centuries. These rigidly controlled command economies ran coercive production schemes, collectivized agriculture, destroyed the lineage of cultures and civilizations, prohibited freedom of worship and other liberties, and rigidly restricted the affairs of independent artistic, literary, civic, cultural, professional, religious, and other social groups. The party-states established under Soviet rule quelled all opposition by eliminating freedom of the press and establishing tightly controlled official news agencies while locking up "dissidents," the name used for any who might criticize the regimes.

As the historian Theodore Ziółkowski (1990, 47) notes, "almost from the moment when the Soviet empire, after Yalta, swallowed up the nations of Eastern Europe, the fight against Communism began." In February 1945, U.S. president Franklin D. Roosevelt and British prime minister Winston S. Churchill met with the Soviet premier, Stalin, at Yalta in the Crimean to discuss the post–World War II reorganization of Eastern Europe and the re-establishment of nations conquered by Germany. Stalin made the case for Soviet influence over eastern Germany as critical to the national security of the Soviet Union. Churchill and Roosevelt disagreed, wanting open democracies throughout Europe, yet they agreed to many of Stalin's demands in an effort to encourage the Soviets to join the war in Asia, where the United States still faced a Japanese campaign that might entail the loss of hundreds of thousands of American lives in the Pacific, and they wanted the Soviet Union to become a member of the United Nations. (Roosevelt could not have forecast that the atomic bomb would render Soviet aid unnecessary.) From Yalta onward, the Soviet Union increased and solidified its influence over Eastern Europe.

As communist regimes took control in Hungary, Poland, and Czechoslovakia, the Soviets augmented these governments' power by backing their security forces; each state developed sizeable secret police forces and could call on Soviet tanks and soldiers when necessary. Soviet authority kept communism intact in Eastern Europe, with the constant threat of military force. In June 1953, the Soviet military put down East German workers' strikes and marches. Soviet tanks successfully crushed a Hungarian uprising in 1956. Soviet forces again intervened, in 1968, leading an "allied socialist" invasion of Warsaw Pact troops to end the Prague Spring in Czechoslovakia. The Warsaw Pact was essentially a series of bilateral agreements between the Soviet Union and each of the member states to further Soviet security objectives.

The communist parties in Eastern Europe also held power through government bureaucracy, controlling state and local officialdom and comprising a ruling class known by the Soviet term *nomenklatura*. In some countries, the nomenklatura consisted of tens of thousands of persons and their families. Over the decades, government suppression required increasing maintenance and exertion. With the communists in power willing to employ all necessary force to maintain stability, violent resistance became impossible. Eastern Europeans thus sought a more effective alternative for fighting for their rights, avoiding the pattern of the courageous-but-doomed leaps toward freedom taken in 1953, 1956, and 1968.

THE BREZHNEV DOCTRINE AND COMMUNIST CONSOLIDATION

Within a month of the August 1968 Soviet-led invasion of Czechoslovakia, the Soviet communist party daily, *Pravda,* justified the incursion by arguing that although various paths to socialism existed, each country's communist party was "responsible not only to its own people but also to all the socialist countries and to the entire communist movement." By invading Czechoslovakia, according to Moscow's logic, the Kremlin was merely asserting the right to intervene in any country in the Soviet bloc in order to prevent counterrevolution or loss of party control. The West dubbed this principle, alternatively, the doctrine of limited sovereignty or the Brezhnev Doctrine. The sovereignty of the Eastern bloc satellite states was in fact limited by their obligations to others in the communist camp. The Brezhnev Doctrine, and its implications for the Soviet Union and other communist countries, cast a long shadow across Eastern Europe.

By the mid-1970s, however, Soviet and Eastern European leaders had come to understand that their model was problematic for effective governance. Economies in the communist bloc were stagnating due to decisions on production or investment driven by political machinery and ideology rather than market forces. Orders came from political hacks and had no basis in global economic commodity prices. With nonconvertible currencies and strict control of foreign trade restricting external market influences, government authorities set prices based on political fiction. Over the years, even as it became clear that the socialist economies were foundering, reform proved to be difficult, if not impossible, because of factory managers' ties to ruling party bosses. Shortages became prevalent. The communist party sought to protect its power and privilege, rather than modify policies based on results. Given this overriding objective, its utopian visions of equity and fairness could not be fulfilled.

The Soviet-backed regimes ruling half a dozen countries in Eastern and Central Europe had little of the precious commodity that all rulers need and only the governed can bestow—legitimacy. The Soviets banned the news media of each country from reporting on the others. This imposition of prohibitions on reports from the diverse countries brought about a certain amount of uniformity in Eastern Europe. Although the people of the countries of the Soviet bloc could not communicate with each other formally, underground publications from other communist countries in the region had important moderating influences on the various mobilizations that got under way in the 1980s. Furthermore, a growing number among the middle classes could discern that their coercive governing and economic systems had been built on a shaky foundation of lies.

THE SOVIET UNION LOOKS OUTWARD

In the late 1960s and 1970s, a number of international agreements began to push the Soviet Union and its constituent and satellite states toward reform and loosen the embargo on information and the communist grip on power. Two sets of treaties—SALT I and II, resulting from the Strategic Arms Limitation Talks, and START, emerging from the Strategic Arms Reduction Talks—began the process of reducing the all-out arms race that had put the Soviet Union and the West on competing paths toward military hegemony. Amid talks of controlling nuclear proliferation, the Helsinki Accords of 1975 turned the spotlight on human rights. As the Soviets began to negotiate and compromise in this series of international agreements, the road toward "revolution" came into view for citizens of the countries that had fallen under Soviet jurisdiction.

Peace and War: SALT I, SALT II, and Afghanistan

After the end of World War II, the United States and the Soviet Union set about building nuclear arsenals with the aim of achieving military supremacy and hegemony in the world. In 1969, the two countries began talks to reduce their nuclear arsenals. Negotiations got under way that year in the Strategic Arms Limitation Talks and in 1972 U.S. president Richard M. Nixon and Soviet premier Brezhnev signed the SALT I treaty. The agreement, a mutual promise to limit certain types of nuclear weapons, helped to temper attitudes toward militarization in both countries as well as improve Soviet relationships with the West. Between 1972 and 1979, the United States and the Soviet Union engaged in further talks to reduce their respective nuclear stockpiles. The resulting SALT II treaty banned new nuclear missile programs and attempted to limit the total number of nuclear weapons to 2,500 for each side. SALT II was a major step toward Soviet reconciliation with the West, but the U.S. Senate never ratified the treaty. Nonetheless, the United States abided by it—decisions on the nation's nuclear arsenal fall under the purview of the presidency—until 1986, when President Ronald R. Reagan withdrew from SALT II after accusing the Soviets of violating the pact.

This period of *détente*—a French term meaning "relaxing" or "easing" used to describe the loosening of tensions between the Soviet Union and United States during the 1970s and 1980s—was not, however, global. In December 1979, the Soviet Union invaded Afghanistan ostensibly to support a communist faction there. For much of the next decade, the Soviet and U.S.-backed forces would engage in a proxy war in Afghanistan's mountainous territory. Using guerrilla tactics against Soviet troops, heavily armed *mujahidin,* holy warriors, were able to raise the financial costs of Moscow's occupation. The growth in defense expenditures by the North Atlantic Treaty Organization (NATO) in the region made clear the resolve of the West. Meanwhile, the financial and military costs of the war raised doubts within the Kremlin about the suitability of maintaining a foreign expansionist policy. This internal conflict advanced the disintegration of the Soviet apparatus.

Human Rights: Helsinki Accords

In 1972, a group of nations launched the Conference on Security and Co-operation in Europe (CSCE). The states of Eastern and Western Europe (with the exception of Albania and Andorra) together with Canada and the United States convened in Helsinki, Finland, that year to discuss four "baskets" of concern: security affairs; economic, scientific, and environmental issues; humanitarian and human rights concerns; and follow ups. The so-called Basket 3 committed all signatories to respect "civil, economic, social, cultural, and other rights and freedoms, all of which derive from the inherent dignity of the human person."

As the talks began, the Soviet Union primarily concerned itself with gaining recognition for the regimes of its satellite nations in Central and Eastern Europe, and toward that end, with obtaining guarantees of the borders resulting from the aftermath of World War II. In addition to securing authority for communist bloc regimes, the Soviets also hoped to negotiate a non-aggression pact with NATO countries and obtain economic rewards. The United States and its Western allies wanted participating states to respect human rights, allow freedom of travel for their citizens, and permit increased contacts with relatives and others living in non-communist bloc countries (of most relevance to separated East German and West German families), and flows of information.

On August 1, 1975, thirty-five European countries, the United States, and Canada signed the Final Act, or Helsinki Accords. The Final Act reflected the interests of the West and the Soviet sphere and in a sense defined the formal end to World War II. The official formation of the CSCE (which later became the Organization for Security and Co-operation in Europe, OSCE) committed all of the signers to recognize and respect human rights and basic freedoms. It was not long before the third basket, pertaining to political freedoms and human rights, surpassed the others in emphasis, and the Helsinki Accords became synonymous with human rights.

Although negotiating with the Soviet leadership, the other participants, including U.S. secretary of state Henry Kissinger, did not invest much seriousness in the process, thinking that the Soviets were merely going through the formalities. Indeed, Soviet general secretary Brezhnev fought against the human rights provisions, but eventually yielded, appearing to treat the Helsinki agreement as something to be signed and then forgotten. Among the documents signed were the International Covenant on Civil and Political Rights and the International Covenant on Social and Cultural Rights. Although not part of a binding treaty, in theory the human rights principles outlined in the agreement were supposed to commit the signatory nations to follow its terms.

The 1975 Soviet signature on the Helsinki agreements sparked a surge in popular defiance. Helsinki "watch" committees appeared across Eastern Europe to monitor adherence to the agreements, the most significant of which was Charter 77 in Czechoslovakia (see **Czechoslovakia, Introduction**; "Prague Detains Five Dissidents after Human Rights Manifesto"). The Helsinki Accords gave citizens in communist countries standards to which they could hold their governments. Within the Soviet Union, a group of "dissidents" were inspired to form a Helsinki Monitoring Committee to publicize through *samizdat* newspapers the Soviet violations of the human rights they had agreed to guarantee in Helsinki. (*Samizdat* is Russian for "self-published.") Unofficial publications were in general called samizdat and were distinct from state-published production, *gosudarstvennoye izdatelstvo* or *gosizdat*. (The name of the official Soviet publisher was *Gosizdat*.)

Many of the activist intellectuals in the Soviet Union who became involved in tracking abuses were arrested or exiled, including Andrei Sakharov, but through their actions were able to lay the groundwork for still more dissent. Eastern Europeans had experienced briefer and less harsh exposure to the barbarities of Stalinism, a more substantial introduction to democracy before World War II, and less severe governments than had Soviet populations, and as a result the seeds of revolution were sown more easily among them.

IDEAS BEGIN TO CREATE REVOLUTION

During the 1970s and 1980s, a broad movement began to emerge to devise alternative institutions free of the corruption pervading the official structures set up by communist parties across Eastern Europe. Citizens began to articulate a vision of a civil society—a sphere of public life with places where citizens can interact unreservedly and without government intrusion—where they could speak and act as if they were free and unsullied by governmental corruption.

The principles that Soviet leader Mikhail S. Gorbachev would later articulate as *glasnost* were first grasped by architects, artists, authors, clergy, journalists, philosophers, scientists, and scholars across Eastern Europe. Activist intellectuals began to share their visions with a broad audience. Some would later become famous, including Christian Führer, Bronislaw Geremek,

Václav Havel, János Kis, George Konrád, Jacek Kuroń, Adam Michnik, and Ludvík Vaculík; hundreds of others were known only in small, local circles. Through their literature and writings, these scholarly activists brought a civil society into being in their imaginations. They dared to conceive of futures that did not yet exist and in which many found it hard to believe. Although "change" in the twentieth century had come to conjure images of bloodshed, these thinkers articulated nonviolent means as the pragmatic way to make their vision possible. Havel (1989, 93) captured this sentiment in 1978, when he stated that dissidents in Eastern Europe "do not shy away from the idea of violent political overthrow because the idea seems too radical, but on the contrary, because it does not seem radical enough."

Most outside observers were shocked by how quickly communism in its Soviet-drawn incarnation ended. Within the span of five years (1989–1994), a once seemingly invincible political force had completely collapsed. The mass movements of nonviolent resistance that had been building behind the scenes over a long period of time were able to effect direct, quick results when the opportunity arose to confront authorities. By adopting nonviolent strategies, the intellectuals pioneering such movements in Eastern Europe faced less resistance and suppression from the Soviet state than they would have had they chosen other methods. Over the preceding half century, assassinations, bloody uprisings, and covert military actions had been futile and had often led to increased repression.

As it has since become possible to access the writings of the playwrights, novelists, historians, philosophers, and poets encountered here, one can see a group of people creating civil society almost undetected—by the Kremlin and by outside observers—in the midst of authoritarianism. Specialists on the Kremlin and experts on communism were in many instances cynical, analyzed the political stability of the communist regimes with economic interpretations, and depended for their analyses on hard-core data. They dismissed the notion that individuals such as those featured in this volume could make a difference. Soviet watchers—with a few notable exceptions, such as the journalist-historian Timothy Garton Ash—did not take the decidedly intellectual writings of the Eastern European activists and the discussions they stimulated with the seriousness they deserved.

The covert distribution of underground publications played a critical role in the democratic transitions of Eastern Europe. In the 1970s, the *samizdat* influential in the Czech and Slovaks' Velvet Revolution involved typing ten carbon copies on onion-skin paper. Illegal printing presses, manifestoes committed to memory, posters appearing overnight on kiosks, journals materializing from nowhere, and an extraordinary outflow of samizdat articles were vital to disseminating ideas, including the need to struggle against communist coercion without violence. In Poland by the 1980s, approximately 2,000 regular samizdat publications were circulating, some in the tens of thousands of copies (Mason 1996, 36). Lithuania's samizdat networks were the most sophisticated among the republics in the Soviet Union, with more then 2,000 books published by its clandestine press. "Appeal for the Hour X," produced in Latvia, was widely shared and provided details on how to behave if a military coup d'état were imposed or unilateral military action undertaken by Moscow.

The ethical sensitivities of common citizens of Eastern Europe were partly shaped by their perceptions of the middle classes in Western Europe. In the late 1980s as the "iron curtain" began to weaken, Eastern Europeans gained a better sense of the Western world. Radio Free Europe, established by the U.S. government and based in Prague, gave opposition leaders and pro-Western commentators airtime. In the 1980s, Gorbachev stopped the practice of jamming Radio Free Europe commentaries unfavorable to the Soviet Union or communist governments (Puddington 2003, 287). By 1990, Radio Free Europe was the most-listened to Western radio station in the Soviet Union (Sosin 1999, 209). Eased travel restrictions between East and

West Germany also increased cross-curtain familiarity. As the Eastern European middle classes became more familiar with Western lifestyles, the contrast made totalitarianism seem even more valid as something worth fighting.

Meanwhile, ideological commitment to communism was waning within the Eastern European communist parties. On the economic front, beginning in the 1970s the Soviet Union increasingly encouraged the Eastern European satellites to participate in Western markets, but the effort failed. For example, the Polish and Hungarian regimes used foreign loans to buy consumer products to prop up their declining political legitimacy. Instead, the opening of new markets and embarrassing inability to keep pace with industrial progress in the West created additional economic problems (Chirot 1999, 29).

The defective communist systems of Eastern Europe did not bring about the even-handedness originally sought in socialism, and when these governments encountered new ideas in their efforts to reform, they came to realize that their top-down models could not work. A large middle class had continued to grow within their states—and, indeed, Marxist ideology favored a substantial middle class—but because of flaws in the socialist system of economic management, the communist middle-income classes remained poorer than their Western European counterparts and were falling even further behind by the 1980s.

Within the Eastern bloc communist regimes themselves and the nomenklatura, the political will to uphold the principles and practices of the party began to diminish. In some situations, reformers emerged within the party apparatus and began to seek liberalization of policies. In country after country, the party began to lose an interest in preserving itself. In autumn 1989 in Hungary, the party decided to dissolve itself. Within the Soviet Union, however, the various republics were not ready to reform from within. The partisanship associated with being a superpower, the gargantuan size of the military forces, and the long record of repression by security forces and police terror kept the governments of the Soviet republics in power.

As the sociologist Daniel Chirot (1999) observes, the academic, artistic, and literary intellectuals who addressed their writings to the middle classes helped them to analyze and comprehend the moral weaknesses of the communist regimes:

> [T]he educated middle classes in a modern society are well informed, and can base their judgments about morality on a wider set of observations than those with very limited educations. The artistic and literary intellectuals who addressed their work to these middle classes helped them to understand and interpret the immorality of the system, and so played a major role. They needed receptive audiences, but it was their work that undid Eastern European communism. Without the social changes associated with the economic transformations that took place in Eastern Europe from 1948 to 1988, these revolutions would not have taken place. But it was not so much that new classes were striving for power as that a growing number saw through the lies on which the whole system was based. That is what utterly destroyed the will of those in power to resist. Once these conditions were set, the massive popular discontent with material conditions, particularly on the part of the working classes in the giant but stagnating industries that dominated communist economies, could come out into the streets and push those regimes over (pp. 38–39).

This book brings to light a relatively small number of persons in each country who helped kindle the emergence of democracies in Eastern Europe. The potency of their ideas about how to resolve their situations is at the center of this account, including a technique for fighting that was unlikely to make things worse.

Collective Nonviolent Action

In understanding how the countries across Eastern Europe made their democratic transitions, *Emerging Democracies in Eastern Europe* lays bare the technique of collective nonviolent action. None of the movements reported on by *The Times* that produced the historic changes documented in this volume were dedicated to nonviolence as a creed. There is no implication of anarchism, charisma, faith, pacifism, religious canons, or spirituality. The Pastors' Movement of East Germany took care to invite believers and nonbelievers to their churches for meetings. What distinguishes the technique is that its adherents attack or undermine the power of the target group, not the lives or well-being of the opponent. In contrast to popular perceptions, the *behavior* of participants defines nonviolent action, not the personal convictions or beliefs of the participants.

Movements that adopt nonviolent action require strategic planning and practical use of specific forms of power. What counts in such mobilizations is adherence to a policy of nonviolent and non-military action. The authors, editors, playwrights, publishers of underground publications, students, university professors, workers, and youth groups in these movements searched for the right strategies to bring about change. In each country, individuals such as Christian Führer, Václav Havel, Adam Michnik, and Lech Wałęsa promoted nonviolent action as the only practical and realistic option for the circumstances of Eastern Europe and advocated methods from a large repertoire of the technique's action steps. The activist intellectuals often played leading roles in the workers' strikes and slowdowns, sit-ins, demonstrations, vigils, marches, and human chains that comprise the collective nonviolent action that was central to the process of democratic transitions in the former communist states.

Civil resistance, another name for nonviolent action, is often misunderstood or goes unrecognized by diplomats, journalists, and observers. To those unfamiliar with the technique, events appear to "just happen." On the contrary, nonviolent struggle requires that those who take deliberate and sustained action against a power, regime, policy, or system of oppression, consciously reject the use of violence in doing so. The unbalanced relationship between the Eastern European nations and other states considered here and the colossal Soviet Union ruled out the use of military methods. On this point there was no disagreement among the scholar activists who were leading the way. As is often the case, the choice of nonviolent civil resistance was one of pragmatism, not idealism. Restoration of independent statehood was a political goal and did not require vanquishing the Soviet masters. Nonviolent political means were thus politically, strategically, and philosophically consistent with popular aspirations for freely independent statehood. Marxist ideologies had long argued that the ends justify the means; the people knew this maxim to be false. Determined to prevent devastating reprisals from Soviet-backed regimes, Eastern European activists believed that the means should be consistent with the ends. "History, said Adam Michnik, had taught them that those who start by storming Bastilles will end up building their own" (Garton Ash 1999b, 111).

Nonviolent action achieves participants' political objectives without harming the lives or limbs of the adversary by altering the power configurations among groups or persons, allowing new formations to occur, thereby creating the political space for social change. At the core of how civil resistance works is noncooperation, that is, withdrawal of obedience to the target group or adversary. Governments require legitimacy to maintain a steady supply of political power. By withdrawing or withholding their acquiescence to that power, the governed can reduce the stock of authority possessed by a government. Withdrawal of *consent* is manifested through strategies implemented with nonviolent sanctions, another term for nonviolent methods. So far, more than 200 specific methods have been identified—more are being developed—and are categorized under three classes: nonviolent protest and persuasion, noncooperation (economic, political, and social), and nonviolent intervention (Sharp 1973).

At points in the various national mobilizations considered here, people migrated westward however they could. Protest emigration is a nonviolent method that dates to the Prophet Muhammad's seventh-century emigration from Mecca to Medina, a potent form of noncooperation called *hijra*, in Arabic "to abandon." Such a deliberate permanent emigration denies the adversary's objectives by self-imposed exile from an intolerable situation, a final physical withdrawal from the reach of unbearable rulers or a corrupt state. In the lexicon of nonviolent action, the term has no religious overtones and was often called "exit" by those emigrating from Eastern Europe. Protest emigration repeatedly came into play as mass popular movements transformed the Soviet bloc during the 1980s and 1990s, where it was an extreme noncooperation method.

In Eastern Europe, the logic behind selecting nonviolent struggle as the way to achieve major social and political transformation was coldly pragmatic. The carnage left by the repression of the 1956 Hungarian uprising led subsequent opposition movements, including Poland's Solidarity and Czechoslovakia's Charter 77, to conclude that nonviolent struggle would be their most effective and realistic option. Any violent struggle would have faltered because of the scale of military weaponry of the adversary regimes. Indeed, any armed uprising in the satellite countries of the Soviet Union would have provided an immediate pretext for crushing counterviolence. The failed Hungarian uprising of 1956 stands in contrast to the successes of the mass nonviolent movements that redrew the map of Eastern Europe within one year after Hungarian reformers on May 2, 1989, cut a hole through the once-impenetrable iron curtain along the Austrian frontier separating East from West. Not only were the activists determined to prevent devastating reprisals from Soviet-backed regimes, they wanted their choice to be ethical and stand in contrast to the ruthlessness of the leaders of those governments.

THEORIES BECOME REALITY

In the mid-1980s, changes within the Soviet Union gave political cover to the underground nonviolent movements that had been percolating for a decade. The rise of Mikhail Gorbachev to power as general secretary of the Communist Party of the Soviet Union in 1985 had led to the opening of "new thinking" in Moscow's foreign policy.

In 1987, Gorbachev published *Perestroika: New Thinking for Our Country and the World*—he claims "at the request of American publishers"—in which he outlines his principles for rebuilding Soviet society. The interconnected reforms fell into four main categories: *perestroika*, or "restructuring," concerning the economy; *glasnost*, meaning "openness" or "publicity"; democratization; and new thinking in foreign policy. Following the death of Brezhnev in 1982, the crises in the Soviet system became undeniable. Gorbachev's proposals were meant primarily to revitalize the stagnating Soviet economy, which had been growing at only 2 percent annually for a decade. At the same time, the new Soviet leader intended to retain the communist party's monopoly of power through managed change. Gorbachev's wisdom was in recognizing that the Leninist system could not be sustained, and unlike all his predecessors, he rejected the Leninist, or *realpolitik*, canon of might makes right. He did not plan to rely on tanks and let this be known. His refusal to condone an unleashing of force against the massive movements of civil resistance of the 1980s (with an exception in Lithuania) led to disarray at senior levels and implosion of the Soviet party machinery.

Some of Gorbachev's reforms initially rang hollow. Glasnost originally alluded to improved publicity and presentation of government policy, but an explosion at the Chernobyl nuclear power station in April 1986 in Soviet Ukraine revealed the limited nature of glasnost, as official news media failed to provide basic information to citizens (see **Ukraine, Introduction**). The nearby Lithuanians learned of the radioactive blast from Polish television. Gorbachev was thereafter able to persuade the Kremlin of the need for greater freedoms of speech and exposure of communist party errors as well as successes.

In military affairs, the Brezhnev Doctrine began to disintegrate. The doctrine's demise meant that the Kremlin's allies in Central and Eastern Europe could no longer assume that they would receive military aid and support in suppressing dissent. The escalating cost of the Afghanistan war reduced the morale of Soviet military officials and the resolve of the Soviet Union to engage militarily to protect other communist countries. Inside the Kremlin, differences and disputes on the suitability of maintaining the spoils from past expansionism and adventurism speeded disintegration of the Leninist canon of might makes right, further leading to disarray at senior levels and implosion of party machinery. Dissension over the use of military force served to help Soviet and Eastern European activists: nonviolent resistance tends to be highly effective in situations when there are internal conflicts within the camp of the opponent regarding the desirability and capacity of maintaining an existing system.

In 1989, Gorbachev himself publicly declared an end to the Brezhnev Doctrine. On October 26, Bill Keller of *The New York Times* reports Gorbachev as saying that "the Soviet Union has no moral or political right to interfere in the affairs of its East European neighbors." Gorbachev's spokesman, Gennadi I. Gerasimov, was quoted as saying, "I think the Brezhnev doctrine is dead." Gerasimov jokingly suggested that Gorbachev had replaced it with the "Sinatra doctrine." "You know the Frank Sinatra song, 'I Did It My Way'?" Gerasimov queried reporters. "Hungary and Poland are doing it their way." His comments were in reference to Hungary having dissolved the communist party and on October 23 announcing a new Hungarian republic and to Poland's parliamentary elections of that year that had put it well on the way to becoming the first democracy in postwar, communist Eastern Europe. After becoming the Czech president, Václav Havel would assert, "Without the changes in the Soviet Union, . . . what has happened in our country would have scarcely happened. And if it did, it certainly would not have followed such a peaceful course" (Havel, 1990).

The Soviets continued to moderate their military stance. In the early 1980s, President Reagan had entered into talks that would lead to the Strategic Arms Reduction Treaty, which barred the United States and the Soviet Union from deploying more than 6,000 nuclear warheads. The treaty's negotiations continued throughout the 1980s, with the potential decline of the Soviet Union consistently cited as a rationale for arms control. The two parties eventually signed the treaty, on July 31, 1991, in the final days of the Soviet Union.

HOLES IN THE IRON CURTAIN

President Jimmy Carter's strong affirmations of the human rights provisions of the Helsinki Accords in the late 1970s had wedged open political space such that mass popular movements of civil resistance could develop in countries under Soviet domination. Unseen, surreptitious political organizing had been under way in parts of Eastern Europe for years, and Carter's resolve in asserting human rights as a central element of U.S. foreign policy facilitated its coming into view. The amalgamation of social and political forces deriving from the peoples of Eastern Europe could expand without obstruction from Moscow's authoritarian compulsions. As Eastern European communist regimes recognized the shifts in policy taking place in Moscow in the 1980s, they found themselves standing isolated against the persistent opposition of their populations. Holes began to develop in the iron curtain.

Subject peoples increasingly viewed the Soviet Union as an imperial power unjustly occupying others' lands. The concept of decolonization got the attention of many activists and scholars, most prominently the Baltic nationalists, who had since 1939–1940 regarded the Soviet Union as a foreign interloper. The despotism of the Soviet party-state's dominion was at issue, yet equally important was the imposing aspect of Soviet rule and the asphyxiating foreign domination that came with it. The popular fronts established in 1988 in the three Baltic nations saw themselves as decolonization movements, not solely as pro-democracy movements. They routinely used the term *decolonization* to characterize their struggle and the vocabulary of empire to depict the Soviet Union. The cry of empire became a rallying call for Eastern Europeans who sought to undermine Soviet jurisdiction over the Eastern bloc and for non-Russian Baltic nationalists seeking independence.

Observers often cite the fall of the Berlin Wall on November 9, 1989, as the moment when Eastern Europe broke the shackles of Soviet domination. The wall became the universal emblem for the nations that disappeared behind what British prime minister Winston Churchill famously called the iron curtain. As *The Times* recalls, on November 10 of that year, as early as 1961 Soviet leader Nikita S. Khrushchev had called the wall an ugly thing ("Clamor in the East; The Berlin Wall"). The wall was symbolic, yet had lost its literal importance earlier in the year because of decisions taken by the ruling party-state to allow the flow of East Germans by train into West Germany. The wall had become the site of almost round-the-clock vigils before it was breached. On November 9, 1989, a spokesperson for the communist party-state declared that all East German citizens could travel abroad at will, without official permission. In recent years, the view shifted, and the wall has become a symbol for the limits of communist control.

The actual turning point for the entire region had come months earlier, in Warsaw, on February 6, 1989, when the so-called Round Table negotiations began between Poland's communist powers and the previously persecuted opposition. These talks led to free elections and eventually to the first democratically elected government in the communist bloc. The implosion of communist regimes throughout Eastern Europe thus got under way at the beginning of the year in which the Berlin Wall would fall. With the exception of the Romanian revolution, which would involve tanks and firing squads, the political and economic transitions in Eastern Europe considered here were effected amid the almost complete absence of violence. The violence that did occur was in the response of police and security systems.

The communist bloc countries discussed in this volume all followed the strategy of the Polish oppositional movement. In each state, the opposition offered communist party officials a choice of the lesser of two evils: either give the people more social independence (which authorities would not be able to control) or smash the democratic awakening with the full coercive powers at their disposal (Smolar 2009, 133). In Poland, the opposition Solidarity union had not set out to overthrow the state or to seize power. Rather, it sought reforms to improve the existing communist system, a free trade union to make life better for workers, a broadening of rights and freedoms, and the opening up of what its theoreticians called civil society. In contrast, two decades after Solidarity began forging democratic change in Poland, the struggle for democratic freedoms in Serbia and Ukraine would strike out at the core of power, as oppositional movements worked to sculpt their state's power structures into democracies.

The activists, thinkers, and theoreticians in each communist bloc country influenced the others. Nonviolent action spread as a technique that evolved across Eastern Europe rather than in compartmentalized individual campaigns.

POLAND

Poland's march toward democracy was slow. Ten years of carefully crafted and organized strikes, leading finally to elections, made Poland the first successful nonviolent victor against totalitarianism in the Eastern bloc. For much of its history, Poland had been subjected to Austrian,

Russian, and German power, and a brief independence between World Wars I and II soon gave way to German control during the latter conflict and Soviet domination thereafter. In no other country did the religious and intellectual elites merge with a popular nonviolent resistance movement as much as they did in Poland.

Of all the countries examined here, Poland counted the largest number of activist intellectuals (Mason 1996, 35). Thinkers such as Adam Michnik developed a framework for nonviolent resistance, but it was the alliance between the theoreticians, the religious elite (including Karol Wojtyła, the former bishop of Kraków and later Pope John Paul II), and political leaders among workers, most prominently Lech Wałęsa, that was able to organize the workers around the causes that the activist intellectuals had adopted as their own.

In Poland, the 10-million-strong Solidarity union staged the largest mass strikes in European history in its campaign in the late 1970s and early 1980s for a free labor union. Women were involved to a large proportion in all activities and actions. Combining the quest for workers' rights with demands for political freedoms gave Solidarity potency and depth across Polish society as a movement for broad social liberation. From running an illegal, noninstitutionalized mass nonviolent movement of opposition, Solidarity moved to playing an instrumental role in the creation of Polish civil society and a new democratic state. For fifty-nine days, from February 6 to April 5, 1989, opposition and government representatives met in round-table negotiations to reach a settlement to legalize free trade unions. Once Solidarity's legal status was secured, union delegates went on to seek concessions concerning reforms in education, the law, local governance, and the media that would lead to parliamentary democracy.

As the communist ruling elites lost confidence in the party, reformers began to doubt their own ability to change the party-state from within and were unable to skillfully manage the changing circumstances. In addition to making Solidarity a legal trade union, the round-table agreement charted a system of semi-free elections that led to political self-determination. The preamble calls the agreement "the beginning of the road to parliamentary democracy." The actions taken by the Poles generated support from the Vatican, the United States, and other key players as well as legitimacy for their own cause.

Hungary

In explaining the alterations of Eastern Europe, Timothy Garton Ash (1999a) notes, "In Poland, it was an election; in Hungary, it was a funeral." Hungarian activist intellectuals used the powerful call of memory and history to organize a national movement toward self-determination. In 1848, the Hungarian people had revolted against the governing Hapsburg dynasty, and within a year the emperor Franz Joseph had exiled or killed most dissenters. More than a century later, in 1956, Imre Nagy led a popular movement for Hungarian independence from and neutrality toward the Soviet Union, free and open elections, and the removal of Soviet forces. Some 200,000 Soviet troops moved on Budapest, with 2,500 tanks. Hundreds of people were executed. The rebellion was crushed, culminating in Nagy's execution.

By the late 1980s, Hungarian academicians and writers began calling for self-determination, using the revolutions of 1848 and 1956 as the emotional referents and political symbols around which to mobilize. Their strategies and messages reawakened Hungary's long history of seeking independence. At first, a small number of rallies were organized around statues of Sandor Petofi, a hero of 1848. Flags commemorating both historical events became salient political statements. The largest national political demonstration in Hungary to date occurred on March 16, 1989, when hundreds of thousands of Hungarians marched in opposition to the communist regime.

Of all the communist parties in Eastern Europe, Hungary's was most inclined toward alteration, having within it reformers and political tendencies that had expressed criticism of how communism had been implemented. On May 2, 1989, Hungarian soldiers, at the behest of reformers inside the communist apparatus, removed the barbed wire fence along the Hungarian and Austrian border. Their cutting through the iron curtain allowed citizens of Hungary, East Germany, and other Eastern bloc countries to "exit" to the West. A strong, coordinated political opposition actively sought to change the country's policies. The reform-minded government concluded that it must open up to multiparty politics—in order to keep the communist party in power. Other factors influenced the transition to democracy in Hungary, including the Soviet government under Gorbachev indicating that it would not oppose Hungarian self-determination. In October 1989, the communist party in Hungary formally dissolved itself.

East Germany

East Germany lay geographically closer to democratic governance than most countries in Central and Eastern Europe. Separated from West Germany, but with the capitalist outpost of West Berlin within its borders, the East German government attempted literally and figuratively to wall off Western influences within East Germans' view. East Germans protested by taking advantage of their proximity to Western territory, as a movement of permanent protest emigration, or "exit," led to the continual westward flow of East Germans to their democratic neighbors in West Germany.

With Germany's Lutheran heritage, the civic role of religious communities played a stronger role in East Germany's transition than in perhaps any other country apart from the Roman Catholic Church's support for Poland's Solidarity movement. While exit captured the attention of authorities, leading to increased surveillance and controls on the population, the most notable and effective organizational strategy was based in the Protestant churches, the one place where free speech and expression might occur in East Germany. The dreaded secret police, the State Security Service, or Stasi, kept tabs on individuals' and organizations' activities through a pervasive network of 85,000 full-time staff and more than 100,000 informers. When in 1992 its records opened to public scrutiny, the scale of the Stasi's surveillance was nonetheless astonishing: files had been kept on 6 million of the population of 16.5 million. It closely monitored dozens of environmental, feminist, and peace groups.

On thirteen consecutive Mondays during autumn 1989 and into 1990, crowds poured from the Reverend Christian Führer's Nikolai Church in Leipzig and from other churches. Their numbers would eventually reach the hundreds of thousands. This so-called Pastors' Movement did not rely on a Mohandas K. Gandhi, a Martin Luther King, Jr., or even a Lech Wałęsa. "There was no head of the revolution. The head was the Nikolai Kirche and the body the centre of the city. There was only one leadership: Monday, 5 P.M., the Nikolai Kirche," said cabaret artist Bernd-Luntz Lange (Dennis 2000, 278). Toward the end of the series of remarkable candlelight demonstrations, some police and authorities had joined in, bringing the final tally to 5 million East Germans who had marched in major processions. In late 1989, the communist party regime yielded to the popular will and decided to open the Berlin Wall. By spring 1990, the two Germanys had become one again.

Czechoslovakia

When the journalist-historian Timothy Garton Ash (1999a) arrived in Prague in November 1989, he remarked to the playwright Václav Havel, "In Poland it took ten years; in Hungary ten months; in East Germany, ten weeks: perhaps in Czechoslovakia, it will take ten days!" (Garton Ash 1990, 78). The case of Czechoslovakia illustrates, most prominently, how years of planning, artistic and theatrical promotion of ideas, and wise political leadership culminated in a transition that appeared to happen almost overnight.

During the Prague Spring of 1968, Alexander Dubček organized reforms of Czechoslovakia's government from within, liberalizing speech and increasing political rights. Under the Brezhnev Doctrine, a fearful Soviet Union sent 750,000 troops and tanks from five Warsaw Pact countries into Czechoslovakia, crushing the revolt. Dubček survived, and memories of his reforms and democratic aspirations remained alive among the country's intelligentsia.

On January 1, 1977, Czechoslovak intellectuals stepped forth as Charter 77, proclaiming themselves a "free, informal, and open association of people of different convictions" united in working for the respect of human and civil rights. Charter 77's text asks Czechoslovak officials to adhere to international agreements, such as the UN Universal Declaration of Human Rights and the Helsinki Accords, as signed by the government. Among the initiators of the "nonorganizational" Charter 77 was Václav Havel, who staunchly advocated collective nonviolent action (see "Václav Havel and Truth"; *nonorganizational* was a term chosen to minimize political confrontation).

When brutal police action violently disrupted a student demonstration on November 17, 1989, the Czechoslovak population initiated the Ten Days. Between November 18 and November 27, the Civic Forum, a citizen pro-democracy group, emerged, with Havel as the guiding light and headquartered in Prague's Magic Lantern Theater. Huge demonstrations filled Prague's Wenceslas Square, and by November 23 more than 300,000 people marched. The party-state started to split and divide. On Day Ten, November 27, 80 percent of the nation's labor force participated in a successful nationwide general strike, after which the Civic Forum and the government began discussions that would lead to a democratic transition of power.

Havel had the assistance of virtually the entire nation's influential theatrical community of actors and dramatists and was aided by Radio Free Europe and workers' unions, catalyzing the organizing of massive national resistance, including immense demonstrations against the actions of the regime. The Civic Forum spanned all viewpoints and opposition groups and included some reform-minded communists. A Slovak group, Public Against Violence, partnered with it. Harsh governmental reprisals to the popular resistance only led to more, daily manifestations of mass civil resistance involving hundreds of thousands of citizens. By Day Nine, November 25, anti-government demonstrations drew 800,000 persons to Prague's Wenceslas Square, while in Bratislava 100,000 marched. The Civic Forum and Public Against Violence led a debilitating general strike that involved almost the entire nation and exerted sufficient pressure on the government to hasten the swift, nonviolent transition of power. On December 29, 1989, the communist-dominated national legislature, the Federal Assembly, unanimously elected Václav Havel as president. Though the events in Prague seemed to happen instantaneously, years of work forming and disseminating ideas, printing thousands of *samizdat* publications, planning in prison cells, and building networks had taught the Czechoslovaks how to withdraw their cooperation from the regime, thereby bending it to the popular will. Benefiting from a more enlightened Soviet policy than in 1968 and having witnessed the popular movements in Poland, Hungary, and East Germany, the Czechoslovaks were able to bring about their 1989 Velvet Revolution with astonishing speed and efficiency.

The Baltic Republics

In Poland, striking became the workers and activists' action of choice, and in East Germany it was public prayers. Citizens of the Baltic states chose singing. Ever since Latvia, Estonia, and Lithuania established themselves as independent republics in 1918, the national identity of their citizens had been under threat. When the Soviet Union annexed the three republics in 1939, it banned traditional national flags, songs, and symbols. Four decades later, citizens began to turn against the Molotov-Ribbentrop Pact and associated secret protocols between Stalin and German leader Adolf Hitler that allowed for the annexation of the Baltic states by the Soviet Union (see "Text of Secret Protocols to 1939 Hitler-Stalin Pact").

In 1986, Helsinki '86, a civic association of young people, workers, and former "dissidents" and political prisoners organized a modest demonstration to commemorate Stalin's 1941 mass deportations of Latvians by the thousands to Siberia. Under the umbrella of the Helsinki Accords, it was the first group openly to reassert the independence of the Baltic republics. By summer 1989, demonstrations were occurring across the Baltic republics.

Most stirring of the countless public rallies was the 400-mile human chain called the "Baltic Way," a "calendar demonstration" that stretched from Estonia's coast across Latvia to the southern border of Lithuania. The event, held on August 23, 1989, marked the fiftieth anniversary of the Molotov-Ribbentrop Pact. Hundreds of thousands of people, and by some estimates 2 million, held hands in an almost unbroken connection across the three republics, where popular fronts had formed in 1988 to lead the mobilization of citizens. They issued a joint statement, also entitled the "Baltic Way," highlighting nonviolent and parliamentary methods for regaining independent nationhood. The human chain represented the peak event for disciplined Baltic nonviolent action during the period 1987–1991. Those forming the chain sang national songs in their call for independence to make clear through symbolic means their verdict: the secret protocols were illegal, and the Baltic peoples would not be part of the Soviet Union.

Rising nationalism—expressed through shared culture and history, flag, language, and song—had led citizens of the Baltic states to conceive of themselves as independent of the Soviet Union. Glasnost made it easier for the authors, academicians, activist intellectuals, artists, musicologists, scientists, and poets to commemorate historical events and anniversaries through "calendar events." The Kremlin condemned the mounting citizen action, but communist party officials in Estonia, Latvia, and Lithuania began siding with their regional identities instead of the Moscow line.

On March 11, 1990, Lithuania became the first former Soviet socialist republic to declare independence. By May, Latvia and Estonia had also declared plans for their transition to independence. Violent efforts to suppress the separation largely failed, in part because of Gorbachev's personal aversion to using violence against peaceful demonstrators (though of note Soviet paratroopers killed fourteen Lithuanian civilians in the capital city, Vilnius, on January 13, 1991, known as Bloody Sunday). In addition, after being elected president of the Russian republic, Boris Yeltsin swiftly allied himself with the Baltic cause and plans for independence and entered into a treaty recognizing Lithuanian sovereignty.

SERBIA

The overthrow of the dictatorial president Slobodan Milošević in October 2000 in Serbia was, at its heart, a youth movement. Nestled in the Balkans, between Europe and Asia, Serbia at the time consisted of various minorities, including Bosnian Muslims, Catholic Croats, Romani Gypsies, largely Muslim ethnic Albanians in Kosovo, and others. It had long been a flashpoint for conflict. After the breakup of Yugoslavia, Slobodan Milošević rose to power in the late 1980s, pledging to protect Serbs wherever they lived in the Balkan Peninsula. He took control of Serbia while envisioning "Greater Serbia," which involved a mix of nationalism, political suppression, and persecution of ethnic minorities including in the Kosovo region. Milošević's goal of Serbianization aroused independence movements in Croatia, Bosnia and Herzegovina, Slovenia, and Macedonia and set in motion drives toward warfare in Bosnia, Croatia, and Kosovo. From 1992 to 1995, ethnic tensions led to war between Bosnia and Herzegovina and Croatia. Milošević's actions prompted NATO-backed military strikes in Bosnia in 1995, and Kosovo in 1999, exacerbating the deterioration of Serbia's economy and unemployment.

The NATO bombings brought the Bosnian Serb army to the negotiating table, but Milošević persisted in implementing oppressive policies, including actions to suppress free speech. In response, in 1998 a group of students in Belgrade founded Otpor! (Resistance!) and pushed for free and open elections. They prepared to bring 1 million demonstrators to Belgrade to confront Milošević and began planning to ensure that Serbian security forces would disobey any order to shoot those participating. In pursuing these goals, Otpor leaders placed priority on maintaining nonviolent discipline among their broadening circles of supporters. They studied the writings of the scholar Gene Sharp that were distributed by the Center for Civic Initiatives, a Serbian nongovernmental organization that made translations into Serbian. In 1999 and 2000 in forty-two Serbian cities, Otpor trained more than 1,000 activists in nonviolent action. Nationwide, youth became involved in the overthrow of dictator Slobodan Milošević.

Toward the end of 2000, Otpor had grown to 70,000 members with 130 branches. Opposition leaders who had previously fought among themselves would unite at Otpor's ever-growing rallies. While groups such as Otpor led collective efforts to vote Milošević out of office, the Center for Free Elections and Democracy sought through research, interviews, and data collection to prevent ballot-box fraud, and when that failed, to document systematic election tampering. The group published its results nationwide to encourage further nonviolent action. On September 24, 2000, voter turnout was high, but after losing by approximately 2 percent, Milošević proclaimed that he would not resign until his term expired in summer 2001. The opposition coalition of eighteen political parties bade civil disobedience until Milošević accepted defeat. As the coalition stood firm against participating in another election, citizens took nonparticipation one step further, as activists urged general strikes to shut down the country. General strikes and civil disobedience spread across the country. Milošević's rule ended in October 2000 as police and state security forces receded from view with hundreds of thousands of people descending on Belgrade, busload by busload and some atop bulldozers and tractors. Citizens took over government buildings in what is now sometimes called the Bulldozer Revolution. Milošević became the first head of government ever asked to answer for charges of war crimes.

Georgia

Unlike the peoples of Poland, Hungary, and East Germany, who came to appreciate that the Soviet Union under Gorbachev would probably not intervene to crush their efforts to gain political freedoms and self-determination in the late 1980s, those of Georgia, on the Black Sea, were explicitly a part of the Soviet Union. Gorbachev actively interposed himself to keep it so. After a coup d'état and an independence referendum, in 1992 former Soviet foreign minister Eduard A. Shevardnadze seized power in Georgia. He ruled as had the totalitarian Soviet leaders of the twentieth century, by suppressing speech, jailing opponents, and rigging elections. Inspired by the actions of other countries in the area, including those considered here, Georgia deposed Shevardnadze in 2003.

Student activists of the youth nonviolence group Kmara (Enough) organized demonstrations, modeling their strategy and leadership styles on Serbia's Otpor. (Kmara's leaders were trained by Otpor activists.) In the spirit of Poland's Solidarity movement and the Czech and Slovaks' Velvet Revolution, Georgian opposition leaders organized massive nonviolent demonstrations in Tbilisi's central square. Unlike in other countries, Georgian activists had the advantage of a relatively free press.

Kmara became the prod for puncturing post-Soviet apathy and passivity, and in recruiting thousands of Georgian youth throughout the country succeeded in giving a national thrust to the substantial desire of the Georgian people to bring Shevardnadze's regime to an end. The youthful leaders knew the potency of symbolism: even though guns were directly pointed at demonstrators, they underscored the power of their nonviolent action by placing red roses down the barrels of the police guns at demonstrations, marking their upheaval as the Rose Revolution.

The main point of contention in Georgia's case was the 2003 parliamentary elections, which were being viewed as a test of Shevardnadze's strength. After the elections were declared to have been rigged, nonviolent resistance intensified. Recognizing that his government was no longer obeying his orders, Shevardnadze resigned on November 23, 2003, clearing the way for an opposition leader, Mikhail Saakashvili, to win 96.2 percent of the vote and take office unopposed.

Ukraine

Ukraine's Orange Revolution at the end of 2005 makes tangible the flow of knowledge on nonviolent civil resistance from the Eastern bloc countries into the heart of the Soviet Union. Moscow had made significant efforts to keep Ukraine under Soviet control, as it had done with Georgia. After the Soviet Union's collapse in late 1991, leaders sympathetic to it controlled Ukraine's government. Ukrainians changed the regime through elections in late 2005.

Opposition leader Viktor Yushchenko, despite near-fatal poisoning that disfigured him, led 1 million encamped nonviolent demonstrators in seventeen days of protest in downtown, Kiev, contesting a rigged presidential election in November 2004. The appearance of the autumnal color orange throughout the campaign across the country—in Yushchenko's scarf, in the clothing worn by millions of activists, and in rock song lyrics—gave rise to the name Orange Revolution.

A youth organization, Pora! (It's Time!) became the galvanizing force behind Ukrainian civil resistance. After fastidious internal organizing by Pora similar to that of Kmara and Otpor (both of which trained Pora members), internal court decisions and international pressure led to a re-vote. The Orange Revolution resembled the Georgian Rose Revolution and the Serbian Bulldozer Revolution in its reliance on extensive civic participation. Yuschenko's victory appeared spontaneous, but it was not. It required months of grass-roots campaigning and civil disobedience, public pressure, and the formation of coalitions followed on by extensive publicity generated by large public demonstrations for the Orange Revolution to overturn electoral fraud and bring about a peaceful handover of power to the opposition movement's presidential candidate. Fastidious internal organizing by Pora helped the path to a re-vote, with Yushchenko and his coalition soundly defeating Prime Minister Viktor Yanukovich.

Viewing Nonviolent Transitions through *The New York Times*

Nonviolent direct action, human agency—the ability of men and women to affect the course of history—and initiative shaped the deep and dramatic forces that had been at work in the Eastern bloc countries for a decade or more. In one extraordinary year, 1989, civil resistance movements redrew the map of Eastern Europe. A number of external and domestic circumstances also intersected to play roles, as without war matériel being used, the Warsaw Pact collapsed.

The central issue in each of the mobilizations chronicled by *The New York Times* and chosen for this work is a popular request for democratic controls over the economic, political, and social life of nations in the shadow of the Soviet Union. To free themselves, the peoples of Eastern Europe needed not an individual emancipator, but what Colin Barker and colleagues (2001, 113) define as collective "self-emancipation—liberating people from the need of liberators." Each country's transition to democracy is viewed through the eyes of *The Times* correspondents on the ground. Quotations, facts, and excerpts from speeches and writings from critical moments and days in each revolution explain how these transitions evolved and register what activists, academicians, artists, and politicians were thinking as they advanced. *The Times* articles cover the entire span of the revolutions, usually from the early seedlings of protest under communism to free elections to the inaugurations of democratically elected leaders. By using *The Times* to analyze these moments, readers can appreciate the thoughts and discern the emotions felt by the revolutions' participants as they made them happen.

BIBLIOGRAPHY

Barker, Colin, Alan Johnson, and Michael Lavalette. 2001. *Leadership and Social Movements.* Manchester: Manchester University Press.

Chirot, Daniel. 1999. "What Happened in Eastern Europe in 1989?" In *The Revolutions of 1989,* ed. Vladimir Tismaneanu, 19–50. London: Routledge.

Conference on Security and Cooperation in Europe. 1975. Final Act. www.osce.org/documents/mcs/1975/08/4044_en.pdf.

Dennis, Mike. 2000. *The Rise and Fall of the German Democratic Republic, 1945–1990.* London: Longman.

Garton Ash, Timothy. 1999a. *The Magic Lantern: The Revolution of '89 Witnessed in Warsaw, Budapest, Berlin and Prague.* New York: Vintage Books.

———. 1999b. "The Year of Truth." In *The Revolutions of 1989,* ed. Vladimir Tismaneanu, 108–24. London: Routledge.

Gorbachev, Mikhail S. 1987. *Perestroika: New Thinking for Our Country and the World.* New York: Harper Collins.

Havel, Václav. 1990. "New Year's Address to the Nation," Prague, 1 January. http://old.hrad.cz/president/Havel/speeches/1990/0101_uk.html.

———. 1990. We the People: *The Revolution of '89 Witnessed in Warsaw, Budapest, Berlin, and Prague.* London and New York: Penguin Books.

———. 1989. "The Power of the Powerless," trans. Paul Wilson. In *Living in Truth,* ed. Jan Vladislav, 36–122. London: Faber and Faber. Originally published in October 1978.

Mason, David S. 1996. *Revolution and Transition in East-Central Europe.* 2d ed. Boulder, Colo.: Westview Press.

Puddington, Arch. 2003. *Broadcasting Freedom: The Cold War Triumph of Radio Free Europe and Radio Liberty.* Lexington: University Press of Kentucky.

Sharp, Gene. 1973. *The Politics of Nonviolent Action.* 3 vols. Boston: Porter Sargent Publishers.

Smolar, Aleksander. 2009. "Towards Self-Limiting Revolution':Poland, 1970–89." In *Civil Resistance and Power Politics: The Experience of Non-violent Action from Gandi to the Present,* ed. Adam Roberts and Timothy Garton Ash. Oxford: Oxford University Press.

Sosin, Gene. 1999. *Sparks of Liberty: An Insider's Memoir of Radio Liberty.* University Park: Pennsylvania State University Press.

Ziółkowski, Janusz. 1990. "The Roots, Branches and Blossoms of Solidarnosc." In *Spring in Winter: The 1989 Revolutions,* ed. Gwyn Prins, 39–62. Manchester: Manchester University Press.

FROM *THE NEW YORK TIMES*

Keller, Bill. 1989. "Gorbachev, in Finland, Disavows Any Right of Regional Intervention." October 26.

McFadden, Robert D. 1989. "Clamor in the East; The Berlin Wall: A Monument to the Cold War, Triumphs and Tragedies." November 10.

POLAND AND THE SOLIDARITY UNION

The Polish constitution, drafted in 1791, characterizes the Poles' vivid history of striving for liberty. It was the first such governing document in Europe and second in the world, after the United States', and is famed as a written body of law that recognizes as inviolable the rights of "personal security" and "personal liberty." The word *democracy* was barely used in the eighteenth-century Polish language; instead, concepts of "rights" and "freedoms" were widespread.

The constitution was biased in favor of the dukes and counts of the landed nobility and cast the nobles as the defenders of liberty. Nevertheless, its proclamations of freedom distressed Poland's three powerful neighbors—Austria-Hungary (the Hapsburg or Austro-Hungarian Empire), Prussia, and Russia—which proceeded to annex most of its territory over more than 120 years, forcing the abandonment of the Polish constitution. With partitions in the 1790s, Poland disappeared to the point that it could no longer be found on the maps of Europe. Banished from political reality, Polish culture endured through its great literature and music by such composers as Frédérick Chopin. Despite their land's long history as a battleground fought over by its neighbors, the Poles viewed themselves as having a distinctive democratic tradition based on individual liberties, personal freedoms, and civil disobedience in opposition to state authority. Polish identity and self-awareness refused to die.

POLAND RESTORED TO EUROPEAN MAPS

Poland's history since the late eighteenth century was largely defined by violent revolts. Bloody insurrectionary rebellions in 1794, 1830–1831, 1863–1864, and 1905 were crushed with force. Yet the Poles of Austria-Hungary and Germany found commonality in the Roman Catholic Church. Polish schoolchildren were forced to study in German—their language was forbidden—but priests at church taught them secretly in Polish. The Poles of Russia were forced to attend Russian Orthodox churches. Poland, strategically located between Germany and Russia, was seized alternately by both throughout modern history.

The 1919 Treaty of Versailles returned Poland to the maps of Europe. Experts at the Paris peace talks formally concluding World War I knew that Poles agreed on one issue: having access to the Baltic Sea. As a result, Poland was given Danzig, at the mouth of the Vistula River, at the northern tip of the so-called Polish Corridor, an arm of territory that allowed Poland to reach the sea. Danzig, remembered as an impressive and free port city under Polish rule, had been under German control since the partitions of the 1790s. By the time of Poland's restoration, some 4 million Poles had migrated to the United States, where they comprised the largest group of immigrants from Central Europe.

Poland's rebirth enraged Germany and set in train the next world war. Germany continued to seek hegemony over Polish lands, and in Moscow, Soviet leader Josef Stalin sought revenge for having lost Polish territory that he regarded as his nation's. Stalin did not intend for Poland to be absorbed into the Soviet Union, unlike the Baltic states, but still wanted it under absolute Soviet control. In September 1939, Germany, now ruled by the National Socialists, bombarded installations in Danzig from a battleship while infantry stormed the Polish Corridor. The brutality of the Nazis' invasion provided the ignition for World War II. That autumn, the Soviet army marched into eastern Poland, ostensibly to liberate the lands that Moscow continued to covet. Poland was more important to the Soviets than other nations on its rim. Although Poles' initial reaction had been relief when the Soviets moved to "rescue" them from the Nazis, their mood was short-lived. The nature of the liberation became evident when Stalin banished 1 million to 2 million Poles to Siberia, and Poland fell under one of the most brutal occupations ever. Some historians argue that the cruelty of the Russians exceeded that of the Nazis.

In June 1941, the Nazis completed their control of Europe by attacking the Soviet Union, a former ally, and driving the Red Army from eastern Poland. More than 6 million Poles lost their lives while waging war for their homeland during World War II or were executed in Nazi death camps. Poland's casualties included 3 million of the nation's 3.5 million Jews, or approximately 10 percent of the country's population. In April 1943 in the Warsaw ghetto, some 7,000 Jews fought to their deaths, knowing that they had no hope of prevailing. In 1944, the Red Army approached Warsaw and prepared to engage in one of the most barbaric urban battles

QUICK FACTS ABOUT POLAND

- The Poles' history of striving for liberty is characterized by their 1791 written constitution—the first in Europe and second in the world, after the U.S. Constitution.

- Soviet leader Josef Stalin banished 1 million to 2 million Poles to Siberia.

- During World War II, more than 6 million Poles lost their lives in defense of their homeland and to Nazi death camp executions. Poland's casualties included 3 million of the nation's 3.5 million Jews, approximately 10 percent of the population.

- By the mid-1950s, the Polish United Workers' Party, the ruling communist party, had fully imposed a Stalinist dictatorship. It controlled central and local government, comprising a ruling class, the *nomenklatura*, which represented perhaps 300,000 jobs. Counting families, approximately 1.5 million Poles depended on party favors for special access and benefits.

- On June 2, 1979, Pope John Paul II celebrated mass in Warsaw's Victory Square, where an estimated 300,000 waited for hours in 90-degree heat. According to church officials, the mass was the largest spiritual observance in Eastern Europe during the communist era.

- On September 22, 1980, delegates from thirty-eight regional labor unions held their first national meeting in Gdańsk and formed a new union, NSZZ "Solidarność," the Independent Self-Governing Union Solidarity. By late autumn 1980, Solidarity had registered 10 million members, representing 80 percent of the Polish workforce.

- In 1981, the communist party-state regime under Gen. Wojciech Jaruzelski jailed 10,000 Solidarity supporters, imposed martial law, and banned Solidarity.

- In January 1983, the Jaruzelski regime established officially registered worker unions and banned strikes. With economic productivity in Poland dropping, the communist party lost approximately half of its 3 million members.

- On July 22, 1983, Jaruzelski ended some aspects of martial law. The government offered partial amnesty to 650 political prisoners, which included all but 60 detainees.

- On June 4, 1989, the communists suffered defeat at the ballot box when Polish voters were able to render judgment on the party for the first time. Solidarity won 160 of the 161 seats for which it was allowed to compete in the lower house of parliament. In the 100-member Senate, Solidarity won all but one seat.

of the war. Up to 200,000 civilians alone, mostly youths, died during the fighting. Poland's wartime losses, tallying Gentiles and Jews, may have amounted to one-fifth of the country's population. In addition to targeting Jews, the Nazis aimed their extermination policies at the Polish intelligentsia, destroying the professional classes (Michta 1997, 71). After the end of World War II in 1945, the Poles retrieved Danzig, which had become the city of Gdańsk. Poland emerged from the war, however, as the most devastated country in Europe, challenged by hunger and starvation, housing shortages, communicable diseases, and thousands of invalids and orphans needing care. At the war's close, Poland's population stood at 24 million, down from 35 million in 1939.

UNDER TOTALITARIANISM

Soviet troops occupied Poland at the end of World War II, but despite Polish fears, Stalin did not intend for Poland to be absorbed into the Soviet Union, as the Baltic states had been. Instead he wanted the country firmly under Soviet control. As the country tried to resurrect itself from the scourges of war, some remnants of opposition were tolerated briefly, before the communists seized complete control of government; they were eliminated soon thereafter or absorbed into the communist party. All armed units were liquidated.

By the mid-1950s, the Polish United Workers' Party (PZPR), as the ruling communist party was called, had fully imposed a Stalinist dictatorship, with the heavy hand of bureaucracy imposing state socialism. The workers had anticipated higher wages and improved working conditions, but instead central planning in this totalitarian system meant that sycophantism and currying favor determined success more than did efficiency. As large factories and industrial cities were created by the state, supervisors, bureaucrats, and party officials interfered in performance and production. Economic growth stagnated, exacerbating acute housing crises and food scarcity. Poland's pollution became the worst in Europe.

The personal liberties for which the Poles longed were denied by a system that sought to destroy the society's social fabric. Existence under postwar communist rule would prove extremely difficult, and freedoms would be systematically suppressed. The mainly Roman Catholic population—85 percent practicing Catholics—yearned to worship freely. The status of the society's intellectuals and artists plummeted. The regime's coercive powers relied on two armored divisions of the Soviet army permanently stationed in Poland. Public corruption became widespread. The party controlled central and local officialdom, comprising a ruling class known by the Soviet term *nomenklatura,* which represented perhaps 300,000 jobs. Counting families, approximately 1.5 million Poles depended on party favors.

In the twentieth century, the Polish concept of resistance to domination would shift dramatically from the violent, failed uprisings characteristic of the eighteenth and nineteenth centuries to the use of nonviolent methods. Poland's struggle against Soviet domination first asserted itself in 1956 in the form of a major workers' movement. In June 1956, the workers of the Cegielski factory in Poznań protested in large demonstrations, displaying placards calling for "Bread and Freedom." Internal security forces put down the revolt with brute force; fifty-three persons were killed. The uprising prompted promises of reforms from government leaders. Władysław Gomułka came to power as the initial postwar communist leader, assuring Stalin's successor, Nikita Khrushchev, and the Soviet Politburo that Poland would remain communist and in the Warsaw Pact, the Soviet-led alliance. The population had high expectations during this period, which they called the October Springtime. The government failed to deliver, however, and food shortages and minimal wages persisted.

The so-called Prague Spring, the rebellion in nearby Czechoslovakia that started in January 1968, gave the Poles new inspiration. Although the Prague Spring ended as 750,000 troops from the Warsaw Pact crossed the border in August (see **Czechoslovakia, Introduction**), Polish students demanded freedom of thought and expression and an end to censorship. They were not seeking power, but self-respect. Gomułka's government ended the student uprising by arresting more than 3,000 persons in March 1968. An additional 30,000 were forced into exile. Innumerable others, caught up in student protests, were killed. Government propaganda took advantage of an apparent lack of support for the students among the broader Polish public, arguing that the cause of the students was different from their own, which, for example, touched a chord with factory workforces who could not understand fighting for free speech when first they needed better wages. One young man, Lech Wałęsa, a mustached electrician, encouraged his fellow laborers in the Gdańsk shipyard to see the student complaints as related to their own anxieties. He tried without success to unite the workers with the students, arguing that all Poles were fighting to lead better lives.

In December 1970, the frustration of workers in Warsaw reached a breaking point. Abrupt price increases without corresponding wage hikes were enacted on December 12. The move left laborers struggling to feed their families before Christmas, a high holy day. More than 9,000 fuming workers emerged in unarmed street demonstrations, to which the government responded with harsh crackdowns. Across Gdańsk, police attacked workers. Some 10,000 shipyard laborers marched on party headquarters and set it on fire, demanding withdrawal of the price rises. In a three-day struggle, at least fifty workers were killed, possibly many more, as tanks and troops moved in. Grieving families were forbidden to bury their dead themselves, and the site of an official burial was soon after obliterated by the regime, as if there had been no mortalities. Worker actions spread across the country, forcing the resignation of Gomułka. Throughout the rest of the decade, the martyrdom of those killed would be memorialized, as socioeconomic conditions worsened under Edward Gierek, Gomułka's successor.

An Alliance of Activist Intellectuals, Roman Catholic Laity, and Workers

Gierek reversed Gomulka's price hikes and tried to introduce liberalization measures that resulted in greater indebtedness to foreign lenders. In seeking to modernize industries and increase consumer goods, Gierek's government ultimately decided that it needed to raise prices in 1976. This led to a period of relative improvement followed by economic downturn, thereby creating a perception of comparative deprivation in the populace. Gierek's "quasi-liberalization" and modernization tentatively opened some political space for an embryonic civil society, but the Polish United Workers' Party remained loath to relinquish its monopoly on power.

Price increases announced in June averaged 60 percent for staple items. Sausage prices rose by 90 percent; sugar costs doubled. The price hikes sparked demonstrations that lasted one day, June 25. The vast majority of the protests—held at more than 100 factories, and at Poland's largest industrial plants—were disciplined and nonviolent. At two places, violence occurred: at the Ursus tractor factory near Warsaw, several thousand workers marched on the transcontinental railways, halting the Paris-Moscow train, and in Radom, southwest of Warsaw, a large crowd marched to the party's headquarters, and reverting to less sophisticated protest methods, set fire to it. Harsh police crackdowns ensued, the marches were brutally repressed, and a dozen workers died. Thousands were arrested, even tortured, and lost their jobs. The regime withdrew the price increases.

The 1976 demonstrations and strikes, and Gierek's crackdown on them, produced the catalytic effect of uniting laborers and intellectuals, who came together in opposition to the regime. Thus a Polish mass workers movement emerged that year in resistance to the PUWP's Soviet-backed oppression. In the next four years, at least 1,000 strikes would occur in large enterprises.

Upon learning that many of the workers had been imprisoned, exiled, or fired from their jobs for the events at Ursus and Radom, and that their families lacked resources for legal defense, a group of writers, professors, and other intellectuals set up Komitet Obrony Robotników (Committee for the Workers' Defense, KOR). Starting with fourteen members, it never exceeded thirty-three people, among whom were authors, historians, lawyers, philosophers, social scientists, and priests. The committee, refusing to operate covertly, launched itself with a series of open letters in September 1976. Its transparency was intended to counter the fearfulness that accompanied totalitarianism. It even made public its members' names, addresses, and telephone numbers. KOR was the first group without ties to a communist regime to organize independently in the Eastern bloc. Influenced by KOR, students began working in partnership with workers, sometimes speaking on their behalf, and laborers harmonized their efforts with the dissident intellectuals. Understanding how the Poles were able eventually to win democracy from the Soviet Union requires an appreciation of KOR as the group's actions help to explain why the Poles rejected the romanticized violent uprisings of their history and instead adopted civil resistance, with its large inventory of nonviolent methods. KOR united intelligentsia associated with the Roman Catholic Church with thinkers of the secular political Left in a fight for tolerance, truth, justice, and human dignity. Activist intellectuals, including Jacek Kuroń, Adam Michnik, Antoni Macierewicz, and Leszek Kolakowski, intentionally forged alliances with such individuals as Jan Zieja, a Catholic priest, and the socialist Jan Józef Lipski. Other scholar activists included Bronislaw Geremek, Zbigniew Bujak, and Bogdan Lis.

During the Nazi era, thousands of Roman Catholic priests had been killed or imprisoned, and in the postwar period the Catholic Church had refused to accept the doctrines of Marxism-Leninism. Polish resistance to authoritarianism was intricately linked to the role of the church in Polish society. Although bishops did not step forward with official pronouncements supporting KOR, the church began to experience a renaissance and in the process express concern for human rights under the deft leadership of Stefan Cardinal Wyszyński. The guidance of Tadeusz Mazowiecki, a leading Catholic attorney and editor (1958–1981) of the liberal Catholic monthly *Więź* (Link), had prepared the way for the alliance between KOR and the church. Thinkers like Mazowiecki and Anna Morawska blended Polish nationalism, prophetic religious activism, and a desire for reform with some Marxist elements. The historian and essayist Adam Michnik would later write in *Letters from Prison* on the significance of Poland's Catholic intellectuals in laying the groundwork for political pluralism. Catholic printing houses, publications, and journals had an independence that they were able to exploit. KOR and the church supplemented each other's efforts, shaping an environment for the growth of the peaceful, nonviolent revolution in the making. Other groups emerged, among them the Movement for the Defense of Human and Civil Rights.

Never intending to be more than a small advocacy group defending workers, KOR aimed to overcome government repression and along the way became a creative center for formulating a doctrine of opposition. Blurring the lines between social activism and political organizing, it called its activities "social work." Its key thinkers adopted a policy of employing strictly nonviolent means for achieving greater freedoms. Although communism rested on the presumption that the ends may justify the means, KOR activist intellectuals wanted to fight for rights and freedoms with ethical standards consistent with the goals they espoused. These ideas echoed the writings of Henry David Thoreau, Leo Tolstoy, Mohandas

Gandhi, and Martin Luther King, Jr. Nonviolent struggle, also called civil resistance—a technique to bring about social and political change without bloodshed—was viewed as the best means for reaching the desired end of a free and democratic society, in part because it would minimize repression. The KOR leadership committed itself to rejecting the tragic failures and repressed bloody uprisings of the Polish past. It sought explicitly a strong civil society—a political space not under government control—with citizen action groups jockeying with each other in democratic disarray. The Poles "had enough of being mere components in a deliberately atomized society," Janusz Ziółkowski, a Solidarity supporter who would be elected to the Polish Senate in June 1989, explained. "They wanted to be citizens, individual men and women with dignity and responsibility, with rights but also with duties, freely associating in civil society" (Ziółkowski 1990).

KOR was not utopian, but practical in shunning the conformism of communist machinery sustained by deception, lies, and violence and backed by the Soviet arsenal. It maintained a flexible structure and never applied for official registration, so it could not be "de-registered." It had members, but operated without bylaws, officers, or fees. KOR relied on self-financing through voluntary contributions, initially to aid the workers and their families, but later embarked on nationwide fund-raising; parish priests helped, as did Polish émigrés living elsewhere.

Jacek Kuroń (1999), having scrutinized the history of Polish resistance over the centuries, had concluded that "the most effective form of resistance is based on solidarity." Among those thinking purposefully about the need for unity and solidarity was the shipyard master electrician Lech Wałęsa, who had been trying since 1968 with little success to bring about labor reforms for his fellow workers. During the 1970s, Wałęsa came to the conclusion that what the Poles most needed to change their circumstances and society was solidarity. The same judgment was being reached during this time by the KOR activist intellectuals and Roman Catholic intelligentsia. Wałęsa was often fired from jobs due to his advocacy for improved conditions and pay. He faced hard times during stretches of unemployment, yet remained insistent in his criticism of the communist government, and in each new position would urge his fellow workers to organize.

Knowledge of how to fight without bloodshed spread quietly and quickly throughout Poland. An underground press of illegal publications and books grew, including two uncensored literary publications and dozens of new periodicals. *Nowa,* an independent publishing house, produced more than 100 works. KOR offered documentation and dissemination of information through *Kommunikat* (Communiqué) and *Biuletyn Informacyjny* (Information bulletin). A Catholic periodical published translations of writings on collective nonviolent action by Gandhi and King. Groups that embarked on hunger strikes expressly cited these two men as influences.

Embodying unification of Polish society, in 1977 KOR widened its membership and targets and accelerated its activities, becoming the Komitet Samoobrony Społecznej (Social Self-Defense Committee, KSS-KOR). With its expanded mission, the organization contested discrimination, toiled to stop unlawful government behavior, and called for full rights and freedoms. Advocating universal goals, the members of KSS-KOR surmounted conventional obstacles that previously had prevented coordination among different groups, starting with workers and intellectuals. Wałęsa in 1978 joined with others in KSS-KOR in creating the Baltic Committee for Free and Independent Trade Unions. One of several KSS-KOR–inspired workers' circles, the surreptitious organization in 1979 published the Charter of Workers' Rights, a 1,000-word manifesto signed by sixty-five persons—mainly professors and writers but also including workers such as Wałęsa—that encouraged people to stand up for their rights. The free trade union committee complemented and received support from KSS-KOR. Its members conducted planning and other activities visibly and publicly, although their refusal to operate secretly led to endless arrests and job losses.

By the late 1970s, the organized opposition involved several thousand persons: workers, authors, university faculty and students, activist priests, representatives of religious orders, and independent publishers. Tadeusz Mazowiecki and sixty-two Polish academicians, including KSS-KOR members, established the Flying University in 1978. It held small, unauthorized seminars in private homes and apartments on Polish culture and history that were officially forbidden; locations sometimes quickly changed to avoid interruption. By the end of the 1970s, small, local movements were growing across Poland, including in factories and in the countryside, validating the stance of KSS-KOR, which maintained an apolitical position and declared itself a simple action group.

Kuroń (1999) expressed KSS-KOR's attitude on self-reliance when he said, "Don't destroy committees [meaning committees of the communist party-state structure], build your own." Respect for the law was emphasized, whether domestic, international, or the Helsinki Accords Final Act of 1975, to which Poland was a signatory, with its focus on human rights (see "**Introduction: Strikes, Sinatra, and Nonviolent Revolution**"). A deepening allegiance to egalitarian ideals accompanied these developments taking root among the Poles.

In addition to the incipient free trade union movement and KSS-KOR, the late 1970s also brought about the formation of ROPCiO (the Polish acronym for Defense for the Human and Civil Rights), a Polish chapter of Amnesty International, and the nationalist Confederation of Independent Poland (KPN). Each of these groups and their offshoots produced their own unofficial publications, or *samizdat* ("self-published," in Russian) (see "**Introduction: Strikes, Sinatra, and Nonviolent Revolution**"). The *samizdat* reported on political arrests, treatment of political prisoners, the party, and state violations of Poland's national constitution. They also carried essays on political freedoms and workers' rights, with commentary on violations of the Helsinki Accords and other international treaties on human rights. The severity of censorship in the state-controlled media meant that samizdat became a vital feature of all the Eastern bloc transition struggles. In Poland, however, the volume published was extraordinary. By the middle of the 1980s, as many as 2,000 regular samizdat publications were circulating in the country, some numbering in the tens of thousands of copies. The sharing of samizdat across borders provided vital links between democracy movements throughout Eastern Europe. The Polish underground publications were especially invigorating to similar fledgling, if smaller, movements of civil resistance in Hungary, East Germany, and Czechoslovakia, because Polish social mobilization was immeasurably more extensive and had solidified earlier than in the other nations of the Eastern bloc.

By the late 1970s, Poland was nearly bankrupt and deeply in debt to the Soviet Union, the sole purchaser of Polish goods. By 1980, more than 80 percent of Poland's income from exports went to servicing its foreign debt. By the following year it had suspended payment on its foreign debt (Mason 1996, 128). Food shortages were rampant. Moreover, within the communist apparatus, dissatisfaction with the failures to achieve socialist ideals had become pronounced. Criticism was growing within the party concerning the contradictions between its ideals and reality; some party members hoped that the party could reform itself. In contrast, within the increasingly influential and growing opposition, few believed that the communist apparatus could reform itself. They determined to take history into their own hands.

On June 2, 1979, Pope John Paul II, head of the Church of Rome and spiritual leader for 720 million Roman Catholics worldwide, had returned to Poland, the land of his birth. Born Karol Wojtyła, in Wadowice, not far from the Nazi concentration camps of Auschwitz and Birkenau, Wojtyła had become a priest and later a bishop, an archbishop, and then cardinal. Elected pope on October 16, 1978, he was a charismatic figure on the world stage, capable of arousing affection among believers and nonbelievers alike. *The New York Times,* on June 6, 1979, notes that daily life in Poland was "beset by many nagging restrictions on religion" ("Pope Calls on Polish Government for Guarantee of Religious Liberty"). Among the constraints it identified "sharp restrictions on religious publications, . . . no regular religious broadcasts on state-owned radio and television, [that] priests are regularly drafted into the army and the government routinely denies permits for building or restoring churches." In the largest peaceful assembly in Poland's postwar history and the first papal visit to a communist country, the first Slavic pope addressed hundreds of thousands of Poles during his nine-day visit. As many as 1 million Poles traveled to Warsaw to see him.

The papal tour would later be labeled a "dress rehearsal" for an independent national workers' movement, Solidarność (Solidarity). The complex logistics involved extensive preparations, which gave power to the opposition movements that had been building since 1970. Members of KSS-KOR and Catholic groups organized the huge gatherings, attendance at masses, and transportation during the papal visit, and found that they could administer intricate schedules, coordinate mammoth events, and get out word through their own self-reliant means of communication (see "Pope Gets Big Welcome in Poland"). The following year, small local strikes broke out across Poland, starting in the coastal areas. The term *strike* did not appear in the official Polish media reports: If communism were a superior system for representing the industrial proletariat and their welfare, why would workers need to undertake such potent collective action as a strike?

Solidarność Established

In June 1980, an explosion in the Lenin shipyard in Gdańsk caused the deaths of eight laborers. On August 14, members of the free trade union committee smuggled handwritten posters and leaflets into the shipyard. At 6:00 A.M. committee members began marching through the enormous shipyard, hoisting their placards and beckoning others to join them. Four years earlier, Lech Wałęsa had lost his job in the shipyard; on this day, he was assisted over its twelve-foot perimeter fence and began to lead the workers, who decided to go on strike.

Instead of walking out and abandoning the shipyard as would be customary in a strike, Wałęsa persuaded the workers to opt for a sit-down strike, in other words, an extended work stoppage during which laborers occupy the workplace. Wałęsa called for the establishment of a strike committee, with delegates from the different sections of the shipyard, to present the laborers' demands to the yard's management and the government representatives who swiftly became involved in the negotiations. The government considered the situation a crisis because of its magnitude and potential severity. The strikers insisted on openness, with the talks broadcast over the plant's radio so that everyone could listen to the discussions.

On August 16, delegates from factories across the country joined their Gdańsk colleagues at the negotiating table, as workers formed the Inter-Factory Strike Committee (known by its Polish acronym, MKS), comprised of two representatives from each plant that had undertaken similar sit-in strikes. Within days, MKS had representatives from more than 250 striking enterprises beyond Gdańsk and would soon speak for 500 workplaces in the Gdańsk area alone. Wałęsa asked Tadeusz Mazowiecki, who would later become the editor of *Solidarity Weekly,* and Bronislaw Geremek, a medieval historian and skilled negotiator, to stay in the yard and bring together a group of academicians and intellectuals to form a six-person "committee of experts" to offer advice. Wałęsa was often surrounded by professors. The workers drafted a list of twenty-one demands that according to a *Times* report of August 18, 1980, reflected specific workers' rights and the philosophical positions of KSS-KOR, which included fighting for workers' rights as well as political freedoms (see "Polish Labor Crisis Deepens As Workers List Their Demands").

KSS-KOR activist intellectuals in Warsaw furnished international news media with advisory reports on the strike, contravening the official state news agencies, which offered almost no coverage. Solidarity counted as key advisers Geremek, Kuroń, Mazowiecki, and Michnik. *The Times* on August 18 identifies Kuroń as acting as spokesperson for the strike committee. He did so until the regime cut the telephone lines, and arrested him and Adam Michnik. Radio Free Europe also covered the strike, based on Kuroń's reports to foreign journalists. On August 17, inside the Lenin shipyard, a priest celebrated mass at an improvised altar. Daily mass would thereafter be celebrated at 5:00 P.M. inside the gate. In addition, Wałęsa would climb onto a truck, stand above a photograph of the pope, and give a talk every evening (see "Polish Labor Crisis Deepens as Workers List Their Demands").

Solidarity was formally founded on September 22, three weeks after the Gdańsk accord, as delegates from thirty-eight regional labor unions held their first national meeting and formed a new union, NSZZ "Solidarność," the Independent Self-Governing Union Solidarity. The striking workers soon began to issue the daily *Solidarność* (Solidarity), a strike information bulletin. The inaugural issue's print run was 40,000. Solidarity chose as its logo thick red jumbled letters resembling demonstrators, carrying the Polish flag. The designer later said that the marchers were to appear to be supporting each other (Craig 1990, 226–227).

KSS-KOR became an active link in union activities, coordinating the actions of factories and shipyards. *The Times* on August 20 reports that the original demands of the strike committee had grown to twenty-three and in addition to the right to form trade unions and the right to strike, included crucial political freedoms, such as improvement of working conditions and freedom of the press. Most accounts continued to cite what became known as the 21 Demands (see "Strikers in Poland Defy Gierek Appeal").

The number of industrial installations joining the strike steadily increased. In eighteen days, Poland's workers achieved a major breakthrough: On August 30, all the workers' demands to date were realized in the historic Gdańsk accord. The government's negotiators agreed to recognize Solidarity's description of itself as an "independent, self-governing union," with a right to strike. The Inter-Factory Strike Committee, having refused to compromise on political rights and freedoms, gained the crucial recognition of free trade unions, rights to organize, and the release of all political prisoners, including activist intellectuals, among them university professors. The agreement drew worldwide attention to abuses under the Soviet-led communist system and raised the profile of the Solidarity movement. Only two weeks after the Gdańsk agreement, Solidarity represented 3 million workers. By late autumn 1980, it had registered 10 million members—80 percent of the Polish workforce (see "Strikers in Poland Defy Gierek Appeal"). As *The Times* would years later observe, on September 4, 1988, the agreement reached in Gdańsk "committed the Warsaw Government to an astonishing agenda of change and captured the dreams of Poles" (see "Workers in Poland Heed Walesa and Agree to End Last of Strikes").

In early 1981, an episode of violence inflicted by the regime brought Solidarity to a moment of crisis and affirmation. On March 19, correspondent John Darnton, relying on Solidarity's news reports, sent a dispatch to *The Times* reporting that riot police in the central Polish city of Bydgoszcz had broken up a demonstration by farmers seeking to form Rural Solidarity ("Polish Police Break up Farmer Protest"). Student Solidarity, Peasant Solidarity, and Prisoner Solidarity had already been established, but 3.5 million private farmers wanted their own organization. Evicting the protesters from a government hall, the police beat some people so severely that they needed hospitalization. On March 28 in *The Times,* Darnton writes of the previous day that "millions of Polish workers had conducted a four-hour nationwide strike, the largest organized protest since communism came to Poland 36 years ago" ("Millions in Poland Go on 4-Hour Strike to Protest Violence"). In response to the police brutality in Bydgoszcz, the time-restricted strike began and ended "exactly on schedule and without reports of major incidents." Within Solidarity, the March 27 strike was deemed a "warning"—if demands for the punishment of police officers were not met, a nationwide general strike would take place on March 31.

The beatings in Bydgoszcz caused strains within the union. Workers began striking almost continuously in defiance of Wałęsa's judgment. Meanwhile, Wałęsa, the union's coordinating committee, and advisers had secretly re-entered negotiations with the government. Torn by fears of civil war, and apprehensive about Solidarity's collapse, Wałęsa appeared on television and, at the recommendation of his advisers, unexpectedly announced the suspension of the pending general strike. Bydgoszcz was a watershed (see "Polish Union Opens Convention"). Despite the chaos that followed events there, Solidarity held its first national convention, September 5–10 and September 16–October 7, 1981, where Wałęsa was elected leader.

As Solidarity's stature grew, it seemed to render obsolete the need for KSS-KOR, whose members concluded that its aspiration of protecting workers within the broader context of political rights could be realized under the unified banner of Solidarity. Leading KSS-KOR members assumed positions in the movement. For its final act, KSS-KOR presented a formal report on the human rights situation in Poland to the Helsinki Watch Committee, which had been established to monitor implementation of the 1975 Helsinki Accords. On September 18, 1981, KSS-KOR formally disbanded. It had successfully shaped a general Polish commitment to fighting with nonviolent resistance and had strenuously worked on behalf of the Polish worker for a healthy civil society beyond government control (see "Polish Union Opens Convention").

Martial Law

Stanislaw Kania succeeded Edward Gierek as communist party chief in autumn 1981. Kania was then replaced by Gen. Wojciech Jaruzelski, who was already prime minister and chief of the armed forces. The new government stealthily undermined Wałęsa and the 10-million strong Solidarity union.

On December 12, 1981, the Jaruzelski government's despised and feared riot police descended on Solidarity buildings, took possession of property, arrested the entire Solidarity leadership and thousands of its sympathizers, and declared the union illegal. Martial law, labeled by Jaruzelski a "state of war," was officially declared. On December 14, *Times* correspondent John Darnton chronicles how Jaruzelski justified such a move as obligatory because "a strict regime was necessary to save Poland from catastrophe and civil war" (see "Poland Restricts Civil and Union Rights" and "As Jaruzelski Leaves Office: A Traitor or a Patriot to Poles?").

On December 15, *The Times* notes that a day after the imposition of martial law, the clandestine information networks of Solidarity reported "strikes and worker resistance in factories, shipyards, steel mills, coal mines, and even academic institutions in Warsaw and other major cities and regions" ("Widespread Strikes Reported in Defiance of Polish Regime"). With all commercial communications lines cut, the international newspapers had to rely on Solidarity's news outlets. *The Times* does not provide a figure, but by mid-1982, some 10,000 Solidarity members were under "preventive detention," with more than 3,000 behind bars for "political crimes" (see "Poland Restricts Civil and Union Rights"). In January 1983, the Jaruzelski regime created officially registered worker unions and banned strikes. Solidarity had been weakened but not broken.

The clandestine, underground publication of samizdat continued, along with aggressive circulation of newspapers, periodicals, books, journals, and factory rags, which were being disseminated on a scale unlike anywhere else in the Soviet orbit. Within Solidarity's ranks, Zbigniew Bujak pressed the case for strictly nonviolent resistance against the regime's martial law reprisals: "The basic principles adopted by Solidarity, and still valid, is the use of exclusively peaceful means. . . . We are against any acts of violence, street battles, hit squads, acts of terror, [and] armed organizations" (Mason 1996, 70).

Solidarity's tenacity would be invigorated by the second visit of Pope John Paul II, June 16–23, 1983. Meeting with Wałęsa, the pope stressed the importance of continuing to rely of nonviolent strategies: "If the world grasps what you are trying to do, if it sees in your movement hope and a way to resolve conflicts, it is precisely because you have renounced violence" (Walesa 1992, 118). Although inside Poland the government had managed to suppress Solidarity, yet externally the union had become recognized worldwide as the first major, mass nonviolent challenge to Soviet domination. Such acclamation became evident when Wałęsa was awarded the Nobel Prize for Peace on October 6, 1983. Flawed, alive, but underground, Solidarity broadened during this period, as its various tiers and circles sought ingenious ways to defy communist rule and express discontent toward the regime. Citizens refused to believe news from official state sources. Others resorted to emigration from Poland as a method of nonviolent noncooperation. Economic productivity in Poland continued to decline, and the communist party lost approximately half of its 3 million members.

As churches across the land provided succor from the repression of martial rule, best recognized was Father Jerzy Popiełuzko's Mass for Poland, held in Warsaw on the last Sunday of every month. At these gatherings, Father Jerzy would state that the Church could not remain neutral in the face of injustice; rather, it had a duty to protect the oppressed. He spoke plainly of "a nation terrorized by military force," of beatings, of persons brought to trial simply for trying to be faithful to the principles of Solidarity. The regime tried to silence him through the Church hierarchy, but the bishops refused to cooperate. On October 30, 1984, the mutilated corpse of Father Jerzy Popiełuzko was found in the Vistula River. The discovery of the body led to international protests. *The Times* on November 4 reports that 200,000 people attended the funeral of the thirty-seven-year-old beloved priest. Jaruzelski claimed that the government bore no responsibility for his killing, yet by February 1985, four officers in the secret police had been sentenced to prison terms between 14 and 25 years for the murder (see "200,000 at Rites for Polish Priest").

Solidarity never sought to destroy the communist apparatus or consider overthrowing the party-state. By its own terminology, Solidarity wanted instead to "repair" Poland by gaining reforms for workers' rights while preserving the economy and liberating civil society (see "Polish Union Opens Convention"). Its momentum was powered by the workers whose lot under communism had gone steadily downhill with high human costs, activist intellectuals from Poland's university faculties and students, the Roman Catholic Church, and writers and editors who vigorously plied their trade in a subterranean press.

The movement's strategy was slowly to enlarge its successes, but without cornering those in power. It sought to offer authorities the lesser of two evils whereby widening social independence for the populace was preferable to belligerent confrontation (Smolar 2009, 133). Within the Polish United Workers' Party were reformist elements that no longer wished to preserve one-party rule. Adam Michnik, among the key KSS-KOR activist intellectuals and later editor of *Gazeta Wyborcza* (Election Gazette), which became Poland's second largest daily newspaper, would afterward write not only about the ethics of Solidarity's way of seeking political change, but spoke of its opposition—the party-state—as comprised of rational actors who could define their own power interests, weigh advantages and shortcomings, and who were able to conclude that it was more disadvantageous for them to exert the coercive powers under their control than to accommodate the changes that were sought by the union. In Poland began the peaceful acceptance of the loss of power by communist party elites in the Soviet bloc.

IN THE SHADOW OF THE SOVIET UNION

A Soviet-led invasion of 750,000 Warsaw Pact troops had marched into Czechoslovakia during August 20–21, 1968, to crush the Prague Spring (see **Czechoslovakia, Introduction**). Within a month of the invasion, *Pravda,* the Soviet Communist Party newspaper, justified the invasion by citing the principle dubbed the Brezhnev Doctrine in the West, named after Soviet premier Leonid Brezhnev. *Pravda* acknowledged various paths to socialism, but maintained that each country's party held responsibility not solely only for its own populace but also for all socialist countries and the whole communist movement. The Kremlin asserted the right to intervene in any country in the Soviet bloc in order to prevent counterrevolution or loss of party control. Thus, sovereignty in the Eastern European satellites was limited by these states' obligations to others in the communist bloc, which is why the Brezhnev Doctrine is sometimes called the "doctrine of limited sovereignty." It cast a long shadow, diminishing resistance to communism across Eastern Europe for the following decade.

The Soviet Union recognized Solidarity's potency. In early December 1980, Brezhnev, who had not taken any action until that point, dispatched fifteen to twenty military divisions to the Polish border, intending at a minimum to threaten Solidarity. U.S. president Jimmy Carter, already exerting sustained pressure on the Soviet Union through his persistence in asserting the human rights provisions of the Helsinki Accords, telephoned Brezhnev and warned him not to send forces into Poland. The troops did not invade.

Soon after taking office in January 1977, Carter had secretly ordered the Central Intelligence Agency to enlarge its support of oppositional groups in the satellite nations of the Soviet Union and to flood the Eastern bloc with books, journals, and periodicals by and about human rights dissidents. The impact of the large Polish underground press therefore broadened across the region. As the Brezhnev Doctrine unraveled, a series of U.S. policies that would be continued under President Ronald Reagan, who advocated further opposition to the Soviet Union, were set in motion.

On March 11, 1985, Mikhail S. Gorbachev assumed power as general secretary of the Communist Party of the Soviet Union and began advocating a policy of *perestroika* ("restructuring" in Russian), a principle he would describe in a 1987 book (see "**Introduction: Strikes, Sinatra, and Nonviolent Revolution**"). Others had tried to reform the Soviet system, but authentic economic reforms inescapably threatened the status of the

Communist Party, and thus were always abandoned. Part of Gorbachev's unique approach derived from his view that Soviet society and the communist party would have to change in order for economic reforms to be effective. This did not mean, however, that the Soviet Union was ready to relinquish control over the region. Gorbachev believed in socialism but did not fully appreciate its moral weakness and ethical implications as interpreted and applied across Eastern Europe and the Soviet Union. He failed also to appreciate the depth of hostility toward it because of its often brutal imposition in Eastern Europe. When the Soviet Union came under the hand of this committed communist reformer in 1985, it heralded an altered atmosphere for Solidarity, though it would take some years to realize. On March 12, 1985, *The Times* comments,

> Coming to power at the age of 54, Mikhail Sergeyevich Gorbachev, the peasant's son from southern Russia, is expected to bring a new style of leadership to the Kremlin. If the expectations prove correct, this leadership will be more open, perhaps, less obsessively suspicious, less burdened with memories of Stalin's terror and the war. He revealed his impatience in a major speech last December when he said, "We will have to carry out profound transformations in the economy and in the entire system of social relations."

Gorbachev faced huge challenges, because as *The Times* reports, the Soviet communist edifice at the time consisted of individuals "who have made their careers in a communist party that has changed from an idealistic elite into an entrenched, privileged and self-perpetuating bureaucracy intolerant of too much independence or non-conformism among its members" (see "A Leader with Style—and Impatience").

Election of a Non-Communist Government

In Poland in 1982—the second year of martial law and before Gorbachev assumed power—the Jaruzelski regime had instituted decentralizing economic reforms but found itself unable to implement them because of bureaucratic lethargy, traditionalist opposition, and lack of popular support. The economy had experienced zero growth, more or less, between 1981 and 1985, and only meager growth after that. Governmental attempts to harmonize pricing structures merely led to higher rates of inflation (60 percent by 1988), increased worker demands for pay raises, and spiraling wage-price indices that further reduced the standard of living. Poland's debt would reach $40 billion by 1988.

Eastern Europe's negotiated end to communism began in 1988, as waves of mutinous strikes spread across Poland that were not called by Solidarity. In response to them, Wałęsa said, "I am not on strike, although I am not against it." (Stokes 1993, 121). The economy had continued to deteriorate, as foreign indebtedness, inflation, and prices continued to rise, while health services deteriorated. Outright economic collapse loomed. Eight years after Solidarity's founding, a new generation was not as unsettled by martial law and less intimidated as well. Movement toward reform had become discernible in the Soviet Union, so it could not automatically be assumed that Gorbachev would support the old regime in Warsaw. From April 21 to May 2, strikes and other acts of noncooperation spread across Poland to protest the latest wage limits and price hikes, as had happened in 1956, 1970, 1976, and 1980. Once again at the Lenin shipyard in Gdańsk, sit-in strikes began with displays of photographs of Pope John Paul II. The workers' principal demands were the legalization of Solidarity and reinstatement of Wałęsa as head of Solidarity. Wałęsa offered his help to end a nine-day Gdańsk work stoppage.

In August, a second wave of wildcat strikes broke out that were larger than the spring strikes, which largely concerned economic demands. The wildcat strikers called more broadly and forcefully for political freedoms as well as the legalization of Solidarity. On August 26, Gen. Jaruzelski told the party's Politburo that he wanted to hold talks with the regime's opponents, with no preconditions. On August 31, the government and Solidarity held their first meeting in seven years, on the eighth anniversary of the 1980 Gdańsk agreement and start of Solidarity, and the interior minister, Gen. Czesław Kiszczak, met with Wałęsa (see "Strikers in Poland Defy Gierek Appeal" and "Polish Union Opens Convention").

The regime had long portrayed Wałęsa as a mere private citizen, yet now the minister in charge of security was offering to discuss legalizing the Solidarity union with him—if Wałęsa could persuade the workers to return to work. In retrospect, this meeting would be seen as the first formal discussion in the so-called round-table talks between Solidarity and the Polish government that would half a year later begin the negotiations that would eventually lead to removal of the communists from power. Months later, on November 30, Wałęsa was invited to debate the head of the communist party's official labor unions. He appeared for forty-five minutes on national television and affably proceeded to trump the regime's representative with his clever arguments, charm, and wit. Some observers later suggested that this moment had been a turning point in legitimizing Solidarity and elevating Wałęsa as a national figure as well as generating psychological power equivalent to the pope's first visit to Poland.

On December 18, Wałęsa formed a citizens' committee within Solidarity consisting of more than 100 leading academicians and writers. Most were Wałęsa's intellectual advisers from the days of KSS-KOR. In a banner moment for nonviolent strategies, Wałęsa and the majority won a debate against a sizable minority who wanted to employ violence in a bloody, anticommunist revolution. Solidarity formally decided to pursue a peaceful solution, which was another step toward the round-table talks that would begin two months later. For the balance of 1988, however, Solidarity and the government were unable to agree on guidelines for their negotiations.

The communist party's Central Committee came under pressure from both Jaruzelski and Gorbachev to recognize Solidarity. After a tempestuous meeting of the Central Committee in January 1989, at which Jaruzelski threatened his resignation if his recommendations were not accepted, the party approved a resolution that would allow political pluralism, a political opposition, and the legalization of Solidarity. This cleared the way for the round-table negotiations, which would mark the moment when the communist regimes throughout the region would begin to implode (see "Workers in Poland Heed Walesa and Agree to End Last of Strikes"). The talks opened in Warsaw in February 1989. Within nine months, the Berlin Wall would fall.

From February 6 to April 5, 1989, in Namiestnikowski Palace, twenty-six Solidarity representatives and Church witnesses met with twenty-nine party representatives around a smooth, round oak table—twenty-eight feet in diameter and able to seat fifty-seven—to discuss the situation in Poland. Zbigniew Bujak, Jacek Kuroń, Bogdan Lis, Adam Michnik, Wałęsa, and other trailblazers of Solidarity were among the fifty-seven principal negotiators in the talks and had a decisive role in the future of the Eastern bloc. Thirteen working groups held ninety-four sessions, often conversing until dawn. Three core working groups discussed union law, economic questions, and political restructuring. Two plenary sessions convened. In addition, four informal summit meetings took place at Magdalenka, a village near Warsaw, between the government's chief negotiator, Interior Minister Kiszczak, Solidarity's Wałęsa, and their most trusted advisers. There, in seclusion, they negotiated the most difficult sticking points, with no more than two dozen persons present. At the round-table, the various sub-tables, and hundreds of specialized subcommittee sessions that accompanied it, former political prisoners sat with their previous jailers. As the talks created bonds, the previously incarcerated and their keepers signed several hundred pages of protocols, records of agreed-upon propositions, in addition to notations of disagreements.

The Polish government and Solidarity signed the round-table agreements on April 5, 1989. The preamble calls the accords "the beginning of the road to parliamentary democracy." At the signing ceremony, Wałęsa declared, "This is the beginning of democracy and a free Poland." According to Jacek Kuroń, one of the influential thinkers who had shaped Solidarity and spent nine years in prison, the talks permitted Polish society to organize itself for democratic governance (see "Polish Labor Crisis Deepens as Workers List Their Demands"). Intensive organization had made the negotiations possible, Kuroń (1999) penned: "[I]t became possible to reach this stage only after the enormous social activity in the legal days of Solidarity [sixteen months] and the widespread clandestine resistance during the years of martial law."

In addition to making Solidarity a legal trade union, the round-table talks created a bicameral legislature with a senate, reestablished an independent judiciary, expanded freedoms of the press and assembly, and charted a system of semi-free parliamentary elections that appeared to protect the interests of the ruling communists, yet the agreements reached beyond the Central Committee's promises of January. Not only would Solidarity be reinstated, the union would also receive airtime on television and radio and be allowed to publish its own national and provincial newspapers. The Polish United Workers' Party and its satellite parties would have a single list to contest 65 percent of the seats in the Sejm, the restructured lower chamber of the Polish parliament. The opposition would be allowed to vie for 35 percent of the Sejm seats. For the newly reconstituted upper chamber, the Senate, elections for all seats would be open and free. The Senate would be able to veto the Sejm, but could be overridden by a two-thirds majority, and the two chambers would elect a president (Stokes 1993, 126).

The Polish agreements were being dissected and discussed elsewhere. *The Times* correspondent in Budapest writes on May 15, 1989, that he had spoken with a Hungarian party official, who indicated that the party there would not preserve its power "by administrative means or military force" (see "In Hungary, the Political Changes Are Tempered by Economic Fears"). Henry Kamm quoted the official as saying that the party "wants to negotiate with the opposition a formula similar to that worked out between the Polish Government and its opposition."

May 1, 1989, Wałęsa, standing on a wooden barrel outside St. Brygid's Church in Gdańsk, initiated the first Polish electoral campaign in more than sixty years that allowed participation by freely nominated candidates. Open, if complex, elections took place on June 4. Almost all the Solidarity candidates met with success in the first round, a landslide for all the "free" seats. Of the 161 seats for which it was allowed to compete in the Polish parliament's lower house, Solidarity won every one. In the second, runoff round of voting, on June 18—the first time that voters were able to render their judgment on the communist party—the communists lost. Solidarity won 99 of the 100 Senate seats. More important perhaps, the party publicly accepted the validity of the results. Although pre-election polls had forecast big victories for the communist party, the results were astonishing: Solidarity swept the seats for which it had stood.

According to the bargain struck and agreed in advance at the round-table, Jaruzelski was elected president by the parliament, by one vote. On August 24, this same legislature elected the first non-communist prime minister in the Soviet bloc in its selection of Tadeusz Mazowiecki, a key member of the Catholic intelligentsia who had helped to shape KSS-KOR and Solidarity. In December 1990, Wałęsa was elected president of Poland (see "To His Volatile Young Allies, Walesa Preaches Conciliation"). *The Times* on December 22, 1990, points out that after Gorbachev had loosened Moscow's reins on Warsaw, Jaruzelski "steered Poland's communist party as it became the first one in Eastern Europe to relinquish power to the opposition," but that he was "pointedly excluded" from Wałęsa's swearing-in as president (see "As Jaruzelski Leaves Office: A Traitor or a Patriot to Poles?").

Poland became the first democracy in postwar, communist Eastern Europe achieved through nonviolent struggle. The Soviet newspaper *Izvestia* reported offhandedly that the opposition "will take their place in the parliament . . . where, incidentally, the PUWP [Polish United Workers' Party] will no longer have a majority." The Kremlin watched with calmness. On July 7, 1989, Gorbachev told the Council of Europe, in Strasbourg, France, that he had rejected the Brezhnev Doctrine. Although he stopped short of endorsing the political developments in Poland and elsewhere in Eastern Europe, the political will for the Soviet Union to remain an empire seemed to have dissipated. "It seems that at that moment, for practical reasons," Janusz Ziółkowski (1990) explains, "Gorbachev wrote off Eastern Europe." The Soviet leadership may have wanted to extricate itself from the Eastern bloc.

That summer, a spokesperson for Gorbachev joked about Moscow's new "Sinatra doctrine," referring to the American crooner Frank Sinatra and his song "My Way." The bold implication was that the Soviet satellite states would be allowed to go their own ways. Shortly thereafter Polish prime minister Mazowiecki visited Moscow, where he was warmly received. The Brezhnev Doctrine had become obsolete.

The daring originality of Solidarity's approach and its generosity of spirit was exemplary. "What was most characteristic and most remarkable about the Solidarność revolution was the complete lack of violence," according to Ziółkowski (1990). "It was a statement about how things should be." Solidarity had staged the largest mass strikes in European history. Women were involved to a large proportion in all activities and actions. The combination of workers' rights and political freedoms gave Solidarity its potency and depth across Polish society as a movement for broad social liberation.

Conclusion

The Solidarity trade union emerged with a strike in the Lenin shipyard in Gdańsk that began on August 14, 1980. Its specific use of power derived from exercising economic noncooperation, principally through the use of sit-in strikes, in which workers occupied workplaces while halting production rather than walking out. This protracted and massive nonviolent movement—an alliance of workers and intellectuals and backed by the Roman Catholic Church—fought Poland's communist government with nonviolent methods for the rights and freedoms of shipyard and factory workers, professors and students, priests, political prisoners, and peasants. Despite seven years of martial law and illegality, Solidarity "survived underground as an ideal of community and a formula for collective resistance to the regime" (Michta 1997, 75). Wildcat strikes in 1988 succeeded in bringing about talks between Solidarity and the party-state. These round-table negotiations marked the moment when the communist regimes of the Eastern bloc began to implode, starting in Warsaw in February 1989, the year that the Berlin Wall would fall. Having employed the largest labor strikes in European history, the Polish workers' movement was able to negotiate the first free elections in the Eastern European countries that had fallen under Soviet control after World War II. It was instrumental in the creation of a Polish civil society and new democratic state. As has occurred before (and since) in history, a nonviolent struggle was required to achieve the negotiations that re-created Polish governance.

Pope John Paul II Visits Poland, Challenges State

On June 2, 1979, Pope John Paul II returned to Poland, the land of his birth, for the first papal visit to a communist country. He had originally wanted to go in May, to celebrate the nine hundredth anniversary of St. Stanislaus, the patron saint of Poland and one-time bishop of his former diocese who, when slain in the eleventh century by the king's hirelings, had retained his dignity. The authorities, according to a *New York Times* article of June 6, 1979, denied him permission to visit in May because they were "worried about the symbolism of a saint martyred because he defied the king" ("Pope Calls on Polish Government for Guarantee of Religious Liberty").

On June 5, 1979, *The Times* editorializes that "Edward Gierek and his colleagues in the Polish communist leadership gave John Paul II permission to come because they had no choice. They recognize in this first Polish pope the most formidable opponent Polish communism has ever faced. His elevation to the papacy touched the Polish soul and to have denied him now would have risked more than Warsaw or Moscow dared" ("The Polish Pope in Poland").

Born Karol Wojtyła, in Wadowice, the future John Paul II became a priest and subsequently a bishop, an archbishop, and then a cardinal. He was elected pope on October 16, 1978, after the very short tenure and death of John Paul I. The new pope emerged as a charismatic figure on the world stage, capable of arousing affection among Catholics, Christians outside the Catholic tradition, agnostics, and even atheists. As archbishop of Kraków, Karol Cardinal Wojtyła had for twenty years refused to go along with the formula espoused by Poland's communist authorities of conceding political matters to the state while restricting the Church to spiritual and moral issues. He also fought a twenty-year battle for permission to build a church in Nowa Huta, near Kraków, a steel town and model of socialism in which the state was determined that religion would have no role. Wojtyła succeeded finally in building his church, but was barred from going to Nowa Huta during his 1979 visit.

Although the Polish constitution protects freedom of religion, according to a *Times* report of June 6, 1979, daily life was "beset by many nagging restrictions on religion" ("Pope Calls on Polish Government for Guarantee of Religious Liberty"). The state refused formal recognition to the Church. *Times* reporter David A. Andelman notes the following:

> In addition to sharp restrictions on religious publications, there are no regular religious broadcasts on state-owned radio and television, priests are regularly drafted into the army and the Government routinely denies permits for building or restoring churches. Television viewers in Warsaw have received only 10 minutes a day of coverage of the Pope's visit. There is widespread discrimination against believers in the top layers of the state and party bureaucracy.

Spiritual education of children was also affected, and the Church was not granted formal recognition. On June 2, at the largest peaceful assembly in Poland's postwar history, the first Slavic pope addressed hundreds of thousands of Poles. *The Times* notes on June 3 that nine days and eight nights of the Pope's visit brought celebrations, ritual, and "a display of the continuing importance of the Roman Catholic Church in this communist land, where

90 percent of the 35 million people are Catholic." From the pulpit of his former cathedral in the ancient university town of Kraków, where the astronomer Copernicus once studied, John Paul II asserted that the future of Poland would "depend on how many people are mature enough to be nonconformists."

Meanwhile, the "delicate planning," as the June 3 *Times* article refers to the series of logistical feats involved in the visit, had unintended effects. The opposition movements that had been forming since 1970—including KSS-KOR, the Social Self-Defense Committee, consisting primarily of academicians and Roman Catholic laity, and other Catholic activist groups—organized the enormous rallies, masses, and internal transportation for the pope's visit and found the experience to be empowering. They discovered that they could organize large events and spread information through their own independent communications networks (see **Poland, Introduction**).

Although *The Times* does not mention this situation, the regime's security forces were nowhere to be seen as the pope visited cities about the land. Volunteer stewards maintained order; no violence occurred. In general, the state authorities attempted to minimize the papal visit and allowed only sparse television coverage. In Kraków's twelfth-century central square, among the largest in Europe, John Paul II held a mass to celebrate St. Stanislaus. At Częstochowa, he openly criticized the regime, reproaching the Soviet-backed government, and he called upon it to recognize fundamental human rights, including the right to religious liberty. After the pope's departure, KSS-KOR, the Flying University, priests, and other groups followed the model of John Paul's studied confrontation with the Polish authorities (see **Poland, Introduction**). Unquestionably, the pope's influence became a factor in the development of Poland's massive nonviolent struggle.

JUNE 3, 1979
POPE GETS BIG WELCOME IN POLAND, OFFERS CHALLENGE TO THE AUTHORITIES
By DAVID A. ANDELMAN
Special to The New York Times

Warsaw, June 2 – Pope John Paul II returned home to Poland to a tumultuous welcome today. . . . He was warmly welcomed by a crowd of 20,000 at the airport, hundreds of thousands lined the 10 miles of streets he traveled into the city, and 290,000 heard his pontifical mass in Warsaw. . . . It was the start of nine days and eight nights of celebrations, ritual and display of the continuing importance of the Roman Catholic Church in this Communist land where 90 percent of the 35 million people are Catholic. The formal reason for the visit is to mark the 900th anniversary of the martydom of St. Stanislaus, Poland's patron.

In his arrival message and in statements at formal meetings with Polish Communist leaders and the afternoon mass, the Pope appeared to carve out a broad area of responsibility for the church.

This area was far broader than is comfortable for the Communist leadership and broader than any statements by the Polish episcopate during the weeks of delicate planning that preceded the Pope's arrival.

"The church wishes to serve people also in the temporal dimension of their life and existence," the Pope told the Polish Communist leader, Edward Gierek, at their afternoon audience at the Belvedere Palace, the presidential residence. . . . This was a challenge to Mr. Gierek, who had just told the Pope: "Cooperation between the church and state should embrace everything that serves the development of Poland, consolidation of her security, and position

Pope John Paul II en route from the airport to Warsaw Cathedral on June 2, 1979, during the first papal visit to a communist country, Poland, his birthplace. Later that day in Warsaw's Victory Square, the pontiff celebrated mass attended by some 300,000 persons. The gathering was the largest peaceful assembly in Poland's postwar history. Many observers considered the pope's visit to be a "dress rehearsal" for the creation of Solidarność—Solidarity—the independent national workers' movement, because of Polish opposition groups' extensive involvement in organizing events for the occasion.
Source: AP Images

on the international arena, all that favors further progress in the life of the society."

Poland's Communist leadership has long held that the church and state could coexist here if the church would restrict its concern to moral and spiritual questions and leave political and temporal matters to the authorities. As Karol Cardinal Wojtyla, Archbishop of Cracow, the Pope for 20 years refused to bend to these demands, and his views today have clearly not changed.

A Polish Catholic editor said: "If anything, he is tougher that he ever used to be."

A Carnival Atmosphere

Warsaw took on a carnival atmosphere. . . . Tens of thousands streamed toward the city's center for a glimpse of the leader of the world's 720 million Roman Catholics.

More than a million people were estimated to have entered Warsaw, nearly doubling the normal population of the capital. The crowds were orderly for the most part, even restrained.

Western diplomats said that roadblocks as much as 70 miles outside the capital prevented millions more from reaching the area. . . . Finally, at 4 P.M., the Pope arrived in Victory Square, where the nearly 300,000 people had been waiting for hours in the 90-degree heat.

Polish journalists said that the crowd was the largest in the postwar history of Poland. Church officials said the mass was also the largest single religious observance in the Communist history of Eastern Europe.

As the Pope stood, his arms spread before the 36-foot high plywood cross that dominates the skyline, thousands wept openly.

Workers Unite and Issue Demands

The shipyard master electrician Lech Wałęsa, who had unsuccessfully attempted to unite students and workers in 1968, concluded that solidarity was the one thing the Poles needed but lacked in order to change their society. In the 1970s, members of KSS-KOR—the Social Self-Defense Committee, composed largely of activist intellectuals and Roman Catholic laity—reached the same conclusion (see **Poland, Introduction**).

While Wałęsa was often fired from jobs, and faced many adversities in unemployment, he remained unrelenting in his criticism of the government. At each new place of employment he urged his fellow workers to organize. In April 1978, Wałęsa and others formed the Baltic Committee for Free and Independent Trade Unions, one of several KSS-KOR–inspired workers' circles. Created in Gdańsk around the magazine *Coastal Worker*, this surreptitious organization in 1979 published a Charter of Workers' Rights. The 1,000-word manifesto was signed by sixty-five persons, mainly professors and writers, and encouraged people to stand up for their rights.

The ideas and activities of this free trade union committee complemented and received support from KSS-KOR. Its planning and activities were conducted openly and publicly, even though this approach led to arrests and job losses. The committee's leadership was always changing, but its message of unity reached the citizens, who were kept abreast of developments in the gradually solidifying resistance by an array of samizdat and independent newspapers and publications in circulation by 1979.

Polish workers had used slowdowns and sit-ins and other nonviolent methods—action steps also called nonviolent sanctions—to protest their worsening conditions. In the late 1970s, small local strikes, part of a large class of economic noncooperation methods, began breaking out across Poland. A strike is a collective, intentional, and usually temporary suspension of labor meant to exert pressure and change relationships with others in an enterprise or unit. State media reports avoided the term *strike* to describe the workers' many and varied strike actions: since communism was supposed to be the best system for representing the industrial proletariat and its requirements, why would laborers need to utilize disruptive collective action to apply pressure, namely, a strike?

In June 1980, an explosion at the Lenin shipyard in Gdańsk killed eight laborers and injured sixty others. Anna Walentynowicz, a crane driver in the shipyards, had campaigned for protective garments and safer techniques of operation. On July 9, after thirty years on the job, she was fired for collecting candle stubs from a cemetery to form new candles in order to memorialize protesting workers killed by government forces in 1970; the police accused her of stealing. In a Gdańsk apartment that summer, a group of Poles discussed the possibility of striking to get Walentynowicz rehired. Wałęsa attended that meeting.

Before dawn on August 14 at the Lenin shipyard, members of the free trade union committee, of which Walentynowicz was a co-founder and spokesperson, smuggled onto the grounds handwritten posters and leaflets calling for Walentynowicz, a widow, to be reinstated and given a raise in pay. Around 6:00 A.M., after the first shift had clocked in, committee members marched through the enormous shipyard, waving their placards and calling for others to join them. Wałęsa, who had lost his job at the shipyard four years earlier, was helped over the perimeter fence and assumed leadership of the movement.

The workers' strike had come alive on August 14, and on August 16 they formed the inter-factory committee, but instead of walking out and abandoning the shipyard as would be customary, Wałęsa proposed that they have a sit-down strike—that is, an extended work stoppage in which the workers occupy the workplace. He also encouraged the workers to coordinate and establish a strike committee, so they could present the yard's management and government representatives a reasoned program of demands. Given the magnitude of the situation, negotiations quickly ensued in the assembly hall of the yard, with Wałęsa sitting across from the yard's director at a long table. The strikers insisted that the talks be broadcast on the plant's radio so everyone could hear the discussions. Wałęsa presented the shipyard director with a list of five demands, including re-employment of Walentynowicz and himself, a wage increase, immunity from reprisals for the strikers, and authorization to build a monument to the martyrs of the December 1970 massacre.

Alina Pieńkowska, the shipyard nurse, spoke movingly of the labor actions that had begun elsewhere and asked that the workers not leave, but instead continue their strike in solidarity with the other shipyards and factories that had heard about what was happening and decided to strike as well. That night, several thousand striking workers settled down to sleep in the yard. The sit-in strike was vital to the maintenance of nonviolent discipline, as all strikers remained together; it also minimized provocations that the regime might use as pretexts to justify reprisals.

Within twenty-four hours of the August 14 dawn action in Gdańsk, strikes spread across the region. On August 16, the strikers formed an Inter-Factory Strike Committee (MKS). As two representatives from some twenty or more plants that had begun to strike elsewhere joined the Gdańsk delegates at the long negotiations table, their list of demands grew to sixteen. Five days after the initial action, by August 19, more than 250 workplaces were represented on MKS.

Wałęsa asked Tadeusz Mazowiecki and Bronislaw Geremek to remain at the yard and create a committee of experts to provide advice. Not for the last time, Wałęsa would be surrounded by professors of history, law, philosophy, and the social sciences who added demands to the workers' roster. By August 17, the list of demands grew to twenty-one, reflecting specific workers' rights and the philosophical positions of KSS-KOR, whose broadened mission included fighting for rights and freedoms. The alliance between the workers and the academicians gave resilience to the unfolding struggle, and the KSS-KOR academicians and Catholic laity were entrusted with acting as spokespersons for the labor action. Though prioritizing independent trade unions, the demands represented all of the aggrieved, whether laborers, students, prisoners of conscience, priests, or people from faith-based groups. Careful references were made to the Polish constitution, as well as to popular social participation, rather than specific political reforms of the state-socialism machinery.

The historian Jacek Kuroń of KSS-KOR acted as spokesperson for the strike committee until the regime cut the telephone lines and arrested him and Adam Michnik, another Warsaw historian and essayist, who like others kept the international news media advised on the facts of the strike. The activist intellectuals' interactions with the press contravened official news agencies, which within Poland offered almost no coverage. Kuroń's reports of events to foreign journalists reached the Polish people through Radio Free Europe.

On August 15, tentative accord was reached as shipyard authorities agreed to a wage increase, the rehiring of Walentynowicz and Wałęsa, and, remarkably, the building of a monument to the workers martyred by the government in 1970 at the front gate of the yard. On August 17, a Sunday, a priest celebrated mass at an improvised altar inside the yard. Loudspeakers carried the prayers across a listening city. Daily mass would thereafter be celebrated at 5:00 P.M. inside the gate. Wałęsa developed a habit of delivering an evening talk each day while standing above a photograph of the pope.

KEY PLAYER IN POLAND
Jacek Kuroń (1934–2004)

Jacek Kuroń was born in Lvov, in modern-day Ukraine. Raised in Poland in a committed socialist family, Kuroń in his youth was a vocal member of the communist party. He studied pedagogy, and like Adam Michnik, became a vocal critic of education policies. His outspokenness on this issue earned him an official reprimand in 1953.

In 1957, Kuroń was graduated from the University of Warsaw faculty of history and became a leading intellectual in Poland's fledgling but little-noticed resistance movement. In 1964, he and a colleague, Karol Modzelewski, co-authored "An Open Letter to Members of the Polish United Workers' Party." The missive scathingly criticized the communist party for its élitist practices. The party expelled Kuroń and sentenced him to three and a half years in prison. After his release in 1967, authorities again arrested him for organizing student strikes.

Kuroń became a key organizer for the opposition. In his role as a professor, Kuroń mentored the Association of Polish Youth, a communist scouting group, where Michnik was among the scouts. During the 1970s, several members of the group followed his lead and left the party to build a movement of political defiance. In a 1974 article, "Political Opposition in Poland," Kuroń wrote that preserving culture, reading literature, and discussing philosophy amounted to political opposition, because they ignored politics in a system that saturated everything with politics (Stokes 1993, 25). As the Committee for the Workers' Defense (KOR) began to form an alliance with workers in 1976, labor leader Lech Wałęsa and Kuroń, called by *The Times* "the senior organizer and guiding spirit of KOR," embarked on an education campaign in the Gdańsk shipyard (Kaufman 2004). Kuroń supervised the distribution of an underground publication, *The Coastal Worker*, which carried articles to teach laborers how to organize against the regime.

During his work in Gdańsk, in September 1980 Kuroń became an adviser for the founding committee of what that month would become Solidarity. He remained a key thinker and organizer until 1982, when, during the implementation of national martial law, Gen. Wojciech Jaruzelski arrested Kuroń for insubordination. Undeterred, Kuroń organized Solidarity activities from prison and was freed after two and a half years, in August 1984, among the last eleven political prisoners released from detention (ibid.).

Having been a key participant in steering Solidarity's cause, Kuroń participated in the round-table talks as a lead negotiator. He ran for parliament as a member of the Solidarity party in 1989. Despite not being of Jewish descent, his campaign was marred by anti-Semitic advertisements aimed at him. Nevertheless, he won a parliamentary seat and from 1989 to 1990 and 1992 to 1993 served as labor minister. He ran for president in 1995, coming in third behind the winning candidate, Aleksander Kwaśniewski, and the runner-up incumbent, Lech Wałęsa. He remained in parliament until 2001.

AUGUST 18, 1980
POLISH LABOR CRISIS DEEPENS AS WORKERS LIST THEIR DEMANDS
STRIKE COMMITTEE IS FORMED
Panel, Agent for 50,000 in North, Seeks to Tie Pay to Prices—Regime Remains Patient
By JOHN DARNTON
Special to The New York Times

Warsaw, Aug 17 – The labor crisis in Poland deepened today as striking workers in three northern cities formed a special organization to consolidate their demands and strengthen their bargaining position with the Government.

The strike committee, which is said to represent at least 50,000 workers in 21 major factories and enterprises in the Baltic region, promptly drew up a list of 16 demands, including automatic pay increases for all workers to compensate for higher consumer prices, guarantee of the right to strike, vacation pay for all strikers, the abolition of Government censorship, free access for all religious groups to the mass media, and an end to interference in union affairs.

The move appeared to bring the rebellious workers onto a collision course with the beleaguered regime of Edward Gierek, head of the Communist Party. But there were no reports of troops getting ready to storm the huge Lenin shipyards seized by thousands of workers in Gdansk three days ago.

Instead, the Government continued to follow a patient course, apparently hoping the crisis would run out of steam. . . . Poland's socialist system theoretically rules out worker protests, but three other times, in 1956, 1970 and 1976, the workers have rioted, and twice they brought down the Government. . . . Telephone communications with Gdansk have been blocked for two days. Some of what is going on there has been reported by dissident sources who monitor the situation and get the reports to the capital the best they can. Resumption of normal telephone service was a precondition for negotiations cited as the first of 16 points by the new organization, called the Inter-Factory Strike Committee.

Visit to Express Solidarity

Jacek Kuron, a spokesman for the dissident group called the Committee for Social Self-Defense, which released the list of demands, said the overall strike committee was formed yesterday when representatives of the shipyard strikers visited 20 other factories in Gdansk and the neighboring towns of Gdynia and Sopot to express solidarity. Dock workers, bus drivers and others have walked off their jobs, bringing maritime activities to a virtual halt.

A document released by Mr. Kuron today said the strike would continue until "all demands of the striking group have been met." It said that the committee was authorized to negotiate with the state in the name of all the strikers and that it would carry on even when the work action was over, as a sort of embryonic "free trade union."

"This committee creates an absolutely new situation," said Mr. Kuron, interviewed in his apartment here. "It is a step toward a free trade union—a very important step." Dissidents in Poland have long pressed for "free trade unions," with members nominated and elected by the workers, in contrast to the current system of state- and management-sponsored workers' unions.

Call for Release of Prisoners

Among other demands on the committee's list, which were still being debated by the strikers this evening, were guarantees of compliance with constitutionally granted freedom of speech and press and a call for all political prisoners to be released. The dissident group maintains there are six such prisoners.

The document also called for the Government to inform and involve all sections of the public in attempting to resolve the crisis. . . .

Strikers Defy the Government

Gdańsk's populace energetically supported the striking workers despite government efforts to cut off the Lenin shipyard from it and the rest of the world. Taxi drivers made free trips to and from the yard carrying strike supporters; families cooked meals and carried baskets to the strikers. Those involved in the strike adhered to discipline: no drinking of alcohol was allowed, and civilized conduct became the rule, so as not to provoke government reprisals. *Solidarność* (Solidarity), the strike information bulletin, began appearing daily, with a first-day printing of 40,000.

News of the strike that started on August 16 spread quickly throughout Poland. KSS-KOR, the Social Self-Defense Committee, professors, activist intellectuals, and Catholic laity acted as the clearinghouse for information. KSS-KOR became an important link, coordinating the actions of factories and shipyards. As word spread to Gdańsk and the Lenin shipyard that factories and shipyards across the nation had joined in the strike in an effort to include the grievances of all Polish workers, hundreds, perhaps thousands of proposals regarding workers' rights were examined and weighed by the strike leaders. The Lenin shipyard strike committee transformed itself into the Inter-Factory Strike Committee, as the spirit of unity spread throughout Poland. The movement then named itself Solidarność, after its bulletin. Its foundations in KSS-KOR and the Church provided the new organization with a stable base.

The New York Times on August 20 reports that the original demands of the Lenin shipyard strike committee, assembled in the early hours of the action, had expanded to twenty-three (see "Strikers in Poland Defy Gierek Appeal; Crisis at an Impasse"). Most historical accounts still famously cite the so-called 21 Demands of the Gdańsk strikes. These stipulations emphasized workers' rights to independent labor unions and to organize strikes, which provided the foundation for all other petitions, including improved working conditions and political demands, such as freedom of the press. They also included the symbolically important right to erect a public monument to commemorate workers killed by government forces in 1970 during labor unrest.

In a televised speech, communist party leader Edward Gierek appealed to the workers' patriotism, which, *The Times* informs on August 20, elicited jeers from workers listening to the broadcast at shipyards. He appeared to misunderstand the determination of the laborers, as 500 industrial installations in the Gdańsk area had joined the strike, with others likely. In an editorial on August 19, *The Times* stresses, "[I]nsurgent workers are not talking of just food and wage increases. They are also demanding the unthinkable—political rights." It called the workers' list of demands "exhilarating," drawing attention to sought-after guarantees of free expression and abolishing special privileges for party officials ("Demanding the Unthinkable in Poland").

Early in Poland's popular awakening in 1980, *The Times* had not fully appreciated the portentous nature of the alliance of workers and intellectuals and often relied on wire services such as Reuters and United Press International. The newspaper shared the general preoccupations generated by the prevailing cold war perspective, which was accentuated by President Jimmy Carter having two Polish Americans, Secretary of State Edmund Muskie and national security adviser Zbigniew Brzezinski, high up in his administration. As with much of the media, the newspaper had episodically carried news of various strikes in 1980, but was slow to recognize the significance of the massive popular upheaval that began with hand-painted posters on August 14. Not until August 18 did the first dispatch from Poland appear in the pages of

The Times about the momentous strike that began in Gdańsk's Lenin shipyard and would subsequently reverberate across the region. Once aware that an unprecedented mobilization was under way for the first time in the Soviet bloc, *The Times* assigned John Darnton, a first-rate correspondent, to Warsaw. In 1982, Darnton would receive the Pulitzer Prize for his reporting from Poland. Many of his stories had to be smuggled from the country.

KEY PLAYER IN POLAND
Anna Walentynowicz (1929–)

World War II left Anna Walentynowicz an orphan as a teenager. Both her parents were killed, and her brother was sent to a Soviet labor camp. In 1950, she became a welder in the Lenin shipyard in Gdańsk and later a crane operator. By the 1960s, some 15,000 individuals were employed at the Lenin shipyard. An exemplary worker, Walentynowicz won medals, attended international youth meetings, and accepted at face value the pledges of communist leaders to build a better society. She became disillusioned with the Polish communist party, however, when she saw it dismiss and deny her fellow workers' concerns and grievances.

In December 1970, the dissatisfaction of workers reached a breaking point as prices rose without corresponding pay raises; laborers were already spending half their wages on food. Walentynowicz emerged among the leaders of a three-day struggle that resulted in forty-four deaths of unarmed laborers at the hands of government forces. The following year saw new strikes erupt along the Baltic coast; again, Walentynowicz was a leader. She became part of a small group that in April 1978, along with Lech Wałęsa and others, formed the Baltic Committee for Free and Independent Trade Unions, created in Gdańsk and linked to *The Coastal Worker* publication, which in 1979 surreptitiously published a Charter of Workers' Rights.

In August 1980, officials at the Lenin Shipyard fired Walentynowicz, who had worked there for thirty years and would have qualified in several months for her pension. She was dismissed for collecting burned-down candle stubs from a cemetery to make recycled tapers in order to commemorate the protesting workers who had been killed by army divisions in 1970; the police accused her of stealing. A keenly determined advocate for the workers, and a widow with a grandmotherly demeanor, Walentynowicz was admired and trusted. She was also a crucial connection to the movement for free labor unions that had been slowly building in Poland throughout the 1970s.

Walentynowicz read the underground publications in circulation and went to lectures of the Flying University. Within days of her sacking, a group of shipyard workers had printed thousands of leaflets demanding her reinstatement, asking for pay raises, and calling for a monument to the laborers who had been killed in 1970. Before daylight on August 14 at the Lenin shipyard, the free trade union committee members, of which Walentynowicz was a co-founder and spokesperson, smuggled in leaflets demanding her reinstatement and a raise in pay. The arrest of Walentynowicz was the spark that ignited the strike at the shipyard, and the strikes throughout Poland that followed, which led to the creation of Solidarity.

Polish authorities ultimately allowed Walentynowicz to return to work. By 1989 the Polish workers had won the right to form independent unions and had negotiated the elections that brought about Poland's path-finding transition to democracy. In 2005, she was awarded the Truman-Reagan Medal of Freedom, which she accepted on behalf of Solidarity from the Victims of Communism Memorial Foundation in Washington, D.C.

Lech Wałęsa, leader of striking shipyard and factory workers, addresses laborers on August 26, 1980, after the signing of the preliminary contract that would lead to the Gdańsk accord. The agreement recognized the labor union Solidarity, the first "independent, self-governing union" in a communist country, and confirmed a right to strike.

Source: AP Images

AUGUST 20, 1980
STRIKERS IN POLAND DEFY GIEREK APPEAL; CRISIS AT AN IMPASSE
MORE PLANTS JOIN STOPPAGE
Government Avoids Negotiations—Delegates of Shut Factories Meet at Gdansk Shipyard
By JOHN DARTON
Special to The New York Times

GDANSK, Poland, Aug. 19 – Defying an appeal by Edward Gierk, the Communist Party leader, to abandon their protest, tens of thousands of striking workers continued to occupy factories in northern Poland today.

The strikes that have plunged the country into its greatest turmoil in a decade spread further. Members of the strike committee, set up two days ago, said 174 plants were now closed in the tri-city area of Gdansk, Gdynia and Sopot. Yesterday there were 130 and the day before 21.

Strikes Extend to Szczecin

The strikes in the north have spread to Szczecin, near East Germany, and Elbiag, 30 miles from the Soviet Union. There were unconfirmed reports of unrest in the Silesian coal-mining region, in the south. . . . Gdansk was virtually paralyzed by the stoppage. There were no taxis or buses, but shops were open.

Throughout the day factory delegates continued to arrive at the shipyards in vans flying the red-and-white Polish flag. As they strode into a grimy, red-brick conference building serving as strike headquarters, they were given a rousing welcome by delegates already there, seated at long tables with makeshift placards identifying their plants.

Last evening a group of five from an electrical factory walked in. A woman carrying a bouquet of carnations approached the microphone somewhat timidly. After she had pledged the solidarity of her co-workers, the entire hall rose for a solemn signing of the national anthem.

Mr. Gierek's television speech, in which he appealed to the workers' patriotism and promised pay increases and more meat, but warned that anarchy would not be tolerated, prompted jeers when it was broadcast over the public-address system at the shipyards. When it was rebroadcast today, it was ignored by hundreds of strikers. . . . "He said nothing new at all," a delegate from the Gdynia dockworkers said. "He talked to us as if we were children."

List of Demands Up to 23 Points

The strike committee, in a statement, called on the authorities to meet their demands, which have grown to 23, and to start talks. As a precondition, they insisted that telephone communications, which have been cut, be restored. . . . Rumors spread that the Government might be moving to break the strikes with force. Jacek Kuron, spokesman for a dissident group in close contact with the strikers, said yesterday that militia troops have been observed moving toward Gdansk. . . .

Gierek's First Direct Intervention

Mr. Gierek, in his speech, appeared to assume some personal blame for the crisis when he referred to "mistakes in economic policy." The 25-minute address was the party leader's first direct intervention in the six weeks of growing labor unrest. By so doing he placed his prestige, and his political future, on the line.

Mr. Gierek rose to power in 1970 when similar protests, centered on the Gdansk shipyards, brought down his predecessor, Wladyslaw Gomulka. The precipitating cause then was that troops opened fire on strikers, killing scores of them.

The lesson of the public outrage that followed has not been forgotten. So far at least, the authorities have gone out of their way to play down the threat of force.

In Gdansk, where every enterprise in sight, even a metal junkyard, flies the defiant Polish flag and where blue-clad workers sit atop gates like watch-tower guards, the few police officers to be seen downtown are mostly women.

Inside the shipyards, there was no sense of an imminent showdown. Organizers worried about collecting money for food, distributing free milk and getting their views across to the public outside.

The proceedings inside the meeting hall were broadcast throughout the yard. . . . Lech Walesa, a longtime shipyard worker and political activist with a gravelly voice, was presiding. He was dismissed after riots in 1976, but slipped into the shipyard to join the latest protest and ended up at its head.

One issue that is emerging as a potential stumbling block is that of independent labor unions. Mr. Wojciechowski, the press spokesman, said the Government considered this a political demand and one that could not be discussed. The members of the strike committee do not represent the workers, he said.

Call for Real Unions Applauded

Those inside the meeting hall indicated another view. They applauded Florian Wisniewski, a strike leader, when he said: . . . "Until we have real trade unions, our only weapon is strikes. We want to restart work as soon as possible, but we must be the real masters of our factories."

Some of the demands are economic, including calls for more meat, wage increases. . . . but other demands reach deep in politics, such as the freeing of political prisoners and the opening of the press to church views.

Some see in this the hand of dissidents, in particular the Committee of Social Self-Defense, which has been active here in the last four years.

Solidarity's Inaugural Convention

In eighteen days, Poland's workers had reached a milestone. On August 30, they signed the Gdańsk accord, an historic agreement with the government realizing their demands. The government's negotiators agreed to recognize Solidarity's description of itself as an "independent, self-governing union," with a right to strike. The Inter-Factory Strike Committee (MKS) had refused to compromise on political rights and freedoms and the right of workers to organize. The shipyard and factory workers had also fought for the university professors and writers in having demanded the unconditional release of all political prisoners, that is, "dissident" activist intellectuals. In addition to meeting the strikers' demands, the Gdańsk agreement also drew worldwide attention to the excesses of communist rule and raised the profile of the fledgling Solidarity movement. Two weeks after the Gdańsk accord, Solidarity represented 3 million workers.

The changes agreed upon in the Gdańsk accord were slow in coming. On September 22, Solidarity was formally founded as, three weeks after the accord, delegates from thirty-eight regional labor unions held their first national meeting in Gdańsk and formed a new union—NSZZ "Solidarność" (Independent Self-Governing Union Solidarity). The government postponed Solidarity's official registration until November 1980, three months later than stipulated. Despite the delay, by late autumn 1980 Solidarity had registered 10 million members—80 percent of the Polish workforce—and established Student Solidarity and Peasant Solidarity. Prisoners also established counterparts. Some 3.5 million private farmers wanted their own union, Rural Solidarity. The Solidarity union chose as its logo thick red jumbled letters resembling demonstrators, carrying the Polish flag. The designer later said that the intention was for the marchers to appear to be supporting each other (Craig 1990, 226–227).

The Polish government found itself at odds with Marxist theory in conceding on representation for workers, a function typically claimed by the party and supposedly historically determined. Solidarity made known its view of history in an April 1981 program: "History has taught us that there is no bread without freedom. What we had in mind was not only bread, butter and sausages, but also justice, democracy, truth, legality, human dignity, freedom of convictions, and the repair of the republic." Solidarity sought to "repair" Poland, not to overthrow the communist system.

An episode in March 1981 had brought a moment of decision to Solidarity, which had defined itself as a nonviolent social movement. On March 19, *New York Times* correspondent John Darnton, relying on Solidarity news reports, sent a dispatch about riot police in the central Polish city of Bydgoszcz breaking up a demonstration by farmers seeking to form Rural Solidarity ("Polish Police Break up Farmer Protest"). While evicting the peaceful protesters from a government assembly hall, the security forces beat some people so severely that they needed hospitalization. Darnton reports this as "the first use of violence in eight and a half months of labor unrest." In several cities, sympathy two-hour strikes were called. The government seemed more concerned with appeasing the Soviet Union than in placating a provoked Polish population, *The Times* editorializes on March 25, in "Beyond Bydgoszcz":

> How can [Warsaw] curb a movement that enjoys such broad support, not only among ordinary workers and farmers but also in the military, the Roman Catholic Church and

the Communist Party itself? . . . [The government] can easily lose [its] balance and trigger a Soviet occupation or a violent revolution, or both. . . . It only looks as if the fate of the Soviet empire and the future tone of East-West relations depend on the actions of a few police thugs in the Polish provinces. In reality, fateful consequences for the diplomacies and economies of many nations are riding on one of this century's most remarkable mass movements—a workers' movement, a national liberation movement and a nonviolent witness rolled into one.

On March 28 in *The Times*, Darnton reports that the previous day "millions of Polish workers had conducted a four-hour nationwide strike, the largest organized protest since communism came to Poland 36 years ago." Originating from anger over police violence in Bydgoszcz, the time-restricted strike began and ended "exactly on schedule and without reports of major incidents" ("Millions in Poland Go on 4-Hour Strike to Protest Violence").

Within Solidarity, the March 27 four-hour strike was deemed a "warning"—if the demands were not met for punishment of the police officers involved in the events in Bydgoszcz, a nationwide general strike would take place on March 31. A general strike is a widespread cessation of labor in an effort to bring all economic activity to a total standstill. One of the most potent noncooperation methods in the repertoire of nonviolent resistance, the general strike must be called judiciously because it loses its effectiveness if overused. Intricate preparations began throughout Poland for the anticipated general strike, as food was hauled by the truckload, sleeping bags stowed, and flashlights stored. Solidarity now had 40,000 regular staff, who were seconded, or transferred, from their workplaces—as was Wałęsa—or paid directly from Solidarity dues of 1 percent of pay.

The possibility of Soviet intervention was openly voiced. The Reagan White House cautioned against Soviet incursion. Appealing for calm, Polish communist leader Gen. Wojciech Jaruzelski turned to Stefan Cardinal Wyszynski; both men called for restraint. Meanwhile, fearing civil war and Solidarity's collapse, Wałęsa, along with the union's coordinating committee and advisers, had secretly begun negotiating with the government. Appearing on television, Wałęsa announced that the general strike would not go forward. "The strike did not take place because Wałęsa's advisers persuaded him not to implement the threat," explains Janusz Ziółkowski in "The Roots, Branches and Blossoms of Solidarność." "There was real fear of Soviet intervention, . . . and still hope that the party itself might reform and adapt itself to the new realities." Yet other union leaders felt betrayed by the decision; some worried that Wałęsa was in league with the regime.

Bydgoszcz was a watershed. The beatings of Rural Solidarity members caused strains in the union's efforts at being unified and democratic. Many members became confused. Workers began striking almost continuously, against advice from Solidarity's leadership and in defiance of Wałęsa's judgment. Some members acted as if the communist party had vanished and were intent on settling scores, while Wałęsa rejected revenge as foolish. Many wanted to purge inept or deceitful factory supervisors and corrupt government officers, yet large numbers of officials were already losing their posts, with dismissals, disclosures, and resignations.

Nicknamed "The Fireman," Wałęsa rushed about quelling combustions across Poland. The intermittent strikes lacked strategy, and the workers' inclination for sporadic strikes perplexed Wałęsa, who believed the union had made its point and now should seek sustained and constructive dialogue. In the course of events, some members began to view the union leader as expendable. Criticism of him weakened Solidarity internally. Wałęsa stood his ground, adhering to the Gandhian perspective that the struggle should be against the antagonism and not the antagonist. He and the essentially moderate leadership of Solidarity wanted to reassure an anxious government that Solidarity had no plans to take power and would not endanger the Warsaw Pact. In talks with the government, union representatives repeatedly maintained that they did not want to dismantle the state, but instead sought to secure more freedoms and better living conditions. Much as had the Roman Catholic Church achieved space for its disagreements with the party-state, Solidarity's national leadership saw itself as a loyal opposition whose purpose was to protect the workers' interests, something best done in a joint enterprise with the government.

As a formality, Solidarity had recognized the "leading role of the party," but the growing number of unsystematic strikes did not persuade the regime that Solidarity sought only altered socioeconomic structures, rather than replacing the individuals upholding the structures. Solidarity's emergence had been so rapid that the populace had not become adept in managing its new freedoms. Workers wanted swift change. Solidarity often extended its goals and escalated demands from one month to the next, instead of aiming to win small conflicts that would build government confidence in their interactions. Solidarity would never again achieve the popular cohesion, mass organization, and discipline that it possessed on the eve of the suspended general strike.

Despite the dissonance and chaos that followed events in Bydgoszcz, Solidarity held its first national convention from September 5 to September 10, and September 16 to October 7, 1981. Wałęsa was elected its official leader. On September 6 at a clubhouse of a sports stadium, 900 delegates gathered. As they heard reports on the growing organization of free trade unions, differences on preferred strategies emerged. Some championed a centralized approach as offering strength in standing up to the regime; others thought decentralized grass-roots entities would be more resilient against government intrusion. The delegates decided to establish a national consultative and advisory group, with all the country's new unions similarly adopting the same approach. They would register with the government as a single entity.

On September 10, *The Times* reports that the convention had voted to send a message to workers throughout the Soviet bloc, declaring support for "those of you who have decided to enter the difficult road of struggle for free and independent unions" ("Polish Party Assails Appeal by Union"). Darnton notes in *The Times* on September 11 that the question of self-management was raised, with workers wanting to choose their own directors and the delegates wanting a national referendum on the subject ("Poland's Union Meeting Asks Free Elections to Parliament"). Summing up, Darnton writes on September 18 that this was the first public gathering of an organization free of party control in post–World War II Poland.

As Solidarity's standing grew, it rendered obsolete the need for KSS-KOR, the Committee for the Workers' Defense, the group instrumental in the formation of Solidarity and its subsequent successes. KSS-KOR members started to believe that its goal of protecting workers within the larger context of political rights might better be realized under the unified leadership of Solidarity. Leading KSS-KOR members assumed positions with Solidarity. On September 18, 1981, KSS-KOR formally disbanded. During the ten-year period prior to the 1980 historic strike, it had forged a strong partnership between the church and activist intellectuals and overcome the problem of workers and intellectuals separately fighting for rights and freedoms that both needed equally, which had doomed workers' demonstrations in 1968 and 1970. KSS-KOR had created a general commitment to fighting with nonviolent civil resistance and had strenuously worked on behalf of the Polish worker for an enduring civil society.

Edward Gierek was retired from office as the communist party leader in September 1981 and died soon after. The regime, led by his successor, Stanisław Kania, persisted in breaking its promises. Workers again began to exhibit their dissatisfaction with random strikes as coordination broke down within Solidarity.

SEPTEMBER 6, 1981
POLISH UNION OPENS CONVENTION

By JOHN DARNTON
Special to The New York Times

GDANSK, Poland, Sept. 5 – Lech Walesa, the union leader, today opened the first national convention of Solidarity with a plea to the independent labor organization to remain united and strong so that Poland will be "the way we have dreamed."

Addressing 900 delegates in a sports stadium converted with banners and ballots into a cavernous convention hall, he said the union's struggle was far from over.

If the union is to win, he said, it must retain its spirit of unity as it grapples with a difficult issue—how far to cooperate with the Communist authorities, which allowed it to come into being in August 1980 but have sought to circumscribe its activities ever since.

"If we do not stay together, we will not win," Mr. Walesa said. "If we remain strong as we did in August, we will win and make Poland the way we have dreamed because there can be no other Poland."

Delegates Leap to Their Feet

The delegates jumped to their feet in applause. It was a sign that Mr. Walesa is likely to be confirmed in office in elections scheduled for a second phase of the convention later this month.

The significance of today's proceedings was not in any decisions it made—it was largely a procedural session devoted to committee selections—but in the simple fact that it occurred. It was the first public gathering in Poland since World War II of an organization that was not under party control.

As if to underline the strained relations with the authorities, the session was not covered by state-run radio or television because its reporters were refused accreditation by the union in a dispute that has defied resolution.

The union wanted either continuous live transmission of the convention proceedings or comprehensive daily programs over which it would have some editorial control. One of its proposals called for twinned television coverage—by government journalists and by union-selected journalists, with viewers given a choice of programs.

Negotiations over the convention coverage, part of the broader issue of union access to the government-controlled news outlets, broke down last week.

Strong Ovation for Walesa

The union's position stems from suspicion that the official outlets manipulate news reports. Mr. Walesa drew the strongest ovation today when he said that the convention would not be carried on television "as long as we have no possibility of authorizing, of checking what they will say about us."

Union leaders say privately that the blackout may also be an effective instrument to mobilize public support for a radio and television strike if such action were to be decided.

"We are now at a better starting point for a strike throughout radio and television," Bogdan Lis, deputy union chairman, said in an interview. "If it happens now after the convention, people will support us more easily."

An Anthem and Church Hymn Sung

The session began when Mr. Walesa strode to the podium, under an emblem of the Polish eagle and a crucifix, to lead the unionists in a rendition of the national anthem, followed by a church hymn. He told the crowd what it wanted to hear—that the union, born after a three-week sit-in at the Lenin shipyard here—would not be split or destroyed.

"We deliberate in a spirit of truth as free and reasonable men," he said, recalling that union and government representatives "talked as Poles to Poles" when they reached an accord a year ago.

"Today, after these 12 months of tension and conflict, we want to know whether this will be the way we are going, whether the moment has come to realize that the path we entered in August cannot be reversed," he added.

The session was an odd hybrid. Its proceedings—with elections of presidiums, reading of reports and voting by raising delegate cards—seemed to spring straight out of Communist-style gatherings. But the trappings had the flavor of a Western convention, with an electronic scoreboard for vote tallies, banners emblazoned with slogans hanging from the rafters, and delegates wearing blue-rimmed beach hats with the Solidarity logo on the crest.

In addition to selecting a new leadership, the convention will also consider modifications of union statutes and programs for economic changes in Poland.

Government Minister Speaks

Among the speakers was Stanislaw Ciosek, Minister for Labor Relations, who read a message asking for "creative cooperation" with the union and stressing the need for social peace.

The union approached the convention in something of a downbeat mood, realizing that even revolution takes time. The mood was captured in an editorial in the first issue of Free Voice, the convention newspaper, which said:

"The hopes that we all attached a year ago to the creation of Solidarity have been shaken. What in August appeared to be the crowning of the great workers' protest was soon shown to be just the beginning of the road." The congress opened amid a perception among Poles that the union has yet to come up with a comprehensive program of its own to overcome the nation's economic difficulties. There is also a sense among union members that, for all the drama of the confrontations over the past year, little has actually been won. Many of the major issues, from access to news outlets to a new trade union law, are still pending.

As one union leader here put it before the convention opened, "We have come a long way, but I am not sure we have really arrived anywhere."

Rights Curtailed, Solidarity Urges a Strike

Stanisław Kania succeeded Edward Gierek as Poland's communist party leader in autumn 1981, and Kania in turn was replaced by Gen. Wojciech Jaruzelski, who was also prime minister and chief of the armed forces. It was a simple matter for the new state-party leadership stealthily to undermine Lech Wałęsa, the leader of the 10-million-strong Solidarity union, and to take advantage of the union's internal uncertainties and inconsistencies.

On December 12, 1981, the Jaruzelski government's despised and feared riot police descended on Solidarity buildings, taking possession of property, arresting members, and pronouncing the union illegal. Declaring a state of war, or *stan wojenny,* on December 13 Jaruzelski officially imposed martial law. The regime jailed Solidarity's leadership and thousands of its sympathizers and designated the union as illegal. *The New York Times* reports on December 14 that Jaruzelski had justified such strict measures as necessary to spare the country catastrophe and civil war. *Times* correspondent John Darnton writes that Solidarity leaders in Gdańsk meeting hours before had proposed a national referendum on the formation of a non-communist government. In addition, a government spokesperson had stated at a news conference that the Soviet Union was aware of the Jaruzelski regime's intention to undertake military measures.

That same day in "Neither Polish Nor a Solution," *The Times* editorializes against Jaruzelski's bellicose action:

> [T]he Polish Government is now determined to decapitate the union opposition, to move against strikers with force and to summon the Polish army and, if it fails them, the Soviet army to put down insurrection. . . . This is no "Polish" solution. For months, the Soviet Union has demanded a crackdown, made to look exclusively Polish. But it could occur only with Soviet help. It requires the threat of Soviet intervention if Polish soldiers side with Solidarity. Only the futility of resisting Soviet forces may prevent massive civil disobedience.

The Times was correctly concerned that Polish armed forces might sympathize with Solidarity. Among the properties of nonviolent resistance is its ability to split the ranks of the target group, such that some of the regime's soldiers, security, and police may become persuaded by the underlying grievances of the nonviolent protagonists. In contrast, violent struggle tends to consolidate the target group against any challenge.

In a December 15 article without a byline, *The Times* notes that a day after imposition of martial law, the clandestine information networks of Solidarity were reporting "strikes and worker resistance in factories, shipyards, steel mills, coal mines, and even academic institutions in Warsaw and other major cities and regions" ("Widespread Strikes Reported in Defiance of Polish Regime; U.S. Postpones All Pending Aid"). With commercial communications lines cut, foreign newspaper reporters had to rely on Solidarity's news. Arguably Poland's finest journalists were preparing the union's news accounts, until they themselves were arrested.

Stirred by reports that Wałęsa, who was being held incommunicado, had refused to divulge any information to his captors, the Poles once again united. Solidarity called for a nationwide general strike to protest the militarization of Poland. According to the December 15 *Times* article, Solidarity issued a declaration from Gdańsk over five signatures: "Our answer to violence is a general strike. We were forced and provoked to stage it because we were deprived of our rights and our leaders have been arrested."

Wałęsa's use of the potent nonviolent method of fasting became a new symbol of resistance. Groups named Without Violence emerged, and clandestine translations of works by the Boston scholar Gene Sharp appeared. Wałęsa smuggled out an appeal reiterated by the rest of Solidarity's leadership that all Polish citizens should resist the regime nonviolently. He often invoked Gandhi's example. Adam Michnik, one of the key activist intellectuals and later editor of Poland's second-largest daily newspaper, *Gazeta Wyborcza* (Election Gazette), would write in *Letters from Prison and Other Essays* (1985) that the ethics of Solidarity, with its consistent rejection of the use of force, "has a lot in common with the idea of nonviolence as espoused by Gandhi and Martin Luther King, Jr." (pp. 88–89).

Flawed, alive, but underground, Solidarity matured during this period, as its various tiers and circles sought ingenious ways to defy communist rule and express discontent with their supposed leaders. Citizens refused to believe news from official outlets. Others resorted to the drastic nonviolent tactic of emigrating from Poland. By mid-1982, some 10,000 Solidarity members were interned in a type of preventive detention, with more than 3,000 locked up for "political crimes."

KEY PLAYER IN POLAND
Wojciech Jaruzelski (1923–)

Born into an aristocratic family in Poland, Wojciech Jaruzelski was an early victim of communist brutality. As a teenager, he and his family were caught in the snares of the invading Red Army and were deported to the Soviet Union in 1940. Years of forced labor in Kazakhstan coal mines resulted in permanent injuries to his back and eyes. From an early age, to protect his eyes, he began wearing the dark sunglasses that would become his trademark.

By 1943, with the Red Army fighting in Europe against Germany, Jaruzelski joined Polish army units being formed under Soviet command. He made his way into a position of influence and quickly earned a reputation as a capable soldier known for his "ruthless suppression" of the Polish wartime resistance movement (Repa 2001). By the end of World War II, Jaruzelski had attained the rank of lieutenant.

Throughout the 1960s, Jaruzelski continued his rise to prominence in his native land. He was appointed chief political officer of the Polish armed forces in 1960 and became chief of staff in 1964. He also rose in rank in the Polish United Workers' Party, the Polish communist party. In 1964, Jaruzelski was elected to the party's Central Committee and in 1968 was appointed minister of defense. In 1971, he became a member of the Politburo.

In a bloody campaign for which he would later stand trial, Jaruzelski and other communist leaders approved the suppression of workers' protests in coastal cities, culminating in December 1970 in the shooting deaths of forty-four striking shipyard laborers in Gdańsk. In the early 1980s, the Solidarity Union gained in strength and in numbers, becoming ever more coherent in pressing for an independent trade union and the right to strike. In December 1981, Jaruzelski, now premier and first secretary of the party, imposed martial law. The regime imprisoned Solidarity's leadership and thousands of sympathizers and declared the union illegal.

Although martial law paralyzed Poland, it did not stop Solidarity. In 1983, Jaruzelski ended some aspects of military rule and offered partial amnesty for most political prisoners. After seven years as a high-ranking member in an increasingly oppressive regime ostensibly attempting to reform communism in Poland, Jaruzelski freed the leaders of Solidarity in 1988 and approved the start of round-table negotiations between the government and the union. He agreed to the major reforms that resulted, culminating in free elections for a restructured parliament. He resigned from the Polish United Workers' Party after the parliament elected him president in 1989, in an understanding arrived at in the negotiations, after which he was succeeded by Solidarity leader Lech Wałęsa.

Jaruzelski continued to defend his record on the 1970 killings and argued that he was not responsible. He was defense minister at the time, but claims that the prime minister bypassed him in giving the orders directing troops and tanks to fire on the strikers. In May 2001, Jaruzelski appeared in court, having been charged with ordering the 1970 shipyard shootings. He also went on trial for ordering martial law in 1981. The general defended his actions, telling *The New York Times*, "I am entirely convinced that if not for martial law there would have been a war" (Green 2001). Often claiming that he had acted out of patriotism, Jaruzelski suggested to *The Times* that allowing Solidarity's strikes to continue would have led to a Soviet invasion resembling that which crushed the revolt in Budapest in 1956. The soldiers involved were acquitted of war crimes in 2006. Jaruzelski's trials for ordering the December 1970 shootings and imposing martial law in 1981 remain pending.

DECEMBER 14, 1981
POLAND RESTRICTS CIVIL AND UNION RIGHTS; SOLIDARITY ACTIVISTS URGE GENERAL STRIKE
WALESA NEGOTIATES
New Army Council Bans Rallies and Sets Wide Ground for Arrests
By JOHN DARNTON
Special to The New York Times

WARSAW, Dec. 13 – Poland's new military leaders issued a decree of martial law today, drastically restricting civil rights and suspending the operations of the Solidarity union. The union's activists reacted with an appeal for an immediate general strike to protest.

A proclamation broadcast by the newly formed Martial Council for National Redemption, now the top authority in the country, also banned all kinds of public gatherings and demonstrations and ordered the internment of citizens whose loyalty to the state was under "justified suspicion."

The military rule was announced in a dramatic broadcast at dawn by Gen. Wojciech Witold Jaruzelski, the Prime Minister and Communist Party leader, who said a strict regime was necessary to save Poland from catastrophe and civil war. Hours before, Solidarity leaders meeting in Gdansk had proposed holding a national referendum on forming a non-Communist government.

No Reports of Violence

Following a provision in the constitution, General Jaruzelski, declared a "state of war," equivalent to a state of emergency in other countries.

There were no immediate reports of any violence, but opposition to the military move seemed in the offing. Union activists, in dozens of leaflets being circulated in the streets, called for an immediate general strike.

Many Solidarity activists were in detention following coordinated police raids across the country after midnight last night. So were several former leaders of Poland's Communist Party.

Among the detained were some of the top leaders and advisers of the Solidarity union who had assembled in Gdansk to work out strategy in the latest confrontation with the Government.

Walesa Flown to Warsaw

Lech Walesa, Solidarity's chairman, who became an international figure by his role in the workers' uprising of last summer, was meeting with Government officials at a site outside Warsaw today, Jerzy Urban, a Government spokesman, said at a news conference.

Mr. Walesa was flown to Warsaw in a Government plane at 4 A.M. to begin talks with Stanislaw Ciosek, the Minister of Trade Union Affairs, according to the Interpress information agency. Mr. Urban said that Mr. Walesa had not been detained at any point.

Mr. Urban also stressed that Solidarity had been suspended, not banned altogether. He said the Soviet Union was aware that Poland was about to mount a military operation, stating, "It's hard to imagine that Poland's allies were not informed of such an action."

General Jaruzelski also announced that several former officials had been "interned" because they were "responsible personally for pushing the country into crisis" by their policies in the 1970's and had been guilty of "abusing their posts for personal profit." He specifically mentioned Edward Gierek, the party chief who was ousted in September 1980, Piotr Jaroszewicz, his longtime Prime Minister, Zladislaw Grudzien, a former party leader from Katowice, and Jerzy Lukaszewicz, a former Politburo member in charge of party propaganda.

Corruption Alienated Public

The abuse of power and corruption were among the reasons for the loss of public confidence in the party and Government. The announcement of the internment was seen as an attempt to gain some support for the military takeover.

The Government moves came hours after the Solidarity leaders meeting in Gdansk had proposed a nationwide referendum on setting up a non-Communist Government and defining Poland's military relationship with the Soviet Union.

The union leaders, assembled at the Lenin Shipyard where their independent labor movement was born 16 months ago, said that, unless the Government met a series of demands, the union would conduct its own national referendum asking four questions:

Are you for a vote of confidence in General Jaruzelski? Are you for the establishment of a temporary government and free elections? Are you for providing military guarantees to the Soviet Union in Poland? Can the Polish Communist Party be the instrument of such guarantees in the name of the whole society?

Reason for Threat Is Unknown

Political sources pointed out yesterday that the mere threat by Solidarity to hold such a referendum on its own could be unacceptable to the Government. Why it made the threat is unknown, but in recent weeks there have been signs that Mr. Walesa's control over the union membership has been weakened. There had been more frequent challenges to his leadership from more militant factions within the union.

Within hours after the meeting in Gdansk, Polish troops surrounded the union's headquarters in Warsaw. Mr. Urban, the Government spokesman, said the events of the last 24 hours had prompted scattered transport strikes around the country but that the bus and trolley workers had returned to their jobs everywhere except in Cracow.

The situation around the country, where most internal and external communications have been severed, remained unclear. The capital was calm and the downtown area was nearly deserted by late this afternoon, as thousands of motorists left, passing through military checkpoints and past armored cars parked at strategic intersections. Soldiers patroling the streets and bridges in pairs had bayonets fixed on their rifles.

Poster Calls for a Strike

A hand-scrawled red and white poster reading "Strajk Generalny," or "General Strike," with today's date, hung on the front door of the five-story former school building that houses the Solidarity chapter in Warsaw. The headquarters was stormed early this morning by policemen who seized 32 people inside, according to a Solidarity worker.

The police returned later today, again in force, wearing plastic riot helmets and carrying riot sticks, to raid the headquarters again. This time they took files, documents, cash and equipment, while an angry crowd of several hundred looked on, jeering and yelling "Gestapo!" The police at one point used a fire hose to disperse the crowd, which quickly gathered again as soon as the policemen had departed.

The measures announced in the proclamation from the new Martial Council were sweeping. They were read out over television by the usual announcers newly dressed for the occasion in military uniforms. The measures grew in number as the day wore on. By nightfall, there were 61 separate points.

All Strikes and Protests Banned

All strikes, demonstrations, protests, meetings and public gatherings other than those for religious services were banned. A curfew from 10 P.M. to 6 A.M. was imposed. The country's airspace was closed to international and domestic commercial flights, the borders were virtually sealed and Poles were told not to travel to border regions.

Western diplomats and foreign correspondents were informed that they could not travel outside Warsaw. The sale of gasoline to private motorists was prohibited. Dissemination of any publications without prior approval of the authorities was made a punishable offense.

Censorship of mail and other communications was legalized. The proclamation also granted the authorities the right to make preventive detention arrests of anyone whose behavior aroused "suspicions that being free, they will conduct activity threatening the security of the state."

Poles were ordered to carry their identification cards at all times.

Regional Broadcasts Suspended

In a move to control the vital centers of mass communication, all regional radio and television broadcasts were suspended, so that only programs originating from Warsaw could be aired. Over half a dozen public service sectors, ranging from transport to post offices and electric power stations, were placed directly under the military, apparently rendering the employees subject to a military-type command structure. Orders from superiors are equivalent to "military orders during a war," the radio said.

A tape of General Jaruzelski's broadcast was played over television throughout the day. He sat stiffly, staring into the camera without his customary dark glasses, next to emblems of patriotism, a shield depicting the Polish eagle and the flag. He declared that what had been done was for the good of the nation.

Poland had reached "the limits of mental endurance," he said. Catastrophe was "not days, but hours" away. History would judge the momentous steps being undertaken to save the country from disintegration at the hands of extremists and "adventurists." Not to have acted would have been "a crime," he declared.

The general insisted that the military's assumption of power was not a military coup or installation of a military dictatorship. The constitutional organs of state will continue to function, he said, and the Martial Council "will be dissolved once the rule of law is reestablished."

'Mortal Danger' to Nation Cited

The military council's proclamation, plastered along with movie posters on walls and concrete pillars lining downtown shopping arcades, insisted that the move had been undertaken to save the country from "mortal danger."

"Forces hostile to socialism" have brought the society to the brink of civil war and "anarchy, lawlessness and chaos," it said. A reactionary coup was openly being prepared, it asserted.

Bystanders who stopped beside dirty snowbanks to read such statements were sometimes handed leaflets by union men. "The attack on our union is aimed at its liquidation," said one, signed by the Solidarity chapter at the Ursus tractor factory. "Do not let them smash our Solidarity."

Public reaction, except among the crowd drawn to the union headquarters, was difficult to gauge. Many people seemed to fear that the move by the Government was a prelude to bloodshed. Monday, when the factories open, will be critical, many said.

'There's Real Trouble Ahead'

"It won't stop here," said a grandmother pulling a young child on a sled. "Solidarity won't accept it and so there's real trouble ahead. For the first time, I'm afraid."

The union had laid plans for a huge demonstration at Victory Square in downtown Warsaw on Thursday. It was to be part of a "national day of protest" that the Warsaw chapter had called out of anger over what it denounced as the Government's confrontational policies. The protest was officially endorsed by the entire union leadership.

Travelers from Gdansk said that several union leaders had been taken by the police from their hotel rooms after the session in the Lenin Shipyard ended shortly after midnight. The only inkling that something was wrong was a statement by Mr. Walesa that communications were down. The arrests started about two hours later.

Troops Stationed on Roofs

Troops were stationed on the roofs of buildings surrounding the Hotel Monopol as union members were taken away in a bus....

The travelers said they had passed a column of about 55 modern T-72 tanks crossing the road at Paslek, about 40 miles south of Gdansk. The tanks were fully equipped for battle, with spare gasoline tanks at the backs.

Rites for Father Jerzy, Priest and 'Martyr'

On November 15, 1982, when Solidarity leader Lech Wałęsa was released after eleven months in prison, Polish party-state officials asserted that he had been forgotten and that his movement was terminated. The enormous crowds that welcomed him home told another story. While incarcerated, Wałęsa had smuggled messages to his colleagues. Upon release, he found that Solidarity had survived underground and that opposition to communist rule had deepened. In December, the government partially lifted martial law, although 5,000 people remained in prison, and laborers could not change jobs without permission. In January 1983, the government moved to create officially registered worker unions and to ban strikes. Productivity continued to drop. The communist party lost approximately half of its 3 million members.

Solidarity's efforts would be invigorated with Pope John Paul II's second visit, June 16–23, 1983. Meeting with Wałęsa, the pope emphasized the Poles' adoption of nonviolent strategies: "If the world grasps what you are trying to do, if it sees in your movement hope and a way to resolve conflicts, it is precisely because you have renounced violence." Although clandestine newspapers, periodicals, books, journals, and factory rags were being disseminated on a scale unlike anywhere else in the Soviet bloc, within Solidarity many were disillusioned by their seeming inability to translate moral authority into political action.

On July 22, 1983, Jaruzelski lifted more elements of martial law. The government offered partial amnesty to 650 political prisoners, that is, all but 60 detainees. Through amnesty, a state restores those who may have been guilty of an offense against it to the status of innocence. More than a pardon, amnesty obliterates the legal remembrance of an offense. In Poland, however, the right of assembly continued to be restricted. Solely official unions were granted permission to meet, and printing presses had to be registered. Anyone working for Poland's underground media faced potential imprisonment.

Solidarity had been effectively crushed, yet externally the union had become recognized worldwide as the first major mass nonviolent challenge to Soviet domination. The Norwegian Nobel Institute awarded Wałęsa the Nobel Prize for Peace on October 6, 1983, for his efforts in the struggle for workers' rights. The citation of the committee of Norwegian former parliamentarians and politicians who choose the winner described him as "an exponent of the active longing for peace and freedom which exists, in spite of unequal conditions, unconquered in all the peoples of the world."

Fearful that he would not be permitted back into Poland if he left, Wałęsa sent his wife, Danuta, and son, Bogdan, to Oslo to accept the award for him. In the acceptance speech delivered by Wałęsa's family, he confirmed his conviction in the practicality of nonviolent struggle: "My most ardent desire is that my country will recapture its historic opportunity for a peaceful evolution, and that Poland will prove to the world that even the most complex situations can be solved by a dialogue and not by force."

In May 1984, with local elections scheduled for the following month, Father Jerzy Popiełuszko, a priest at the parish of St. Stanisław Kostka in Warsaw, warned that the Polish people themselves were responsible for their enslavement when, either out of fear or avoidance of trouble, they allowed authorities to sponsor evil. Solidarity decided to boycott the June elections. Boycotting, a method of political noncooperation, expresses doubt about validity or fairness, in this case of the balloting.

When the government instated martial law in December 1981, the youthful Father Jerzy asserted that the duty of a priest was to stand with the people, particularly when they are wronged, dishonored, and mistreated. Despite poor health, Popiełuszko worked to his limits as medical chaplain in Warsaw; steelworkers there adopted him as their chaplain. When students at the Warsaw Fire-Fighting School, a division of the military sector, conducted sit-ins, and riot police expelled them, Father Jerzy acted as their unofficial chaplain. Under martial law, he took advantage of the exemption that allowed assemblies by the Church and worked to provide food, clothing, and money.

Despite the threat of the death penalty for anyone speaking against the party and state, Father Jerzy became famous for his Masses for Poland, his sermons on the last Sunday of every month often staunchly in support of Solidarity. One Sunday, he alluded to suppression of the freedom of speech and asked the people therefore to pray in silence. He asserted that the Church could not be neutral in the face of injustice; it must instead become the protector of the oppressed. He spoke plainly of "a nation terrorized by military force," of beatings, of persons brought to trial simply for trying to be faithful to the principles of Solidarity. The regime tried to silence him through the Church hierarchy, but the bishops refused to cooperate.

On October 30, 1984, the mutilated corpse of Father Jerzy Popiełuszko was found in the Vistula River. The discovery of the body led to international protests. *The New York Times* on November 4 reports that 200,000 turned out for the funeral of the thirty-seven-year-old priest. Thousands of delegations from factories and offices attended the ceremony, officiated by Jozef Cardinal Glemp, the Roman Catholic primate. Young people formed human chains to facilitate the entry of journalists, nuns, priests, and special guests to the grounds of Father Jerzy's parish church.

Jaruzelski claimed that the government bore no responsibility for Popiełuszko's death. By February 1985, however, four police officers had been sentenced to between fourteen and twenty-five years in prison for the murder. "After this terrible act," Janusz Ziółkowski notes in "The Roots, Branches and Blossoms of Solidarność," "the State's remaining shreds of credibility in the eyes of the people were gone."

NOVEMBER 4, 1984
200,000 AT RITES FOR POLISH PRIEST; CARDINAL LAUDS HIM AS A 'MARTYR'
By MICHAEL T. KAUFMAN
Special to The New York Times

WARSAW, Nov. 3 – An enormous throng of Poles stood and prayed for more than three hours today as a slain Roman Catholic priest was buried with eulogies from the leaders of the church he served and the Solidarity movement he championed.

The slayers of the priest, the Rev. Jerzy Popieluszko, have been identified as three security police officers. On Friday the Government said two others had been detained and a general had been suspended in connection with the case.

As people clung to trees and perched on canted roofs to glimpse the plain coffin in front of a parish church, Jozef Cardinal Glemp, the Primate, praised the 37-year-old priest as a martyr who had entered Polish history.

Throng Gathered Overnight

Though the gathering was solemn, political professions were being made. As the day broke cold and misty, a crowd that had gathered overnight and then grew to 200,000 thronged the streets for six and seven blocks in every direction.

Scattered throughout were the forbidden banners of Solidarity held aloft by members of outlawed chapters at factories, schools and shops from every city and region of Poland.

The most direct political symbolism came when Lech Walesa, the Solidarity founder, rose to deliver a eulogy from the balcony of the church. He arrived from Gdansk on Friday, and today, before going to the church, he visited the Indian Embassy to sign a condolence book for Indira Gandhi.

In a powerful voice, he addressed himself to Father Popieluszko. "We bid you farewell, servant of God, pledging that we shall never bow to oppression," Mr. Walesa said.

He was interrupted as the crowd took up the chant, "We pledge, we pledge." Weeping priests and older women joined young people in the promise.

"We shall act in solidarity with service to the fatherland and we shall respond with truth to lies and with good to evil," Mr. Walesa went on.

Shouts and V-for-Victory

"We bid farewell to you solemnly and with dignity and hope for a just social peace in our country. Rest in peace. Solidarity is alive, for you have given your life for it."

There were shouts of "Solidarity! Solidarity!" as a sea of hands rose in the V-for-Victory salute.

Cardinal Glemp paused several times during his eulogy to gain control over his emotions and cracking voice. He described the activist priest as a man whose life and death had inspired the nation. . . . "[L]et Poles of different social groups meet not crying over the coffin of a martyred priest, but at the table of dialogue to strive toward peace. The church has wanted this for a long time. [H]is voice wavering, he added, ". . . and the church repeats this desire today.". . .

The Cardinal asked people to forgive the priest's killers.

Other eulogies included statements from an actor speaking for artists, a nurse who had worked with the priest during visits by Pope John Paul II, and a priest who had been in Father Popieluszko's seminary class. There was also Karol Szadurski, an engineer from the Warsaw steel mill, where Father Popieluszko had been chaplain.

Mr. Szadurski stirred many in the crowd to tears with his quietly delivered words.

"My friend," he said, "I believe all of Warsaw is here. Do you hear how the bells of freedom are tolling? Do you hear how our hearts are praying? Your ark of solidarity of hearts sails on and carries more and more of us. Let the Lord accept you among Polish martyrs. For the Fatherland you have suffered the most. You are already victorious with Christ. It is this that you wanted the most. Jerzy, our priest, farewell."

Thousands of Delegations

In the crowd were thousands of delegations from factories, offices and schools who checked in with the priests and factory workers serving as volunteers at the church in a quiet riverside residential neighborhood.

Passageways through the crowd were maintained by Boy Scouts, Girl Scouts and university students in their distinctive peaked caps. They held hands to form human barriers, allowing priests, nuns, journalists and special guests to enter the grounds of Father Popieluszko's parish church, St. Stanislaw Kostka.

There the guests gathered in groups by occupations, with Andrzej Wajda, the movie director standing with film workers, and Zbigniew Herbert, the poet, standing with writers. The heads of diplomatic missions of the United States, Britain, France, Belgium and Ireland were applauded when their presence was announced.

Silence Greets Officials

There was silence when a priest reported that there were also official representatives. Among them were Zenon Komender, a member of Pax, a pro-Communist Catholic group, who is one of half a dozen Deputy Prime Ministers, and Kazimierz Morawski, a member of the Council of State, the collective presidency. Mr. Morawski is chairman of the Christian Social Association, another officially sanctioned Catholic group.

The pallbearers were coal miners and steelworkers. Some miners wore their work clothes with lamps in their helmets burning. Others wore the ceremonial clothes of their social organization, black-braided costumes and hats with black and purple plumes. The steelworkers were recognized by their own ceremonial garb—white suits with large white, wide-brimmed hats.

They carried the coffin around the church with the priest's parents, farmers from eastern Poland, following, and then the Cardinal and the bishops, and laid him to rest in a grave dug under a still green willow.

Through the night, people had waited in line as long as five hours to pass before the coffin inside the church. After the requiem mass and burial, another line formed as people carrying flowers came to make their offerings. There was not much room for the floral displays and one man carrying a wreath inscribed "From the discharged workers of the Meteorological Institute" reluctantly placed it on other wreaths.

During the service, there were no signs of police. Speakers said security was being provided "by ourselves." In the city center, police vehicles, including water cannon trucks, were parked at key intersections.

After the service most of the crowd scattered but one group of about 20,000 began to walk to the city center, chanting "There can be no freedom without Solidarity." The police stood by, but made no attempt to scatter the mourners, who eventually dispersed themselves.

• •

Enter Gorbachev: *Perestroika* and *Glasnost*

On March 11, 1985, Mikhail S. Gorbachev rose to become general secretary of the Communist Party of the Soviet Union and began advocating the principle of *perestroika*, Russian for "restructuring" (see **Introduction: Strikes, Sinatra, and Nonviolent Revolution**").

Others before him had tried to reform the Soviet system, but any authentic economic reform inevitably threatened the status of the communist party and thus was always set aside. Part of Gorbachev's unique approach was the view that both the society and the party would have to change in order for economic reform to be effective. This did not mean, however, that the Soviet Union stood ready to give up hegemony over Eastern Europe and the Soviet republics. Gorbachev believed in socialism, could not see its ethical weaknesses, and failed to appreciate the depth of hostility toward its imposition in Eastern Europe. The nature of the one-party state meant that he could not have received accurate assessments of popular perceptions, because the party determined who received ambassadorships as well as who reported the news.

No one anticipated Gorbachev's readiness to confront the Eastern bloc's leading political and social problems. His 1987 policy of *glasnost* (openness) had the effect of relaxing censorship. This meant that failures of the Soviet system to provide for the basic welfare of its citizens could be exposed. It was still unthinkable that major transformations could occur, or that the Soviet Union would ever abandon its dominion in Eastern Europe. *The Times* reporter delightedly observes that Gorbachev had brought his granddaughter with him to the polling station to cast his ballot in parliamentary elections and that he also bantered with foreign journalists on this occasion.

With Gorbachev's selection as general secretary, the Soviet grip began to loosen on its communist-ruled satellites. The emergence of Gorbachev suggested that Moscow's uncertainty about Poland—revealed as early as 1981, when Soviet premier Leonid I. Brezhnev pulled back troops from the Polish border after a phone call from U.S. president Jimmy Carter—might be exacerbated within the Soviet Union. Although the appearance of Gorbachev on the scene indicated a move toward reform in Poland and the Soviet Union, this evolution was not immediately perceptible in Poland. On September 14, 1986, nearly five years after Jaruzelski had crushed Solidarity under martial law, *The New York Times* editorializes,

> Poland has remained a society in sullen stalemate. The Soviet Union has watched its largest East European ally converted into a strategic question mark and an economic burden. Millions of Poles suffer continued spiritual demoralization and physical poverty along with official brutality of both word and deed.

Solidarity had not sought to destroy the communist apparatus or overthrow the party-state. By its own terminology, Solidarity sought to "repair" Poland (see "Polish Union Opens Convention"), liberate civil society, and obtain workers' rights while preserving the economy. Adam Michnik, a key activist intellectual and later editor of Poland's second-largest daily newspaper, would after Solidarity's peak write not only about the ethics of the union's way of seeking political change, but would speak of its opposition—the communist party-state—as consisting of rational actors who could define their own power interests, weigh advantages and shortcomings, and eventually conclude that it was more disadvantageous for them to exert the full force of its coercive powers than to accommodate the changes being sought by the union.

Even if Gorbachev had not assumed the reins of power, Poland's alliance of workers and intellectuals would have pressed for Solidarity to be legalized in order to pursue its fundamental purposes of free trade unions, rights and freedoms, including the right to strike, and better standards of living. Its momentum was powered by the workers whose lot under communism had gone steadily downhill with high human costs, scholar activists from Poland's university faculties and students, the Roman Catholic Church, writers and editors who robustly plied their trade in a subterranean press, and committees upon committees. As incarcerated Solidarity protagonists were released from prison, they simply returned to their workplaces, classrooms, typewriters and printing presses, and their committees.

In October 29, 1987, the Jaruzelski regime proposed policies of economic and political reform. The following month, it held a national referendum to win support for its reform program, which included price hikes. Polish voters rejected the modifications through a circuitous process. The referendum process included a provision that no fewer than 51 percent of the registered electorate must vote affirmatively for a proposal to pass. With the program's destruction built in, it became a foregone conclusion that when abstentions and negative votes were combined, the majority would effectively defeat the proposed new policies. Jaruzelski allowed the rejection of his own proposals, because the regime sought to appear to be more democratic in contrast to Solidarity, which had been trying to govern itself democratically even while illegal. The government announced that the reforms would proceed anyway.

Regarding the balloting, John Tagliabue notes in *The Times* on December 1, 1987, "It appeared to be the first time that the Communist leadership of an East-bloc country was handed a decisive vote of no-confidence in a popular referendum on a major governmental program" ("Nationwide Vote in Poland Rejects a Party Proposal"). For the first time since 1945, a vote within the Soviet bloc had been free and fair.

MARCH 12, 1985
A LEADER WITH STYLE—AND IMPATIENCE
Special to The New York Times

MOSCOW, March 11 – Coming to power at the age of 54, Mikhail Sergeyevich Gorbachev, the peasant's son from southern Russia, is expected to bring a new style of leadership to the Kremlin. If the expectations prove correct, this leadership will be more open, perhaps, less obsessively suspicious, less burdened with memories of Stalin's terror and the war. . . .

He revealed his impatience in a major speech last December when he said, "We will have to carry out profound transformations in the economy and in the entire system of social relations."

'Intensive Development'

There was an echo of that today when he said, "We are to achieve a decisive turn in transferring the national economy to the tracks of intensive development."

He added, "A good deal is to be done."

What remained to be seen, however, was how Mr. Gorbachev . . . would translate his impatience into action by the enormous bureaucracy that manages the Soviet Union's ponderous, creaky, centralized economy.

For all the fervor, style and obvious achievement he has displayed in reaching the highest position in the Soviet power structure, Mr. Gorbachev and the generation he represents remain an untested and largely unknown political force.

These are people who were reared after the war and after the Stalinist terrors, who grew up in a state more secure in its power and potential, men who got better educations than their predecessors and had more contact with the outside world.

Yet these are also men who have made their careers in a Communist Party that has changed from an idealistic elite into an entrenched, privileged and self-perpetuating bureaucracy intolerant of too much independence or nonconformism among its members.

Under [Yuri V.] Andropov, Mr. Gorbachev worked under a seasoned politician who knew the power structure intimately from within as a consequence of his 15 years at the head of the K.G.B., the internal security and intelligence agency. And though he himself rose to the peak of Soviet power, Mr. Gorbachev's political biography did not conclusively prove his ability to wage the sort of brutal political struggle that is required to get change through the bureaucracy.

After a steady and apparently uneventful climb through the provincial party apparatus in the Stavropol region of southern Russia, north of the Caucasus, Mr. Gorbachev was brought to Moscow to take over as Communist Party secretary for agriculture, a post that became vacant with the death of Fyodor D. Kulakov. He apparently benefited from the patronage of Mikhail A. Suslov, the powerful party ideologist, who also came from Stavropol.

Disastrous Harvests

In the years when Mr. Gorbachev managed agriculture, the Soviet Union suffered a series of disastrous grain harvests, and actually stopped publishing crop statistics. Yet when Mr. Andropov came to power in November 1982 on the death of Leonid I. Brezhnev, he evidently found in the young party secretary the energetic aide he needed to help launch his programs.

As Mr. Andropov's health declined, he delegated more and more of his responsibilities to Mr. Gorbachev. It was Mr. Gorbachev who managed changes in the party ranks and new experiments in industrial management, and who acted as a go-between for Mr. Andropov and the Politburo.

When Mr. Andropov died, however, the senior members of the Politburo evidently concluded it was too early to hand power to the younger generation and selected Mr. Chernenko. But Mr. Gorbachev emerged as the No. 2 man in the party structure, as the bearer of Mr. Andropov's legacy and evidently as the heir-apparent.

Following Succession Route

Everything in the procedures today suggested that the succession had been decided long before Mr. Chernenko died, and if Mr. Gorbachev had opposition this time, it was not apparent in the smooth and swift transition.

One advantage Mr. Gorbachev has is that the depleted Politburo, now down to 10 members, has ample vacancies to bring up protégés like Yegor K. Ligachev. Mr. Gorbachev also will be able to use the party congress that is said to be scheduled for before the year's end to bring new blood into the Central Committee, the pool from which the Kremlin draws its senior managers and party executives.

Mikhail Sergeyevich Gorbachev was born March 2, 1931, in the village of Privolnoye in the Stavropol region. Official biographies list his parents as peasants, and as a teen-ager he worked at a machine-tractor station.

His break came in 1952 when he entered the law school of Moscow State University. There he joined the party and became a Communist Youth League organizer. He returned to Stavropol to start a career in party work, broken only by a correspondence course in agricultural economics, for which he received a degree in 1967. He enjoyed a steady rise until 1970, when he was named first secretary of the regional organization, a post that also brought him into the Central Committee.

A Big Move to Moscow

In 1978 Mr. Gorbachev was brought to Moscow, where he became party secretary for agriculture. In October 1980 he became a full member of the Politburo.

Under Mr. Andropov, Mr. Gorbachev expanded his responsibilities to the economy and party cadres, and under Mr. Chernenko he further took charge of ideology and party affairs.

Mr. Gorbachev has made several trips abroad, but the most celebrated was his visit to Britain last December. He and his wife, Raisa Maksimovna, won over the British press and many British politicians with their easy style, their flashes of humor, their curiosity—and, above all, with the contrast they presented to the classic image of the rumpled, boorish Soviet leader.

At the end of the visit, Prime Minister Margaret Thatcher declared: "I like Mr. Gorbachev. We can do business together."

Mr. Gorbachev's early priorities are likely to be in internal economic policies, which are based on some decentralization of decision-making, more incentives for workers and managers and other efforts to loosen the stranglehold of the central bureaucracy on far-flung enterprises.

Foreign policy is likely to remain the domain of Foreign Minister Andrei A. Gromyko, and to undergo no immediate change.

On human rights, Soviet history shows that the Government has been least tolerant when it is seeking to make significant changes. Mr. Gorbachev, in any event, has never demonstrated more or less tolerance for dissent than his Politburo colleagues, and his pronouncements on culture and ideology have followed standard Kremlin lines.

If substantial change may take some time, Mr. Gorbachev is expected to act quickly to change the style of leadership. He has called several times for more and better public information, and he has not demonstrated the obsession with personal secrecy of older leaders.

His trip to Britain gave one glimpse of his political style. More recently, casting his ballot last month in the single-candidate Soviet parliamentary elections, he brought his granddaughter with him and bantered easily with foreign correspondents.

· ·

WORKERS CALL A HALT TO STRIKES

Eastern Europe's negotiated end to communism got under way in 1988 as waves of strikes spread across Poland. The economy had continued to deteriorate, as foreign indebtedness, inflation, and prices rose, and health services declined. Outright economic collapse loomed. From April 21 to May 2, workers held the first of two rounds of nationwide strikes over wage limits and price hikes. At the Lenin shipyard in Gdańsk, sit-in strikes began with gates once again festooned with flowers and photographs of the pope. The workers' principal demands included the re-legalization of Solidarity and Lech Wałęsa's reinstatement as its leader. Workers chanted, "Nie ma wolnoscki bez Solidarnośći!" (There's no liberty without Solidarity!)

On May 3, a strike organizer told *The New York Times* that all 12,000 employees in the Gdańsk shipyard supported the strike, while 3,000 workers were actually occupying the yard ("Thousands at Gdansk Shipyard Join Polish Strike"). The regime responded by locking up regional Solidarity leaders in Warsaw, Gdańsk, Lodz, Torun, and other cities. That night, *The Times* reports, police sealed off the gate of the Lenin shipyard, where banners announced "Sit-in strike." With a full moon, some workers slept on the ground while others created makeshift shelters. When asked whether the political demands, such as the legalization of Solidarity, were as important as financial requests for higher pay, one replied, "We want to be free."

In August, a second wave of wildcat strikes broke that were larger than the spring's economic noncooperation actions, with strikers calling even more widely and forcefully for the legalization of Solidarity and for political freedoms. On August 31, the first meeting in seven years took place between the regime and Solidarity, interestingly the day after the eighth anniversary of the 1980 Gdańsk accord at the start of Solidarity (see "Strikers in Poland Defy Gierek Appeal" and "Polish Union Opens Convention"). For the negotiations, the interior minister, General Czeslaw Kiszczak, met with Wałęsa. The regime came offering to discuss legalizing Solidarity if Wałęsa could persuade laborers to return to work. In hindsight the meeting was the first formal session of round-table talks between Solidarity and the government (see "To His Volatile Young Allies, Wałęsa Preaches Conciliation").

Wałęsa in the end employed his personal influence to end the strikes. *The Times* on September 4 reports that some strikers were angry about returning to work empty-handed. Wałęsa appeared for forty-five minutes on national television on November 30, 1988, stealing the show from the regime's representative with the cleverness of his arguments, his charm, and his wit. Some observers detected an equivalency in psychological power between the pope's first visit to Poland and Wałęsa's ability to outmaneuver the government spokesperson on television.

On December 18, Wałęsa formed a citizens' committee within Solidarity that consisted of more than 100 prominent academicians and writers. Most were long-time intellectual advisers to Wałęsa from the days of KSS-KOR, the Social Self-Defense Committee (see "Polish Labor Crisis Deepens as Workers List Their Demands"). In a banner moment for nonviolent struggle, Wałęsa and the majority won a debate against a sizable minority who wanted a bloody revolution against the communist regime. Solidarity's reassertion of pursuing a peaceful solution cleared the way for the historic round-table talks held outside Warsaw that would begin two months later.

For the balance of 1988, however, Solidarity and the government were unable to agree on ground rules for their negotiations. In January 1989, after a tempestuous communist party Central Committee meeting—where Jaruzelski threatened to resign if his recommendations were not adopted—the party approved a resolution that would allow political pluralism, a political opposition, and the legalization of Solidarity. This opened the door to the round-table discussions where, in retrospect, it can be said that the collapse of communism began throughout the region.

SEPTEMBER 4, 1988
WORKERS IN POLAND HEED WALESA AND AGREE TO END LAST OF STRIKES
By JOHN TAGLIABUE
Special to The New York Times

GDANSK, Poland, Sept. 3 – A fragile labor peace settled over Poland today for the first time in 20 days after striking coal miners in the south of the country and dock workers and bus drivers in the north agreed to return to work.

The rest of Poland was quiet after nearly three weeks of strikes to demand the return of the outlawed Solidarity trade union, as well as economic and political changes.

Workers at the July Manifesto coal mine in Jastrzebie, near the Czechoslovak border, and in Szczecin, a Baltic Sea port, bowed to the urging of Lech Walesa, the leader of Solidarity.

New Talks Awaited

With the last strikes ended, Mr. Walesa is expected to begin talks with the Government on preparing for new roundtable discussions. The authorities have set no conditions on topics to be discussed or on who can take part in the talks.

As he had earlier among the Gdansk shipyard workers, Mr. Walesa encountered anger and resentment in Jastrzebie and acccusations that the strikers were returning to work empty-handed. . . .

"We found it hard to understand his reasoning," the strike leader [Andrezej Szczesniak] was quoted as saying. "He was talking about the state of the country's economy, but our economic situation was also very difficult."

Mr. Szczesniak said the miners applauded the 44-year-old Solidarity founder on his arrival, but the discussion quickly turned bitter and ended in charges of betrayal.

Today was the eighth anniversary of the signing in Jastrzebie of the last of three agreements establishing Solidarity. Those accords committed the Warsaw Government to an astonishing agenda of change and captured the dreams of Poles until those hopes were dashed by the imposition of martial law in 1981.

On Wednesday, in the first meeting between Government officials and Solidarity in seven years, Mr. Walesa received assurances that the authorities would consider restoring legal status to Solidarity if the strikes ended. Solidarity was banned in 1982 after the Polish leader, Gen. Wojciech Jaruzelski, imposed martial law and suppressed the union.

On Friday, Mr. Walesa drove the 440 miles from Gdansk to Jastrzebie in a Mercedes-Benz made available to him by the Roman Catholic Church. Mr. Walesa visited the mine after the workers refused to heed his back-to-work appeal, demanding instead to talk with the union leader face to face.

First Talks in 7 Years

Earlier, workers at the steel and machinery complex at Stalowa Wola, southeast of the capital, and shipyard and dock workers in Gdansk agreed to heed Mr. Walesa's call to end their work stoppages. The end of the strikes removed the last barriers to the first official talks between Solidarity's leadership and the Government since 1981.

In a statement broadcast on the state television on Aug. 26, the Interior Minister, Gen. Czeslaw Kiszczak, offered to open roundtable discussions with workers and other social groups. Mr. Walesa responded that he was "unconditionally" prepared for such talks.

Late Friday, the striking miners met with mine managers. The Government press agency reported that the miners left the grounds they had been occupying at 6 A.M. today after statements were issued by the local public prosecutor and the political leadership that the miners would face no disciplinary penalties.

The report said losses from the 20-day work stoppage totaled 250,000 metric tons of coal that was not mined.

Solidarity organizers who traveled with Mr. Walesa later quoted him as telling the miners: "Thank you for your fantastic struggle. I think it is a victory, but we will see how big it is."

The talks with the Government will pose a major challenge for Mr. Walesa's legendary negotiating skills, which led in large measure to the 1980 agreements that founded Solidarity.

"This time we must succeed in achieving a compromise," an exhausted Mr. Walesa told reporters this morning at St. Brygida's Church, a Solidarity stronghold, after his return from the coal fields. "Talks at the table mean compromise."

'Minimizing the Strikes'

The union leader said his activity was aimed "at minimizing the strikes."

"I did so with a view to minimizing the economic losses," he said, "but also to push Poland toward reform and agreement."

"The nation's economic situation is hard, and strikes do not help," he said. "But until now, we have been unable to reach agreement. We did not strike for the fun of it. We struck so that there would be no need to strike tomorrow, or the day after."

The decision to end the strikes, which ended a potentially serious threat for the Communist leaders, came after intense discussions in which church leaders played a mediating role.

It was the second wave of serious labor conflict this year. Five strikes in Poland from April 25 to May 10, and brief work stoppages or strike threats in 25 other work places, constituted the worst labor unrest in the country since martial law.

At their high point, the strikes idled 14 coal mines and 9 industrial enterprises, and Interior Ministry officials said a further 39 enterprises in 14 provinces were threatened by stoppages.

The strikes idled 12 percent of Poland's coal production and severely hampered its two largest ports.

Beyond the challenge of resumed strikes, the Communist leadership is preoccupied with how to address the social unrest that has spawned the protests.

• •

Solidarity and Wałęsa Rebound

By all accounts, no one had expected that Solidarity would be able to rebound from seven years of martial law. Yet after the wildcat strikes of 1988, the ruling communist party invited Solidarity to discuss Poland's future, implying that the union would become legal again. Solidarity's national commission—as close as the still-illegal union could get to self-governance given that under martial law it was not permitted to hold elections—accepted the invitation. The Citizens Committee of 100 preeminent professors and intellectuals, formed in December 1988, assembled the negotiating team (see "Workers in Poland Heed Walesa and Agree to End Last of Strikes").

In the Namiestnikowski Palace in Warsaw from February 6 to April 5, 1989, Solidarity and government representatives negotiated around a large oak table, leading the process to be called the round-table talks. Two plenary sessions convened and four informal summit meetings took place at Magdalenka, near Warsaw, between the government's chief negotiator, Interior Minister General Czesław Kiszczak, Lech Wałęsa, and their most trusted advisers. In the secluded Magdalenka retreat, they negotiated the most difficult sticking points, with no more than two dozen persons present. A total of thirteen working groups held ninety-four sessions, often conversing until dawn. At the round-table and various sub-tables, former political prisoners held discussions with their former jailers. They went on to sign several hundred pages of protocols. The round-table agreement between Poland's regime and the opposition movement was signed on April 5. The preamble calls it "the beginning of the road to parliamentary democracy." At the signing ceremony, Wałęsa declared: "This is the beginning of democracy and a free Poland." Totalitarianism in Poland had ended.

The round-table talks allowed Polish society to organize itself for democracy, according to Jacek Kuroń, one of the influential thinkers who helped to shape Solidarity and who had spent nine years in prison (see "Polish Labor Crisis Deepens as Workers List Their Demands"). Concerted organization made the talks possible, Kuroń asserted in 1999 in "Overcoming Totalitarianism": "[I]t became possible to reach this stage only after the enormous social activity in the legal days of Solidarity and the widespread clandestine resistance during the years of martial law" (pp. 198–201).

The negotiations brought legitimacy to Solidarity, whose interest had been focused on its legalization. With its legal status secured, Solidarity delegates proceeded to promote reform in education, the law, local governance, and the media. Ironically, government officials themselves sought early elections, thinking that briefer campaigns would hasten the defeat of a disorganized opposition. The regime had hoped to bring the opposition leaders into the ruling party without making meaningful changes to the political power structure in Poland. Solidarity reluctantly agreed to early contests.

Regarding the governmental decision to allow Solidarity's reinstatement, after having crushed it under martial law in 1981, *The New York Times* states on March 2, 1989, that Wałęsa and his critics had agreed that the regime was motivated not by altruism, but a desire to co-opt Solidarity and encourage the union to help relieve the nation's economic calamity, while ensuring the communists' continued existence as a political player. In addition to making Solidarity a legal trade union, the agreement charted a system of semi-free elections that appeared to protect the interests of the ruling communists, but went beyond Central Committee's promises of January that year. Not only would Solidarity be reinstated, but the union would have airtime on television and radio, and its own national and provincial newspapers. New parliamentary elections would be announced, and Solidarity would be allowed to vie for 35 percent of the seats in the Sejm, the restructured lower chamber of the Polish parliament. Elections for the reconstituted upper chamber, the Senate, would be open and free. In actuality, the agreement redesigned the government. "These were important but still limited concessions by the communist regime," Alexander Smolar notes; "[h]owever, they triggered its rapid collapse" (Smolar 2009, 140).

On May 1, Wałęsa, standing on a wooden barrel outside St. Brygid's Church in Gdańsk, initiated the first Polish electoral campaign in more than sixty years to allow participation by freely nominated candidates. Open, if complex, elections were held on June 4, just two months after the round-table agreement. Solidarity was permitted to compete for 161 of the 460 Sejm seats (35 percent) and all 100 Senate seats. The Polish United Workers' Party (PZPR), as the communist party was known, reserved 38 percent of the seats for itself, while the rest (27 percent) went to its allies in the government. Solidarity was at a disadvantage in having to transform itself quickly from an illegal underground opposition to a free electoral contender.

Although pre-election polls forecast big victories for Solidarity, the results were astonishing. Polish voters soundly rejected the communists in their first chance to render judgment on the party. Solidarity won all 161 Sejm seats for which it contended. Most embarrassing, the communists lost all but two of 35 seats for which their leaders ran unopposed. The leading reformer, Mieczysław Rakowski, secured the 50 percent required for his seat. In the 100-seat Senate, Solidarity won all but one seat. Most important, the communist party publicly accepted the validity of its losses. (It still controlled the army, police, party, and *nomenklatura*.)

A second round of elections occurred on June 18. As agreed at the round-table talks, Gen. Wojciech Jaruzelski was elected president by the parliament, by one vote, the minimum required, in an attempt by Solidarity to keep the communist party and police from opposing Solidarity. In the balloting for prime minister, the communist party's flank refused to support the communist candidate and instead supported Solidarity. With this surprise move, the party no longer had a majority in the parliament, and the communist contender for premier, Czesław Kiszczak, who replaced Rakowski, could not gain enough support to form a government. He had been instrumental in negotiating the round-table agreement, but this was superseded by memories of his role as dreaded interior minister under martial law.

At last, on August 24, a coalition cabinet was formed under Tadeusz Mazowiecki, a key member of the Catholic intelligentsia who had helped to shape KSS-KOR and Solidarity and the first non-communist prime minister in the Soviet bloc. The other two candidates, also from Solidarity, had been Bonislaw Geremek and Kuroń. As with most of Solidarity's senior leadership, Mazowiecki had been imprisoned under martial law, in his case for a year, but now pledged a "thick line" between his administration and the communist past. The Leninist idea that the rule of the communist party could not be reversed by peaceful means was invalidated. In December 1990, Wałęsa was elected president of Poland.

Thus, Poland became the first democracy in postwar, communist Eastern Europe through successful nonviolent struggle. The Soviet newspaper *Izvestia* reported offhandedly that the opposition "will take their place in the parliament . . . where, incidentally, the PUWP [Polish United Workers' Party] will no longer have a majority." The Kremlin watched with calmness, perhaps approval.

KEY PLAYER IN POLAND
Adam Michnik (1946–)

The grandson of Jews murdered by the Nazis, Adam Michnik was born in Warsaw to staunch communists of Jewish and non-Jewish extraction; he describes himself as a Pole of Jewish origins.

Michnik's early political affiliation was also as a committed communist. While a student in secondary school, Michnik became a member of the Club of the Crooked Circle, a Warsaw discussion group. Through the club, Michnik connected with other prominent progressive thinkers and expanded his thinking on politics. Michnik was expelled from school for advocating educational reform.

From 1965 to 1986, Michnik was jailed six times for political dissent. His first arrest came in 1965 after criticizing the communist party when he was student at the University of Warsaw. After his release, he was ordered to work as a welder for two years at the Rosa Luxemburg Light Bulb Factory. He later told *The New York Times* that he felt the stint had given him "proletarian credibility" (Kaufman 1987). He then spent time traveling in Europe as an employee of the Polish poet Antoni Słonimski.

In 1968, in response to student unrest and protest, the communist government arrested dissidents, a disparaging term, many of whom were Jewish, including Michnik. Although he had often written and spoken critically about the party, this arrest led him to cease identifying as a communist. During the 1970s, Michnik helped to found the Committee for the Worker's Defense (KOR) along with other activists who would later become prominent members of the Solidarity union. As an author and organizer, he helped to build the infrastructure of ideas for Poland's political transition to democracy.

In 1977, authorities arrested Michnik for challenging the deaths of protesting students in Kraków. He became a national figure as a nonviolent organizer in early 1981, when he intervened to prevent a riot in the town of Otwock, calming a crowd and saving police officers from physical assault. Michnick got the attention of hard-line proponents by the way he calmly negotiated with the party-state, rather than violently rejecting it (Tighe 1997).

The declaration of martial law by Gen. Wojciech Jaruzelski in 1981 led to Michnik's last arrest and six years of imprisonment. He spent most of his time behind bars writing political essays that were published outside of Poland and garnered support for Solidarity. In 1986, the communist government freed Michnik, who once again became active in the reconstitution of the Polish state. Lech Wałęsa, who headed Solidarity, persuaded Michnik to found *Gazeta Wyborcza* (Election Gazette) in 1989, in order to earn support for Solidarity during the crucial historic elections that would transform Poland. Michnik did so and became editor in chief.

In 1990, Michnik was elected to the Polish parliament. In the same year, he broke politically with Wałęsa. In balloting for the presidency, he and the *Gazeta* supported Wałęsa's opponent. Wałęsa won the election. Michnik continued to serve as editor of the *Gazeta* until his retirement in 2004. His role as a journalist, public intellectual, and organizer has earned Michnik recognition, respect, and accolades around the world. He has remained an influential thinker and activist for democratization in Eastern Europe, and his determination and beliefs in the necessity of nonviolent collective action have earned him the nickname "the Sisyphus of Democracy" (Dement 2001).

MARCH 2, 1989
TO HIS VOLATILE YOUNG ALLIES, WALESA PREACHES CONCILIATION
By JOHN TAGLIABUE
Special to The New York Times

WARSAW, March 1 – Whether haranguing students in Cracow, churchgoers in the port of Gdansk or workers in the gritty textile town of Lodz, the Solidarity leader Lech Walesa these days resembles no one as much as an itinerant preacher.

"I'll negotiate with Satan himself," the portly, mustachioed Mr. Walesa shouted last week at a worker rally in Lodz, "if he'll recognize heaven!"

The remarks, carried by an undergound newspaper, gave insight into Mr. Walesa's attitude about the Government representatives with whom Solidarity leaders have been negotiating recently on the shape of political and economic change in Poland. The statement also gave a revealing glimpse of the deep differences dividing Mr. Walesa and the followers who criticize him.

While the Government and Solidarity profess to have agreed on key issues, like provisions to let Solidarity control about two-fifths of a future parliament's seats, the fragile unity of Mr. Walesa's flock has become glaringly apparent. . . .

'There'll Be a Big Brawl'

. . . Walesa, having left the narrow negotiating tables in Warsaw to his senior aides, has gone on a tour to carry a message of unity to factories, churches and universities throughout Poland. The message for the workers and the Government is that Poland needs agreement—and that if some agreement does not come quickly the disastrous economic situation, with its social repercussions, will renew worker unrest.

Mr. Walesa's task is a delicate one. The aggressive young workers he is now seeking to rein in are the very ones who carried out the strikes last spring and summer that catapulted Solidarity and its leader back into the political arena. The union leader knows that if he alienates them he has lost his most loyal and effective constituency.

"If the round table does not succeed," Mr. Walesa, half warning, half predicting, told the Lodz workers, "then in April, May, an avalanche begins—big strikes, inflation, the strongest man wins. Young people will say 'enough,' and start marching forward, and there'll be a big brawl."

Eight years ago Mr. Walesa was an electrician, a worker who climbed over his shipyard's fence to join other workers who struck for more pay and better working conditions on the wind-swept hulls of the Lenin shipyard in Gdansk where he worked. Today, he has become a national and international symbol, the leader of the largest and best-organized opposition movement in the Eastern bloc, a man who negotiates with Government ministers and is given prime-time television exposure to air his views.

Recently, he was invited to the Soviet Union, and only the pressing negotiations prevented him from accepting the invitation. Tonight he addressed university students in Warsaw, with some of his remarks broadcast on television, as they so often are these days.

There was little sense of mission when he began his career as leader of the strikes that spawned Solidarity nearly nine years ago, and little of the trappings of success. Then, an electrician in blue-denim overalls, he was chosen by other shipyard workers to argue their case, not least because of an innate rebelliousness and quick tongue.

A New Walesa Bent on Compromise

A combination of things brought about the transformation from shipyard leader to national figure. One is the influence of the Roman Catholic Church, whose leaders—including the Bishop of Gdansk, Tadeusz Goclowski, a close personal adviser—have urged him where possible toward accommodation. Most important, however, was the experience of martial law and months of internment that followed. In speeches, he often laments the eight years he says were lost to Poland; the experience appears to have hardened in him the conviction that compromise is essential.

Perhaps the most startling aspect of the current talks is the Government's decision to allow the return to power of Solidarity, a movement it sought to crush with martial law in late 1981. But Mr. Walesa and his strongest critics agree that the Government moved not out of altruism, but rather in an attempt to co-opt Solidarity and induce the union to help ease the nation's economic crisis, thus assuring the Communists' survival as a political force.

But Mr. Walesa and his critics disagree over the possible consequences of the strategy. While Mr. Walesa's harshest detractors accuse him of selling out the union, those closest to him say they believe that over the long term the party's concessions will help the Solidarity-based opposition build support throughout the country, heightening opportunities for further change in the Soviet Union's largest and most populous Eastern-bloc ally.

"We want to begin a certain process," said Adam Michnik, the essayist who is a principal Walesa adviser. "We want democracy, but step by step."

The three alternatives, he said, would be either "Minor Apocalypse," an allusion to a book by a Polish novelist, Tadeusz Konwicki, that describes a descent into anarchy; an Iranian-style dictatorship "with populist slogans but no real democracy," or "Spain, with both sides realizing that the only solution consists in a process leading to democracy."

Communists' Plans for Solidarity

Curiously, of late the word "Spain" has become a kind of byword in the political discourse of Eastern Europe as opposition strategists in Poland and party officials in Hungary evoke the example of a European nation that ended nearly 40 years of dictatorship with free parliamentary elections—all within 19 months of the death of Franco.

Some Communist leaders, predictably, say they are offended by the comparison. When Mr. Michnik raised it recently in a televised discussion, Janusz Reykowski, a Central Commitee member who is also a Government negotiator at the Solidarity talks, rejected it as "unseemly." Party leaders bristle at the idea that they are trying to co-opt Solidarity. . . .

[A senior party leader said,] "It's not a question of absorbing the opposition, but of creating something new. There will be an opposition. It's only an organizational question." . . .

Opposition leaders also recognize the limits of the Spain comparison.

For one thing, they note that Spain, having never dismantled the principal features of a competitive economy, was in a far better position to resolve its economic problems than is Poland, where centralized planning, artificial pricing and the elimination of competition laid the economy to waste. . . .

Thus, Solidarity's negotiators have accepted—at least in principle—an accord that will allow the opposition to control as much as 40 percent of the seats in a future parliament, under a kind of gentlemen's agreement by which each side will contest only its share of the seats.

In exchange, Solidarity is being asked to provide popular support for distasteful Government economic policies; ultimately, the union would be accorded a form of legality.

"What is the Government looking for?" said Mikolaj Kozakiewicz, a university sociologist and a deputy in the present parliament. "It's looking for a partner willing to share responsibility for unpleasant measures that are necessary for improvement. They don't want a situation where they are the sole party responsible. They want in Solidarity a kind of fireman specializing in preserving social peace. The price of that, of course, is the recognition of Solidarity."

For the party, the plan to admit about 100 opposition deputies to Parliament is a considerable departure from past procedure. But senior party officials, who briefed reporters on progress at the talks, have made it clear that the Communists will not permit a coalition that excluded the ruling party to form a government.

Parliamentary sessions are infrequent and, by Western standards, brief. Despite the talk about increasing the parliament's power, it essentially merely ratifies party decisions. Still, it is probably the liveliest in the Eastern bloc.

The opposition's ultimate weapon, it is pointed out, would be to walk out of Parliament en masse.

At the Government's center—and much of the time above the fray—is the Polish leader, Gen. Wojciech Jaruzelski, who has kept largely out of the public eye since the Government-opposition talks began. On Monday, in a rare public appearance, he addressed army officers at a military school in Bydgoszcz, in central Poland, warning opposition extremists and party hardliners alike that Poland would "not be pushed from the path of socialism," nor would it cave in to conservatives who he said were "clutching at the party's throat" to obstruct change.

Judiciously, however, he refrained from defining what he meant by socialism, nor did he spell out in detail how hardliners were blocking change.

The Economy: Unabated Erosion

It is clear that the key impetus for the bargaining by Prime Minister Mieczyslaw Rakowski and his colleagues is the enduring economic crisis.

Some foods, like meat, are still abundant, but the very abundance may be a harbinger of shortage: the official price for meat is lower than what farmers must pay for feed, fuel and equipment, so they are killing their pigs and cows wholesale.

Last year the Government poured out 90 billion zlotys, about $180 million at the Government's official exchange rate, in milk subsidies to consumers to keep the price down. That has led farmers to begin slaughtering their milk cattle and selling the meat. Agricultural experts say prices would have to go up by 120 percent to 130 percent to correct the market.

The cost of living went up 70 percent last year, causing workers throughout Poland to seek higher wages. Income growth, which reached an annual rate of 135 percent in December, still appears to be rising. The result is that supplies are thin but wallets are bulging, and many experts say they believe that the overall inflation rate will pass 100 percent this year.

Brief strikes over wages, illegal but unhindered, are widespread. They are usually settled by pay increases, which are often illegal but useful in keeping social peace.

In a country where 10,000-zloty notes have only recently come off the printing press, a 20,000-zloty bill has just been announced. The joke making the rounds of Warsaw is that the next big denomination will bear the likeness of the Pope, since it is probably only his prayers that are capable of healing the ailing economy.

Jaruzelski Exits

The language of Marxism had so distorted and corrupted the ruling party-state apparatus that the Polish workers' movement needed another vocabulary. Fortuitously, Solidarity's association with the Roman Catholic Church, university-based activist intellectuals, and writers and editors of the huge underground press had over a decade developed new semantics, avoiding the hackneyed clichés of socialist lexicons. Hence, some observers say that Solidarity won its struggle through the news media as much as through strikes.

The daring originality of Solidarity's approach stands out. The union's generosity of spirit was, if not unique, exemplary. "What was most characteristic and most remarkable about the Solidarność revolution was the complete lack of violence," states Janusz Ziółkowski, a Solidarity supporter elected to the Senate in 1989. "It was a statement about how things should be," he writes in "The Roots, Branches and Blossoms of Solidarność." Solidarity had staged the largest mass strikes in European history. Women were involved to a large proportion in all activities and actions. The combination of workers' rights and political freedoms had given Solidarity potency and depth across Polish society as a movement for broad social liberation.

From running an illegal, noninstitutionalized mass nonviolent movement of opposition, Solidarity moved to playing an instrumental role in the creation of both Polish civil society and the new democratic state. The union's ability to articulate achievable goals, and choose means consistent with those ends, became a model, followed to a greater or lesser degree, in transitions throughout Eastern Europe.

Solidarity was a flexible, 10-million-strong, loose amalgam of local unions, regional groupings, a national commission, and citizens' committees. After Solidarity organized for 1989 election campaigning, its disparate groups were swelled by physicians, teachers, engineers, and professionals who had not been visibly active in the past but who wanted to help preparations for governance and would become constituencies for the fledgling members of parliament.

The union had, Jacek Kuroń stressed in 1999 in "Overcoming Totalitarianism," "disproven the assumption that totalitarianism can be broken only from the outside, that there are no internal forces capable of overcoming a totalitarian system" (see "Polish Labor Crisis

Deepens as Workers List Their Demands"). Ahead lay uncertainties of how to implement the rights, freedoms, and liberty that Solidarity had won and that would now require the arduous construction of democratic institutions.

An unresolved question remains: Why did the Soviet Union not interpose itself, starting with Poland, as the communist regimes of Eastern Europe began to implode? *The New York Times* on December 12, 1990, wades into this aspect of Solidarity's story in its reporting on the departure of General Wojciech Jaruzelski from his predetermined position as Poland's president (see "To His Volatile Young Allies, Walesa Preaches Conciliation").

The Soviet Union never invaded Poland, even before Mikhail S. Gorbachev came to power in 1985. The country had been in decline at least since its invasion of Afghanistan in late 1979. Within a few months of the Gdańsk accord being signed, U.S. president Jimmy Carter had threatened sanctions against the Soviet Union on December 3, 1980, on the White House "hot line," the telephone instrument reserved for communication with the Soviet premier. The Soviets had dispatched fifteen to twenty military divisions to the Polish border, when Carter, already pressuring them by asserting the human rights provisions of the 1975 Helsinki Accords, telephoned Soviet premier Leonid I. Brezhnev and warned him not to send forces into Poland. Earlier, Carter had secretly ordered the Soviet bloc to be flooded with publications by and about the new opposition writers, amplifying the impact of the Polish activist intellectuals across the region. As the Brezhnev Doctrine unraveled, U.S. policies that would be sustained under President Ronald Reagan were put into play.

Scholars have since shown, *The Times* notes, that the regime in Warsaw had considered imposing martial law when Jaruzelski first became prime minister. When he did so, in late 1981, he claimed the initiative was essential to avert catastrophe and civil war (see "Poland Restricts Civil and Union Rights"). Did "catastrophe" refer to Soviet invasion? Stephen Engelberg's December 22 article cites Jaruzelski as having told an Italian newspaper that imposition of martial law in 1981 was the only alternative to an invasion by Soviet and other Warsaw Pact troops. Engelberg also quotes the Tadeusz Mazowiecki government, freely elected as a result of the 1989 historic round-table agreement, to the effect that martial law had been planned from Solidarity's birth in August 1980 and that preparations had been under way before any recorded instances of Soviet pressure (see "To His Volatile Young Allies, Walesa Preaches Conciliation").

According to political scientist Mark Kramer, under supervision by Soviet intelligence and military officials, "[p]reparations for a violent crackdown by Polish internal security commandos were launched in mid-August 1980, . . . elaborate planning was initiated in October 1980, . . ." As the moment loomed for imposing martial law in December, Soviet leaders were uneasy about Jaruzelski's resolve because he was asking Moscow to send troops to help him. They did not want to afford him any excuse for failing to act as forcefully as they thought he should (Kramer 2009, 98).

Jaruzelski's martial law meant that no Soviet soldier had to cross the border into Poland. On July 7, 1989, Soviet premier Gorbachev told the Council of Europe, in Strasbourg, France, that he rejected the Brezhnev Doctrine. He stopped short, however, of endorsing the political developments in Poland and elsewhere in Eastern Europe. Nonetheless, the political will of the Soviet Union to remain an empire seemed to have dissipated; perhaps the Soviet leadership wanted to extricate itself from Eastern Europe. That summer, a spokesperson for Gorbachev joked about Moscow's new "Sinatra Doctrine," referring to the American crooner, Frank Sinatra, and his song, "My Way." He suggested that the Soviet satellite states would be allowed to choose their own course. Shortly thereafter, Prime Minister Mazowiecki visited Moscow and was warmly received. The Brezhnev Doctrine was no more.

Evaluating Soviet intentions and policy alternatives will remain important for scholars because of a haunting possibility: If martial law had not been imposed in 1981, might Solidarity have brought about democracy in communist Poland some years earlier?

DECEMBER 22, 1990
AS JARUZELSKI LEAVES OFFICE: A TRAITOR OR A PATRIOT TO POLES?
By STEPHEN ENGELBERG
Special to The New York Times

WARSAW, Dec. 21 – There was no fanfare or ceremony today at the Belweder Palace as Gen. Wojciech Jaruzelski, the last of Eastern Europe's old-guard Communist leaders, stepped down as Poland's President.

Nonetheless, this snowswept winter day marked the passing of an epoch in which the general presided over the long retreat of the Communist Party.

As he steps down, the ambiguous record he leaves behind has become the object of a growing debate. Was he essentially a Soviet satrap who happened to be in office when Moscow's power ebbed, or was he primarily a Polish patriot who actively and cunningly set the pace of the transition from totalitarian rule?

As the Communist leader who imposed martial law in December 1981 to crush Solidarity as a free trade union, General Jaruzelski was widely condemned by Poles as a traitor. Yet eight years later, after Mikhail S. Gorbachev loosened Moscow's reins on Warsaw, it was General Jaruzelski who steered Poland's Communist Party as it became the first one in Eastern Europe to relinquish power to the opposition.

For most of his tenure he has maintained the posture of a stiff military man who kept his feelings behind the dark glasses he wore as a result of retinal problems. The corset he wore to ease old war wounds added to the impression of unyielding rigidity. But in taking his leave over the last few weeks, the stoic military officer for the first time offered his countrymen some sense of his emotional responses to the storms of the last decade.

In a televised address last week, the general declared that the suffering caused by his decisions "hurts me like a thorn in my flesh."

A Different Kind of Communist

"As a soldier, I know that the commander is responsible for every man and everything," he continued. "The words 'I apologize' may sound banal. But I cannot find any other words."

The general has been pointedly excluded from Saturday's ceremony swearing in Lech Walesa, his old Solidarity adversary, as the next President. Mr. Walesa, who was imprisoned for nearly a year under martial law, will receive the office from representatives of Poland's last pre-Communist Government, an act that symbolically underscores the belief of many Poles that the succession of Communist leaders were illegitimate, having been essentially installed and maintained by Soviet force. . . .

. . . Czeslaw Bielecki, an architect, journalist and underground Solidarity activist who was imprisoned for 20 months in the mid-1980s, found General Jaruzelski's words of apology insufficient.

Admiring Opinion Growing

"Too late, too late, it's simply too late," said Mr. Bielecki, who in 1985 went on a hunger strike in prison that lasted 11 months. "He is saying this in the moment when he's completely powerless, without any real political cost. It's not that I demand vengeance. But this is not an efficient satisfaction for a society to which he told so many lies, so many false justifications."

There are, however, a number of Mr. Bielecki's old Solidarity allies, who share in the growing weight of Polish opinion that credits General Jaruzelski with changing his views and with playing a substantial role in the transition to democracy.

"In the cold assessment which history will make in, say, 10 years, there will be a positive balance sheet," asserted Piotr Nowina-Konopka, a Solidarity figure who served on General Jaruzelski's staff during the Government of Prime Minister Tadeusz Mazowiecki.

Mr. Nowina-Konopka said the general's main achievements as President were to smooth the path to democracy. He led the Communist Party to the "round table" talks that led to free elections in June 1989, and was leader of an army that respected Solidarity's resulting victory.

Much Is Mysterious

In his 15 months in office after the Communists lost control of the government, he interposed no objections as the tools of the Communist state—the police, the army, the courts, the local governments—were wrested one by one from party domination. Last fall, he announced that he would leave office with four years remaining on his term as President to make way for a popularly elected chief executive.

"Yes, he was a man who for 45 years participated in totalitarian power, and that cannot be forgotten," Mr. Nowina-Konopka said. "When he finally decided to let go, he did not do it halfway. He accepted wholly the results of the June elections, and everything that followed."

In many important ways, General Jaruzelski remains a man of mystery. He was born into a family of Polish gentry in 1923, the only East bloc Communist leader to claim such social origins. Shortly after the Soviet Union invaded Poland in 1939, his family was deported to Siberia, where his father died. Nonetheless, Mr. Jaruzelski joined the Soviet Army, and after the war rose rapidly through the ranks of the Polish Army, which was formed and led by Soviet generals.

Zbigniew Brzezinski, the former United States national security adviser who was born in Poland, said . . . in a phone interview from Washington that in the 1930s his older brother attended boarding school with the future general, who was a devout Catholic and nationalist as a youth.

"Why was he trusted by the Soviets?" Mr. Brzezinski asked. "This was a period when social origins automatically disqualified you from holding such a position. He must have convinced them. But how?"

Two 'Fundamental Changes'

"He told me, 'Not many people go through a fundamental change of values in their lives, but I had two,'" Mr. Brzezinski said, recounting a recent three-hour conversation he had in Warsaw with General Jaruzelski. "He went through that in 1939–40 when pre-war national Poland collapsed and again in the last few years when it became clear to him that the promises of Marxism-Leninism were an illusion."

Questions about General Jaruzelski's relationship with the Soviet Union are likely to persist for years. He has indicated in his public statements and one brief interview this year with an Italian newspaper that martial law was imposed in 1981 as the only alternative to an invasion by Soviet and other Warsaw Pact troops.

In the interview, he recounted that he was put on a Soviet plane, was told that its destination was a Polish city but was instead flown to the Polish-Soviet border, where he was met by Leonid I. Brezhnev, the Soviet leader. Mr. Brezhnev said the Soviet Union was prepared to invade if the Polish Communist Party did not initiate the crackdown itself, General Jaruzelski said.

On the other hand, it was recently disclosed by the Mazowiecki Government that martial law had been in planning from virtually the moment the Solidarity movement was born in August 1980. It appears that preparations were under way well before the first recorded instances of Soviet pressure.

Bibliography

Ackerman, Peter, and Jack DuVall. 2000. "Poland: Power from Solidarity." *In A Force More Powerful: A Century of Nonviolent Conflict*, 113–74. New York: St. Martin's Press.

Barker, Colin. 1987. "Poland, 1980–81: The Self-Limited Revolution." In *Revolutionary Rehearsals*, ed. Colin Barker, 169–216. London: Bookmarks.

Barker, Colin, Alan Johnson, and Michael Lavalette. 2001. *Leadership and Social Movements*. Manchester: Manchester University Press.

Bernhard, M. H. 1993. *The Origins of Democratization in Poland*. New York: Columbia University Press.

Chirot, Daniel. 1999. "What Happened in Eastern Europe in 1989?" In *The Revolutions of 1989*, ed. Vladimir Tismaneanu, 19–50. London: Routledge.

Conference on Security and Cooperation in Europe. 1975. Final Act. www.osce.org/documents/mcs/1975/08/4044_en.pdf.

Congressional Quarterly. 1984. "Walesa Peace Prize Acceptance Address, December 11, 1983." In *Historic Documents of 1983,* ed. Carolyn Goldinger and Margaret C. Thompson, 925–932. Washington, D.C.: Congressional Quarterly.

Craig, Mary. 1990. *Lech Walesa: The Leader of Solidarity and Campaigner for Freedom and Human Rights in Poland.* Milwaukee, Wisc.: Gareth Stevens.

Dement, Phillipe. 2001. "Adam Michnik: The Sisyphus of Democracy." *UNESCO Courier.* September.

Dennis, Mike. 2000. *The Rise and Fall of the German Democratic Republic, 1945–1990.* London: Longman.

Dobbs, Michael, K. S. Karol, and Dessa Trevisan. 1981. *Poland: Solidarity: Walesa.* New York: McGraw-Hill Book Company.

Falk, Barbara J. 2003. *The Dilemmas of Dissidence in East-Central Europe: Citizen Intellectuals and Philosopher Kings.* Budapest and New York: Central European University Press.

Garton Ash, Timothy. 2002. *The Polish Revolution: Solidarity.* 3d ed. New Haven, Conn.: Yale University Press.

———. 1999a. *The Magic Lantern: The Revolution of '89 Witnessed in Warsaw, Budapest, Berlin and Prague.* New York: Vintage Books.

———. 1999b. "The Year of Truth." In *The Revolutions of 1989,* ed. Vladimir Tismaneanu, 108–24. London: Routledge.

———. 1990. "Eastern Europe: The Year of Truth." *New York Review of Books* (February 15): 17–22.

Gates, Robert. 1996. *From the Shadows: The Ultimate Insider's Story of Five Presidents and How They Won the Cold War.* New York: Simon and Schuster.

King, Mary E. 2002. "The Polish Fight for Freedom." In *Matatma Gandhi and Martin luther King, Jr.: The Power of Nonviolent Action,* 2d ed. 397–407. New Delhi: Indian Council for Cultural Relations and Mehta Publishers; orig. Paris: UNESCO,1999.

Kramer, Mark. 2009. "The Dialectics of Empire: Soviet Leaders and the Challenge of Civil Resistance in East-Central Europe, 1968–1991." In *Civil Resistance and Power Politics: The Experience of Non-violent Action from Gandhi to the Present,* ed. Adam Roberts and Timothy Garton Ash, 91–109. Oxford: Oxford University Press.

Kuroń, Jacek. 1999. "Overcoming Totalitarianism." In *The Revolutions of 1989,* ed. Vladimir Tismaneanu, 198–201. London: Routledge.

Lazo, Caroline. 1993. *Lech Walesa.* New York: Dillon Press.

Lipski, Jan Jozef. 1985. *KOR: A History of the Workers Defense Committee in Poland, 1976–1981.* Berkeley: University of California Press.

Mason, David S. 1996. *Revolution and Transition in East-Central Europe.* 2d ed. Boulder: Westview Press.

Michnik, Adam. 1985. *Letters from Prison and Other Essays.* Berkeley: University of California Press.

Michta, Andrew A. 1997. "Democratic Consolidation in Poland after 1989." In *The Consolidation of Democracy in East-Central Europe,* ed. Karen Dawisha and Bruce Parrott, 66–108. Cambridge: Cambridge University Press.

Paulson, Joshua. 2005. "Poland's Self-Liberation, 1980–1989." In *Waging Nonviolent Struggle: 20th Century Practice and 21st Century Potential,* ed. Gene Sharp, 223–29. Boston: Porter Sargent Publishers.

Puddington, Arch. 2003. *Broadcasting Freedom: The Cold War Triumph of Radio Free Europe and Radio Liberty.* Lexington: University Press of Kentucky.

Repa, Jan. 2001. "Profile: Poland's Last Communist Leader." BBC World News. May 16.

Roberts, Adam. 1991. *Civil Resistance in the East European and Soviet Revolutions.* Monograph series, no. 4. Cambridge, Mass.: Albert Einstein Institute.

Sharp, Gene. 1980. *Social Power and Political Freedom.* Boston: Porter Sargent Publishers.

———. 1973. *The Politics of Nonviolent Action.* 3 vols. Boston: Porter Sargent Publishers.

Smolar, Aleksander. 2009. "Towards 'Self-Limiting Revolution': Poland, 1970–1989," In *Civil Resistance and Power Politics: The Experience of Non-violent Action from Gandhi to the Present,* ed. Adam Roberts and Timothy Garton Ash, 127–143. Oxford: Oxford University Press.

Sosin, Gene. 1999. *Sparks of Liberty: An Insider's Memoir of Radio Liberty.* University Park: Pennsylvania State University Press.

Stokes, Gale. 1993. *The Walls Came Tumbling Down: The Collapse of Communism in Eastern Europe.* New York: Oxford University Press.

Tighe, Carl. 1997. "Adam Michnik: A Life in Opposition." *Journal of European Studies* 27:323–366.

Wałęsa, Lech. 1992. *The Struggle and the Triumph: An Autobiography.* With the collaboration of Arkadiusz

Rybicki, trans. Franklin Philip and Helen Mahut. New York: Arcade Publishing.

———. 1987. *A Way of Hope.* New York: Henry Holt and Company.

Walker, Martin. 1994. *The Cold War: A History.* New York: Henry Holt and Company.

Zielonka, Jan. 1989. *Political Ideas in Contemporary Poland.* Aldershot, England: Avebury, Gower Publishing Company.

Ziółkowski, Janusz. 1990. "The Roots, Branches and Blossoms of Solidarność." In *Spring in Winter: The 1989 Revolutions,* ed. Gwyn Prins, 39–62. Manchester and New York: Manchester University Press.

From *The New York Times*

Andelman, David. 1979. "Pope Calls on Polish Government for Guarantee of Religious Liberty; Freedom Sharply Restricted." June 6.

Darnton, John. 1981. "Polish Police Break up Farmer Protest." March 19.

———. 1981. "Millions in Poland Go on 4-Hour Strike to Protest Violence." March 28.

———. 1981. "Polish Party Assails Appeal by Union." September 10.

———. 1981. "Poland's Union Meeting Asks Free Elections to Parliament." September 11.

———. 1981. "Poland Restricts Civil and Union Rights; Solidarity Activists Urge General Strike." December 14.

Green, Peter. 2001. "An Aging Ex-Dictator Who Refuses to Recant." May 27.

Kaufman, Michael T. 2004. "Jacek Kuron, of Solidarity, Dies at 70." June 18.

———.1987. "Poland's Plucky Activist." April 26.

Tagliabue, John. 1988. "Thousands at Gdansk Shipyard Join Polish Strike." May 3.

———. 1987. "Nationwide Vote in Poland Rejects a Party Proposal." December 1.

Unsigned. 1981. "Beyond Bydgoszcz." March 25.

Unsigned. 1981. "Neither Polish Nor a Solution." December 14.

Unsigned. 1981. "Widespread Strikes Reported in Defiance of Polish Regime; U.S. Postpones All Pending Aid." December 15.

Unsigned. 1980. "Demanding the Unthinkable in Poland." August 19.

Unsigned. 1979. "The Polish Pope in Poland." June 5.

HUNGARY: COLLECTIVE MEMORY AND A NEGOTIATED REVOLUTION

In the 1980s, Hungarians held in their national, collective memory the bloodshed of two revolutionary movements in 1848 and 1956. Whereas Poland's Solidarity union chose to challenge the communist party-state through economic non-cooperation in the form of strikes, the Hungarian democratic opposition used the commemoration of national history in its call to collective action to reform the communist regime.

The Magyars, a people whose language is unrelated to the Indo-European languages (except Finnish and Estonian), originated thousands of years ago in the Ural Mountains area and are the principal ethnic group of Hungary. The kingdom of Hungary was independent under Saint Stephen (1000–1039), but over the centuries its boundaries repeatedly altered as a result of European conquests and wars. In the sixteenth century, Hungary fell to the Turks and was administered as part of the Ottoman Empire.

The Austrians eventually usurped Hungary into the Hapsburg dominions, as a consequence of Ottoman invasion and rule, as well as religious dissent and feudal power struggles. The Protestant Reformation had won over a majority of Hungarians, who became Calvinist or Lutheran. Feuds between individual (particularly Magyar) groups and a Hapsburg strategy of divide-and-rule helped shape the ethnic composition of the Hungarian basin.

In the mid-nineteenth century, protracted nationalist struggle by Hungarians against the Hapsburgs culminated in the 1848 revolution during a year of upheaval across Europe. Rising nationalism, yearning for freedoms and popular involvement in governance, social developments resulting from the Industrial Revolution, and hunger after crop losses in the 1840s had contributed to growing tumult across Europe. The Hungarians' struggle was ended as more than 300,000 troops of Czar Nicholas I marched into Hungary. The czar was anxious that the Hapsburg monarch should not disintegrate and feared that unrest would spread to Russia. Austrian supremacy was restored. Emperor Franz Joseph had by 1849 had leaders of the Hungarian struggle executed or exiled and imposed unsparing martial law. Following a compromise in 1867, the emperor of Austria was king of Hungary in a "dual monarchy" with a single diplomatic service.

World War I not only shattered and weakened the general structure of the Habsburg lands, but also revived efforts by individual nationalities, such as the Hungarians, to break loose from Austrian rule. Hungary remained in the Austro-Hungarian Empire until 1918, when it proclaimed itself an independent republic following the empire's defeat as a member of the Central Powers at the close of the war. The collapse of the Hapsburgs in 1918 led to Hungary's dismemberment and a reduction of territory by two-thirds.

During World War II, Hungary allied with Germany until its leader, Admiral Nicholas Horthy, tried to reverse course; the Germans, who occupied the country, arrested him. Budapest unconditionally surrendered to Soviet forces in early 1945. In an armistice with the Allied powers, Hungary relinquished territory acquired through the 1938 dismemberment of Czechoslovakia and agreed to return to its 1937 borders. After the war, in free elections in November 1945, the Hungarian communist party got 17 percent of the vote. Yet with Soviet troops omnipresent, the party's ruthless "salami tactics," which sliced up the country's fledgling democratic institutions piece by piece, and a 1948 communist takeover consolidated control.

The introduction of a Soviet-type government system secured communist party dominance over the legislative and executive branches of government and the legal system. Other political parties were eliminated. In 1948 the Communist Party and the Social Democratic Party merged into the Hungarian Workers Party, which after 1956 reorganized into the Hungarian Socialist Workers Party (Magyar Szocialista Munkáspárt, MSzMP).

From 1949 to 1953, the government advanced forced industrialization and collectivization, along with the deportation of "class enemies" to rural areas. "Those who are not with us are against us" was the slogan of the party's general secretary, Mátyás Rákosi. Informers riddled the society during a phase of violent turmoil, torture, and executions. "Social life, civil society and social networks were deliberately sabotaged and destroyed by the communists," according to Hungarian philosopher Elemer Hankiss (1990).

QUICK FACTS ABOUT HUNGARY

- In the 1956 Hungarian uprising, Soviet forces removed Imre Nagy from power and crushed the rebellion, killing 20,000 Hungarians and wounding 150,000.

- In the late 1980s, between 65,000 and 80,000 Soviet troops were stationed in Hungary.

- By the 1980s, 20 to 30 percent of Hungarians lived in poverty, and 80 percent held second and third jobs. An unreported decline in life expectancy had begun in the late 1970s, attributable to overwork.

- By 1988, Hungary owed $18 billion in foreign debts.

- In January 1988 in the People's Park in Budapest, 600 people met in the Jurta Theater for the first session of the Hungarian Democratic Forum. The police did not break up the meeting.

- On March 16, 1989, *New York Times* correspondent Henry Kamm reports that 75,000 persons marched in opposition to the communist regime. Most accounts suggest the number was in excess of 100,000.

- On May 2, 1989, Hungary officially removed a manifestation of the iron curtain by cutting the barbed wire fence demarcating the Hungarian-Austrian border. This allowed citizens of Hungary, East Germany, and other Soviet bloc countries to begin their "exit" to the West.

- The June 16, 1989, reburial of former prime minister Imre Nagy in Budapest attracted 250,000 demonstrators and spectators.

- On October 7, 1989, the Hungarian communist party formally dissolved itself.

- On October 23, 1989, the thirty-third anniversary of the 1956 uprising, Mátyás Szűrös announced the new Hungarian Republic from the balcony of the parliament building. That evening, three memorial marches, each with approximately 100,000 demonstrators, converged in front of the parliament building.

- By November 1989, approximately 200,000 East Germans had exiled themselves in the West.

- In free elections in April 1990, the Hungarian Democratic Forum won more than half the seats in the parliament.

THE 1956 UPRISING

Having undertaken some liberalization starting in 1953, the Stalinist Mátyás Rákosi was replaced as general leader in July 1956. Demonstrations and a tidal wave of popular revolt demanded the transfer of power to Imre Nagy, a former prime minister regarded as a moderate communist. Soviet politburo members flew to Budapest to oversee the transfer of power to Nagy as premier and János Kádár as party leader. Responding to public demands, Nagy began to call for free elections, multiparty politics, negotiations to withdraw Hungary from the Warsaw Pact, and recall of Soviet forces. On November 1, Nagy proclaimed the country's neutrality, going well beyond what the Kremlin was willing to tolerate. On November 4, some 200,000 Soviet forces launched a massive attack against Budapest using 2,500 tanks and armored cars. The Soviets removed Nagy from power, killed 20,000 Hungarians, and wounded 150,000 people. Kádár had briefly supported the uprising, but after being installed by the Soviets as prime minister during their suppression of the revolt, he betrayed Nagy. Rákosi was reinstated. In 1958, the state hanged Nagy and buried him face-down in an unmarked mound, alongside the unidentified mounds of 300 others killed for political reasons. Thousands were arrested. Nagy's execution would become central to the historical memory and shape the events of 1989.

The 1956 uprising and its brutal suppression sent shockwaves across the globe and solidified the Soviet bloc. The world came to accept Eastern Europe as part of the Soviet sphere of influence and merely rued the Hungarian tragedy. Hungarian troops participated in the 1968 Warsaw Pact invasion of Czechoslovakia that crushed the Prague Spring (see **Czechoslovakia, Introduction**). By the late 1980s, between 65,000 and 80,000 Soviet troops were based in Hungary, in some 40 garrisons. Nonetheless, of all the Eastern European communist parties, the Hungarian party was the most inclined toward reform. Stalin did not destroy it with purges and brutality as had happened to the Polish party.

In 1982, Prime Minister Kádár introduced measures to decentralize the economy. These brought Hungary to a level of relative economic contentment and limited freedoms unmatched in the Soviet bloc. By the early 1980s, Hungary had the most pro-liberalization government in the Warsaw Pact, but Kádár acknowledged the declining economic situation in the country.

Within the Soviet Orbit

Until World War II, Hungary was largely agrarian, but once under Soviet hegemony, Hungary became the most economically successful of the Eastern bloc satellites. Agriculture was coercively collectivized, from 1958 to 1961. After the 1956 carnage, Prime Minister Kádár made efforts to gain legitimacy for the party. It launched cautious liberalization and economic modifications beginning in 1968, marking the transition from a centrally planned system to one with partial freedoms and piecemeal market reforms. Hungary was more attractive to foreign investment than its neighbors. Despite its relative successes, however, the system continued to suffer from internal problems. Semi-independent businesses still relied on cooperatives for supplies and distribution. Such industries as developed were energy-intensive, inflexible, polluting, and wasteful.

During détente—the general loosening of tensions between the Soviet Union and United States and a thaw in the cold war from the late 1960s into the 1980s—the Soviets encouraged their satellite countries to leap into Western markets to try to alleviate some of their economic problems. Hungarian party-state leaders borrowed to purchase advanced technology and then tried to sell their outmoded products to the West in order to service their debts. With managers pushing loans and increasing investments into obsolete enterprises, the plan ultimately failed. The Stalinist economic systems were too rigid and stymied by ideology. Foreign loans were used by the Magyar state to buy consumer goods to boost the deteriorating economy and political legitimacy of the party that controlled what had become a backward society.

Visible inequities between a new entrepreneurial class and urban sectors that were still dependent on socialist schemes for production of basic goods and services exacerbated the situation and led to quasi-reforms that would eventually contribute to the downfall of Hungary's system. Aside from encumbering major indebtedness, the reforms failed to address the basic weaknesses of Stalinist institutions, which continued to entrench corruption, further spreading pessimism, cynicism, and disillusionment while awakening popular curiosity and interest in Western ideas and comparative prosperity (see **"Introduction: Strikes, Sinatra, and Nonviolent Revolution"**).

By the 1980s, 20 to 30 percent of Hungarians lived in poverty. Eighty percent held more than one job. An unreported decline in life expectancy developed in the late 1970s, attributable to overwork. By 1988, Hungary owed $18 billion in foreign debt. *The New York Times* reports on May 29, 1988, that for Hungarians this was "an era in which the boom of the 1970s soured . . . to stagnation, inflation of about 20 percent a year, the painful introduction of capitalist-style income- and value-added taxes, falling real wages and the threat of unemployment. Hungarians have been pained in recent years to see the shrinkage in the purchasing power of their wages and extra earnings in their second and third jobs, as well as in the tolerated but marginal private sector" (see "In Hungary, Flexibility as Doctrine").

Calls for a "Social Contract"

The calls for workers' rights and political freedoms echoing from Poland in the 1980s revived the Hungarians' revolutionary spirit. The years 1848 and 1956 provided strong rhetorical points for rallying public consciousness. In 1986, Hungarians began holding demonstrations in Budapest on the anniversary of the first Hungarian revolution in 1848, the nation's unofficial independence day.

The Budapest School played a contributing role in the eventual disintegration of state socialism in Hungary. The school was named for a group of philosophers at Budapest University who had gathered in the late 1960s around György Lukács, a Marxist theoretician with an international following who argued that Hungarian communism had deviated from its original concerns. He coined and popularized the slogan "Back to Marx." Lukács helped young philosophers close to him find in the early writings of Karl Marx the footing for their own critiques. Despite persecution and exile, the members of the school persisted and in 1977 were among the thirty-four Hungarian intellectuals who publicly supported Charter 77 in solidarity with Czechoslovak activist intellectuals (see "Prague Detains Five Dissidents after Human Rights Manifesto").

Despite Soviet efforts to inhibit communications among satellite populations, cross-border awareness grew. At the same time that KOR-KSS (Committee for the Workers' Defense, KOR, and Social Self-Defense Committee, KSS) began in Poland in 1976 (see **Poland, Introduction**), Hungary's opposition intellectuals also coalesced, although in smaller numbers. Hungary's first typewritten *samizdat* ("self-published," in Russian) passed from hand to hand. In 1978, the Hungarian variation of Poland's Flying University sponsored its inaugural lecture. Monday night talks persisted for years in Budapest parlors, with up to 400 listening in separately wired rooms. At weekly "samizdat boutiques" in private flats, readers could buy publications without identifying themselves. In winter 1980–1981, inspired by Solidarity, twenty-five intellectuals in Budapest openly founded the journal *Beszélö* (Speaker). János Kis, a member of the Budapest School, played a central role at the journal and became a principal thinker guiding the opposition. In 1987, *Beszélö* editors called for a new "social contract," including political and civil rights, rule of law, constitutionalism, freedom of the press, and checks on the communist party's power. The journal focused on a social contract to promote civil society as the only sound basis for democracy.

As creative ideas penetrated Eastern-bloc borders, worsening living conditions meant some Hungarians had less to lose by resisting indifferent party elites. In the wake of the August 1, 1975, signing of the Final Act of the Helsinki Accords, some Hungarian minorities were openly pressing for human rights through independent organizations (see **"Introduction: Strikes, Sinatra, and Nonviolent Revolution"**). The Hungarian activist intellectuals who would eventually deem themselves the "democratic opposition" numbered only a few hundred in the early 1980s. The relative liberalism of the Kádár regime facilitated the ability of educated Hungarians to share in samizdat from their sister countries, follow the democratizing upsurges in Poland and Czechoslovakia, and even to travel openly to Prague for meetings.

The oppositional movements throughout the Soviet bloc, including in Hungary, would generally follow the strategy of the Poles in Solidarity: offer the authorities a choice between the lesser evil of increasing independence for the people or aggressive confrontation. This was far more than "dissidence," János Kis later explained: the point was to place those in power in a predicament. Either they could clamp down with brutality, or they could accept their loss of control of the civil society under construction. Political scientists call this dynamic "the king's dilemma": the monarch must liberalize to stay in power, yet the more the king sponsors reforms, the less power he possesses.

Reform-minded Communists

Mikhail S. Gorbachev rose to power as the Soviet Communist Party general secretary in 1985 and within a few years introduced changes meant to revitalize a stagnating Soviet economy that for a decade had been growing at only 2 percent annually. Gorbachev's reforms, while interconnected, fell into four main categories: *perestroika* (restructuring of the economy); *glasnost* (openness or publicity); democratization; and new thinking in foreign policy.

In Hungary, the number and influence of reformers inside the communist party were growing. They may have become a majority by the mid-1980s. *The Times* observes on May 29, 1988, that after Gorbachev came to power, communist leaders who were "seeking Soviet approval as the best way of rising to the top, have been inspired not only to be nondogmatic but even to let it be known that they are 'pragmatists'" (see **"In Hungary, Flexibility as Doctrine"**). The first of the new pragmatists was Prime Minister Károly Grósz, who replaced Kádár as general secretary of the Hungarian Socialist Workers' Party in 1988.

Grósz wanted to weaken the role of the party and style a less inhibited approach by the news media while allowing "interest organizations," such as agricultural associations and trade unions, more sway. He realized that Hungary lagged behind the Soviet Union in political reforms. *The Times* on April 2, 1989, reports on Grósz's visit to Moscow on March 23 and March 24, 1989, and his meeting with Gorbachev for four hours (see "Gorbachev Said to Reject Soviet Right to Intervene"). Briefing the Hungarian party's Central Committee, Grósz reported that Gorbachev "indicated to him that safeguards must be provided to prevent a repetition of the Soviet invasions of Hungary and Czechoslovakia." What these protections might be was not clarified, but *The Times* correspondent Henry Kamm quotes an unnamed Hungarian as saying, somewhat humorously, that "the only necessary safeguard would be a Soviet leader who will not order his armies to march into other countries." Grósz also indicated he had "obtained a promise from Moscow that Hungarian historians would be granted access to Soviet documents related to the 1956 uprising." As Kamm fittingly notes, "a reinterpretation of the events of October and November 1956 has become one of the benchmarks of the degree of liberalization under way in Hungary."

After the August 1968 Soviet-led invasion of Czechoslovakia by Warsaw Pact troops, the Soviet Communist Party daily *Pravda* justified the incursion by citing a principle that in the West was dubbed the Brezhnev Doctrine, named for the party leader Leonid I. Brezhnev. *Pravda* acknowledged a variety of paths to socialism but maintained that each country's communist party was "responsible not only to its own people but also to all the socialist countries and to the entire communist movement." In other words, the Kremlin was asserting the right to intervene in any country in the Soviet bloc in order to prevent counterrevolution or loss of party control. The Brezhnev Doctrine darkened the prospects for change and resistance across Eastern Europe for the following decade (see **"Introduction: Strikes, Sinatra, and Nonviolent Revolution"**). In the April 2 *Times,* Kamm quotes Hungarian party spokesman Laszlo Major as saying, "[T]he Gorbachev-Grosz talks showed that what Western news organizations have called the 'Brezhnev doctrine,' was dead."

Harbingers of Change

A tangible harbinger of change became visible in Budapest on March 15, 1986, as a crowd gathered around a statue of the poet Sandor Petofi, a hero of the 1848 revolution. Those assembled excitedly realized that they had an impressive turnout—approximately 3,000 persons. For decades, students had been keeping the nation's unofficial independence day alive after its abandonment by the communist regime following World War II. Carrying high a Hungarian flag, the mostly young, teenaged demonstrators clapped as they walked slowly through Budapest, marching from one monument to another, singing nationalist songs (see "The Hungarians, Gingerly, Recall Day in '56 When It All Changed").

Another omen indicating broad shifts under way was evident in a *Times* story from Michael T. Kaufman on October 19, 1986, that illustrates the developing cross-border awareness among the generative intellectuals of the subjugated countries (see "122 in East Europe Proclaim Praise of Hungarian Uprising"). Despite Soviet bans on communications between the satellite states, 122 Eastern Europeans issued a signed proclamation in Budapest, East Berlin, Prague, and Warsaw. The statement extolled the 1956 Hungarian uprising as "our common heritage and inspiration" and was timed to commemorate the anniversary of the Hungarian uprising that had begun thirty years earlier. Kaufman calls it the "boldest open document ever issued in the East bloc." The four-paragraph proclamation connected the samizdat authors, organizers against totalitarianism, and human rights activists in four of the six Warsaw Pact allies of the Soviet Union. In its portrayal of the turbulent start of Hungary's doomed popular revolt, the declaration discloses the consternation of a generation of Eastern Europeans, some of whom were beginning to rise against state-controlled media, official concealment, and suppression of debate: "On the 23d of October 1956, workers, students and soldiers stormed the radio building in Budapest because they were fed up with the official lies and wished to hear the truth and to voice their demands."

By 1987, Hungarian activist intellectuals had gone beyond asking that the state honor the Helsinki Final Act and human rights and were calling on the government to let society define state limits. That was the same year that *Beszélö* called for a new "social contract" with civil society as the basis for democracy. By 1988, a number of new, independent groups had begun organizing openly and suggesting that they should share in power, although this concept was not tightly defined. The civil society for which Poland's Solidarity union had been fighting for eight years manifested itself more quickly in Hungary.

In January 1988, in the Jurta Theater in the People's Park in Budapest, 600 persons met for the first session of the Hungarian Democratic Forum (Magyar Demokrata Forum, MDF) (see "In Hungary, Flexibility as Doctrine"). Discussion focused on parliamentary democracy; reformers within the communist party attended. MDF had been founded in 1987 in Lakitelek by 160 intellectuals, many of whom had links to Imre Pozsgay, the leading communist reformer. By late 1988, the MDF would have 10,000 members. The Alliance of Free Democrats (Szabad Demokraták Szövetsége, SzDSz) at the time had 1,500 members.

In March, law students organized Fiatal Demokraták Szövetsége (FIDESz, pron. fee'-dess), the Alliance of Democratic Youth, which became the first autonomous group to declare its purpose as a "political organization." Students were among the most militant proponents of democratic freedoms. Membership in FIDESz, conceived as an alternative to the official communist youth organization, was limited to persons between the ages of sixteen and thirty-five. The government soon declared it illegal. In May, workers formed the Democratic Union of Scientific Workers, the first independent trade union. The Network of Free Initiatives followed. The Democratic Forum, Free Democrats, and Democratic Youth were the three main Hungarian political parties that formed in the late 1980s, yet dozens more were jockeying to become players. By December, the League of Independent Trade Unions was formed. The Democratic Forum, the largest of the independent groups, would a year later claim 12,000 members.

By late 1988, more than fifty independently organized civil society groups existed. With the economy exhausted, inflation rising, and unemployment looming, reformers inside the government had begun advocating cooperation and dialog with the various "autonomous organizations," as they called them, and a need for institutional changes to generate societal support for the party's economic policy changes. Yet as sociologists Lászlo Bruszt and David Stark put it, "the reformers were still too weak to speak in the name of the regime, and the opposition was much too weak to speak in the name of society" (1992, 26). No single organization could embody the democratic opposition and confront the communist party on its own, as with Solidarity in Poland.

On May 31, 1988, *The Times* comments that Prime Minister Grósz had appointed "aggressive reformers to the new Politburo" and had "managed an orderly rotation at the top, a difficult feat in any one-party state." Yet, the newspaper editorializes, "A more daring feat would be to set a limit on [Grósz's] own term in office, a truly revolutionary notion in geriatric Eastern Europe."

By September, the democratic opposition had become more coherent. Official media published accounts of strikes and other collective nonviolent actions. Environmental activists organized a demonstration of 30,000 in Budapest, in front of the parliament building, in opposition to the construction of a dam on the Danube River. The main independent groups endorsed the rally in what was the first major outspoken public questioning of the legitimacy of the National Assembly, whose members had previously been "elected" in name only. Protesters chanted "Democracy or Dam!"

By December, Grósz had decided to attempt to marginalize the opposition. He informed parliament that from 1989 onward, March 15, the anniversary of the 1848 revolution, would be a national holiday. Grósz sought to appease critics and hoped to weaken the government's democratic opponents by incorporating the alternative organizations into the party's newfound embrace of the collective memory of 1848. The national celebration was supposed to salute national unity, in which all Hungarians wanted "democracy" and a "multiparty" political system and banded together under the party's catchphrase, "renewal."

On January 26, 1989, the government announced that Imre Nagy and his comrades would be reburied. As October 1989 and the thirtieth anniversary of the 1956 uprising neared, authorities grew visibly uneasy. Everyone knew that after Soviet troops had crushed the revolt, Kádár ordered Prime Minister Nagy executed, along with 300 others. On February 10, the Central Committee of the communist party issued a determination that the 1956 uprising had been a "popular uprising against an oligarchic rule that had debased the nation" and agreed that multiparty democracy was needed. The party aligned itself with the democratic opposition in this regard. Inside the party, reformers had been fighting for this capitulation. Also in February, the government yielded on a bit of important symbolism. Not only would it permit celebrations on March 15, but it would also give Nagy a state funeral with reburial on June 16, 1989.

On March 16, *The Times* correspondent Henry Kamm reports the conservative estimate of 75,000 persons having marched in opposition to the communist regime on the day of independence, the day before (see "Thousands of Hungarians March to Commemorate Revolt in 1848"). Kamm notes that the government "urged the members of various informal, but no longer clandestine, opposition groups to join in one national celebration, but did not object when 31 such organizations staged their own joint commemoration." The thirty-one independent groups probably collectively brought out a crowd in excess of 100,000. (Journalists habitually underestimate such numbers, to be safe.) Their rally, which paralleled official March 15 events, started at the Petofi statue, which also marks the point at which the demonstration of October 23, 1956, began. Hungarian television broadcast the official and alternative events, making evident which was the better attended. By eclipsing the official event, the democratic opposition came into its own that day. The parallel event and demonstration made clear that Hungarians now had a choice: the party-state or what had cohered into a fully fledged opposition.

Hungary Cuts through the Iron Curtain

On April 25, *The Times* quotes Hungarian foreign minister Gyula Horn as saying that genuine democracy was Hungary's main goal, the top priority being "to institutionalize pluralism and establish a real role for Parliament." He said the end result "must be of revolutionary nature." He would soon turn his words into action.

On May 2, 1989, Hungary removed the barbed wire fence demarcating the Hungarian and Austrian border, cutting a "hole" in the iron curtain, a central event in the chronicle of the former Soviet states' transition to democracy, a momentous saga of the twentieth century. This allowed citizens of Hungary, East Germany, and other Soviet bloc countries to begin their "exit" to the West. The event was attended by Hungarian leaders and filmed by Western media. Previously, it had been impossible for Hungarians to cross into Austria. The repercussions from the Hungarian decision, influenced by reform elements within the communist party, would be spectacular. The regimes in East Germany and Czechoslovakia would have to choose between prohibiting their citizens from visiting Hungary as tourists or risk their permanent departure.

By mid-July 1989, as anticipated, thousands of East German tourists traveled via Czechoslovakia to Hungary, where they then crossed the newly opened border with Austria and thence to West Germany. The East German government complained that existing requirements for exit visas were being violated by the Hungarian government. When Budapest sought to enforce the exit permission obligations in regard to its border with Austria, East Germans who had entered Hungary in order to leave the Eastern bloc found themselves stranded. By September, some 3,000 of them were camped out at the West German embassy in Budapest, with perhaps 100,000 more elsewhere in Hungary mulling over their options.

After weeks of diplomatic activity, on September 10 Horn resolved the crisis matter-of-factly by announcing that the East German refugees had the right of free movement. A week later, Prime Minister Miklós Németh declared the border permanently open. The government ordered all barriers on the Austrian border removed to let the Germans leave. The East German government forbade travel to Hungary, which resulted in new floods of tourists traveling "westward" through Poland and Czechoslovakia, from whence they could enter West Germany, with comparable encampments in those countries.

The Times, on September 11, 1989, reports that on the previous night, East Germans seeking to make their way to West Germany through Hungary had departed their homes (see "Hungary Allows 7,000 East Germans to Emigrate West"). By November, approximately 200,000 East Germans had exiled themselves in the West.

Multipower Politics

Of all the communist parties in Eastern Europe, the Hungarian party was the most disposed to reform. By 1988, "reform circles" in local branches of the party were manifest. They began to pressure the party leadership, championing a view that the party's hard-line policies had become, in the words of Bruszt and Stark, "a most damaging liability" (1992, 37). Reformers in parliament were also showing independence from the party line. On April 25, Prime Minister Németh, who had been appointed by party general secretary Grósz, appeared on evening television and repudiated a speech by Grósz, thus distancing himself from the party hierarchy. Even the government was beginning to differentiate itself from the party.

On May 1, 1989, the communist party convened its customary May Day event in Budapest's central park, where Grósz spoke. Much as on March 15, the League of Independent Trade Unions held a parallel rally. Tens of thousands attended, as a new federation, the Opposition Round Table (Ellenzéki Kerekasztal, EKA), made its first public appearance as an umbrella under which the most significant of the democratic opposition groups could act in unison. Its creation had begun when on March 23, under the sponsorship of the Association of Independent Lawyers, representatives from eight opposition groups had met to create a coordinating mechanism. EKA argued, "The political and economic crisis cannot be solved by any kind of 'power sharing.' The solution . . . is for power to be legitimated by genuinely free, fully contested, elections." The demise of the concept of reforming the existing system was in sight.

Henry Kamm's interview of Grósz in *The Times* on May 15, 1989, reveals that the communist party-state had concluded that to remain in power it had to open the arena to multipower politics (see "In Hungary, the Political Changes Are Tempered by Economic Fears"). As János Kis would later note, the democratic opposition had sought to create a dilemma for the party: it either could clamp down with deadly coercive measures or accommodate the reality that the party was steadily losing control of the civil society under construction.

On June 16 in Budapest, the reburial of former prime minister Nagy attracted 250,000 demonstrators and spectators who filed somberly through Heroes' Square before six caskets bearing the exhumed remains of Nagy, his defense minister Pal Maleter, and three of their colleagues. The sixth coffin was empty, a symbol chosen to commemorate *all* 20,000 Hungarians who had been killed in 1956. Many came to the event from Poland, including Adam Michnik, essayist and adviser to the Solidarity union.

On the occasion of the reburials, leaders from the democratic opposition called for liberalization. *Times* correspondent Henry Kamm on June 17, 1989, reports Viktor Orban of the Alliance of Young Democrats, known as FIDESz, as decrying, "We cannot . . . understand that the party leaders, who made us study from books that falsified the revolution, now rush to touch the coffins as if they were charms of good luck." He appealed for Soviet troops to leave Hungary. Kamm recounted seeing in the audience tearful emotion attesting to the sorrowful burdens of impotence and dishonor that Hungarians had borne since 1956 (see "Hungarian Who Led '56 Revolt Is Buried as a Hero").

The memorializing and rehabilitation of Nagy played a decisive role in solidifying public support for the rebuilding of Hungarian popular sovereignty. Shown on television and covered by national newspapers, the memorial service rallied Hungarians across the country. A week later, Károly Grósz was downgraded from general secretary, put under the tutelage of the party's three main reformers, and replaced with a presidium of four (that included himself) created within the government to ride over a party now rife with divisions. He became one among equals: Grósz, Németh, Pozsgay, and Rezso Nyers. Pozsgay's role as a reformer had been a public one; he was known for emphasizing a wider scope for civil society organizations authentically autonomous from the party. Nyers, a key architect of the 1988–1989 reforms, had been working for months internally to encourage the party to accept its diminishing status and loss of power.

On June 13, 1989, negotiations for free elections in Hungary began, with a few similarities to the Polish round table's fifty-nine days of talks, from February 6 to April 5, 1989. Government officials wanted a round table in the Polish sense (see "To His Volatile Young Allies, Walesa Preaches Conciliation"), yet the fact that an "Opposition Round Table" existed that was, figuratively speaking, already circular, led to a compromise—a three-sided table. The democratic opposition had one side, the quasi-official state entities, such as trade unions, sat at another, and the third side was occupied by Mátyás Szürös, president of the parliament. At a second round of talks on June 21, Pozsgay promised democratic elections, in which the communist party would be competing on an equal basis with other political parties.

On July 6, Kádár died at the age of seventy-seven. Only then was the party-state willing to act on the unresolved historical dilemma of 1956 that had placed in power those who had ridden into office along with Soviet tanks. Within hours, the supreme court rehabilitated Nagy posthumously along with those killed with him. The democratic opposition's focus on commemorating national history had taken a major stride. The official reassessment of 1956 opened the sluice gates to Hungary's negotiated revolution.

On July 30, *Times* correspondent Henry Kamm ruminates on the distance yet to be traveled to democracy in Hungary. He judges, "Unlike Poland, the other East European bastion of reform Communism, Hungary does not present a contest between a ruling party and a formidable opposition movement that quickens the pace of change. The struggle in Hungary is instead among various party leaders who differ on the methods and pace of change and an opposition far more diffuse than Solidarity" ("Hungary Is Far From Democracy, and Even From Poland"). To Kamm, "Hungary has no equivalent for Lech Walesa." Indeed, none of the independent groups in Hungary had achieved the legitimacy of Solidarity and its ability to speak for society.

The trilateral talks advanced in fits and starts, during which time those at the table turned out to be the highest deliberative political body in the land. The negotiations were reconfiguring the political system and creating a new political class. The delegates reached agreement on September 18, providing in intricate formulations new draft laws for free elections and democratic governance. A presidential election would be held in November and balloting for parliamentary elections three months after that.

The agreement envisioned free parliamentary elections, but if conducted under the newly proposed draft laws, the old guard, including corrupt parliamentarians, would likely win and thus get to choose the president. The most fervently anticommunist groups in the growing democratic opposition refused therefore to sign the agreement: the Alliance of Free Democrats (chaired by János Kis), the Alliance of Democratic Youth, and the independent trade unions. *The Times* on September 20 summarizes the opposition's stance: "Electing a powerful president first would put into question the Parliament's powers." The Free Democrats stood on street corners and obtained 200,000 signatures requesting a referendum to postpone the presidential election until after parliamentary balloting in March 1990. The Free Democrats' petitioning succeeded, and the presidential election was rescheduled to follow the free general election, slated for March 25, 1990. In the referendum, 58 percent voted to delay the presidential election (see "Hungary Allows 7,000 East Germans to Emigrate West").

The September 18 agreement resulted in six bills to be submitted to parliament, the National Assembly, described by *The Times* on September 20 as providing "a more democratic electoral law, a new office of President, . . . a law legalizing and guaranteeing rights of political parties, a constitutional court and amendments that would liberalize the penal code and rules of criminal proceedings." Seeking to persuade all the opposition groups to approve the agreement, Pozsgay, the communist party's reform candidate for president, was reported in *The Times* as announcing that the party would hand over to the government property valued at approximately $33 million to finance all of the parties' election campaigns ("Communists and Foes Back a Multiparty Hungary"). On October 7, the Hungarian communist party formally dissolved itself.

On October 18, 1989, no longer a rubber stamp for the communist party, the National Assembly debated and passed the constitutional amendments agreed to at the negotiations one month earlier that would take the nation to parliamentary democracy. Noteworthy was the elimination of "People" from the name of the state and altering the preamble to the constitution to declare "the Hungarian republic is an independent, democratic state based on the rule of law, in which the values of bourgeois democracy and democratic socialism are equally recognized." Although socialism remained, freedoms of assembly and association were legalized, along with other liberties. The new legislation established a "state of law," in which persons' rights are protected by law and all institutions are answerable to the law. Yearning for this protection had guided the country's would-be democrats at least since 1986. As Hungary started shifting away from communism, new parties started to bud.

On October 23, the thirty-third anniversary of the 1956 uprising, Mátyás Szürös announced the new Hungarian Republic from a balcony of parliament. That evening, three distinct memorial marches with 100,000 demonstrators each converged in front of parliament, proclaiming free, independent elections. Former political prisoners made speeches; youths scrambled onto statues. *Times* correspondent Serge Schmemann reports on October 24 that "commemorative rallies were held openly for the first time across Hungary on what was proclaimed a 'day of national reconciliation'" (see "New Hungary Marks '56 Uprising: 'Gorby!' and 'Russians Out!' Mix"). Schmemann notes that the Soviet Union, which by then had some 65,000 troops in Hungary, would withdraw two of its four divisions. The next day Schmemann observes, "Hungarians have never really accepted the status of 'Eastern European.' For 40 years, they have sustained the dream that they were full-fledged Europeans who would rejoin the fold as soon as the Soviets let them go" ("Hungary Hits Ruts on Road to Pluralism").

On March 25, 1990, Hungarians held the first round of a general election. In the country's first free elections since November 1945, more than 60 parties competed in an infant democracy still fragile, experimental, and tentative. The Hungarian Democratic Forum, established but two years earlier, and the Alliance of Free Democrats became the major parties in the new legislature (see "In Hungary, Flexibility as Doctrine"). Both advocated a free market economy and privatization, with the Free Democrats pushing for a rapid changeover. A third party, the Independent Smallholders, also did well; it had been the biggest vote-getter in the last free elections of 1945 and now sought the return of state-appropriated farmlands to their pre-1947 owners. Partly due to proportional representation, no single party received a majority of seats in the National Assembly.

Times reporter Celestine Bohlen states on April 9, 1990, that fewer than 50 percent of Hungary's 7 million eligible voters turned out to cast ballots for the second time in two weeks. The Hungarian Democratic Forum won more than half the seats in parliament (see "Roofless Ghost Mocks Exiting Soviet Troops"). The forum's leader, Jozsef Antall, would become prime minister and establish a conservative coalition, including the Independent Smallholders and Christian Democrats. Cumulatively, they would command more than 60 percent of the seats in the new legislature. A librarian and scholar of medical history, Antall, then 58 years old, addressed "an ebullient crowd" at the communist party's Budapest headquarters, where half a year earlier the building had housed the workers militia, a prop of communist rule (see "Hungary Allows 7,000 East Germans to Emigrate West"). János Kis of the Alliance of Free Democrats told *The Times* his party would be "part of a responsible opposition," because Hungary needed strong government.

According to Bohlen, Antall was a former pariah, the offspring of prominent anticommunists and a youthful participant in the 1956 uprising who had been "marked as politically suspect, periodically interrogated, and until 1974 denied the right to travel abroad, even to the Soviet Union." Antall described the forum as a "European center party," with connections to other Christian Democratic parties, and "committed to a new and rational European order."

Starting in 1989, Poland, then Hungary, and then the rest of the Eastern bloc rejected their communist regimes and pressed for disbanding the Warsaw Pact, formed in 1955 through Soviet prodding as a counterweight to the North Atlantic Treaty Organization. The pact was in essence a series of bilateral agreements between the Soviet Union and its satellites, each of which belonged to the pact, in support of Soviet security objectives (see **"Introduction: Strikes, Sinatra, and Nonviolent Revolution"**). The Hungarians and Soviets signed a pullout agreement on March 10, 1990. According to a *Times* report of June 17, 1991, it had "been strictly followed by the Soviet Army, with a steady convoy of troops and equipment heading eastward across the border . . . ahead of schedule" (see "Roofless Ghost Mocks Exiting Soviet Troops"). "In a move that pushed the cold war further into history," *The Times* reports on July 2, 1991, "the Soviet Union and the five other countries in the Warsaw Pact formally agreed today to dissolve the political and military alliance that long enabled Moscow to dominate Eastern Europe" ("Death Knell Rings for Warsaw Pact").

In late 1991, members of the Hungarian democratic opposition formed Charter 91, a project similar to Charter 77 in Czechoslovakia (see "Prague Detains Five Dissidents after Human Rights Manifesto"). Responding to perceptions that the conservative Hungarian Democratic Forum threatened Hungary's new constitutional liberties, Charter 91 proffered seventeen points in favor of liberal democracy. In less than two months, 5,000 persons had signed on to them. György "George" Konrád—one of the charter's signers who had also signed the October 1986 proclamation commending the 1956 Hungarian revolt (see "122 in East Europe Proclaim Praise of Hungarian Uprising")—described the charter as part of the toolbox of democracy, where "civil society continually searches for and experiments with appropriate forms of expressing itself." The charter sought not to replace institutionalized parliamentary democracy, according to Konrád, but to make sure that government does not become "some far-off chattering on high" (Isaac 1999, 147). Another initiative, the Helsinki Citizens' Assembly, an outcome of international networks between Central European intellectuals and peace movements in Western Europe, sought to bring about alterations in society through citizen action rather than governmental programs. The assembly operated under the assumption that governments would either have to change or become less relevant.

Conclusion

Having dared to cut through the electrified installations of the iron curtain along its border with Austria in May 1989, Hungary by autumn had dashed ahead of Poland on the road to democratization in the sense that on October 7, the Hungarian communist party formally dissolved itself. Hungary would become the first Eastern bloc country to conduct unfettered, multiparty parliamentary elections in spring 1990.

The lines between the democratic opposition and the reformers inside the party were thinner in Hungary than anywhere else in Eastern Europe. This is not to ignore constant persecution by the party-state, but to emphasize the narrowing of differences on ideas about reform in the respective camps. By 1988, Hungarian reformers in the party were supporting extensive social and political change, some even advocating the abandonment of the one-party monopoly altogether. The more tolerant, less repressive environment in Moscow under Gorbachev reflected the Soviet leader's own reasons for wanting political transformation. The leading thinkers of the democratic opposition in Hungary had avoided backing the party-state into a corner. Their refusal to condone violence meant greater sympathy for their political aspirations; they found friends inside the communist apparatus.

Elemer Hankiss explains another factor that played a major role in Hungary: the party elite lost interest in preserving the party. A philosopher and political scientist at the University of Budapest and Academy of Sciences, later head of Hungarian television, Hankiss observes that during the late 1980s a considerable portion of the Hungarian communist party and bureaucracy "discovered a way of converting their bureaucratic power into lucrative economic positions and assets (and indirectly also into a new type of political power)" in Hungary's partially modernizing system based on freer markets and political democratization. Under early, postwar communism, "the Bolshevik leaders coming back from Moscow needed to exercise dictatorial power in order to protect themselves as the ruling élite." By 1965, they were strongly established and "controlled all the economic, political, social, and cultural institutions, resources, and interactions." They "co-opted large numbers of activists and experts," building a constituency that realized it could profit from the existing system. "In this situation, the over-centralised and despotic rule exercised by the party leadership became anachronistic. It was time to decentralise power and to reward the faithful. With this, the development of oligarchic and neo-feudal structures began in Hungary."

When in the late 1980s these new oligarchies saw that they could transfer their power into novel, more efficient socioeconomic developments, to become "part of an emerging new and legitimate ruling class or *grande bourgeosie,* they lost their interest in keeping the communist party as their instrument of power and protection. And, as a consequence, on the night of 7 October 1989 they watched indifferently, or assisted actively in, the self-liquidation of the Party" (Hankiss 1990, 30–31).

Thus the Hungarians negotiated their transition from one form of government to another. In light of communist elites who no longer sought to defend the party, it is not a complete surprise that the democratic opposition held the trump card.

The Soviet troops departed from Hungary on June 19, 1991. On May 1, 2004, Hungary joined the European Union.

The Truth about 1956

Soviet forces installed János Kádár in power after he suddenly changed sides in the middle of the 1956 uprising. He was relatively popular during the 1960s and 1970s due to the government's comparatively liberal stance and somewhat rising standard of living. Kádár's regime seemed solid, but it was heavily indebted, borrowing to compensate for the inflation and unemployment that would otherwise challenge the communist reverie of having devised a superior economic system. In 1985 at the communist party congress, Kádár admitted that standards of living had declined. Many Hungarians held his ministers responsible for their problems but did not blame him. Within the party, a robust discussion on reform strategies had begun; among the Hungarian people, currents were churning below the surface.

A tangible harbinger of change was visible in Budapest on March 15, 1986, as a crowd gathered around a statue of the poet Sandor Petofi, a hero of the 1848 revolution. Those assembled were excited when they counted approximately 3,000 persons, more than they had expected. Students had been keeping alive the nation's unofficial independence day after the communist regime abandoned it following World War II.

Those mingling were mostly young, many of them teenagers. At noon, they began moving slowly, carrying high a Hungarian flag of red, white, and green bands. Clapping as they walked the old passageways of Pest, on the left bank of the Danube River, they marched from one monument to another, singing nationalist songs. A few speakers called for democracy. Those watching from windows who remembered the uprising of 1956, crushed by Soviet tanks, must have felt anxiety, but the largely youthful marchers evinced no fear. That evening, police broke up a smaller march on the Chain Bridge, beating demonstrators and spectators with truncheons in what the university-based academicians and students call the "battle of the bridge." *The New York Times* did not report on the 1986 demonstration nor did Hungary's official media publish anything about it.

As October and the thirtieth anniversary of the 1956 uprising neared, Hungarian authorities became visibly uneasy. All Hungarians knew the details of the rebellion: Soviet troops had crushed the revolt, and in 1958 the Kádár government executed Prime Minister Imre Nagy and 300 others and disposed of their bodies in unmarked graves.

On November 5, *The Times* ponders the disagreements over what had happened in 1956. Thirty years on, some contested that history had been rewritten. After Soviet forces subdued the street fighting, the Kádár-led Hungarian Socialist Workers Party judged the uprising to be an upheaval in response to mistakes by the postwar Stalinist government of Mátyás Rákosi. This view holds that communists led by Prime Minister Imre Nagy had used the events as justification for trying to withdraw Hungary from the Warsaw Pact, and in declaring Hungary's neutrality were thus guilty of treason.

János Berecz, an historian quoted by *The Times*, said that the workers had erected barricades from which to attack Soviet patrols with weaponry given to them by Hungarian soldiers, and that on November 1, Kádár had commended those who had fought in the streets. Within three days, however, Kádár, it is claimed, had parted ways with Nagy. Leading a new party, Kádár disparaged as "counterrevolutionaries" the same students, laborers, and peasants he had earlier praised. What happened during those three days was, *The Times* observes, not yet understood. Asked at a news conference about holes in the historical account, Berecz acknowledged that the Hungarians were not in possession of the truth.

NOVEMBER 5, 1986
THE HUNGARIANS, GINGERLY, RECALL DAY IN '56 WHEN IT ALL CHANGED
By MICHAEL T. KAUFMAN
Special to The New York Times

SZOLNOK, Hungary, Nov 4 – The Hungarian Government of Janos Kadar today modestly recalled its origins in this provincial town where it proclaimed itself 30 years ago as Soviet tanks rumbled past to quell a popular uprising in Budapest. . . .

[T]he ceremony was overwhelmed and muted by the national flags, red banners and posters of Lenin being installed all over this country to celebrate the anniversary Friday of the Russian Revolution.

"For us this is not a festival," said Janos Berecz, a party secretary who was the main speaker here. "Because the Hungarian experience of 30 years ago includes bitter memories, we lower our flags modestly when we mark the day, and we do not make it a holiday." . . .

[M]aneuvering through a carefully abridged account of the events of 30 years ago, Mr. Berecz said: "From the beginning our party has declared that the uprising was counterrevolutionary from a social point of view. The basic objective was to crush the power of the workers, to change the pattern of ownership and to tear the ties of the Socialist People's Republic of Hungary from its socialist allies." . . .

In his address, Mr. Berecz alluded to the losses suffered in 1956 in terms of clear distinctions. . . .

But the categories of behavior could not have been so clear at the time, when workers set up barricades from which to attack Soviet patrols with weapons turned over to them by Hungarian soldiers. On Nov. 1, 1956, Mr. Kadar himself praised those who had battled in the streets in the previous week.

In the radio address, Mr. Kadar declared: "In a glorious uprising, our people have shaken off the [Mátyás] Rakosi regime. They have achieved freedom for the people and independence for the country without which there can be no socialism. We can safely say that the ideological and organizational leaders who prepared this uprising were recruited from among your ranks.

"Hungarian Communist writers, journalists, university students, thousands and thousands of workers and peasants and veteran fighters who had been imprisoned on false charges fought in the front line against the Rakosite despotism and political hooliganism. We are proud that you, permeated by true patriotism and loyalty to socialism, honestly stood your ground in the armed uprising and led it."

And yet, according to official accounts of the day now being circulated here, Mr. Kadar is said to have broken with [Prime Minister Imre] Nagy some hours after the address. Three days later he was in this town, 60 miles southeast of Budapest and 120 miles from the Soviet border, heading a new party and denouncing the same students, workers and peasants as counterrevolutionaries or their agents.

What happened in those three days is still not fully known. There are some reports that Mr. Kadar had been locked in long discussion with Yuri V. Andropov, then the Soviet Ambassador to Hungary. There is a report circulating in the West that Mr. Kadar was even taken to the Ukraine to meet with Nikita S. Khrushchev and that only after this conversation was he persuaded to take leadership of the new party that gained Soviet backing.

At a news conference after his address here, Mr. Berecz was asked about the gaps in the historical account. "We still do not have a minute-by-minute account of what happened between the first and fourth of November," he said.

In Praise of 1956: Eastern Europeans Speak Out

Hungary had a corps of activist intellectuals like Poland's, but much smaller in number. Poland's Social Self-Defense Committee (KSS-KOR) had created the framework for a broad movement of social liberation, to be achieved through nonviolent resistance, and advised the potent alliance of workers and intellectuals of the 10-million-member Solidarity union (see "Polish Labor Crisis Deepens as Workers List Their Demands"). At the time that KSS-KOR came into existence in 1976 in Warsaw, uniting the Roman Catholic intelligentsia with the secular political Left, Hungary's first typewritten *samizdat* surfaced. The samizdat ("self-published" in Russian) of the Hungarian opposition was also much smaller than Poland's and reached perhaps 10,000 readers. By the mid-1980s in Poland, as many as 2,000 regular samizdat publications were circulating, some in the tens of thousands of copies (see **Poland, Introduction**). KSS-KOR members had developed the strategy that would essentially be utilized throughout the Eastern bloc (see **Hungary, Introduction**).

Hungary's opposition of teachers, journalists, academicians, and professionals often simultaneously worked with or for the government of János Kádár while criticizing the regime. In other words, an official Hungarian intellectual class guided monitoring and assessment of major social issues, such as inequality and economic injustice. In 1978, Hungarian intellectuals began a "Flying University," as did the Poles, at which they gathered in private apartments to discuss topics that could not be addressed openly (see **Hungary, Introduction**). The seminars were "flying" because locations could be quickly changed. It would be another decade before Hungarian opposition leaders began to work collectively.

Although the Soviet Union banned communications between the populations of its satellite states, *The New York Times* on October 19, 1986, illustrates the growth of cross-border awareness among the generative intellectuals of Eastern Europe. Despite "difficult communications between the countries," 122 activists released a signed proclamation in Budapest, East Berlin, Prague, and Warsaw extolling the 1956 Hungarian uprising. *Times* correspondent Michael T. Kaufman notes the signers' reference to the uprising as "our common heritage and inspiration." He calls the four-paragraph statement the "boldest open document ever issued in the East bloc." It reveals the connections established among samizdat authors, organizers against totalitarianism, and human rights activists in four of the six Warsaw Pact allies of the Soviet Union and a common awareness of their shared circumstances.

The Poles were acutely aware of Hungarian dilemmas. *The Times* on November 10 reports that 500 persons gathered in a Roman Catholic church in a Warsaw suburb to mark the thirtieth anniversary of the 1956 Hungarian uprising. Its correspondent asserts that the mass and ceremony were "much more passionately outspoken than any Hungarian observance of the revolt." Letters from the Hungarian democratic opposition were read aloud from the pulpit, citing connections between the Polish, Czechoslovak, and Hungarian upheavals. Photographs of Budapest during the 1956 revolt were displayed in the church basement, and poetry books in Polish and Hungarian about the insurrection sold out. A marble plaque was unveiled to commemorate the 20,000 Hungarians killed in the uprising.

OCTOBER 19, 1986
122 IN EAST EUROPE PROCLAIM PRAISE OF HUNGARIAN UPRISING
By MICHAEL T. KAUFMAN
Special to The New York Times

WARSAW, Oct. 18 – A proclamation extolling the 1956 Hungarian uprising as "our common heritage and inspiration" was issued today in Budapest, East Berlin, Prague and Warsaw, along with the names of its 122 prominent Eastern European signers.

The four-paragraph statement, the boldest open document ever issued in the East bloc, linked dissident writers, anti-totalitarian organizers and human rights activists from four of the six Warsaw Pact allies of the Soviet Union.

After weeks of often difficult communications between the countries, the document was issued in time to mark the anniversary of the Hungarian revolt, which began 30 years ago next Thursday. It was quashed after brutal street fighting when Soviet tanks arrived 12 days later.

The signers included members of the outlawed Charter 77 movement in Czechoslovakia, the illegal Solidarity free trade union federation in Poland, East German independent peace and human rights activists, as well as 54 Hungarian writers, scientists and workers. Some of the Hungarians, such as Miklos Vasarhelyi, a journalist, and Imre Mecs, an engineer, were among those arrested and, for a while, sentenced to hang for their role in the revolt.

The declaration begins with a description of the tumultuous beginning of the popular uprising.

'Were Fed Up With Official Lies'

"On the 23d of October 1956, workers, students and soldiers stormed the radio building in Budapest because they were fed up with the official lies and wished to hear the truth and to voice their demands," it said.

"They destroyed Stalin's statue and the credibility of the regime, which had called itself the dictatorship of the proletariat and the republic of the people. The struggle made it clear that what the Hungarian people really wanted was independence, democracy and neutrality. They wanted to live in peace, in a free and decent society."

The statement ties the aspirations of the Hungarians in 1956 to the yearnings of people and the growth of anti-totalitarian movements elsewhere in Eastern Europe. It said widespread hopes for change were still unfulfilled.

"The Hungarian revolution as well as the uprising in East Berlin, the Prague spring and the social movement of the free trade union Solidarity in Poland were suppressed either by Soviet intervention or domestic military violence," the statement said. "Over the last 30 years life has become easier for many. Some people speak up without being thrown into jail, but the basic demands of the revolutionaries have not been realized."

The document concluded with the signers from each of the four countries appealing for and pledging support for one another's efforts to develop greater independence and democracy.

In the most recent social upheaval in Eastern Europe, the period of Solidarity's growth in Poland, the Soviet leadership as well as the rulers of Poland's East bloc allies found the free union movement's occasional gestures of reaching out to the people of neighboring countries particularly troublesome.

. . . . [A]s the most assertive and broadest-based public call for change in the Soviet Union's European buffer zone, [the proclamation's] challenge to both the entrenched rulers of Eastern Europe as well as to Mikhail S. Gorbachev, the Soviet leader, is unmistakable.

"We declare our joint determination to struggle for political democracy in our countries, pluralism based on the principles of self-government, peaceful reunification of divided Europe and its democratic integration as well as the rights of all minorities," it said.

No Rumanians or Bulgarians

The signers were grouped by country: 54 Hungarians, 28 Poles, 24 Czechoslovaks and 16 East Germans. No Rumanians or Bulgarians signed because, as one Polish signer said, "there are no organized opposition groups in those countries, and there no one could sign something like this without taking enormous risks."

Among the Hungarian signers were dissident writers such as Janos Kis, Gaspar Miklos Tamas and Istvan Eorsi and the novelist Gyorgy Konrad. Also signing was Sandor Racz, who as a 23-year-old elected representative of the workers' council spent months after the rebellion negotiating with the Soviet-installed Government before being imprisoned.

Another signer was Laszlo Rajk, an architect, whose father, a Foreign Minister with the same name, was hanged in 1949 after an anti-Semitic show trial and then seven years later posthumously rehabilitated. . . .

The Polish group includes Adam Michnik, the essayist. . . .

A New Generation of Communists

At a Hungarian communist party conference in 1988, János Kádár was forced to step aside and accept a ceremonial presidency after serving thirty-two years as the party's general secretary. Károly Grósz replaced him as premier. A Hungarian *perestroika* ("restructuring" in Russian) had begun, as Grósz promised more openness (*glasnost*) in government.

Grósz inherited the leadership of a party-state in which funds borrowed from the West had been used to modernize industry but was unable to produce goods considered desirable in the West; as a result, the burden of servicing Hungary's debt was crippling. Grósz introduced taxes. He also increased the authority of the government, as opposed to the party.

The pace of forming new political groups outside the communist party's structure accelerated. Urbanist and populist intellectuals had met in 1985 at Monor, near Budapest. A year later, the Writers' Union reasserted its customary position of leadership, recalling its role in articulating demands in the 1956 uprising. In September 1987, a group of intellectuals sent a "Letter of 100" to 380 members of parliament presenting a Magyar-language version of arguments on "no taxation without representation." Also in 1987, *Beszélö* (Speaker), the main journal of the democratic opposition, published a special issue bidding a new "social contract," with basic political and civil rights, constitutionalism, rule of law, freedom of the press, and checks on the communist party's power. By 1988, a number of new groups in the democratic opposition were organizing with relative openness and suggesting that they should share in power, although the concept of power sharing was not tightly defined (see **Hungary, Introduction**).

On May 31, 1988, *The New York Times* would comment that Prime Minister Károly Grósz had appointed "aggressive reformers to the new Politburo" and had "managed an orderly rotation at the top, a difficult feat in any one-party state." Yet, the newspaper editorializes, "A more daring feat would be to set a limit on [Grósz's] own term in office, a truly revolutionary notion in geriatric Eastern Europe" ("A Hungarian for Too Many Seasons").

MAY 29, 1988
IN HUNGARY, FLEXIBILITY AS DOCTRINE
By HENRY KAMM

BUDAPEST – The Hungarians have often been quick to take advantage of changes blowing in from the East. They proved that again last weekend when a new generation of Hungarian Communist leaders succeeded in seizing power.

When the idea of changing the system was first allowed to be discussed in Eastern Europe in the 1960's, the talk was of replacing highly dogmatic Stalinist leaders with Communists who were ideologically sound but undogmatic—ready to experiment with their economies to increase production. A bit of borrowing of ideas from the West was tolerated.

In those days, Janos Kadar, Hungary's leader since 1956, became the first of the nondogmatists, the deviser of "goulash Communism," the party chief who allowed his economists some freedom to allow changes based on the capitalist notion that producers and consumers are better able than a central planning bureaucracy to stimulate an economy.

Hungarian economic efforts had their ups and downs under Mr. Kadar, dictated not so much by Hungary's needs or Mr. Kadar's wishes as by the Soviet Union's increasing or decreasing fear of the political effects of movements for change in its dependencies in Eastern and Central Europe.

Since Mikhail S. Gorbachev came to power in 1985, Communist leaders, seeking Soviet approval as the best way of rising to the top, have been inspired not only to be nondogmatic but even to let it be known that they are "pragmatists." Last Sunday, the first of the new pragmatists reached the pinnacle. Prime Minister Karoly Grosz replaced Mr. Kadar as General Secretary of the Communist Party. Only 15 years old when Communism came to Hungary with the conquering Soviet Army, the new leader reached maturity with the first generation of Eastern Europeans for whom there has never been an alternative to Communism. Nothing about the 57-year-old Mr. Grosz ... shows his pragmatism more clearly than his newfound devotion to downgrading ideology.

Until the ascendancy of Mr. Gorbachev in Moscow, Mr. Grosz had been counted as a leader in the orthodox wing of the party bureaucracy. He had overseen the ideological purity of the press and broadcasting and served as a tough party chief before becoming Prime Minister last June.

For most Hungarians, the removal of Mr. Kadar, who retains a ceremonial role in the newly created position of party President, appears to be a psychological boost. They see it as the end of an era in which the boom of the 1970's soured in this decade to stagnation, inflation of about 20 percent a year, the painful introduction of capitalist-style income- and value-added taxes, falling real wages and the threat of unemployment. Hungarians have been pained in recent years to see the shrinkage in the purchasing power of their wages and extra earnings in their second and third jobs, as well as in the tolerated but marginal private sector. . . .

Toughness and Ambition

The vast majority of Hungarians, who have never been persuaded that Communism is the road to well-being, believed that Mr. Kadar's nondogmatic ideology was not the worst, but not good enough. They would like to believe that the new official talk about pragmatic approaches and the emphasis on decentralization and market mechanisms is sincere. . . .

Since he became Prime Minister, Mr. Grosz has made himself a spokesman for the market system and relations with the West. He has paid official visits to West Germany, . . . [and] won the pragmatic approval of Prime Minister Margaret Thatcher. . . . President [Ronald] Reagan is looking forward to his visit to Washington. . . . A supporter of Mr. Grosz has called his efforts "realpolitik." Mr. Grosz has invited American businessmen such as Edgar M. Bronfman, Ronald S. Lauder and George Soros to visit Budapest. . . .

Mr. Kadar did not meet the customary East European fate of either holding power until death or being overthrown by a Politburo coup and disappearing into oblivion. His election to a ceremonial post and the public handshake—no matter how sincere—between the new and old leaders, are seen as accomplishments of the era of Gorbachev and pragmatism.

COMMEMORATING 1848

The Hungarians hold the national independence movements of 1848 and 1956 at the center of their collective memory. Their choice of nonviolent mobilization to overthrow communist rule in 1989 can be largely attributed to their attachment to this history.

On January 26, 1989, the government announced that former prime minister Imre Nagy and comrades executed following the 1956 uprising would be reburied; it did not, however, state that he and his associates had been falsely accused. The National Assembly passed the

Law of Associations, which legitimized organizations that were in any case already determinedly at work. On February 10, the Central Committee of the communist party issued a determination that the 1956 uprising had been a "popular uprising against an oligarchic rule that had debased the nation." It also concluded that multiparty democracy was needed. The party had aligned itself with the stance of the democratic opposition in this regard. Inside the party, reformers, among them Imre Pozsgay, had been fighting for this capitulation. In February, the government yielded on points of important symbolism: Not only would it permit celebrations on March 15—to commemorate the 1848 revolution—it would also adopt the date as the national holiday and disinter Nagy and give him a state funeral with reburial on June 16.

On March 16, *The New York Times* correspondent Henry Kamm notes the conservative estimate of 75,000 persons marching in opposition to the communist regime at the official observance of the newly authorized holiday. According to Kamm, the government "urged the members of various informal, but no longer clandestine, opposition groups to join in one national celebration, but did not object when 31 such organizations staged their own joint commemoration." The thirty-one independent groups probably brought out more than 100,000 people.

The parallel rally started at the statue of celebrated poet Sandor Petofi, hero of the 1848 revolution. His statue also marked the point from which the demonstration of October 23, 1956, began, setting in motion the uprising violently crushed by Soviet troops. Eclipsing the official event, the democratic opposition came into its own that day and made clear that Hungarians now had a choice, between the party-state or a fully fledged opposition.

Organizers scrupulously planned the march so that in five hours it would pause at six points of interest in Budapest connected historically to the revolutions of 1848 and 1956. Emboldened, they demonstrated without interruption, commemorating the 1848 uprising against Austrian rule, which had been put down with lives lost, carnage, and the help of 300,000 Russian army troops. The crowd listened as the philosopher-sociologist János Kis spoke. He was part of the Budapest School, named for a group of academicians at Budapest University who in the late 1960s began an earnest challenge to Marxist ideals that had gone astray and whose ideas would fuel the democratic opposition (see **Hungary, Introduction**). Kis said that history had delivered its verdict on socialism, by which he meant failure. The last pause was at Batthyány Square, the terminus of demonstrations in 1956. The speakers touched the chords of a national memory injured by wars and communism. The march was so peaceful that not even the flowerbeds were ruffled.

MARCH 16, 1989
THOUSANDS OF HUNGARIANS MARCH TO COMMEMORATE REVOLT IN 1848
By HENRY KAMM
Special to The New York Times

BUDAPEST, March 15 – Tens of thousands of opponents of the Communist Government demonstrated freely in the streets of Budapest today to commemorate the 1848 uprising against Austrian rule, which was put down with much bloodshed and the help of the Russian Army.

The marchers, estimated by Western diplomats to number 75,000, listened to speeches by opposition leaders beneath monuments to heroes of the 1848 revolution and from the steps of the national television headquarters.

KEY PLAYER IN HUNGARY
János Kis (1943–)

János Kis is a former leading member of the Hungarian democratic opposition to the communist regime and cofounder and first chairman of Hungary's liberal party.

Kis graduated in 1967 with a degree in philosophy from Eötvös Loránd University in Budapest, his birthplace. He spent the next few years conducting research at the Institute of Philosophy, Hungarian Academy of Sciences, but was banished from academia after penning a criticism of the Marxist concept of socialism. In his youth, Kis identified with leftist values, yet was critical of how such ideals had been implemented, and risked his personal safety in joining the opposition in Hungary. His primary goal became democracy in Eastern Europe.

A key intellectual leader and strategist of the slowly growing opposition, Kis in 1981 cofounded the most influential underground political journal, *Beszélö* (Speaker), and was its editor in chief until 1989. In 1988, he cofounded and became the first chairman of the Alliance of Free Democrats, one of the major parties that would be voted in to the new legislature after free elections in 1990. In 1989, he spoke at a rally commemorating the 1848 Hungarian revolt against the Hapsburgs; thousands attended, exercising their freedoms under the newly self-liberated regime. Having become internationally recognized for his originality and leadership in the Hungarian transition to democracy, in 1990 Kis was invited to teach at the New School for Social Research in New York. In 1991, Kis returned to Budapest to teach at the Central European University. Since 1996, he has been a visiting professor of philosophy at New York University. He writes in the fields of philosophy and politics and continues to play a key role in supporting human rights and political freedoms.

For the first time, the annual highlight of the opposition calendar received explicit permission from the authorities. As recently as three years ago, the marchers were still met by policemen blocking their way, and tear-gassing, beatings and confiscation of identity cards resulted.

In 1987, for the first time, about 1,500 marchers met no hindrance. In fact, the police stopped traffic to give them clear passage through main streets on the Pest side of the Danube and across Margaret Bridge to the hilly Buda section. The number taking part rose to several thousand last year.

A Holiday Is Declared

This year the leadership of Karoly Grosz legitimized the march by restoring to March 15 its former status of a national holiday. It urged the members of various informal, but no longer clandestine, opposition groups to join in one national celebration, but did not object when 31 such organizations staged their own joint commemoration.

In a speech at the television headquarters, Denes Csengey, a leader of the Democratic Forum, the largest non-Communist grouping, explained the refusal to take part in the official commemoration. "Our goal is true, lasting national unity, but this cannot be built on a system of masters and servants," he said. "The political partners must be equals."

Gaspar Miklos Tamas, a philosopher, said, "If next year this country is a state ruled by laws, we hope we will celebrate together."

No uniformed police officers were in sight, and no interference or counterdemonstration marred the event.

Political Freedom Debated

Janos Kis, a philosopher and principal opposition figure, [spoke] from the base of the statue of Lajos Kossuth, the 1848 revolutionary hero, opposite Parliament. . . .

The liberalization of the last months has caused much debate here about the state of political freedom. The thousands who marched today and cheered the speakers clearly believed that the Communist Party continues to hold virtually exclusive power, although it hesitates to exercise it to the full. . . .

In a particularly bold address, Viktor Orban, a 26-year-old representative of the major independent youth organization, recalled that until some months ago the present leadership had demonstrators who demanded independence and democracy beaten in the streets.

"They speak differently now and say, 'Forget what happened before, because what we say now is the truth, not what we said earlier,' " Mr. Orban said in an interview summarizing his speech. "We can't believe that."

THE DEMISE OF THE BREZHNEV DOCTRINE AND REVISITING 1956

In early April 1989, Károly Grósz, as head of the Hungarian communist party, reported to the Central Committee on a meeting he had had with Soviet leader Mikhail S. Gorbachev in Moscow. The account of Gorbachev's comments was brief. The Hungarian party spokesman, Laszlo Major, interpreted the Gorbachev-Grósz talks to indicate the death of what had been called the Brezhnev Doctrine, according to which all communist nations had the duty to act when a communist regime faced internal threats. The doctrine served as justification for the Soviet Union, under the premiership of Leonid I. Brezhnev, invading Czechoslovakia in 1968 (see **"Introduction: Strikes, Sinatra, and Nonviolent Revolution"**). As the death rattle of the Brezhnev Doctrine could be heard, and the Kremlin's prerogative to intervene anywhere in the Soviet bloc in order to prevent counterrevolution or loss of party control was no longer imminent, the fear of another bloody Soviet intervention as in 1956 began to subside.

The New York Times fittingly notes that the reinterpretation of the 1956 uprising sought by Hungary's emerging democratic opposition, and supported by party reformers such as Imre Pozsgay, had become a reference point for the speed of liberalization under way in Hungary. It also notes that gravediggers were seen in a potter's field at Budapest's largest cemetery, searching among 300 unidentified mounds—the graves of men and women hanged for participating in the revolt.

APRIL 2, 1989
GORBACHEV SAID TO REJECT SOVIET RIGHT TO INTERVENE
By HENRY KAMM
Special to The New York Times

BUDAPEST, April 1 – Karoly Grosz, General Secretary of the Hungarian Communist Party, reported to his Central Committee this week that Mikhail S. Gorbachev had indicated to him that safeguards must be provided to prevent a repetition of the Soviet invasions of Hungary and Czechoslovakia.

Mr. Grosz visited Moscow on March 23 and March 24 and met with the Soviet leader for four hours.

"Surveying the experiences of 1956 and 1968, Mr. Gorbachev said that all possible safeguards should be provided so that no external force can interfere in the domestic issues of socialist countries," . . . the official Hungarian press agency quoted from Mr. Grosz's report to the Central Committee on Wednesday.

Soviet troops stationed in Hungary intervened in 1956 to crush a widespread popular uprising. In 1968, Soviet armed forces, supported by troops from Hungary, East Germany, Poland and Bulgaria, invaded Czechoslovakia to stamp out the liberalization movement led by Alexander Dubcek.

Mr. Grosz apparently offered no details on the kind of "safeguards" Mr. Gorbachev had in mind....

[T]he Hungarian party spokesman, Laszlo Major, said Thursday that the Gorbachev-Grosz talks showed that what Western news organizations have called the "Brezhnev doctrine," was dead. This was the label used for the Soviet justification of the invasion of Czechoslovakia; Leonid I. Brezhnev, the Soviet leader at the time, asserted that it was the duty of all Communist nations to act when a Communist regime faced internal threats. In the world today, interference in the domestic affairs of a smaller country is unthinkable, Mr. Major said.

Mr. Grosz said he also obtained a promise from Moscow that Hungarian historians would be granted access to Soviet documents related to the 1956 uprising. A reinterpretation of the events of October and November 1956 has become one of the benchmarks of the degree of liberalization under way in Hungary.

Party liberals, led by Imre Pozsgay, a Politburo member and minister of state, have adopted as their own the widely held view that the movement crushed by Soviet troops was a genuine popular uprising. Mr. Pozsgay is regarded as Mr. Grosz's chief rival. Mr. Grosz has not publicly varied from the official line, which labels the rising a Western-inspired "counterrevolution."...

Unmarked Graves Searched

Meanwhile, in a potter's field at the outer reaches of Budapest's largest cemetery, gravediggers are searching among 300 unmarked mounds, mainly graves of men and women hanged for their participation in the uprising, for the remains of Prime Minister Imre Nagy and his four closest associates, who supported the 1956 uprising. They were executed or, in the case of Geza Losonczy, killed in an attempt to force-feed him during a hunger strike....

The Government ruled in January that after 31 years in which there was no public knowledge of which mounds ... cover whose remains, burials in marked graves would be allowed. Only representatives of a recently formed Committee for Historical Justice and family members of the victims have been admitted to observe the exhumations.

The committee plans a reburial ceremony on June 16 and the laying of a groundstone for a monument to honor those executed for taking part in the rising. June 16 is the 31st anniversary of the hanging of Mr. Nagy.... At the families' wish, reburial will take place in Plot 301.

Changing Economic and Political Winds

On May 2, 1989, Hungary removed the barbed wire fence that demarcated the Hungarian and Austrian border, a manifestation of the iron curtain. This allowed citizens of Hungary to go shopping in Austria or to travel there for any other purpose. East Germans and others in Soviet bloc countries could also begin their "exit" to the West via this route. *The New York Times* did not report the making of the hole in the iron curtain, although it was attended by Hungarian leaders and filmed by Western media. Repercussions from this Hungarian decision would be spectacular. The regimes in East Germany and Czechoslovakia would have to choose between prohibiting their citizens from visiting Hungary as tourists—or risk their permanent departure.

Of all the communist parties in Eastern Europe, the Hungarian party was the most inclined to reform. By 1988, "reform circles" in local branches of the party surrounded the senior leadership. Reformers in parliament exhibited their independence from the party line. Even at the prime ministerial level, displays of distancing the government from the party were visible, as for example when Prime Minister Németh, who had been appointed by party general secretary Károly Grósz, appeared on evening television on April 25 and repudiated a speech by Grósz.

An interview of Grósz by *Times* correspondent Henry Kamm shows that the communist party-state had concluded that it must open up to multiparty politics, a reform calculated to keep the party in power. Reading the interview, it is possible to discern the basic strategy first employed by the Polish Solidarity movement of seeking reform, freedoms, and rights, yet of limited scope, so as not to threaten authorities with a total loss of power (see "Polish Union Opens Convention"). Grósz essentially concedes the strategy's success, when he tells Kamm that the party seeks "to shape the political system" through establishing a multiparty system. Grósz told Kamm that "in proposing to create a system that would eventually allow the party to be voted out, he foresaw no loss of power." He thus confirms the motivation of ushering in reforms in order to hold on to power.

On June 13, negotiations for free elections in Hungary began, with some similarity to the talks leading to the Polish round table of the same year (see "To His Volatile Young Allies, Walesa Preaches Conciliation").

MAY 15, 1989
IN HUNGARY, THE POLITICAL CHANGES ARE TEMPERED BY ECONOMIC FEARS
By HENRY KAMM
Special to The New York Times

BUDAPEST, May 14 – In an atmosphere of increasing freedom of expression, Hungarians are looking forward to a possibility that after 44 years of Communist rule the party may permit free elections that could one day drive it from power. . . .

The Communist Party, led by Mr. [Karoly] Grosz since last May, has dictated Hungary's fate since 1945, eliminated all other parties and built a centralized economy. . . .

Four of the political parties that were dissolved by the Communists four decades ago have come back to life, and new political organizations that intend to constitute themselves as parties have been legally formed. Only one of the reborn or new groups claims more than 4,000 members.

Mechanisms are being prepared that are to lead this year or next to a law establishing the rights of parties, parliamentary elections and the framing of a more democratic constitution.

New Economics: Amid Decline, Brave Hopes

The main concern for the majority of Hungarians is the steadily declining standard of living, and to them the constantly echoing word "reform" means mainly the threat of an end to Government subsidies, with unemployment and higher prices.

The announced economic changes, which still await definition and enactment, foresee elimination of the state subsidies that make consumer prices artificially low and protect jobs by keeping alive unproductive enterprises.

The economic plight of the average Hungarian has not reached the poverty that has become common to many Poles and Yugoslavs. But the standard of living, long among the highest in the Communist world, has suffered steady attrition through the 1980's. . . .

Stock Market in Embryo

. . . While little has been done to ease the pressure on most Hungarians, the Government this year introduced the eye-catching device of creating the first stock exchange in Communist Europe. Because foreign investment capital is not rushing into Hungary, it has done virtually no trading. . . .

[T]he public mood is unexcited, with little of the enthusiastic mass participation that marked the popular movements here and in Poland in 1956, the "Prague spring" of 1968 and the Polish Solidarity movement of 1980–81.

'Dissidents' Now Lionized

. . . With exceptional civic courage, a small group of dissidents, as they were called until recently, had over the years asserted their civil liberties and preached them to the nation through illegal publications, often seized, and meetings in private homes, frequently raided by secret police. Now their views are being proclaimed not only in new, unofficial dailies and weeklies but also in the official press, which a few months ago denounced or ignored them.

Writers and philosophers who less than a year ago, under the same regime, experienced the force of police truncheons on their backs now find themselves in demand for talk shows and university symposiums, contributions to the press and the right to publish their books in translation.

New Politics
Defining 1956 Is the Touchstone

At the center of an intense reexamination of the past, fraught with present-day political significance as Communist leaders compete in an unacknowledged power struggle, is the uprising of 1956, its crushing by the Soviet Army with the help of Hungarian supporters and the execution of its leader, Imre Nagy.

Within the ruling party, whose leaders all owe their rise to the former General Secretary, Janos Kadar, installed by Moscow as it put down the revolt, "liberals" and "conservatives" can be identified by the view they have adopted on 1956.

The 55-year-old Mr. [Imre] Pozsgay, in whom non-party liberals as well as reform-minded Communists place their best hope for leadership, has identified himself with the opinion that the rising was an authentic national movement.

Mr. Pozsgay has built a reputation for enthusiastic support of the innovations of Mikhail S. Gorbachev, the Soviet leader.

A National Uprising?

... Mr. Grosz, 58 years old, who throughout his political life represented strict Communist orthodoxy, first adhered to the view that 1956 was a "counterrevolution." As the significance of the issue in the power contest rose, however, he moved to a centrist position. Mr. Grosz engineered a compromise in which the 1956 events were said to have begun as a "national uprising" and degenerated into "counterrevolution."

In what many Hungarians saw as a gratuitous act intended to use the 76-year-old Mr. Kadar to deflect blame from today's leaders, the party this month cast him into virtual disgrace. Pronouncing him physically and mentally ill, it completed his downfall, begun when Mr. Grosz replaced him a year ago. It expelled him from the honorary post of party president and membership on the central committee.

Mr. Kadar's consent to Hungarian participation in the Soviet-led invasion of Czechoslovakia in 1968 is one of the charges now laid against the former leader in the columns of the press and on the air.

New Parliament
Election May Come In November

Many Hungarians look forward to the expected parliamentary elections, perhaps as early as November, as the first step toward dislodging the Communist Party from power. This is not a view shared by Mr. Grosz, his advisers or his associates, even some in whom liberals place faith to transform the autocratic party into a democratic body ready for power-sharing or even a change of rule.

In a 90-minute interview in his spacious office at party headquarters in Pest on the left bank of the Danube, overlooking the green hills of Buda across the river, Mr. Grosz defined his view of a multi-party system and made clear that he regards the replacement of Communist government by another party as a long-term prospect at best.

The General Secretary, who expressed pleasure at receiving President [George H. W.] Bush here in July, placed the institution of a multi-party system in the context of creating confidence among the Western lending institutions and private investors that Hungary must convince of its credit worthiness.

In the view of Hungarian critics and defenders of the regime, as well as diplomats from East and West, Hungary's economic plight, its declining standard of living and rising inflation, even more than Mr. Gorbachev's liberalizing innovations in the Soviet Union, are the principal motives for the transformation under way. ...

[Said Grosz,] "[One] element of creating confidence [in the West] is political reliability and stability, because nobody would invest in a place where they had to fear civil war breaking out the next day or have on their minds a fear that 'those communists' will change their minds and in five years nationalize it.

"To create safeguards, we try to shape the political system, the political superstructure in such a way that its operation would give guarantees for preventing events like that. One of the main ways of doing that is the establishment of a multi-party system. ... [W]e put our own party under social control by taking it out of the existing mechanism, which is a one-party system.

"We create a situation in society, a mechanism of checks and balances, so that every day we would be able to report on actions and results and check whether there is coincidence between intent and results."

Mr. Grosz made clear that he had no intention of presiding over a loosening of his party's hold over the country by allowing the proposed checks and balances to develop quickly into a method of transferring power.

New Communists
Strategy Is Based On Realism

..."If we are unable in a period of six to eight years to acquire through political efforts the confidence of society that we need to carry out our program, then we deserve to lose its faith."

The party chief said that although he was sincere in proposing to create a system that would eventually allow the party to be voted out, he foresaw no loss of power....

The Rehabilitation of Imre Nagy

On June 16, 1989, in Budapest, a funeral emblematically marked the passage from one era to another, as the reburial of former prime minister Imre Nagy attracted 250,000 demonstrators and spectators. Nagy, regarded as a moderate communist, was installed as premier with popular assent in 1956, during the upheaval that would end with Soviet suppression. Calling for free elections and multiparty politics, Nagy had begun to negotiate the withdrawal of Hungary from the Warsaw Pact and had asked for Soviet troops to be recalled. After he proclaimed the country's neutrality, 200,000 Soviet forces on November 4 crushed Budapest with 2,500 tanks and armored cars. The Soviets removed Nagy from power, arrested thousands of Hungarians, killed 20,000, and wounded 150,000.

Nagy was charged with treason, hanged by the party-state, and buried face-down in an unmarked mound alongside the unidentified mounds of 300 others killed for political reasons. Now, thirty-three years later, Hungarians in large numbers filed somberly through Heroes' Square before six caskets bearing the exhumed remains of Nagy, his defense minister Pal Maleter, and three of their colleagues, coming to pay tribute to the fallen and to renounce the still-occupying Soviet army. The sixth coffin was empty, a symbol chosen by the Historical Justice Committee that organized the interment to commemorate all 20,000 Hungarians who had been killed in 1956.

In attendance were four government figures: Prime Minister Miklós Németh; Minister of State Imre Pozsgay, representing the government; Deputy Prime Minister Peter Megyessy, and President of the Parliament Mátyás Szürös. *The New York Times* reporter Henry Kamm notes their presentation to the crowd by their government titles, because they would not have been welcome as communist party representatives.

The rehabilitation of Nagy was a decisive act in public support for the rebuilding of Hungarian popular sovereignty. Shown in an eight-hour national television broadcast and covered by national newspapers, the memorial service rallied Hungarians to become publicly vocal. Leaders from the democratic opposition gave speeches calling for liberalization. Viktor Orban, of the Alliance of Young Democrats (FIDESz), called for Soviet troops to leave Hungary. Many people attended from Poland, including Adam Michnik, essayist-adviser to Solidarity. Tearful emotion reported by Kamm attested to the sorrowful burdens of impotence and dishonor that the Hungarians had borne since 1956.

On July 6, János Kádár died at the age of seventy-seven. His passing provided the party-state the opportunity to act on the unresolved historical question of 1956, with its implicit condemnation of the party as made up of those who came to power alongside Soviet tanks.

Kamm, on July 30 in *The Times,* reflects on the expanse yet to be traversed to achieve democracy in Hungary, as the effects of the reburial of Nagy were contrasted in the same month by "a great massing of orthodox Communists to pay final honors to Mr. Kadar." ("Hungary Is Far From Democracy, and Even From Poland"). Within hours of Kádár's death, the supreme court ruled that Nagy and those tried with him had been innocent. The official reassessment of 1956 opened the floodgates to the negotiated revolution that would follow.

KEY PLAYER IN HUNGARY
Imre Pozsgay (1933–)

• •

Imre Pozsgay was one of the reformers in the Hungarian Socialist Workers Party and played a significant role in Hungary's transition to democracy.

Pozsgay was born in Kony and was graduated with a degree in English from the Lenin Institute in Budapest. A poised orator, he would become known as the Hungarian Socialist Workers Party's most logical hope for continued existence and revival, as he rose from the local to the national level.

In 1975, Pozsgay held several ministerial portfolios, including culture and education, and in 1983 became a member of parliament. His emphasis on a broad scope for civil society organizations that might function independently of the party and his calls for reform led to a falling out with the party's general secretary, János Kádár; in 1988, Kádár was removed from power due to shifting viewpoints in the party and given the largely ceremonial title of party president. By the time Pozsgay replaced Kádár as minister of state in 1988, he had become, with the assistance of the news media that he had largely controlled, a commanding and popular politician. As with many in the reform wing of the party, Pozsgay had come of age in the apparat but was unsullied by the brutal crushing of the 1956 Hungarian uprising. He became deputy president in 1989 and especially concerned himself with the alterations needed for Hungary to become a democracy.

In January 1989, as chair of a committee studying Hungary's postwar history, Pozsgay publicly announced the panel's conclusion that the 1956 uprising crushed by the Soviets had been "a people's uprising," not a counterrevolution, a finding not in keeping with the party line. Unafraid of taking initiative, he had the nerve to rebut the party's ideologists. The Central Committee of the communist party reached a compromise, declaring that the revolt had begun as a legitimate uprising but then disintegrated into a revolt against communism. It quietly endorsed the committee's findings. Pozsgay's comments about the 1956 revolt led to the reburial of Imre Nagy, former prime minister and reform movement hero, who was executed for treason after the subjugated uprising.

Pozsgay played a critical role leading up to the Opposition Round Table talks in spring 1989. On June 21, he pledged "fully free and democratic elections, in which the communist party would compete on an equal basis with other parties." In August, Pozsgay and Otto von Habsburg, the former crown prince of Austria, Hungary, Croatia, and Bohemia, sponsored the "Pan-European Picnic," which allowed hundreds of East Germans to cross into Austria. In 1990, Pozsgay was elected leader of a faction in the new parliament called the Hungarian Socialist Party, which emerged from the crumbling of the Hungarian communist party. He resigned in November, but continued serving in the National Assembly as an independent. He formed the National Democratic Alliance, which folded in 1994. After his retirement from parliament in 1994, he began teaching at Kossuth Lajos University of Science in Debrecen.

Hungarian Prime Minister Miklós Németh, left, and Imre Pozsgay, a leader of the Hungarian reform movement, pay their respects at the coffin of former Hungarian prime minster Imre Nagy. Soviet troops crushed the 1956 revolt, and in 1958 the Moscow-installed government of János Kádár executed Prime Minister Nagy and 300 others and disposed of their bodies in unmarked graves. The state reburial and posthumous legal rehabilitation of Nagy and his associates on June 16, 1989, became an event of major symbolic importance in Hungary's transition to a democratic system.

Source: AP Images/Dieter Endlicher

JUNE 17, 1989
HUNGARIAN WHO LED '56 REVOLT IS BURIED AS A HERO
By HENRY KAMM
Special to The New York Times

BUDAPEST, June 16 – Thirty-one years after he was hanged and his body thrown into a prison grave, Imre Nagy, who led the 1956 uprising against Soviet domination, was given a solemn funeral today on Budapest's largest square, followed by a hero's burial.

The ceremonies were organized by the opposition, which worships the former Prime Minister as a national hero, but four leading members of the ruling Communist Party came to pay tribute.

They were announced to the crowd by their Government titles, because it had been made clear that they would not have been welcome as party representatives. . . .

Eulogies and Condemnations

The four top party officials, Prime Minister Miklos Nemeth, Minister of State Imre Pozsgay, Deputy Prime Minister Peter Megyessy and Matyas Szuros, the president of Parliament, laid wreaths and stood briefly as honorary pallbearers flanking Mr. Nagy's coffin.

They left before a succession of eulogies to Imre Nagy . . . that were unsparing in their condemnation of the Communist Party and its ally, the Soviet Union.

The Soviet Army crushed the uprising after feigning a withdrawal from Hungary on Nov. 4, 1956. Its tanks began rolling after Mr. Nagy, yielding to an aroused nation, formed a coalition government to replace one-party rule, declared Hungary's neutrality and withdrew from the Warsaw Pact.

Moscow secretly put Janos Kadar, whom Mr. Nagy had earlier freed from prison, in full charge of the country, which he dominated until he was deposed last year. Mr. Kadar has been relegated into oblivion by his successor, Karoly Grosz. . . .

Many in the crowd looked up in shock and seemed to be holding their breath to hear at so public a ceremony, in so sumptuous a setting, words of such astonishing candor. The Government network televised the ceremony live from 9 A.M. to 6 P.M.

Victor Orban, a spokesman for the Federation of Young Democrats, paid tribute to Mr. Nagy as a man who, although a Communist, "identified himself with the wishes of the Hungarian nation to put an end to the Communist taboos, blind obedience to the Russian empire and with the dictatorship of a single party."

As though speaking of the party leaders who shortly before had bowed before the coffins of Mr. Nagy and his colleagues, Mr. Orban continued: "We cannot . . . understand that the party leaders, who made us study from books that falsified the revolution, now rush to touch the coffins as if they were charms of good luck."

Sandor Racz, who led the Budapest Workers' Council during the uprising and spent seven years in prison, condemned the Soviet Army and the Communist Party as "obstacles for Hungarian society." Looking toward the coffins, . . . Mr. Racz said, "These coffins are a result of the presence of Russian troops on our territory." He said the party was . . ."responsible for the damaged lives of Hungarians."

Budapest experienced a day full of anomalies and contradictions. No state funeral could have been more solemnly and publicly marked or held in a more prestigious setting, but for the Hungarian Government and the ruling party, Mr. Nagy and the four companions who were sentenced to death and reburied with him remain traitors and counterrevolutionaries.

A review of their trial is under way, and after today's rites it can hardly end with anything short of restitution of their civil dignity and full rehabilitation as victims of judicial murder. But their sentences still stand. . . .

On the 30th anniversary of the hangings last year, the police broke up with considerable violence a small tribute organized by dissidents on a Budapest square.

It was an anomaly also that the Soviet Union and Hungary's other Communist friends sent diplomats, but not their ambassadors, to attend the ceremony. . . . [O]ther Communist countries—China, North Korea, Rumania and Albania—stayed away.

The Heroes Square ceremony was staged, in one more irony, by the son of another executed Communist, Laszlo Rajk, who was Interior and Foreign Minister. Mr. Rajk, a loyal Communist, was hanged after a show trial in 1949 at the height of the Stalinist period.

The younger Laszlo Rajk, an architect and movie set designer, draped the neo-classical facade of the art museum and a tall column in the center of the square's vast expanse fully in black and white, traditional mourning colors among the Hungarians of Transylvania, annexed by Rumania.

He devised strikingly modern wood and metal structures as a setting on which to display the five coffins, as well as a sixth, empty one commemorating the more than 300 victims of judicial retribution after the uprising.

Tall, flaming torches stood between the coffins, and a permanent rotation of honorary pallbearers—including widows, children and other relatives of the five victims being buried—flanked them. Each coffin was inscribed with the name of the executed man and his dates, all ending in 1958.

Like all of the victims, Mr. Nagy was a lifelong Communist and friend of the Soviet Union, where he spent nearly one-third of his 62 years. The others were his Defense Minister, Gen. Pal Maleter; Minister of State Geza Losonczy; Jozsef Szilagyi, the head of the Prime Minister's staff, and Miklos Gimes, a leading journalist and close associate of Mr. Nagy.

General Maleter and Mr. Gimes were executed with Mr. Nagy, Mr. Szilagyi was tried and put to death separately, and Mr. Losonczy died in prison.

Mr. Nagy was buried in secret in a prison lot while his wife and daughter were interned in Rumania. He was reburied, again in secret and in an unmarked grave a few years later and exhumed this year when the party leadership finally yielded to demands for a decent burial.

Today, after the wreath-laying and eulogies, a procession of hearses, followed by cars and buses, set out for the huge public cemetery next to the prison where the hangings took place.

Potter's Field Is Landscaped

Plot 301, the once desolate potter's field that contains the graves of perhaps 260 of the victims, had been turned in recent weeks . . . into a landscaped funeral park.

Fresh grass and trees now grow where weeks ago there was only dirt and weeds. Paved paths led through the field to five open graves aligned in a row that had been dug for Mr. Nagy's companions and for the symbolic coffin.

Beyond them, in an adjoining field full of mainly unmarked graves, a tomb had been dug for Mr. Nagy. His daughter had requested that he be laid to rest amid the bulk of those who paid with their lives for following his lead.

Two actors read in alphabetical order the names of the 260 victims, who were executed from 1956 to 1961, their occupations and their ages. At each name, a torch-bearer stepped forward, held high the flame and replied, "He lives in us; he has not gone."

When the name of one of the five was called, surname first, in the Hungarian fashion, like "Nagy Imre, Prime Minister, 62 years," his coffin was carried to the grave and a friend delivered a eulogy. Then, supporting one another, his nearest relatives stepped to the grave to put down flowers and stand, with bowed heads, allowed for the first time to mourn in public, together with those who share their grief.

Political Alterations and a Hole in the Iron Curtain

In *The New York Times* on April 25, 1989, Hungarian foreign minister Gyula Horn is quoted as saying that democracy was Hungary's main goal, reflecting the extent to which hard-line communists in the party-state had lost their effort to control political liberalization. Speaking on the need for change, he said the end result "must be of revolutionary nature." He soon turned his words into action.

By mid-July 1989, an anticipated flow of thousands of East German tourists in Hungary began fleeing the country—and the Soviet bloc—crossing the Hungary-Austria border, which had been opened in May, with a final destination of West Germany. The East German government complained of violations by Hungary of existing requirements for exit visas. When Budapest began to enforce the exit permission obligations, East Germans who had come to Hungary to leave the Eastern bloc found themselves stranded, as they couldn't return to East Germany at will. By September, some 3,000 East Germans were camping at the West German embassy in Budapest, with perhaps 100,000 more elsewhere in Hungary deciding if and how to return home.

After weeks of diplomatic activity, on September 10 Horn resolved the crisis by announcing that the East German refugees would have rights of free movement. A week later, Prime Minister Miklós Németh declared the border permanently open. The government ordered all barriers on the Austrian border pulled down to let the East Germans leave. The East German government forbade travel to Hungary, which resulted in new floods of tourists traveling westward through Poland and Czechoslovakia, with comparable encampments in those countries.

The Times on September 11, 1989, reports that on the previous night, East Germans seeking to make their way to West Germany through Hungary had departed their homes. *Times* reporter Serge Schmemann is appropriately objective, but with human emotion evident just below the surface. He asserts that the Hungarian decision was "wrenching." By November, approximately 200,000 East Germans had exiled themselves in the West.

Within Hungary, big developments were afoot. The negotiators at the Opposition Round Table talks had the summer out of the limelight, as they essentially built a new structure for Hungary's political system and opened the space for a newborn political class. Agreement was finally reached on September 18. In a complex formulation, a series of draft laws and codicils provided for free elections and democratic governance. A presidential election would be held in November. This balloting would be followed in three months by parliamentary elections, employing a formula mixing proportional representation (parties gain seats in proportion to votes cast for them) and constituencies (areas represented in a legislative body) based on a system in use in West Germany. The agreement envisioned a free parliamentary election, but this meant that the old, possibly corrupted parliamentarians would choose the president.

Three fervently anti-communist groups in the opposition refused to sign the agreement: the Alliance of Free Democrats (chaired by János Kis), the Alliance of Young Democrats (FIDESz), and the independent trade unions. The Free Democrats stood on street corners and obtained 200,000 signatures requesting a referendum on four issues: disbanding the armed workers militia, official accounting for the party's assets, withdrawing communist party cells from workplaces, and most important, postponing the presidential election until after parliamentary balloting in March 1990. This became known as the "Four Yeses" referendum. The last question established the democratic precedent. At a news conference, the organizational spokespersons denounced the sequencing of electing a president by popular vote before electing the first democratically selected parliament. Henry Kamm in *The Times* on September 20 would report that "they believed that no voting should take place under present circumstances, in which Communist-imposed rules dominate political life. Electing a powerful president first would put into question the Parliament's powers" ("Communists and Foes Back a Multiparty Hungary").

The Free Democrats achieved their referendum. The plebiscite's results were honored; 58 percent voted to delay the presidential election. As a result, the presidential election was rescheduled after the free general election, slated for March 25, 1990.

The September 18 agreement had resulted in six bills, to be submitted to parliament, described by *The Times* on September 20 as providing "for a more democratic electoral law, a new office of President to replace the virtually powerless Presidential Council, a law legalizing and guaranteeing rights of political parties, a constitutional court and amendments that would liberalize the penal code and rules of criminal proceedings."

The Times also notes on September 20 the demand by the Free Democrats and FIDESz for disbanding the workers militia, "considered hostile to democratization," and a full accounting of the party's assets: "The vast holdings of the communist party, which for 44 years has had unhampered access to public property, have become a subject of increasing criticism not only from opposition groups but also from the public." The Free Democrats and FIDESz also objected to what they called "continued Communist domination of more than 90 percent of the press and the party's refusal to dissolve its cells at places of work."

Seeking to persuade all of the diverse opposition groups to approve the agreement, Imre Pozsgay, the communist party's reform candidate for president, was reported in *The Times* on September 20 as announcing that the party would hand over to the government property valued at approximately $33 million, with which to finance all of the parties' election campaigns. He furthermore announced that the party's paramilitary workers militia would be reduced from 60,000 to 40,000 members in 1990, its weapons placed under control of the defense ministry, and its armed exercises discontinued.

SEPTEMBER 11, 1989
HUNGARY ALLOWS 7,000 EAST GERMANS TO EMIGRATE WEST
Scenes of Joy and Relief
Tough Decision by Budapest Severely Strain Solidarity of Soviet Bloc Allies
By SERGE SCHMEMANN
Special to The New York Times

BUDAPEST, Sept. 10 – Hungary announced today that it is allowing thousands of East Germans who have refused to return home to leave for West Germany. It was another chapter, and a dramatic one, in a summer-long exodus through the new Hungarian gap in the Communist frontier.

The announcement cleared the way for more than 7,000 East Germans, who have said they wanted to go west, to do so beginning at midnight. But it was possible that this number might substantially increase as other East Germans, now in Hungary as tourists, take advantage of the new opportunity. Hungary's Foreign Minister said there are 60,000 people in this category.

A declaration by the Hungarian Government said that because of the "unbearable situation" created by the tide of East Germans trying to leave their country, Hungary has decided to temporarily suspend a 20-year-old agreement with East Germany and to allow the refugees free passage "to a country of their choice."

Tears of Joy

. . . Late last night, the first of the departing East Germans, honking their car horns and cheering wildly, began pouring across the Hungarian border. For virtually all those who are refusing to return to East Germany, the destination is West Germany, where they are eligible for automatic and instant citizenship.

[The Associate Press reported that the first of the cars crossed from Austria into West Germany before dawn on Monday.]

Split Within East Bloc

The agreement marked the first break by a Warsaw Pact country in the customary cooperation in blocking citizens from going to the West. . . .

All indications were that the decision was wrenching for the Hungarians, who are among the leaders of East European nations in adopting some Western standards of democracy and human rights. Still, the Hungarians have been reluctant to break openly with neighbors and major trading partners in the East. . . .

"Under the guise of humanitarian thinking, an organized trade in humans is being carried out," the [official East German news] agency said, implying that Hungary was being paid by West Germany for the release. "With regret it has to be stated that representatives of the Hungarian People's Republic have been led to support this action that has been long prepared by the Federal Republic of Germany in violation of treaties and agreement."

Outside the Holy Family Church, on a residential hillside of Budapest, at the oldest of the four camps set up for the East Germans, hundreds of refugees crowded near a television set placed outdoors broke into loud cheers and sobs of joy, relief and anguish as Foreign Minister Gyula Horn made the long-awaited announcement that they were free to move on at midnight.

A few left immediately for their cars to be first in line at the Austrian border, blaring their horns in excitement, and some left for the rail station. Half the East Germans were expected to leave in perhaps 1,000 private cars, and the rest were to travel west on Austrian trains and buses over the next few days, all headed for West German reception camps long prepared in Bavaria. . . .

In Bavaria, the new settlers will follow about 6,000 countrymen who have already fled, crossing what has been called the "green border" between Hungary and Austria. The flow began shortly after Hungary began to tear down the barbed wire and other fortifications along the border with Austria in May, and swelled at the end of August when East German school holidays ended and vacationing East Germans had to choose whether to remain in Hungary or go home.

Mr. Horn said Hungary was ready to release the East Germans last week, but delayed the movement to enable East Germany to try to talk its citizens into coming home. Officials at the refugee camp in Hungary said no East Germans had accepted the offer, and none even contacted East German diplomats who set up an office in a trailer near the church.

Both Mr. Horn and the West German Foreign Minister, Hans-Dietrich Genscher, who appeared on West German television at the same time that Mr. Horn spoke in Budapest, denied that there was a financial arrangement. . . .

Almost No Restrictions

The East Germans were told they could travel on virtually any document, be it East German, West German or provided by the International Red Cross. Austria announced that it was lifting all visa restrictions for this transiting, and that it had trains standing by to help.

The East Germans arrived in Hungary after receiving routine tourist visas from the East German Government. Some flew to Budapest, while others obtained transit visas to drive through Czechoslovakia. Once in Hungary, they massed near the Austrian border, seeking entry to the West. East Germany, angered by the emigration, has since suspended its travel agreement with Hungary. . . .

[Hungary's] official declaration said that Hungary had initially hoped to see the problem resolved between the two Germanys, but that negotiations had failed. At the same time, it said, the number of East Germans declaring their desire to head West increased steadily, and an "alarming situation" developed on the Austrian border, where hundreds of East Germans continued to cross illegally.

• •

THE THIRTY-THIRD ANNIVERSARY OF THE UPRISING

On October 18, 1989, parliament enacted constitutional amendments settled at the round table talks that had ended one month earlier. "People" was omitted from the name of the state and the preamble to the constitution changed to declare "the Hungarian republic is an independent, democratic state based on the rule of law, in which the values of bourgeois democracy and democratic socialism are equally recognized." Although socialism was still viewed as an implicit force, freedoms of assembly and association were made legal, with other liberties. The phrase "state of law" was included in new legislation, so that individual rights would be protected by law and institutions governed by it. A quest for this particular protection had been expressed by Hungarian would-be democrats at least since 1986, as Hungary started to move away from communism.

On October 23, the thirty-third anniversary of the 1956 uprising, Mátyás Szürös stood on the balcony of the National Assembly building and proclaimed the new Hungarian Republic. Within a few hours, three separate memorial processions with 100,000 demonstrators each converged at the parliament building, asserting that they wanted free, independent elections. Political prisoners released from incarceration offered speeches; youths clambered onto statues. The next day, October 24, *The New York Times* correspondent Serge Schmemann reports "commemorative rallies were held openly for the first time across Hungary on what was proclaimed a 'day of national reconciliation.'" The following day, Schmemann would muse, "Hungarians have never really accepted the status of 'Eastern European.' For 40 years, they have sustained the dream that they were full-fledged Europeans who would rejoin the fold as soon as the Soviets let them go" ("Hungary Hits Ruts on Road to Pluralism"). He notes that the Soviet Union, which had 65,000 troops based in Hungary, would pull out two of its four divisions. On October 7, the Hungarian communist party formally dissolved itself.

The Free Democrats, having achieved their referendum, saw 58 percent vote to delay the presidential election. As a result, the presidential election was rescheduled after the free general election, slated for March 25, 1990. Some were confused by the pell-mell disorder of the new situation. Others said Hungary had multi-party politics, before it had democracy.

OCTOBER 24, 1989
NEW HUNGARY MARKS '56 UPRISING: 'GORBY!' AND 'RUSSIANS OUT!' MIX

By SERGE SCHMEMANN
Special to The New York Times

BUDAPEST, Oct. 23 – Hungary today marked the 33d anniversary of the violent uprising against Soviet rule in 1956 by peacefully scrapping the "socialist people's" label and proclaiming itself a republic.

Bells tolled from Budapest's churches at noon, memorial plaques were unveiled at sites of key battles, wreaths were laid and patriotic poems were read. About 100,000 Hungarians with lighted candles, banners and flags gathered outside Parliament again in the evening to cheer emotional speeches from veterans of the uprising and to vent an old anger with chants of "Russians go home!"—punctuated at times by "Gorby! Gorby!"

As is often the case in demonstrations in Eastern Europe, some Hungarians in the crowd seemed to draw inspiration from President Mikhail S. Gorbachev of the Soviet Union, whose policies have opened the way to Hungary's new boldness in asserting its independence.

Hammer and Sickle Torn Out

Many people wore armbands in the national colors of red, white and green or carried flags with the Communist hammer and sickle torn out of the middle, just as the insurgents did in 1956.

Hungarian leaders continued to caution against too much haste in breaking all ties with the Soviet Union, especially membership in the Warsaw Pact military alliance. Matyas Szuros, the Acting President, drew some jeers when he said it was in the interest of the new republic to maintain "undisturbed and balanced relations" with the Kremlin.

Tens of thousands of Hungarians had packed the square outside the Gothic Parliament buildings to cheer the announcement of Hungary's status as a republic, made at the stroke of noon by Mr. Szuros, and to commemorate a rebellion that until recently was branded a "counterrevolution" but is now hailed as the wellspring of democracy.

'A New Historical Age'

"This is a prelude to a new historical age," Mr. Szuros declared from the same balcony where 33 years earlier Prime Minister Imre Nagy inspired a throng of rebellious Hungarians, setting off the uprising that would soon be crushed by Soviet tanks.

"The Hungarian Republic is going to be an independent, democratic and legal state in which the values of bourgeois democracy and democratic socialism are expressed equally," Mr. Szuros said, with a banner reading "Freedom—Independence" and a portrait of Mr. Nagy behind him.

The Acting President traced the newly proclaimed republic to the yearning for a "free, democratic Hungary" that arose in 1956 and to the "national independence movement" that survived the uprising. . . .

As recently as last year, the police broke up a peaceful rally to mark the uprising. . . .

Today, commemorative rallies were held openly for the first time across Hungary on what was proclaimed a "day of national reconciliation." Opposition parties and veterans of the rebellion organized gatherings at major sites associated with the uprising, all shown live on national television.

"It took 33 years for those behind thick walls to hear the cries for democracy," declared Jeno Fonay, a veteran of the uprising who spent six years in prison.

Moscow Doesn't Interfere

So far, Moscow has not interfered in the changes, as Prime Minister Miklos Nemeth acknowledged in a televised speech on Sunday when he said Hungary no longer had to fear foreign intervention. "This time, our hands are not tied down," he said.

There were Hungarians who also recognized that much of the country's new-found freedoms stemmed from the liberalized policies introduced by Mr. Gorbachev.

One speaker at the Parliament rally, Gyula Obersovszky, who was editor of the first revolutionary newspaper in 1956 and whose death sentence was commuted to imprisonment, told the crowd: "I'm rooting for Gorbachev. I'm rooting and worrying about him. Our freedom is an illusion until Moscow becomes free."

The crowd responded with chants of "Gorby! Gorby!"

Before Mr. Gorbachev announced unilateral cuts last year, the Soviet Union had about 65,000 troops in Hungary, according to the International Institute of Strategic Studies. It is now withdrawing two of its four divisions in Hungary. As of summer, the Soviets had announced that they had withdrawn one division and some additional units involving 10,000 troops.

The proclamation of Republic of Hungary was the latest of a series of dramatic steps by which Hungary has moved from the Stalinist model imposed on it by Soviet occupiers after World War II toward a Western-style parliamentary democracy....

THE SOVIETS DEPART

The backdrop for the drama of eventual Soviet troop withdrawals was as important as the military occupation ending at center stage. More than sixty parties contested the first free elections held in Hungary since November 1945. The first round of the general election took place on March 25, 1990. The multiplicity of parties and complexity of the voting system may have affected turnout; only 65 percent participated in the first round of voting, and a week later in runoffs, 46 percent voted.

On March 25, 1990, *The New York Times* anticipates that two of the main parties contending would be the Alliance of Free Democrats, described by the newspaper as a party of liberals and free-market economists supported by "urban intellectuals and disaffected workers," and the Hungarian Democratic Forum, "a coalition of center-right forces with a tinge of nationalism," whose strength was in the professional middle classes. It notes a third party, the Independent Smallholders, which had surfaced quickly and was promising to return land seized by the communists. Parliament's 386 seats were to be filled under a hybrid proportional-representation procedure, based on party lists collected in Budapest and the country's nineteen counties ("Upheaval in the East; A Democratically Evolving Hungary Heads Into Unknown at Polls Today").

The Times reporter Celestine Bohlen notes on April 9, 1990, that fewer than 50 percent of Hungary's 7 million eligible voters turned out to cast ballots for the second time in two weeks. In the new parliament, the Hungarian Democratic Forum won more than half the seats. Its leader Jozsef Antall would become prime minister at the head of a conservative coalition, which incorporated the Independent Smallholders and Christian Democrats. All together, they would hold more than 60 percent of the seats in the new parliament. At age fifty-eight, a librarian and scholar of medical history, Antall spoke to "an ebullient crowd" at the communist party's Budapest headquarters. The Alliance of Free Democrats lagged behind, but János Kis told *The Times* that his party would play the role of "a responsible opposition" (see **Hungary, Introduction;** "In Hungary, the Political Changes Are Tempered by Economic Fears," "Thousands of Hungarians March to Commemorate Revolt in 1848").

The Democratic Forum and the Alliance of Free Democrats became the mainstream parties in the new legislature (see "In Hungary, Flexibility as Doctrine"). Both promoted free-market economies and privatization, although the Free Democrats made a rapid changeover a priority. A third party, the Independent Smallholders, showed well. It had been the largest vote-getter in Hungary's last free elections, in 1945, and hoped for the return of farmlands appropriated by the communist state to their pre-1947 owners. The vagaries of proportional representation meant that no single party received a majority of seats in the National Assembly.

The new government began a program leading to liberalization and democratization, normalization of relations between church and state, redirecting its foreign policy toward the West, and setting up a State Property Agency to manage privatization. As elsewhere in the region, the principal issues were economic, as Hungarians were witnessing 12 percent unemployment, inflation rates in excess of 20 percent, a declining gross national product, and rises in crime.

On April 28, 1991, Bohlen reports in *The Times* that negotiations were underway over a new bilateral treaty between Budapest and Moscow ("Hungary Resisting Moscow's Shadow"). Hungary "resisted language proposed by Moscow that would ban either country from joining any alliance that could be considered hostile to the other, or from allowing its national 'infrastructure' to be used by a potential aggressor against its neighbor." The potentially hostile alliance doubtless alluded to Hungary's joining the North Atlantic Treaty Organization (NATO), although Bohlen cites Western officials as putting "a damper on Eastern European hopes that the NATO umbrella might soon be extended eastward." Prime Minister Antall said his concern was Hungarian pursuit of membership in the European Community. Pointing out that the main threat in the region was not military attacks, but instability due to economic crises, social stress, and nationalist eruptions, Bohlen reports, "Its solution is to criss-cross the region with bilateral treaties, and add a thin protective layer of loosely-defined groups pledged to mutual cooperation" ("Hungary Resisting Moscow's Shadow").

As Poland, Hungary, and eventually the rest of the Eastern bloc turned out their communist regimes beginning in 1989, they also began applying pressure for the disbanding of the Warsaw Pact, established in 1955 with Soviet prompting to counterbalance NATO. The pact was basically a series of bilateral agreements between the Soviet Union and its satellites, each of which was a member state of the pact, to support Soviet security objectives (see "**Introduction: Strikes, Sinatra, and Nonviolent Revolution**"). A Hungarian-Soviet withdrawal agreement had been signed on March 10, 1990, *The Times* reports on June 17, 1991, and had "been strictly followed by the Soviet Army, with a steady convoy of troops and equipment heading eastward across the border . . . ahead of schedule."

On July 2, 1991, *The Times* reports, "In a move that pushed the cold war further into history, the Soviet Union and the five other countries in the Warsaw Pact formally agreed today to dissolve the political and military alliance that long enabled Moscow to dominate Eastern Europe" ("Death Knell Rings for Warsaw Pact"). The last Soviet troops left Hungary on June 19, 1991. On May 1, 2004, Hungary joined the European Union.

JUNE 17, 1991
ROOFLESS GHOST MOCKS EXITING SOVIET TROOPS
By CELESTINE BOHLEN
Special to The New York Times

BUDAPEST, June 16 – Among the mementoes left by the Soviet Army as it withdraws from Hungary is a half-completed building on the edge of Budapest's 16th district, a roofless symbol of a rapid departure.

Local inspectors, who made a tour of the base as soon as the Soviet military vacated it last month, have no idea what the building was meant to be. No documents were left behind, and nothing can be deduced from the piles of pockmarked concrete slabs and broken bricks, gaping stairwell, uneven floors and dangling wires. But judging from the building's condition, the inspectors were able to conclude that construction had continued during the last 15 months—that is to say, after Hungary and the Soviet Union signed an agreement for the total withdrawal of Soviet troops by June 30 of this year.

Such wasted effort is not unusual in the Soviet economy, where projects are built according to plans drafted years earlier. But at a time when Soviet generals are complaining bitterly about being left in the lurch by diplomats who negotiated the withdrawal from Eastern Europe, the building off Ujszasz Street would seem to mock their grievances. The building, the unused materials, even the crane looming over the skeletal structure, will have to be swept away by Hungarian bulldozers.

Meanwhile, many of the Soviet soldiers and officers heading home from Budapest will live in tents until the Soviet Army comes up with the materials and the money to build new housing for its troops.

The Hungarian-Soviet pullout agreement, signed on March 10, 1990, has been strictly followed by the Soviet Army, with a steady convoy of troops and equipment heading eastward across the border. Last week, Budapest was informed that the last troops would cross the border on Wednesday, 10 days ahead of schedule.

The last scheduled Soviet troop train crossed the border today, . . . leaving behind only a skeleton staff led by the Soviet commander. . . .

"The trucks, the trains have been going day and night," said Gabor Fekete, Mayor of the 16th district, where housing for the Soviet forces was concentrated. . . .

"It was all so quick," said a [Soviet] officer headed for the troubled Soviet republic of Georgia. "But the decision was not ours. Our President decided to free Europe and he gave his word. "

About a week ago only 500 members of the Soviet military remained in Budapest's 16th district, which once housed 9,000 Soviet soldiers, officers and their family members. The 60 acres that were once the exclusive domain of the Soviet Army—no Hungarian was allowed to set foot inside the fenced-off areas—were being relinquished to the local authorities, one parcel at a time. . . .

The atmosphere is of a town just evacuated after a disaster. The children's playgrounds are silent, with weeds already growing high among the swings. . . .

The city of Budapest is planning to celebrate the Soviet departure with daylong street parties on June 30. In the 16th district the party will start on June 29, with a band playing at the airport where Soviet helicopters used to land. "We are calling it 'Bye-Bye, Sasha,' " said Mr. Fekete, a 27-year-old electronics specialist elected last year. . . .

BIBLIOGRAPHY

Bruszt, László, and David Stark. 1992. "Remaking the Political Field in Hungary: From the Politics of Confrontation to the Politics of Competition." In *Eastern Europe in Revolution*, ed. Ivo Banac, 13–55. Ithaca, N.Y.: Cornell University Press.

Chirot, Daniel. 1999. "What Happened in Eastern Europe in 1989?" In *The Revolutions of 1989*, ed. Vladimir Tismaneanu, 19–50. London: Routledge.

Falk, Barbara J. 2003. *The Dilemmas of Dissidence in East-Central Europe: Citizen Intellectuals and Philosopher Kings.* Budapest: Central European University Press.

Garton Ash, Timothy. 1999. *The Magic Lantern: The Revolution of '89 Witnessed in Warsaw, Budapest, Berlin, and Prague.* New York: Vintage Books.

———. 1990. "Eastern Europe: The Year of Truth." *New York Review of Books* (15 February):17–22.

Hankiss, Elemer. 1990. "What the Hungarians Saw First." In *Spring in Winter: The 1989 Revolutions*, ed. Gwyn Prins, 13–36. Manchester and New York: Manchester University Press and St. Martin's Press.

Isaac, Jeffrey C. 1999. "The Meanings of 1989." In *The Revolutions of 1989*, ed. Vladimir Tismaneanu, 125–164. London: Routledge.

Kis, János. 1989. "Turning Point in Hungary: A Voice from the Democratic Opposition." *Dissent* (Spring).

Konrád, George. 1990. "Chance Wanderings: Reflections of a Hungarian Writer." *Dissent* (Spring).

Mason, David S. 1996. *Revolution and Transition in East-Central Europe*. 2d ed. Boulder: Westview Press.

Stokes, Gale. 1993. *The Walls Came Tumbling Down: The Collapse of Communism in Eastern Europe.* New York and Oxford: Oxford University Press.

FROM *THE NEW YORK TIMES*

Bohlen, Celestine. 1991. "Hungary Resisting Moscow's Shadow." April 28.

———. 1990. "Upheaval in the East; A Democratically Evolving Hungary Heads into Unknown at Polls Today." March 25.

Greenhouse, Steven. 1991. "Death Knell Rings for Warsaw Pact." July 2.

Kamm, Henry. 1989. "Hungary Is Far From Democracy, and Even From Poland." July 30.

———. 1989. "Communists and Foes Back a Multiparty Hungary." September 20.

Schmemann, Serge. 1989. "Hungary Hits Ruts on Road to Pluralism." October 25.

Unsigned. 1988. "Editorial: A Hungarian for Too Many Seasons". May 31.

EAST GERMANY AND THE PASTORS' MOVEMENT

East Germany, created after World War II, included within its borders what had in the sixteenth century been Saxony. Frederick III, the Saxon elector, made Wittenberg, fifty-five miles southwest of Berlin, a center of learning and pilgrimage. Frederick's collection of Christian holy relics, purportedly including remains of infants slaughtered by Herod and fragments of swaddling clothes, attracted pilgrims to Wittenberg. Martin Luther, a theology professor at Wittenberg University, objected to the sale of special indulgences from the Church of Rome that were sold to pilgrims by papal agents. He believed that such deals exploited the poor, and that the Grace of God could not be purchased. To Luther, faith was the source of salvation. In 1517, he challenged what he saw as abuses and corruption by Rome and nailed ninety-five theses to the door of Wittenberg's Castle Church, an accepted way to stimulate public debate. Luther's theses ignited controversy. Frederick gave Luther protection and made Saxony the cradle of the Protestant Reformation and a Protestant tradition of individual dissent.

At the end of World War II, as Germany unconditionally surrendered to the Allies on May 8, 1945, no peace treaty was possible because the rout of Nazism meant that Germany was an occupied country without a government. During the war, discussions in Tehran (1943), London (1944), Yalta (1945), and Potsdam (1945) had produced agreement among the Allies to divide Germany into occupation zones. At Yalta, France got one zone, in addition to those of Britain, the United States, and the Soviet Union. Differences were glossed over at meetings in Potsdam in July and August 1945, when the Americans, British, and Soviets agreed on Germany's denazification, demilitarization, and democratization.

On October 7, 1949, the Soviet occupation zone in eastern Germany became a separate, ostensibly sovereign nation, the German Democratic Republic (GDR), or East Germany. The Soviet sector of East Berlin became its capital. In May 1949, four years after the collapse of the Third Reich, western Germany had become the Federal Republic of Germany (FDR), or West Germany, aligned with Western Europe. The two countries shared an 860-mile border, which was heavily fortified on the GDR side.

At the war's end, some 14 million dislocated persons had been on the move. Moscow-trained political operatives, among them German communists led by Walter Ulbricht, had flown into Berlin before Germany surrendered and with Soviet backing wielded influence beyond their numbers in configuring government institutions to serve communist needs. East Germany's licensing of political parties entrenched the German communist party, although it proclaimed to be a "multiparty" state. In April 1946, the party—the Socialist Unity Party of Germany (Sozialistische Einheitspartei Deutschlands, SED)—took charge of a Stalinist party-state. All parties had come under the SED's "leading role" by 1948. The party controlled the GDR citizenry, creating a secretive, passive society. All large estates and those previously belonging to Nazis were expropriated and the land redistributed to peasants and landless workers. Banking, industry, and mining were nationalized and small businesses administratively wrung dry.

The most heavily policed state of Eastern Europe after Romania, East Germany became the core of the Warsaw Pact. This pact, a series of bilateral agreements between the Soviet Union and each member state, was fundamentally created to protect Soviet interests and promote its security objectives. Some 400,000 Soviet troops plus their families lived in East Germany. The East German party-state employed repression, propaganda, and fierce surveillance against any opposition to the SED, which, under the Brezhnev Doctrine, could count on the Soviet military and Warsaw Pact to subjugate any revolts (see "**Introduction: Strikes, Sinatra, and Nonviolent Revolution**").

The Staatssicherheitsdienst (State Security Service, or Stasi) operated a deeply feared network of spies and other agents that penetrated and intimidated the entire society. *The New York Times* on October 31, 2001, reports that the Stasi consisted of 90,000 full-time staff and received information from some 175,000 informers ("Zirndorf Journal: Germans Piece Together Nation's Stasi-Riven Past"). When the Stasi's files were opened to public scrutiny in 1992, the scale of its surveillance was no less than astounding: it had files on 6 million of the population of 16.5 million. The Stasi kept close watch on 160 opposition organizations, including

QUICK FACTS ABOUT EAST GERMANY

- The German Democratic Republic (GDR), or East Germany, was the pivot of the Soviet-backed system of communist governments in Eastern Europe. Some 400,000 Soviet troops were permanently based there with their families.

- With the exception of Romania, East Germany was the most heavily policed of the Soviet-bloc Eastern European states. The Stasi, the secret security agency, gathered information from 175,000 informants. When the agency's files were opened to the public in 1992, the scale of its surveillance activities staggered many: dossiers had been maintained on 6 million persons out of a population of 16.5 million. With 90,000 full-time staff members, the Stasi kept close watch not only on individuals but also on 160 organizations, among them environmental, feminist, and peace groups.

- A total of 2.69 million East Germans fled their country from 1949 to 1961 (Naimark 1992, 77). At least 191 were killed trying to get across the Berlin Wall; some 5,000 persons made it over, under, or through the wall beginning in 1961 ("Clamor in the East; The Berlin Wall: A Monument to the Cold War, Triumphs and Tragedies"). To halt this human flow, the original Berlin Wall—consisting of cinder blocks and barbed wire erected overnight in August 1961—was replaced systematically with a series of concrete fortifications topped with barbed wire and guarded from watchtowers and gun emplacements. It became a sober symbol of communist oppression and the physical embodiment of the iron curtain. A twenty-nine-mile stretch of the wall divided Berlin's eastern and western sectors. Built entirely on East German territory, the wall eventually stretched for another 103 miles around West Berlin, isolating it from East Germany.

- An estimated 90 percent of East Germany's population had been able to receive West German television programs beginning in the 1970s. These broadcasts undermined the credibility of reports by the ruling Socialist Unity Party (SED) about East German prosperity and rights.

- Protest emigration was a major nonviolent sanction employed by the East Germans, as they departed for West Germany into self-imposed exile. In doing so, they were exercising a form of noncooperation called *hijra* in the vocabulary of nonviolent struggle and termed "exit" by East Germans (see "**Introduction: Strikes, Sinatra, and Nonviolent Revolution**"). Those who fled jeopardized themselves and those they left behind.

- During August 1989, some 500,000 East Germans crossed the Hungary-Austria border, ostensibly for vacation. By September, some 3,000 self-exiled East Germans were camped out at the West German embassy in Budapest seeking asylum, with another 100,000 East Germans in Hungary as tourists likely deciding whether to return home. By October, 2,000 East Germans were exiting the country each day.

- The other significant nonviolent method employed in East Germany—massive demonstrations—resulted in a series of thirteen consecutive Monday night demonstrations in Leipzig, from September 25 to December 18, 1989, and generated the largest public gatherings in German history. Waves of demonstrators flowed from the Protestant churches of Leipzig and other cities, calling on the government to reform and liberalize. Five million East German citizens would participate in these marches, exerting political pressure that would lead to the collapse of the communist regime. On the

(Continued)

(Continued)

- third weekend of October 1989, demonstrators marched in Chemnitz, Dresden, Erfurt, Magdeburg, and other cities.
- During autumn 1989, Leipzig was called the *Heldenstadt* (City of Heroes). On October 23 at the Nikolai Church, some 320,000 persons—more than half of Leipzig's population—demonstrated. On October 30, the crowds in Leipzig exceeded 350,000, despite police efforts to obstruct their gathering.
- Covering a November 5, 1989, demonstration in East Berlin, *The New York Times* correspondent Serge Schmemann reports that a million people may have marched, with conservative estimates putting the crowd at 500,000. This was the largest demonstration of the forty-two nationwide that took place on Mondays between 1989 and 1991, but the numbers in Leipzig—the ignition for the massive candlelight processions—were larger in the aggregate and as a percentage of the population that became involved (Lohmann 1994, 65 and 67).
- On January 30, 1990, the government of the Soviet Union agreed to the reunification of the two Germanys. On October 3, 1990, unification was completed with the annexation of East Germany by West Germany, making it the only Warsaw Pact country to disappear among the Eastern European revolutions of the 1980s and 1990s.
- On December 18, 1990, *The Times* reports that the SED had lost more than half a million of its 2.3 million members since September.

environmental, feminist, and peace groups (see "300,000 Reported to March in Largest East German Protest").

On June 17, 1953, construction workers in East Berlin went on an unplanned, effectively leaderless strike to fight new controls, in effect pay cuts, instituted by the party-state. More strikes followed, with a declared general strike and massive march led by the labor movement through East Berlin to oppose governmental persecution of the churches, constant food shortages, and increased work standards that effectively reduced wages. A general strike is part of a large category of economic noncooperation methods of nonviolent action and aims at near-total economic shutdown. Approximately 500,000 workers went on strike, and 480,000 demonstrated.

Although expressive of the protesters' views, the strikes and marches lacked strategy. The East German government brutally suppressed the demonstrations, with the help of Soviet troops stationed in the country. At least fifty-two people died, although documents released after German unification suggest hundreds of deaths. Purges within the SED followed, from which Ulbricht emerged stronger and able to eliminate internal party opposition to his Stalinist approaches. The West showed little or no interest in intervening and appeared willing to abandon East Germans to their fate.

During 1952–1953 and 1959–1960, East Germany collectivized agriculture. Although a few concessions were allowed for consumers after the 1953 uprising, the state's industrial policies stressed heavy industry. The government announced a succession of impracticable plans, revised them when they showed few results, and then dropped them. By the start of the 1960s, it had become evident that East Germany's centralized economy could not match West Germany's accomplishments.

The *Wende* and Leipzig, "City of Heroes"

An underlying Judeo-Christian legacy of resistance, nurtured from Roman antiquity onward, urged that one's allegiance not be given to rulers: "Put not your trust in princes," the Old Testament psalmist scribed. Assertion of an individual's right to voice disagreement with authority derived from the Protestant Reformation, initiated by Martin Luther in 1517. Within East Germany, the tradition of the Protestant Church—the German Evangelischekirche, or Evangelical Church, also known as the Lutheran Church—encouraged individual dissent on the basis of conscience. Also persuasive were the principles of the German Reformed Church, which was theologically aligned with the Swiss reformers John Calvin and Ulrich Zwingli. For four centuries, the German Reformed Church, smaller than the Lutheran Church, embodied Calvinist traditions calling for personal freedom to deviate from governmental positions and resist unscrupulous rulers.

Protestant resistance to Hitler originated from these same traditions. During the Nazi era, the Reformed League, an attempt to preserve the Reformed heritage on the four hundredth anniversary of Zwingli's birth, joined with the Confessing Church, an organization formed by German Protestants to resist efforts by the National Socialists to control the churches. The Confessing Church was among the few German resistance movements against Nazism, but it avoided advocacy for the Jews. Although defiance based on conscience was deeply rooted in the Protestant tradition, some influential theologians supported Hitler. Many other clergy and laity later felt guilt and remorse over having failed to mobilize to resist the Nazis. With the rise of the SED state, various Protestant bishops accepted the party's authority but espoused "the church in socialism," meaning that the clergy would criticize the regime without challenging the socialist order. This was not true of all churches, however.

Anyone aware of the Protestant legacy of dissent might not have been surprised that a Pastors' Movement would emerge in the 1980s and be crucial in bringing down the communist regime and the Berlin Wall, the worldwide symbol for the cold war. By one estimate, 52 percent of East Germans were affiliated with the predominant Evangelical Church. The Evangelical and Calvinist Protestant traditions meant that a pastor in Leipzig or Dresden, in East Germany, might find it more feasible to take a stand divergent from the communist regime than might a priest of a Roman Catholic parish in Cologne or Munich, in West Germany, where more than 40 percent of the population was Catholic.

From 1953 onward, opposition activities against the regime were limited to the writings of intellectuals, who sustained a powerful critique in the realm of ideas and kept alive independent thought, or subdued efforts by activists within small circles. Out of sight, a peace and anti–nuclear war movement developed unofficially. Any rising leaders were arrested and dispatched to West Germany.

Throughout the 1980s, East Germans held quiet discussions in churches, which by the late 1970s had solidified their role in East German society and had carved out space for serious conversations about issues of concern. By the end of the decade, East Germans had begun to express their opposition to the party-state through two principal nonviolent methods, also called nonviolent sanctions. The first method, street demonstrations, is from the category of protest and persuasion, which comprises a large repertoire of recognizable action steps used around the world. Under the protection of the Protestant churches, huge marches emerged from the Nikolaikirche (Nikolai Church), an historic church of Gothic architecture named for St. Nicholas in the center of Leipzig.

East Germany's democratic transition lacked an individual exemplar, such as a Mohandas K. Gandhi, Martin Luther King Jr., Lech Walesa of Poland, or Václav Havel of Czechoslovakia. The Lutheran Church strongly endorsed nonviolent resistance, however, and had a minister, the Reverend Christian Führer of the Nikolaikirche, who facilitated the church's leadership. By 1983, Pastor Führer's church was sponsoring Monday prayers for peace on a regular basis (see "Security Forces Storm Protesters in East Germany").

In 1988, occasional demonstrations took place after Monday peace prayers. Active resistance against the regime became visible with a form of political noncooperation—a boycott against manipulated local elections in May 1989. Fifteen percent of voters abstained while some cast ballots that they invalidated to show their disapproval (see "East Germany Faces Unrest among Youth" and "Security Forces Storm Protesters in East Germany").

In autumn, a series of thirteen consecutive mass demonstrations, held on Mondays in Leipzig from September 25 to December 18, 1989, became the largest public gatherings in German history. Waves of protests spread from Leipzig to other churches and cities. Eventually, more than 5 million GDR citizens would march in autumn 1989 (Lohmann 1994, 62). During this season of intense political revolt, Leipzig became known as the "city of heroes," or *Heldenstadt*. The churches and the people came together in an upsurge against totalitarianism, creating what Germans call the *Wende*—a turning, turnabout, or policy reversal—that would soon sweep across the Soviet satellite states. The protesters' demands included political freedoms, open borders, and eventually unification of the two Germanys (see "500,000 in East Berlin Rally for Change").

A turning point came on October 9, when security police backed down from inflicting violent reprisals against a demonstration surging from the Nikolai Church in Leipzig (see "300,000 Reported to March in Largest East German Protest"). The day before, Soviet president Mikhail S. Gorbachev had ended a visit to East Berlin, having said that "matters relating to the German Democratic Republic are decided not in Moscow, but in Berlin" (see "Gorbachev Lends Honecker a Hand"). In other words, the era of the Brezhnev Doctrine had come to a close. In December, the SED regime renounced its Stalinist past and began democratization processes (see "Leipzig Marchers Tiptoe around Reunification"; "Upheaval in the East"). Another cycle of demonstrations occurred from January 8 to March 12, 1990, pressing for rapid formal unification and free elections, balloting that would eventually transpire on March 18 (see "Two Germanys Unite after 45 Years with Jubilation and a Vow of Peace").

Protest emigration was the second major nonviolent sanction employed by the East Germans. For years, a steady flow of East Germans had departed for West Germany, into self-imposed exile, exercising a form of noncooperation known as *hijra*. No more irrefutable method of noncooperation can be identified than hijra ("to abandon" in Arabic)—to deny an antagonist's objectives (see "**Introduction: Strikes, Sinatra, and Nonviolent Revolution**"). The term may not have been uttered by those fleeing, but the exercise of hijra, called "exit" by East Germans, was significant in the Eastern European revolutions of 1989, and nowhere more so than in East Germany (see "500,000 in East Berlin Rally for Change").

At great risk to themselves and those they left behind, individuals permanently exiled themselves; others perished in the effort. In 1961, to stanch the exodus of what the government called "illegal exit," the SED state built a wall to separate East Berlin from West Berlin as well as to surround West Berlin and prevent access to that portion of the city from elsewhere in East Germany. Closing off West Berlin along the western borders of the city blocked the sole route of escape for East Germans into West Germany. One million Germans fled the eastern sector between 1945 and the creation of East Germany in 1949. During the 1950s, skilled personnel, often young men, constantly fled the dreary and authoritarian air of East Germany. They carried few possessions with them, so as not to raise suspicion and to appear to be making only a short visit. Instead, they were in effect "voting with their feet," making their way into permanent exile. Between 1949 and erection of the Berlin Wall, another 2.5 million East Germans "exited." Nearly 200 died trying to get across the wall.

On May 2, 1989, Hungarian soldiers cut an opening in the fence along the Austria-Hungary border, setting off a hemorrhage of East Germans fleeing to the West through this hole in the iron curtain (see "Exodus Galls East Berlin"). This exodus, combined with huge candlelight marches, led to the crumbling of the pillars of support for the communist regime, including its hated secret police (see "500,000 in East Berlin Rally for Change"). The Berlin Wall fell on November 9, 1989 (see "East Germany Opens Frontier to the West for Migration or Travel"; "Clamor in Europe").

One of the most recognized mass nonviolent movements against communist rule in Eastern Europe had by spring 1990 achieved its primary goals of political liberalization and open borders. Official unification of the two Germanys followed in October, as the five East German states agreed to annexation by the Federal Republic of Germany (see "Two Germanys Unite after 45 Years with Jubilation and a Vow of Peace").

Under the heavily militarized Soviet presence and a vast surveillance system, East Germany's opposition had expressed itself in 1953 through strikes and demonstrations. Collective action subsided after the 1961 erection of the Berlin Wall, as East Germans were trapped, apart from the westward flow of those choosing self-exile through protest emigration and managing to get out. The Protestant churches offered those who remained the only safe haven for speaking openly about oppression in East Germany's rigidly closed society. By autumn 1989, the combination of hundreds of thousands marching in church-sponsored protests for political freedoms and open borders, and thousands more withdrawing their cooperation with the communist regime by emigrating, undermined the power of the party-state. The government opened the gates of the Berlin Wall on November 9 and by year's end would announce complete freedom of travel for East Germans.

By spring 1990, East Germany's democratic opposition had achieved its goals, as transition to democracy and reunification of the two Germanys accelerated. The fall of the Berlin Wall became the symbol for the end of the cold war era. In actuality, the civil resistance of 5 million marching in immense candlelit demonstrations and the exit of thousands of fleeing citizens, along with the decision of a now-reforming communist party to open the barrier, were the decisive events.

"Stay and Change Things"

The German Democratic Republic (GDR), or East Germany, emerged from communist totalitarianism in part because of the courage and ethical clarity of the Lutheran Church. Protestant churches in East Germany had been encouraging reform efforts in small circles since the late 1940s, sanctioning resistance based on individual conscience. They were the only sizeable, independent institutions not directly controlled by the communist state-party. They possessed buildings, credibility, congregational networks, organizational capacity, their members' skills, and inspiration unavailable elsewhere. The great proportion of the populace trusted the churches. While their edifices provided safe meeting rooms, their pulpits communicated issues. For more than 400 years, the Protestant tradition in Germany had encouraged a dichotomy between the corruptions of the secular state and the private spiritual realm (see **East Germany, Introduction**).

Germany's Lutheran heritage was formally recognized in the constitution of East Germany, ratified in 1968: "Every citizen of the GDR has the same rights and duties regardless of his nationality, race, world outlook, or religious faith." Bishops, pastors, and laity employed this shield to the fullest in their forthright criticism of the system. Houses of worship offered protective auspices and provided sanctuary. Their doors were open to any inquiring spirit, even if not observant. Religious journals and church newsletters were not censored to the same degree as secular news media. Many nonbelievers viewed free-thinking clergy as worthy guides. The study of theology was one of the few university degree programs that did not require party-state approval or membership. The Protestant ministry "provided natural leaders of opposition," in the words of historian Charles S. Maier. Some ministers "possessed a natural political vocation, but most would learn politics on the job," he notes. "What motivated them through the 1980s was an ethical earnestness. . . . [T]hey believed in an engagement for lofty social and political goals, including disarmament, and they radiated an aura of reformist sincerity that was familiar to those who had seen American pastors active in the civil rights struggle" (Maier 2009, 266, 267).

The Protestant churches tended to argue that East Germans should remain in their country rather than exile themselves. In February 1988, the Reverend Christian Führer, pastor of the Nikolai Church (Nikolaikirche) in Leipzig, East Germany's second largest city, invited 50 persons to his church to discuss their involvement in a movement advocating international travel for East Germans. More than 600 persons attended the evening's event, titled "Living and Staying in the GDR." *The New York Times* did not cover the gathering, but an article from February 4 recognizes the relevance of such mobilizing. The reporter, John Tagliabue, mentions that while some young East Germans were organizing groups to swap information on emigration to West Germany, "what marks the new movements is a desire to stay and change things." Young congregations were torn between attempting to emigrate on the one hand and staying to improve life in East Germany on the other.

KEY PLAYER IN EAST GERMANY
Christian Führer (1943–)

Christian Führer, whose name translates as "Christian leader," was born in Leipzig, Germany, during World War II and followed his father into the ministry. He studied Greek and Latin and went to the University of Leipzig, at the time Karl Marx University, to study theology. While a student, he worked in a car factory and as a delivery boy. In 1980, he became the pastor of the Nikolaikirche (Nikolai Church or Church of St. Nicholas) in Leipzig.

The Nikolai Church and the Reverend Führer became the focal point for the East German opposition movement in the 1980s. By 1982, Führer had begun providing a room at the church where up to two dozen persons gathered to discuss nuclear disarmament. One year later, a pattern had developed whereby on Monday evenings at five o'clock, people walked through the cobbled yard en route to the church's Gothic interior, where Führer led "prayers for peace" sessions. In his sermons, Führer would criticize the arms race and advocate peace and nonviolent action. In 1983, the first demonstration against communist rule emerged from the church after the Monday peace prayers meeting.

In 1988, the Nikolai Church hosted what it thought would be a discussion among fifty activists at the church, but nearly six hundred attended. Thereafter the number of East Germans taking part in the Monday night meetings grew. After the sermons and discussions, those in attendance would march through Leipzig with lighted candles to express their opposition to communist policies. News spread of the Monday processions by word of mouth. The demonstrations always reflected the *keine Gewalt* (no violence) policy of what became known as the Pastors' Movement and were disciplined and restrained. The number of marchers increased by the thousands, so alarming government officials that in 1989 they ordered the police to begin blocking the streets to the church.

A large proportion of those who attended the prayers for peace and the marches following them were not necessarily committed Christians. Yet they found in the church a safe place where they could voice their opposition to oppression. Führer stressed that the church was "offen für alle" (open for all), including nonbelievers. According to one source, "On one occasion, the pews were filled with government officials and university students who had been sent to foil the demonstration. But the pastor shrewdly 'reserved' the balconies for the demonstrators" (Wall 1996, 283).

On September 25, 1989, the first "formal protest" occurred in a cycle of thirteen major demonstrations held on consecutive Mondays, culminating on December 18. The Leipzig protests were the kindling for waves of popular demonstrations in towns and cities throughout East Germany (Lohmann 1994). The marchers fluidly separated and merged to avoid becoming a single target for the security services. They moved toward Karl Marx Square in front of City Hall to issue calls for open borders, foreign travel, democratic liberties, political liberalization, and as the demonstrations proceeded during the autumn, German reunification. On September 25, some 8,000 people marched, singing "We Shall Overcome," the signature anthem of the U.S. civil rights movement.

On October 9, 1989, two days after the fortieth anniversary of East Germany, more than 70,000 persons participated in the Monday demonstration, chanting "Wir sind das Volk!" (We are the people). Rumors swirled about Leipzig that the party-state planned a "Chinese solution," alluding to the June 1989 massacres of student demonstrators in Tiananmen Square. *The New York Times* reports on November 19,

1989, that the regime's leadership had given orders to shoot if necessary (see "How the Wall Was Cracked"). Führer, and other Protestant clergy who had opened their churches and joined the so-called Pastors' Movement, continually admonished the large crowds to avoid violent expressions, in part to prevent providing police a pretext for breaking up the gatherings.

At 5:45 P.M. on October 9, the security police conspicuously began to pull back and did not use force. "[Un]named, frightened, yet very determined people" poured from Führer's church and marched steadfastly, according to political scientist Susan Lohmann, in a demonstration that "broke the back of the regime" (Lohmann 1994, 71). Encouraged by the absence of police reprisals on October 9, thousands more arrived the following Monday and each one after that until the Berlin Wall fell on November 9.

Between 1989 and 1991 in Leipzig, East Germans held forty-two major Monday evening demonstrations, which played a significant role in bringing about the collapse of the communist regime (Lohmann 1994, 65). As the government's power imploded in the face of massive popular defiance and other nonviolent methods, Führer traveled to West Berlin to learn what his church could do to help others. In the 1990s, he began a permanent, church-based initiative to assist the poor. Führer retired from the Nikolai Church in 2008, having reached the mandatory retirement age of sixty-five. In an interview, he told *The Times* that he plans to write a book ("A Clergyman of the Streets Leaves His Historic Pulpit").

FEBRUARY 4, 1988
EAST GERMANY FACES UNREST AMONG YOUTH
By JOHN TAGLIABUE
Special to The New York Times

EAST BERLIN, Feb. 3 – East Germany, long insulated from critical calls for change, is facing an increasingly assertive human rights movement among the young. . . .

Throughout the country, small independent groups print and circulate underground leaflets and books on environmental, social and political topics.

Artists in cities like Dresden and Jena publish art folders and prints outside the pale of state surveillance.

Alternative Service Sought

Anti-war groups work for the recognition of alternative service in hospitals and homes for the elderly, in place of service in the army.

Some young East Germans are organizing groups to trade information on emigration to West Germany.

But mainly, what marks the new movements is a desire to stay and change things.

In part, the movement was stirred by the warm winds of change from Moscow now blowing in the Soviet bloc.

Allies in the West

But opponents of change in this tightly ruled country point accusing fingers at what they call Western instigators as well. Across the wall in West Berlin, the alternative newspaper Tageszeitung has broken a leftist taboo and begun publishing once weekly a page of news "by and about people" in East Germany. A private network called Radio 100 broadcasts one hour a month of similar material under the name Radio Glasnost.

But the consensus that emerged from recent conversations with East Germans active in dissident movements, as well as with church leaders under whose auspices many groups operate, is that the germ of criticism is indigenous. . . .

Role of Protestant Church

Crucial also is the role of the main Protestant group, the Evangelical Church, where a new generation of pastors has initiated an opening to change. . . . [T]he church has taken dissident groups under its wing, putting at risk its improved relations with the authorities.

When the police raided the Zion Evangelical Church in East Berlin in November, arresting two members of an environmental group and confiscating printing equipment, protest vigils were held under church auspices until the equipment was returned and criminal investigations against church campaigners dropped.

100 Dissidents Arrested

In January, the authorities struck. Human rights advocates sought to unfold banners calling for change at a Communist Party rally Jan. 17 in East Berlin, and 100 or so persons were rounded up. Night after night, first in East Berlin and then in some 30 towns all over East Germany, people flocked to Protestant churches to demonstrate for those in prison.

The Rev. Manfred Becker, head of the Berlin and Brandenburg Synod, told youths at East Berlin's Galilee Church, "Much hope in our country is linked with the name Gorbachev."

"Glasnost and perestroika," he went on, using the Russian slogans for Mikhail S. Gorbachev's liberalization program, "belong on the agenda in our country too."

Expulsions to the West

The party leadership, unsettled by such rumblings, has repeated a surgical procedure it used before to remove symbolic figures of protest movements, first arresting and then expelling them to West Germany.

Thus, while this week's vigils continued, representatives of the church and the regime negotiated the release of 20 or so opposition leaders who remained in prison after the Jan. 17 events. . . .

FEARS OF FREE EMIGRATION

On May 2, 1989, Hungarian soldiers cut through the barbed-wire barrier along the mostly forested boundary between Austria and Hungary. A reform-oriented government had decided that it must accept multiparty politics to keep itself in power (see "In Hungary, the Political Changes Are Tempered by Economic Fears"). The key strategy first employed by the Solidarity union in Poland—seeking limited reforms, freedoms, and rights, so as not to threaten authorities' loss of power—had been followed in Hungary. The democratic opposition in Hungary also offered the regime a choice between the lesser of two evils: it could choose to open up the system and grant social autonomy to the people, in essence a civil society, avoiding aggressive confrontation with a democratic opposition that it could no longer control, or it could employ the full panoply of coercive measures it possessed and crush the opposition (see **Hungary, Introduction**).

East Germans had generally been allowed to travel to other Soviet-bloc countries. In the summer of 1989, however, East Germans ostensibly on holiday crowded into Czechoslovakia and Hungary while actually seeking a roundabout route to the West. Some East Germans fled in desperation. They made their way in an eastward loop, down through Czechoslovakia into Hungary behind the iron curtain—and thence into Austria and up into West Germany. Others sought physical protection inside the West German embassies and diplomatic missions in Budapest, Prague, Warsaw, and East Berlin. In their *hijra,* a centuries-old nonviolent method of permanent protest emigration called "exit" in East Germany, 10,000 East Germans might leave on a given day, resulting in disrupted industry, labor, and public services (see "500,000 in East Berlin Rally for Change").

Liberalizing reformers in the Hungarian government were increasing in number and influence and had decided to violate a preexisting travel agreement with East Germany stipulating that all travelers only be allowed to enter or return to a neighboring Eastern bloc nation. On August 20, a country fair near the Austrian border provided the chance for 500 East German citizens to escape. On August 22, *The New York Times* reports 1.5 million East Germans having applied for exit visas, while 5 million out of the population of 16.5 million were ready to leave if they could. During August, 500,000 East Germans crossed the Hungary-Austria border. By September, some 3,000 self-exiled East Germans were encamped at the West German embassy in Budapest, with another 100,000 already in Hungary as tourists likely contemplating whether to return home. *The Times* on September 7, 1989, reports that 1.25 million East Germans annually visited Hungary as tourists.

On September 10, the Hungarian foreign minister announced that the exiles in Hungary had the right of free movement; a week later the prime minister declared its border permanently open. All barriers on the Austrian border were ordered pulled down. Hungarian officials let East Germans cross electrified barbed wire, security stations, fences, guard posts, and installations of the iron curtain along the Austrian border while unilaterally terminating Hungary's agreement with the East German regime (see "Hungary Allows 7,000 East Germans to Emigrate West").

The Hungarian decision posed a dilemma for East German officials. To allow free emigration would bleed the country of its youthful population and intellectuals and reduce the population in general. To forbid travel would accelerate the pressures building in the country. The government dithered. On September 11, the Hungarian authorities decided that adherence to a United Nations agreement preventing the return of refugees to their country of origin took precedence over a 1956 bilateral accord with East Germany to surrender "illegal" visitors and those breaking GDR laws by trying to escape. No longer traversing through a cut hole, in only seventy-two hours a mass exodus of 15,000 East Germans arrived in the West.

In the background was the principle of "one Germany," enshrined in the West German constitution, entitling any East German to automatic West German citizenship. *The Times* notes that for the GDR this provision was an "infuriating mockery of its sovereignty and legitimacy, and a permanent enticement for East Germans to flee." West Germans considered it, Serge Schmemann writes, "politically unthinkable to abandon the principle of one German nation, and with it the official dream of reunification." This also explains why East Germany maintained the most stringent travel restrictions of the Warsaw Pact.

SEPTEMBER 14, 1989
EXODUS GALLS EAST BERLIN
Nation's Sovereignty Seems to Be Mocked
By SERGE SCHMEMANN
Special to The New York Times

EAST BERLIN, Sept. 13 – To the East German Government, the drain of its citizens to the West, by way of Hungary, has been both an economic loss and a source of acute embarrassment. But what seems to provoke the sharpest anger is the open challenge posed by the exodus to East Germany's shaky legitimacy.

As the drain of its citizens through Hungary continued at a reduced rate, East Germany's main Communist Party daily, Neues Deutschland, devoted a long article to arguing that the exodus was a major violation of international laws and conventions.

The culprit, however, was not Hungary, which announced on Sunday that it was suspending an agreement with the East Germans restricting the movement of their nationals to the West. The target, rather, was West Germany and its claim to represent all Germans, East and West.

Principle of One Germany

That claim, enshrined in the West German Constitution, entitles any East German to automatic West German citizenship.

To East Germany the claim is an infuriating mockery of its sovereignty and legitimacy, and a permanent enticement for East Germans to flee. It is also, therefore, the reason East Germany feels compelled to maintain some of the most stringent travel restrictions of the Warsaw Pact.

The West Germans, while not anxious to attract tens of thousands of new citizens, say it would be politically unthinkable to abandon the principle of one German nation, and with it the official dream of reunification. . . .

Moscow Criticizes Bonn

Diplomats said there was never a real chance of an agreement between Budapest and East Berlin. Hungary, having embarked on a westward-looking program of change, had no choice but to find a way to let the Germans go west. . . .

East Germany's predicament appeared evident to Moscow, which focused the bulk of its few comments on the affair on bolstering East Germany's claim to sovereignty and criticizing West Germany's claim to represent all Germans.

Yegor K. Ligachev, the hard-line Soviet Politburo member who is visiting East Germany in his capacity as overseer of Soviet agriculture, lauded East Germany today as a reliable ally, but made no direct comment on the exodus.

The approach suggested to diplomats that Moscow had little interest in stepping directly into the affair, but was anxious to bolster East Germany and to soothe the tensions among its allies.

Focuses of Disquiet

. . . . To the old men who rule East Germany, some of whom have been in leadership ranks since its founding, Hungary's decision to open its border seemed to contribute to an aggressive defensiveness and insecurity already heightened by the serious illness of Erich Honecker, East Germany's 77-year-old leader. Their reaction was a flurry of statements that seemed to consider any concession as a sign of weakness.

"The old men up there seem unable to understand that something needed to be changed," a Western diplomat said. "They confuse status quo with stability. Sometimes status quo breeds instability, and change is required to restore it, but they are no longer capable of seeing that."

Bloc's Best Standard of Living

What probably galled the leaders was that they thought they had met the most pressing yearnings of their people. The standard of living in East Germany is the best in Eastern Europe. Millions of East Germans have been allowed to travel to the West in recent years. In the first eight months of this year, 59,320 East Germans had emigrated legally, according to West German figures. Given this flow, the additional 15,000 or so who had fled or were expected to flee through Hungary did not pose a really serious problem.

What they did was to disrupt a delicate order East Berlin thought it had achieved, letting people go without openly admitting they were dissatisfied or were being enticed by West German citizenship.

Now, beyond the international humiliation, the exodus spread new insecurity through the land. People spoke gloomily of the prospect that travel even to other Eastern European countries would now be cut, and those who had lost relatives or friends to West Germany spoke with anger both of being abandoned, and of the Government that made people want to leave. . . .

EAST GERMAN AFFAIRS: "DECIDED NOT IN MOSCOW, BUT IN BERLIN"

In 1989, Erich Honecker, the Socialist Unity Party (SED) leader and head of the party-state for the previous eighteen years, had been ill during the summer's wave of East Germans traveling into Hungary and thence to West Germany. *The New York Times* on September 26 reports that Honecker had undergone gall bladder surgery on August 18. Although a 1974 amendment to the East German constitution proclaimed the state "irrevocably allied" with the Soviet Union, not only had Honecker rejected *perestroika* ("restructuring" in Russian), he had also censored reports of the new policy to insulate East Germany from the reformist tendencies of Soviet leader Mikhail S. Gorbachev (see "**Introduction: Strikes, Sinatra, and Nonviolent Revolution**"). *The Times* on September 14 observes, "To the old men who rule East Germany, some of whom have been in leadership ranks since its founding, Hungary's decision to open its border seemed to contribute to an aggressive defensiveness and insecurity already heightened by the serious illness of Erich Honecker, East Germany's seventy-seven-year-old leader. Their reaction was a flurry of statements that seemed to consider any concession as a sign of weakness" (see "Exodus Galls East Berlin"). As *Times* correspondent Serge Schmemann would explain in an article published on October 8, the main problem was that "45,000 East Germans had made a frenzied exit over the past month from the 'Democratic Republic,' reviving questions about the legitimacy of the old men who had been assigned by the Kremlin 40 years earlier to build a Stalinist state in the Soviet area of occupation" ("A Sympathy Card on East Germany's Birthday").

In fact, Gorbachev's arrival in Berlin on October 6 with his wife, Raisa Maksimovna Titarenko, to mark East Germany's fortieth anniversary celebration, was not covered live. What Gorbachev found during the festivities was far from a country "moving forward to strengthen socialism," as Honecker had penned to the Soviet leader from his sickbed a month earlier. Instead, he encountered job vacancy notices on factory walls, unmet production targets, scaled-down transportation services, closed building sites, dysfunctional hospital departments, and 2,000 citizens a day exiting the country.

Gorbachev made the stunning declaration upon his arrival in East Berlin that Moscow would not interfere in East Germany's affairs. Schmemann writes in the October 7 *Times* that Gorbachev won applause on the eve of the gala when he declared, "First I should tell our Western partners that matters relating to the German Democratic Republic are decided not in Moscow, but in Berlin."

OCTOBER 7, 1989
GORBACHEV LENDS HONECKER A HAND

At East Berlin Rally, He Says East German Communists Run Their Own Affairs
By SERGE SCHMEMANN
Special to The New York Times

EAST BERLIN, Oct. 6 – President Mikhail S. Gorbachev of the Soviet Union arrived in East Berlin today to offer the East German Communists a measured show of solidarity and to declare that Moscow would not interfere in East Germany's problems.

In a line that won a particularly loud burst of applause from an elite congregation gathered in the glittering Palace of the Republic for a special meeting on the eve of East Germany's 40th anniversary, Mr. Gorbachev declared:

KEY PLAYER IN EAST GERMANY
Erich Honecker (1912–1994)

Erich Honecker was born in Neunkirchen, Germany, a small industrial town. As the son of a staunch communist who worked as a miner, his upbringing was a formal introduction to the Communist Party. Honecker was a Young Pioneers member at ten years of age, a member of the Communist Youth Association at fourteen, and a full-fledged party member by seventeen in 1929. By trade he was a roofer.

After the National Socialists took power in 1933, Honecker organized underground activities by communist youth in various parts of Germany. Arrested by the Gestapo in 1935, he was sentenced to ten years hard labor for "preparing treason." Refusing to repudiate his communist beliefs, Honecker spent the time in solitary confinement. The Soviet Red Army freed him in 1945 as it moved across eastern Germany.

Honecker rapidly connected with the German communists who had been training in the Soviet Union in preparation for establishing a communist government in the Soviet-occupied zone. He ultimately joined the group of Bolsheviks associated with the Moscow-trained Stalinist Walter Ulbricht that was planning a Soviet-style regime for East Berlin. There, Honecker worked his way up the party ranks. He helped drive more liberal Berlin administrators out of power in 1948 and end a workers' uprising in 1953 that was brutally crushed.

During this time, he married Edith Baumann, a communist three years his senior, and they had a daughter; the marriage ended in divorce. Soon after, he married the twenty-six-year-old communist activist Margot Feist, with whom he had another daughter. Feist, too, held political aspirations, rising to the position of minister of education in 1963.

Elected a member of the Central Committee of the Communist Party in 1946, Honecker became a pivotal figure in fusing the Communist and Social Democratic Parties in East Germany into the Socialist Unity Party (SED). He also cofounded the Free German Youth movement (Freie Deutsche Jugend, or FDJ), which recruited militant cadres for the party. He would chair this movement from 1946 to 1955. In 1958, Honecker became a member of the Secretariat of the party's Central Committee, where he assumed responsibility for security, a role that included devising and managing the Berlin Wall in 1961. Ten years later, in 1971, Honecker rose to first secretary of the SED, replacing Ulbricht and effectively becoming head of state.

In 1972, East Germany signed the Basic Treaty with West Germany, pledging both countries to civil relations. Honecker managed to maneuver East Germany into joining the United Nations in 1973 at the same time West Germany became a member. He worked to keep relations cordial with West Germany and to keep economic resources flowing through trade. He set out to stabilize East Germany economically by making it industrially sound.

Honecker distrusted Soviet leader Mikhail S. Gorbachev's push for more openness that began in the late 1980s. In October 1989, after a series of large demonstrations and the flight of hundreds of thousands of East Germans to West Germany, Gorbachev reportedly warned Honecker of waning Soviet support. According to *The New York Times*, a crossroads was reached on October 7, after Honecker gave orders for security forces to be ready to open fire on demonstrators in Leipzig. Bloodshed was averted when Egon Krenz, the Politburo member in charge of security, flew to Leipzig on October 9 and canceled Honecker's orders, allowing marching protesters to proceed unmolested. Honecker resigned under pressure ten days later, on October 18, 1989, and the East German communist party began to undertake significant changes. Weeks later, the government decided to open the Berlin Wall (see "How the Wall Was Cracked").

After his resignation, Honecker had been scheduled to stand trial for treason and forty-nine counts of manslaughter in connection with ordering guards at the Berlin Wall to shoot anyone trying to escape. He took refuge at a Soviet military installation near Berlin and in 1991 fled to Moscow, where he was granted asylum in the Chilean embassy. He was deported to the newly reunified Germany in 1992. Honecker was tried in Berlin and spent time under house arrest and in prison. In January 1993, a Berlin court ruled that he was too sick to stand trial. He rejoined his family in Chile, where he died in 1994.

"First I should tell our Western partners that matters relating to the German Democratic Republic are decided not in Moscow, but in Berlin."

Without referring directly to the exodus that has cost East Germany 45,000 citizens and enormous humiliation this summer, Mr. Gorbachev acknowledged that East Germany had problems "that demanded solutions," and that these were related to the modernization and renewal sweeping much of the Communist world.

But the Soviet leader said he had full confidence that the East German Communists would themselves find solutions, "in cooperation with all powers of society."

Stands With Honecker

After the gala meeting, Mr. Gorbachev stood late into the night shoulder to shoulder with Erich Honecker, the East German leader, reviewing a torchlight parade of 100,000 members of the Free German Youth, the German Communist youth organization.

The image of the two leaders side by side, smiling and waving to a flood of loyal German youths flowing down the grand Unter den Linden boulevard under a thicket of flags and torches, was shown constantly on East German television.

It appeared to be what Mr. Gorbachev had come for, to demonstrate to East German Communists that he would not abandon them in a period of crisis, while at the same time suggesting that the problem demanded a new approach. Though neither Mr. Gorbachev nor Mr. Honecker made any direct reference to it, the summerlong exodus permeated all the anniversary rites. . . .

Defiant Formulas Repeated

. . . Speaking with a gusto that belied reports of ill health and the serious surgery he underwent this summer, Mr. Honecker, who is 77 years old, repeated the defiant formulas that have led many East Germans to doubt that any real changes can come under his leadership.

"The unbridled defamation campaign that is being internationally coordinated against East Germany is aimed at confusing people and sowing seeds of doubt in the power and advantages of socialism," he said.

Mr. Gorbachev, by contrast, took care while declaring support for a major ally to stop well short of Mr. Honecker's hard line. Soviet officials traveling with Mr. Gorbachev said his primary mission was to soothe the brittle nerves in East Berlin and to help prevent the crisis from increasing to a level at which it might destabilize Moscow's most important ally.

But while expressing confidence in the East German Communists, Mr. Gorbachev also injected a distinct plug for renewal and emphasized that solutions to East Germany's problems would be found in cooperation with all of the East German society.

"The G.D.R. of course has its problems, demanding solutions," he said. "They arise from the internal demands of a society moving toward new horizons and the gradual process of modernization and renewal in which the socialist world now finds itself."

He is confident, he said, that the East German Communists "will know how to find answers to the questions on the agenda of the day in cooperation with all the powers of society." The Soviet Union, he said, wants East Germany to "strengthen, grow and develop."

Inevitably, the Soviet leader drew cheers and chants of "Gorby, Gorby!" at his limited stops around the city, and young Germans parading past him in the night gazed at him with evident admiration and sometimes burst into spontaneous greetings.

. . . Last Monday, some 10,000 demonstrators in Leipzig chanted "Gorby, Gorby!" as a code word for the reforms they are demanding of their unyielding Government.

In his speech, Mr. Gorbachev rebutted accusations that Moscow was alone responsible for the division of Europe, and . . . specifically assailed demands that Moscow dismantle the Berlin wall—a call made by Presidents Reagan and Bush. . . .

DEMONSTRATIONS GREET FORTIETH ANNIVERSARY CELEBRATIONS

As Protestant churches provided moorings, popular opposition activities were being openly organized and an alternative culture was emerging in East Germany. In 1985, activist intellectuals in Berlin founded the Initiative for Peace and Human Rights (Initiative für Frieden und Menschenrechte), to work on democratization, and published a *samizdat* ("self-published" in Russian) newsletter. The concerns of the small civic movements emerging included questions of peace (heightened by the deployment of nuclear weapons), environmental preservation, the place of religious institutions in public life, draft resistance and conscientious objection, and public participation (including, as time went on, the status and role of women). Debate of these issues was enacted in novel and unsanctioned behaviors that bypassed the established order, unofficial living arrangements, unauthorized peace meetings, and actions to encourage environmental conservation. Meanwhile, the Protestant Church assumed a role similar to that of the Solidarity union in Poland during 1980–1981 (see "Strikers in Poland Defy Gierek Appeal"). The slogan "Peace Without Weapons" became an informal motto for diverse groupings.

Protected by the churches, groups that materialized almost overnight coordinated protest demonstrations in different cities. The New Forum (Neues Forum), founded September 9–10, 1989, in Grünheide, was a network of local, democratic, and decentralized initiatives to spur debate. Set up by six physicians, four physicists, three clergy, three students, and fourteen other activist intellectuals, the forum appealed for "awakening '89" and declared its purpose as a "political platform." *The New York Times* reports on September 26 that the New Forum gathered 4,200 signatures on its founding appeal.

The historian Charles S. Maier notes that the New Forum sought institutional reforms, including "rights of political association, an end to violence and secret policing, entrepreneurial independence but without Western-style competitive capitalism." The forum offered an "organizational network that excited previous fence-sitters and prompted an explosion of political meetings and organization," using the terminology of "dialogue," as opposed to the Lutheran bid for conscience. A major organization involved in demonstrations from Leipzig to Berlin, the network itself was "a product of the self-emancipation already underway" (Maier 2009, 271).

On September 28, a physicist, an historian, a pastor, and a film director founded Democracy Now! (Demokratie Jetzt). Bidding "peaceful democratic renewal," they invited Christians and critical Marxists to join "an alliance of all reformers." The United Left similarly called for critical reappraisal of East German socialism. On October 1, the Democratic Awakening (Demokratischer Aufbruch) was formed, calling for "a socialist society on a democratic basis" with human rights, travel, market freedoms, and independent trade unions. Composed of Protestant clergy, its outlook was more cautious than the stance of the mushrooming secular organizations. Availing itself of the auspices of the Protestant Church, it attracted a disproportionate share of Western news coverage.

With this broad civic mobilization overlooking the concerns of women, a feminist movement emerged to fight gender inequality. Although constitutionally equal with men in East Germany, the pressures of daily life meant that women were bowed down in servitude by restrictive customs, exceedingly long working hours, and discriminatory pay. By December, the Independent

Women's Association had coalesced. The Democratic Awakening raised environmental issues, and the Green Party had come into existence by late autumn, partly motivated by fear that ecological concerns had faded from deliberation. On October 24, formation of an independent trade union would be mentioned in *The Times* (see "300,000 Reported to March in Largest East German Protest").

The church leaders sheltering these movements propounded *gewaltloser Widerstand* (nonviolent resistance) or *keine Gewalt* (no violence) as the only option for the opposition. The conviction of the ministers was partly ethical, yet it was also highly strategic and grimly logical, rooted in a determination to break the regime's use of violence and its surveillance of citizens. They concluded civil resistance, or nonviolent action, to be the only force that could work against the government's solidly militarized system of force. So strictly did they instill the discipline of nonviolent struggle that burning tapers and votive candles, originally a testimony of adherence to nonviolent means, soon became the overall symbol for resistance against the regime.

Soviet leader Mikhail S. Gorbachev arrived in East Berlin on October 6 and on October 7 addressed ceremonies to mark the fortieth anniversary of the East German communist state. He subtly encouraged reforms while asserting a principle of noninterference. East German leader Erich Honecker relayed to Gorbachev no intimation of changing course and offered no acknowledgment of the public's rising discontent. *The Times* on October 9 would quote Gorbachev as having told Honecker "those being late will be punished by life itself," which was interpreted as a reprimand to Honecker and tacit support for the proponents of change (see "Security Forces Storm Protesters in East Germany").

With Gorbachev still in the country, demonstrations broke out across East Germany on October 7, as protesters held mass rallies, marches, and demonstrations in cities urging democratic changes. Wherever he went, East Germans greeted Gorbachev with cries of "Gorby! Gorby!" On October 8, *The Times* reports on the October 7 demonstrations that took place in Leipzig, Potsdam, Halle, and other East German cities. As Gorbachev was leaving that night for Moscow, tens of thousands of East Berliners had walked to Alexanderplatz in the middle of the city, carrying candles and flashlights. Those in attendance chanted, "No violence!" "We're staying here!" "We Are the People!" Their proclamations referenced specifically the adoption of *keine Gewalt* (no violence) as the policy of the Pastors' Movement and the decision by some young East Germans to stay and fight for reform and democracy rather than emigrate. Security police severely attacked the participants in the candlelight vigil, and chased them into Prenzlauer Berg, a section of the city where many adherents of New Forum lived. Hundreds were beaten and arrested.

The journalist-historian Timothy Garton Ash describes the ruthlessness of the October 7 party-state's actions despite the presence of Gorbachev: "[T]he police used force, indeed gratuitous brutality, to disperse these protests and intimidate any who might have contemplated joining in. Young men were dragged along the cobbled street by their hair. Women and children were thrown into prison. Innocent bystanders were beaten" (Garton Ash 1999, 67). The events of October 7 and the next two days would represent a milestone. By October 8 the demonstrations by East Germans had become more widespread, grown larger, and become politically more pointed.

OCTOBER 8, 1989
POLICE AND PROTESTERS CLASH AMID EAST BERLIN FESTIVITY
By SERGE SCHMEMANN
Special to The New York Times

EAST BERLIN, Oct. 7 – East Berlin ended its 40th anniversary celebrations tonight with clashes between demonstrators demanding change and police troops.

Callers to Western news reporters told of other demonstrations, in Leipzig, Potsdam, Halle and other East German cities, but initial details were sketchy.

The clashes in East Berlin began under a display of fireworks that lit up the night sky, underscoring the contrast between the state-ordered festivities and the crisis shaped by the flight of more than 45,000 citizens this summer.

Frustration Shifts to Streets

With the flight curtailed by the closing of the Czechoslovak border earlier this week, the focus of popular frustration seemed to shift to the streets. Large demonstrations and outbursts of violence were reported earlier this week in Leipzig and Dresden.

In East Berlin, what began as a clutch of about 100 demonstrators mingling with [a] crowd of holidaymakers at a fair set up on the vast Alexander Square turned into a march of thousands through the center of the city, first toward the Palace of the Republic, where President Mikhail S. Gorbachev of the Soviet Union and other visiting Communist chiefs were attending a gala reception, and then through the dark, cobbled streets of the working-class Prenzlauerberg district.

Thousands of police officers, plainclothes security forces and volunteer militia ringed the marchers, estimated at about 5,000, and drove them down the side streets of Prenzlauerberg, where the police periodically charged seized individual protesters.

Their chants were those that were sounded in the demonstrations in Leipzig and Dresden this week: "Freedom," "We want to stay," and "New Forum," the name of a newly formed reform group. They also again shouted "Gorby, Gorby," invoking the name of Mr. Gorbachev, which has become a rallying cry for those demanding change.

Many demonstrators said they were followers of New Forum, whose founders said they were dedicated to staying in East Germany and campaigning for change along socialist lines.

In Prenzlauerberg, the police, plainclothes security forces and volunteer militia drove the protesters down side streets, seizing dozens and beating some. Several Western reporters and photographers were detained and beaten. There were no immediate estimates of arrests or injuries.

Barricades at Checkpoint Charlie

As they walked, the marchers called to people watching from windows to join them. Some clapped and shouted their support, some came out to join the protest.

A group of several thousand marchers eventually was driven to the Gethsemane Church, where dissenters have been holding a vigil demanding the release of protesters arrested at earlier demonstrations. The church was the site of a peaceful gathering tonight, and candles burned at its main entrance.

The police brought three water cannons and massive reinforcements, but the cannons were not used as the security forces finally dispersed the throng. . . .

In a move that surprised Western officials, East Germany erected heavy concrete-and-metal barricades outside the crossing at Checkpoint Charlie last night and prevented most visitors from crossing through the day.

Resident foreigners, diplomats and correspondents were allowed through. But the visitors who routinely receive a daylong permit to visit East Berlin were turned back. Diplomats surmised that the aim was to prevent West Germans and foreigners from joining or witnessing any demonstrations. . . .

• •

THE NIKOLAI CHURCH AND THE *WENDE*

As the twin forces of the churches and the people converged, the *Wende*—the change or turnabout—began in Leipzig at the Nikolaikirche (Nikolai Church or Church of St. Nicholas) and would soon sweep the Soviet satellite of East Germany.

An important city in Saxony's past and home to a respected university, Leipzig was called "little Paris" during Goethe's time. By 1982, the Nikolai Church, built in 1165 and rebuilt in the sixteenth century, had begun providing a room for fifteen to twenty persons to meet and discuss nuclear disarmament. One year later, a pattern had emerged: on Monday evenings at five o'clock, people would walk pensively through the church's cobbled yard to the church's grand baroque interior, where the Reverend Christian Führer had made available space for regular "prayers for peace." In 1983, the first demonstration emerged from the Nikolai Church following peace prayers in opposition to the deployment of missiles by the North Atlantic Treaty Organization (NATO) (Pfaff 2001 292). Originally conversing about the nuclear arms race, the weekly meetings became a symposium for contesting numerous issues. Pastor Führer made clear that the church welcomed persons of all persuasions, not only believers.

Erich Honecker, the leader of the Socialist Unity Party (SED) since 1946, had never been pleased by the Soviet deployment of short-range missiles in East Germany to counter the cruise missiles and Pershing-2 rockets of NATO. He did not immediately order the party-state's security apparatus to interrupt the antinuclear meetings as long as they were small protests directed at NATO and Moscow. By spring 1989, however, the Monday prayer meetings were normally brought to a close with participants filing out of the church and into public demonstrations against the government.

The East German government described the state as "multiparty," but in truth, the SED ran a one-party regime of Stalinist origins. When East Germany held national elections in May 1989, some 10 to 15 percent of voters invalidated their ballots. (By failing to fill out a ballot correctly or writing in a name not officially on the ballot, a voter can express disapproval and exert political noncooperation.) East German officials reported a 98.77 percent turnout, with the ruling party receiving 98.85 percent of the vote. The notion that 98.85 percent of voters favored the communists turned skepticism to anger, which in Leipzig was expressed at one entrusted location—the Nikolai Church. Known as a safe haven, the church welcomed the debate and led in voicing grievances over electoral tampering. More than 100 were arrested for protesting the elections. From that point on, even more East Germans converged on this house of worship on Monday evenings.

The Monday gatherings at the Nikolai Church became the symbolic center for civil resistance in East Germany as the number of people attending steadily increased that autumn. Open to everyone, the prayer meetings established the precedent for holding regular nonviolent mass meetings, at which "We Shall Overcome," the signature anthem of the U.S. civil rights movement, was often sung. The Leipzig assemblies at the Nikolai Church grew, even though on September 18 after a peace meeting authorities arrested 100 demonstrators. As police trucks shifted gear to transport the detained, they drove directly into the crowd, injuring many people. The security services sought to suppress the democratic rising with brutality and force. The imprisonments only invigorated the demonstrations that followed.

September 25 marked the first "formal protest" in a cycle of thirteen major Monday demonstrations that would occur. Protesters would form, break up, and re-form into fluid groups to avoid presenting a single, easy target for the security forces as they moved toward Karl Marx Square in front of City Hall to demand rights to foreign travel, democratic freedom, freedom of expression, and others. Approximately 8,000 persons marched on September 25, singing

"We Shall Overcome." Security forces put scores under arrest, as marchers blocked traffic in downtown Leipzig. The demonstration occurred hours after communist authorities refused to register New Forum, foremost of the growing civil society opposition groups, and demanded that its members cease all activities.

Prior to the visit of Soviet leader Mikhail S. Gorbachev, more than 25,000 nonviolent activists gathered on October 2 outside the Nikolai Church in the largest demonstration since the 1953 uprising. Some chanted "Gorby! Gorby!" As the demonstrators marched toward Karl Marx Square, the police blocked their way and began dispersing them by force. Some found refuge in St. Thomas Church, where Johann Sebastian Bach is buried. Five days later, on October 7, the peaceful demonstrators in East Berlin and other cities were violently interrupted by police brutality; in Leipzig police arrested and beat unarmed peaceful protesters outside the churches.

On October 9 in *The New York Times*, Serge Schmemann writes about celebrations and demonstrations on the night of October 7 in East Berlin marking the fortieth anniversary of East Germany. It was a crucial moment in the East German struggle, when police brutality, still routine at this stage, reached its height. Chronicling the storming of unarmed demonstrators by armed security forces, Schmemann shows how popular defiance was spreading from Leipzig to East Berlin and Dresden, where police hit demonstrators with riot sticks and threatened them with water cannons. Security forces broke up an East Berlin candlelight vigil of nearly 1,500 participants, who were chanting "No violence!" and "We're staying here!" In Leipzig, police used dogs and truncheons to attack more than 20,000 marchers. In all three cities, police used batons and rubber riot sticks to separate demonstrators, whereupon they beat the smaller groups. In Dresden, witnesses told *The Times* of demonstrators being struck or dragged away.

East Germany's demonstrations of 1989 were distinguishable by their deliberate prohibition on violence, despite their eventually massive size. The predictability of East German police violence in early autumn 1989 actually fortified the resolve of demonstrators not to contaminate their goals with violence. By and large, those demonstrating not only rejected provocations by agents of the secret police who attempted to create pretexts for reprisals, and rowdies who intruded, they also held to the implicit connection of the means and ends (see "**Introduction: Strikes, Sinatra, and Nonviolent Resistance**"). This is not to say that there were no breakdowns of discipline. Informed and sophisticated analysts sometimes observe nonviolent mobilizations and conclude that they "just happen." Long periods of behind-the-scenes development and organization often antedate the appearance of civil resistance.

What became known as the Pastors' Movement gave birth in East Germany to mass demonstrations—one of the key methods of nonviolent resistance—organized by the groups that had been protected by the churches. Cabaret artist Bernd-Luntz Lange recalled, "There was no head of the revolution. The head was the Nikolaikirche and the body the centre of the city. There was only one leadership: Monday, 5 P.M., the Nikolaikirche" (Dennis 2000, 278). The regular Monday assemblies attracted more citizens each week, from which the street demonstrations of thousands emanated. "We didn't start this, but we protected it," Pastor Führer stated. "We were the catalysts" (Banta 1989, 41). Meanwhile, the East German police, growing increasingly concerned about the large crowds attending Führer's weekly prayer meetings, began sealing off access roads around the church.

OCTOBER 9, 1989
SECURITY FORCES STORM PROTESTERS IN EAST GERMANY
Worst Unrest Since '53
2d Day of Violence Follows Communists' Celebration of 40th Anniversary
By SERGE SCHMEMANN
Special to The New York Times

DRESDEN, East Germany, Oct. 8 – Protesters clashed with the police and security forces today in cities throughout East Germany as the Communist Government's efforts to celebrate its 40th anniversary ignited rallies and demonstrations urging changes in the country's hard-line system.

Spurred on in part by the presence of the Soviet President, Mikhail S. Gorbachev, who came for the celebrations, protesters took to the streets late Saturday and again today, often mingling their calls for greater freedom with chants of "Gorby! Gorby!"

In East Berlin, Dresden, Leipzig and elsewhere, the police beat back defiant protesters, swinging riot sticks and menacing them with water cannon. In East Berlin late tonight, a candlelight vigil was broken up by the security police, who set upon some of the nearly 1,500 people there as the protesters shouted, "No violence!" and "We're staying here!"

"We Are the People!"

When the police and security forces ordered the protesters to leave a street near Gethsemane Church, Reuters reported, the demonstrators drowned out the order, chanting, "We are the people! We are the people!" The church is a center for pro-reform groups.

Police trucks blocked streets around the church, Reuters said, and the Rev. Gottfried Forck, the Lutheran Bishop of Berlin-Brandenburg, went to the church to meet a police colonel.

It was the second night of violence in East Berlin, and it came at the end of a week of sporadic and spontaneous protests in other parts of the country. The demonstrations, which flared and subsided in short bursts, marked the biggest anti-Government protests since a failed workers' uprising in June 1953. For a Government already smarting from the flight of nearly 45,000 of its citizens in the last few weeks, the protests were a further embarrassment.

Police Are Jeered

In the Prenzlauer Berg district of East Berlin and in Dresden, protesters told of older people leaning out windows to jeer the police, and the demonstrations displaced the exodus of their compatriots as the main topic of conversation.

"That's all we're talking about at our factory," said a middle-aged worker in Dresden. Communist Party members reported a flood of queries, and in the streets people gathered around cars on the hour to hear radio reports from West Germany about the outbreaks.

The East German authorities made only a terse mention of the weekend disorders, which for them marred the swirl of parades, speeches and fireworks marking the 40th anniversary. "The violence caused by the hooligans who were provoked by international media was stopped by the People's Police and order was restored," the official ADN press agency said in a report read over the East German radio and television.

Challenge to Honecker

Diplomats said the protests could become a greater challenge to Erich Honecker, the Communist Party chief, than the exodus because the protesters are overwhelmingly people who want to stay but who are demanding change.

"I don't want to leave," said a 17-year-old youth on his way to a demonstration in Dresden with a candle in his hand. "Those who fled were selfish. They only wanted to have more material things. We want to stay. This is our country. But we want it to be democratic and really socialist."

Though several groups advocating change have formed, most notable among them the New Forum, none have asserted any recognizable leadership or coordination over the novel resistance, nor any unified program.

New Forum, whose 30 founders have been surprised by the flood of support they have received, has in essence called for socialist change. The group's name has become a standard chant, along with "Gorby! Gorby!" at demonstrations, and its platform of reform is posted in churches.

During the weekend's festivities, even when prodded gently by Mr. Gorbachev, Mr. Honecker gave no indication of any intention to change course. According to Mr. Gorbachev's spokesman, the Soviet leader said to Mr. Honecker at a private meeting yesterday that "those being late will be punished by life itself."

To this, the spokesman said, Mr. Honecker repeated his stock formula, that he stood for "continuity and renewal."

At the demonstration today in Dresden, no sooner had the crowd gathered than the police came, forming double rows around the historic Theater Square. From loudspeaker trucks on either side they began to shout: "This is the German People's Police! This is an illegal gathering! You must move!"

Police Wield Rubber Truncheons

Slowly the crowd of 2,000 began to move under the bombed-out ruins of the old Saxon royal palace, some holding lighted candles, while the policemen, armed with long rubber riot clubs, tightened the cordon and occasionally snatched a protester.

Within an hour, several hundred youths had quickly swelled into a throng of thousands moving toward the main railroad terminal in Lenin Square, chanting "We want to stay!" and "Freedom!"

In Leipzig, a demonstration on Saturday night reportedly turned violent when policemen charged more than 20,000 marchers with dogs and truncheons. Today, sympathizers came silently to place candles and flowers outside Leipzig's central Nikolai Church, where protest vigils are held every Monday.

As in East Berlin and Leipzig on Saturday night, policemen in Dresden used batons to separate the demonstrators and attack the smaller groups. Many witnesses reported demonstrators being beaten or dragged away. . . .

HUNDREDS OF THOUSANDS CHOOSE "SELF-EMANCIPATION"

An October 9 climax approached in Leipzig. On October 7, antigovernment demonstrations faced violent police reprisals across East Germany. In East Berlin, police attacked some of the thousands of unarmed marchers. Erich Mielke, the head of the Staatssicherheitsdienst (State Security Service, or Stasi), allegedly fomented the violent reprisals, saying "give those pigs a sound beating" (as cited in Naimark 1992, 90). Many were injured and scores arrested. (On the Stasi, see **East Germany, Introduction**.)

The following day, October 8, in the face of fears of imminent violence and displays of security and police presence, East Germans held still more large demonstrations in Berlin, Dresden, Leipzig, Potsdam, and elsewhere. Mielke again commanded crackdowns and interruptions of the processions out of concern for what Norman M. Naimark calls the regime's view of "enemy-negative and rowdyesque forces" seeking to disrupt state security and public order, thus "endangering the state and social order of the GDR" (Naimark 1992, 90).

On Monday, October 9, rumors began flying across Leipzig that the government planned a violent "Chinese solution"—a reference to the June 1989 assault against protesters camped out on Beijing's Tiananmen Square in which an estimated 2,600 persons were killed; exact numbers have never been confirmed (Paulson 2005, 266). The gossip and speculation in Leipzig were accompanied by reported movements of army troops, armed factory militia, and tanks. Large security forces deployed near the Nikolai Church. Armored vehicles circled Leipzig. The New Forum, the leading opposition group, counseled discipline, but impending violence hung in the air; the police were armed and appeared to have orders to shoot. Schools had closed early; hospitals stocked up on blood. It was later confirmed that Erich Honecker, the East German leader, had signed shoot-to-kill orders (Lohmann 1994, 69).

According to *The New York Times*, witnesses in Leipzig reported packed prayer meetings at the Nikolai Church and three other churches in the city center on October 9. In the largest demonstration to date, as many as 70,000 of Leipzig's 500,000 residents joined the Monday evening demonstration that poured from the Nikolai sanctuary and other churches. The sheer size, anonymity, and restraint of the multitude were the crowd's best defense. Loudspeakers called for dialogue and interaction. *Times* correspondent Serge Schmemann recounts that when the services let out, the protesters marched around the city center, chanting, "We want to stay!" "Gorby! Gorby!" "On to Perestroika!" "We are the people! We are the majority!" ("East Germans Let Largest Protest Proceed in Peace")

The ruling Socialist Unity Party (SED) had dispatched a large security contingent to halt the October 9 demonstration, but at 5:45 P.M. the police conspicuously began to pull back. Security bosses awaited orders from East Berlin directing them to subdue the huge demonstrations forcefully, but they never arrived. Somewhere a decision had been made—perhaps several—and catastrophe was averted.

While flickering candles reminded onlookers that the opposition was nonviolent, their numbers revealed that the SED regime no longer controlled the people. "We planned everything," one security head sighed; "we were prepared for everything, except for candles and prayers" (Wall 1996, 283). According to political scientist Susan Lohmann, the "unarmed, frightened, yet very determined people" marched peacefully, and "the demonstration broke the back of the regime" (Lohmann 1994, 71). As it became apparent that the government would not crush the demonstrations, timidity in the populace, an essential requirement for the SED's power, was transformed into the unflinching resistance that Charles S. Maier calls "self-emancipation." The candles compounded the government's quandary: the marchers' refusal to obey, or yield to fear, undermined the SED regime's predilection for using brute force. Some police doubtless felt stirrings of identification with the marchers. Large demonstrations erupted all over East Germany.

By several accounts, Honecker had ordered "the counterrevolutionary demonstrators" in Leipzig put down "with any force necessary." His successor, Egon Krenz, would later be credited by *The Times* with halting the crushing of this pivotal Leipzig demonstration, in which local SED leaders Helmut Hackenburg and General Major Gerhard Strassenburg ordered the retreat of their forces to avoid a possible massacre. German newspapers later reported that consultations between local SED officials and opposition groups, especially with Kurt Masur, famed maestro in the grand German symphonic tradition, brought about the October 9 march ending without police violence (see "How the Wall Was Cracked").

The Times reports on October 10 that a statement from three members of Leipzig's communist leadership had been read aloud in churches at the beginning of the previous day's demonstration and also broadcast by radio and loudspeakers. It read, "'We all need free dialogue and exchanges of views about the further development of socialism in our country" and that those making the appeal "promise all citizens to apply all our authority so that this dialogue will be conducted not only in Leipzig, but also will be taken up by our government."

Serge Schmemann reports on a meeting in Dresden of the Lutheran bishop of Saxony, the Reverend Johannes Hempel, twenty active participants in the marches, and Mayor Wolfgang Berghofer and City Council members. According to accounts from Dresden, the party-state officials were presented with a list of demands, including the legalization of the New Forum, freedom of the press, and greater freedom to travel. News of that gathering was publicized in four Leipzig churches, where thousands had gathered for the weekly Monday peace prayers on October 9 and broadcast by radio and from public loudspeakers in the streets. Schmemann reports that the statement contributed to the subsidence of violence against the march ("East Germans Let Largest Protest Proceed in Peace").

From October 9 forward, SED authorities allowed mass demonstrations to proceed peacefully. The protests grew in number and scale, as hardcore officials within the party-state were gradually replaced. On October 16, more than 100,000 marched, starting at the Nikolai Church; on October 23 in Leipzig, 245,000 persons—nearly half the city's population—demonstrated (Lohmann 1994, 71). On October 24, Schmemann reports on the hundreds of thousands of East Germans marching peacefully through Leipzig, citing their demands for democratic change, legalization of opposition movements, independent labor unions, and separation of powers between the communist party and the government. On October 30, crowds in Leipzig would exceed 350,000. By the third weekend of October, demonstrators were marching in Dresden, Chemnitz, Magdeburg, Erfurt, and other cities.

The processions were leaderless. At first they consisted mostly of the young, but their makeup evolved during autumn 1989. Next to become involved were intellectuals and white-collar employees who promoted human rights, followed by thousands of traditionally skilled laborers. Finally, hundreds of thousands joined from formerly apolitical sectors. Word spread, facilitated by crudely printed action flyers and announcements in churches. Soon collective nonviolent actions were being staged in virtually every city in the country. Sometimes the marchers placed candles in front of Stasi headquarters (see **East Germany, Introduction**). They often had to restrain skinheads from introducing violence.

Despite governmental efforts to quarantine East Germans from contact with Poland—as if the Solidarity union were a communicable disease—Solidarity's lessons penetrated, as unauthorized publications—*samizdat* ("self-published" in Russian)—spread across Eastern Europe through underground channels. Solidarity's success was regarded as proof of the effectiveness of civil resistance in challenging a communist regime (see "Poland Restricts Civil and Union Rights").

Since the 1970s, perhaps 90 percent of the East German populace had been able to receive West German television programs that undermined the credibility of SED reports about East German prosperity. Viewers could see for themselves the economic gap between the East and the West. Western news media magnified the phenomenon of the massive marches as they reported on East Germany's growing candlelit demonstrations, and their reportage stimulated still more processions as broadcasts were received by East Germans from West Germany. Televising the marching East Germans enlarged a local demonstration into a seemingly ubiquitous event. Schmemann refers to East German news corps, radio, and television as "newly awakened" and as becoming a source of excitement for a populace that had previously trusted news solely from West German media. Now, East German television displayed theatrical artists and rock stars confronting the Politburo's chief ideologist to demand the freedom to express opinion and an end to censorship.

Within a week of the decisive October 9 Leipzig demonstration, the Politburo would meet, and on October 18 Honecker, who had ruled in the Stalinist mold since 1971, would resign for health reasons, though ousted by his own former associates. *Times* reporter David Binder subsequently wrote of Honecker's "bizarre and disgraceful legacy" and how he had prevailed until cast out for "massive embezzlement," corruption, "police brutality, lying and cheating." Binder notes that "it had become clear to the rest of the party that Mr. Honecker was no longer able to cope either with the mass migration of 200,000 East Germans to West Germany—another 100,000 have left since then—or with this country's economic misery and its suddenly awakened citizenry, who were demonstrating in the streets of every city and some villages, several million strong" ("Clamor in Europe").

OCTOBER 24, 1989
300,000 REPORTED TO MARCH IN LARGEST EAST GERMAN PROTEST
By HENRY KAMM
Special to The New York Times

EAST BERLIN, Oct. 23 – Hundreds of thousands of East Germans marched peacefully through Leipzig tonight, demanding democratic changes, including legalization of opposition movements, independent labor unions and separation of powers between the Communist Party and the state.

East German television, which showed the demonstration on its main news programs, put the number of marchers at more than 150,000. But in a telephone interview with West German television, a Protestant pastor, the Rev. Christoph Wonneberger, said more than 300,000 people marched. This would make it the biggest

East German citizens gather in Leipzig on October 23, 1989, to demand democratic change. An estimated 300,000 people, more than half of Leipzig's population, participated in the march. The banner on the right reads, "Gorbi, Gorbi, Help Us." The banner on the left reads, "Without visa from Rostok to Shanghai."

Source: AP Images

opposition demonstration since the protests began last month.

Smaller demonstrations took place in at least five other cities—East Berlin, Magdeburg, Dresden, Halle and Schwerin. All demonstrations were reported to have ended peacefully, with the police showing exceptional restraint....

Union Reported Formed

News broadcasts today did not refer to conflicting reports from the Wilhelm Pieck factory in the East Berlin suburb of Teltow where some workers were reported to have formed an independent trade union. There is acknowledged discontent, however, about the subservience of the official union to the party, and in union meetings at work places members were reliably reported to have demanded a rupture in the link between the two....

Welcome News for Many

Many East Germans were pleased to learn from their newly awakened press, radio and television last weekend that not only would [Egon] Krenz [communist party choice to replace Erich Honecker] soon visit Mr. Gorbachev but also that he had thanked the Soviet leader for the opportunity to study recent Soviet developments....

The press and news broadcasts have for the first time become a source of pleasant excitement for a public that over many years had learned to receive the news it believed in from West German television and radio. The change is remarkable in a country where even orthodox Communists, including journalists, have conceded for years that their press and broadcasts were unnecessarily dull and predictable.

"Now people run to be home every evening to catch the 7:30 news on television," a historian said, and the waitress who was serving coffee agreed. "And sometimes now," the historian said, "we think we are seeing Western television when it's our own."...

Tonight's television news, for example, showed theater artists and rock and pop musicians in discussion with the Politburo's chief ideologist, Kurt Hager. For once, Mr. Hager was not lecturing but on the defensive. The performers demanded an end to censorship and freedom of opinion.

Television reports from the northern town of Schwerin showed people confronting party and government leaders with items from what has become the general catalogue of grievances—the treatment of citizens like children, the shortage of housing and the meager supplies of consumer goods....

Until earlier this month, demonstrators were vilified as minions of West German manipulation, calls for an end to censorship never reached the public and few deficiencies in the Government's performances in any sector were admitted. Now the press and broadcasters seem to have changed direction completely.

Today, East Germans were demanding that in Tuesday's session of Parliament, which was called to confirm Mr. Krenz as President of the country, another candidate be put forward to prevent one person from holding both of the country's most powerful positions.

• •

"Revolution from Below"

Provision had been made by the end of September 1989 for special trains to carry East Germans to the West. In secret negotiations under UN aegis, East Germany agreed to expel by train East Germans who had sought sanctuary in embassies in East Germany. The citizens of East Germany heard through West German television broadcasts the timetables of departing "refugee trains." Officials of the ruling Socialist Unity Party, SED, termed these departures "expulsion" to mask the shock of mass desertion, but its net effect was to legalize *hijra*, permanent protest emigration. Hijra—"to abandon" in Arabic—is perhaps the most undeniable form of noncooperation, denying an antagonist's objectives. Although the term might not have been spoken by those who fled, the exercise of hijra, called "exit" in East Germany, was significant in the Eastern European revolutions of 1989 (see "**Introduction: Strikes, Sinatra, and Nonviolent Revolution**").

After the government in Budapest opened Hungary's borders on May 2, 1989, East Germany restricted travel there. Czechoslovakia became the sole Eastern European country that East Germans could visit without permission. In short order, thousands who sought to become émigrés and inquired about permission to travel to West Germany via Czechoslovakia were stuck in the West German embassy in Prague. Wanting to clear the embassy before a visit to East Germany by Soviet leader Mikhail S. Gorbachev in early October, Honecker on October 1 gave authorization for the refugees there to leave; he obliged them, however, to journey on special trains through East Germany to fulfil his government's stipulation that they first return home.

Violence intruded when the SED began requiring visas to travel to Czechoslovakia. Some 2,000 persons without visas were thrown off trains. Hundreds of enraged youths blocked rail tracks and tried to leap onto refugee trains speeding toward the West. On October 4, when citizens of Saxony heard that a special train from Prague was carrying East Germans and traveling westward through Dresden, Leipzig, and Plauen, they stormed stations along the way and tried to throw themselves onto the train. In Dresden, 3,000 would-be émigrés brandishing cobblestones skirmished with police using water cannons, damaging the central train station. Church pastors and the growing numbers of groups calling for nonviolent action swiftly subdued the violence.

Tensions grew between the "stayers" (*Dableiber*) and the "leavers" (*Weggeher*). Groups like the New Forum hoped that the East German government could be reformed from within, but mass exodus made effective internal solutions unlikely. It verified what East Germans already knew in their hearts: physical blockades propped up their society. Exit further emboldened antigovernment opposition, as more people withdrew cooperation with the regime through demonstrations or flight.

On November 5, *The New York Times* discloses reports from Prague that East Germany had decided to let its citizens leave for West Germany through Czechoslovakia by merely showing their internal identity documents. The judgment, as yet unannounced in East Germany, marked the first time that the SED regime had permitted unrestricted emigration to West Germany. Covering a November 4 demonstration of 500,000 East Berliners, *Times* reporter Serge Schmemann allows that a million may have marched. He describes how, in passing the SED Council of Ministers headquarters, many protesters posted demands on the wall. Christa Wolff, a literary figure recognized beyond East Germany, described the opposition as "revolution from below." Schmemann notes "a cordon of actors and artists, wearing sashes that read 'No Violence,' helped keep order." The authorities held their fire, as they had since the crucial October 9 Leipzig demonstration (see "Hundreds of Thousands Choose 'Self-Emancipation'").

In Schmemann's account, demonstrators carried "a thicket of placards." Most of the November 4 posters and speakers called for free speech, free elections, an end to the communist party's "leading role," and settling scores with the despised secret police of the State Security Service, the Stasi (see **East Germany, Introduction**). A rebirth of personal self-respect drove the pro-democracy movement as much as the desire for political freedoms. As East Germans rejected silence, the messages in their banners, chants, and signs changed to reflect deeper transformations among the populace. Slogan writers broadened their meaning to reflect popular sentiment. By November, chants went from "We want to leave" to "We are staying here." Others proclaimed popular sovereignty: "We are the people!" (Wir sind das Volk). Soon the signs would proclaim of the two Germanys, "We are one people!" (Wir sind ein Volk). The slogan alluding to the unification of the two Germanys first appeared in Leipzig, the "city of heroes."

The presence of armed security forces no longer elicited apprehension over SED repression. The actions of the Pastors' Movement and discipline of the resisters threw the regime off balance when its totalitarianism provoked nothing but more marches. East Germans were no longer intimidated.

NOVEMBER 5, 1989
500,000 IN EAST BERLIN RALLY FOR CHANGE
Emigres Are Given Passage to West
Prague Removes Barriers to Departing East Germans
By SERGE SCHMEMANN
Special to The New York Times

EAST BERLIN, Nov. 4 – Four weeks to the day after a few thousand East Berliners took to the streets to demand political change, at least a half million demonstrators jammed the heart of the East German capital today for the largest rally so far in what one speaker called a "revolution from below."

At the same time, reports from Prague, the Czechoslovak capital, said East Germany had agreed to let its citizens leave for the West from Czechoslovakia by simply producing their internal identity documents.

The decision marked the first time that East Germany allowed its citizens free passage to West Germany, and in essence it opened a door through the wall that for so long has stood as the foremost symbol of Communist control, the dividing line between East and West.

March to Alexanderplatz

. . . [T]he throng in the East German capital marched down broad boulevards through the city center with a thicket of placards, finally engulfing Alexanderplatz, a vast plain of concrete at the heart of East Berlin, to hear a series of speeches. As the marchers passed the headquarters of the Council of Ministers, many demonstrators posted demands on the wall or laid them on the ground, and they remained there long after the demonstration ended.

Authorities Do Not Interfere

Some estimates put the crowd at more than a million, and by any count it posted another milestone in a mass movement that has filled the streets of East Germany virtually daily in numbers unknown in its 40-year history.

And like all the demonstrations since the state first reined in the police on Oct. 9 and allowed people to protest unmolested, the authorities did not interfere and the four-hour rally was disciplined and peaceful. . . .

. . . [T]he demonstration was broadcast live on the East German radio and television.

Most of the placards, and the statements from the 17 speakers that drew the loudest cheers, called for free speech, free elections, an end to the "leading role" of the Communist Party and—a demand that prompted the most boisterous whoops—and a settling of accounts with the hated security police. . . . There was also a banner linking "monopoly of power by the Communist Party" and "mass flight" by emigres.

Cars Arrive at Border

The agreement between East Germany and Czechoslovakia, first announced by West German officials, meant that an East German had only to show an internal identity document to cross Czechoslovakia to West Germany. Almost immediately, sputtering East German Trabant cars began arriving at the Czechoslovak–West German border, along with trainloads of East Germans who had thronged to the West German Embassy after East Berlin first lifted restrictions on travel to Czechoslovakia on Nov. 1.

East Germans still could not travel directly to West Germany. But the announcement of the East German–Czechoslovak arrangement stressed that it would be in force only until East Germany enacts a promised new travel law, which reportedly will enable East Germans to travel abroad with relative ease.

The march in East Berlin had been organized by the official Union of Actors, and a cordon of actors and artists, wearing sashes that read "No Violence," helped keep order.

Unimpressed by Promises

Most marchers seemed largely unimpressed by the promises of "far-reaching" changes and the dismissal of five Politburo members announced Friday evening by Egon Krenz, the new party chief. The new program and the resignations are to become formal at a meeting of the Communist Party's Central Committee next week.

It seemed a measure of the remarkable pace of events in East Germany that even while Mr. Krenz was announcing measures that would have been breathtaking only four weeks earlier, he now seemed to trail behind the demands of a popular movement still without real leadership.

"He's learned a lot, he's gaining pace, but I'm not sure whether he's quick enough to keep up with events," said Jens Reich, one of the founding members of the New Forum opposition group and a speaker at the rally. . . .

Many of the placards carried by the crowd were laced with a humor that seemed to reflect a growing confidence in the popular movement. "Always forward, never backward—Erich Honecker, roofer," read one, referring to the fallen party leader and his original trade. . . .

Other banners called for dismantling the security police and demanded free trade unions and new faces at the top. One simply read, "Thanks, Hungary." It was Hungary's opening of its borders that prompted a mass migration last summer, which in turn was a catalyst for the movement for change at home.

The 17 speakers included actors, opposition leaders, party officials, church leaders, writers and other prominent figures. . . .

'Revolution From Below'

"I don't like the words 'change of course,' " said one of the most popular speakers, the prominent writer Christa Wolff, referring to the term by which the Communist Party has repeatedly referred to its new openness. "It sounds like a sailor changing direction with the prevailing wind," she said. "I would rather say 'revolutionary renewal,' a 'revolution from below.' " . . .

Shouts of 'Shut Up'

. . . Among the last speakers was an elderly and popular actress, Steffie Spira, who alone stayed within the five-minute limit set on addresses, and who raised a roar of laughter when she concluded her remarks by saying: "I want the Government to do what I am about to do. Step down." And she did.

OPENING OF THE BERLIN WALL

Berlin, and Germany, had been divided by the Allied powers after World War II. The city lay geographically within East Germany. Citizens of East Germany could move to the West by walking from East Berlin into West Berlin, and from there find transportation to West Germany. Waves of East Germans fled their country in the years after World War II in a population-diminishing brain drain, as tens of thousands from every walk sought new lives in the West. To halt the flow of East Germans to West Germany, the East German communist government built the Berlin Wall.

The ruling Socialist Unity Party (SED) in June 1961 ordered construction of the wall. Work on it began on August 13, 1961, with backing from the Soviet Union and the endorsement of the Warsaw Pact. Erected overnight of cinder blocks and barbed wire, the original barrier was later replaced with a series of concrete walls topped by barbed wire and guarded with watch towers and gun emplacements.

The twenty-nine-mile wall dividing Berlin became the physical embodiment of the iron curtain and austere symbol of the communist oppression fatefully consigning East Germans to a closed society under extensive secret police surveillance. Located entirely on the eastern, Soviet-occupied portion of Germany, the wall eventually stretched for another 103 miles around West Berlin, sealing it from the rest of East Germany. Escaping to West Berlin meant hurling oneself across a killing field of barbed wire, concrete impediments, and minefields.

Enclosing East Germans by force, the SED sought to diminish the numbers otherwise taking flight to West Germany. East Germany lay as if under a shroud, rarely in the news except for the occasional death of a person desperately daring fortifications and electrified fences. For twenty-eight years, the situation continued, until, unexpectedly, East Germany became a major arena for propulsive political change in 1989. During all those years, West Germany summoned its estranged countrymen and women like a beacon.

The New York Times reports that West German sources counted 191 shot to death or killed by exploding mines while trying to get across the Berlin Wall; 5,000 more within sight of freedom were hauled in and taken into custody ("Clamor in the East; The Berlin Wall: A Monument to the Cold War, Triumphs and Tragedies"). Possibly 1 million Germans had fled westward between the end of World War II and the establishment of East Germany in October 1949. From 1949 to 1961 and the building of the Berlin Wall, 2.69 million more registered as refugees and moved to the West. After the erection of the wall, a quarter of a million "legal immigrants," such as pensioners and "special cases," were allowed to leave. German publications, among them *Der Spiegel* and *Die Zeit*, reported in 1984 that from 1961 to 1984, 176,714 East Germans had risked death and incarceration to escape illicitly. Their perilous journeys included crawling through tunnels, darting through forests, hiding in trucks, and swimming rivers. At least 177 East Germans were killed at borders during these years, generally shot, while 17,000 were imprisoned for "political crimes," normally meaning attempted flight (as cited in Naimark 1992, 77–78).

President John F. Kennedy had gone to Berlin on June 26, 1963, and declared, "Ich bin ein Berliner" ("I am a Berliner"). On June 12, 1987, U.S. president Ronald Reagan stood in front of the Brandenburg Gate and Berlin Wall and issued an exhortation to the Soviet leader Mikhail S. Gorbachev: "Mr. Gorbachev, tear down this wall." Some observers developed a mythology in which Reagan's confrontational enunciation brought about a convergence of forces that caused the wall to collapse. Others interpret the speech as having offered cover for Reagan's diplomacy, an anti-communist spectacle that preserved support in the political base of a conservative president who was seeking to improve U.S. relations with Moscow and end the cold war.

Some consider that Gorbachev's accession to leadership in 1985 "provided the essential precondition for the subsequent upheaval in eastern Europe" (Roberts 1999, 7). Still others believe that Reagan and Gorbachev were part of the backdrop to what was an intense, internal drama of self-liberation being played out within East Germany. The sociologist Jeff Goodwin observes, "[M]ass protest did not so much *result* from expanding political opportunities as it gradually revealed and indeed helped to *create* such opportunities. Gorbachev or no

Gorbachev, regime opponents . . . feared, for good reason, that public demonstrations would be violently repressed by local authorities. After all, Communist hard-liners were in charge in these [Eastern bloc] countries, reform Communists were largely invisible, and the authorities threatened protesters and violently attacked them virtually until the moment when these authorities abruptly capitulated" (Goodwin 2001, 278–279).

After conferring with Soviet leader Mikhail S. Gorbachev in Moscow, Egon Krenz, who succeeded Erich Honecker as the new East German head of the communist party-state, returned home and pleaded for the citizenry to stop fleeing the country, promised reforms, and dismissed five senior Politburo members (see "500,000 in East Berlin Rally for Change"). *The Times* on November 4 reports Krenz, in a televised address, imploring, "To those who 'think about emigrating,' put trust in our policy of renewal" ("East Germans' New Leader Vows Far-Reaching Reform and Urges an End to Flight"). The regime began appointing moderates to government positions.

After hundreds of thousands of protesters formed a nonviolent human chain across East Germany and on November 4 more than 1 million demonstrators packed East Berlin, on November 7 the forty-four-member Council of Ministers resigned and preparations got under way for members of the Politburo and Central Committee to step down. The headline of *The Times* dispatch that appeared on November 8 told the whole story at a glance: "East Germany's Cabinet Resigns, Bowing to Protest and Mass Flight." More than 2,000 East Germans a day were removing themselves from the SED's authority, or, as *Times* reporter Serge Schmemann put it, at a rate of 200 per hour. "East Germany's Great Awakening," a *Times* editorial of November 10, states, "Once people sense the hope for change, their impatience and courage increase with each concession." The potency of two nonviolent methods used by the opposition—street demonstrations and protest emigration—brought the SED government and Politburo to resign.

As the leadership of the communist party stepped down, governmental and party commissions and newly assertive party newspapers, radio, and television stepped up to reveal abuses by the Honecker regime. The disclosures outraged the population of 16.5 million East Germans, especially the party's 2.3 million members, of whom 10 percent resigned.

International relations expert Adam Roberts tells a "tragicomic" tale of a gentleman who departed East Berlin in early November 1989, via the transit camp at the West German embassy in Prague, then traveled to Hungary, to Austria, and on to West Germany, where he took an airplane into West Berlin in time to see the Berlin Wall opened. Had he waited, he could have arrived at the same destination on foot (Roberts 1999, 41*n*40).

On November 9, its authority undermined by massive processions and waves of emigration, what was left of the SED changed its central policy. An East German official spokesperson, Günter Schabowski, member of the Politburo and party secretary for East Berlin, declared that all East German citizens could travel abroad at will, without official permission. As this news was broadcast on television, multitudes gathered. That night the Berlin Wall was breached. The barrier had become the object of almost round-the-clock vigils, and with its collapse began the end of communist East Germany.

NOVEMBER 10, 1989
EAST GERMANY OPENS FRONTIER TO THE WEST FOR MIGRATION OR TRAVEL; THOUSANDS CROSS
A Jubilant Horde
Berlin Wall Is Rushed by Easterners as Travel Limits Are Lifted
By SERGE SCHMEMANN
Special to The New York Times

EAST BERLIN, Friday, Nov. 10 – East Germany on Thursday lifted restrictions on emigration or travel to the West, and within hours tens of thousands of East and West Berliners swarmed across the infamous Berlin Wall for a boisterous celebration.

Border guards at Bornholmer Strasse crossing, Checkpoint Charlie and several other crossings abandoned all efforts to check credentials. . . . Some guards smiled and took snapshots, assuring passers-by that they were just recording a historic event.

Politburo Announcement

The mass crossing began about two hours after Gunter Schabowski, a member of the Politburo, had announced at a press conference that permission to travel or emigrate would be granted quickly and without preconditions, and that East Germans would be allowed to cross at any crossing into West Germany or West Berlin.

"We know this need of citizens to travel or leave the country," Mr. Schabowski said. "Today the decision was taken that makes it possible for all citizens to leave the country through East German crossing points."

Mr. Schabowski also said the decision ended the agreement to let East Germans leave through Czechoslovakia and other countries. Some 50,000 East Germans have left through Czechoslovakia. . . . Since September, thousands more have left through Hungary and Poland.

Flag Waving in the West

Once Mr. Schabowski's announcement was read on radio and television, a tentative trickle of East Germans testing the new regulations quickly turned into a jubilant horde, which joined at the border crossings with crowds of flag-waving, cheering West Germans. Thousands of Berliners clambered across the wall at the Brandenburg Gate, passing through the historic arch that for so long had been inaccessible to Berliners of either side. . . .

All through the night and into the early morning, celebrating East Berliners filled the Kurfurstendamm, West Berlin's "great white way," blowing trumpets, dancing, laughing and absorbing a glittering scene that until now they could glimpse only on television. . . .

The extraordinary breach of what had been the most infamous stretch of the Iron Curtain marked the culmination of an extraordinary month that has seen the virtual transformation of East Germany under the dual pressures of unceasing flight and continuing demonstrations. It also marked a breach of a wall that had become the premier symbol of Stalinist oppression and of the divisions of Europe and Germany into hostile camps after World War II.

The immediate reason for the decision was evidently a recognition by East Germany's embattled authorities that they could not stem the outward tide by opening the door a crack and hoping that rapid liberalization at home would end the urge to flee. . . .

The Berlin wall—first raised on Aug. 13, 1961, to halt a vast hemorrhage of East Germans to the West—evolved into a double row of eight-foot-high concrete walls with watchtowers, electronic sensors and a no man's land in between. Frequent attempts to breach the barrier often ended in death, and the very sophistication of the wall became a standing indictment of the system that could hold its people only with such extraordinary means.

The decision to allow East Germans to travel freely came on a day when Egon Krenz, the new East German leader, was reported to have called for a law insuring free and democratic elections, [and] . . . new laws on freedom of assembly, association and the press. . . .

Mr. Schabowski's announcement about the unimpeded travel was greeted with an outburst of emotion in West Germany, whose Constitution sustains the hope of a reunited Germany. . . . Mr. Schabowski abandoned the customary East German reference to the barrier as an "anti-fascist protection wall," and instead called it a "fortified border."

His statement underlined that the new regulations did not change the status of Berlin, which is still formally occupied by the victorious Allies of World War II, with East Berlin as the Soviet zone. . . .

East Germans began almost immediately to test the new measure. One couple crossed into West Berlin at the Bornholmer Strasse crossing with only their identity cards just two hours after Mr. Schabowski spoke. After a gleeful exchange with some West Berliners, they returned to their side of the wall....

Some Are Skeptical

Other East Berliners were more muted in their reaction, reflecting the skepticism fostered by the dizzying rate of change in East Germany in recent weeks....

The new measures also raised some questions, including how much currency East Germans would be allowed to change into Western money. The East German mark is not freely convertible, and up to now East Germans have been allowed to exchange just 15 of their marks, about $8 at the official exchange rate....

The official East German press agency, A.D.N., said the new measures took effect immediately....

. . . . The main novelty in the new regulations was that permission to travel to the West would be virtually automatic. Though millions of East Germans have traveled to the West in the past, the permission was always conditional and difficult to obtain.

The excitement over so momentous an opening failed to conceal a growing anxiety on both sides of the border over the swelling size of the exodus from East Germany.

More than 50,000 East Germans fled over only the last weekend. West German estimates have put the figure of East Germans yearning to settle in the West at up to 1.4 million, out of a population of 16 million....

Marked 40th Anniversary

The announcement of the travel measures was the latest in an extraordinary chain of events that has profoundly transformed East Germany since it marked its 40th anniversary on Oct. 7.

Shocked into action by the mass flights that gathered pace all through the summer, hundreds of thousands of East Germans have taken to the streets in the last months to press with increasing urgency for profound change in their society, which under Erich Honecker ranked among the most iron-clad Communist strongholds in Eastern Europe.

The double pressures of the mass exodus and mass demonstrations has sent the Communist Party into headlong retreat. Mr. Honecker was ousted Oct. 18, and ... the entire Politburo resigned.... The Government had already resigned....

PEACEFUL REVOLUTION LEADS TO A PARTY COUP

The end of the wall's usefulness on November 9, 1989, was a consequence of a number of converging factors, including Moscow's decision not to intervene in East German decisions. Of all the forces at work, however, the most consequential were the massive nonviolent demonstrations throughout autumn 1989 in cities across the land and the *Ausreisewelle* (wave of exits), as thousands of East German citizens fled to the West each day. When the wall came down, it dragged the communist state with it.

What happened behind the scenes that brought the keystone of the Soviet bloc to bend to the popular will? *The New York Times* tasked three of its foremost foreign correspondents to write a special report answering lingering questions, and eliminating perplexities, on what had taken place inside the Socialist Unity Party (SED) as the government made crucial decisions of autumn 1989. In the report, which evokes cold war thrillers, the young successor to the grizzled head of the East German party-state flies into Leipzig on the pivotal night of October 9 and cancels the order to shoot; the former head of the SED's spy agencies testifies to plans for a "Chinese solution"; an internationally esteemed conductor and party officials huddle in urgent discussions at his home; an eighty-two-year-old security chief pleads that they cannot savage hundreds of thousands of people; the chief ideologist of the communist party allies himself with the country's youth; and district communist leaderships recognize that "the grassroots wouldn't stand for things to continue the way they were." Moreover, an East German diplomat told The Times that during the visit of Soviet leader Mikhail S. Gorbachev to East Berlin on October 6 and 7, Gorbachev not only would not prescribe what the East Germans should do, but said that the sight of thousands fleeing the country and of violent measures being the sole means to keeping them in was unhelpful for his own circumstances.

NOVEMBER 19, 1989
HOW THE WALL WAS CRACKED—A SPECIAL REPORT; PARTY COUP TURNED EAST GERMAN TIDE; CLAMOR IN THE EAST

The following article is based on reporting by Craig R. Whitney, David Binder and Serge Schmemann and was written by Mr. Whitney.
Special to The New York Times

The turning point came on Oct. 7, after the Communist Party leader, Erich Honecker, ordered security forces to be prepared to open fire on demonstrators in Leipzig—a "Chinese solution" to the rising tide of dissent in East Germany.

But violence and killing were averted when Egon Krenz, then Politburo member in charge of security, flew to Leipzig on Oct. 9 and canceled Mr. Honecker's order, allowing the protesters to march unmolested. Mr. Krenz [had] become the new party chief on Oct. 18.

What could have become a bloodbath as terrible as China's June crackdown instead became a peaceful revolution that is changing the face of East Germany and Eastern Europe. Within 10 days, Mr. Honecker had resigned under pressure and the Communist Party was pledging profound changes. Within a month, the Berlin wall was broken.

Although this sequence of events would tend to bolster the image of Mr. Krenz, it is supported by the accounts of several members of the East German party, most of whom do not owe their current positions to Mr. Krenz.

Krenz Given the Credit

They said Mr. Krenz reversed the order to shoot because he feared that hundreds of dead and wounded would be a fatal blow to the East German party's standing at home and abroad.

The critical events of Oct. 9 are part of a drama that began in May, when Hungary decided to dismantle the barbed wire from its border with Austria, and continues to this day with the steady dismantling of the rigid Stalinist system for which Mr. Honecker was reportedly willing to shed his people's blood.

What follows is the story of what the East Germans call their "Wende," the turning point that abruptly pulled their state from the rear guard of Stalinism to the front ranks of change in the Eastern bloc.

The storm had been gathering through the summer. With every week, more and more East Germans flowed westward through Hungary. But with Mr. Honecker stricken by a gall bladder ailment, the East German leadership seemed frozen, capable only of snarling at the West Germans.

A Frenzied Exodus

The flow grew to a flood and finally into a frenzied exodus at the end of September, when Hungary threw open its borders. In East Germany, the crisis stoked long-gathering discontent into open protest. Violence broke out in Dresden in early October when people tried to storm trains carrying their compatriots to West Germany.

Then on Oct. 7, with Mikhail S. Gorbachev in East Berlin, crowds took the streets of the capital, chanting "Gorby! Gorby!" and "We want to stay!" With many foreign reporters looking on, the police waded into the throngs, and their actions were recorded and immediately played back to the rest of East Germany on West German television.

More violence followed on Sunday, and by Monday, Oct. 9, the suspense was tangible. A weekly Monday peace service, held in the Nikolai Church in Leipzig, had in recent weeks become the launching point for broad protests, and after the weekend clashes, huge crowds were expected at the church.

According to Manfred Gerlach, the leader of the small Liberal Democratic Party, and others, a huge force of soldiers, policemen and secret police agents was assembled in Leipzig and issued with live ammunition. Their order was to shoot if necessary, and the order had reportedly been signed by Mr. Honecker himself.

"There was a written order from Honecker for a Chinese solution," said Markus Wolf, the retired head of East Germany's spy agencies, who has emerged as a leading advocate of reform. "It could have been worse than Beijing."

But by then many in the Politburo had come to the decision that Mr. Honecker must go, and that the situation was explosive. In Leipzig, Kurt Masur, the director of the Gewandhaus musical theater, and some local party officials opened urgent discussions on averting a clash.

Finally, Mr. Krenz and Wolfgang Herger, the Central Committee department chief under him, flew to Leipzig's Schkeuditz Airport. They drove into the city to meet with local Communist officials at the home of Mr. Masur.

"I was in Leipzig," Mr. Krenz later said. "I helped there to see to it that these things were solved politically."

When tens of thousands took to the streets of Leipzig that night, the police did not interfere. The "revolution from below" was under way.

The Exodus Begins Stirrings First, Then Floodgates

The frustration that erupted in October had been long in gathering. Mikhail S. Gorbachev, the Soviet President, had set loose yearnings for change throughout Eastern Europe, but in East Germany the old loyalists around Mr. Honecker sat entrenched in their isolated villas on Lake Wandlitz, refusing to acknowledge any reason to change.

The words perestroika and glasnost could not be uttered over the airwaves or printed in the East German press, either in Russian or German, and Soviet publications were banned.

East Berlin continued to flaunt its rigidity. Local elections on May 7 were plainly rigged. After the massacre in Tiananmen Square in Beijing on June 4, Mr. Krenz sent a message to the authorities in China congratulating them on their firmness.

But a new threat was growing in the south: the rapid drives by Poland and Hungary toward Western models of democracy. When Hungary began to snip away at its stretch of the East-West divide, the East German Interior Ministry warned the Politburo in a report that such action could spell serious trouble for East Germany, many of whose citizens vacationed in Hungary.

No Action by Politburo

The Politburo took no action, evidently afraid that closing its borders with Hungary would be more dangerous than allowing a few East Germans to flee. And at first the exodus was a trickle—a few East Germans sneaking across the border, a few others seeking asylum at the West German Embassy in Budapest.

Soon East Germans were filling West German embassies in Prague, Warsaw and East Berlin. By late August, thousands of East German refugees were camped in Budapest. The Hungarians declined to force them home. Then, on Sept. 10, Budapest said it would let the emigres go to the West in defiance of a 1967 agreement with East Berlin to prevent East Germans from doing so without East Berlin's authorization.

Hungary's decision marked a momentous breach in Eastern European unity. For the first time, a Communist Government declared that international covenants on human rights were more important than treaties with other Warsaw Pact nations.

The gates were open. Eventually, more than 30,000 East Germans swept out to West Germany through Hungary. In all, more than 200,000 have left East Germany.

Gorbachev Arrives; Honecker, Isolated, Loses Another Ally

Mr. Honecker was back at work, and his attention was on the celebrations planned for Oct. 7, the 40th anniversary of the German Democratic Republic. Mr. Gorbachev was to lead a retinue of Communist leaders to East Berlin.

But the moment of triumph was shaping rapidly into a disaster. East Germany had quickly curtailed travel to Hungary, and Czechoslovakia remained the only Eastern European country where East Germans could go without permission. Before long, thousands of would-be emigres seeking permission to travel to West Germany via Czechoslovakia were jammed into the West German Embassy in Prague.

Desperate to clear the West German Embassy in Prague before his guests arrived, Mr. Honecker granted permission on Oct. 1 for the refugees to leave the embassy, although he insisted that they ride special trains through East Germany to satisfy East Berlin's demand that they first return home.

That solution proved disastrous. Even as the first group left, more East Germans flooded the embassy in Prague, forcing Mr. Honecker to authorize a second release and finally to shut his southern border.

Mobs Follow the Trains

Worse, the trains riding through Dresden drew thousands of East Germans desperate to join the exodus. On Oct. 4, violent clashes erupted with the police, who tried to clear the Dresden station, and the trains were sealed to prevent them from being mobbed by others hoping to flee.

Against that backdrop, Mr. Honecker went to Schonefeld Airport on Oct. 6 to greet Mr. Gorbachev, walking with a deliberate jauntiness to show that he was in good health.

Mr. Gorbachev seemed intent, publicly at least, not to inflame the opposition. But it did not take much. It was enough that he said that East Germany had to decide its own future to signal to many that Soviet troops would not interfere. When he said that those who did not change with the times would see life punishing them, the comment was seen as a direct reference to Mr. Honecker. Wherever he went, the crowds chanted "Gorby! Gorby!"

Mieczyslav Rakowski, the Polish Communist Party leader, sat next to Mr. Gorbachev on the reviewing stand at the Oct. 7 military parade. He later said with some irony that when he heard the chants he remarked to Mr. Gorbachev, "It looks as if they want you to liberate them again."

Direct Comments to Politburo

The Soviet leader was more direct when he met in private with the East German Politburo. An East German diplomat said Mr. Gorbachev did not try to prescribe what the East Germans should do. "He made it very clear that the spectacle of thousands of people running away from the country and of violence being the only way to keep them in was not helping him in his own difficult situation," he said.

According to a wide range of party insiders, Mr. Honecker was incapable of grasping the situation. He reacted with stubborn insistence that he was on the right course and would brook no leniency. He told a Chinese visitor that any attempt to change his course was "nothing more than Don Quixote's futile running against the steadily turning sails of a windmill."

On Saturday night, Oct. 7, as Mr. Gorbachev was leaving for Moscow, tens of thousands of East Berliners moved from the anniversary ceremonies to Alexanderplatz, the vast square at the heart of the city. Bearing candles and torches, they began chanting slogans demanding change.

The East German police, armed with riot sticks, chased them out of the square and north into the heavily populated and dilapidated Prenzlauer Berg section, a hotbed of the growing New Forum opposition group. Hundreds were beaten and jailed. The scene was played out again on Sunday night in the same area of East Berlin, as well as in Leipzig and Dresden.

Krenz Takes Charge; Old-Line Ideologues Are Out in the Cold

Mr. Krenz, at 52 the youngest member of the Politburo, was hardly a predictable architect of change. He had followed Mr. Honecker's path from the Communist youth league to take charge of security and youth affairs, and his statements had given no sign that he was anything but a hard-liner.

But he was considered sharp, and he was young. And it was he who took the fateful step on Oct. 9 to avert violence in Leipzig.

Back in East Berlin, the Politburo gathered for its regular Tuesday meeting. Nobody knew how Mr. Honecker or his ideological allies would react to the unilateral order by Mr. Krenz barring the Leipzig crackdown.

It was Erich Mielke, the tough 82-year-old security chief, who told Mr. Honecker, "Erich, we can't beat up hundreds of thousands of people."

But the 77-year-old Communist leader would not be swayed. Earlier in the day, three members of the Central Committee had handed Mr. Honecker a report on the unrest among the country's youth and its causes, with a request for a special session of the leadership to deal with it. Mr. Honecker flew into a rage, calling the report "the greatest attack on the party leadership in 40 years."

Protests by Youths Defended

Now Kurt Hager, the 77-year-old chief ideologist, raised his voice. The young people were right, he said. The mood on the streets was more defiant that he had ever seen it. Gunter Schabowski, the respected party secretary for East Berlin, concurred.

Only two members firmly took Mr. Honecker's side: Gunter Mittag, the 63-year-old Economics Minister, who had dominated East German planning since the era of Walter Ulbricht, the first Communist Party chief, and Joachim Hermann, the 61-year-old secretary for propaganda.

Others wavered or kept silent. With the Politburo deadlocked, the secretaries of East Germany's 15 districts, including Hans Modrow, the party chief for Dresden who had a reputation as a reformer favored by Moscow, were called in for an unusual expanded meeting of the leadership. The meeting went late into the night of Oct. 10 and continued on Oct. 11.

"The district leaders said that the grassroots wouldn't stand for things to continue the way they were," a Central Committee member said.

Statement to Nation

The leaders began discussing a conciliatory statement to the nation. According to several accounts, Mr. Honecker resisted this too, fuming instead about his betrayal by Hungary.

Over his objections, the statement was issued Oct. 11, declaring that the Politburo was ready "to discuss all basic questions of our society," and acknowledging that those who had fled may have had valid reasons.

From that day, the press suddenly became more open, with panel discussions on major public complaints. The small "parties," traditionally subservient to the Communists, suddenly gained a voice of their own, and Mr. Gerlach, the Liberal Party chairman, even suggested in his party paper that the "leading role" of the party should be reconsidered.

The Politburo met again on Oct. 17. By now it was clear to most of the other 17 Politburo members that Mr. Honecker no longer understood what was happening. One Communist official said Mr. Honecker had been so infuriated by Mr. Gerlach's statement and considered taking action against him.

This time, several Central Committee members said, only Mr. Mittag and Mr. Hermann still supported Mr. Honecker. Some officials said Mr. Mittag was holding out in the hope of securing the party leadership for himself, after having filled in for the ailing Mr. Honecker through the summer.

An important defector was Mr. Hager. "Without Hager, nothing would have gone through in the Politburo," a party official said.

Finally, Willi Stoph, the 75-year-old Prime Minister, told Mr. Honecker that the time had come for him to resign, a Central Committee member said.

That was the decisive push. On the next day, Oct. 18, Mr. Honecker announced to the Central Committee that he was resigning for reasons of health, and the Politburo moved that Mr. Mittag and Mr. Hermann be ousted. Mr. Krenz was the new party chief, head of state and Defense Council chairman.

The meeting was brief. Mr. Krenz read a speech promising an "earnest political dialogue," and then urged the Central Committee to quickly close its proceedings so he could go on nationwide television.

The Pace Quickens

Mr. Krenz immediately set about trying to establish himself, within the party and outside, as the leader of real change. "We see the seriousness of the situation," he said. "But we also sense and recognize the major opportunity we have opened for ourselves to define policies in dialogue with our citizens."

The pace quickened. Mr. Krenz and other Politburo members met people in factories and in the streets. On Oct. 27, the Government announced that it would restore free travel through Czechoslovakia, for people wanting to go to West Germany. On Nov. 1, Mr. Krenz flew to Moscow to meet Mr. Gorbachev and endorsed a version of perestroika—economic and social restructuring—in East Germany.

Still, demonstrations swelled. Huge crowds marched in Leipzig, East Berlin, Dresden and other major cities, and thousands of East Germans perhaps seeing this as their last chance to flee resumed their efforts to get into the West German Embassy in Prague.

Finally, on Nov. 4, Mr. Krenz announced that East Germans who wanted to settle in West Germany could travel freely through Czechoslovakia. More than 10,000 a day began quickly surging across the border into the West.

That same day, more than a half million East Germans demonstrated for democracy in the largest protest that East Berlin or East Germany had ever seen. The crisis was not over.

The Frontier Opens: A Crude Barrier Is Breached at Last

Hoping to slow the exodus, the Government hastily drafted a law on travel that said East German citizens would be free to go abroad, but for only 30 days a year and after applying at police offices. The bill was promptly denounced, and in a sign of the rebellious mood, the Legal and Constitutional Committee of the normally docile Parliament dismissed it as unacceptable.

The pace of change gathered speed. On Nov. 7, the entire Council of Ministers resigned and called on Parliament to choose a new government. The Central Committee convened on Nov. 8, and this time the entire

Politburo resigned, to be replaced by a smaller group, still headed by Mr. Krenz, with five new members. Among them was Mr. Modrow, the party leader from Dresden, who would soon become the next Prime Minister.

Thousands of Communist Party members demonstrated outside, demanding a party congress to install an entirely new leadership.

On Nov. 9, a Thursday, the Central Committee continued to sweep the ranks of the leadership. Four new members of the top leadership were swept out after their regional party organizations rejected them.

New Travel Law Announced

Mr. Mittag came under intense criticism and was expelled from the Central Committee for "the most egregious violations of internal party democracy and of party and state discipline, as well as damaging the reputation of the party."

In the evening, Gunter Schabowski came to brief reporters. Toward the end of the session, he announced that a new travel law has been drafted, giving East Germans the right to leave the country through any border crossings. The Berlin wall, already circumvented, was beginning to crumble.

The measures had been drafted by the Politburo, officials later said. It was still fresh, and the details were not immediately clear, although it later became evident that citizens did have to obtain exit visas from local police stations before going across. But when Mr. Schabowski was asked directly if East Germans could freely go West, his answer was yes.

Soon after, a young East German couple went to the Invalidenstrasse crossing to test the announcement. To their amazement, the guards, who had heard Mr. Schabowski and had no instructions, let them cross. After 28 years, 2 months, 27 days, and the deaths of 80 killed trying to cross it, the wall was open. The astonishing event was reported on West German television, and within an hour tens of thousands were streaming into West Berlin for one of the most extraordinary reunions ever held. Over the weekend two million visited the West, bought chocolates, and, for the most part, returned home to East Germany. Only a few thousand remained.

Not even the Soviet Government, one of the four World War II Allied powers who hold occupation rights in Berlin, was told of what the East Germans were doing, an East German Government official said.

Looking to the Future Can Europe Cope With Reunification?

The quiet revolution in East Germany is not over. Mr. Krenz has promised free elections. Mr. Modrow, the new Prime Minister, has named a Government with far fewer ministers and many more members of smaller parties, and he has called for a broad program of change.

New border crossings are opened daily, and soon the Brandenburg Gate might become a passage from East to West. On Monday, demonstrators again came out in Leipzig, fewer in number but still in a throng vast enough to demonstrate that public pressure has not been eased by the open wall. A party congress is scheduled for December.

Beyond it all, German reunification still hovers on the horizon, a giant question mark that troubles Europeans in the West as well as those in countries until recently referred to as Soviet bloc nations. Washington is watching closely. But on one thing all agree. East Germany will never be the same; nor will Eastern Europe.

"The Locomotive of East German Renewal" and Reunification

In November 1989, after the fall of the Berlin Wall, the slogan "Wir sind das Volk!" (We are the people) became "Wir sind ein Volk!" (We are one people, or We are one nation). Popular fervency made reunification seem inevitable. Constricted by the protests of massive demonstrations and noncooperation of mass exit, the power of the ruling Socialist Unity Party (SED) had fragmented during late autumn 1989.

The collapse of the wall has gone into human memory as the symbolic watershed bringing the cold war era to a close. In actuality, however, the civil resistance of large candlelight demonstrations and the ceaseless exit of citizens, along with the decision of the communist party to lift blockades, were the influential events. The years since have not brought to light reports of deaths caused by police or security forces in the East German nonviolent revolution. In Munich, nevertheless, Roman Catholic bishop Karl Lehmann challenged the political leaders of the newly reunified Germany during a mass in the Marienkirche: "Now that the wall of stone has tumbled, the barrier in our heads must also come down (Jarausch 1994, 178)."

Chancellor Helmut Kohl of West Germany recognized earlier than others that although he did not know exactly how to do it, the two Germanys must unify. On November 28, he proffered a modest plan of confederation to create common agencies. Contemplating the altered situation, the ambassadors of France, the United Kingdom, the United States, and the Soviet Union—the four powers technically still in control of Berlin—met to examine the city's future as well as that of Germany.

On December 4, Egon Krenz resigned as SED head, having been "whistled, shouted and booed into silence," as *The New York Times* phrases it on that day in an article by David Binder on the high-level corruption in the regime ("Clamor in Europe; For East Germany's Party, a Gamble Out of Desperation to Erase Disgrace"). Describing internal upheaval in the party, Binder writes that "workers and peasants have turned on the masters who ruled them for the last 43 years in the names of Marx, Engels and Lenin—the creators of Communist doctrine—and with a vengeance unheard of in the history of the Communist movement." Arrests were made of the senior-most lieutenant for the economy of the Erich Honecker government, and his trade union chief, "on charges of embezzlement of state and party funds for their personal pleasures," while an associate who had gone into hiding was placed on an international police "wanted" list. The response in the lower ranks of the party to the disclosures was one of "contempt, fury and disgust," Binder records, and at this lower level "the rebellion against Mr. Honecker's now intermediate successors began." Agitation over the newly laid-bare dishonesty in the leadership continued into the streets. "There is a smell of anarchy in the air," Binder stated.

Krenz was replaced by Gregor Gysi, who was soon supplanted by Hans Modrow, a reform-inclined economist. Replacements for the members of the Politburo and Central Committee that resigned on November 7 began attempting to develop democratic processes, as was concurrently proceeding in Poland and Hungary.

On December 16, the SED, its power spent and its legitimacy gone, agreed to break with its Stalinist past. By December 18, according to *The Times* on that day, the SED had lost more than half a million of its 2.3 million members since September. The party changed its name to the Party of Democratic Socialism at a congress that had opened on December 8 and which *The Times* describes as a "mass purification ceremony." The "exhausting exercise" was intended to make, as a law professor put it, "an absolute break with the Stalinist system" imposed in October 1949 ("Upheaval in the East").

Although unprepared for the enormity of change experienced in a few months, the East German parliament voted to end the leading role of the communist party and promised free elections in the spring. Just as the tide from East and West started flowing toward unification, contradictory pressures arose. Communist totalitarianism was breaking down, as fledgling democratization moves began; conflicts were unavoidable. *The Times* on December 19 covers the regular Monday demonstration in Leipzig, yet this time the demonstrators set aside their banners and marched silently with candles only. Their silence was in commemoration of "victims of Stalinism" and to reduce fevers over German reunification. Much of the friction was over the speed of reunification, enough to trouble a Roman Catholic priest, the conductor Kurt Masur, and others who called for a moratorium on large Leipzig demonstrations until January 8, 1990.

During Christmas 1989, responding to the continuing westward flow of East German citizens, Modrow's government, with assistance from West Germany, introduced complete freedom of travel across the two countries' borders for the first time since June 1946. One of the major goals of the East German opposition had been achieved.

DECEMBER 19, 1989
LEIPZIG MARCHERS TIPTOE AROUND REUNIFICATION
By SERGE SCHMEMANN
Special to The New York Times

LEIPZIG, East Germany, Dec. 18 – The marchers at the regular Monday demonstration in Leipzig today exchanged most of their banners for candles and their chants for silence—to commemorate "victims of Stalinism" and to cool passions that have begun to flare in recent weeks over the issue of German reunification.

The march came on the eve of the first official visit by a West German head of government to East Germany. Chancellor Helmut Kohl is scheduled to meet with Prime Minister Hans Modrow in Dresden . . . to announce a multibillion-mark package of assistance to East Germany. . . .

In anticipation of Mr. Kohl, some 10,000 demonstrators marched in Dresden tonight demanding unity. Many carried West German flags. . . . There were also reports of a demonstration by 30,000 in Karl-Marx-Stadt demanding reunification.

A Warning on Sovereignty

In East Berlin, the second session of the round-table discussions between governing parties and opposition movements was held. A resolution was issued calling on Mr. Kohl and Mr. Modrow to expand economic cooperation but adding that "the sovereignty and state identity of each of the two German states must not be questioned by either side."

The cautionary note reflected the position of the Communist Party and its allies, as well as of the main opposition group, New Forum, which favors the transformation of East Germany into a democratic socialist state. Other East German groups, like Democratic Awakening, which formally became a political party yesterday, have taken a more ambivalent stand. . . .

Calls for Reunification

While most of the 150,000 people who turned out in Leipzig for what has become the weekly weathervane of the East German mass movement against Communist rule heeded the appeal of the church and secular opposition leaders for a silent march, several dozen carried West German flags and one clutch of several hundred demonstrators chanted defiantly for one Germany.

Among their chants was "Get the Reds out," a reference to some left-wing opposition groups that have come out against reunification.

The chant had sounded first last Monday, and at the vigil service at the Nikolai Church that has traditionally preceded the march, a Roman Catholic priest, the Rev. Gunter Hanisch, said today that it had troubled him.

"Here a sack is opened, a label is stuck on it and everyone I disagree with is stuffed into it," he said. "At the beginning we were in agreement, but now conflicting camps are emerging."

Moratorium on Marches Urged

Father Hanisch's concern was evidently behind the call by church leaders and Kurt Masur, the director of the Gewandhaus musical theater and one of the most respected civic voices in Leipzig, for a moratorium on the Leipzig marches until Jan. 8, as well as for reflection on their purpose.

In the past two weeks, marchers demanding reunification, including some espousing openly nationalist sentiments, have become increasingly visible, and some angry confrontations took shape last week between them and demonstrators opposing what they argue would be absorption in West Germany.

The differences reflected a discord that has entered the popular movement in East Germany now that most of the demands that initially united the vast majority of East Germans have been effectively satisfied—freedom to travel, the dismantling of the secret police apparatus, the retreat of the Communist Party and the promise of free elections.

In their wake, the debate—in East Germany as in West Germany—has shifted to the sensitive question of reunification, or rather the timing of reunification. The emerging majority view, expressed recently by West German President Richard von Weizsacker and repeated at the Nikolai Church today by Father Hanisch, was that "what belongs together will grow together, but it should not be forced to grow frantically."

Argument for Fast Reunification

But a vociferous minority in East Germany has begun demanding quick reunification, arguing that this is the only cure for East Germany's relative backwardness....

Watching from the sidelines with a candle in her hand was 20-year-old Anja Richter. She said she was against quick reunification, and this was the reason she definitely would be back when the marches resumed in January. "I'll be here because there are so many banners for reunification," she said....

Faith in the Marches

On one point everyone seemed to agree: The Leipzig marches remain the locomotive of East German renewal, and must go on. "If we stop now, everything will be for nothing," said Thomas Schadt, a teacher who walked with a large West German flag on a broomstick. "The Government will see no reason to act anymore."

In an appeal read on public loudspeakers and at the vigils in churches, Mr. Masur tried to strike a note of calm and reason. He said all of Europe hoped that the Leipzig marches would resume Jan. 8 as peacefully as they had been until now, "and that through them the great idea of a united Europe can be realized...."

Joining in the appeal was Friedrich Magirius, a superintendent of the Protestant Church in Leipzig, who urged that today's march be dedicated to the "victims of violence and spiritual suppression under the Stalinist Government."

Many marchers left their burning candles by the walls of the headquarters of the state security force [Stasi], bathing the austere granite building in a bright glow. The building used to be a focus of anger during the marches, but two weeks ago it was taken over by a "citizens' committee" that has kept it sealed with the help of the police....

The Two Germanys Unite

For years in East Germany, any opposition figures thought capable of generating dissent had been arrested and exiled to West Germany, draining the society of commanding personalities. Throughout autumn 1989, events had proceeded at breakneck pace as several opposition organizations formed, and Protestant churches became the crucible for the nonviolent revolution against communist despotism. Yet East Germany's civil society was weak; independent environmental, human rights, peace, and women's groups were still adolescent, and worse, were divided among themselves. Within two weeks of the fall of the Berlin Wall, the government had entered into talks with the opposition to chart a new course (see "East Germany Opens Frontier to the West for Migration or Travel"). In the second round of negotiations in mid-December, eleven groups joined with three churches and five political parties for discussions with the tenuous government.

Prime Minister Hans Modrow had set May 1990 as the date for free elections, but was slow to proceed, and only took tangible steps after the New Forum opposition group had threatened a general strike, to bring all economic activity to a total standstill. His delays fired doubts about the communists' willingness to yield power and contributed to turmoil that boiled over in mid-January, as throngs in East Berlin invaded the headquarters of the loathed Staatssicherheitsdienst (State Security Service, the Stasi) and seized documents, strewing the streets with them. Citizens in other cities followed suit, and by month's end the Stasi had been disbanded (see **East Germany, Introduction**).

On January 30, 1990, Moscow agreed to the reunification of the two Germanys—the German Democratic Republic, or East Germany, with the Federal Republic of Germany, or West Germany.

By February 5, negotiations between East German authorities and the opposition had yielded a government of national responsibility that could with some credibility claim to be representative of the changed circumstances. Eight new government ministers without portfolio joined with their communist colleagues to begin dismantling their country.

A second series of demonstrations took place between January 8 and March 12, seeking rapid reunification and urging free national elections. Virtually all of the demands of the nonviolent challengers who had poured out of the Nikolai Church every Monday after peace prayers had been met by spring 1990. The first free, multiparty elections were moved up to March 18, ending the Monday demonstrations, which had diminished in size in the new year. Voter turnout was more than 93 percent. Between January 1990 and the March balloting, another 150,000 East Germans departed for the West. Free elections constituted the second major achievement of the opposition, after free travel abroad, yet the import of the balloting with competition among several parties for what would in effect be an interim government, was soon outstripped by impending reunification.

In the summer, the West German deutsche mark was introduced into East Germany, as the meshing of the two economies got under way. On October 3, the unification was completed by annexation of East Germany by West Germany, making it the only Warsaw Pact country to disappear, which it did through merger and incorporation into its residual and historical nation-state. A national festival celebrated the reunion and the creation of the new Federal Republic of Germany, its tone intentionally restrained.

The citizens of East Germany had destroyed the communist apparatus on their own by withdrawing their cooperation from it, revealing the regime's dependency on popular consent even though its authoritarian structures controlled the means of coercion, but they could not build a reunited Germany by themselves. Geopolitical support was provided by the West German chancellor Helmut Kohl and his foreign minister, Hans-Dietrich Genscher. Within one year of the fall of the Berlin Wall, East Germany had vanished. The former headquarters of the Stasi reopened as a museum.

OCTOBER 3, 1990
TWO GERMANYS UNITE AFTER 45 YEARS WITH JUBILATION AND A VOW OF PEACE
A Million in Berlin

Flag at Reichstag Marks Start of New Era at Center of Europe

By SERGE SCHMEMANN

Special to The New York Times

BERLIN, Wednesday, Oct. 3 – Forty-five years after it was carved up in defeat and disgrace, Germany was reunited today in a midnight celebration of pealing bells, national hymns and the jubilant blare of good old German oom-pah-pah.

At the stroke of midnight Tuesday, a copy of the American Liberty Bell, a gift from the United States at the height of the cold war, tolled from the Town Hall, and the black, red and gold banner of the Federal Republic of Germany rose slowly before the Reichstag, the scarred seat of past German Parliaments.

Then the President, Richard von Weizsacker, drawing on the words of the West German Constitution, proclaimed from the steps of the Reichstag: "In free self-determination, we want to achieve the unity in freedom of Germany. . . . We want to serve peace in the world in a united Europe."

Singing of Anthem

With that, a throng estimated at one million joined in the West German national anthem, now the anthem for united Germany. . . .

The moment marked the return of a nation severed along the front line between East and West to the center stage of Europe, this time as an economic powerhouse vowing never again to bring grief to a continent it had so terribly ravaged in the past century. . . .

Beer and Revelry

Hundreds of German flags waved and firecrackers snapped in the chilly autumn night. Beer and sparkling wine flowed freely and the strains of divergent bands mingled in a rowdy cacophony. Soon bottles began smashing on the pavement and celebration turned to intoxication, and by early morning the center of the new capital was deep in smashed bottles and weaving revelers.

A force of about 5,000 police officers had been massed in case radicals tried to disrupt the festivities, and the police reported seven arrests. But what protests there were passed with no major incidents.

Unity essentially meant that the German Democratic Republic with its 16 million citizens acceded to the Federal Republic of Germany, which expanded to become a state of 78 million souls and 137,900 square miles. The accession meant that the name, anthem, Constitution and Government of the Federal Republic became those of all Germany, that Chancellor Helmut Kohl became the first Chancellor of the reunited state and Mr. von Weizsacker the first President.

Berlin Is Capital

Berlin, a city divided by the infamous wall into a gray Communist capital and a glittering capitalist enclave, became once again the political and spiritual capital of Germany. . . .

'Farewell Without Tears'

. . . [T]he East German Prime Minister, Lothar de Maiziere, at the final "state act" of the East German Government in the grand Schauspielhaus concert hall, . . . the first and last democratically elected leader of East Germany, committed his state to history with the words: "In a few moments the German Democratic Republic accedes to the Federal Republic of Germany. With that, we Germans achieve unity in freedom. . . . It is the end of many illusions, . . . a farewell without tears."

Then Kurt Mazur, the conductor from Leipzig and a hero of the peaceful revolution last fall, rose to conduct Beethoven's Ninth Symphony. . . .

Address by Kohl

Mr. Kohl, capping a year of political successes, addressed the nation on television several hours before unity. . . . "After 40 bitter years of division, Germany, . . . will be reunited . . . one of the happiest moments of my life. . . . "

'It Is Really Moving'

The Chancellor also made a point of thanking and reassuring Germany's allies and neighbors. "In particular," he said, "we thank the United States of America and above all President George Bush." Mr. Bush was among the first world leaders to abandon reservations about German unity....

In recent weeks, the process of unity had drawn growing grumbles from both East and West as Germans came to realize the huge cost of the undertaking. But for the hundreds of thousands who had gathered from across Germany and abroad, this was a night not to moan, but simply to celebrate.

"It is really moving," said Heinz Schober, a Berlin shopkeeper who had come with his wife. "We were here when the wall went up and we were here when it came down, and now we see something children will read about in history books."

Hundreds of stands along the Unter den Linden peddled everything from bratwurst and beer to "Day of Unity" T-shirts and chunks of the Berlin wall. Musicians ranging from rock bands to a Soviet military band to Wolf Biermann, a onetime East German dissident, blared from 16 stages set up among the beer and sausage stands, and all along the mile-long avenue the mood was festive and joyous....

The most serious trouble was reported in Gottingen, a West German city near the former border, where about 1,000 radical youths went on a rampage, smashing windows and denouncing unity.

Year of Rapid Change

Unity came to the Germans barely a year after streams of East Germans began pouring out through newly porous borders in Hungary and Czechoslovakia, forcing the East German leader, Erich Honecker, to confront a crisis just as he prepared to preside over the celebrations of his state's 40th anniversary.

A year before unity came, on Oct. 3, 1989, a flood of East German refugees had all but overwhelmed the West German Embassy in Czechoslovakia, and the East German Government finally gave permission for the refugees to go west....

The celebration of East Germany's anniversary four days later marked the beginning of the state's undoing. The Soviet leader, Mikhail S. Gorbachev, gave the first indications that he was not prepared to prop up the East German Government....

...[D]emonstrations rapidly grew, driving the Government into disarray until it took the fateful action on Nov. 9 of opening the Berlin wall a crack, touching off a rush to unity. By March 18 East Germany held its first democratic elections, and by July 1 its economy was merged into West Germany's. The pace accelerated through the summer, bringing formal unity up to Oct. 3 and setting the scene for the celebration.

The pace of events also required a rapid termination of the vestigial occupation under which both the Germanys and the Berlins existed, and the moment of unity was preceded by a flurry of final arrangements and actions to end the Allied controls.

The commanders of the Western Allied forces, the United States, Britain and France, which merged their occupation zones of the city after the war to form West Berlin and defended it against Communist encirclement in ensuing years, met for the last time and ceded authority over the city.

"I now close this final meeting of the Allied Kommandatura with a good, solid bang," said the British commander, Maj. Gen. Robert Corbert, pounding the gavel at the Allied headquarters with a solid thump.

BIBLIOGRAPHY

Banta, Kenneth W. 1989. "Leipzig: Hotbed of Protest." *Time*. November 27, 41.

Bleiker, Roland. 1993. *Nonviolent Struggle and the Revolution in East Germany*. Cambridge, Mass.: Albert Einstein Institution.

Chirot, Daniel. 1999. "What Happened in Eastern Europe in 1989?" In *The Revolutions of 1989,* ed. Vladimir Tismaneanu, 19–50. London: Routledge.

Darnton, Robert. 1991. *Berlin Journal, 1989–1990*. New York: W. W. Norton and Company.

Dennis, Mike. 2000. *The Rise and Fall of the German Democratic Republic, 1945–1990*. London: Longman.

Funder, Anna. 2003. *Stasiland: Stories from Behind the Berlin Wall*. London: Granta Books.

Garton Ash, Timothy. 1999. *The Magic Lantern: The Revolution of '89 Witnessed in Warsaw, Budapest, Berlin and Prague*. New York: Vintage Books.

Goodwin, Jeff. 2001. *No Other Way Out: States and Revolutionary Movements, 1945–1991.* Cambridge: Cambridge University Press.

Jarausch, Konrad H. 2007. "Democratizing Democracy: Civil Resistance in West Germany, 1960s to 1980s." Conference on Civil Resistance and Power Politics, St. Antony's College, University of Oxford, March 15–18.

———. 1994. *The Rush to German Unity.* Oxford: Oxford University Press.

Keithly, David M. 1992. *The Collapse of East German Communism: The Year the Wall Came Down.* Westport, Conn.: Praeger.

Lohmann, Susanne. 1994. "The Dynamics of Informational Cascades: The Monday Demonstrations in Leipzig, East Germany, 1989–91." *World Politics* 47:42–101.

Maier, Charles S. 2009. "Civil Resistance and Civil Society: Lessons from the Collapse of the German Democratic Republic in 1989." In *Civil Resistance and Power Politics: The Experience of Non-violent Action from Gandhi to the Present,* ed. Adam Roberts and Timothy Garton Ash, 260–276. Oxford: Oxford University Press.

Mason, David S. 1996. *Revolution and Transition in East-Central Europe.* 2d ed. Boulder: Westview Press.

Naimark, Norman M. 1992. " 'Ich will hier raus': Emigration and the Collapse of the German Democratic Republic." In *Eastern Europe in Revolution,* ed. Ivo Banac, 72–95. Ithaca, N.Y.: Cornell University Press.

Neckermann, Peter. 1991. *The Unification of Germany or the Anatomy of a Peaceful Revolt.* Monograph no. 33. Boulder, Colo.: East European Monographs.

Paulson, Joshua. 2005. "Uprising and Repression in China–1989." In *Waging Nonviolent Struggle: 20th Century Practice and 21st Century Potential,* ed. Gene Sharp, 253–267. Boston: Porter Sargent Publishers.

Pfaff, Steven. 2001. "The Politics of Peace in the GDR: The Independent Peace Movement, the Church, and the Origins of the East German Opposition." *Peace and Change* 26: 280–300.

Roberts, Adam. 1999. *Civil Resistance in the East European and Soviet Revolutions.* Monograph Series no. 4. Cambridge, Mass.: Albert Einstein Institution.

Stokes, Gale. 1993. *The Walls Came Tumbling Down: The Collapse of Communism in Eastern Europe.* New York: Oxford University Press.

Wall, James M. 1996. "Rough Transitions: Churches in Political Struggles." *Christian Century,* March 13, 283–284.

From *The New York Times*

Binder, David. 1989. "Clamor in Europe; For East Germany's Party, a Gamble Out of Desperation to Erase Disgrace." December 4.

———. 1989. "Upheaval in the East; At Confessional East Berlin Congress, 'An Absolute Break' With Stalinism." December 18.

Erlanger, Steven. 2001. "Zirndorf Journal: Germans Piece Together Nation's Stasi-Riven Past." October 31.

Kulish, Nicholas. 2008. "A Clergyman of the Streets Leaves His Historic Pulpit." January 12.

McFadden. Robert D. 1989. "Clamor in the East; The Berlin Wall: A Monument to the Cold War, Triumphs and Tragedies." November 10.

Schmemann, Serge. 1989. "A Sympathy Card on East Germany's Birthday." October 8.

———. 1989. "East Germans Let Largest Protest Proceed in Peace." October 10.

———. 1989. "East Germans' New Leader Vows Far-Reaching Reform and Urges an End to Flight." November 4.

———. 1989. "East Germany's Cabinet Resigns, Bowing to Protest and Mass Flight." November 8.

Unsigned. 1989. "Editorial: East Germany's Great Awakening." November 10.

CZECHOSLOVAKIA'S VELVET REVOLUTION

The 1989 Czechoslovakian struggle for personal freedoms and self-governance, known as the Velvet Revolution, was rooted in the history of bloodless transitions by the Czechs and Slovaks, related peoples who speak similar languages. Since the seventeenth century, lacking other alternatives, both ethnic groups accepted their status as subjects of foreign monarchies under the Austro-Hungarian Empire while retaining hopes of independence. World War I offered the prospect of independence, which finally came in 1918 as a byproduct of the war rather than as the fruit of their struggles. The two peoples who had so long sought autonomy were joined together by the Allies as one nation—Czechoslovakia.

The unification of the Czechs and Slovaks was generally welcomed by both peoples as a positive development. Czechoslovakia's population of 14 million consisted of 3 million Germans, 700,000 Hungarians, and others, including Poles and the Roma people. Czechs and Slovaks comprised the balance of two-thirds. Bohemia, with its Czech population, formed the western section, Moravia occupied the center, and Slovakia lay to the east. Although animosities between the two peoples made the unification somewhat unstable, the bloodless transition to independence was regarded as the "first velvet revolution" of these two Central European nations in the twentieth century. Czechoslovakia became a democratic country of cultural and economic accomplishment; many still view their democracy in the interwar years as unique to Central and Eastern Europe. Recognizing the unpredictability of Germany toward her neighbors, the new nation oriented itself with the United Kingdom and France.

In 1938 at a conference in Munich, the major powers of Europe decided the future of Czechoslovakia—which had no representatives at the table—in response to territorial demands made by the German leader Adolf Hitler. On October 1, 1938, the Munich agreement, called the Munich *diktát* or the Munich betrayal, by Czechs and Slovaks, dismembered Czechoslovakia. Signed by Germany, France, Britain, and Italy, it allowed the Germans to annex Czechoslovakia's Sudetenland—areas along the border with Germany that were largely inhabited by Czechs of German descent.

The Sudetenland was strategically important for Czechoslovakia because most of its border defenses were situated there. At Munich, France reneged on its military alliance with Czechoslovakia. Czechs and Slovaks still regard the Munich agreement as a diplomatic failure by Western democracies and a betrayal by allies. To them it was an act of humiliating totalitarianism which only made easier the submission of Czechoslovakia to Nazi occupation. "No Czechoslovak is unaware that the Western democracies let their country be politically dismembered in 1938 and swallowed by Nazi Germany the next year," as *The New* York Times puts it on November 30, 1989 (see "Spirit of 1968 Is Still Alive, Still Distinct").

With the onset of World War II and invasion by Nazi troops, freedom was not the only thing crushed by the advancing Germans. Czechoslovakia lost land, alliances, independence, and hopefulness. "Liberation" of most of Czechoslovakian territory by the Red Army in 1944 enhanced the standing of the small communist party there, legal since 1921 and active in parliament. The communists did not employ violent force to become the most powerful party, although the people's militia, or workers' militia, a paramilitary arm of the communist party, played a coercive role in 1948 in helping it to power. The party found support among industrial workers and amid peasants, who favored communist land-reform programs that redistributed the properties of the 3 million expelled Sudeten Germans. Key army and security sectors also championed the party. Dishonor at Munich and doubts about the defense of democracy—devastating setbacks for the democratic political parties—prepared the way for the communist takeover. Mass purges soon began, along with reducing the number of permitted political parties. In February 1948, the communist party staged a bloodless coup d'état and seized power.

CZECHOSLOVAKIA UNDER STALINISM

As the Soviet Union flexed its military muscle, Josef Stalin—the all-powerful, ruthless communist marshal of the Soviet Union—insisted that Czechoslovakia be brought completely

QUICK FACTS ABOUT CZECHOSLOVAKIA

- At the time of the Velvet Revolution, Czechoslovakia's 14 million persons consisted of 3 million Germans, 700,000 Hungarians, and others, including Poles and Romanies. Czechs and Slovaks made up two-thirds. Bohemia, with its mainly Czech population, comprised the western section, Moravia dominated the center, and Slovakia was to the east.

- On September 30, 1938, in Munich, the United Kingdom, France, and Italy agreed to German demands that it be allowed to annex the Sudetenland in western Czechoslovakia, the home of a large number of Czechoslovakians of German heritage. On October 1, Czechoslovakia was dismembered.

- In February 1948, the Czechoslovak communist party staged a bloodless coup d'état and established a new Stalinist-style regime, which subdued all internal opposition and imposed its communist political and economic policies. Those who resisted were executed, imprisoned, and made to suffer otherwise.

- By the early 1950s, the monastic orders of the Roman Catholic Church had been abolished, and 8,000 of the church's monks shipped to labor camps. Priests, bishops, and theologians were imprisoned for up to fifteen years. The church suffered the worst persecution in largely Catholic Slovakia.

- On the night of August 20–21, 1968, after the government of Alexander Dubček refused to reverse the reforms of a period of liberalization known as the Prague Spring, 750,000 Soviet-led troops from the five Warsaw Pact countries—Bulgaria, East Germany, Hungary, Poland, and the Soviet Union—invaded Czechoslovakia.

- On January 16, 1969, Jan Palach, a student at Charles University, committed suicide by self-immolation in the center of Prague's Wenceslas Square to protest the persistent replacement of reformers in the government with reactionaries. His act shocked Czechoslovaks.

- After the crushing of the Prague Spring, Miloš Jakeš, chairman of the communist party's Control Commission from 1968 to 1977, personally supervised the destruction of the careers of 800,000 persons, who lost their jobs as part of the re-Stalinization of the country that had begun under Gustáv Husák. The purges by Jakeš expelled half a million members from the communist party and destroyed their reputations.

- From 1968 to 1988, more than 500,000 of Czechoslovakia's 15 million citizens fled the country. Such flight violated the law, so they could not return.

- On January 1, 1977, 243 signatories issued a document called Charter 77, which indicted the Czechoslovakian party-state for violations of human rights provisions provided by the nation's 1960 constitution and various treaties, including the Helsinki Final Act. Its sponsors included leaders from the Prague Spring, academicians, actors, artists, clergy, journalists, and playwrights. Declaring themselves a "free, informal, open community of people of different professions," they described Charter 77 as a "nonorganization" because forming an independent organization was considered criminal.

- On October 22, 1978, the Polish archbishop of Kraków, Karol Cardinal Wojtyla, was installed as pope of the Roman Catholic Church. Taking the name John Paul II, he would become a unique figure in providing encouragement for the Eastern European nations in their resistance to communism.

(Continued)

(Continued)

- In the 1980s, state enterprises accounted for 30 percent of Czechoslovakia's industrial production. By 1988, the government instituted an economic decentralization experiment but produced only negligible results. By 1990, the country's per capita spending on education was among the lowest in Europe. Mortality rates continued to rise and life expectancy fell below most European states'.

- In June 1989, "Just a Few Sentences," an inconspicuously entitled text, appeared, calling for democratization. The initial statement was signed by both official, regime-supported artists and authors and artists of the growing opposition. Within a few months, more than 40,000 citizens had signed it.

- In Prague, on November 17, 1989—Day One of what would be called the Ten Days of the Velvet Revolution—police crushed a student demonstration chanting anticommunist, antigovernment slogans and singing the Czech rendering of "We Shall Overcome." By Day Four, 200,000 marched on Wenceslas Square in the largest protest demonstration since the Prague Spring.

- Within a week following a general strike on November 27, 1989, the nationwide noncooperation action had exerted such pressure on the communist regime that it was forced to agree to the formation of a coalition government, free elections, and open travel to the West. On November 29, the Federal Assembly rescinded the constitutional article that provided the communist party a monopoly.

- On December 7, 1989, the government resigned rather than meet the demands of nonviolent challengers. The next day, an amnesty was granted for all political prisoners, and a new government was sworn in. On December 9, the one-party system ceased to exist. Ten days in reality took twenty-four.

within the communist sphere, with a totalitarian system of government. In 1947, he had refused to allow Czechoslovakia to receive post–World War II assistance through the Marshall Plan, created by the United States to help rebuild Europe.

Stalin ordered that all remnants of democracy be crushed in Eastern Europe. In the process, the economy, the environment, and virtually every aspect of Czechoslovak life were mismanaged, almost to the point of destruction. On a comparative basis, Czechoslovakia's economy had suffered the least of the Central and Eastern European states and retained a relatively strong economic infrastructure. Yet the mismatch between the relatively developed Czechoslovak economy and the centralization of communist planning schemes was greater than with other, less industrialized Eastern bloc nations. As the communists implemented their economic policies after 1948, it took a relatively longer time to realize the resulting vulnerabilities because the country had started on a higher plane. Moreover, the communist party-state set up large industrial complexes, despite advice from its own economists, to mollify a communist constituency beholden to the party for status and jobs.

The effort to crush internal opposition to the communist regime and its failing economic policies led to hundreds of executions and tens of thousands of imprisonments. Millions were left to suffer under Stalinism. The private sector disappeared, as the state owned everything. All employees became state workers, including those of the Roman Catholic Church, which was placed under party-state control and became known in Czechoslovakia as the "underground" or "catacomb" church.

The church in Czechoslovakia lacked the influence possessed by the Roman Catholic Church in Poland. More was at work than the doctrinal antipathy of communism toward organized religion and freedom of worship. Historically, Czechoslovakia had been divided between Catholics and Protestants. Protestant influence ran deep. Jan Hus was the most significant Czech religious reformer of the fifteenth century, whose work bridged the medieval period and the Reformation, antedating the Protestant Reformation by a century. He was convicted of heresy, burned at the stake in 1415, and remains a defining figure in Czech history. Tomas Masaryk, another iconic figure exemplifying Protestant traditions, served as Czechoslovakia's first president (1918–1935),

In earlier times, the Roman Catholic Church had been identified with the Hapsburgs' counter-Reformation and restoration of Catholicism, and was associated with Austro-Hungarian dominion over Czech lands and society. By the early 1950s, the party-state had abolished the monastic orders associated with the Church of Rome and sent 8,000 of the church's monks to labor camps. Priests, bishops, and theologians received terms of imprisonment up to fifteen years. Slovakia, with the densest Catholic population in the country, suffered the worst persecution. Protestant churches, in the minority, also experienced coercive pressures.

Czechoslovak clergy, effectively state employees, were salaried by the government, which retained the final say on all appointments. In Poland, the Roman Catholic Church could function with independence and provide protection to the workers and intellectuals in the Solidarity union alliance (see "Pope Gets Big Welcome in Poland"). In East Germany, the status of the Protestant churches allowed them to offer auspices for marches that would eventually involve 5 million East Germans, particularly in Leipzig (see "Security Forces Storm Protesters in East Germany"). In Czechoslovakia, however, the official churches suffered from corruption along with the rest of the society. The Roman Catholic Church continued secretly to consecrate priests.

The constant threat of mass terror and Soviet military intervention subdued the Czechoslovaks into relinquishing their independence. Stalinism perpetuated despotism, in which a few ruled arbitrarily, from the narrowest of self-interested perspectives. The majority of Czechoslovaks conformed. Inflexible communist economic thinking, stultifying bureaucratization of every aspect of life, and continual shortages meant that survival inside the communist party was often through venality and by creating shortcuts around the rules and regulations. Those who went along with routine corruption—the vast proportion of managers and professionals—often found themselves subjected to blackmail and mired in lies. The extent of active collaboration with the party-state, as opposed to submission, is unknown and may never be fully detailed. The Czechoslovak situation was not as severe as in East Germany, where the ratio of informers to those being observed was higher even than in the Soviet Union. The East German state kept surveillance files on 6 million out of a population of 16.5 million (see **East Germany, Introduction**).

Silence was the price for survival, under a regime that meted out humiliation at every turn. The gap between socialist visions of equity, evenhandedness, and advancement and the cruel reality was felt most acutely by the educated classes of authors, academicians, and artistic and theatrical figures who lived in a miasma of corruption, official lies, despotism, and breakdown of basic human trust and integrity; for them, the betrayals of ideology cut the most deeply. Hundreds of gifted musicians, writers, actors, and artists were either forced to flee their homeland or act the role of loyal party members. Thousands of scholars and highly educated individuals could find only menial labor, jobs as janitors, doorkeepers, furnace stokers, night watchmen, or window washers.

Yet while most may have accepted such distressing circumstances and loss of freedoms out of fear or need, a small community preserved its memories of how Czechoslovaks had earlier in history refused to cooperate with their own subjugation. These traditions, forged over time, would reemerge with renewed strength. The Stalinist system never completely suppressed the yearning for freedom, especially in the cultural and academic communities.

By the late 1950s, it had become evident that the communist party, although firmly in command, lacked absolute unity, as cracks began to appear in the communist front. The first audible rumblings for reform could be heard within the party. Splitting into factions, some announced an aversion to orthodox Stalinist economics, while others maintained a hard line. The atmosphere began to change as some students and intellectuals began publicly to voice their concerns and as party members became disaffected with the leadership of Antonin Novotný, Czechoslovakia's communist leader since 1957. Novotný lost his allies, as his fellow communists joined rival factions.

In 1967, the Writers' Union convened a congress of authors, playwrights, and writers at which Milan Kundera spoke, author of *The Incredible Lightness of Being,* a novel (and later a film) about how Czechoslovaks under communism had turned inward to lead private, introspective lives. The party-state responded by abolishing the union. Student unrest climaxed late that year, as young Czechoslovaks marched and were brutally repressed by Novotný. He was quickly replaced. His party comrades offered no support and were eager to see him, and his policies, go.

THE PRAGUE SPRING OF 1968

On January 3, 1968, Alexander Dubček replaced Novotný as first secretary of the Czechoslovak communist party. Although Dubček had few major ideas for improving the country's leadership, he recognized the benefits of reform. Political prisoners had been released intermittently during previous years, and in 1968 the state freed the last of them. In a political maneuver encouraged by revelations by Soviet leader Nikita Khrushchev about the abuses of the Stalin era, Dubček encouraged Czechoslovaks to voice their opinions against strict Stalinist policies. The public took part in debates over the resulting deterioration and impact from failing economic policies, twenty years before Mikhail S. Gorbachev would promote the principle of *glasnost,* or openness. The communist party intelligentsia and elites led the deliberations because the "leading role" of the party remained unquestioned.

Dubček began to liberalize the country. He launched an Action Program of reforms in April, which included freedom of speech, the press, and movement and emphasized consumer goods and multiparty elections. His regime sought to build what he called "socialism with a human face," as he eagerly exploited what he considered to be liberal leanings in the Czechoslovakian communist party. He even went so far as to experiment with a free market economy. Within the party, some dismissed the criticism. Yet by and large, hopes abounded that the party could transform itself.

Many Czechoslovaks, especially intellectuals and those around urban centers, were excited about Dubček's reforms and believed his promises. They threw their energy into efforts to support liberalized policy reforms. Citizens, academicians, artists, authors, lawyers, and politicians soon began to actively challenge government policies, outpacing the party-state in the speed of proposed reforms. In July 1968, the manifesto "Two Thousand Words Which Belong to Workers, Farmers, Officials, Artists and to Everyone" appeared, calling for stepped-up efforts to rid the government of its Stalinist attributes. "Two Thousand Words" as it came to be known, articulated a fear of hard-line conservatives within the party and candidly contemplated a Soviet invasion. Yet, the tone was not provocative and called for civic engagement.

Officials sometimes formally instituted reforms after realizing that the people had already put them into practice. One such striking example occurred when the government endorsed more open news media, after recognizing that the press was already operating freely. Intellectuals and students informed the public of new freedoms, inspiring further change. These heady days of liberalization in 1968 became known as the Prague Spring.

Although Dubček positioned himself as a symbol for change and liberalism in the minds of Czechoslovaks, he was not the originator or regulator of new policies and soon lost control of the situation. The populace in general had few independent means of supporting the regime's attempted reforms. According to Jan Urban, a Czech educator, "The terrified leadership of the communist party of Czechoslovakia could not even partially institutionalize reform" (Urban 1990, 108). Dubček tried to present the reforms to the watchful Soviets as a variation of communism, but the leadership in Moscow, also hearing reports of chaos and democratic commotion, did not believe him. Party apparatchiks, by some accounts, were the ones who asked the Soviets to intervene militarily to suppress the liberalization movement. Regardless, in summer 1968, Moscow decided to stop Dubček and his reform-minded citizenry. The Brezhnev Doctrine provided the justification and use of force with which to do so.

Within a month of the August 1968 Soviet-led invasion of Czechoslovakia, *Pravda,* the Soviet communist party daily, justified the military occupation of Eastern Europe by citing the principle named for the party leader Leonid I. Brezhnev. *Pravda* acknowledged the existence of various paths to socialism, yet maintained that each country's communist party was "responsible not only to its own people but also to all the socialist countries and to the entire communist movement." In other words, the Kremlin asserted the right to intervene in any country in the Soviet bloc to prevent counterrevolution or loss of party control (see **Introduction: Strikes, Sinatra, and Nonviolent Revolution**"). The Czechoslovak leadership, hearing of the impending invasion, was quick to condemn it. Nonetheless, in late summer, the Soviets, supported by factions of the Czechoslovak party, moved to crush the Action Program with military force. On the night of August 20–21, after the Dubček government failed to reverse the reforms of the Prague Spring, 750,000 troops from five Warsaw Pact countries—Bulgaria, East Germany, Hungary, Poland, and the Soviet Union—crossed into Czechoslovakia.

Crushing of the Prague Spring

True to their history of bloodless revolutions, the Czechoslovaks resisted without violence. When troops arrived on August 21, they were greeted with peaceful demonstrations. "One of the most amazing factors in Czechoslovakia after the night invasion . . . was the spontaneous introduction of passive resistance by the entire population, which assumed the character and had the effect of unarmed combat on a nationwide scale," observes Josef Jøsten, a journalist and writer of Czech origin, recalling the stunning popular response to the assault (Jøsten 1977, 4). By "passive resistance," he was referring to a nineteenth-century term for nonviolent, or civil, resistance.

Czechoslovak soldiers, along with their fellow citizens, resisted the invaders. When ordered out of their barracks to make room for the occupying troops, Czechoslovak armed forces removed windows and doors, disengaged electrical systems, and cut water lines, making the barracks nearly uninhabitable for the new arrivals. In Prague, students surrounded Soviet tanks and offered peace gestures. Leaflets encouraged nonviolent resistance, and occupying soldiers were asked to search their hearts for mercy and understanding.

The disciplined restraint of hostility threw the Warsaw Pact soldiers off balance. Before long, the troops' mental strain and confusion made them undependable. Regiments began to alternate the time spent on duty in Prague, leaving every four days to escape the pressures of the civil resistance. As noncooperation with the occupiers spread across Czechoslovakia, soldiers had to be rotated in and out of other cities and regions as well. On the first Sunday of the occupation, August 25, factory workers reported for an extra shift of work and called it "Dubček's Sunday." This is a rare form of economic intervention known as a reverse strike, in which workers labor for additional hours, unpaid, to press their point. They reasoned that a normal strike would damage their own economy, rather than that of the occupiers. Czechoslovaks quickly developed ingenious resistance methods across the country.

The foreign troops were not uniformly unnerved by the Czechoslovaks' unarmed actions. As Soviet tanks filled Prague's streets, some Czechoslovaks rushed to blockade the entrance to Prague Radio with trucks, vans, and buses. The tanks proceeded to roll over them and drive into the multitude, killing and wounding those in their path.

On January 16, 1969, Jan Palach, a student at Charles University, committed suicide by self-immolation in the center of Prague's Wenceslas Square, named for the tenth-century King Wenceslas, a prince and patron saint of Bohemia, the ancient kingdom and seat of learning that is now the central and western portion of the Czech Republic. Occurring where it did, near the statue of St. Wenceslas, who is celebrated in the Christmas carol "Good King Wenceslas," Palach's fiery death could not be missed. It had a traumatic effect. Czechoslovaks compared him to Jan Hus, the Protestant martyr burned at the stake. In taking his own life in this horrific protest, Palach sought to send a fervent message against the continued replacement of reformers in the government with reactionaries.

Large demonstrations erupted. Citing the huge rallies as proof of Dubček's inability to rule effectively, the Soviet leadership forced him to resign on April 17, 1969. The Czechoslovakian season of hope ended. Dubček and the party architects of the country's reforms were handcuffed and forcibly flown to Moscow. There, they signed the so-called Moscow Protocols, recognizing their acceptance of the invasion and the military occupation. Their reforms were rescinded, and communist hard-liners assumed leadership in Czechoslovakia.

The crushing of the Prague Spring represents the moment when the meaning of the Brezhnev Doctrine became definitively clear in Eastern Europe: basic political reforms would not be allowed under Soviet suzerainty. This was particularly biting, because communist party leaders had led the Czechoslovak liberalization. By year's end, the hopes of artists, activist intellectuals, and literary figures about the future of communism had been dashed. Reform-minded Czechoslovaks had generally accepted the leading role of the party in the pursuit of reforms. Two decades of Stalinism had severely weakened civil society in Czechoslovakia, reducing it primarily to those in the arts. It lacked freestanding centers of power and multilayered independent institutions, and could never have mounted the program in sight during the eight months prior to the August invasion. Only the communist party and Dubček had the political heft to launch the April 1968 Action Program of reforms. Party reformers had also encouraged and supported emotional unity during the August troop movements. The populace that had seen Dubček and the leading reformers dragged unwillingly to Moscow was now demoralized and fearful. The removal of the party elite tolled the final death knell for the Prague Spring.

Gustáv Husák replaced Dubček as first secretary. Dubček was expelled from the party in 1970 and relegated to a humble forestry post. The hard-line Husák overturned previous reforms and promoted "normalization," a euphemism for bringing the country under Soviet control as pressured to do so by Moscow. Without mobilization from a popularly based opposition in support of reforms, and lacking independent centers of power outside the party to encourage restructuring, by April 1969 the party had succumbed to re-Stalinization under Husák. The party adopted a stance of antagonism toward the nationalist and benevolent forces within the society and aligned itself with repressive communist parties elsewhere in Eastern Europe. "Reform" became a dirty word. The party-state asked for conformist behavior and nonparticipation in politics, offering state-subsidized comforts in return. In the darkness of the country's theaters and cinemas, viewers could laugh and find double meanings in ambiguous phrases, while returning to the anonymity of meaningless chatter when the lights came up. By February 1971, practically half the country's journalists had been purged for refusing to sign a loyalty oath to the party-state.

Despite Husák's efforts to end the reform movement and restrict the media and free expression, small groups, generally in the arts, continued to work clandestinely for peaceful change. Those spotlighting disapproval of Husák's repression were often intellectuals, writers, poets, artists, and students, who were subsequently punished. Their endeavors appeared ineffectual because of the small numbers involved, the immediate arrest of any organizational leaders who surfaced, and constant surveillance by Husák's security forces. The government confiscated their property; made it illegal for their work to be published, produced, or displayed; strangled the organizations that nourished them; and drove individual "dissidents" into the oblivion of manual labor in remote rural areas.

The government could not, however, stop all activity opposing it. Despite the regime's placement of cultural and social activities under strict official censorship, authorities could not silence all its critics. Theatrical productions moved into private apartments. Rock groups banned from cities held concerts in countryside barns.

Husák's 1969 program of Soviet-style reforms was continued by his successor, Miloš Jakeš. As chairman of the party's Control Commission from 1968 to 1977, Jakeš personally presided over the destruction of the careers of 800,000 people. His purges drove half a million from the communist party's roll of 1.5 million members. Economic conditions worsened. Equipment and infrastructure received little investment. Industry plundered the environment. Transportation systems worsened. A nation once proud of its high educational standards and learning found itself in the lower ratings of national investment in education in Eastern Europe. Mortality rates rose. Life spans dropped. Nonetheless, the Prague Spring of 1968 continued to hold symbolic value throughout the communist world as a moment of openness and reform and became an iconic influence for Czechoslovakia's later Velvet Revolution.

The "Ten Points Manifesto" and Underground Publications

On August 21, 1969, the first anniversary of the Soviet-led invasion, defiance reasserted itself in the "Ten Points Manifesto." The document, which appeared unbidden, was a program for noncooperation in which Czechoslovaks were to cease using public transportation, stop shopping, and avoid patronizing restaurants and theaters. They were to halt work at noon, festoon certain monuments and graves, and spread word throughout the country and beyond about nonviolent resistance to repression. The government launched preventive arrests and other repressive measures to thwart these calls on August 20, but it could do nothing about the impressive showing on the so-called Day of Shame, marking the implementation of the manifesto's program.

For some time, a number of Czechoslovaks had expressed their opposition through protest emigration, deliberately and permanently fleeing their homeland. In the two decades after 1968, more than 500,000 of the country's 15 million citizens fled the country. Their flight violated laws, so they could not return. The predominantly Roman Catholic population gathered in churches and at other religious functions to share their collective desire for change and to circulate bulletins about venturesome civil resistance aimed at testing the communist bureaucracy. In houses of worship, cautious and reserved members of the community found the resolve to take action against the government's repressive measures despite Stalinist-style efforts to break the spine of the church.

In the 1970s, position papers and manifestoes began to appear on kiosks and walls. Citizens copied or memorized them to transmit to other areas of the country. Growing numbers of unlawful printing presses and publications began cultivating fearlessness, as clandestine publishing houses and journals flourished with communication beyond government censorship. Musicians, unauthorized rock bands, and other entertainers and artists spread ideas through society. Meanwhile, one popular strategy bogged down government officials in an endless sea of protest letters from concerned citizens.

Unofficial publications were called *samizdat* ("self-published" in Russian) and were distinct from state-published works, or *gosudarstvennoye izdatelstvo,* abbreviated to *gosizdat.* (The name of the Soviet official publisher was *Gosizdat.*) Czechoslovaks had begun using samizdat as a means of assertion, after the country fell under Soviet domination in 1948. Such publications included letters, appeals, books, periodicals, editorials, and summaries detailing government persecution. They were also disseminated outside the country in the hope that international attention would lead to the acquisition of more freedoms.

On February 15, 1977, *The New York Times* quotes Ludwík Vaculík, a publisher of samizdat, in an interview: "My poor wife has been at the typewriter most of the night. . . . [I]t is a crime for a private Czechoslovak to operate a copying machine. So we have to type everything and press our friends and relatives into service." Often ten carbon copies were typed on yellowed onionskin paper. The samizdat literature was crucial to the sharing of ideas that underpinned the Velvet Revolution. "Issues go from hand to hand, and many people in the chain make their own copies and circulate them among their own friends," Vaculík clarified. A typewritten samizdat was not technically illegal, Vaculík stressed, "but the system views it with extreme distaste." Vaculík in 1972 had become involved in publishing when the playwright, dramatist, and actor Václav Havel created Edice Petlice (Padlocked Editions), a semi-clandestine press. Edice Petlice produced typescripts of typewritten (allowed under the law) fiction, philosophical works, and other literature. By 1987, it had issued more than 400 unsanctioned and manually typewritten volumes. As one of twenty individuals running the semi-clandestine "publishing ring," Vaculík had become what *The Times* calls a "literary outlaw" after he produced "Two Thousand Words," the 1968 manifesto that appeared a month before the Soviet-led invasion to encourage liberalizing reforms. It describes Padlocked Editions as "an outlet for authors who are blacklisted by the government and cannot have their works printed." The journalist-historian Timothy

Garton Ash later judged that the finest contemporary Czech writers were published in samizdat.

The sharing of samizdat also established vital links between democracy movements throughout Eastern and Central Europe. Disenchantment continued to fester, along with growing awareness of insufficient results from the limited economic reforms being tried in Poland and Hungary in the 1970s (see **Poland, Introduction; Hungary, Introduction**).

The Helsinki Final Act

Even into the 1970s, the Soviet Union continued to seek guarantees of the borders resulting from its post–World War II hegemony over Eastern Europe; in return the United States and its Western allies wanted Soviet respect for human rights, freedom of travel, and increased contacts and flows of information. The Final Act of the Helsinki Accords—signed on August 1, 1975, and popularly known simply as the Helsinki Accords—reflected both these interests (see "**Introduction: Strikes, Sinatra, and Nonviolent Revolution**").

The accords committed signatories to the formation of the Conference on Security and Cooperation in Europe (CSCE, later the Organization for Security and Co-operation in Europe, or OSCE) and recognition of and respect for human rights and basic freedoms. The human rights provisions soon supplanted all others, and "Helsinki Accords" became synonymous with human rights. Though the accords were not a binding treaty, the human rights principles outlined were incorporated into the laws of the signatory nations. In Czechoslovakia, however, the process of "normalization," Gustáv Husák's cagey euphemism for re-Stalinization, proceeded with an implicit rejection of the Helsinki tenets. Even so, the Helsinki Final Act, signed by the Kremlin, provided cover for those who wished publicly to criticize curtailments of human rights. In that same year, a number of reform-minded Czechoslovaks founded the Democratic Initiative.

The late 1970s were portentous for innovation and creativity in the "dissident" communities of Czechoslovakia. The Committee for the Defense of the Unjustly Prosecuted, usually referred to by the Czech acronym VONS, was founded on April 27, 1978. VONS was similar to Poland's Social Self-Defense Committee, KSS-KOR, comprised of activist intellectuals and Roman Catholic laity who advised the Solidarity union. KSS-KOR had begun two years earlier with similar inspiration and focused on cases of injustice, providing documentation and advice for individuals (see **Poland, Introduction**, and "Polish Labor Crisis Deepens as Workers List Their Demands"). VONS concentrated on identifiable injustices and offered documentation and recommendations to individuals.

Václav Havel had been among the first Czechoslovaks to voice refusal to conform. On August 9, 1969, he sent a private letter to Alexander Dubček—after Dubček had signed the Moscow Protocols, but prior to being deposed—urging him to take a stand against government capitulation to the Soviet Union. The regime had blacklisted Havel's writings and arrested and imprisoned him for subversion without trial. In April 1975, Havel expressed publicly his concern over the government's brazen disregard of the Helsinki principles by releasing his "Open Letter to Gustáv Husák" to protest the general secretary's policy of normalization.

In his letter, Havel asks Husák to consider the issues about which he has written and to "act accordingly." Havel had done what the party-state most hated—broken the rule of silence. Havel asserts, "We cannot remain silent in the face of evil or violence; silence merely encourages them." Havel sent the letter by regular mail but also released it to foreign news agencies. His first serious philosophical writing, it focuses on fear and moral decay. As the letter's contents became known by way of samizdat, waves of dissent began anew, to be followed by repression. Actions to suppress youth and cultural activities sparked petitions. Civic dissent groups began rapidly to form throughout 1976. Havel was often incarcerated. *The Times* of January 2, 1990, notes, "In a series of prison terms beginning in 1977, Mr. Havel served more than five years for refusing to surrender his conscience to the dictates of the Communist state" (see "Václav Havel and Truth").

Charter 77

The 1976 arrest of musicians from the Plastic People of the Universe, an underground rock group, channeled the energies of a loose coalition of former party reformers, artists, authors, and Roman Catholic intellectuals who set out to defend the musicians' right to free expression. Milan Hlavsa had formed the band in September 1968, soon after the Warsaw Pact's August invasion, and took the name from the song "Plastic People," by the American musician Frank Zappa. The Plastics' long-haired and aggressively rebellious aura was not unusual when compared to rock bands in the West, but it shocked the straitened, conformist, and coercive authorities of Czechoslovakia.

The Plastics had played a number of illegal concerts after authorities revoked their permits in 1970, but by 1976 the crackdowns had grown more ruthless. Incensed by the regime's coarse attacks on the musicians, Václav Havel and his colleagues expressed solidarity and rallied support for the jailed musicians among their extensive circle of European activist intellectuals and writers. The Plastics' catalytic effect in Czechoslovakia is represented in the contemporary play *Rock 'n' Roll* by Sir Thomas Stoppard, who was born in Czechoslovakia and fled with his family in 1939. According to Stoppard's drama, the Plastics had no desire to bring down communism; instead, they sought to create freedom within a communist society.

Despite a huge outcry, and a chorus of condemnation across the nation, the Plastics were convicted for spreading "antisocialist ideas" and imprisoned. The band became an emblem of liberties. Encouraged by the ready response of their European counterparts, twenty to thirty Czechoslovak intellectuals began meeting in late 1976 to discuss their options in response to the party-state's reprisal of putting the Plastics behind bars. The group included the Catholic writer Václav Benda, writer Pavel Kohout, former party official Zdeněk Mlynář, radical socialist Petr Uhl, educator Jan Urban, and Havel, who had never been a member of the communist party. Notwithstanding their mixture of viewpoints, they agreed on what they considered an antipolitical strategy, the details of which they released on January 1, 1977, in the form of Charter 77.

Under any other circumstances, such a document's release would have heralded the emergence of an oppositional movement, but its creators downplayed its explosive thrust by describing it as "antipolitical." Muted in wording, its writers—referring to a civic initiative—express kinship among "people who share concern for the fate of the ideals to which they have linked their life and work." Charter 77 proclaimed itself a "free, informal, open association of people of different convictions, different faiths and different professions, who are linked by the desire . . . to insist on the respecting of civil and human rights in our country and throughout the world, rights recognized . . . [by] enacted international pacts, the Final Act of the Helsinki Conference and . . . the United Nations Declaration of Human Rights." The Helsinki Accords had been signed by the Czechoslovak regime in 1975.

The language of the founding document is historical, literary, and philosophical. In Husák's Czechoslovakia any independent organization would be criminal, hence its writers chose the following wording: "Charter 77 is not an organization, it has no statutes, no permanent organs and no organized membership. Everyone who agrees with the idea behind it, participates in its work and supports it is a member. . . . [I]t is not a base for opposition activity." It lays out its purpose as "constructive dialogue with political and state power" and offers to submit proposals for deepening rights.

According to Urban, Charter 77 had been inspired by the work of Poland's KSS-KOR. Like Charter 77, KSS-KOR never applied for official registration and thus could not be de-registered; although it had members, it functioned without bylaws or officers (see **Poland, Introduction** and "Polish Labor Crisis Deepens").

The basic principle of Charter 77 was that society cannot be transformed through orders from above. The literary figures, actors, and intellectuals involved held the strong conviction that change must be generated from the citizenry, and that the people are the best defense against totalitarian power and conformity. The signers were persuaded that human beings generally and initially form associations on a cultural level, where, within the context of art and imagination, they can exert political pressure as a consequence of their innermost needs. Although not intended as a politicized opposition, and not a direct political challenge to the regime, it nonetheless had political impact. According to political analyst Janusz Bugajski, "[A]s an essential ingredient of an authentic campaign for fundamental political, civil, economic, cultural, and national rights, the Charter's existence undermines the principles of the totalitarian communist system" (Bugajski 1987, 1).

Charter 77 was signed by 243 citizens, including leaders from the Prague Spring, academicians, actors, artists, clergy, journalists, and playwrights. Agreeing to live "as if" they were free, they also provided their addresses. A few months earlier, in September 1976 in Warsaw, KOR had similarly announced its members' names, addresses, and telephone numbers (see **Poland, Introduction**).

Jan Potočka—among the influential Central European philosophers of the twentieth century, banned from teaching in Czechoslovakia, and viewed as the founding father of the charter—is one of the three spokespersons designated in writing in Charter 77, who had been selected by the Chartists to speak for the others. Professor Potočka intimated that persecution might follow. The other two "entrusted" spokespersons were Václav Havel and Jiři Hájek, a lawyer and diplomat who in the pivotal year of 1968 was Alexander Dubček's minister of foreign affairs. The East-West détente, or relaxing of cold war tensions in the 1970s and 1980s, had offered some shelter to KOR leaders until 1980—because Poland was heavily indebted to the West and therefore concerned about its image—but it provided no comfort to the Chartists.

The regime launched campaigns of disinformation, smears, and vilification against the instigators of Charter 77. Ludwík Vaculík, an original signer of Charter 77, told *The Times* in February 1977, "They clearly want to separate the organizers of Charter 77 from the mere adherents" (see "Czech Underground Literature Circulating from Hand to Hand"). Czechoslovak authorities administered beatings, fired hundreds from their jobs, and jailed others. In many workplaces, employees were forced to sign denunciations of

Charter 77, called the "anti-socialist pamphlet," even if they had not seen its contents. The resulting lists of signatures were delivered to party secretariats.

After the founding of Charter 77, publishing of illegal samizdat exploded. Political trials instituted by the regime were to some degree neutralized by international awareness of the Helsinki Accords. During August and September 1978, representatives of Poland's KSS-KOR and Charter 77 held clandestine meetings in the forested frontier between their countries to exchange ideas and share experiences. Those attending included Adam Michnik and Jacek Kuroń, advisers to Solidarność (see "Strikers in Poland Defy Gierek Appeal," "Adam Michnik," and "Jacek Kuroń"). In 1984, six years after their first meeting, these Polish and Czechoslovak resisters would form Friends of Czechoslovak-Polish Solidarity.

On October 22, 1978, the Polish archbishop of Kraków, Karol Cardinal Wojtyla, was installed as pope of the Roman Catholic Church and took the name John Paul II. The Church of Rome, the "underground" or "catacomb" church, thereafter began to raise its voice on human rights. The new pope would play a unique role in connecting and providing support for Eastern European nations in resisting communism (see "Pope Gets Big Welcome in Poland"). In 1979, eleven of the leading Chartists were arrested, six of whom, Havel included, were given prison terms of two to five years.

In August 1988, twenty years after the 1968 Soviet-led occupation of Czechoslovakia, 10,000 people marched to Wenceslas Square in Prague in a demonstration organized by the Independent Peace Initiative (Nezávislé Mírové Sdružení, or NMS). A new generation had grown up with less fear than their forebears and turned out to mark the memory of the humiliations of the Warsaw Pact occupation of their country. In October 1988, the authorities declared that the seventieth anniversary of Czechoslovakian independence from the Hapsburgs of October 28, 1918, would be nationally celebrated as a holiday. Thousands took part in the festivities. Also in 1988, 500,000 Roman Catholics and non-Catholics signed a petition for religious rights and liberties after encouragement from František Cardinal Tomášek of Prague, whose concern for the worsening condition of the Catholic Church had been noted by *The Times* on June 23, 1985 (see "Pope and Polish Aide Have 'Cool' Talk"). Cardinal Tomášek said Catholics were being "hindered, pursued and controlled." From his pulpit, he urged Czechoslovaks to sign the petition.

GORBACHEV AND *PERESTROIKA*

In 1980, the regime had acknowledged for the first time that Czechoslovakia had negative economic growth and admitted that only 2 percent of the nation's technological outputs matched the quality of goods produced in advanced industrialized countries. In 1988, it implemented an economic decentralization experiment in state enterprises, which constituted 30 percent of the country's industrial production. The results were negligible. By 1990, per capita expenditures on education were among the lowest in Europe. Mortality rates had continued to rise with the passage of time, and Czechoslovakia had a lower life expectancy than most European states.

The communist intelligentsia and elites in Czechoslovakia had been hesitant to inaugurate the more fundamental changes suggested by Mikhail S. Gorbachev after he took the helm of the communist party of the Soviet Union in 1985. They were persuaded that any repudiation of the past would represent self-rejection; they could no longer blame Stalin. Adopting reforms would imply accepting responsibility for the ill performance of the country's economy and for any resulting confusion or chaos. The educated middle classes, particularly those reading the samizdat, knew of the spirit of reform emanating from the Soviet Union. Reports of uncertainties, debates over dogma, and divisions of opinion in Moscow were eagerly seized upon as new opportunities in Prague and elsewhere in Central and Eastern Europe. *Times* correspondent Serge Schmemann notes the awakening across the Eastern bloc on November 28, 1989:

> The marching masses in the streets demanding democracy, the Communists belatedly showing remorse and desperately jettisoning old leaders, [East Germany's] New Forum reappearing as [Czechoslovakia's] Civic Forum, press organizations suddenly abloom with candor and everyone around declaring in wonder, "This could not have happened a month ago." The parallels are not entirely chance. As the death knell of Communism spread from state to state, each revolution seemed to learn and gather strength from the last. (see "'Replay' in Prague: Popular Uprising Echoes the Experience of Neighbors")

According to Jan Urban, who lost his teaching post for signing Charter 77, "Gorbachev and *perestroika* changed the situation in a fundamental way." Gorbachev's coming to power "accelerated the erosion of the [communist] system in all Eastern European countries." In addition, the Czechoslovak party leadership had become ingrown and isolated from the rest of the communist world. To Urban, it "answered in the only way it knew—with increased repression" (Urban 1990, 113). The government remained intransigent. Despite changes advancing rapidly throughout Eastern Europe, the regime maintained its hard line. It went so far as to congratulate China for its deliberately murderous crackdown on the nonviolent student demonstrations of Tiananmen Square in June 1989.

The Prague Autumn of 1989

In 1989, Central Europe began pulsating with a revolutionary fervor. In March, Karoly Grósz, the communist party chief in Hungary, met with Gorbachev in Moscow. To the Hungarian party, what emerged from the talks pointed to the death of the Brezhnev Doctrine. By autumn, astonishing changes in Poland, Hungary, and East Germany had proved how much could be accomplished by collective nonviolent action, especially when abetted by internal communist party reformers who no longer wished to preserve the party or believed that it could not be reformed: Solidarity moved toward round-table negotiations with the party-state in Poland. Hungarian officials, having dismantled the electrified barrier on their border with Austria, abetted the prospect of thousands fleeing to the West. Socialists across Eastern Europe called for more freedoms. As awareness spread of the speed of reforms represented by the Polish and Hungarian developments, the Czechoslovak regime found itself in a problematic position.

Tensions grew in Czechoslavakia as news arrived of advances in the rest of Eastern Europe but not in their country. *The Times* picks up on this on November 21, 1989: "In general, the Czechs and the Slovaks appeared to be moving more cautiously and more hesitantly than their Polish, German and Hungarian neighbors in challenging Communist rule" (see "200,000 March in Prague as Calls for Change Mount"). Younger Czechoslovak generations watched during September, October, and November, as East German exiles passed through their country and they learned of enormous nonviolent demonstrations pouring out of the churches in East Germany. In Leipzig on October 9, East German police and security forces had backed down from retaliatory violence against demonstrators in a watershed moment. Not so in Prague, where three weeks later police suppression was brutal (see "Police in Prague Move to Break Up Big Protest March").

Aided by samizdat and broadcasts from Radio Free Europe, Czechoslovaks, particularly in institutions of higher learning and the theater, were aware that hundreds of thousands of protesters had formed a nonviolent human chain across East Germany, and on November 4 more than 1 million demonstrated in East Berlin. On November 5, West German officials announced an agreement between East Germany and Czechoslovakia allowing East Germans to show only an internal identity document to cross into West Germany from Czechoslovakia. East Germans began arriving almost immediately at the Czechoslovakia–West German border. Moreover, thousands of East Germans were encamped at the so-called Prague Embassy, in West Berlin, when the Czechoslovak government relented and permitted them to travel across Czechoslovakia by train to West Germany without any prerequisite (see "500,000 in East Berlin Rally for Change" and "Hungary Allows 7,000 East Germans to Emigrate West").

Czechoslovak citizens were comparatively more conscious of regional developments than had been their counterparts in Poland and Hungary; they could see with their own eyes the trains carrying East Germans across their lands. They knew that on November 7 the entire East German government had resigned, elections were in the offing, and on November 9 the Berlin Wall was breached (see "East Germany Opens Frontier to the West for Migration or Travel" and "Clamor in the East").

These dramatic events heightened domestic pressure on the Czechoslovakian regime. On August 11, authorities had rejected any communication with groups advocating change, dismissing them as "illegal structures." By late August, as officials continued to rebuff demands for change, 30 percent of Czechoslovak industries were moving toward collapse. Communist managers were themselves recommending sites to be shut and facilities closed. The government found itself unable to deliver on its bargain in which the cooperation and acceptance of the people were swapped for governmental subsidies.

R. W. Apple, Jr., in *The Times* on November 17, 1989, contemplates the failed deal:

> Two generations ago, at the time of World War I, this was a rich country, with two-thirds of the industrial capacity of the entire Austro-Hungarian Empire concentrated in Bohemia and Moravia, which make up the western two-thirds of Czechoslovakia. The Skoda armaments works and the Bata shoe factories were world famous. The region was comparable to Pittsburgh. . . .

> Now Czechoslovak industry is inefficient, old-fashioned and undercapitalized. Soft coal still turns many wheels; its soot and its smell are everywhere. The famous glass industry, which once taught the world, is trapped in the styles and technology of the 1930s. The machine-tool industry cannot supply the computer-driven elements that can be ordered

from Japan or West Germany. Things are getting worse. If the communist government cannot halt the rot, and many of its own economists doubt that it can, it will eventually be unable to deliver on its side of the bargain that has kept the Czechoslovak public quiet for the last two decades: We'll keep your standard of living up, and you leave the political decisions in our hands. ("Prague's Shaky Bargain")

On November 12, Miloš Jakeš threatened that protests in Czechoslovakia would not be permitted. Five days later, nearly 50,000 marched on Wenceslas Square. Jakeš's threats prompted more forms of protest and demonstrations that grew larger with each day.

"Just a Few Sentences"

In June 1989, a document unassumingly called "Just a Few Sentences" (Několik vět) had appeared. Clearly reminiscent of Ludwík Vaculík's "Two Thousand Words," the manifesto that materialized a month before the 1968 Soviet-led invasion encouraging liberalizing reforms, it was originally signed by official, state-subsidized artists and unofficial artists, independent figures working outside the party framework. It called for democratization and religious freedom. It also advocated freedom of assembly, release of political prisoners, environmental assessments of industrial enterprises, and open discussion of the Prague Spring and the so-called normalization policies that followed. Within a few months, 40,000 citizens had signed "Just a Few Sentences," including workers and police officers, apart from the predictable university-based academicians and students.

As the movement to speak out gained in popularity, artists who had signed "Just a Few Sentences" were joined by journalists, literary figures, playwrights, and cultural leaders in a boycott of Czechoslovakian television to protest the persecution of the document's signers. In its wake, new groups arose, some expressing democratic political objectives, others dedicated to environmental preservation or grouping themselves under the broad rubric of peace. Of note was the Movement for Civil Liberties (Hnutí za Občanskou Svobodu, or HOS), established with a specific goal of building the infrastructure needed for "normal" political activities. Its purposes included economic and political pluralism, a reorganized legal system, a new constitution, and protection of fundamental freedoms. Among HOS proponents were signers of Charter 77 who wished to undertake a more overtly political role.

On October 28, the anniversary of the founding of the Czechoslovak Republic, the streets of Prague filled with citizens demonstrating for rights and democracy. In addition to their political goals, thousands were also eager to protest the destructive environmental degradation caused by the unchecked dumping of industrial wastes into rivers and streams, air pollution, unregulated ecological devastation, and policies that degraded natural resources. Approximately 350 people were arrested at the independence day commemoration, with another 100 detained for parallel protests against Czechoslovakia's destruction of its environment.

In late September 1989, with the Soviet satellites undergoing major transformations, Hungary's parliament issued an ex post facto condemnation of the 1968 invasion of Czechoslovakia by Warsaw Pact troops. On November 4, as more than a million demonstrators jammed Berlin's streets, the East German Politburo resigned, along with hundreds of other officials; elections were in the planning stages. Two days later, Hungarian television aired an interview with Václav Havel in which he associated himself with the popular cause; the Czechoslovak party-state condemned the interview. By mid-November in Prague, the Democratic Initiative declared itself the first independent political party since 1948.

The Ten Days of November 1989

When the journalist-historian Timothy Garton Ash arrived in Prague in November 1989, he remarked to Václav Havel, "In Poland it took ten years, in Hungary ten months, in East Germany ten weeks: perhaps in Czechoslovakia it will take ten days!" (Garton Ash 1990, 78.)

November 17, Day One of what became the Ten Days, pinpoints the start of the 1989 Velvet Revolution. It began with a group of students that had been active for perhaps a year and decided to protest in Prague to condemn the Nazi occupation of Czechoslovakia and to honor publicly Jan Opletal, a student killed by Hitler's forces half a century earlier. On the day of the demonstration, some 15,000 students marched to Opletal's grave at Vysehrad Cemetery. As they walked, they chanted anticommunist, antigovernment slogans and sang the Czech adaptation of "We Shall Overcome." Banners read "Democracy, Freedom, and Free Elections," "Democracy for All," and "We Don't Want Violence." The action could have concluded at the graveside, but some called out, "To Wenceslas Square," and turned down the hill and alongside the Vltava River, toward the city center.

As they moved past the National Theater and onto Narodní Avenue, by several accounts the students were directed by agents provocateurs toward riot police in full gear who cornered them in archways near the square. White-helmeted riot police carrying shields and truncheons, along with antiterror squads recognizable by their red berets, began clubbing the students. Police blocked escape routes and beat the young demonstrators, some of whom cried, "We are unarmed," and "No violence." Hundreds were injured. Their numbers grew to 50,000 by some accounts. Those who went to the square sat on cobblestones and sang songs, gathering around impromptu, makeshift shrines to the injured, posies in hand. Soldiers smashed the candle-lit shrines and stomped on bouquets. Toward nine o'clock at night, riot police accosted the students, clubbing them again.

During the night of November 17 and into Saturday, November 18, some of the students resolved to go on strike. By Saturday morning (Day Two), they had gotten word to most of Prague's Charles University and other colleges and universities. The students were the first to call for strikes, but by Saturday afternoon the theater people had declared their support and proposed a national general strike for November 27. The students immediately endorsed the proposed general strike and would persist for six weeks in striking on their own, extensively backed up by similar noncooperation measures by theatrical actors and dramatists. Throughout the weekend, tens of thousands of mostly young people and students took over Wenceslas Square, carrying flags and posters. They chanted slogans, including "Freedom" and "Resign." One of their catchphrases was "Now's the Time," another "This Is It."

The following day, Sunday, November 19, a crowd of 200,000 gathered for a demonstration in Prague to protest the police brutality against the students. That night at 10:00 P.M., on Day Three, a citizen pro-democracy group called the Civic Forum (Občanské Fórum) emerged. Many of its members had led in Charter 77. Over the following three days, throngs occupied Prague. The forum made four demands: resignation of communist officials responsible for preparing for the 1968 Warsaw Pact incursion, including President Gustáv Husák and the party chief, Miloš Jakeš; resignation of the federal minister of the interior, František Kincl, and the first secretary for Prague, Miroslav Štěpán, both of whom were seen to be responsible for the crushing of the initial nonviolent demonstrations; establishment of a special commission to investigate such police behavior; and the release of all prisoners of conscience (Garton Ash 1990, 82–83).

Václav Havel became the guiding light and exemplar of the Civic Forum, which used the Magic Lantern Theater as its headquarters. He addressed the crowds on Tuesday, November 21, Day Five, two days prior to Alexander Dubček making his first public appearance in twenty years. The Socialist Party's publishing organ made available its balcony, conveniently positioned mid-square, for this and subsequent remarks. In Bratislava, Havel spoke to 50,000 people enlisted by the Civic Forum's Slovak partner, the Public Against Violence (Verejnosť proti Nasiliu, or VPN), which had arisen four days earlier, comprised of Slovak authors, playwrights, cultural artists, and actors. *The Times* on November 21 notes that besides the Slovak capital, Bratislava, demonstrations had begun in Ostrava and Brno, with several thousand marchers (see "200,000 March in Prague as Calls for Change Mount"). By Thursday, November 23, Day Seven, the numbers in Wenceslas Square had risen to more than 300,000.

On Friday, November 24, Day Eight, Alexander Dubček met with the Civic Forum, and 350,000 turned out in Wenceslas Square to greet him and Havel. That same evening, former general secretary Jakeš and the entire Politburo resigned. The communist apparatus was showing splits and divisions.

After the passage of ten days, on Monday, November 27, Czechoslovaks mounted a successful nationwide general strike in which 80 percent of the nation's labor force participated. The party began to yield. The Civic Forum and the government began to talk. The "leading role" of the communist party, protected in a constitutional clause, was formally rescinded.

On December 3, communist party secretary Husák nominated a new coalition government, headed by Ladislav Adamec. Fifteen of the twenty ministers were to be communists, but the Civic Forum and Public against Violence rejected the formula. The potency of the Civic Forum and Public Against Violence came from their ability to catalyze huge street mobilizations of hundreds of thousands; they now called for more demonstrations and another general strike. In seventy-two hours, the communist party ceded and accepted a new government with a communist prime minister, but a noncommunist majority. The next day, the party expelled Jakeš, who was quoted by *The Times* on November 21 to the effect that organizers of the 200,000-strong demonstrations that day were "seeking to create chaos and anarchy . . . [which would] seriously endanger the implementation of necessary changes and bring socialism into crisis, with unforeseeable consequences" (see "200,000 March in Prague as Calls for Change Mount"). Miroslav Štěpán, the Prague city party chief, was also ousted. Štěpán was one of eight whose dismissal had been demanded by the Civic Forum, *The Times* notes on November 24 (see "Prague Rivals Vie for Favor on Eve of Party Meeting"). Jakeš and Štěpán had been blamed for the police brutality of November 17 against the student demonstrators that had resulted in the party's loss of legitimacy.

Havel demonstrated the caliber of his leadership when he spoke to multitudes in Wenceslas Square on November 24, the seventh consecutive day of enormous antigovernment rallies. He invited the police and army to join the opposition. In the November 24 *Times,* correspondent John Tagliabue quotes Havel as telling the enormous crowds, "We are against violence.... We want to live as peaceful and dignified people who do not think only of themselves, but also consider the fate of generations to come." Havel portrayed Czechoslovakia as poised at "historic crossroads" and accused the communist party-state of taking the nation to the edge of "spiritual, moral, political and economic catastrophe." We want "to live in a free, democratic and prospering Czechoslovakia, returned to Europe, and we will never give up this ideal" (see "Prague Rivals Vie for Favor on Eve of Party Meeting").

Turning the Page of History

Despite the changes being implemented by the regime, nothing guaranteed that the communist party would not reorganize, regroup, and propel itself back into control. As a new government assembled under Marián Čalfa, the sentiment grew that President Husák should be replaced by a non-communist president, so that all centers of power—political, military, and the fledgling civil society—could be brought under democratic control. One candidate stood out: Václav Havel.

Demands accelerated for Havel to be nominated to the presidency. On December 10, Husák presided as Čalfa was sworn in, accompanied by a majority of non-communist ministers, and thereafter resigned. The ten days had in reality taken twenty-four. At meetings, gatherings, marches, and rallies nationwide, popular sentiment favored Havel moving into Prague Castle and assuming the presidency. On December 16, Havel agreed to his candidacy.

By the end of December, the Federal Assembly, the parliament, followed in the footsteps of the rest of the Czechoslovak regime in taking the reins from the communists. On December 28, Dubček was seated in the Federal Assembly and sworn in as Speaker. The assembly on December 29 unanimously elected Havel as president of what was still called the Czechoslovak Soviet Republic, in one of the most brisk, dramatic, and highly symbolic political reversals in history. Havel had linked Dubček's election to his own, to please the Slovaks and to retain support by communist party reformers. Seeing that Havel's election met their stipulations, the students called off their six-week strike. As 1990 approached, changes considered inconceivable but sixty days earlier had been achieved.

Reporting on Havel's New Year's address as president, *Times* reporter Craig R. Whitney on January 2, 1990, notes a double entendre from Czechoslovak history at the conclusion of Havel's speech. In it, the new president paraphrases a prayer by the seventeenth-century Moravian church leader John Amos Comenius that Tomas Masaryk, Czechoslovakia's first president, had adopted: "Your government, my people, has returned to you" (see "Havel Tells Festive Czechoslovaks that Honesty Is Key to Recovery"). The Czechoslovak citizens had finally determined their own history.

Conclusion

The Helsinki Accords of 1975 facilitated Czechoslovaks' criticism of the Prague regime on human rights; official authorities' actions could be held against their signing of the Final Act. A cultured nation in which civil society had not been permitted to flourish was during the 1970s and 1980s quietly developing such a sphere, a domain not under governmental control. There, artistic, academic, drama, journalism, and literary communities—and those who had been forced into manual labor as window-washers or furnace stokers, downgraded to clerks, banned as authors, or thrown into jail—could interact freely and work to set themselves free from the rot of economic, moral, and political decay.

Czechoslovakia benefited greatly from the democratic civil insurgencies in Poland and Hungary. News about events in Poland, Hungary, and East Germany was reaching Czechoslovaks through samizdat and Radio Free Europe. The midnight typists of samizdat churned out information. Soviet leader Gorbachev's principles and reforms signaled the permissibility of challenging the established order. Word had spread that in October 1989 Gorbachev had declared in a visit to Berlin that matters relating to East Germany were to be "decided not in Moscow, but in Berlin" (see "Gorbachev Lends Honecker a Hand").

Not only did the actors, artists, authors, playwrights, students, university faculties, and theatrical communities of Prague understand that any violence would create a pretext for repression, but "[F]rom the first moment [of the Civic Forum], we wanted to be aggressively nonviolent in our stance—to make a power of our lack of weapons," Jan Urban (1990, 119) recalls. Moreover, living in the shadow of the Soviet Union, the activist intellectuals and artists understood a great irony, which Václav Havel explained: the dissident movements of the Soviet bloc "do not shy away from the idea of violent political overthrow because the idea seems too radical, but on the contrary, because it does not seem radical enough" (Havel 1989, 93).

The artists and intellectuals wanted truly revolutionary change, to transform Czechoslovakia permanently and create a lasting democracy. More violence would have been a counterproductive throwback and would not have resulted in durable change. Their years of cautiously building a capacity in the civil society under construction would culminate in mounting a successful national general strike. Combined with the effective voices of the Civic Forum and Public Against Violence, they brought about a swift transition of power. As Urban put it, "In the course of one week, in November 1989, Winter blossomed into Spring in Czechoslovakia. A nonviolent mass movement, . . . triumphed . . . in transition from the negation of the old to the building of the new" (Urban 1990, 100).

CHARTER 77

On New Year's Day 1977, a group of 243 Czechoslovak citizens released a signed document that asked for "constructive dialogue" on, among other things, "the system of the virtual subjection of all institutions and organizations in the state to the political directives of the apparatus of the ruling party and the arbitrary decisions of the influential individuals." It suggested that the Soviet-imposed system had no social mandate. The declaration's appearance was the most important development in the country since the 1968 Prague Spring, during which Alexander Dubček, who had come to power in January, led reforms and liberalization that ended in August with a Soviet-led invasion of 750,000 Warsaw Pact troops into Czechoslovakia. The signers included professors, engineers, journalists, artists, clergy, and leaders from the Prague Spring. Also among the signers was Václav Havel, author of the 1975 "Open Letter to Gustáv Husák." After the Warsaw Pact incursion on August 21, 1968, Husák had been installed as general secretary of Czechoslovakia's communist party and set about instituting a program of "normalization," meaning a return to Soviet control (see **Czechoslovakia, Introduction**). In his open letter, Havel spoke out against the effects of the normalization policy, writing, "We cannot remain silent in the face of evil or violence; silence merely encourages them." He asks Husák to consider the issues he raises in the letter and encourages him to "act accordingly." Havel had been among the earliest Czechoslovaks to refuse to conform to communist strictures and was the progenitor of Charter 77.

In its statement, Charter 77 calls itself a "free, informal, open community of people of different professions," who have united to work human and civil rights. "Charter 77 is not an organization," it offers; "it has no rules, permanent bodies, or formal membership. It embraces everyone who agrees with its ideas, participates in its work, and supports it. It does not form the basis for any oppositional activity." Thus the issuance of the Charter 77 document also signaled the formation of a community by the same name. It was not, however, an organizational entity, and it had no official membership.

The literary figures, actors, and intellectuals involved in it held the strong conviction that change must be generated from the citizenry; the basic principle of Charter 77 was that society cannot be transformed by orders from above. The signers considered the convictions of the people the best defense against totalitarian power and conformity. They were persuaded that people initially form associations on a cultural level, and that within the context of art and imagination, human beings can exert political pressure as a manifestation of their innermost needs. Although Charter 77 was not intended to play the role of a politicized opposition or pose a direct political challenge to the Czechoslovak regime, it nonetheless had a political impact.

Charter 77 was inspired by the Helsinki Final Act and guided by the need to respect human rights (see "**Introduction: Strikes, Sinatra and Nonviolent Revolution**"). Among these entitlements was a citizen's right to a dialogue with his or her government. The gist of Charter 77 was to assert that the Czechoslovak government should honor all international agreements, including the UN Universal Declaration on Human Rights, and particularly the Helsinki agreements that it had signed in 1975 with regard to human rights. Agreeing to live "as if" they were free, the 243 charter signatories even provided their addresses on the document. They selected three spokespersons to bring human rights abuses to the public's and the government's attention, the first being Jan Potočka, a philosopher viewed as the founding father of the charter.

In short order, the government moved against the Chartists, among which were a few hundred active adherents and several thousand nominal associates. *The New York Times* reports on January 8, 1977, that five key signers of Charter 77 had been arrested by the Czechoslovak authorities following the charter's appearance in Western European newspapers. Havel, a playwright whose dramas address the constraints and pressures of living in an authoritarian system, was among those arrested. Never a member of the communist party, his writings and efforts at speaking out had established him as a respected moral philosopher outside government circles (see "Václav Havel and Truth").

Other organizers of Charter 77 included the Catholic writer Václav Benda, playwright Pavel Kohout, former party official Zdeněk Mlynář, radical socialist Petr Uhl, novelist-essayist Ludwík Vaculík, and educator Jan Urban. They unified their diverse perspectives in what has been called an antipolitical strategy in releasing Charter 77.

The Husák regime also instituted campaigns of disinformation in the state-controlled news media, smears, and vilification aimed at the Chartists. *Times* reporter Malcolm W. Browne was waiting for an interview outside the Prague apartment of Pavel Kahout, a communist critical of the party, when Czechoslovak police seized Kahout from his residence. "The pattern is to arrest signers of the rights petition and question them after searching their homes," Browne writes in his dispatch, which appears on the front page of *The Times* of January 11, 1977. "The arrests thus appear intended mainly as harassment," he added ("Czech Police Hold a Dissident Writer; Kahout Is Seized in the Presence of a Visiting Reporter").

Ludwík Vaculík was shortly thereafter arrested and subsequently told *The Times* on February 15, "They clearly want to separate the organizers of Charter 77 from the mere adherents" among the full contingent of signers (see "Czech Underground Literature Circulating from Hand to Hand"). Beatings were administered to signers, hundreds were fired from their jobs, and others were jailed. In a number of workplaces, employees were forced to sign denunciations of Charter 77, which was disparaged as the "anti-socialist pamphlet." This they did, even if they had not seen its contents.

Charter 77 created a new arena for political activity simply by declaring its existence. Although not a mass movement, its presence, influence, and offer of constructive dialogue kindled the sparks of what would eventually become a mass mobilization to bring about the transition to democracy. Its potency was irrefutable. The appearance of Charter 77 created an outpouring of underground publications and encouraged other such endeavors. For instance, on April 27, 1978, the Committee for the Defense of the Unjustly Prosecuted, more commonly referred to by its Czechoslovak acronym VONS, was founded. Like Poland's KSS-KOR (Social Self-Defense Committee)—comprised largely of activist intellectuals and Roman Catholic laity and central to the alliance of workers and intellectuals in the Solidarity union—VONS began similarly by responding to specific instances of injustice and provided documentation and advice to individuals.

According to Jan Urban, Charter 77 had itself been inspired by the work of KSS-KOR. For example, like the Polish committee, the Chartists never applied for official registration and functioned without bylaws or officers (see **Poland, Introduction,** and "Polish Labor Crisis Deepens"). Representatives of KSS-KOR and Charter 77 had held clandestine meetings on the forested frontier between their two countries during August and September 1978, to exchange ideas and share experiences. Six years after their first meeting, these Polish and Czechoslovak resisters would in 1984 form the Friends of Czechoslovak-Polish Solidarity.

JANUARY 8, 1977
PRAGUE DETAINS FIVE DISSIDENTS AFTER HUMAN RIGHTS MANIFESTO
By MALCOLM W. BROWNE
Special to The New York Times

PRAGUE, Jan. 7 – At least five dissident Czechoslovakian intellectuals have been detained for questioning in the last 24 hours, and the Communist Party newspaper Rude Pravo warned other dissidents that "those who lie on the rails to stop the train of history" must expect to get their legs cut off.

The detentions followed the publication yesterday by several West European newspapers of a new manifesto signed by 241 prominent Czechoslovaks in support of human rights.

At the same time, the Prague leadership appeared to be intensifying publicity intended to link the United States not only with dissident activity here but also with Nazi war criminals and an espionage campaign against the Soviet bloc.

Dissident sources said that the police had picked up Vaclav Havel, one of the country's best-known playwrights; Ludvik Vaculik, Pavel Landovsky, and Zdenek Urbanik, writers, and Frantisek Pavlicek, director of Prague's Vinohrady Theater.

In each case, the residence was apparently searched as well. All were released, but Mr. Pavlicek was picked up by the police again today and by nightfall, eight hours later, he had still not returned home.

Called 'Son of a Millionaire'

Mr. Havel was attacked by name in the Rude Pravo today as the "son of a millionaire who have never forgiven the working class."

Mr. Havel, one of the organizers of the manifesto published in Western Europe yesterday under the title "Charter 77," is known for such plays as "The Garden Party," "So Difficult to Concentrate," and "Butterfly on the Aerial."

The Government statement attacked all those who had signed various petitions in recent years, especially supporters of Alexander Dubcek, the former Czechoslovak Communist Party leader who was removed from office eight months after the 1968 Soviet-led Warsaw Pact invasion of the country. He was assigned briefly to Turkey as Ambassador before ending up in a lowly job.

Rude Pravo said that dissident human rights petitions purported "to be addressed to Czechoslovak authorities, are in fact commissioned by anti-Communist and Zionist centers and published by the most reactionary information media."

Prague TV Shows U.S. 'Spying'

Prague television tonight continued a four-part series on alleged American espionage activities against Czechoslovakia.

The second of four installments was broadcast tonight, featuring an interview with a man identified as Glen Roy Rohrer, who purports to be an American intelligence agent who had taken asylum in Czechoslovakia. . . .

Samizdat Propel Pro-Democracy Movements

Unofficial, underground publications were called *samizdat* ("self-published" in Russian). The name distinguished them from state-published production, *gosudarstvennoye izdatelstvo*, or *gosizdat*. Czechoslovaks had begun using samizdat as a means of assertion after the country fell under Soviet domination in 1948. These took the form of letters, appeals, books, periodicals, editorials, and summaries detailing instances of government persecution. Samizdat were also disseminated to an international audience, in hopes that world attention would induce freedoms. Often typed on yellowed onionskin paper with ten carbon copies, they passed among Czechoslovaks, from hand to hand, and along the way additional copies were sometimes made. The samizdat literature would be crucial to the sharing of ideas that underpinned the Velvet Revolution.

Ludwík Vaculík, a publisher of samizdat, had in July 1968, one month before the Soviet-led incursion by Warsaw Pact troops against the Prague Spring, issued a manifesto entitled "Two Thousand Words Which Belong to Workers, Farmers, Officials, Artists and to Everyone." Also known as "Two Thousand Words," it called for liberalizing reforms and accelerated efforts to rid the government of its Stalinist tendencies. In 1972, Vaclàv Havel, Vaculík, and others had created a semi-clandestine publishing enterprise called Edice Petlice, or Padlocked Editions, to publish typewritten fiction, philosophical works, and other literature. By 1987, it had more than 400 manually typed underground productions to its credit. One of twenty literati running the "publishing ring" of Padlocked Editions, Vaculík was what *The Times* on February 15, 1977, calls a "literary outlaw," one of a number of writers whose work was banned by the government. He was also among the signers of the politically influential Charter 77 (see "Charter 77").

The journalist-historian Timothy Garton Ash concluded that practically all the finest contemporary Czech writers were published solely in samizdat. The underground publications often probed deep philosophical questions. Havel chose "living in Truth" as his leitmotif, having in his youth repudiated unthinking subservience to those in authority. Instead, he had determined to search for Truth in forbidden books and thinking freely in private. Havel's Truth was not an abstraction: "[Truth] can be any means by which a person or a group revolts against manipulation: anything from a letter by intellectuals to a workers' strike, from a rock concert to a student demonstration, from refusing to vote in the farcical elections, to making an open speech at some official congress, or even a hunger strike" (Havel 1989, 59).

The sharing of samizdat provided vital, energizing connections between the pro-democracy movements throughout Eastern and Central Europe. Journals and periodicals published elsewhere were also essential sources of information and circulated actively. The Czechoslovaks and others improvised complex and elaborate systems for transporting materials across borders.

KEY PLAYER IN CZECHOSLOVAKIA
Ludwík Vaculík (1926–)

The New York Times on February 15, 1977, describes Ludwik Vaculík as a "literary outlaw" (see "Czech Underground Literature Circulating From Hand to Hand"). If so, his turn to the pen instead of the sword started early. Vaculík was born in Brumov, in south Moravia, in 1926, before Czechoslovakia came under the heel of first the Nazis and then the Stalinists. By age thirteen, he was keeping a diary that forty-five years later would be published as *The Indian Book*.

In 1967, he gave a speech attacking the communist party at the Fourth Congress of the Writer's Union. His comments led to his expulsion from the party. In June 1968, just prior to the Prague Spring, Vaculík urged the end of dictatorship with his manifesto titled "Two Thousand Words Which Belong to Workers, Farmers, Officials, Artists and to Everyone." What famously came to be known simply as "Two Thousand Words" expressed fear of hard-line apparatchiks within the party and contemplated a Soviet invasion. The tone was not provocative, however; Vaculík called for civic engagement. Seventeen-year-old Jan Urban, later an educator, commented at the time, "The 2000 words manifesto was the first public show of discontent or opinion unconsulted with the communist authorities since 1948 when the communists took power. So it is important both emotionally and politically on one hand, and on the other it was devastating for the old style communists, and accepted and perceived as a tremendously important show of new public self-confidence. It is a truly historical document, and I think that its importance should not be forgotten" (Jůn 2008). The party condemned Vaculík and banned his writings; he would not be officially published for another twenty-one years.

Nonetheless, Vaculík continued to speak out against the government. In 1972, along with the dramatist Václav Havel (eventually elected three times to presidential office as a result of Czechoslovakia's Velvet Revolution), he established Edice Petlice, or Padlocked Editions, a publishing outfit that he ran until 1989. It became the most famous of Czechoslovakia's underground publishing enterprises. Semi-clandestine and uncensored, Padlock produced *samizdat* (Russian for "self-published") typescripts and banned titles, including typewritten fiction and philosophical works. They were typewritten because it was a crime for a private Czechoslovak to operate a copying machine. Usually typed on yellowing onionskin paper atop ten carbon copies, this samizdat literature was vital in allowing Czechoslovaks to share the ideas that would underpin their Velvet Revolution. Vaculík and his twenty literary cohorts were instrumental in producing more than 400 manually typed underground publications.

In 1977, Vaculík was one of the 243 individuals who signed Charter 77, a manifesto criticizing the government for its failure to implement human rights provisions of the Helsinki Accords, which the Czech regime had signed in 1975. In short order, the charter sparked a number of autonomous initiatives for civic renewal, as new groups materialized, some seeking to democratize Czechoslovak society, others focusing on environmental preservation or banding together under the broad umbrella of advancing peace.

Vaculík, a novelist and essayist, wrote about Czech daily life as well as political issues. On May 20, 1977, *The New York Times* published "A Cup of Coffee at the Interrogation," in which he and the lieutenant colonel who has him under surveillance for the secret police discuss Vaculík's artful persistence as he remains within the contours of what was legal with his writing, while still yearning for complete freedom of expression. The essay in *The Times* made him an internationally recognized literary figure and proponent of democratic freedoms.

During the late 1970s and 1980s, Vaculík's writings were smuggled out of Czechoslovakia through underground networks to be published abroad. Critics praised them. Some of his most notable works include "The Axe" and the allegorical "The Guinea Pigs." "The Czech Dreambook," a diary of real and fictional events, is perhaps his best-known work; it appeared as a samizdat at the beginning of the 1980s and is yet to be published in English. In 1987, a book of twenty-three essays and feuilletons appeared under a title similar to his *Times* piece: *A Cup of Coffee with My Interrogator*. It concerns the Prague Spring and subsequent political upheaval in Czechoslovakia.

Recognized in Czechoslovakia for his earlier role as editor of the communist party daily *Rudé Právo* (The Red Light, or Red Law) and *Literarni Noviny* (Literary News), and also known to audiences as a radio journalist, Vaculík's samizdat writings inspired the growing civil society and resistance movement. It also helped to encourage the June 1989 document modestly entitled "Just a Few Sentences," which appealed for democracy, freedom of religious conviction, freedom of assembly, release of political prisoners, environmental assessments of industrial enterprises, and public discussion of the Prague Spring and the so-called normalization policies that followed with coercive programs of re-Stalinization. In short order, 40,000 citizens had signed "Just a Few Sentences."

The government lifted the ban on Vaculík's writings in late 1989 as the Velvet Revolution realized its sought-after restoration of democracy. He continues to write a weekly column for a newspaper and is active in the Czech literary world. In 2002, he brought out a collection entitled *The Last Word;* however, as Gerry Turner, his translator into English, observes, the last word has not been uttered by this literary outlaw.

FEBRUARY 15, 1977
CZECH UNDERGROUND LITERATURE CIRCULATING FROM HAND TO HAND
Blacklisted Writers Find Outlet in Typescripts Similar to Soviet Union's Samizdat
By PAUL HOFMANN
Special to The New York Times

VIENNA, Feb. 14 – A middle-aged Czech in a Prague park the other day pulled a few yellow onionskin sheets out of a sheaf in his briefcase and presented them to a foreigner who was walking with him.

"My poor wife has been at the typewriter for most of the night," said the man with the briefcase, a well-known writer. "You know, it is a crime for a private Czechoslovak to operate a copying machine. So we have to type everything and press our relatives and friends into service.

The writer is among a group of about 20 who run a two-year-old semiclandestine publishing venture known as "Padlocked Editions." The project, which will start its third year on March 21, may be compared to the Samizdat (self-published) underground literature in the Soviet Union.

The Czechoslovak enterprise provides an outlet for authors who are blacklisted by the Government and cannot have their works printed.

Copies Move From Hand to Hand

"I can't tell you what the circulation of Padlocked Editions is, honestly," said Ludvik Vaculik, a member of the publishing ring, in an interview. "Issues go from hand to hand, and many people in the chain make their own copies and circulate them among their friends."

Mr. Vaculik, who also signed Charter 77, a plea for broader human and civil freedoms in Czechoslovakia, had been a literary outlaw since July 1968, when he published a manifesto that became known as the "2,000 Words," urging a stepped-up liberalization drive. A month later Soviet and allied troops invaded Czechoslovakia.

Many of the writers and artists who endorsed "2,000 Words" in 1968 also signed Charter 77, which appeared at the beginning of this year. This circumstance apparently led the authorities to believe that Mr. Vaculik helped write the new document.

In the interview he would not discuss his role in Charter 77. He said that the police had questioned him for six to eight hours a day for an entire week last month, wanting to know above all how Charter 77 had been drafted.

"They clearly want to separate the organizers of Charter 77 from mere adherents," Mr. Vaculik remarks. "It seems just signing the manifesto is not considered an offense. But I didn't tell them anything."

The writer said he had written an account of his interrogations for Padlocked Editions. According to Mr. Vaculik, the typewritten literature is not exactly illegal, "but the system views it with extreme distaste."

Copy Confiscated at Border

Mr. Vaculik gave a copy of his account to this reporter for possible use on the Op-Ed page of The New York Times. The three-page article, titled "A Cup of Coffee With the Inquisitor," was among papers seized by the Czechoslovak police on Saturday during a prolonged inspection of the reporter's luggage at the Austrian border.

The article is apparently widely circulating in Prague these days. A student, a clerk in a state foreign trade agency, and a painter all told this correspondent independently that they had read a copy and passed it on.

To avoid trouble with the authorities, contributors cultivate an Aesopian and allusive style that leaves many things unsaid and relies on being read between the lines. In this respect, the underground literature continues a genre that goes back to Jan Neruda, a 19th-century essayist and poet, who had to be careful not to run afoul of the censorship of the Hapsburg monarchy, and to such writers as Eduard Bass and Karl Capek,

Mr. Vaculik said in the interview that in connection with his part in Padlocked Editions and in Charter 77 he was the subject of police blackmail. "The subject, not the victim, because I didn't cave in," he said, referring to photos showing him in the nude that foreign correspondents in Prague found in their mailboxes last month. The pictures were then published by some magazines in Czechoslovakia and by some pro-Soviet newspapers elsewhere.

Mr. Vaculik said the pictures were seized in his home during a police raid two years ago. Later he was warned that they would be made public if he continued criticizing the Government. The time evidently came when he refused to cooperate with the police in the recent interrogations.

"And nothing has happened," Mr. Vaculik remarked. "The people in my building keep saying hello, my friends stand by me, and people whom I hardly know tell me the police disgraced themselves by the illegal use of material that was illegally seized...."

THE VATICAN VERSUS THE COMMUNISTS

During August and September 1978, Polish and Czechoslovak opposition figures quietly met on the frontier between their respective countries to exchange ideas and share their experiences. Those convening clandestinely included representatives of Poland's KSS-KOR (Social Self-Defense Committee), comprised of activist intellectuals and Roman Catholic intelligentsia essential to the Solidarity union, and of Charter 77. After the gathering, the Roman Catholic Church in Czechoslovakia, known as the "underground" or "catacomb" church, began publicly expressing its concern for human rights (see **Poland, Introduction** and "Polish Labor Crisis Deepens"; see **Czechoslovakia, Introduction** and "Prague Detains Five Dissidents after Human Rights Manifesto").

A month later, on October 16, the Polish archbishop of Kraków, Karol Cardinal Wojtyla, was elected as pope and took the name John Paul II. He traveled to his native Poland in January 1979 as head of the Church of Rome and spiritual leader for 720 million Roman Catholics worldwide (see "Pope Gets Big Welcome in Poland"). The profoundly revitalizing regional impact of the first Slavic pope's message was revealed as, in early 1985, 30,000 Czechoslovaks signed a petition inviting him to visit them. František Cardinal Tomášek of Prague saw that the pope received the invitation, but the government led by Gustáv Husák denied John Paul permission to enter.

On March 11, 1985, Mikhail S. Gorbachev became general secretary of the communist party of the Soviet Union. Two years later, in March 1987, he visited Prague and raised hopes of reforms along the lines of *perestroika*, the concept of "restructuring" that he had described in a 1987 book, and *glasnost*, a policy of openness, which he believed was essential for reforming society and the communist party so that new economic policies could be effective. The Czechoslovak government remained inflexible, however.

Communist leaders in Prague were reluctant to make the changes suggested by Gorbachev because they were persuaded that repudiation of the past would represent invalidation of themselves. Put another way, accepting reforms would mean that they accepted responsibility for the country's economic chaos. At the street level, advantage was taken of the mood of reform emanating from the Soviet Union, although many worried whether Gorbachev would survive. In Prague and elsewhere in Eastern Europe, people seized upon divisions of opinion in Moscow as openings.

František Cardinal Tomášek had begun taking a more public role in the 1980s, as John Paul II offered moral and spiritual encouragement to all the countries of Eastern European nations to resist communism. Slovak Catholics in particular made much of his leadership. On June 23, John Paul II met with the Polish foreign minister in a session described by one Vatican official as "rather cool." The immediate cause of the Pope's interventions was the trial of incarcerated members of Poland's Solidarity union. Poland was at the time under martial law declared by General Wojciech Jaruzelski, communist party leader, prime minister, and chief of the armed forces (see "Poland Restricts Civil and Union Rights" and "Wojciech Jaruzelski").

Solidarity's mass social movement for free trade unions and political freedoms remained under martial law for seven years; by mid-1982 some 10,000 Solidarity members were subjected to a type of preventive detention, with more than 3,000 imprisoned for "political crimes." The activists about whom the pope was concerned had been charged with "calling for a strike" and had received sentences ranging from two to three and a half years. *Times* reporter E. J. Dionne, Jr., on June 23, 1985, describes John Paul as angered over their trial and declaring "what is regarded in Italy and some countries as a right is in other places considered and punished as a crime." Dionne explains that the Vatican's secretary of state would travel on behalf of the pope to Czechoslovakia and Yugoslavia the following month.

The Times reporter ponders the trip to Czechoslovakia by Agostino Cardinal Casaroli, the Vatican secretary of state, because among the Soviet satellites, church-state relations were at their lowest in Czechoslovakia. František Cardinal Tomášek of Prague had expressed concern for the worsening situation of the Roman Catholic Church and the party-state's intrusion on Catholics. Dionne explains the Czechoslovak authorities' agreement to the cardinal's visit as suggesting in Prague that the regime was not utterly rigid in its dealings with the church. He wonders whether the conclusion to receive Cardinal Casaroli as the pope's special representative might be a function of Czechoslovakia's building better ties with the Vatican.

JUNE 23, 1985
POPE AND POLISH AIDE HAVE 'COOL' TALK
By E. J. DIONNE JR.
Special to The New York Times

ROME, June 22 – Pope John Paul II met with the Polish Foreign Minister today in an atmosphere that one Vatican official described as "rather cool."

Officials said that the Polish-born Pope had expressed his concern over charges brought against Solidarity activists by the Polish Government and that John Paul effectively closed off the immediate possibility of improved relations between Poland's Communist Government and the Holy See.

At the same time, the Vatican announced that its Secretary of State would travel on behalf of the Pope to Czechoslovakia and Yugoslavia next month.

The Polish Foreign Minister, Stefan Olszowski, later issued a statement describing the talks as "frank and constructive" and said at a news conference that he did not believe the discussions had suffered from the trial of three dissidents in Gdansk. The dissidents were charged with calling for a strike and were given sentences ranging from two to three and a half years earlier this month.

John Paul had expressed his anger over the trial last weekend, saying that "what is regarded in Italy and some countries as a right is in other places considered and punished as a crime."

Meeting with Craxi Canceled

Mr. Olszowski had been scheduled to meet earlier this week with the Italian Prime Minister, Bettino Craxi. But Mr. Craxi canceled the meeting to protest the jailing of the Solidarity leaders.

The visit to Czechoslovakia by Agostino Cardinal Casaroli, the Vatican Secretary of State, is significant because church-state relations there are among the worst in Eastern Europe. Frantisek Cardinal Tomasek of Prague, 85 years old, said earlier this year that the situation of the Roman Catholic Church was growing steadily worse and that Catholics were being "hindered, pursued and controled."

The Pope had accepted Cardinal Tomasek's invitation to attend celebrations in Czechoslovakia for the 1,100th Anniversary of the death of St. Methodius. But the Czech authorities vetoed the Pope's visit.

St. Methodius and his brother St. Cyril brought Christianity to the Slavic countries and are especially revered by John Paul.

Reasons for Czech Move

Accepting Cardinal Casaroli's visit was seen here as an effort by the Czech authorities to avoid appearing entirely inflexible in their relations with the church.

Cardinal Casaroli will go to Croatia in western Yugoslavia on July 4–5 and then to Velehrad in Czechoslovakia's Moravia region on July 7.

The decision to receive Cardinal Casaroli as the Pope's special representative could be part of an effort by Czechoslovakia to improve ties with the Vatican. But a top Vatican official cautioned that the Holy See's relations with Eastern Europe are at a difficult stage and that any change would be part of "a long process."

The announcement of Cardinal Casaroli's trip and the Pope's meeting with the Polish Foreign Minister were part of a period of intense maneuvering in the Holy See's relations with the Soviet bloc.

Encyclical Is Planned

John Paul, the first Slavic Pontiff and a strong foe of the Communist authorities in his homeland, is planning to issue an encyclical next month expounding his views on Eastern Europe and on what he has referred to as the "artificial" division of Europe into blocs.

The encyclical will be in honor of Saints Cyril and Methodius, and Vatican officials have said the letter will express the Pope's concern about the persecution of Catholics in Communist countries.

An encyclical is one of the most important forms of papal communication and represents a way for a pope to underscore ideas and teachings that he regards as particularly important. John Paul, who has given hundreds of speeches and put forward a variety of special documents, has issued only three encyclicals in his six-and-a-half-year papacy.

Czechoslovaks Stir

On August 21, 1968, the Soviet-led invasion of 750,000 Warsaw Pact troops crushed Czechoslovakia's Prague Spring, a period of reform from within the communist party led by Alexander Dubček, first secretary of the party. Twenty years later, 10,000 Czechoslovaks marched to Wenceslas Square in Prague to commemorate the military occupation of their country in a demonstration organized by new groups called the Czech Children and the Independent Peace Initiative (Nezávislé Mírové Sdružení, or NMS). In two decades, a generation had grown up with less fear than their forebears; they turned out in large numbers to memorialize the humiliation of 1968. Hungarian law student activists from FIDESz (acronym for Fiatal Demokraták Szövetsége, Alliance of Democratic Youth) traveled to Prague and issued a statement of support (see "In Hungary, Flexibility as Doctrine"). Shortly thereafter, in October 1988, the regime announced that the seventieth anniversary of Czechoslovakian independence from the Hapsburgs would be nationally celebrated as a holiday. Thousands turned out on October 28.

Half a million Roman Catholics and others outside the Church of Rome signed a petition for religious rights and liberties, in the wake of encouragement from František Cardinal Tomášek of Prague, whose earlier concern for the worsening condition of Catholics had been noted by *The New York Times* on June 23, 1985. Cardinal Tomášek described Catholics as "hindered, pursued and controlled." From his pulpit in 1988, Tomášek urged Czechoslovaks to sign (see "Pope and Polish Aide Have 'Cool' Talk").

That same year, Czechoslovak proponents of democratic reforms, many of them active in Charter 77, held periodic meetings with their Polish counterparts in the mountains along their border. The Poles included Adam Michnik and Jacek Kuroń, activist intellectuals in KSS-KOR (Social Self-Defense Committee), comprised largely of university faculty and Roman Catholic laity. Michnik and Kuroń were also key advisers to the alliance of workers and intellectuals of Solidarność, the Solidarity union (see "Strikers in Poland Defy Gierek Appeal," "Adam Michnik," and "Jacek Kuroń").

By 1988, a Czechoslovak variation on the theme of *glasnost* permitted publication of some formerly banned authors, including, for example, Franz Kafka. In December, the party-state stopped jamming broadcasts of Radio Free Europe, as the Kremlin had done in the Soviet Union months earlier. The regime let Alexander Dubček, whose "socialism with a human face" had ushered in the Prague Spring, give interviews to Western media. As in Poland, Hungary, and East Germany, the internal relaxation resulting from actions and principles advocated by Soviet leader Mikhail S. Gorbachev stirred thinking on political liberalization in Czechoslovakia. In a 1987 book, Gorbachev had laid out his thinking on *perestroika* ("restructuring") and *glasnost* ("openness") in regard to society, the party, and economic reform (see "**Introduction: Strikes, Sinatra, and Nonviolent Revolution**").

In January 1989, several thousand persons commemorated the self-immolation of Jan Palach, a Charles University student who on January 16, 1969, had committed suicide in Prague's Wenceslas Square to protest Soviet interventionism (see **Czechoslovakia, Introduction**). The Czechoslovak people compared Palach to Jan Hus, a Protestant burned at the stake in 1415 whose martyrdom still resonates with the Czech people. Palach's taking of his own life in horrific protest sent a fervent message against the ongoing removal of reformers from the government and their replacement with reactionaries.

Shortly after the honoring of Palach, large demonstrations erupted. Miloš Jakeš, considered a hard-line communist, was called upon to replace Gustáv Husák as general secretary of the Czechoslovak communist party in an effort to subdue rising voices of dissent; Husák remained as president. Structural weaknesses in the Czechoslovak economy were becoming unmanageable. Mild attempts at economic decentralization had been made, but fell short of producing serious alterations, which might have lessened the party-state's control. Jakeš ignored calls from Gorbachev for reform. His maintenance of "normalization," with its coded meaning of Stalinist-style control, led to the spontaneous protests on January 16, 1989, the twentieth anniversary of Palach's death.

The street rallies and public protests lasted for another six days. The police responded harshly, using batons and gas. Václav Havel, a dramatist and actor who had been arrested for his role in Charter 77, was arrested again and sentenced to nine months in prison. His incarceration was tinder for still more demonstrations and brought international attention to Prague (see **Czechoslovakia Introduction**; "Prague Detains Five Dissidents after Human Rights Manifesto" and "Václav Havel and Truth").

As a result of the demonstrations, the parliament enacted legislation to increase the penalties for disturbing the peace. Petitions protesting police brutality began to circulate, signed not only by artists, writers, and others in the growing community of opposition to the regime, but by official figures as well. The ranks of the communist apparatus were starting to split. The neo-Stalinist sympathizers in Prague were increasingly isolated from their communist counterparts in other Eastern bloc countries. They were also indignant at Gorbachev, whose principles and precedents were unsettling to them. Hungary had opened the iron curtain on May 2, 1989, and tens of thousands of East Germans were fleeing through it, moving westward (see "In Hungary, the Political Changes Are Tempered by Economic Fears" and "500,000 in East Berlin Rally for Change").

Concurrent with the volatile political atmosphere within party circles, the Czechoslovak economy continued to sink; state industries that had begun to decline were starting to fail. Although the government sought to maintain its policy of subsidizing enterprises, citizens increasingly recognized the diminishing advantages of the communist regime. Pressing for adjustments and reforms from within the party-state's political and economic infrastructure, a new communist revisionist group, Obroda (Rebirth, or Revival, also called the Club for Socialist Restructuring), materialized in February 1989. It comprised officials who had been active communist reformers during the Prague Spring (see **Czechoslovakia, Introduction**). Notwithstanding their communist loyalties, they strongly supported Gorbachev's liberalism and endorsed perestroika and glasnost. Obroda was soon leading calls for reform. Its members articulated their positions, disseminated their ideas, and argued their viewpoints through the journal *Dialog 89*.

In June 1989, a document appeared under the unassuming title "A Few Sentences." It reaffirmed the sentiments of "Two Thousand Words," a manifesto that had appeared in July 1968, just before the Soviet-led invasion, asking for accelerated efforts to rid the government of its Stalinist attributes. *The Times* on February 15, 1977, had identified the publisher of "Two Thousand Words Which Belong to Workers, Farmers, Officials, Artists and to Everyone," its full title, as Ludwík Vaculík, who had been publishing semi-clandestine typewritten materials since 1972 with Václav Havel and who was part of the substantial flow of *samizdat* (Russian for "self-published") (see "Czech Underground Literature Circulating from Hand to Hand"). These ideas conveyed in the underground publications were central to the chronicle of the democratic transitions in late 1980s Eastern Europe.

"A Few Sentences" became a statement calling for democratization. It was initially signed by official, state-supported artists and unofficial oppositional authors and artists. Of significance, in just a few months, more than 40,000 citizens had signed it. Havel and twenty-two of the original signers on September 15, 1989, sent a letter to Prime Minister Ladislav Adamec requesting talks between the regime and the opposition on reforming and liberalizing Czechoslovak politics. The landscape of the Czechoslovak opposition now ranged from Obroda, with its communist reformers, to Charter 77, with its avowedly nonpolitical and nonorganizational stance calling for adherence to the human rights clauses of the Helsinki Final Act (see **"Introduction: Strikes, Sinatra, and Nonviolent Revolution"**), to smaller opposition, student, literary, and theatrical groups.

The influence of the expanding and diverse array of Czechoslovak civil society organizations increased as news spread through samizdat about the changes taking place throughout the Soviet bloc. Tensions flared as such groups realized that one way or another, such reforms had gone astray in Czechoslovakia. On August 11, the party-state authorities rejected any exchange with emergent groups advocating democratic transformation and dismissed them as "illegal structures." *The Times* notes, on October 29, 1989, that on August 21, the twenty-first anniversary of the crushing of the Prague Spring, the police had arrested more than 350 people taking part in a commemorative demonstration on Wenceslas Square. Those detained included citizens of other Eastern European states.

By late August, as government authorities persisted in rejecting the clamor for change, 30 percent of Czechoslovakian industries were on the brink of collapse. Communist managers in some failing industries were recommending that sites be shuttered. The government was no longer able economically to meet its end of the bargain in which the cooperation, silence, and acceptance of the people would be swapped for governmentally subsidized necessities. The various fledgling civil society groups taking public stands were, in retrospect, developing into a movement, but not yet in a distinct sense. Those who had signed "A Few Sentences" were soon joined by writers and journalists in boycotting Czechoslovakian television in a show of noncooperation to protest the persecution of the document's signers.

On October 28, 1989, the anniversary of the founding of the Czechoslovak Republic, the boulevards and streets of Prague were filled with citizens demonstrating for human rights and democracy. In addition to citing political goals, thousands also protested the environmental degradation caused by the dumping of industrial waste into rivers and streams, air pollution, unregulated ecological destruction, and policies that mismanaged natural resources. Approximately 350 were arrested at the informal Independence Day commemoration, with another hundred detained for protesting Czechoslovakia's destruction of its environment. In the October 29 *Times*, correspondent John Tagliabue—who also reported from East Germany on the mounting popular mobilization protected by the Protestant churches there—writes of the regional upsurge tangible by autumn 1989 and the hopes it stimulated in Czechoslovakia.

OCTOBER 29, 1989
POLICE IN PRAGUE MOVE TO BREAK UP BIG PROTEST MARCH

10,000 Gather at Square
Eastern Bloc Upheaval Raises Czech Hope for Reform—'We Want Democracy!'
By JOHN TAGLIABUE
Special to The New York Times

PRAGUE, Oct. 28 – Czechoslovakia's hard-line Government used heavily armed policemen today in an effort to crush protests by thousands of Czechoslovaks who marched in the capital calling for freedom and an end to Communism.

Despite warnings by the Communist authorities, about 10,000 Czechoslovaks gathered in Wenceslas Square, long the focal point of both joy and protest in the capital, singing and chanting "Freedom!" and "We want democracy!"

The confrontation here today came almost a month after large-scale demonstrations in neighboring East Germany that have led to changes in the leadership there. The German protests raised the hopes of many Czechoslovaks that the leadership here might also be changed. The East German leader, Erich Honecker, was replaced by Egon Krenz on Oct. 18.

Wide Basis of New Hope

Hopes have also been raised by the political liberalization taking place in Hungary, Poland and the Soviet Union.

The leadership in Prague has found itself increasingly isolated as political turmoil grips most of the Soviet bloc, including East Germany, until recently Czechoslovakia's closest ally in an informal grouping resisting change.

Invoking a Czech saying, a young demonstrator today described Milos Jakes, the Communist Party leader here, as being "as alone as a slat in a fence." "The slat must go," he added. On Friday, the police rounded up some of the country's major dissidents, including Vaclav Havel, Czechoslovakia's most prominent writer and a founder of the Charter 77 human rights movement, in an effort to pre-empt today's demonstrations.

Riot Police Charge Crowds

After refusing to heed warnings to disperse issued over loudspeakers, the protesters today faced an attack by streams of riot police officers in white helmets, who charged the crowds with clubs. At the same time, young men in casual dress who were obviously working with the uniformed police seized demonstrators, beating them and dragging them into waiting buses.

Within about 10 minutes the police had cleared the square, an immense pedestrian mall. But groups of hundreds of demonstrators gathered along side streets and in front of hotels that line the square, which is the city's most prominent shopping district.

One crowd of demonstrators, cornered by rows of riot policemen in front of the Grand Hotel, challenged the officers for more than half an hour, chanting "We want no violence!" and shouting to the young troopers, "Boys, come with us!"

They sang hymns, including the Czechoslovak national anthem and other patriotic songs.

Through most of the early evening, the city resembled an armed camp, as crowds of hundreds of demonstrators roamed through the streets, while large numbers of policemen pursued them, seeking to keep them from the main squares.

Combat at a Famous Bridge

At the Charles Bridge, an imposing yet graceful edifice of soot-black stone lined with the statues of saints, hundreds of young demonstrators were trapped by two bands of riot policemen at either end. Together with their confederates in civilian clothes, the uniformed officers charged and beat the trapped demonstrators with clubs.

At least 250 people were detained, the state television reported. It was not clear how many demonstrators were injured, but some were beaten unconscious, and the sirens of ambulances racing through the city sounded into the night.

Crowds of thousands of demonstrators marched through the narrow lanes of the city's old quarter toward the hospital where Mr. Havel was being kept under close guard. They chanted "Free Havel!" and appealed to people in surrounding buildings to join them with shouts of "Czechs, Come With Us."

To the masses of policemen who blocked their path at every turn, the demonstrators shouted, "Gestapo!" and, "The World Is Watching!"

There were also shouts of "Dialogue!" and "Free Elections!"

Centerpiece of Resistance

The demonstrations began on one end of Wenceslas Square, at the foot of the equestrian statue of the sainted King who is the patron of Czech lands. Demonstrators unfurled banners reading "The Truth Will Prevail" and "We Will Not Allow The Disruption of the Republic." The last is a frequent slogan of the Communists, and appears to have been unfurled on red cloth to mock the Government.

The demonstrations came in response to urgings by human rights leaders that the Czechoslovaks turn out on the day their republic was founded in 1918 from the rubble of the Austro-Hungarian Empire.

This morning, the Communist rulers had their hour. Several hundred recruits for the army, the Communist militia and the border guards were sworn in at a ceremony in the square, to which only people with special-entrance tickets were admitted.

Tonight, most of the city center was secured by troops of the People's Militia, recruited from Communist cells in the factories. Czechoslovak observers said they believe the Government had enough policemen to deal with such demonstrations but used the militia symbolically to underscore their readiness to defend Communism with arms.

By late this evening, the cobblestoned square, and the imposing buildings surrounding it, made up a ghostly sight that seemed to reflect the sullen spirit of the nation. It lay deserted under evening mists that shrouded softly glowing street lamps.

The leaders of Poland and Hungary, with the approval of the Communist parties there, have condemned their countries' roles in the 1968 Warsaw Pact invasion of Czechoslovakia, a drive mounted to prevent changes far less sweeping than those now transforming the East bloc.

In August, on the 21st anniversary of the invasion that crushed the Prague Spring of renewal under Alexander Dubcek, the police arrested 376 people, including many from other Soviet bloc countries, when they gathered on Wenceslas Square for a commemorative demonstration.

Authorities Have Been Adamant

The Government's attitude until now has been to refuse to talk with opposition and human rights groups, insisting that any measures leading to political or economic change must be orchestrated solely by the leadership.

Unrest is coming particularly from the small parties, the People's Party and the Socialist Party, which have long been satellites of the Communists. This month, at a meeting of more than 70 People's Party members, a movement called Living Stream was established within the party to work for faster change.

But the Government was perhaps left most vulnerable by the decision this week by Czechoslovakia's most prominent musical conductor, Vaclav Neumann, director of the Czechoslovak Philharmonic Orchestra, not to play on the state radio or television as a way of protesting the blacklisting of actors and other artists who have been demanding political change.

The decision by the 69-year-old Mr. Neumann was later supported by the orchestra members in a vote in which 90 musicians voted in favor, 3 abstained and only 1 was opposed.

Ten Days of Revolution

Throughout 1989, Czechoslovaks learned by word of mouth and underground publications about communist regimes making portentous alterations elsewhere in Eastern European Soviet satellites. That summer, contacts between the pro-democracy activist intellectuals of Poland and Hungary became more overt. Czechoslovak security services could no longer prevent Polish and Hungarian opposition leaders from visiting their Czechoslovak counterparts. In September, Hungary's parliament issued an ex post facto condemnation of the 1968 invasion of Czechoslovakia by the Warsaw Pact militaries.

In early November, Czechoslovaks, particularly in institutions of higher learning and theatrical circles, learned that hundreds of thousands of protesters had formed a nonviolent human chain across East Germany and that on November 4 more than a million demonstrators had packed East Berlin. On November 5, *The New York Times* reports an agreement between East Germany and Czechoslovakia—but announced by West German officials—to allow East Germans merely to show an internal identity document to cross Czechoslovakia into West Germany (see "500,000 in East Berlin Rally for Change").

Czechoslovakia was geographically situated between East Germany and Hungary, and East Germans soon arrived at the Czechoslovak–West German border. Meanwhile, thousands of East Germans were bunked in the so-called Prague Embassy in West Berlin when the Czechoslovak government relented and allowed them to travel across Czechoslovakia by train to West Germany without prerequisites (also see "Hungary Allows 7,000 East Germans to Emigrate West"). Czechoslovaks were attentive to the trains transporting East Germans to the West and other developments. On November 6, Hungarian television aired an interview with the Czech dramatist Václav Havel in which he aligned himself with the popular causes sweeping Eastern Europe. The Czechoslovak regime immediately denounced the broadcast.

Many Czechoslovaks would have learned through underground publications or Radio Free Europe that the East German government had resigned on November 7 and that elections were in the offing. In a headline of November 8, 1989, *The Times* succinctly tells the story in a few words: "East Germany's Cabinet Resigns, Bowing to Protest and Mass Flight." On November 9, the Berlin Wall fell (see "East Germany Opens Frontier to the West for Migration or Travel"). Such dramatic events, along with others unfolding concurrently, heightened domestic pressure on the Prague regime.

When the journalist-historian Timothy Garton Ash arrived in Prague in November 1989, he remarked to Havel that Poland's struggle of ten years, Hungary's ten months of upheaval, and East Germany's ten weeks of massive demonstrations might in Czechoslovakia take only ten days. The first stage of the Czechoslovaks' Velvet Revolution took place between November 18 and November 27, 1989. Events on November 17 provided the catalyst.

On November 16, in conjunction with International Students Day and to commemorate Jan Opletal—a Czech student killed half a century earlier in an uprising against the Nazis during World War II—some students organized a demonstration in Bratislava, in what is now Slovakia, without incident. A local municipal council had rejected another student request for permission to march the following day, a Friday, in Prague to condemn the wartime Nazi occupation and its resulting bloodshed. The Prague students decided to proceed regardless, and on November 17, considered Day One of the Ten Days, a peaceful student rally turned into a demonstration that some would later call a massacre.

Journalists said tens of thousands attended the rally; the government news agency downplayed the crowd's size to 15,000. The students marched to Opletal's grave at Vysehrad Cemetery, chanting anticommunist, antigovernment slogans and singing the Czech rendition of "We Shall Overcome," the signature anthem of the U.S. civil rights movement. Banners read "Democracy, Freedom, and Free Elections," "Democracy for All," and "We Don't Want Violence." The action could have concluded at the graveside, but a group of students called out "To Wenceslas Square." The march turned toward the city's center. In what had become the country's largest demonstration since the Prague Spring, approximately 50,000 were marching (Flint et al. 1990, 102).

By some accounts, agents provocateurs led the students up Narodni Street toward a wall of white-helmeted riot police and special forces in red berets who cornered them and began beating them with heavy truncheons. Two students at Charles University, Pavlina Rousova and Otto Urban, recounted: "We sat down and sang hymns, the national anthem, even old Beatles hits. We chanted: 'We have no weapons.' The only things we had with us were candles and some flowers, which we gave to the police. They used loud-hailers to shout 'Go home,' but they had blocked our path" (Flint et al. 1990, 103). Other demonstrators called out, "We are unarmed," and "No violence."

Another squadron of riot police had encircled the students from behind. Those who had gone to Wenceslas Square were trapped. They sat down on cobblestones and began singing songs. At approximately 9:10 P.M. a police car drove into the throng, as riot police lunged, clubbing students as they dispersed. Wax that had fallen from candles made the ground treacherously slippery. Martin Polach, an art student, later said, "You could literally hear the bones cracking" (Flint et al. 1990, 103).

Paula Butturini, a Warsaw-based correspondent for the *Chicago Tribune*, was beaten and required fifteen stitches on the head, her newspaper reported. Edward Lucas, a journalist for *The Independent* (London), was knocked to the ground, unconscious. An *Atlanta Journal and Constitution* photographer, Michael Schwarz, told the Associated Press that he had gone with the crowd trying to march to Wenceslas Square, but was beaten on the head by police. He reported glimpsing many bleeding faces, and seeing twelve ambulances taking people to hospitals and at least three busloads escorted away by police.

Government television said the march participants had "misused the mass gathering for anti-socialist performances" and that those who went to the square had "attempted to violate public order"; the standard justification for police intervention had long been the "attempted violation of public order." While the regime acted as if everything were normal and called again for "normalization," the code for a return to Stalinist practices, the young, unarmed demonstrators beaten on November 17 and onlookers bonded in outrage. From the standpoint of history, it may have been fortuitous that what the students called "the massacre" happened on a Friday, which gave them the weekend to remobilize. That same night of "Bloody Friday," from Prague's theater district, actors consulted by phone with their counterparts in other cities. The authorities' brutality would be met with boycotts and strikes.

Overnight, students determined to strike. By Day Two, Saturday, November 18, they had spread word throughout Prague's Charles University and other institutions of higher learning. Students originally called for strikes. By Saturday afternoon, some 500 actors, playwrights, stage directors, and theater managers, among them communist party members, met in Prague's Realistic Theatre. They demanded an impartial investigation into the police brutality and announced a week-long strike to protest the violence. They also proposed a national general strike for November 27. Prague's theaters were ideal for robust political engagement and discussion. Instead of offering performances, the actors would lead audiences in deliberations of the situation. Signs reading "We Strike" or "On Strike" immediately appeared in theaters across the country, making an emotional impression, because of the esteem in which the arts were held. Theaters in Bratislava, Brno, and Ostrava went on strike the next day. Wherever there were actors and dramatists, they joined the noncooperation action.

The students straight away endorsed the proposed general strike. The timing would give them a week and a day to mobilize popular adherence. Indeed, the students would for six weeks stay on strike; they were expansively supported with comparable noncooperation methods by theatrical actors and dramatists. During the weekend, tens of thousands of young people and students milled about Wenceslas Square, boosting flags and posters. Their rallying cries included "Freedom" and "Resign," directed at the communist party leader, Miloš Jakeš, and "Jakeš to the shovel." The students' slogans also, fetchingly, read, "Now's the Time" and "This Is It."

Students in Prague began meeting intensively with actors at the Realistic Theatre. The actors released a pamphlet entitled "Don't wait—act!" Academicians and theater people joined with growing numbers of students to demand a boycott and call for a general strike on November 27, a week away. With Prague's Magic Lantern Theater serving as headquarters, within twenty-four hours commitments were on hand across the republic for strikes, including students at the Academy of Performing Arts.

The students issued releases announcing their strikes; the theatrical managers and actors distributed theirs. Radio Free Europe broadcast texts, received by telephone. The official media, having previously deferentially toed the government line, started to condemn the authorities' violence of November 17. Employees at television stations asserted themselves against slanted coverage, protesting that the news reports were not truthful. Broadcasters displayed the first photographic images of the Prague demonstrations. Showing these scenes proved to be crucial, because they enabled thousands in remote areas to see what was actually occurring in their own country.

On Day Three, Sunday, November 19, the Civic Forum (Občanské Fórum) was established in Prague. It resulted from a late-night theatrical gathering of approximately 400 persons organized by Václav Havel, who brought together the principal opposition groups, including Obroda (Rebirth, or Revival), consisting of communists seeking reforms (see "Police in Prague Move to Break Up Big Protest March"). The Magic Lantern became the Civic Forum's nerve center, partly because of its proximity to Wenceslas Square. Its wardrobes and changing rooms were allocated to committees. Envisaged as a citizens' group to promote democracy, the Civic Forum would act "as a spokesman on behalf of that part of the Czechoslovak public which [was] increasingly critical of the existing Czechoslovak leadership and which [had] been profoundly shaken by the brutal massacre of peacefully demonstrating students" (Garton Ash 1990, 82).

Havel was the author and final arbiter for the Civic Forum's statements and positions. Throughout the Velvet Revolution, the forum would act as the speaker for the Czechoslovak people, while coordinating the collective nonviolent actions of the broad opposition. Among its earliest demands were the resignations of Miloš Jakeš, party general secretary, and Gustáv Husák, who had become president. The forum was comprised of a far-reaching spectrum of opposition organizations—student groups, artistic, drama, and literary circles, and various socialist political entities interested in reform; it emerged in public view simultaneously with a large demonstration in Prague on November 19, as 200,000 gathered to protest the police brutality of November 17. So revolted had observers of the police attacks become that even the cautious or reluctant among them now joined the resistance. Even the official news agency and state television were reporting the crowd of 200,000, signifying cracks in the mask of the regime. Over the following three days, throngs occupied Prague. Fearfulness dissipated, as thousands streamed into Wenceslas Square. Videotapes of the events were circulating in Slovakia, in Bratislava, Brno, and other cities.

Although R. W. "Johnny" Apple, Jr., had been in Prague reporting for *The Times* on November 17, it appears that no *Times* correspondent was based in Prague and reporting on the events of Days One, Two, and Three (see **Czechoslovakia, Introduction**). By year's end, however, the paper would have more than one correspondent in Prague. On Monday, November 20, Day Four, John Tagliabue began a series of dispatches.

On November 20, Public Against Violence (Verejnost' proti Nasiliu, or VPN) emerged in Bratislava, Slovakia, as a partner for the Civic Forum comprising Slovak authors, playwrights, artists, and actors. This was Day Four, and it saw the entire country's student population go on strike, along with students in Prague's institutions of higher learning and the city's theatrical personnel, actors, and staff who were already on strike. They publicized their demands through a computerized network.

While the Prague demonstrations drew 200,000, smaller numbers were marching in Bratislava, Brno, Liberec, and elsewhere. In Teplice, northwest of Prague, where 8,000 turned out to condemn the air pollution in the North Bohemian coal-producing area, demonstrators castigated the district government, shouting, "No one trusts you anymore."

The crowd moved upward when the space on the ground was filled, perching on tree boughs, hanging off scaffolding, dancing atop telephone coin boxes. Banners were pointed: "It's the end, Miloš," referring to party leader Jakeš, and "Jakeš in the bin." The throngs started ringing bells and jangling key rings, giving a magical quality to the mounting resistance.

Meanwhile, students by the handful began to mobilize the entire country, visiting factories and villages to spread the word. The effect of small teams of amiable students speaking words that had never been publicly voiced was potent. It was only amplified when joined by recognized actors and theater personalities. That night, hundreds of thousands crammed into Wenceslas Square chanting, "This is it!" and "Now is the time!" In seventy-two hours, the Czechoslovak communist colossus would start to crumble.

Tuesday, November 21, marked Day Five. The Civic Forum held official meetings with Prime Minister Ladislav Adamec, who guaranteed that no violence would be used against Czechoslovak citizens. Student representatives also met with Adamec. Although the government report said "socialism was not up for discussion," no one missed the significance of the encounter. The regime was emitting contradictory signals. In Wenceslas Square in Prague and in Hviedoslav Square in Bratislava, mass demonstrations again took place. The crowds ratified calls for a general strike on November 27 and demanded the release of a political prisoner, Ján Čarnogurskỳ. František Cardinal Tomášek, the Roman Catholic primate, declared his support for the mounting student demonstrations and issued a statement criticizing the government. Bells were ringing. One journalist said 200,000 sets of key rings were jangling. The crowds chanted "Today Prague, tomorrow the whole country!" and "Time's up!" According to *The Times*, striking students closed down some schools in the university, as banners announced sit-in strikes at institutions of higher learning throughout Prague.

Václav Havel addressed the multitude, this time as the luminary and exemplar of the Civic Forum. As the Reverend Vacláv Malý, an admired banned priest, spoke to the crowd, everyone could hear, because rock groups had lent huge loudspeakers. A message from Cardinal Tomášek was read, calling for democracy and declaring, "We cannot wait any more." The cardinal's text pointedly mentioned that Czechoslovakia was surrounded by countries that "had broken the back of totalitarianism," referring to Poland, Hungary, and East Germany. Havel's speech was blunt and less courtly than usual. He repeated the Civic Forum's demands: resignation of the leaders, including Gustáv Husák and Miloš Jakeš, who had laid the groundwork for the 1968 Warsaw Pact invasion; resignation of the interior minister, František Kincl, and the Prague first secretary, Miroslav Štěpán, who were considered responsible for the carnage of November 17; creation of a commission to investigate police actions; and the immediate release of prisoners of conscience. Havel pledged a national general strike for the following week, on November 27. Thunderous applause resounded.

The Times account notes official state media reports of related marches in at least three other cities: Ostrava; the Slovak capital, Bratislava; and Brno, site of the second-largest demonstration, in which several thousand marched. In Brno, Havel spoke to 50,000 enlisted by the Public Against Violence. In a nationally televised address, Jakeš, the party general secretary, responded by declaring that order must be preserved, as "socialism" was the only option for Czechoslovakia. The implacability of the party-state in the face of ascending popular defiance lay partly in the enormity of the purges after 1968. Jakeš had personally been responsible for ruining the careers of 800,000 people after the Prague Spring, many of them talented intellectuals and artists, and he had purged half a million from the communist party rolls. Hence communists who had been optimistic about reforming the party were long gone from its deliberations.

On Wednesday, November 22, Day Six, following nonstop meetings at the Magic Lantern Theater, the Civic Forum formally announced a two-hour general strike for Monday, November 27. The first live broadcasts from the Wenceslas Square demonstrations appeared on federal television, but were quickly cut off, when a participant denounced the regime in favor of Alexander Dubček, who had guided the 1968 Prague Spring before the reform movement was crushed by the Soviet-led military invasion (see **Czechoslovakia, Introduction**). Demonstrations continued, as students circled round the statue of King Wenceslas in the square named for him. Workers and laborers began adding their backing to the growing mobilization.

NOVEMBER 21, 1989
200,000 MARCH IN PRAGUE AS CALLS FOR CHANGE MOUNT
Largest Protest in Two Decades
Officials Resist Pressure—East German Visit Put Off
By JOHN TAGLIABUE
Special to The New York Times

PRAGUE, Nov. 20 – More than 200,000 marchers called today for freedom and a change in government in the largest and most vociferous public demonstration since the euphoric Prague Spring that preceded the 1968 Soviet-led invasion of Czechoslovakia.

At the same time, party and Government officials pointedly reaffirmed their opposition to introducing political change in the face of the protests.

Nonetheless, they at least tacitly acknowledged a changed political climate by postponing an official visit here by Egon Krenz, the new East German leader, which was to have begun Tuesday. Prague's official press agency said that on the "basis of a mutual agreement," Czechoslovakia and East Germany had decided to call off the visit indefinitely.

Mostly Young People

The demonstrators, most of them young people, gathered initially at Wenceslas Square, the half-mile-long pedestrian plaza sloping down from the National Museum. The square has repeatedly been the forum for expressions of Czechoslovak nationalism. And today, the crowd waved flags and chanted anti-Government slogans.

As the group, which included striking university and high school students, set out to cross the Vltava River on the way to Hradcany Castle, which houses the President's office, their shouts became bolder. Cries demanding "freedom" and "free elections" mingled with calls for a general strike and chants of "Jakes out!," a reference to the country's orthodox Communist Party General Secretary, Milos Jakes.

Marchers Are Sent Back

The gigantic crowd moved slowly through the narrow, curving streets of the baroque city. But as the marchers headed onto several bridges, they were confronted by large numbers of heavily armed police officers. The protesters reversed course and dispersed soon after they returned to the north shore, avoiding the kind of violence with which club-wielding policemen scattered a smaller group of demonstrators on Friday night.

The march through Prague was reminiscent of the mass protests in 1967 that swept out Antonin Novotny, then the hard-line Communist leader, replacing him with the reform-minded Alexander Dubcek.

Demonstrations over the last six months have mustered several tens of thousands, and on some occasions, no more than a few hundred people responded to calls for a candlelit vigil. In general, the Czechs and the Slovaks appeared to be moving more cautiously and more hesitantly than their Polish, German and Hungarian neighbors in challenging Communist rule.

Though the tremendous size of the crowds—which seeped through crooked squares and broad shopping streets, and then snaked along the open stretches of the river shore—made it difficult to determine how many people marched, the official radio estimated that more than 200,000 Czechoslovaks had taken to the streets.

National television, which reported extensively on the demonstration, also gave news of similar marches in at least three other cities—the northern center of heavy industry, Ostrava; the Slovak capital, Bratislava, and Brno, the site of the second-largest protest, with several thousand marchers.

In Prague, schools of the university were closed by striking students, and banners declar[ed] sit-in strikes at institutes of higher learning throughout the city.

Dissident leaders repeated a call for a two-hour general strike on Nov. 27. Vaclav Havel, the playwright and leading Czechoslovak dissident, reported that he had received a message from coal miners at a small pit in northern Bohemia, who expressed support for the requested stoppage. But the extent to which industrial workers might join the swelling protest remained both critical and, as yet, unanswered.

Essential Question of Unity

Western diplomats and Czechoslovak dissident leaders believe that if workers were to join in with students and intellectuals, it would spell the almost certain collapse of the Government.

At various sites throughout the city tonight, groups of young people, students and workers could be seen milling around columns of police vehicles, in animated discussion with the young officers. Apparently, the security authorities had given orders for the police to use restraint today. But that decision did not appear to signal any lessening of the leadership's will to resist political change.

Mr. Jakes, in a statement that rang with a sense of warning, accused the protest-march organizers of "seeking to create chaos and anarchy."

Such efforts, he said, would "seriously endanger the implementation of necessary changes and bring socialism into crisis, with unforeseeable consequences."

Even more striking than the statement by Mr. Jakes, a widely acknowledged hard-liner, was another by the Cabinet today that endorsed the measures taken by the Communist Party leadership to put down protest last Friday. Many demonstrators were injured in that action.

The Cabinet said it approved of "measures whose purpose is to renew order, protect property and protect the lives of the citizens."

Its remarks were notable because Ladislav Adamec, the 62-year-old Prime Minister, has emerged in recent weeks as the principal rival to Mr. Jakes. He has adopted a relatively moderate stance in his apparent maneuvering to succeed the party leader.

An example of the Communist Party's declining authority came . . . when the leader of the hitherto satellite Socialist Party, Jan Skoda, broke ranks and turned up along with Mr. Havel and other dissidents at the founding assembly of a new political group, the Civil Forum.

That gathering, held in a Prague theater, heard another leading dissident, the Rev. Vaclav Maly, a Roman Catholic priest banned by the state from performing his priestly duties, read a declaration calling for the removal of hard-liners like Mr. Jakes and threatening a general strike.

Earlier today, Mr. Havel announced that he had refused a Government offer of a passport to travel to Sweden and accept an award there "because the situation at home is becoming dramatic."

• •

Protesters Call for Communist Leaders to Step Down

Thursday, November 23, 1989, was Day Seven of the Czechoslovaks' Velvet Revolution. When journalist-historian Timothy Garton Ash arrived in Prague that month, he commented to Václav Havel, the playwright who would play a crucial role in the democratic transition of Czechoslovakia, "In Poland it took ten years; in Hungary ten months; in East Germany, ten weeks; perhaps in Czechoslovakia, it will take ten days!"

In Prague by mid-November, the Democratic Initiative—formed in 1975 around the time of Czechoslovakia's signing of the Helsinki Final Act—declared itself the first independent political party established since 1948. Citizens with no record of taking public roles were participating in the demonstrations igniting Prague and sweeping the nation. On November 19, the Civic Forum (Občanské Fórum) had been formed, a broad-based citizens' pro-democracy group, with Havel as its leader. Throughout the Ten Days, the Civic Forum would stand in for the Czechoslovak people and coordinate their nationwide collective nonviolent action.

In Bratislava, now in the Slovak Republic, Civic Forum's partner, Public Against Violence (Verejnost' proti Nasiliu, or VPN), spread word that a peaceful revolution was under way. Representatives from the Forum and VPN visited factories and workplaces in towns across the nation and appeared at schools to present their viewpoints and urge listeners to express nonviolently their dissatisfaction with the government. Strike committees were forming to prepare for an upcoming two-hour general strike formally announced on November 22 by the Forum.

Making his first public appearance in twenty years on November 23, Alexander Dubček, first secretary of the Czechoslovak communist party who had led the Prague Spring season of hope and reform in 1968, appeared at a rally in Bratislava, his first speech since 1969. Known for the slogan "socialism with a human face," he had been forced by government officials to work in obscurity in a state forestry service for two decades (see **Czechoslovakia, Introduction**). Now he re-emerged to speak to 2,000 who were protesting the trial of a human rights advocate. Evening news broadcasts showed factory workers booing the Prague city party chief, Miroslav Štěpán. When Štěpán tried to incite the laborers against the students, who were seeking their support for the upcoming general strike, he stated, "We do not intend to be dictated to by children." Enraged workers shouted back, "We are not children." The Ministry of Defense that day announced that the Czechoslovak military forces would not be deployed against Czech and Slovak peoples.

KEY PLAYER IN CZECHOSLOVAKIA
Alexander Dubček (1921–1992)

Shortly before Alexander Dubček's birth, his parents were living in Chicago, Illinois. His father's refusal, as a pacifist, to serve in the U.S. military led the family to return to Czechoslovakia, so Alexander was born in the town of Uhrovec in 1912. When he was three years old, the family moved to the Soviet Union because of a scarcity of jobs in Czechoslovakia and aspirations to build socialism. Alexander received his early education in Kirgiziya (Kyrgyzstan) in Soviet Central Asia, where his father, Stefan Dubček, a member of the Czechoslovak communist party, had settled the family.

The family returned to Czechoslovakia in 1938. Dubček trained as a locksmith and at age 18 joined the then-outlawed communist party. He became part of the underground resistance to the German occupation during World War II. He was wounded twice, and his brother was killed. After the war, Dubček worked in a yeast factory and became more involved in politics, rising through the ranks of the communist party and becoming a party secretary in Trencin in 1949. In 1951, he became a member of the Central Committee of the Slovak communist party in Bratislava, where he was studying law at Komensky University, and a member of the National Assembly, the parliament. He rose to chief secretary of the regional committee in Bratislava in 1958 and subsequently became a member of the communist central committees of the Slovak and the Czechoslovak parties.

The party sent Dubček to Moscow Political College, from which he was graduated, with honors, in 1958. In 1962, he became a member of the Czechoslovak party Presidium and a year later succeeded the Stalinist Karol Balicek as first secretary of the Slovak communist party. In 1964, he became chairman of the Slovak communist party.

When a recession hit, the Czechoslovaks grew more restless. Antonin Novotný, first secretary of the party, made some liberalizing concessions, but they were slow to take effect, and in 1968 the party called for his removal. Dubček took his place in January 1968 by a unanimous vote of the Central Committee of the communist party, in part because of his moderate political views.

Upon becoming first secretary, Dubček began rigorously implementing a series of liberal reforms and expressed the need for democratization. He worked to increase free speech, relaxing restraints on writers and censorship of news media. Dubček's reforms were groundbreaking, but at the same time he stressed that Czechoslovakia would not be leaving the Warsaw Pact. Despite these assurances, Moscow thought the reforms too radical and threatening. Warsaw Pact members discussed the "Dubček problem" in July 1968 at a meeting without Czechoslovak representation.

In August 1968, after Dubček's refusal to return to party policies, forces from Bulgaria, East Germany, Hungary, Poland, and the Soviet Union invaded Czechoslovakia. The troops were met with civil resistance. Some students and workers when confronted by Soviet troops offered flowers and pleas for them to go home. During the occupation, many small villages named themselves "Dubček" in a show of solidarity with the country's leader. Street names were changed to confuse the occupying forces. Hundreds of Czechoslovaks were wounded and many killed.

During the invasion, the Czechoslovak communist party secretly elected a Central Committee and Presidium, filled its ranks with allies of Dubček, and re-elected him as first secretary of the party. The Kremlin forced Dubček to resign on April 17, 1969. The Prague Spring of hope ended as Dubček

(Continued)

(Continued)

and party reformers were handcuffed and flown to Moscow. There, they signed the Moscow Protocols, accepting the Warsaw Pact incursion and occupation. Their reforms were annulled, and communist hard-liners assumed positions of leadership. In January 1970, Dubček was appointed ambassador to Turkey. After being expelled from the party, he was recalled and relegated to a low post in the forestry administration, based in Bratislava, where he remained until 1987.

In 1989, Dubček was returned to public life at the behest of Václav Havel and the Civic Forum, which were piloting the Velvet Revolution. Born in what is now Slovakia, Dubček appeared at a rally in Bratislava, the Slovak capital, to lend his support to Havel, whose family roots were in Bohemia, in what is now the Czech Republic, thereby symbolically linking both peoples in the struggle. On November 24 (Day Eight), as Dubček stepped onto the balcony to speak to the throngs in Prague's Wenceslas Square, the crowds roared, "Dubček-Havel!" the leading figures of 1968 and 1989. After the communist party-state yielded to the demands of the Civic Forum, Dubček was elected Speaker of the Federal Assembly and received the Sakharov Peace Prize. In 1990, he published *The Soviet Invasion* and later penned his autobiography, *Hope Dies Last*. Dubček succumbed in 1992 to injuries sustained in an automobile accident.

In fact, the first talks between the Czechoslovak prime minister, Ladislav Adamec, and representatives of the Civic Forum were taking place by Day Seven. The delegation did not include Havel, who told Timothy Garton Ash that the prime minister had sent word that he did not want yet to "play his trump card," referring to Havel. Instead, Havel was communicating with the premier through mediators who called themselves "the bridge": Michal Horáček, a reporter for a youth newspaper, and Michael Kocáb, a rock star (Garton Ash 1990, 84).

Workers in factories began speaking out against the communist party. Representatives from 500 plants announced that they agreed with the demands of the Civic Forum and would strike. Soccer players from the national team told reporters, "We support the students. . . . We have signed the declaration against violence."

The potency of the Czechoslovak insurrection was undeniable, as the numbers demonstrating on November 23 rose to more than one-third of a million. In Prague's Wenceslas Square, speakers bade the country's hard-line communist chiefs to step down. A roll call of factories joining the opposition was read, including large engineering enterprises, defense groups, and steel works. *The New York Times* of November 23, 1989, notes that Dubček drew the loudest response when he personally called for resignations. For the first time, Czechoslovaks were able to watch the event, at least partially, broadcast live from Wenceslas Square on state television.

Václav Havel, his voice hoarse, implored the throngs not to use violence and appealed to the soldiers to break ranks from their commanding officers. He pledged, "No matter what happens in the next few days, we are positive that Monday's general strike will be crucial for the lonesome group of Stalinists who want to hold onto power" (Flint et al. 1990, 119). This was a signal that the opposition would reject a modest reshuffling of officials; the whole lot had to go. The Civic Forum issued a statement outlining renewed commitment to a Czechoslovak tradition: "We are against violence and do not seek revenge."

Havel especially recognized contributions from younger generations: "Our gratitude goes to the students for giving this revolution a beautifully peaceful, dignified, gentle and I would say loving face, which is admired by the whole world. This was a rebellion of truth against lies, of purities against impurities, of the human heart against violence." A 25-year-old teacher cheered, "Gandhi would have been proud of us" (Simmons 1991, 187). *The Times* on November 23 confirms this spirit on Day Seven. It was important on that day for the growing opposition movement to show that it not only had numbers but could lead the crowds in carefully planned actions. The crowds obliged with disciplined noncooperation. One man gave a high-wire display of anticommunist fervor: he hung, spider-like, above the throngs and did not fall. The stage was being set for the removal of Miloš Jakeš as communist party general secretary.

The question of whether hard-pressed laborers could afford to strike still loomed. Some 60 percent of Czechoslovakia's working population was comprised of blue-collar industrial laborers, and no one knew if they would identify with the actors, artists, activist intellectuals, university students, and theatrical communities of the capital city who were leading the mobilization. Yet, chronicling shifting support from major sectors of Czechoslovak society, *Times* correspondent John Tagliabue reports that it had become evident that portions of the work force were drifting away from the party-state toward support for the student-led opposition. Tagliabue questions whether employees of semiconductor plants near Prague and at the huge Tesla electronic works were among those publicly endorsing the strike call. He notes that laborers in the northern Bohemian coal fields and the steel works of Ostrava, or Kladno, seemed hesitant. Such smokestack enterprises might be endangered were major political or economic changes to occur, resulting in a loss of subsidies.

NOVEMBER 23, 1989
250,000 CZECHS, HAILING DUBCEK, URGE OUSTER OF HARD-LINE LEADERS
By JOHN TAGLIABUE
Special to The New York Times

PRAGUE, Nov. 22 – More than 250,000 Czechoslovaks who gathered in Wenceslas Square for a sixth consecutive day of protest shouted "Resign! Resign!" today when speakers called for the country's hard-line Communist leaders to step down.

The loudest cheers came when the urging was made in the name of Alexander Dubcek, the reformist leader who was forced from power after Soviet tanks invaded Czechoslovakia 21 years ago. Mr. Dubcek emerged today from the obscurity to which he had been officially consigned to ask that President Gustav Husak and Milos Jakes, the party leader, give up their posts.

First Address in 2 Decades

Mr. Dubcek also spoke in public today for the first time since his efforts to introduce "Socialism with a human face" were crushed in 1968. In Bratislava, he addressed 2,000 people protesting the trial of a human-rights advocate, urging calm. Mr. Dubcek, who has been officially ignored while working in a state forestry office for much of the last two decades, was shown on state television tonight as he met protesters. Mr. Dubcek's message, read to the crowd in Prague, noted that he hoped to visit the capital soon and to appear in person at Wenceslas Square. When this was announced, the crowd began chanting, "Dubcek, Dubcek."

The pressure generated by the huge rallies on the capital's central square appeared to have forced the ruling Communists to move up to this Friday a crucial Central Committee meeting originally planned for December. There were growing indications that major leadership changes might come at the meeting.

A Possible Replacement

Tonight, the party's ruling Presidium met, as it has every evening since the recent wave of protest marches began last Friday, amid recurring reports that the stage might be set for the removal of Mr. Jakes and his replacement by a more liberal politician, possibly the Prime Minister, Ladislav Adamec.

As the party leaders planned their meetings and the demonstrators shouted and chanted in glee, the struggle between the intellectuals and students in the street and the party stalwarts was increasingly becoming a contest for the hearts and minds of Czechoslovakian industrial workers.

The people in the street, mostly intellectuals, students and artists, have sought to have the workers join in a two-hour general strike set for next Monday. The Communist leadership is seeking to avert or minimize the walkout at all costs.

At today's rally, Vaclav Havel, the playwright and dissident, told cheering crowds that he sought to reach "especially all the workers in our country who are for reform."

As cheers of "Long live the workers" echoed through the floodlit square, Mr. Havel continued, "Those who have been taking bloody vengeance against all their rivals for so many years are now afraid of us."

"But we are not like them," he said, from a balcony high above the square. "We don't want to take vengeance on anyone. We only ask to take control of our country."

A Mission Among the Workers

Students in Prague who have been striking since Monday, demanding free elections and a change in government, sent hundreds of their numbers into the countryside to visit industrial plants in an effort to enlist support for the general strike.

And for the first time, parts of the work force appeared to be tilting away from the Communist Party and toward the student-led opposition movement.

Mostly the reports of support came from white-collar workers in industries that would most easily survive a major overhaul of the economy.

Workers at semiconductor plants near the capital and at plants of the giant Tesla electronic works were listed prominently among those backing the strike call.

By contrast, workers in the northern Bohemian coal fields, and steel works in places like Ostrava, in the north, or Kladno, near the capital, appeared to hesitate.

Many of these smokestack industries might be threatened with curtailment or even closing down if major political and economic changes were undertaken and subsidies were trimmed.

A delegation of several carloads of workers from Kladno who came to Prague for the demonstration was led, typically, by workers from the industrial city's plant for electronic measurement instruments.

Several steel workers from the big Poldi steel foundries who lingered on the square after the demonstration said they had succeeded in gathering several hundred signatures on a petition in support of the strike, and expected many more.

But they acknowledged that many workers were troubled by a possible drop in living standards if strikes become the rule in Czechoslovakia. Bearing a banner that said, "Kladno Is With You," they recounted how the steel mill's director had stressed this argument in an address to the workers over the internal public-address system, warning them that strikes and destabilization would produce "Polish conditions."

The Government's Warning

The Government argues that Poland's moribund economy has dissuaded workers from labor action.

Not all the workers bought that argument.

"Two hours of strike can hardly do as much damage as the last 40 years," said one Kladno worker, bundled against the bitter cold in a tan parka.

To counter the Communist argument, the opposition leaders in the newly founded Civic Forum movement availed themselves of official economic experts whose loyalty they have gained.

In recent days, the staff of the prestigious National Forecasting Institute, a leading economic research group that has been in the forefront of criticism of Government economic policy, has thrown its weight to the opposition.

Vaclav Klaus, a senior economist at the institute, said a large number of "foremost Czech economists" would seek to form a program "for the day after" that would attempt to transform Czechoslovakia's economy "without economic chaos, without inflation and without the disintegration of basic economic structures."

But dire warnings of economic disintegration were hardly the only means the Communist Government was using to persuade workers not to join a strike.

Reporters who traveled to the CKD machinery works, near Prague, found that busloads of the Communist militia had secured the plant and were preventing students from approaching the workers or distributing leaflets.

Changes in Party Leadership Foreseen

The second stage of the Czechoslovak Velvet Revolution was reached as the government agreed to talk with the Civic Forum—a broad, citizens' pro-democracy group established on November 19, 1989, as a representative of the opposition calling for democracy. It was led by the dramatist Václav Havel. In a sense he was the playwright for the unfolding drama. The forum also coordinated the nationwide collective nonviolent actions of the growing opposition movement (see "200,000 March in Prague as Calls for Change Mount" and "Václav Havel and Truth").

November 24, a Friday, was Day Eight of the Ten Days of the Velvet Revolution. On this day, as many as 350,000 gathered in Prague's Wenceslas Square to cheer Alexander Dubček and Havel. A previously banned singer sang "The Times, They Are A-Changin'." Dubček had been communist party secretary in 1968 when the Soviet-led invasion of 750,000 Warsaw Pact troops militarily occupied Czechoslovakia and was subsequently forced into obscurity by the communist regime (see **Czechoslovakia, Introduction**). Crowds chanted "Dubček-Havel!" By now, security services and police forces were routinely surrounding the rallies and marches, but nevertheless allowing them to proceed. Reproaching the security forces, Dubček called, "Don't be traitors to your people" (Flint et al. 1990, 119). At the close of the rally, the 350,000 demonstrators took out their key chains and shook them in unison, filling the square with the sound of jangling keys.

Milos Jakeš, the communist party secretary who came to power in December 1987, had pledged Czechoslovakia's confidence in *přestavba*, Czech for *perestroika* (Russian for restructuring), a principle being articulated by Soviet general secretary Mikhail S. Gorbachev. Little if anything, however, was ever restructured. As the number of protest actions and participants continued to grow daily, demands for Jakeš to resign topped the list of formal demands. On November 24, *The Times* reports correspondent John Tagliabue as having spoken with an old hand in the communist party who implied that Jakeš's departure had been sealed when he met in Prague with the Soviet ambassador, Viktor P. Lomakin. According to *The Times,* diplomats and officials in Prague believed that Gorbachev wanted a resolution to the strained situation in Czechoslovakia before an upcoming meeting with U.S. president George H. W. Bush and that Jakeš had failed to comprehend how his persistent hard-line control worked against Soviet interests. Tagliabue learned from sources close to the party that basic decisions had already been made, and the party leadership had determined not to use force against the "mounting wave of demonstrations." The party's goal had shifted to retaining the appearance of having the advantage despite calls by the Civic Forum for a two-hour national general strike. Tagliabue states that the party-state had already forfeited jurisdiction of many of the country's daily newspapers.

NOVEMBER 24, 1989
PRAGUE RIVALS VIE FOR FAVOR ON EVE OF PARTY MEETING

Leadership Shifts Seen
Police Secure a TV Center—Ally of Communists Calls for Profound Changes
By JOHN TAGLIABUE
Special to The New York Times

PRAGUE, Nov. 23 – On the eve of a pivotal Central Committee meeting that is expected to make major changes in Czechoslovakia's Communist Party leadership, factions inside and outside the party appeared today to be openly jockeying for support from the nation's security forces.

The police were called in to secure the central television station in Prague today, and other security units were bused into the capital, . . . only to be turned around.

It appeared possible that the hard-line leadership might be seeking to secure a major means of communication on the eve of the party meeting after having lost control of many of the nation's daily newspapers.

Ouster of Hard-Liners Sought

But despite the police presence, the evening news . . . broadcast scenes of workers at a meeting with Miroslav Stepan, a member of the ruling Presidium, demanding the ouster of the hard-line leadership.

"No doubt evaluations will be discussed, though we've had enough evaluations," Mr. Stepan, one of eight orthodox leaders whose resignation has been demanded by the new Civic Forum opposition group, said of the party meeting. "But a concrete course of action for the near future will also be discussed. There will also be concrete personnel changes."

His listeners, workers at the big CKD machinery works near the capital, responded with chants of "Resign! Resign!"

Demonstrators were also enthusiastic in Bratislava, where some 70,000 people heard Alexander Dubcek, the Communist Party chief ousted in the Soviet-led crackdown in 1968, as he threw his support today to the anti-Government movement.

Havel Addresses Throng

In Wenceslas Square in central Prague, more than 250,000 people gathered for the seventh straight day of huge anti-Government rallies. Reflecting the skittishness among opposition leaders, Vaclav Havel, the playwright and dissident, appealed to the police and army to side with the popular movement in a crisis.

"We are against violence," Mr. Havel said. "We want to live as peaceful and dignified people who do not think only of themselves, but also consider the fate of generations to come."

Describing Czechoslovakia as lying at a "historic crossroads," he accused the Communists of leading the nation to the brink of "spiritual, moral, political and economic catastrophe."

"We want to live in a free, democratic and prospering Czechoslovakia, returned to Europe, and we will never give up this ideal," he told the throng, which cheered wildly and waved Czechoslovak flags.

The director of state television, Libor Batrla, acknowledged tonight that he had requested that the police guard the station's doors. He also said he had sought the advice of Matej Lucan, a Deputy Prime Minister who is considered a hard-liner, on running the station in tense times.

At a news conference organized by Civic Forum, a young woman who identified herself only as a television employee said members of the civilian militia, considered solidly aligned with the hard-liners, had joined police officers in occupying "all technical points" of the broadcasting center.

The . . . meeting of the Central Committee, a kind of party parliament, was called suddenly this week under intense pressure from the huge turnouts at the daily anti-Government demonstrations in Prague.

In a profound sign of crumbling Communist authority, the head of the Socialist Party, Jan Skoda, long a loyal Communist ally, told the crowds, "It is our view that things here have gone so far that we need profound changes, including those of personnel."

The remarks, which were greeted with thunderous shouts of "Too late! Too late!" appeared to be a call for the removal of the orthodox leadership around the Communist Party chief, Milos Jakes.

Meeting With Soviet Envoy

An experienced Communist Party official said the stage may have been set for Mr. Jakes's departure on Wednesday, when the party leader met here with the Soviet Ambassador, Viktor P. Lomakin.

Nothing was officially disclosed about the meeting, which was not attended by aides to the two men.

But the Communist official, assessing what he believed to be the thrust of the encounter, said: "The message was clear and simple, but not very concrete: Make the changes and listen to the streets."

The politician, speaking on condition that he not be identified, said he believed that Mr. Jakes would come "under attack from all sides" at the Central Committee meeting, and that a successor would be expected to produce a program of changes....

Gorbachev's Desires Cited

Many diplomats and officials believe that the Soviet President, Mikhail S. Gorbachev, wants a resolution to the tense situation in Czechoslovakia before he meets with President [George H. W.] Bush next week, but that Mr. Jakes has failed to recognize that his continued hard-line control runs against Soviet interests.

"It is beyond his capacity," a party adviser said of Mr. Jakes, "to understand that the Soviets are ready to sacrifice Communists to get Western technology and assistance, to create little Finlands in this part of the world."

Officials familiar with the workings of the party said they believed that the fundamental decisions were made . . . at one of the recent daily meetings of the party's Presidium, when the leadership resolved that force could not be used to stop the mounting wave of demonstrations.

The goal of the Communists has been to maintain a semblance of initiative in the face of calls by the opposition around Civic Forum for a two-hour general strike.... The planned strike is emerging as a kind of referendum on Communist rule.

Today, there were major demonstrations in at least five cities besides Prague, including Ostrava, the coal and steel center; Bratislava, the capital of Slovakia, and Kosice, also in Slovakia, all calling for the Communists to go.

Militia Is Sent Back

. . . [A]ccording to reports in Communist-controlled newspapers, several units of the civilian militia, a corps of armed factory workers loyal to the Communists, were bused to Prague from cities in southern and western Bohemia, but were sent back to their towns later in the day, after the Presidium decided against the use of force.

In several factories, the civilian militia appeared and tore down posters put up by supporters of the general strike.

But the view of those who prevailed in the party leadership appears to be that only by announcing dramatic changes at the conclusion of the Central Committee meeting—such as the replacement of Mr. Jakes and a program of accelerated political change—can the party prevent a landslide defeat if workers support the general strike in large numbers.

That appeared more and more likely as reports poured in from around the country of large industrial enterprises willing to support the strike. At the demonstration in Wenceslas Square here, the Rev. Vaclav Maly, a Catholic priest who is the spokesman for Civic Forum, said workers at more than 500 enterprises had agreed to strike.

The man considered most likely to succeed Mr. Jakes if he is ousted is Ladislav Adamec, the Prime Minister.

Security Boss Praises Premier

Recently, the 62-year-old Mr. Adamec has begun to challenge the formula repeatedly stated by Mr. Jakes, that major economic changes must be undertaken first, and that political adjustments could wait.

In what was believed by some to be a harbinger of political change, a senior Central Committee official responsible for security, Rudolf Hegenbart, was quoted as praising Mr. Adamec's stewardship as Prime Minister.

Appealing for a "profound spiritual and moral restoration" of the party, Mr. Hegenbart used terms reflecting the openness endorsed by Mr. Gorbachev but rejected up to now by the Prague leadership.

"Part of that," Mr. Hegenbart said of the party's restoration, "is harmony between deeds and acts, to learn to call things by their right names, to learn to tell the truth eye to eye, to stand behind your word and to honor the opinions of others, to give up demagogy and simplified and primitive interpretations of a complicated reality with all its interconnections."

6,000 Strike Committees Ready a Nationwide General Strike

The Civic Forum stood at the helm of preparations for a general strike on November 27, 1989. A citizens' pro-democracy group established on November 19 and led by the dramatist Václav Havel, the forum's organizational members included virtually the entire Czechoslovak opposition to the communist regime (see "200,000 March in Prague as Calls for Change Mount" and "Václav Havel and Truth"). The forum acted as the representative for the Czechoslovak public, coordinated the collective nonviolent action of the opposition, and had become a national force. Conducting itself in a practical, ethical, and purposely open, if slightly chaotic, way, the Civic Forum usually met at the Magic Lantern Theater in Prague, whose dressing rooms had been allocated for specific committees to meet. It called its program "What We Want" and focused on civil and human rights, an independent judiciary, multiparty electoral democracy and political pluralism, economic and free-market reforms, and changes in the nation's environmental and foreign policies.

On November 24, Alexander Dubček met with the Civic Forum. Later, as Dubček and Havel gave a news conference in the Magic Lantern Theater, they learned that Milos Jakeš and the entire Politburo had resigned. The regime's readiness to change personnel and policies did not go much further, however, as Karel Urbánek, considered another hard-line communist, became the new general secretary. The forum and its component groups viewed these concessions as unsatisfactory. The nationwide demonstrations widened. Even Czechoslovak sportsmen and sportswomen joined the boycotts and strikes in a time-tested nonviolent sanction: refusal to participate in competitions.

On Saturday, November 25, Day Nine, the Civic Forum declared the upcoming national general strike a "referendum" on communist rule. In Prague, antigovernment demonstrations attracted 800,000 persons, and in Bratislava 100,000 marched. In a nationally televised address, Havel announced that the planned November 27 national general strike would proceed.

Also on November 25, Agnes Přemyslid, a patron saint of Bohemia, was canonized. Pilgrims trekked across the nation to a Prague ceremony, where František Cardinal Tomášek, who had been persecuted during the 1950s, celebrated a commemoration mass at St. Vitus Cathedral (see **Czechoslovakia, Introduction**). Thousands more watched the televised event, broadcast live. After the observance, 750,000 persons gathered in a park on Prague's Letná Plain. Havel cited the popular slogan, "The time is at hand!" The crowd roared back as one, "It is here!" Challenged by the enormity of the assemblage, Urbánek announced publicly that the government was ready for talks. In response, a few reactionaries in the communist party resigned from their positions.

In a striking moment, on Sunday, November 26, Day Ten, three riot policemen wearing uniforms appeared at a demonstration to beg forgiveness for themselves and their colleagues, confessing that they had clubbed unarmed students on November 17 during the violent episode that launched the Ten Days. At Prague's city hall, government delegates led by Prime Minister Ladislav Adamec met formally for the first time with the Civic Forum, including Havel. The main agreement was for further talks. As half a million Czechoslovaks assembled on Letná Plain, Adamec assured the forum that the communist party's monopoly would be abolished, and he would present a compromise to the people no later than December 3. The editorial staff of Slovakia's *Pravda*, the central newspaper of the communist party of Slovakia, joined the opposition.

A human chain formed, similar to one assembled in East Germany just days earlier (see "East Germany Opens Frontier to the West for Migration or Travel"). Hands interlocked, the chain stretched from the Letná Plain to Prague Castle, the seat of the presidency. As individuals physically linked arms, they whispered to each other that they wanted to make sure that promises were not broken.

A general strike followed ten extraordinary days—November 17 to 26—in which hundreds of thousands of young and old Czechoslovaks had participated in ever-growing daily demonstrations and rallies in the baroque capital city of Prague. Approximately 6,000 strike committees were now working to prepare for the strike, a widespread cessation of labor that seeks to bring all economic activity to a total standstill. As noon approached on November 27, a Monday, Czechoslovakia stopped working to the ringing of church bells. Just before noon, a television anchor declared that he would join the strike and go off the air. Taxi drivers positioned themselves to block Prague's ring road with a two-mile string of cabs. This exquisitely implemented national noncooperation action lasted from noon until two o'clock—that is, during lunch, so as not to jeopardize jobs.

The mammoth industrial strike manifested no divisions between Czechoslovak groups and classes, and no breaches occurred between the workers and the intellectuals, students, and artists orchestrating the movement. Steven Greenhouse, reporting for *The New York Times* on November 27, quotes Petr Muller, a labor leader from a large industrial complex: "The strike is intended as a demonstration of political will. . . . It is not designed to bring political pressure by hurting the economy" ("Prague Premier Sees Top Foes"). In a rally at Wenceslas Square, Václav Klaus, an economist concerned about the country's future free market, and the Civic Forum called for the government's resignation (see "Spirit of 1968 Is Still Alive, Still Distinct"). Having been active in the forum, he stated that the forum "considers its basic objective to be the definitive opening of our society for the development of political pluralism and achieving free elections" (Garton Ash 1990, 107).

Town squares across the country bulged as strikers gathered; students from Prague had traveled beforehand to villages and hamlets bringing news of the national democratic upheaval. As students teamed with citizens from a hodgepodge of backgrounds in remote neighborhoods, the protesters were transformed into a solid mass movement capable of altering the future of Czechoslovakia. As the Czechoslovak people held to their commitment to nonviolent means, peaceful crowds bearing nothing but candles and flowers were sometimes met by battalions of police wielding truncheons. Greenhouse on November 27 reports on a human chain of thousands extending from Wenceslas Square to Hradcany Castle in Prague. He also observes that if the general strike succeeds, it "will be read as the workers' vote of no confidence in the leadership of a self-proclaimed workers' state" ("Prague Premier Sees Top Foes").

An estimated 80 percent of the Czechoslovak labor force participated in the strike. Ringing bells, jangling keys, honking horns, and blaring sirens, in addition to issuing political demands, they celebrated their ability to unite. Public libraries served as resources for disseminating anticommunist literature. On the day of the strike, the Ministry of Culture released books and films that the authorities had long banned for political reasons. Realizing that they were wielding the power to transform their country, crowds chanted, "Truth Shall Prevail." Increasingly assertive because of the immense show of popular strength represented by the strike, the Civic Forum and its Slovak partner, Public Against Violence (Verejnost' proti Nasiliu, or VPN), now asked for full political pluralism and representation in a new government.

The Civic Forum halted the daily demonstrations as it geared up for its second round of discussions with the regime, Serge Schmemann reports on November 28 in *The Times,* while also judging that the strike was the first general strike in the country since laborers had enacted similar economic noncooperation on August 23, 1968, in protest of the Soviet repression against the Prague Spring (see **Czechoslovakia, Introduction**).

The Civic Forum unabashedly took the helm of talks with the party-state leadership, while Public Against Violence did the same with Slovak leaders. Formal negotiations began over management for various agencies with the government, led by Prime Minister Ladislav Adamec. The regime set up a commission to investigate the provocative November 17 police violence against demonstrating unarmed students (see "200,000 March in Prague as Calls for Change Mount"). Adamec offered to discuss with Soviet authorities the withdrawal of their troops from Czechoslovakian territory. Greenhouse reports Adamec as promising to present to the central committee the list of demands proffered to him earlier in the day by a nine-member Civic Forum delegation.

Within 72 hours of the general strike and start of talks between the government and the Civic Forum, the party-state accepted a new government with a communist prime minister but a non-communist majority. The entire leadership resigned. The next day, the party expelled its general secretary, Miloš Jakeš. On November 27, the Prague city communist chief, Miroslav Štěpán, was dumped. Štěpán was one of eight whose ouster had been demanded by the forum, according to *The Times* of November 24 (see "Prague Rivals Vie for Favor on Eve of Party Meeting").

NOVEMBER 28, 1989
'REPLAY' IN PRAGUE: POPULAR UPRISING ECHOES THE EXPERIENCE OF NEIGHBORS
By SERGE SCHMEMANN
Special to The New York Times

PRAGUE, Nov. 27 – It seemed at times almost a replay of East Berlin, only a month later and a bit faster.

The marching masses in the streets demanding democracy, the Communists belatedly showing remorse and desperately jettisoning old leaders, New Forum reappearing as Civic Forum, press organizations suddenly abloom with candor and everyone around declaring in wonder, "This could not have happened a month ago."

The parallels are not entirely chance. As the death knell of Communism spread from state to state, each revolution seemed to learn and gather strength from the last. And in the end, what seems most remarkable is how brittle the East European Communists have proved to be once stripped of Moscow's muscle.

Once it was clear that the Soviet President, Mikhail S. Gorbachev, had no intention of propping up his erstwhile allies, it was only a matter of time before the Poles had installed Solidarity in power, the Hungarians had proclaimed a republic, the East Germans had punctured their wall and even the Bulgarians had ousted their longtime Communist chief.

With so much precedent to draw on, it took the Czechs a scant week of demonstrations to throw Milos Jakes out of power and to have the party in retreat. Now after

11 days of demonstrations, it seems difficult to find anyone in Prague who had not been for reform for a long time.

When Czechoslovakia's new Communist Party leader, Karel Urbanek, took to television and factories over the weekend to intone, "We were far from the people, we made many mistakes" and to pledge renewal, it seemed more pathetic than bold.

It is too early to tell whether, or at least how quickly, the Czech or East German Communist Parties will go the way of their comrades in Poland and Hungary. But the unavoidable image is of Mr. Urbanek's falling glumly in step behind Egon Krenz of East Germany, Reszo Nyers of Hungary and Mieczyslaw Rakowski of Poland—the others tapped at the eleventh hour to salvage their parties—in what The Financial Times called "doing the Gorbachev": desperately admitting error, promising renewal, pledging reforms, opening dialogues and, inexorably, surrendering their "leading role."

In each state, disparate social groups seemed to unite in common hatred for the Soviet-installed Communists, and each had at least one moment of defiance enshrined in underground history—the East German uprising in 1953, the Hungarian uprising in 1956, the "Prague Spring" of 1968 and the suppression of Solidarity in Poland in 1981.

And in each state, once the Communist leadership was put on the defensive, it seemed to fall to pieces. The facades quickly crumbled, leaving behind [a] chain of ravaged economies.

There are differences, too, and these are certain to become more pronounced as each newly loosened East European state shapes its separate destiny and confronts the economic ravages of 40 years of Communism.

Most important among these is that the Czechs marching through Wenceslas Square with their forest of red-white-and-blue Czech flags have no wall to breach, no wealthy cousins with whom to contemplate reunification.

If the chance for "free elections" in East Germany means a referendum that stands to change the alignment of Europe, Czechoslovakia—like Poland, Hungary or Bulgaria—stands to change only the governing system, not the national or geographic composition.

'From Below' vs. 'From Above'

There are more immediate differences, too. East Germany's "revolution from below" remains largely a spontaneous movement, with opposition groups like New Forum lacking nationally accepted leaders and even a headquarters.

In Prague, by contrast, Civic Forum seemed swiftly to gather real authority from its basement headquarters in the Lanterna Magica Theater. And while the two Forums share a predominance of artists and intellectuals among their founders, Civic Forum in Prague could rally behind recognized leaders such as Alexander Dubcek, the party leader during the 1968 Prague Spring; Vaclav Havel, the dissident playwright, and Walter Kamarek, the head of the Prognostics Institute, who has been touted as a potential Prime Minister.

After demonstrating its power by calling a two-hour nationwide strike today, Civic Forum called a halt to daily demonstrations and prepared for its second round of talks with the Communist authorities. The strike was the first general strike in Czechoslovakia since workers put down their tools on Aug. 23, 1968, to protest the Soviet suppression of the Prague Spring.

This time, however, the show of strength seemed to dash the Communists' last hope, that workers could somehow be prevailed upon not to join a rebellion led initially by students and intellectuals. Instead, wave after wave of workers marched under banners identifying their state-owned enterprise, chanting, "We're with you."

It seemed only yesterday that Czechoslovakia ranked at the forefront of the neo-Stalinist "rejection front," and now it seems entirely plausible that Mr. Jakes could be replaced by his two nemeses, Mr. Dubcek and Mr. Havel.

But it is a season when the incredible has become routine, when dissidents lead governments and acts that meant prison are a common privilege. East Germans pour daily through the Berlin Wall, and West German Chancellor Helmut Kohl is about to set out a blueprint for a form of confederation. . . .

"Moral Reparations Would Be Enough"

The general strike of November 27, 1989, had paralyzed the country for two hours, as such a strike is intended to do, yet without harming the economy, since it occurred between noon and two o'clock. Within one week, it had forced the regime to agree to the formation of a coalition government, free elections, and more open travel westward. (On November 5, an agreement between East Germany and Czechoslovakia was announced by West German officials, allowing an East German simply to show an internal identity document to cross Czechoslovakia to West Germany.)

As Czechoslovaks extolled their Velvet Revolution, discussions with opposition representatives were broadcast on official television. Since November 29, the Civic Forum had enjoyed guarantees of airtime on Czechoslovak radio, the result of huge numbers of participants in public rallies. The Civic Forum, a citizens' pro-democracy group established on November 19, had incorporated virtually the entire spectrum of Czechoslovak opposition to the regime, with Václav Havel as its leader (see "200,000 March in Prague as Calls for Change Mount"). Also on November 29, the constitutional article that designated a monopoly for the communist party was formally rescinded by the parliamentary Federal Assembly. Ending the constitutional guarantee of the party's "leading role" had been an uppermost priority for the students at the heart of the Ten Days of demonstrations held November 17 to 26. The speaker of the assembly resigned. Prime Minister Ladislav Adamec, as a result of negotiations with the Civic Forum, promised to put together a new coalition government by December 3.

On November 30, the Presidium of the Slovak government resigned. The Adamec regime declared that the barbed wire barriers at the country's borders should be removed, and Czechoslovak citizens no longer needed exit visas in order to emigrate. In *The Times* of November 30, 1989, correspondent Henry Kamm reports concerns of some Czechoslovaks about a possible military coup, which might reverse the advances that had been made. Kamm reports that although the chances of such an event were remote, leaders of the Civic Forum took the concerns seriously enough to meet with members of the military.

Kamm, in the same article, offers readers a sense of the character of the Velvet Revolution, as he contemplates the "enduring lack of vindictiveness" shown by victims of communist vengeance after the 1968 invasion, as tens of thousands of academicians, artists, writers, and professionals were forced out of their jobs and into manual labor far from their professional training. Leaders of the Civic Forum were asked at news conference if they would seek reinstatement for such opposition figures, who had for two decades toiled in the menial jobs to which they were consigned. The spokesperson, Jiří Dienstbier, responded with the magnanimity that characterized the Velvet Revolution, saying that this would be hard to do after such passage of time; instead, "moral reparations" would be satisfaction enough. Dienstbier, a leading broadcaster covering foreign affairs until the 1968 Soviet-led Warsaw Pact invasion, had often been arrested for his struggle for human and civic rights for Czechoslovakians. For years after being dismissed from his post, he stoked a factory furnace, except for four years in prison, during which time he shared a cell with Havel. "What is going on is sufficiently satisfactory for all of us," Kamm quotes him as saying. Dienstbier was referring to the marches, rallies, and processions of hundreds of thousands—the "reawakening," as Kamm puts it—that had resulted in democratic governance.

NOVEMBER 30, 1989
SPIRIT OF 1968 IS STILL ALIVE, STILL DISTINCT

By HENRY KAMM
Special to The New York Times

PRAGUE, Nov. 29 – "You remember the spirit of 1968," said a science writer who left her country that year for exile in West Germany. She came back last weekend for three days, bringing her young daughter, so that she, too, could see "our second revolution."

"The same spirit is here today," she continued. "The aims are so high. This is what I saw written on a subway wall, among all the political satire." She spoke as if reciting a poem, her eyes glistening: "We have already learned to fly like the birds and to swim like the fish. Isn't it time we learned to live like humans?"

Now as in 1968, when people in Prague talk about the drastic changes they have set in motion, they speak less in the political terms used in Poland, in Hungary and to a lesser extent in East Germany, and more in the language of truth and beauty, or in words that might describe a work of art.

"We're living our youth once again," said a journalist, her voice barely able to contain her joy. She was, indeed, a young reporter recording her nation's awakening in 1968.

To many of her generation, the events of the last few days represent the liberating light of the Prague Spring without the ominous shadow of the threat of Soviet military intervention.

After liberalization grew in the mid-1960's, the Soviet shadow began to hang darker over the nation's joy in January 1968, even though tentative steps toward freedom under new Communist leaders met surprisingly little resistance. The shadow of intervention kept the steps from becoming long strides in the spring and early summer, and became a crushing reality in August, when the tanks of the Warsaw Pact nations rolled in.

The fear of invasion gave a desperately intense quality to the elation of 1968. And still—one could not tell how—it remained light-hearted and self-mocking rather than sentimental or vindictive. It brought about a sense of mutual affection among a not visibly warm-hearted people, which seemed based on a sense that to be a Czech or a Slovak at that time was to share a common joy.

A Special Bond

As in 1968, today's striving appears to be free of the heightened nationalism and xenophobia that have been both a motive force and a consequence of national liberation movements in this region.

A reporter who witnessed both cheerful revolutions recognizes, even on arrival on a cold and dark night, that this special bond among the usually undemonstrative people has once again been forged. Strangers wave to each other, exchange V-for-victory signs and laugh together at the many witty slogans pasted to walls and shop windows.

They gather again at the Wenceslas Monument at the head of the long, broad pedestrian mall that is strangely called a square, and cheer impromptu speakers or light candles of celebration. But being a realistic people, they also remember that after the invasion they lighted candles at the same place in mourning.

Czechoslovaks who remember the fine months of 1968—and to most who lived then, those months seemed to grow in beauty as the years passed—are quick to remark that today, when the pace of freedom's progress is much faster than in 1968, hardly anyone even mentions the Soviet Union.

The Threat This Time

"For the time being, at least," a skeptic remarked. He said the place of the Soviet threat is taken today by rumors of a possible military coup. Remote as that chance is believed to be, it is taken seriously enough by leaders of the Civic Forum for them to have arranged an informal meeting with the military and to issue a statement of warm greeting to the soldiers tonight.

Several Czechoslovaks also noted, with slight bitterness usually softened by apologetic smiles, that since this revolution is an internal affair, they run scant risk of being again disappointed by their supposed friends.

No Czechoslovak is unaware that the Western democracies let their country be politically dismembered in 1938 and swallowed by Nazi Germany the next year. They have not forgotten the world's inaction when a Soviet-sponsored coup in 1948 made their country a dependency, and similar inaction when the freedom they achieved for themselves 20 years later was stolen by armed might.

A contradiction seen by many in Prague is that when the Communist Party brought about Czechoslovakia's radical renewal in 1968, the Soviet Union and four Warsaw Pact allies stamped it out. Now that renewal is being pressed forward over the heads of an unwilling Communist Party, Moscow has raised no known objections.

Bridge between Generations

In fact, as a sign of changing times in both countries, Soviet television today asked for an interview with Vaclav Havel, the playwright never performed in his own land, who in 1989, as in 1968, represents more fully than anyone else the striving for democracy and freedom of non-Communist Czechoslovaks.

Today, after years of imprisonment for defending freedom when it was forbidden to do so, Mr. Havel has become the principal leader of the reawakening.

He is the bridge between the 1968 generation and the young people of today whose demonstrations and continuing strikes started the dismantling of the Communist stranglehold on this nation of 15 million. As uncontroversial for the moment as a leader of a mass movement can be, he appears to enjoy the support of the nation and the grudging respect of the Communists with whom he has negotiated their retreat from absolute power.

A Contrasting Case

This is not entirely true for Alexander Dubcek, the party leader who, often reluctantly, let the Prague Spring happen and paid the price of official banishment and humiliation. For the 1968 generation, Mr. Dubcek is the symbol, as many say, of a dream of spring that did not die in the next 21 years of winter.

They wish for the poetic justice that would have Mr. Dubcek replace Gustav Husak as President. In 1969, Mr. Husak ousted his fellow Slovak as party chief and banished him to the first stage of his exile by sending him as Ambassador to Turkey. A demotion to Government clerk in Slovakia followed.

Many of the young do not share this nostalgia. A Civic Forum leader said ruefully that his son, a university student, berated him angrily for Mr. Dubcek's speech to an enthusiastic public here. "You are pushing him for President," the son said. "Why don't you leave Husak in place, who doesn't do anything? Dubcek will try to do things, and we don't want any more Communists doing things to Czechoslovakia."

In 1968, the Communist Party rapidly gained mass support as its striving for freedom was recognized as genuine. Today, the party has no noticeable credit. To party diehards, it is betraying its principles and past by surrendering its power. But the majority of the nation considers the party leaders stodgy, humorless oppressors who are slow to recognize that their time has ran out.

A Lack of Hatred

As in 1968, little hatred marks either demonstrations or private conversations.

Just as Antonin Novotny, the unpopular party and state leader until 1968, was allowed to retire to his villa outside Prague and tend his roses, no one today is calling for the head of Milos Jakes, the deposed party leader, although it is known that he was one of the few who prepared the invasion, or that of Mr. Husak, who led the process of restoring a repressive regime that was called, with unintended irony, normalization.

This enduring lack of vindictiveness was shown tonight by three of the victims of Communist vengeance after the 1968 invasion. Tens of thousands of professionals were dismissed not only from their jobs, but from their professions. And yet, when leaders of the Civic Forum were asked at [a] news conference whether they would insist on the reinstatement of those condemned for two decades to menial jobs, Jiri Dienstbier, the spokesman, said this would be difficult after so many years.

Moral reparations would be enough, the spokesman said. Mr. Dienstbier was a leading broadcaster until the invasion and has spent the years since stoking a factory furnace, except for four years in prison and many briefer arrests for his struggle to restore the human and civic rights of his nation.

"What is going on is sufficiently satisfactory for all of us," he added. And two others who lost their work, Vaclav Klaus, an economist, and Rita Klimova, the news-conference interpreter, volunteered, "For me, too."

Mr. Dienstbier's reaction typifies an attitude that prevailed in 1968 as it does now and that distinguishes Czechoslovakia from other countries in this region. Czechoslovaks shy away from grand romantic statements or from giving vent to resounding patriotic effusions.

Mr. Klaus and Mr. Dienstbier vied tonight in the self-deprecation often characteristic of their countrymen. Asked about further innovations in the program that has already brought so many changes so quickly, one replied, "We in Czechoslovakia are already last in so many things that we don't want to be first in anything."

President Václav Havel Delivers New Year Address

On December 1, 1989, Vasil Mohorita, the Czechoslovak communist party central committee secretary, admitted that the invasion of 1968 had been "a mistake." On December 3, the people's militia, or workers' militia, a paramilitary arm of the communist party, was disbanded. It had played a coercive role in 1948 in bringing to power the communist party. It issued formal apologies to the people of Czechoslovakia for errors made since 1968.

Also on December 3, President Gustáv Husák nominated a new coalition government, headed by Ladislav Adamec, consisting of fifteen communist ministers out of twenty. The Civic Forum and its Slovak partner, Public Against Violence (Verejnost' proti Nasiliu, or VPN), rejected the concept and called for more demonstrations and a general strike on December 11. The next day, 300,000 crammed Wenceslas Square to exclaim their sense of betrayal, protest Adamec's proposal, and support another national strike. The party-state yielded.

On December 5, communist party leaders traveled to Moscow for a Warsaw Pact meeting, during which Bulgaria, East Germany, Hungary, Poland, and the Soviet Union—the five countries that had participated in the 1968 military invasion of Czechoslovakia—announced a condemnation of their own action. Negotiations continued between the government and the opposition. On December 7, Prime Minister Adamec and his government resigned, rather than meet the demands of the challengers. The next day, President Husák, in his capacity as head of state, granted an amnesty for all political prisoners and swore in a new government that had been elected by a chastened communist Federal Assembly, the parliament. After the swearing-in, in a long-awaited move, exactly according to the Civic Forum's time limit, Husák resigned. On December 9, Czechoslovakia's one-party system ceased to exist.

A younger and more liberal communist party leader, Marián Čalfa, agreed to reopen talks with the opposition. Advances were made, and on December 10, International Human Rights Day, a "government of national understanding" was announced. For the first time since 1948, the communists were not the sole governing party in Czechoslovakia. The Ten Days of the Velvet revolution had in actuality taken more like twenty-four.

On December 12, Čalfa became prime minister of a government comprised primarily of non-communists. He spoke of intentions to lead the transition of the country into a full market economy. In just hours, Jiří Dienstbier—among the activist intellectuals who shaped the opposition and had been sent to oblivion as a coal stoker—became the new foreign minister. It took two weeks for Ján Čarnogurský to move from being a prisoner of conscience to becoming the country's vice premier, in charge of the secret police in whose cells he had languished (see "200,000 March in Prague as Calls for Change Mount").

In Prague, citizens gathered in Wenceslas Square to celebrate their new government. The intellectuals and artists, watching the entire political structure collapsing, nonetheless did not want the state to cease functioning. Most groups called off their boycotts and strikes. Only students, still fearful of residual communist strength, followed through by sitting-in and refusing to leave university buildings and with strikes. Crowds hoisted signs and posters reading "Havel na Hrad!" meaning that Havel should go to Hradcany Castle, or Prague Castle, the seat of the presidency.

Václav Havel and Truth

Václav Havel is a playwright, dramatist, and actor, born in Prague in 1936, two years before Nazi Germany occupied the Central European nation of Czechoslovakia. Havel's father was a restaurateur whose property was confiscated after 1948 by the communist regime of Czechoslovakia. Denied straightforward access to education due to his "bourgeois" background, Havel was nonetheless able to complete high school and reach the university level. In 1959, he was given employment as a stagehand in a Prague theatrical company and soon started writing plays with Ivan Vyskocil. By the late 1960s, Havel had become a resident playwright of the Balustrade theatrical company.

He was one of the first Czechoslovaks openly to refuse to conform to the totalitarianism that subsumed his country after 1948. *The New York Times* on January 2, 1990 , draws attention to his having served "a series of prison terms beginning in 1977." Authorities imprisoned him for more than five years for "refusing to surrender his conscience to the dictates of the communist state" (see "Havel Tells Festive Czechoslovaks that Honesty Is Key to Recovery").

On August 9, 1969, Havel sent a private letter to Alexander Dubček, first secretary of the Czechoslovakian communist party, urging him to take a stand against party-state capitulations to the reintroduction of harsh one-party rule, following the Soviet-led invasion by 750,000 Warsaw Pact troops in response to the reforms led by Dubček and during what came to be called the Prague Spring of 1968 (see "**Czechoslovakia, Introduction**"). In 1969, the state blacklisted Havel's writings and charged him with subversion.

Under Stalinism, the Havel family's farmhouse in northern Bohemia served as a secluded retreat for discussions that became relaxed authors' conferences. There, writers and theatrical personalities found repose and reinforcement after being alienated from each other when authorities destroyed their articles, novels, and plays or as they struggled to overcome cultural stagnation.

For more than a century, rulers in the name of Marxism had claimed that their way was the true foe of repression and injustice. When Havel and his contemporaries attempted to reveal the emptiness of that pretension with a strategy coined by Havel as "living in Truth," it challenged the vaunted claims of the communists, who over a period of years had begun to lose their ability to coerce the population. Eventually, the undermining of the legitimacy of the party-state by these activist intellectuals would be among the forces leading the communist party to relinquish its efforts to preserve its hegemony.

In April 1975, Havel departed from what had been an essentially private witness to express publicly his concern for the government's barefaced disregard of the principles outlined in the Helsinki Accords Final Act of that year (see "**Introduction: Strikes, Sinatra, and Nonviolent Revolution**"). In "Open Letter to Gustáv Husák," general secretary of Czechoslovakia's communist party, he protested the effects of "normalization," the code word for re-imposition of harsh Soviet control after the crushing of the Prague Spring. Havel, articulating the deep ethical, social, and spiritual crises faced by communist Czechoslovakia, wrote, "We cannot remain silent in the face of evil or violence; silence merely encourages them." He asks Husák to consider the issues about which he has written and "act accordingly."

In his letter, Havel had done what the party-state most despised: he shattered the rule of silence. He had sent the letter by regular mail, but also released it to international wire services and news agencies. In this, his first serious philosophical writing, Havel focuses on fear and moral decay. As the letter's contents became known by way of underground publications, waves of dissent, to be followed by

Václav Havel speaks in Prague on December 10, 1989, on the announcement of a "government of national understanding." Havel, a playwright and former political prisoner, had been the guiding light of the Velvet Revolution that toppled the Soviet-backed, Czechoslovak communist regime. On December 29, 1989, the soon-to-be-obsolete communist parliament would unanimously elect Havel as interim president of Czechoslovakia, and in July 1990, Havel would become the country's first noncommunist leader since 1948.

Source: AP Images

repression, began anew. The regime's moves to suppress youth and cultural activities sparked petitions; civic defiance groups began rapidly to form throughout 1976.

By the early 1970s, Havel had become an active member of a dissenting community of university-based academicians and the actors, playwrights, and staff of Czechoslovakia's admired theatrical companies. In 1972, he and others founded Edice Petlice, or Padlocked Editions, a semi-clandestine press that published typescripts of fiction, philosophical works, and other literature. Copy machines were prohibited, but typing was permitted. By 1987, Padlocked Editions had produced more than 400 manually typed works (see "Czech Underground Literature Circulating from Hand to Hand"). Havel grasped what his biographer, Michael Simmons, calls "an extraordinary opportunity to spell out the details of a new moral code of good social behaviour." Rather than denouncing a particular type of governance, Havel damned the communist party-state "not because it was Communist, but because it was bad" (Simmons 1991, xii, 3).

On New Year's Day 1977, a document signed by 243 citizens appeared. The most important development since the 1968 Prague Spring, Charter 77 challenged "the system of the virtual subjection of all institutions and organizations in the state to the political directives of the apparatus of the ruling

(Continued)

(Continued)

party and the arbitrary decisions of the influential individuals." It notes that decisions are "mainly exercised behind the scenes, often only verbally" and that their "originators are responsible to no one but themselves and their hierarchy." In short, the Moscow-imposed and communist party-driven system had no popular mandate. Its signers included leaders from the Prague Spring, professors, engineers, journalists, artists, clergy, and its progenitor, Václav Havel. The essence of Charter 77 is to assert that the Czechoslovak regime should honor all international agreements, including the UN Universal Declaration on Human Rights and the Helsinki Accords that it (and the Soviet Union) had agreed to uphold in 1975 (see "Prague Detains Five Dissidents after Human Rights Manifesto"). Two years later, eleven of the leading Chartists were arrested, six of whom, Havel included, were given prison terms of two to five years.

In 1979, Havel was locked up under a four-and-a-half year sentence. Having once secreted his manuscripts in a tree-trunk to prevent confiscation by the party-state authorities, Havel's letters from behind bars and other prison writings became a source of inspiration for all of the pro-democracy communities throughout Eastern Europe. Among his major works are four complete plays and three one-act dramas (see "Prague Detains Five Dissidents after Human Rights Manifesto"). Havel's plays include The Garden Party (1963), The Memorandum (1965), The Increased Difficulty of Concentration (1968), Audience (1975), Private View (1975), Protest (1978), Largo Desolato (1985), and Tomorrow (1988). *The Times* on November 30, 1989, calls Havel "the playwright [who] never performed in his own land, who in 1989, as in 1968, represents more fully than anyone else the striving for democracy and freedom of non-communist Czechoslovaks" (see "Spirit of 1968 Is Still Alive, Still Distinct").

Havel's writings often contemplate the explanations given by individuals who obey a repressive system and are therefore forced to reconcile, within themselves, their cooperation with a malevolent order. In his dramas, he depicts persons who are fearful and accepting of what they know to be wrong and destructive. Avoiding the trap of excusing individuals as powerless against state forces, he penned essays on dissent, the origins of power, and totalitarianism. His dramas address the pressures of living in an authoritarian system of rampant corruption, tyrannical decisions, absence of accountability, constant moral compromise, arbitrary violence, brutality, police maintenance of communist parties unable to reform themselves in power, and most significantly for Eastern Europeans, the necessity of "living in Truth" as a way of breaking a vicious cycle.

The concept of "living in Truth" established Havel as a moral philosopher and playwright. He never joined the communist party. The Beatle John Lennon had become a symbol of witty defiance for the burgeoning opposition in Czechoslovakia during the 1970s, especially to the young, who were to become so important to the Velvet Revolution. Havel said he was a Lennonist, not a Leninist.

Accepting an honorary doctorate in 1984 from Toulouse University, Havel explained that he viewed politics "as a practical morality, as service to the truth." Connecting the ethical and practical, Havel writes, "It is my responsibility to emphasize, again and again, the moral origin of all genuine politics, to stress the significance of moral values and standards in all spheres of life."

Havel's years in prison, and an even longer period of being banned and censored, made him into an emblem for those who prevailed despite pitiless Eastern bloc regimes. He profoundly understood the importance of the news media and prolifically wrote articles and tracts on political responsibility, relying on the covert circulation of unofficial, underground publications called *samizdat* (Russian for "self-published," as opposed to state-published) to spread his writings and ideas. Samizdat, often typed on yellowed onionskin paper onto ten carbon copies, was critical to the sharing of ideas leading to the Velvet Revolution (see "Czech Underground Literature Circulating from Hand to Hand"). Havel's fellow countrymen and -women constantly sought him out in their quest for a leader who understood honor and honesty.

Havel's "living in Truth" concerns the ability of persons who regard themselves as powerless to understand that they possess a form of power and can act upon it. The obverse of this situation is to live within a lie, a double existence, which means mutely functioning while in the midst of injustice, official lies, and corruption—doing nothing to bring about change and thus supporting an unjust structure through one's silence. To cease living within a lie, one must refuse to cooperate with systems of oppression that degrade humanity, speak one's mind, and express commonality with other human beings who are oppressed.

"Living in Truth" allows citizens to repossess their humanity and assume responsibility for their world. It is compatible with the repertoire of nonviolent collective action in its understanding that means and ends are linked. Havel put this concept into plain words: those who live in Truth "create a situation in which the regime is confounded, invariably causing panic and driving it to react in inappropriate ways." He often expressed his conviction that the power that resides in "living in Truth" is the power to overturn repressive power structures and undermine dictatorships; such power resides within each person. When individuals live in Truth, he insisted, they can achieve a certain peace despite their objective circumstances.

THE POWER OF THE POWERLESS

Havel's "The Power of the Powerless," an essay originally written in October 1978, became the single most significant piece of writing prior to 1989 in the various Eastern bloc movements that led to democratic transitions. Circulating across borders in samizdat, it also appeared overseas in several forms. In this parable, Havel writes of a typical seller of fruits and vegetables who exposes a falsehood as a lie and is thus regarded by the authorities as menacing and hostile. The power of the powerless, according to Havel, lies in Truth, which also represents the political power residing within every person. Hence, "living in Truth" is an effective weapon against totalitarianism and at the heart of opposition to its structures. Havel describes the force of Truth as "bacteriological," similar to contagion.

The activist intellectuals shaping democracy movements across Eastern Europe appreciated the futility of violence and bloody uprisings and the realities of the cold war. Havel's conceptualizing of "living in Truth" with his colleagues and counterparts constituted the development of civil society, whose disparate, small power centers and multilayered institutions could counter the pillars of power that sustain authoritarian systems. Ultimately, the playwright would assume a pivotal role in rejuvenating the nation's resistance to communist oppression. As large demonstrations began in early 1989, the authorities arrested Havel and sentenced him to nine months in prison. His incarceration sparked still more demonstrations across the country and brought international attention to Prague, possibly a factor in the regime's decision to parole him in May of that year.

The journalist-historian Timothy Garton Ash had arrived in Prague on November 23, 1989, and observed to Havel that Poland's Solidarity union had taken ten years to achieve its goals, Hungary needed ten months to reach its target, East Germany took ten weeks, but that in Czechoslovakia it might take ten days. Havel delightedly seized upon this reflection and beckoned a samizdat video team to spread the word. Indeed, on November 19 (Day Three) Havel brought together the principal opposition groups, including reform-minded communists, and, led by signers of Charter 77, initiated the Civic Forum (Občanské Fórum), a citizens' pro-democracy initiative seeking democratic changes. Prague's Magic Lantern Theater served as the forum's headquarters.

Comprised of a broad spectrum of actors and theatrical personalities, organizations, student groups, artistic and literary circles, and a selection of socialist political entities, the Civic Forum soon emerged

(Continued)

(Continued)

into public view and remained there until decisive steps toward democratic governance had been accomplished. Havel was the author and final arbiter for the group's statements and positions. The forum was immediately accepted as speaker for the Czechoslovak people and coordinated the collective nonviolent actions of the swiftly growing opposition. Public Against Violence (Verejnost' proti Nasiliu, or VPN), a counterpart group, rapidly materialized in Slovakia.

On Day Seven of the Ten Days, speaking to a Prague demonstration of more than 300,000, Havel purposely acknowledged the contributions of the younger generation: "Our gratitude goes to the students for giving this revolution a beautifully peaceful, dignified, gentle and I would say loving face, which is admired by the whole world. This was a rebellion of truth against lies, of purities against impurities, of the human heart against violence" (see "250,000 Czechs, Hailing Dubcek, Urge Ouster of Hard-Line Leaders").

The success of a November 27 nationwide general strike attracted the participation of 80 percent of the Czechoslovak labor force. Members of the theatrical community had first called for the *national* strike, which was crucially endorsed by Czech students, and the Civic Forum launched the effort, with Havel leading, and its Slovak partner Public Against Violence. Within seventy-two hours of the general strike, followed by the start of talks between the government and the Civic Forum, the communist party began to acquiesce; the entire party-state leadership resigned (see "'Replay' in Prague: Popular Up-rising Echoes the Experience of Neighbors"). The old-guard communist parliament on December 29 unanimously elected Havel as president of what was still called the Czechoslovak Soviet Republic in one of the most brisk, dramatic, and highly symbolic political reversals in history.

Havel became the country's first noncommunist leader since 1948. According to *The Times* on January 2, 1990, President Havel in his New Year's address told the citizens of Czechoslovakia that "their communist leaders had lied to them for 40 years, that their country was in a serious economic and environmental crisis, and that only a return to the values of honesty, decency and mutual respect could lead to recovery" (see "Havel Tells Festive Czechoslovaks that Honesty Is Key to Recovery"). *The Times* quotes him:

> For 40 years you have heard on this day from the mouths of my predecessors, in a number of variations, the same thing: how our country is flourishing, how many more millions of tons of steel we have produced, how we are all happy, how we believe in our Government. . . . I assume you have not named me to this office so that I, too, should lie to you. We have become morally ill because we are used to saying one thing and thinking another.

His New Year's speech stressed that the Czechoslovak citizens had relied on themselves, acted to change their condition, and at last determined their own history (see "Havel Tells Festive Czechoslovaks that Honesty Is Key to Recovery"). Havel declared, "Your government, my people, has returned to you." Communism, Havel asserted, "was overthrown by life, by thought, by human dignity."

Havel was reelected as president in July 1990. As Czechoslovakia in 1992 confronted dissolution into two nation-states, the Czech Republic and the Slovak Republic, Havel, who opposed the dissection, resigned. By the following year, he had again been elected, as president of the new Czech Republic. His political sway was, however, limited by Prime Minister Václav Klaus (1993–1997), a free-market economist who had been involved in the Civic Forum and who by then held much of the political power. In 1998, Havel was again elected, by a narrow margin. Under his presidency, the Czech Republic in 1999 joined the North Atlantic Treaty Organization. Constitutionally banned from seeking a third term, he stepped down as president in 2003. *Odcházení* (Leaving), Havel's first new drama in more than two decades, is a tragicomedy that autobiographically draws on his terms as president. It premiered in 2008 and depicts a chancellor leaving his position while struggling with a political opponent.

In the new environment, the communist party re-examined its role. A few days after the formation of the new government, Defense Minister Miroslav Vacek announced that all communist party activities in the armed forces had been halted. The party convened a conference at which it fundamentally altered the structure of the party and announced its support for a multiparty electoral system.

Some Federal Assembly parliamentarians resigned from their seats, to make room for opposition representatives to serve in the national legislature. The first session of the incoming parliament, on December 28, elected a new (but not really new) speaker in Alexander Dubček. The Federal Assembly, as yet communist, on December 29, unanimously elected Václav Havel as president of what was still named the Czechoslovak Soviet Republic, in one of the most brisk, dramatic, and highly symbolic political reversals in history. Havel had linked Dubček's election to his own, so as to please the Slovaks and retain the support of the country's few communist party reformers. Seeing that Havel's election had met their stipulations, the students called off their six-week strike. Mass was celebrated at St. Vitus Cathedral after Havel's installation as president.

In the new year, *The Times* of January 2, 1990, pinpoints Miroslav Štěpán as having been party head in Prague when riot police in the capital violently repressed student demonstrations on November 17—the tinder for the Prague Autumn of 1989—and cites the state-run press agency in reporting Štěpán's arrest on December 23. Both Milos Jakeš and Štěpán were blamed for the mistakes of November 17. Their violent reprisals and police brutality against mostly young nonviolent challengers had backfired, causing in response what *The Times* calls "a shake-up."

With the new year, changes had occurred that would have been inconceivable sixty days earlier. Havel had replaced the hard-line communist secretary Gustáv Husák, who had been instated after the Soviet-led crushing of the 1968 Prague Spring (see **Czechoslovakia, Introduction**). Only two months earlier, Havel had been behind bars, denounced as a "dissident" playwright. *The Times* on January 2 notes that Havel had since 1977 served a number of prison terms, spending more than five years incarcerated for "refusing to surrender his conscience to the dictates of the communist state."

On Monday, January 1, 1990, President Václav Havel, Czechoslovakia's first noncommunist leader since 1948, gave a forty-minute address that began by looking back over forty years. *The Times* reporter Craig R. Whitney points to Havel's allusion to a pervasive bitterness toward the Soviet Union but also his telling Czechoslovaks that they too were responsible for their past. Havel's writings had shown that he understood how obedience by the ruled is required for a despot to succeed and that *Czechoslovak* communists had conspired with the Soviets for forty years. Havel remarked, "If I speak about a spoiled moral atmosphere I don't refer only to our masters. . . . I'm speaking about all of us. For all of us have grown used to the totalitarian system and accepted it as an immutable fact, and thereby actually helped keep it going. None of us are only its victims; we are all also responsible for it" ("Havel's Vision").

Recognizing the serious problems to be confronted in years ahead, the new president offered an amnesty, yet it was not unlimited. In an amnesty, a nation-state restores those who may have been guilty of an offense against it to the status of innocence. More than a pardon, the state erases the legal remembrance of the offense, a step often required in democratic transitions from tyrannical regimes, because of former political prisoners, who must be reintegrated into the nation.

Whitney notes a double entendre from Czechoslovak history in Havel's conclusion to his speech. Havel evoked Tomas Garrigue Masaryk, Czechoslovakia's first president, who is credited for founding the country after the Austro-Hungarian Empire collapsed during World War I. In his inaugural address, Masaryk had used a prayer by the seventeenth-century Moravian church leader John Amos Comenius. Havel paraphrased it: "Your Government, my people, has returned to you." The thrust of Havel's address was that Czechoslovaks had been able to rely on themselves, change their condition, and enact their own history. In office in Prague Castle, time and again Havel would entreat the Czechoslovaks not to seek retribution, but to pursue reconciliation. He believed that rebuilding the country required truthfulness, readiness to forgive, and the taking of personal responsibility.

In June 1990, Czechoslovaks would vote in their first free parliamentary elections since 1946. Havel's appeals for reconciliation, ethics, forgiveness, and Truth were not effortlessly attainable. Hard work on political and economic reconstruction awaited. Difficulties lay ahead. Under communism, a childhood friend of Havel's mused, "Differentiating between good and evil was much easier" (Simmons 1991, 209).

At the end of Havel's first year in office, the name of the country would be legally changed from Czechoslovakia to the Czech and Slovak Federal Republic. In 1993, three years after Havel became president, the Slovaks voted to secede. Havel opposed the divorce of Slovakia from Czechoslovakia, but eventually acceded. He became instead the president of the Czech Republic.

A number of forces had converged in the Velvet Revolution. After Havel became Czech president, he said, "Without the changes in the Soviet Union, Poland, Hungary, and [East Germany], what has happened in our country would have scarcely happened. And if it did, it certainly would not have followed such a peaceful course" (Havel 1995). One factor had been Soviet general secretary Mikhail S. Gorbachev's disinclination to use the violence that the Moscow had employed in 1968 to destroy Czechoslovakia's Prague Spring (see **Czechoslovakia, Introduction**). With the party's subsequent return to neo-Stalinism under Gustáv Husák, the party had been unable to address the country's severe economic problems, caused in Czechoslovakia as elsewhere in the Eastern bloc partly by failed policies and partially by prevalent corruption, as party elites sought to protect their positions and status. Despite lip service to Gorbachev's principle of *perestroika* (restructuring), Husák had opposed any reforms.

The 1975 Helsinki Final Act had provided a framework within which Czechoslovaks could pressure their own government to fulfill commitments that came with the agreement's human rights provisions (see **"Introduction: Strikes, Sinatra, and Nonviolent Revolution"**) and which inspired the formation of Charter 77 (see "Prague Detains Five Dissidents after Human Rights Manifesto"). Despite the persecution of academicians, artists, authors, and theatrical people who signed the charter and went on to form groups like the Civic Forum and Public Against Violence, such organizations, based on ideas of democracy and freedom, mushroomed and gained adherents. Their power derived from numbers—their ability to rally hundreds of thousands for disciplined demonstrations, with candles and jangling key rings. Virtually the entire country participated in the November 27, 1989, general strike, in a textbook example of how to withdraw cooperation from a system of oppression. Of all these factors that made the Velvet Revolution so constructive and smooth, however, the most important was the strategic vision of Václav Havel and his fellow activist intellectuals and their prudent development of citizen-organized initiatives in a blossoming civil society.

JANUARY 2, 1990
HAVEL TELLS FESTIVE CZECHOSLOVAKS THAT HONESTY IS KEY TO RECOVERY
By CRAIG R. WHITNEY
Special to The New York Times

PRAGUE, Jan. 1 – President Vaclav Havel told the citizens of Czechoslovakia today that their Communist leaders had lied to them for 40 years, that their country was in a serious economic and environmental crisis, and that only a return to the values of honesty, decency and mutual respect could lead to recovery.

"For 40 years you have heard on this day from the mouths of my predecessors, in a number of variations, the same thing: how our country is flourishing, how many more millions of tons of steel we have produced, how we are all happy, how we believe in our Government," the author and playwright began, wearing glasses and reading from a manuscript. "I assume you have not named me to this office so that I, too, should lie to you.

"We have become morally ill because we are used to saying one thing and thinking another," Mr. Havel said. His televised message seemed to be aimed at sobering a people who spent the New Year's holiday in delirious celebration of his election and the new freedom that it symbolized.

A Sadness 'Inflicted on Ourselves'

But in an allusion to widespread Czechoslovak resentment of the Soviet Union, he said, "It would be very unwise to think of the sad heritage of the last 40 years only as something foreign, something inherited from a distant relative." On the contrary, he said, it is "something we have inflicted on ourselves."

Mr. Havel, who was elected by the national Parliament on Friday, repeatedly called in his 40-minute address for mutual respect among the Czechs, Slovaks, and other nationalities in this Central European country, without directly comparing ethnic tensions with similar problems in the Soviet Union.

He announced an amnesty for thousands of prisoners who have been protesting overcrowded conditions, poor food, and the lack of rehabilitation in more than a score of jails across the country.

He also called for trials to assess responsibility for the Stalinist style of repression in Czechoslovakia over the past 40 years; said he hoped that diplomatic relations could soon be restored with the Vatican and Israel; and invited Pope John Paul II and the Dalai Lama, the winner of last year's Nobel Peace Prize, to visit Czechoslovakia.

Amnesty for Lighter Offenses

Mr. Havel is to visit East Germany and West Germany on Tuesday. "I want to contribute to the cause of peace," he said, "by my short visit tomorrow to our two mutually related neighbors: the German Democratic Republic and the Federal Republic of Germany."

"I have decided to proclaim a relatively broad amnesty," he said of the prison inmates, "but I appeal to the prisoners to understand that 40 years of degraded justice cannot be done away with all at once. By uprisings they will help neither the republic nor themselves."

He urged Czechoslovak citizens "not to be afraid of released prisoners, but to help them in a Christian spirit after their return among us, to find in themselves what our prisons could not instill: repentance and a desire to lead a good life."

Officials said later that the amnesty would free all prisoners serving sentences of two years or less and reduce longer terms by as much as one half. It would not affect people convicted of terrorism, murder, robbery, rape or other sexual abuse, or misuse of public office. The country's jails hold about 50,000 people.

Ex-Party Chief in Custody

The highest-ranking Czechoslovak official known to have been taken into custody on charges of abusing his office is Miroslav Stepan, who was the head of Prague's Communist Party organization when the police in the capital moved in to repress demonstrations on Nov. 17. He was arrested on Dec. 23, the Government press agency said.

Mr. Havel also replaced the Prosecutor General and the Interior Minister today, continuing a shake-up in response to the Nov. 17 crackdown.

In a series of prison terms beginning in 1977, Mr. Havel served more than five years for refusing to surrender his conscience to the dictates of the Communist state.

He told his listeners today that he would be "a President that would speak less but work harder, who will be permanently present among his fellow citizens and listen to them well."

He said that the most difficult work, of insuring that freedom will last, was only beginning, like the cleanup of champagne bottles and broken streamers from Wenceslas Square, Prague's main gathering place.

From Revelry to Reflection

The cobblestones were literally wet with champagne Sunday night as tens of thousands of people came out to celebrate the New Year with whatever beverage came to hand, often sparkling wine made in the Soviet Union. Friends and lovers embraced on the square, firecrackers exploded in salutes and the crowd burst into song, marking the end of a year that also brought new freedom to Poland, Hungary, East Germany and Rumania.

"You have had freedom always," said a gray-haired man, Jaroslav Baraban, amid the din, "but we have only known it for a month."

Like many who filled the vast square, half a mile long and 200 feet wide, between midnight and dawn this morning, the man was nearly weeping. He joined in the repeated chants of "Havel, Havel," "Long Live Havel" that demonstrate how much of a symbol the new President has become.

The celebrations turned more solemn and dignified today as church bells pealed from the medieval towers and baroque domes of the golden city. The gilded baroque interior of the Church of St. James filled with worshipers who flocked to hear a high mass and a performance of Mozart's Coronation Mass by a choir and orchestra. Tonight Mr. Havel and his wife attended a concert of Dvorak's Slavonic Dances in the Municipal Building, where the independence of Czechoslovakia was first proclaimed in 1918.

A Farewell to Cynicism

"Everywhere in the world," Mr. Havel told the nation in his address this afternoon, "people were surprised at how these malleable, humiliated, cynical citizens of Czechoslovakia, who seemingly believed in nothing, found the tremendous strength to cast off the totalitarian system in an entirely peaceful and dignified manner within a few weeks.

"Humanistic and democratic tradition slept on after all somewhere in the unconscious of our nation and national minorities," he said.

But Czechoslovakia also owed its freedom, Mr. Havel said, "to the courage of those in the Soviet Union, East Germany, Hungary and Poland who had fought for theirs."

"All human suffering concerns each human being," he said. He acknowledged that without recent political changes in the Soviet Union, Czechoslovakia's revolution would have suffered the same fate as the Prague Spring of 1968, the reform movement that was cut short by a Soviet-led Warsaw Pact invasion.

Mr. Havel ended his speech with a double echo of Czechoslovak history. He recalled that Thomas G. Masaryk, Czechoslovakia's first President, had taken a prayer by the 17th century Moravian churchman, John Amos Comenius, and paraphrased it: "Your Government, my people, has returned to you."

The crowd in Wenceslas Square last night also echoed Comenius, breaking into a song made popular by the artist Marta Kubicova during the brief Prague Spring. "May peace be with this land," they sang. "Let hate, envy, fear and conflict pass. May they pass, may they pass."

Warsaw Pact Dissolves

The Czech and Slovak peoples were no strangers to great narratives of history. For more than a thousand years, they had experienced foreign monarchies, empires, bloody revolts, Nazism's wanton degeneracy, brutal Soviet hegemony, and the intemperance of unaccountable communist despots. A strong tradition of fighting for freedom runs through the annals of Czechoslovakia, however, and precedents of nonviolent resistance to oppression stand out in its historical chronicle. When the Czechoslovaks finally consolidated themselves in opposition to the communism that had deadened and destroyed their cultural history, popular adamancy against violence and determination not to lose lives made it all the more effective. The "second" Velvet Revolution, so named for the 1918 unification of Czechs and Slovaks after World War I, blended both the ethical and the practical (see **Czechoslovakia, Introduction**).

One of the signers of Charter 77, Jan Urban, said about the Prague Autumn, "A nonviolent mass movement, led by the Civic Forum, triumphed . . . in transition from the negation of the old to the building of the new" (Urban 1990, 100). The dramatist Václav Havel, elected president on December 29, in his first address as president, *The New York Times* of January 2, 1990, reports, partly credited Czechoslovakia's freedom "to the courage of those in the Soviet Union, East Germany, Hungary and Poland who had fought for theirs" (see "Havel Tells Festive Czechoslovaks That Honesty Is Key to Recovery"). The end of the Warsaw Pact, to which these nations once belonged, ensued. Eventually, what became the Czech Republic, alongside the Slovak Republic, would be accepted into the North Atlantic Treaty Organization and membership in the European Union in 2004.

JULY 2, 1991
DEATH KNELL RINGS FOR WARSAW PACT
At Meeting in Prague, the Six Remaining Members Vote to Kill Off the Alliance
By STEVEN GREENHOUSE
Special to The New York Times

PRAGUE, July 1 – In a move that pushed the cold war further into history, the Soviet Union and the five other countries in the Warsaw Pact formally agreed today to dissolve the political and military alliance that long enabled Moscow to dominate Eastern Europe.

"As of noon today, the Warsaw Pact no longer exists," President Vaclav Havel of Czechoslovakia said after leading the organization's final summit conference. "We are saying goodbye to the era when Europe was divided by ideological intolerance."

Last February, Warsaw Pact foreign and defense ministers agreed in Budapest to end all military cooperation. The meeting today was of the pact's political consultative committee. Under today's agreement, the pact will formally end after ratification by each country's parliament. Mr. Havel said this should take less than six months.

The Eastern European leaders at the meeting, which included the Presidents of Czechoslovakia, Poland, Romania and Bulgaria and the Prime Minister of Hungary, said the dissolution of the Warsaw Pact could help hasten the formation of a united, peaceful Europe.

In Prague today for the signing ceremony, Gennadi I. Yanayev, Vice President of the Soviet Union, said dismantling a powerful institution of the cold war should be followed with the dissolution of its Western counterpart, NATO. Officials at the meeting said President Mikhail S.

Gorbachev of the Soviet Union did not attend because he was occupied by domestic problems.

Soon after the nations of Eastern Europe ousted their Communist governments beginning in 1989, they started calling for disbanding the pact, which was founded in 1955, through Soviet prodding, as a counterweight to the North Atlantic Treaty Organization.

"I'm very glad that we're taking part today in the funeral of this institution," President Lech Walesa of Poland said. "I hope we will use this chance to build the united Europe that has been the dream of generations."

Havel Notes Symbolism

In a news conference after the signing ceremony, President Havel noted the symbolism of signing the Warsaw Pact's death warrant in Czechoslovakia, which Soviet-led forces invaded in 1968 in what was the pact's only military action other than troop exercises.

"Prague, once the victim of the Warsaw Pact, is the city where the Warsaw Pact is meeting its end as an instrument of the cold war," he said.

The Warsaw Pact originally had eight members. Albania quit in 1968; East Germany withdrew in September before merging with West Germany.

Referring to NATO, Mr. Yanayev said, "The Soviet Union believes that the existence of instruments that served the policy of confrontation in the cold war have become obsolete."

Prime Minister Jozsef Antall of Hungary said: "The rejuvenated NATO represents a warranty for European security, and the same holds true for the presence of the United States in Europe. European integration and the Atlantic Alliance are very compatible."

'Friendly Hand' to Moscow

Mr. Antall said the end of the Warsaw Pact—as well as the agreement last Friday to dissolve Comecon, the Soviet-dominated trading bloc—could mean closer ties with Moscow. He said, "Now that the shackles are off our hands, we can extend a friendly hand."

The agreement to consign the Warsaw Pact to history's attic leaves Eastern Europe with no security apparatus of its own at a time of bitter strife in Yugoslavia. Many in Europe fear that the forces tearing at the Balkans will stir instability elsewhere in the east.

President Havel expressed concern that the organization that aims to insure peace in Europe now, the 35-nation Conference on Security and Cooperation in Europe, might not provide enough of a security umbrella for Eastern Europe. He said nations in the region would pursue bilateral and multilateral pacts, but Czechoslovak officials expressed frustration that they were not being admitted to NATO.

A Czechoslovak official said: "The main threat isn't from any military alliance. The main threat may be from some unprovoked situation in the destabilized part of Europe where nationalism, economic misery and lack of democratic political structures make for a very volatile environment."

Four days ago, the Soviets withdrew the last of 73,500 troops from Czechoslovakia. A week ago, Moscow withdrew its troops from Hungary. Soviet troops remain in Poland and the former East Germany.

Bibliography

Bradley. John F. N. 1992. *Czechoslovakia's Velvet Revolution: A Political Analysis*. New York: Columbia University Press.

Bugajski, Janusz. 1987. *Czechoslovakia: Charter 77's Decade of Dissent*. Washington Papers 125. New York: Praeger.

"Declaration of Charter '77." 1977. http://libpro.cts.cuni.cz/charta/docs/declaration_of_charter_77.pdf.

Falk, Barbara J. 2003. *The Dilemmas of Dissidence in East-Central Europe: Citizen Intellectuals and Philosopher Kings*. Budapest and New York: Central European University Press.

Flint, Julie, Nigel Hawkes, Peter Hillmore, Ian Mather, Mike Power, Denise Searle, John Sweeney, and Nick Thorpe. 1990. "Czechoslovakia: The Velvet Revolution." In *Tearing down the Curtain: The People's Revolution in Eastern Europe by a Team from* The Observer, ed. Nigel Hawkes. London: Hodder and Stoughton.

Garton Ash, Timothy. 1999. "Czechoslovakia under Ice." In *The Uses of Adversity: Essays on the Fate of Central Europe.* London and New York: Penguin Books. Essay originally written in 1984.

———. 1999. *The Magic Lantern: The Revolution of '89 Witnessed in Warsaw, Budapest, Berlin and Prague.* New York: Vintage Books.

———. 1990. *We the People: The Revolution of '89 Witnessed in Warsaw, Budapest, Berlin and Prague.* London and New York: Penguin Books.

Havel, Václav. 1995. *Toward a Civil Society: Selected Speeches and Writings of Václav Havel, 1990–1995,* ed. Paul Wilson. Prague: Lidové Noviny. See also http://old.hrad.cz/president/Havel/speeches/1990/0101_uk.html.

———. 1990. *Disturbing the Peace,* ed. and trans. Paul Wilson. New York: Vintage Books.

———. 1989. "The Power of the Powerless." In *Living in Truth,* ed. Jan Vladislav, trans. Paul Wilson. London: Faber and Faber. Essay originally written in October 1978.

Jøsten, Josef. August 1977. "Czechoslovakia: From 1968 to Charter 77–A Record of Passive Resistance." *Conflict Studies* 86.

Jůn, Dominik. 2008. "The Two-Thousand Words that Started the Prague Spring." Radio Praha, Current Affairs, June 27. www.radio.cz/en/article/105579.

King, Mary E. 2002. *Mahatma Gandhi and Martin Luther King, Jr: The Power of Nonviolent Action.* 2d ed. New Delhi: Indian Council for Cultural Relations and Mehta Publishers; orig. Paris: UNESCO, 1999.

Kriseová, Eda. 1993. *Václav Havel: The Authorized Biography,* trans. Caleb Crain. New York: St. Martin's Press.

Simmons, Michael. 1991. *The Reluctant President: A Political Life of Václav Havel.* London: Methuen.

Urban, Jan. 1990. "Czechoslovakia: The Power and Politics of Humiliation." In *Spring in Winter: The 1989 Revolutions,* ed. Gwyn Prins, 99–136. Manchester and New York: Manchester University Press.

Whipple, Tim D. 1991. "From 1968 to 1989: A Chronological Commentary." In *After the Velvet Revolution: Václav Havel and the Leaders of Czechoslovakia Speak Out,* ed. Tim D. Whipple. New York: Freedom House.

Williams, Kiernan. 2009. "Civil Resistance in Czechoslovakia: From Soviet Invasion to 'Velvet Revolution', 1968–89." In *Civil Resistance and Power Politics: The Experience of Non-violent Action from Gandhi to the Present,* ed. Adam Roberts and Timothy Garton Ash, 110–126. Oxford: Oxford University Press.

FROM *THE NEW YORK TIMES*

Apple, R. W., Jr. 1989. "Prague's Shaky Bargain; The Government Seeks to Stop the Decline in Industry before It Leads to a Rebellion." November 17.

Browne, Malcolm W. 1977. "Czech Police Hold a Dissident Writer; Kahout Is Seized in the Presence of a Visiting Reporter." January 11.

Greenhouse, Steven. 1989. "Prague Premier Sees Top Foes, Shares Platform With Dubcek; Party Calls Special Congress." November 27.

Unsigned. 1990. "Havel's Vision; Excerpts from Speech By the Czech President." January 2.

INDEPENDENCE OF THE BALTIC STATES

Estonia, Latvia, and Lithuania sit on the eastern shore of the Baltic Sea, one of the grand waterways of civilization. Here, Eastern and Western Christianity met, and Germans, Poles, Russians, and Swedes fought wars for political and economic dominion. Estonia and Latvia, with major rivers, face west on the sea. Lithuania, more shielded by marshes and forests, has less access to the sea than its Baltic neighbors. These geographic variations contribute to some of the differences among these three states.

Estonia, whose capital is Tallinn, is the most northern, sitting on the Gulf of Finland. Adjacent to Estonia's southern border lies Latvia, where its coastal capital, Riga, dominates. South of Latvia is Lithuania, whose capital is Vilnius.

In 2008, Estonia's national population of 1,307,605 was the smallest of any of the former Soviet states; its citizens numbered fewer than those of New Hampshire and Vermont combined. Latvia in 2008 was home to 2,245,423 persons, the size of West Virginia's population. According to the Lithuanian State Department of Statistics, its population in 1989 was 3,875,000, and twenty years later, in 2009, is 3,340,000. Large communities of non-indigenous peoples—Belorussians ("White Russians"), Poles, Russians, Slavs, and Ukrainians—also reside in the Baltic states, comprising 38 percent of Estonia's population and 48 percent of Latvia's. According to the 2001 population census, 16.5 percent of Lithuania's people are correspondingly minorities.

The Baltic nationalities descend from some of the oldest European tribes; they are not Slavs. Estonians speak a language related to Finnish and the Hungarians' Magyar language, unrelated to most European languages. Latvians and Lithuanians speak languages that are related to Scandinavian tongues and are similar in type to those spoken in Europe. The Lithuanian and Latvian languages constitute the Baltic languages group, a principal subdivision of the Indo-European languages. The three Baltic states use the Latin, rather than Cyrillic, script.

Century after century, the German, Russian, Polish, and Scandinavian armies swept back and forth across the fields of the Baltics. The Poles, situated south of Lithuania, had been pushing north for centuries. The cities along the eastern seaboard were largely settled by Germans. Lithuania has its roots in the thirteenth century, when it was the Great Dukedom of Lithuania. (The southwestern part of ethnic Lithuania was conquered by the Livonian order in the thirteenth century.) In the size of its territory and population at that time, it ranked fourth largest in Europe, while Poland was eleventh. By the fifteenth century, the country was among the most powerful European states. In 1565, the Lublin Union between the Great Dukedom of Lithuania and the Kingdom of Poland was created, forming the Commonwealth of Lithuania and Poland, which became a major power.

Latvia and Estonia suffered foreign rule for long periods; their ruling classes from the twelfth to the nineteenth century were German. When they would subsequently demarcate their independent nations in the 1990s, Estonians and Latvians would thus concentrate on linguistic and ethnic factors in the countryside—sidestepping their sizeable Russian and German city populations—while the Lithuanians would choose to blend ethnic, linguistic principles with historical boundaries from old Lithuanian principalities. The Estonians perceive their land to have had Estonian integrity for millennia, their people having emigrated from the Ural Mountains in approximately 500 C.E.

By the late eighteenth century, Estonia, Latvia, and Lithuania had been devoured by czarist Russia. After 1710, imperial Russia became the master of the Baltic provinces. (Lithuania came under czarist rule after 1795, until a fleeting era of national independence starting in 1918.) Nonetheless, Germans and Poles remained landowners, and Germans and Jews dominated commerce. The indigenous peoples were largely peasants.

Estonians are mainly Lutheran, a Protestant denomination also known as the Evangelical Church in Germany, or they are Russian Orthodox. A majority of Latvians are Lutheran, with some Russian Orthodox and Roman Catholics. Lithuanians have for centuries been predominantly Roman Catholic. Culturally, Estonians are inclined toward Sweden and Finland. Latvians have strong German cultural affiliations. Lithuania has Slavic cultural attachments, dating to the country's union with the Polish commonwealth. The Soviet Union's divide-and-conquer policy in the twentieth century had the effect of emphasizing these distinctions.

In the thirteenth century, Danish monarchs established Tallinn, Estonia's medieval capital. A gem of German and

QUICK FACTS ABOUT THE BALTIC STATES

- The three Baltic republics moved toward independence from the Soviet Union at different rates. Estonia led off with economic proposals for autonomy and was the first to establish a popular front. Latvia, considered to be more cautious, initiated calendar events that characterized all three struggles. Lithuania, however, was the first to achieve independence.

- On June 14, 1987, in Riga, Latvia, the fledgling human rights group Helsinki '86 organized one of the earliest unofficial, peaceful assemblies of the postwar period. A thousand people marched to memorialize the Stalinist mass deportation of 14,000 Latvians in 1941 to Siberia. Between 2,000 and 3,000 Latvians also observed the gathering, standing near the Liberty Monument but too afraid to join. The march succeeded in publicly commemorating a painful historical moment. Estonian and Lithuanian activists in attendance vowed to organize similar efforts in their home countries.

- Also in summer 1987, discussions began in the three republics about publishing the 1939 Molotov-Ribbentrop Pact and the accompanying secret protocols that had divided Eastern Europe into German and Soviet spheres of influence and resulted in giving Stalin a free hand in the Baltics. Large gatherings in Estonia, Latvia, and Lithuania memorialized the anniversary of the signing of the secret 1939 clauses, the moment from which Baltic residents date their loss of independence.

- In 1988, "popular fronts" came into being in Estonia, Latvia, and Lithuania. These coalitions of reformist, nationalist, and nonviolent action groups included reform-minded communists inside and outside the governing regimes of the Baltic republics.

- On August 23, 1989, a human chain of hundreds of thousands of Estonians, Latvians, and Lithuanians linked hands across 400 miles, connecting the capital cities of the Baltic republics. As many as 2 million may have taken part, directly and indirectly, in what they called the Baltic Way. The participants, of all ages, demanded the right to restore their independent statehood, and sang folk and nationalist songs. The Estonian independence movement is called the Singing Revolution.

- On February 2, 1990, an assembly of Estonian leaders declared limited independence. The declaration passed with a vote of 138 in favor, none opposed, 1 abstention, and 57 deputies refusing to vote in protest. Meanwhile, Latvian parliamentarians petitioned Soviet leader Mikhail S. Gorbachev to start talks with them about their own independence.

- On March 11, 1990, Lithuania became the first Soviet socialist republic to declare independence. Proclaiming Lithuania a sovereign state, the Lithuanian Supreme Soviet, similar to a legislature for the local communist party, voted 124 to 0, with 9 abstentions and absentees, to restore the independent statehood broken by Soviet annexation half a century earlier. Simultaneously, it changed its name to the Republic of Lithuania and renamed the Supreme Soviet the Supreme Council. Soviet tanks soon thereafter rolled into the capital, Vilnius. In Moscow, Soviet officials pronounced Lithuania's declaration illegal and called for the restoration of "order and legitimacy" in Vilnius.

- On January 12, 1991, between 7,000 and 9,000 unarmed Lithuanians assembled at the parliament building and television broadcasting tower. Singing national folk songs and playing music, they encircled the tower and building, creating a human barrier to defend the structures from Soviet soldiers.

(Continued)

(Continued)

- On Bloody Sunday, January 13, 1991, Soviet paratroopers used live ammunition against unarmed Lithuanian citizens in Vilnius. Fourteen persons were killed, some crushed by tanks, as elite security and intelligence units stormed the broadcasting tower in the early morning. The elected Supreme Council would not surrender. Vytautas Landsbergis of Lithuania, Anatolijs Gorbunovs of Latvia, and Arnold Rüütel of Estonia—the three presidents of the democratic transition era—had also stood unarmed against the Soviet Union. The events of Bloody Sunday ultimately precipitated a chain of events that by December 1991 would lead to the end of the Soviet Union.

Scandinavian Gothic architecture and cobbled streets, its name means "Danish fortress." Tallinn accepted Swedish rule in 1561 and would later be captured by Peter the Great. It is today home to approximately half a million persons. Latvia's capital, Riga, founded in 1201 near the mouth of the Daugava River, has roots in Germany, although it attracted immense wealth under the Russian Empire, of which it was a major port and trading center. Of Riga's current population of 1 million, only one-third are Latvian. Germans and Russians were influential in Tallinn as well as Riga. Vilnius, the baroque capital of Lithuania, is first mentioned in written records in 1323. Sitting to the country's extreme southeast, it has two cleared spaces in its Old Town where the Nazis dynamited the Jewish ghetto. Its population today numbers approximately 600,000.

The First Republics

By the late nineteenth century, the predominantly Lutheran Estonian and Latvian churches as well as the Lithuanian Church of Rome had helped enliven an intelligentsia articulating a growing national consciousness among the Baltic peoples. Intellectual centers developed for Baltic nationalisms, one for Estonians and Latvians and another for Lithuanians. In 1632, the Swedes founded an academy in Tartu—Estonia's second largest city after Tallinn, the country's cultural and intellectual center—that became a university, which recruited Estonians and Latvians. Lithuania's counterpart was a Jesuit college in Vilnius established in 1579. Jewish institutions of learning also thrived in Vilnius, where Poles and Jews dominated.

The first choral fête in Tartu in 1869 celebrated the fiftieth anniversary of the emancipation of the serfs through the singing of folk songs. The collecting of folk songs became associated with early national awakenings of the nineteenth century and more than a century later would inspire similar singing festivals by all three Baltic peoples.

The Baltic provinces were by the early twentieth century economically among the more developed in the Russian Empire. Even so, in 1905 when imperial Russia collapsed as more than a century of capricious rule by autocratic czars culminated in revolution, some of the worst political unrest occurred in the Baltics, where a desire for national self-determination was thwarted by economies that were weak compared to those of nearby European and Nordic nations. World War I destroyed the last vestiges of the czar's legitimacy and weakened the state's ability to rule. The Russian Revolution of October 1917 swept aside imperial power and ended Russia's involvement in the war. With its center weakened by military defeat, rising prospects of civil war, indigenous movements jockeying for independence, and continual German offensives, the Bolshevik regime was obliged to withdraw the Russian military from the periphery of its diluted empire.

In November 1917, the Bolsheviks issued the Declaration on the Rights of the Peoples in Russia, recognizing an equality of nations and formally allowing secession by the various subjugated peoples. Finland broke away in 1917; Estonia and Lithuania declared independence in February 1918. From 1918 to 1920, the Baltic lands were frenzied military battlegrounds over which Baltic nationalists, Bolsheviks, Germans, Poles, and White Russians fought for control. In 1918, Bolshevik Russia went one step further and renounced its sovereignty over the Baltic lands. Tattered by revolution and war, the Soviet Union signed peace treaties with the three independent Baltic states in 1920, recognizing the secession of Estonia, Latvia, and Lithuania. Bolshevik leader Vladimir Lenin claimed to want "peace without annexations or indemnities on the basis of self-determination of the peoples" and granted Baltic independence "voluntarily and for ever," promising respect for their independence. The three Baltic states became members of the League of Nations. The Western powers liked having a buffer zone adjacent to the Soviet Union, and the three small nations occupied strategically important pieces of land between the major powers of Germany and Russia, which had exhausted themselves in hostilities, but could again rise. Remembrance of the wars of independence remains a focal point of Baltic nationalist thinking to this day, as does the memory of their two decades of independence.

Newly independent Estonia, Latvia, and Lithuania created constitutions that provided universal suffrage for men and women, parliamentary rule, multiparty systems, and a president as head of state; they elected unicameral legislatures every three years. Yet in the young, inexperienced Baltic states, the parliaments were fractious as too-numerous political parties jockeyed; their cabinets were unstable. Communists, viewed as unfriendly toward the sovereignty of the Baltic states, were generally excluded from participation. As national minorities gained civil rights and authorities implemented land reforms, many of the mostly German large landowners, called Baltic barons, moved to Germany. The moderate political left, initially popular, lost support after instituting the land reforms, which originally appealed to rural voters. Moderately right-wing and populist parties gained ground, but were fragmented. As fascist movements grew during the post-1929 global economic depression, the Baltic regimes became less democratic and more authoritarian.

The three Baltic states, although different from each other, pursued policies of neutrality and emphasized their belonging together, with mutual celebrations of each others' independence holidays. The Baltic peoples refer to the period of independence from 1918 to 1940 as the First Republics.

"Dirty Booty"

The Soviet and German governments overturned the illusory freedoms evoked by the Bolsheviks' 1920 relinquishment of claims to the Baltic republics when they authorized the signing of the Molotov–Ribbentrop Pact of nonaggression and friendship on August 23 and September 28, 1939. The August 23 document reads, "[T]he two parties discussed in strictly confidential conversations the question of the delimitation of their respective spheres of interest in Eastern Europe." Further, "This protocol will be treated by both parties as strictly secret." Although the treaty is named for its signatories, both Vyacheslav Molotov and Joachim von Ribbentrop were acting on behalf of their bosses, Soviet leader Josef Stalin and German führer Adolf Hitler. Most significant in the August 23 agreement, signed in the presence of Stalin in Moscow, was a secret protocol that provided for the partitioning of Poland, Finland, and the Baltic states between Nazi Germany and the Soviet Union (see "Text of Secret Protocols to 1939 Hitler-Stalin Pact"). The protocol served as the trigger for Germany's attack on Poland that began on September 1, 1939, launching World War II.

On September 28, 1939, the Soviets compelled the Baltic republics, under threat of military incursion, to arrange defense and mutual assistance pacts through a confidential protocol. The Soviet Union received rights to establish naval facilities, bases, and airfields and to house troops. Estonia signed the pact on September 28, the same day as the second Soviet-German pact. The September 28 protocol clarified the borders of Lithuania, which came into the Soviet realm. Shortly thereafter, the Soviets signed mutual assistance pacts with Latvia and Lithuania on October 5 and October 10, respectively.

On June 15–18, 1940, the Red Army—the military force created after the 1917 Bolshevik Revolution by the communist government of the Soviet Union—invaded the independent republics of Estonia, Latvia, and Lithuania. The Soviets had accused the Baltic states of violating the pacts and plotting against the union. Moscow demanded unlimited entry of Soviet forces and formation of pro-Soviet governments. Bullying, threatening, and interposing Soviet troops, Stalin forced out the independent Baltic governments. He thus broke Lenin's pledge and forcibly annexed them as constituent republics of the Soviet Union. The annexations, the last to be carried out by the Soviets, were never officially recognized by the international community.

Under Stalin's bidding, new communist governments and communist sympathizers rigged parliamentary balloting. Applications for admission to the Soviet Union were granted, naturally, and on August 3–6, 1940, the Baltic republics became socialist republics of the Soviet Union. Under duress and Soviet manipulations, new governments were installed. The former presidents of Estonia and Latvia were jailed and dispatched to Soviet Russia, where they died. Lithuania's president, Antanas Smetona, fled to Germany on June 15, 1940, and died four years later in the United States.

In an August 23, 1991, editorial, *The New York Times* recalls that "the United States has never recognized the forcible annexation of the Baltic States by Stalin, the dirty booty in a secret protocol of the 1939" ("Baltic Freedom in a New Light"). In its August 24, 1989, edition, *The Times* publishes the secret protocols from texts translated by the U.S. government from microfilm copies of original German Foreign Ministry documents turned over to the Allies at the end of World War II. The Soviet Union would refuse for five decades to acknowledge the existence of the agreements (see "Text of Secret Protocols to 1939 Hitler-Stalin Pact").

"An Appalling Toll of Baltic Victims"

Under ruthless Soviet totalitarianism after June 1941, the new Soviet-installed regimes in the Baltic nations carried out mass deportations of "class enemies" to Siberia. The deportees together comprised 4 percent of Estonia's population and approximately 2 percent each of Latvia's and Lithuania's. In Lithuania alone, some 20,000 partisans were killed, 140,000 were put in concentration camps, and 118,000 were deported, mostly to Siberia. The Soviet-installed commands in the Baltic republics claimed that these mass banishments were the result of Baltic resistance against Soviet rule.

The application of draconian policies of Russification and Sovietization led to bank accounts being frozen, land expropriated, cattle and grain confiscated, industry nationalized, industrial plants transferred to the Soviet Union, education systems thrown into upheaval with mass firings of teachers, and textbooks replaced. The traumas had led many Baltic residents to view the Germans as liberators, when Nazi troops occupied the region in the first stages of its invasion of the Soviet Union that began June 22, 1941. The German occupation cost hundreds of thousands more in Baltic lives. Almost all the Jews there were murdered, with assistance from connivers and sympathizers among the Lithuanians, Latvians, and Estonians. Of Lithuania's prewar population of 250,000 Jews, only 40,000 survived the Holocaust. Following the German invasion, the Red Army withdrew from Baltic lands, and nationalist uprisings erupted in all three republics.

In 1944, with the Nazis facing defeat, the Soviet Union regained jurisdiction of the Baltic lands. Terror and deportations recommenced. Of a total population of 6 million, more than half a million disappeared. The Soviets reestablished communist regimes in the Baltics that would last nearly five decades. The regimes implemented twin economic policies of agricultural collectivization and rapid industrialization. Each of the three republics was cut off from the others. Official cultural interchanges were routed through Moscow, as were the republics' hierarchical, centrally planned economic systems. All roads led to Moscow. Relationships among the Baltic republics were alienated by Moscow's policies of poor communications, severely limited railway connections, restricted flights between the three Baltic capitals, and an imposed provincialism. Large numbers of Russians emigrated during the late 1940s and 1950s to the Baltics to set up new factories and establish large-scale industrialization. Soviet military personnel were also deployed. The Soviet collectivization process led to still more deportations; 220,000 peasants were deported to Siberia from 1947 through 1949 from Lithuania alone. More than a quarter of a million fled westward from the Baltics. Soviet industrialization policies gave Moscow 90 percent control of Baltic industry.

As the policy of Russification was instituted, systematic efforts were undertaken to eliminate independent civil society. In the process of being collectivized, Russianized, and Sovietized, the histories of the three nations were rewritten. The period of independence known as the First Republics was declared fascist, and the Soviet republics that replaced them extolled as the faithful expression of the yearning, laboring masses. Stalin's ruthless Russification meant eradicating minority languages, forbidding national symbols, and banning customary songs and flags. Local cultures were repressed and folklore groups smothered.

Balts—a collective term for the people of Estonia, Latvia, and Lithuania—had fought the Soviet occupation forces with guerrilla tactics in the early years of Sovietization. By 1952, it was evident, however, that such resistance would not be effective. The 1987–1991 turn to nonviolent resistance in the Baltic republics considered here was thus a logical, pragmatic conclusion. In the mid-1950s Soviet forces defeated the Forest Brotherhoods, killing 20,000 partisans who had taken advantage of the refuge offered by the area's wild forest while resisting Soviet military occupation. Subsequently, opposition to Soviet hegemony became less conspicuous and more dispersed. It ranged from underground groups' refusal to cooperate with officially imposed behaviors and norms to intermittent acts of local protest; the Baltic area became a major source of anti-Soviet "dissident" activity in the Soviet Union. With Stalin's death in 1953, some relaxation occurred. For the next three decades, limited nonviolent action was employed through refusal to join communist youth organizations, speak Russian, and vote in Soviet elections. Some communist officials resisted Russification policies by defending the Baltic cultures.

In 1959, Nikita Khrushchev, first secretary of the Communist Party of the Soviet Union (1953–1964) and premier of the Soviet Union (1958–1964), accused the Latvian communist party of "Latvianizing" local bureaucracies. The party was purged, and as Latvian nationalists were driven out, it became the most pro-Soviet of the three Baltic regimes. Latvia, as one history puts it, "had been laid waste by war and robbed by both German and Russian troops" (Bleiere 2006, 128). In Latvia alone, historians estimate that the number of victims of the communist political repressions of arrests, incarcerations, and deaths in the 1940s and 1950s tallied between 140,000 and 190,000; other estimates suggest 240,000. Figures from the Latvian state security committee show 47,218 arrested and sentenced for political "crimes" between 1940 and 1986. As annexation by the

Soviet Union proceeded in 1940, called "the year of horror," an underground prison was built in Riga, at 37/39 Freedom Street, in the basement of the Home Affairs Ministry. For five decades in the infamous "house on the corner," Latvian nationalists were tortured.

Nationalist Opposition Slowly Builds

Self-awareness of the Baltic nations as distinct entities is perhaps a century old, in part molded by the broadening, educated classes shaping national culture. During the 1970s, nationalist opposition stirred. In 1971 in Estonia, a popular front organized and carried out the first major Baltic protests of students and schoolchildren against Russification. Labor unrest in Poland stimulated more upheaval in Tallinn and Tartu (see **Poland, Introduction**). Estonians had access to Finnish television and could see the Finns' economic prosperity for themselves. *The Times* on October 4, 1988, reflects, "The conditions that have made Estonia a laboratory for independent politics—a tolerant Communist Party, an intense sense of ethnic pride, and a longtime affinity for the ways of other Europeans—are so far unlike those in the [Soviet Union's] 14 other republics" ("Estonia Ferment: Soviet Role Model or Exception?"). The Soviet Union consisted of fifteen republics, each of which had its own communist party subordinate to the Central Committee of the Communist Party of the Soviet Union.

In 1969, critics, widely referred to as dissidents, from all three Baltic republics had signed a joint document. Seventeen Latvian communists signed a petition in 1974 against Russification; among them was Eduards Berklavs. A member of the Latvian communist party, in the 1950s Berklavs had opposed the Soviet policy of Russification, advocated wider use of the Latvian language, and wanted to limit immigration from other parts of the Soviet Union to Latvia. His stance led to his being tagged as a Latvian nationalist. Party head and Soviet premier Nikita Khrushchev reprimanded and dismissed him in 1959, expelling him from the party and sending him into exile in Russia. In the late 1980s, Berklavs would reemerge as a proponent of Latvian independence and retain leadership in Latvia throughout the independence process.

More documents appeared in 1979 and 1980 denouncing the Molotov-Ribbentrop Pact and its secret protocols and appealing to the United Nations to condemn the Soviet occupation and annexation of the Baltic republics. An August 23, 1979, appeal, on the anniversary of the German-Soviet pact, was signed by forty-five Balts, of whom thirty-six were Lithuanian. By the early 1980s, Baltic popular dissent had become more vocal than previously and further organized than anywhere else in the Soviet Union.

Gorbachev Assumes Power

At the Soviet Union's Communist Party congress in October 1961, Khrushchev presented a new, two-stage national policy. The first consisted of a "rapprochement" of the Soviet nations as they learned to cooperate; the second, national "fusion," involved the disparate nations coming together under the umbrella of a supranational Soviet identity. In reality, "fusion" meant the acquiescence of "minor" nations to the dominant Russian nation.

The rise of Mikhail S. Gorbachev to power as general secretary of the Communist Party of the Soviet Union in 1985 led to the introduction of "new thinking" in Moscow's foreign policy. In 1986, Gorbachev freed Andrei Sakharov, a prominent critic of Soviet policies, from exile in Gorky. Release of other Soviet political prisoners in 1987 included leading Baltic opposition figures, who would now be able to strengthen fledgling organizations in their homelands. In 1987, Gorbachev explained his principles for reform, which were interconnected and fell into four main categories: *perestroika,* or "restructuring" of the economy; *glasnost,* "openness"; democratization; and a new course in foreign policy (see **"Introduction: Strikes, Sinatra, and Nonviolent Revolution"**). Following the death of the longtime Soviet leader Leonid I. Brezhnev in 1982, the crises in the Soviet system became undeniable. Gorbachev's proposals were meant to revitalize the system, particularly the stagnating economy, which had been growing at only 2 percent annually for a decade. Gorbachev hoped through managed change to safeguard the Communist Party's monopoly on power.

Of all the nationalities brought together in the Soviet Union, the Baltic republics were the best positioned to take advantage of Gorbachev's new principles. By the late 1980s, developments there were moving toward democratization and the pursuit of independence from the Soviet Union. In the process, it was understood that any use of violence would redound to Moscow's advantage. All three states experienced expansion of unofficial publications, called *samizdat* ("self-published" in Russian, as opposed to state-published production, *gosudarstvennoye izdatelstvo,* or *gosizdat*) (see **"Introduction: Strikes, Sinatra, and Nonviolent Revolution"**). As the tempo of opposition gained speed in 1986 and built momentum in 1987–1988, the communist parties in the Baltic states began to divide and splinter.

The three Baltic republics shared a general outlook of common interests and historic realities, but differences among them also played roles in their collective saga. A Latvian group sparked the calendar events that came to characterize open, popular civil resistance to Soviet rule. The terms *calendar events* and *calendar demonstrations* were chosen by Balts in all three countries to describe their fastening of major actions onto commemoration of historical events. Estonia early took the lead in mobilization by putting forth economic proposals for autonomy. Yet, as time passed, Lithuania would bypass the two northernmost republics and become the first to obtain independence.

Calendar Events, 1986–1987

Often considered the most cautious of the three republics, Latvia emerged as the harbinger of the Baltic nationalist quest for independence in 1986, despite the high proportion of Russian and other immigrants dominating its communist party membership and regime. Latvians comprised only 52 percent of the republic's population. Of the remainder, 34 percent were Russian. By 1990, the Soviet Union had 223 armed forces, navy, and border guard units totaling 70,000 to 80,000 persons in Latvia

A Lithuanian group that sought to monitor adherence to the Helsinki Final Act was established in 1976 with a manifesto emphasizing restoration of an independent Lithuanian state; it folded in 1981 following the arrest of its members. Another critical step in the Baltic's transition to democracy was the formation in Latvia of Helsinki '86 to monitor adherence to the Helsinki Final Act of 1975 and its human rights provisions (see **"Introduction: Strikes, Sinatra, and Nonviolent Revolution"**). Helsinki '86 was established in 1986 in the port city of Liepāja by three young workers—Martins Bariss, Raimonds Bitenieks, and Linards Grantins. The group made a point of operating openly. In their first public statement, its founders explained its purpose as monitoring "how the economic, cultural, and individual rights of our people are respected." Its activities included a series of open, signed letters of protest to Soviet officials, including Gorbachev, and sent to various international organizations. The missives raised the issue of Latvian independence in tentative terms. These communications drew attention to the Latvian situation and protested ongoing Russification, including discrimination against Latvians, and questioned politically oppressive policies.

In February 1987, immediately preceding the announcement of new phosphorite mining in Estonia, Gorbachev visited Riga and Tallinn. In Riga, on February 17, he attacked "Baltic émigré circles and their Western supporters" for "their hate-filled lies" and praised Russian soldiers as defenders against foreign invaders and liberators. In Tallinn, on February 19, he spoke of strengthening "internationalist" education, code for Russification, and called for eliminating "extreme nationalist tendencies in some parts of the Soviet Union." Gorbachev des-cribed Estonia as an economic burden to the Soviet Union that annually received 3 billion rubles but contributed only 2.5 billion. To the contrary, Estonians believed Soviet prices for Estonian "exports" to the union to be below the world market level, while Estonian "imports" were fixed above world market levels.

After Gorbachev's visit, Estonian academicians and intellectuals became skeptical of the prospects for political rebirth and apprehensive of major ecological degradation and immigration by even more Russians. Criticism of Russian influence and their numbers, previously modulated, began to be expressed more vocally.

"Decolonization" evolved as an important metaphor for the Baltic nationalists, who had since 1939–1940 regarded the Soviet Union as a cruel, foreign, and asphyxiating interloper. The Baltics' popular fronts saw themselves as decolonization movements, not solely as pro-democracy movements. They routinely used the term *decolonization* to characterize their struggle and depict the Soviet Union, although the Soviet Union was not technically a colonial state. The Baltic republics fastened their cause to the international norms against conquest and colonization enshrined in the UN Charter and subsequent conventions and resolutions in order to chip away at Soviet control. In 1989, the popular fronts appealed directly to the United Nations in an effort to generate international support (see "Baltic Independence Fronts Plead to U.N."). The question of language was linked to the perception of the Soviet Union as an imperial power and became an issue when it was decided to change street names from Russian to Estonian. Changing street names is a time-honored nonviolent method and was used by the Czechoslovaks in resisting the incursion of Soviet-led Warsaw Pact forces—confusing the troops after they invaded in 1968 (see **Czechoslovakia, Introduction**).

Nationalism first materialized over environmental degradation. In Latvia, citizens founded the Environmental Protection Club in February 1987. Major environmental demonstrations had occurred in 1986 in Riga, where air pollution, toxic waste storage, and lack of potable water had become major issues. Summer and autumn 1987 represented high points for Latvian environmental groups, as the Club for the Defense of the Environment (Videz Aizsardzibas Klubs, VAK) emerged, prompted by successful rallies against the Daugava River hydroelectric power project. By November, the Soviet Union Council of Ministers had decided to reject the plant's construction to sidestep additional negative publicity on environmental matters.

In Estonia in February 1987, a "phosphorite war" had broken out following a television exposé of increased Soviet mining in Estonia of phosphorite ore, half of which came from one site in the republic. The technique used to extract phosphorite, needed for fertilizers for out-of-date Soviet agricultural production, was ecologically destructive. The mining process contaminated groundwater with radioactive substances, and persons living near the main mines suffered from high rates of diseases and deformities. Close to a year earlier, in April 1986, a meltdown at the Chernobyl nuclear power station in Soviet Ukraine had directed attention toward Lithuania's Ignalina nuclear reactor, which was the same as Chernobyl's. Thousands of Estonians had been sent involuntarily, and without adequate protection, to take part in the rescue efforts in Ukraine. The free hand that had been given to Stalin in 1939 meant that exploitation of natural resources had proceeded for decades, with no accountability, no price paid, even for human loss, and no cleanup. A firestorm of environmental protests blazed as glasnost facilitated flows of information. An archbishop issued a prayer to be read in Estonian churches. The indifference of the Estonian government enraged the population and led to the removal of Prime Minister Bruno Saul. Estonian demonstrations culminated in 1987 in the postponement of the environmentally degrading phosphorite mining expansion, and stimulated more oppositional organizing.

On June 14, 1987, in Riga, Helsinki '86 organized the first open and unofficial assembly of the postwar period, at the Freedom Monument—a column topped with the Lady of Liberty holding three stars outstretched toward the sky honoring Latvia's independence between the wars—to memorialize the Stalinist mass deportation of 14,000 Latvians in 1941. The monument had been erected in 1935, five years before the Soviet Union annexed Estonia, Latvia, and Lithuania. *The Times* does not cover the rally, the significance of which became apparent only in retrospect. Some 1,000 marched to the monument, readied for police interruption. Another 2,000 to 3,000 watched near the monument, too afraid to join. To everyone's surprise, the march proved to be a success. Estonian and Lithuanian activists in attendance vowed to organize similar efforts in their respective capitals. It was the first of many calendar demonstrations commemorating critical historical moments of the early independence period or betrayals of the 1940s; such actions would become too numerous to count during the next three years in the Baltic republics. As the days passed, demonstrators returned to the Freedom Monument to leave flowers, which a few years earlier would have been a certain route to prison.

Although some sympathizers remained aloof, other Latvians took courage from the June 14 event, including discussion clubs, small political groups, and cultural and religious organizations. Rebirth and Renewal (Atdzimsana un Atjaunosanas), a religious association that would later play a role in the revitalization of the Lutheran Church in Latvia, established itself on June 14, 1987. An assortment of cultural, environmental, political, religious, and social groups began meeting weekly. Soviet authorities tolerated loyal opposition that functioned within the framework of perestroika and glasnost, but other groups—such as members and supporters of Helsinki '86—were regarded as "radical," thereby justifying criticism and persecution. Members of Helsinki '86, distant followers, and even children were harassed, beaten, and sometimes deported. Regardless, more Latvians joined.

On August 15 in Estonia, a small committee formed to begin work on publishing the 1939 Molotov-Ribbentrop Pact. At the time, the Soviet Union continued to deny the existence of secret protocols. The committee was able to secure official permission for a demonstration, although hopes for a decent turnout were slim. In the end, a respectable 5,000 to 7,000 took part. In Latvia, Helsinki '86 organized Black Ribbon Day, referring to the Stalin-Hitler nonaggression pact. In Estonia, open public protest against the regime called for publication of the secret accords. Official media denounced the organizers as "national extremists," and the communist party organ said only a few hundred had attended the demonstration. In one of the first visible signs of the spread of popular nonviolent dissent in Lithuania, protest groups gathered in Vilnius as the August anniversary of the Molotov-Ribbentrop Pact neared. On August 23, the anniversary of the secret Soviet-Nazi protocol, major demonstrations were held in the three Baltic capitals.

Estonia's leading role in economic reforms came to the fore when on September 26, 1987, four mid-level Estonian members of the communist party, two of whom were economists, presented principles for Estonian economic autonomy within the contours of the Soviet Union. Its signatories would later call it the IME project, from Ise Majandav Eesti, or Self-Managing Estonia. The Soviet bosses may not have understood that *ime* in Estonian means wonder. Consisting of nine points, the program advocates Estonian control of the republic's economy, market principles, a convertible ruble, budgeting separate from the Soviet Union's, economic self-determination, competition, independent enterprises, and abolition of controlling bureaucracies. How to achieve political autonomy was not considered. Truly controversial issues, such as private ownership of land or a separate currency, went unmentioned. IME would not be implemented, but the independence struggle was now fully under way. In Riga, on November 18, the anniversary of Latvia's declaration of independence in the early 1900s, police attacked and injured demonstrators attending a rally. Authorities deported some members of Helsinki '86 to the West. Despite being slandered in public and vilified by news media, the group's members refused to bow.

Popular Fronts

The emergence of "popular fronts" in Estonia, Latvia, and Lithuania made 1988 a euphoric year. These groups, unlike political parties, were broad-spectrum coalitions of reformist, nationalist, and popular dissent groups, including communists from inside and outside the governing regimes of the Baltic republics.

During the glasnost era in the Soviet Union, the Baltic movements distinguished themselves by the swiftness and magnitude of scale with which entire populations mobilized around nationalist issues. The possibilities suggested by glasnost were grasped first by intellectuals, including academicians, architects, artists, authors, clergy, journalists, philosophers, scientists, and scholars. Glasnost offered a framework for imagining, conceptualizing, and mounting broad civil resistance. It opened political space, and helped to make the independence movements' collective nonviolent action effective. Political scientist Mark R. Beissinger (2009) explains:

> In a regime in which the fiction of public support had long been a central narrative of reigning ideology, glasnost created a new set of vulnerabilities for the Soviet state. Large-scale protest punctured the regime's central legitimating myths, such as the claims that it had "solved" the nationalities problem or represented the interests of "toilers." Even if located thousands of miles from Moscow, protest violated long-standing norms of behaviour in Soviet politics, exposed the weakness of the Soviet state, and created tensions within governing circles. . . . [C]ivil resistance exploited two fundamental weaknesses of a semi-liberalized Soviet state: it attacked the gap between the regime's pretense that it represented genuine public will and the reality of widespread antipathy to Soviet rule; and it exploited the new information milieu in which criticism of a once secretive and infallible regime had grown normalized (p. 240).

For the first time since a 1921 prohibition against factions within the Communist Party, alternative political entities took shape. It is easy to underestimate the importance of the development of the popular fronts, but it is they who ushered in the nonviolent transformation of the Baltic republics.

Estonia's Popular Front

On April 8, 1988, Estonian intellectuals released a declaration asking for "real restructuring," playing on the term perestroika. On April 13, Edgar Savisaar, an economist and former party planning committee official, appeared on Estonian television and proposed the formation of an Estonian popular front "in support of perestroika." The Estonian regime endorsed his idea, and Esstimaa Rahvarinne, the Estonian Popular Front—officially the Popular Front for the Support of Perestroika—came into being on October 2. *The Times* on November 17, 1988, reports, "While Latvia and Lithuania also have strong nationalist movements, Estonia's Popular Front has in a way served as a model for nationalists in the two other republics" ("Estonia Asserts a Right of Veto on Soviet Laws").

Throughout 1988, the communist parties fragmented, and members of a reform wing comprised of native Baltic peoples gained significant positions in the state and party bureaucracies. Citing perestroika and glasnost, editors and journalists joyfully cruised from one banned topic to another. As fear dissipated, outspoken citizens organized political activities. The broad nationalist independence movements made use of national symbols, flags, cultural events, revival of the churches, and singing festivals.

On February 2, 1988, in Tartu, a university town and Estonia's cultural center, locals held a demonstration to mark the 1920 peace treaty between Latvia and Soviet Russia that sought "to end the state of war between them." The event was a conscious reminder of the 1869 choral fête in Estonia's second largest city, which celebrated the eradication of serfdom with the collecting of folk songs, as national awareness awoke in the nineteenth century. For the first time since the fleeting period of independence after World War I, Estonians openly flew the original blue, black, and white national flag, despite its official banning. Police responded with harsh reprisals. This would be the last such violent crackdown in the Baltics until autumn 1990, when terror would be introduced into Latvia by special troops of the Otryad Militsii Osobovo Naznacheniya (Militia Unit for Special Assignments, OMON, or black berets) from the Soviet Interior Ministry (see "Latvia Lawmakers Move to Dissolve Links to Moscow"). On February 24, however, 10,000 were able to march peacefully in the streets of the Estonian capital to honor the nation's independence day. The police did not intervene.

In Estonia in spring 1988, "creative unions" of artists, writers, and journalists met on April 1–2 and called for protection of the Estonian language and culture, reinstitution of national symbols, and progress toward independence. They openly criticized the mismanagement of the party's leadership by party chief Karl Vaino. The session represented a benchmark and produced a firm resolution addressed to those who would be attending a Soviet party conference slated for June 28 in Moscow.

In Tallinn in early June, a song festival evoked national pride in this nineteenth-century cultural tradition. (More than 370,000 national songs have been registered by the Estonian National Folklore Archives.) Approximately 100,000 assembled at Lauluväljak, Song Square, or Singers' Field. Heinz Valk, an artist, dubbed the occasion the Singing Revolution, and the name stuck. Live singing in massive choral festivals became a chief method through which ideas of resistance and independence spread.

Some 600 Estonian candidates had been nominated for the thirty-two slots for delegates to the Moscow party congress. At the gathering, Karl Vaino submitted a list of thirty-two candidates for secret balloting that was accepted, although protested; this later came to be regarded as the last gasp of the old system. On June 14, proposals circulated among activist intellectuals and local party reformers for Estonian to be restored as the official language of the republic, along with restitution of the original flag. Vaino's response to the popular clamor was to ask for military assistance from Moscow, a move inconsistent with the direction being taken by Gorbachev. On June 16, the Estonian communist party central committee gathered to appoint a new first secretary. Vaino Väljas replaced Karl Vaino (who disappeared into Moscow's bureaucracy).

On June 17 in Song Square, 150,000 congregated in the largest political assemblage in Estonian history to send a message to the thirty-two delegates soon departing for the Moscow congress. Everywhere, the traditional Estonian flag flew. When the delegates left Tallinn, they carried proposals that went far beyond their original remit. Across the fifteen republics of the Soviet Union, anticipation ran high for the Moscow party congress. Multicandidate elections were planned for the Baltic delegations, with nominations to be presented by republican communist party central committees. The Baltic peoples hoped that this development spelled a possible advance toward eventual free elections. In Moscow, an initial reception of hostility gave way to approval for the Estonians to try their "four-man" IME proposal, with the congress noting, "The notion of transferring the republics to economic self-management deserves attention."

Historian Alfred Erich Senn calls the Baltic mobilizations of summer 1988 a "primordial explosion," because of the rapidity with which huge surges of popular defiance materialized. At long last, in early August the secret protocols of the Molotov-Ribbentrop Pact appeared on paper. In August 1988, the Estonian National Independence Party formed, representing the first self-declared opposition political party in the Soviet Union.

On September 8–10, the Estonian Supreme Soviet and communist party central committee gathered. Väljas, the party first secretary, announced that the demands of the people and the Estonian Popular Front would become the party's demands. On September 11, on Estonia's Song Square, one-third of Estonia's population, some 300,000 persons, assembled in an unparalleled demonstration. Singing and dancing went on throughout the night.

On October 1–2, the Estonian Popular Front held its inaugural congress, marking the first phase toward independence. Concerns over environmental degradation and matters of ethnic pride had morphed into economic programs and political aspirations and led to the formation of a group that could speak for the Estonians with Moscow. *The Times* on October 2, 1988, refers to the front's first congress as "an independent force that is perhaps the most interesting experiment in political pluralism ever tolerated in the Soviet Union" ("The Estonians Say, Let Us Be Estonian"). *The Times* on October 4, 1988, notes:

> With the christening on Sunday of an independent movement for political and economic autonomy, the republic of Estonia became the mecca for aspiring democrats throughout the Soviet Union. From the neighboring Baltic republics of Latvia and Lithuania, from the more distant republics of Armenia, Byelorussia, the Ukraine, Moldavia and Kazakhstan, from the Russian cities of Moscow, Leningrad and Kuibyshev, leaders of like-minded movements sat here in the Lenin Palace of Culture and applauded as 3,000 delegates of the Popular Front of Estonia formally launched their campaign. Similar gatherings have been scheduled to create popular fronts in Latvia next weekend and in Lithuania at the end of the month ("Estonia Ferment: Soviet Role Model or Exception?").

At this stage the popular fronts were calling only for autonomy within the Soviet system, not independence, despite some voices calling for secession. They generally couched their appeals as being in line with Gorbachev's reform processes.

On November 16, 1988, however, the Estonian Supreme Soviet, as the parliaments in all the Baltic states were called, voted to grant itself the right to veto the laws of the Soviet Union, reacting against suspected efforts in Moscow to circumscribe rights of secession from the Soviet Union under a proposed new constitution. The Soviet Supreme Soviet condemned the Estonian legislation as unconstitutional, but nonetheless, as one observer noted, the Estonians' declaration, and later those of the other two Baltic republics, served to chip away "at the legal cement holding the Soviet Union together." Estonia led, but could not alone bring about the remarkable accomplishment of the Baltic peoples.

Latvia's "Awakening" and the Latvian Popular Front

Latvia proceeded more slowly than the other Baltic states, partly because of its larger Russian minority, the result of systematic Soviet policies. Throughout 1988, Latvia's Helsinki '86 produced political documentation, some of it broadcast on Radio Free Europe and Voice of America, or published in *Auseklis* (Dawn) magazine. Its Memorandum to the Central Committee of the Communist Party of Latvia, the first in-depth democratization program for Latvia, proposed ten initiatives, including economic autonomy and restoration of the Latvian language.

On March 25, two demonstrations memorialized the 1949 deportation of 43,000 Latvians to Siberia. A rally organized by Helsinki '86 and allied groups drew harassment and surveillance by the KGB and only a few thousand participants. The second event—the first officially approved demonstration—drew more than 25,000 demonstrators in Riga. It was assembled and well publicized by the creative unions, which presented themselves as moderates; the event intensified their impact.

A psychological breakthrough against fearfulness occurred during June 1–2 in Riga, where a joint conference of Latvian creative unions of artists, writers, poets, scholars, and journalists for the first time engaged in free public discussion about social, political, and economic problems. The issues addressed included Russification, cultural hunger, distortions of Latvia's history, and living conditions. Mavriks Vulfsons, a communist known for obsequious adherence to the regime, drastically altered his position, asserting that Latvia in 1940 had not voluntarily joined the Soviet Union, as communist doctrine maintained, but had been militarily occupied.

As with Estonia's April 1–2 meeting of creative unions, the session proved to be a turning point. The members considered nominations for the upcoming Communist Party conference in Moscow. Those present took full advantage of their interpretation of glasnost and pushed for previously unarticulated disclosures of Soviet obfuscation. Janis Peters, a leader of the Writers' Union, led in the issuing of a series of demands generally expressive of the bids being made by the Baltic nationalist oppositions that year: sovereignty of the republics, economic autonomy, controls over immigration, designation of Latvian as the official language, diplomatic rights, and a separate military force. The term *sovereignty* was not accidental; it had been used historically in the strictly Soviet context. When published, the conference papers generated an intellectual upheaval that journalists called the Awakening. The meeting and subsequent activities, although initially acceptable in Riga and Moscow because of perestroika and glasnost, became the foundation for the Latvian Popular Front. Thereafter, two commissions were created to address rehabilitation for the victims of Stalinism.

On June 14, emboldened by the audacity of the scholar activists and reformers, at least 100,000 persons—as opposed to 1,000 a year earlier—marched to memorialize the victims of Stalin's deportations. The officially approved demonstration far exceeded expectations. Speakers and placards exuded self-confidence. The sight of the national flag hoisted by Helsinki '86 members exhilarated the crowds. Olgerts Eglitis, a Latvian philosopher and participant in the events chronicled here, notes, "From that day on, large-scale peaceful demonstrations of up to 500,000 participants became one of the principal traits of the Latvian national liberation movement" (Eglitis 1993, 14).

Police and army intervention continued against Latvians organizing events and mobilizing citizens in late spring 1988. A campaign was mounted for the release of Modris Lujans, who had been arrested in June for carrying a placard calling Latvia's communist officials "traitors." Pro-democracy and independence activists saw the Lujans case as potentially precedent setting. Determined not to allow the full return of totalitarianism, their petitioning letters, collective declarations, and passing of resolutions gave way to picketing. The Latvians' main action method became standing up and lining streets, carrying posters expressing their bids and objections. Communist authorities did not bend; picketers were beaten or detained. Lujans—changed with "hooliganism" and "slandering the Soviet state"—was put on trial. Three "public advocates" were selected by various groups to defend Lujans, whose acquittal became one of the first victories in the independence struggle.

On June 17, determined nationalists established the Latvian National Independence Movement (Latvijas Nacionalas

Neatkaribas Kustiba, or NIML) under the leadership of Eduards Berklavs. In short, it advocated the resignation of the Latvian government if it could not fulfill its obligations to the people. From the start, it called for full independence for Latvia. Its confrontational tone meant that its membership grew more slowly, but by 1989, it had attracted 11,000 members.

The NIML bridged the gap between faster moving proponents of independence and what would become the Latvian Popular Front. The so-called radicals and moderates developed a division of labor formed between themselves whereby the more militant handled street organizing and the moderates spoke to the media. On October 8–9, the formal congress of the Latvian Popular Front drew hundreds of thousands of people carrying Latvian flags. The mood was elated.

In 1988, Latvians held three calendar events: on June 14, marking the anniversary of the 1941 Stalinist deportations; on August 23, commemorating the Molotov-Ribbentrop Pact; and on November 18, memorializing the pronouncements of independence of the First Republics. The 1987 political rallies had been assembled mainly by the youths who had organized Helsinki '86, but by 1988 their ranks had grown to include activist intellectuals and communist party members and progressive officials. The moderates, proponents of perestroika, sought autonomy within the Soviet Union.

The initiative shifted to the new organizations emerging from the grassroots and organized by youths, environmentalists, artists, activist intellectuals, and communist reformers. The reappearance in a leadership role of Eduards Berklavs—the communist party reformer and former Latvian party secretary dismissed in the 1950s after attempting to introduce political and economic autonomy—symbolized three lost decades. Natvijas Tautus Fronte, the Latvian Popular Front, made its formal appearance on October 9. Prominent academicians, authors, and journalists were joined by critics of the regime and victims of repression in being elected to its council and board. On October 10, 1988, *The Times* reports the front's establishment as follows:

> Latvians created an independent political organization . . . to demand sovereignty in governing their republic. The group, calling itself the Latvian Popular Front and claiming a membership of over 100,000, stopped short of calling for secession from the Soviet Union. But in a meeting attended and often applauded by local Communist Party officials, the group advocated complete economic independence for Latvia, including the right to create its own currency, the right to establish independent relations with other countries, an end to the teaching of atheism in schools and the right to control migration and foreign travel ("Latvians Establish a Movement to Seek Sovereignty").

More than 200,000 would soon count themselves members, initially including some Russians who saw the front as a loyal opposition. Its activities included collecting signatures for petitions and organizing demonstrations. Although the Baltics' mobilization had started in Latvia with Helsinki '86 and VAK, the Latvians were initially surpassed by the Estonians and then would be outflanked by the Lithuanians.

The Lithuanian Popular Front: Sąjūdis

Why Lithuania would be the first to achieve independence among the three Baltic republics may be related to its demographic composition: 79.6 percent Lithuanian, 9.4 percent Russian, and 7 percent Polish. With a majority, the question of nationality was more relaxed. In contrast to Estonia and Latvia, the Lithuanians did not fear being reduced to minority status.

Lithuania's underground *samizdat* networks were the most elaborate in the Soviet Union and the largest on a per capita basis of all of Eastern Europe. More then 2,000 books were published by its clandestine press. The secret protocols to the Molotov-Ribbentrop Pact were first published, covertly, in Lithuania in 1972 (see "Text of Secret Protocols to 1939 Hitler-Stalin Pact"). The following year, authorities imprisoned more than 100 persons in Vilnius, Kaunas (the country's administrative and diplomatic center), and in the Latvian capital of Riga for copying and disseminating the protocols.

In 1978, Antanas Terleckas established the Lithuanian Freedom League, which was considered a "radical" organization because it explicitly advocated independence. The group was among the first to raise openly the issue of the Hitler-Stalin protocols. The league addressed a petition to UN secretary-general Kurt Waldheim and various governments, asking for the pact's nullification, withdrawal of military troops from the Baltic republics, and rights to develop freely. Its thirty-eight Lithuanian signatories were arrested and imprisoned, including Terleckas (for a third time).

Lithuanian demonstrations during the 1970s generally concerned freedom of religion. In 1972, a student named Roman Kalanta killed himself by self-immolation in a Kaunas square to protest Russian control. Riots ensued, with throngs chanting "Freedom!" as they removed street signs with Russian names and burned communist party headquarters and police offices. (In 1969, a student at Prague's Charles University, Jan Palach, had committed suicide by self-immolation in the center of Wenceslas Square and became a similarly symbolic figure in Czechoslovakia's Velvet Revolution; see **Czechoslovakia, Introduction,** and "Police in Prague Move to Break up Big Protest March.")

After the Soviet Union signed the Helsinki Final Act of 1975, committees to monitor its implementation sprouted (see **"Introduction: Strikes, Sinatra, and Nonviolent Revolution"** and "Lithuanians Rally for Stalin Victims"). Lithuania's Helsinki watch group—formed in 1976 by priests, poets, and scientists to scrutinize the country's adherence to the Helsinki accords—voiced a key theme that would echo as the Baltic nationalist mobilizations accelerated during 1987–1988: "restoration of the independent Lithuanian state as it existed before its illegal occupation by the Soviet army on June 15, 1940." The Lithuanian monitoring group was decimated by arrests in 1981, although some stalwart individuals continued to write letters and organize petitions for political prisoners in the early 1980s. In 1982, U.S. president Ronald Reagan proclaimed June 14 Baltic Freedom Day in remembrance of Stalin's mass deportations to Siberia. In 1985, Reagan signed an act that reminded the Soviet Union of its obligations under the 1945 Yalta agreements to permit free elections in countries it had occupied.

On February 16, 1988, on the seventieth anniversary celebration of Lithuanian independence, Reagan issued a statement of support for an expected demonstration, and a large number of U.S. senators wrote letters to Mikhail S. Gorbachev cautioning against interference. Demonstrators filled the churches for commemorative services as cordons of security forces lined the streets. Also in 1988, the Lithuanian Writers' Union condemned the country's environmental policies. Approximately 5,000 Lithuanians signed a petition to the Soviet Union Council of Ministers concerning ecological threats to the Baltic Sea.

By spring 1988, the intellectual cornerstones had been laid for the Lithuanian nationalist movement. On June 3 at the Academy of Sciences, 500 influential Lithuanians met to chart a course of action. They elected a coordinating group of thirty-six intellectuals and scholars who were tasked with organizing a movement in support of perestroika, glasnost, and democratization. It consisted of architects, artists, authors, journalists, philosophers, scholars, and the coordinating group also included seventeen members of the Lithuanian communist party. In October it would officially adopt the name Lietuvos Persitvarkymo Sąjūdis, or simply Sąjūdis, meaning "co-movement" or "joint movement." Sometimes called the Lithuanian Perestroika Movement, or the Lithuanian Movement for the Support of Perestroika, the organization used perestroika as its protective rubric, but Sąjūdis more accurately sought consensus. With its precepts of "openness, democracy, and sovereignty," Sąjūdis would act as a galvanizing group within the larger Lithuanian nationalist movement. According to Lithuanian political scientist and former Sąjūdis member Gražina Miniotaitė, "Sąjūdis began its activities with no funds, no rooms, nor any means of communication with the public, but within three months it would become an alternative power structure" (Miniotaitė 2002, 26).

Sąjūdis organized its first mass event for June 24 in historic Gediminas Square in Vilnius near a centerpiece classical cathedral with white columns. The square was named for the Grand Duke Gediminas, described by *Times* reporter Philip Taubman as the fourteenth-century founding father of the city and hero in Lithuanian history. He notes, "Under Gediminas, Lithuanian power was extended from the Baltic Sea to the Black Sea and east to the Dnieper River. At the time, Lithuanians like to note, Russia was an inchoate state of warring fiefdoms" ("In Lithuania Too, Nationalism Surges").

Twenty thousand people showed up for the Sąjūdis event, having learned of the rally from handwritten notices posted on city walls. Speakers included two individuals who would later play leading roles in the democratization movement: Vytautas Landsbergis, a music historian and member of the Sąjūdis coordinating group, and Algirdas Brazauskas, a member of the central committee of Lithuania's communist party. The gathering bestowed public mandates on the Lithuanian delegates who were departing shortly for the aforementioned nineteenth Communist Party conference in Moscow.

Party bosses picked the delegates to the Moscow conference, so, as in Estonia and Latvia, Lithuanian political activists concentrated on influencing the delegates to take certain stands at the gathering. The June 24 event became a "bon voyage" with a mission. The delegates were briefed on Sąjūdis's demands, which included observance of human rights, release of political prisoners, recognition of Lithuanian as the national language, and cessation of Soviet "colonialism." In *The Times,* Taubman remarks on the early support by the Church of Rome for Sąjūdis's activities:

> Vincentas Cardinal Sladkevicius . . . named a few days before by Pope John Paul II, is the first Lithuanian Catholic to reach that rarified level in the church, and his selection was considered a great honor here. The Roman Catholic Church has long played an important role in Lithuanian life, and while this has been reduced under Soviet rule, the church continues to serve as a rallying point

of pride. Church leaders, according to Lithuanian believers, have quietly encouraged the development of a grass-roots political group that in recent weeks grew out of the resurgence of nationalist activity. Formation of the organization, called the Initiative Group [or Movement] in Support of Perestroika, followed by several weeks the establishment of a political-action group in Estonia ("In Lithuania Too, Nationalism Surges").

Regarding the thinking and size of Sąjūdis, Taubman reports that of Lithuania's population of 3.6 million, 80 percent were Lithuanian (with some 2.5 million Roman Catholics claimed by the church). Sąjūdis asserted a membership of 180,000 (see "Lithuanians Move to Limit Moscow Ties").

The nineteenth party conference in Moscow provided Sąjūdis with a boost. The conference strengthened Gorbachev's hand in promoting reforms and ended with a commitment to perestroika, which was welcomed in Lithuania as helping the popular fronts and offering possibilities for democratic change in the Soviet Union. Brazauskas, in addressing the conference, said the Lithuanian party authorities were ready to meet some popular hopes. Topping the list was ending further funding for construction of the nuclear reactor in Ignalina, which after completion would have been the largest in the world. He also announced that the Lithuanian language would be recognized.

Mobilization steadily increased, and neutral groups that had been watching from the sidelines became Sąjūdis supporters. In the following days, a rock-and-roll march began through the country, as musicians and bands traveled to raise awareness of the Sąjūdis quest for independence. In addition, a hundred cyclists launched a "ride for ecology" to the Baltic Sea and along the route held twenty-four rallies in support of Sąjūdis.

After a July 1988 rally called by Sąjūdis, Lithuanian communist leaders who were fearful that Sąjūdis would elude party control informed Moscow with "panicky characterizations of Sajudis" and asked for intervention (Senn 1990, 86–92, 102). Gorbachev in response dispatched Aleksandr N. Yakovlev, his chief ideologist and most trusted Politburo ally, to Vilnius and to Riga in early August 1988 to investigate the situation. Yakovlev, a Politburo member given the glasnost portfolio, stunned his local hosts when he publicly supported the popular fronts against the local party apparatchiks. Meeting with various groups on what Soviet officials called the "nationalities question," Yakovlev admitted that the Soviet Union had, indeed, tried to suppress all national characteristics.

Described by *The Times* as the "architect of many of Mr. Gorbachev's key foreign and domestic policies," Yakovlev was reported in an interview as observing that the "grass-roots political movements that recently developed in the three Baltic republics had legitimate grievances, and should, in general, be encouraged. 'We believe a new status should be elaborated for the constituent republics, and we're working on this,' he said. But Mr. Yakovlev said that . . . any expectation that the republics could regain the independent status they had before Soviet annexation in 1940 is 'simply unrealistic' " ("Gorbachev Associate Rejects Baltic Independence Moves"). *The Times* also sheds some light on the nationalities question: [T]he Soviet Union is made up of many ethnic groups that have been forcibly put under Moscow's control. In the past, rumblings of independence were crushed because the government felt that if one nationalist group was given its way, others would agitate for change. Even in the days of the Czars, Russian forces had to deal with local revolts in the Caucasus and in Central Asia ("How Patient Is Moscow?").

Yakovlev acknowledged to Rimgaudas Songaila, the Lithuanian party chief, that party hostility toward manifestations of national awareness had been a serious political error. For Sąjūdis, Yakovlev's visit was a turning point, after which it became difficult for party officials to harass, repress, or ignore the movement any longer. It also would result in a reversal of the Russification policy concerning education in Lithuania and confirmation of the decision to suspend construction of the Ignalina nuclear power station.

On August 21, the secret protocols associated with the Molotov-Ribbentrop Pact were reproduced for public consumption for the first time. *The Times* presents the documents in its editions of August 24, 1989 (see "Text of Secret Protocols to 1939 Hitler-Stalin Pact"). In Vilnius, a three-hour calendar event on August 23 memorialized the forty-ninth anniversary of the undisclosed Hitler-Stalin arrangement and attracted 250,000 Lithuanians (approximately the number attending the U.S. March on Washington of August 28, 1963, a milestone in the struggle for racial equity in the United States). A wide array of speakers, including party members, attacked the secret clauses. Sąjūdis members thereafter chose music historian Vytautas Landsbergis to lead their group. According to Alfred Erich Senn (1990), "Sajudis now stood almost as a second government in Lithuania. . . . [I]t had moral authority to which the population responded" (p. 136). In plain words, the Lithuanian people wanted to salvage and recapture what they could of the missing Truth and History of their nation. These Lithuanians wanted not only to nullify the falsifications of their history by the Soviet Union, but to celebrate their own rediscovery.

In September, environmental activists—15,000 in Estonia, 50,000 in Latvia, and 100,000 in Lithuania—formed human chains symbolically to embrace the Baltic Sea, to protect it from the pollution linked to government policies. During September 16–17, Sąjūdis encircled the nuclear power station at Ignalina and demanded cessation of its construction. (Despite Brazauskas's earlier pronouncement, construction had continued.) Also, on September 17, the first Sąjūdis newspaper appeared in print, opening a floodgate that would lead to nearly 150 independent publications. On September 19, the Sąjūdis coordinating group appeared for the first time before a national television audience.

By September's end, local party leaders had begun unsuccessful attempts to recapture command of the situation and targeted the unauthorized rallies of the Lithuanian Freedom League, which had been uncompromising in its advocacy of national independence since the 1970s. Open conflict erupted on September 28, when the league commemorated the Molotov-Ribbentrop Pact at a rally of 15,000 violently attacked by police wielding batons. The actions of the security forces shocked Lithuanians. The following day, Sąjūdis held a joint rally with the Freedom League. Landsbergis urged calm in the face of provocation. In Moscow, the violent response at the Freedom League rally was viewed as threatening to the legitimacy of Lithuania's communist party. The Kremlin expanded the degree to which pluralism would be permissible.

During October 23–24, Sąjūdis held its official founding congress. *The Times* on October 24, 1988, reports, "Cheered by thousands of supporters who attended the meeting at the indoor sports arena in Vilnius, the Lithuanian capital, and a crowd of more than 200,000 that gathered Saturday evening for a torchlight rally downtown, the delegates seemed, in a single weekend, to vent decades of Lithuanian anger and frustration." Correspondent Philip Taubman further notes, "Rewriting the book on permissible political activity in the Soviet Union, the movements have made demands for political, economic and cultural autonomy acceptable that only a few months ago were considered tantamount to treason. The movements, rooted in long-suppressed nationalist sentiment, have thrown local party organizations on the defensive."

The Autumn Watershed

The Latvian popular front had solidified later than the Estonian and did not cohere significantly until after Yakovlev's visit, but with the Estonian and Latvian fronts now engaged, and Sąjūdis mobilizing in Lithuania, in autumn the tempo of oppositional activities increased throughout the Baltics. In general, academicians, artists, clergy, communist reformers, human rights proponents, writers, and activist intellectuals from all branches of knowledge led the three popular fronts. They began holding large national festivals, in which national songs were sung, long-banned national flags were flown, and other time-honored symbols displayed. The Estonian front's positions were the most far-reaching, explicitly calling for a mechanism for secession from the Soviet Union. The founding congress of Sąjūdis in October 1988 reflected a profound change for the cautious Lithuanians, who had come abreast of the Estonians and were no longer asking for autonomy. Their bid was for independence.

The Communist Party conference of June–July 1988 had approved Gorbachev's principle of democratization and ushered in the election of a range of party officials via secret balloting. Moscow, in its relationships with the Baltic republics, seemed to be saying that it wanted an association based on law, common interests, and reciprocal consent. By October, calls had been made for the resignation of Rimgaudas Songaila, as first secretary in Lithuania. He had assumed leadership of the Lithuanian communist party in late 1987 and was one of the conservative apparatchiks who dismissed the "alien philosophies" of the "nationalist extremists." Moscow in 1988 replaced him with Algirdas Brazauskas, a Sąjūdis supporter whose party-state had recently declared Lithuanian the official language. This was symbolically important, but of limited effect.

The Baltic communists' response to the gathering steam of mobilizations varied, as many of them joined the popular fronts. *Times* reporter Esther B. Fein on November 18, 1988, observes, "Popularly based national movements . . . formed recently in all three republics . . . have begun calling openly for more political and economic autonomy, often with the support of local Communist Party officials." The Latvian and especially the Estonian communist parties were intent on minimizing the separation between the fronts and the party. Half the Estonian front's 106 members were also members of the Estonian communist party; 30 percent of the Latvian front's members were party members, beyond their proportion in the population of 5 to 6 percent (Beissinger 2009, 234). The Estonian regime legalized the Estonian national flag, but the Lithuanian party-state had remained unmoved and staunchly conservative ("Moscow Calls for Talks with Estonians").

After eighteen months of debating, the Estonian "four-man" IME program was accepted by the Estonian leadership, and came to be known as the "Baltic model" for economic reform. Estonian premier Bruno Saul endorsed the ideas, claiming that he had proffered similar proposals in 1984. In September, economists from the three republics convened to resolve details of applying the "Baltic model" to all their economies. The model explicitly challenged Marxist theory in holding that the economy should be based on market principles, the republics' natural resources should be under their own control, and Moscow's economic centralization should be replaced with Baltic administration, including the levying of taxes.

In Lithuania, Sąjūdis drafted amendments for its constitution, and the local party appeared unrattled by this development. Changes toward republican sovereignty were readied for presentation to the Supreme Soviet in November. In the few months after the founding congresses for the Estonian and Latvian popular fronts and Sąjūdis's establishment, Latvia and Lithuania had seen their communist parties' first secretaries change.

The three popular fronts expanded the meanings of perestroika and glasnost, as if stretching a giant rubber band, testing its breaking point. Gorbachev had initially seen the popular fronts as building support for his desired reforms. Even so, on October 22 Gorbachev responded with amendments to the all-Union constitution to weaken representation of the Baltic republics and make it difficult for them to secede from the union. Other than military action, this was the most confrontational action that Moscow could take. The Baltic peoples reacted with fury and despondency. The Estonian and Latvian popular fronts and Lithuania's Sąjūdis issued joint statements calling for legal guarantees for economic autonomy. An astonishing 3.7 million persons signed a petition supporting this demand. On November 8, representatives of the three popular fronts met with three Politburo members who had been dispatched to the Baltics from Moscow. In Tallinn, they stated that the purpose of perestroika was to strengthen the unity of the Soviet Union.

On November 17, the Estonian Supreme Soviet, with persuasion from the popular front, passed a constitutional amendment and issued a Declaration of Sovereignty that would permit them to reject Soviet Union legislation pertaining to their territory. This represented the first serious Baltic challenge to the Soviet colossus and was the first feat in what would be called the "parade of sovereignties"; comparable declarations of sovereignty would be promulgated by Lithuania in May 1989 and Latvia in July 1989. Gorbachev was reportedly furious. Perhaps to prevent similar defiance from Lithuania, the new party secretary, Brazauskas, was immediately called to Moscow for consultations. On November 18, the Lithuanian Supreme Soviet had retracted its planned statement of sovereignty. Brazauskas had pulled out all the stops to halt its issuance, prompting protests from Sąjūdis, which on November 20 issued a declaration of "moral independence" proclaiming that "Lithuania's will is the highest law . . . [and] only those laws will be respected in Lithuania that do not restrict Lithuania's independence."

On November 26, the Soviet Union's Supreme Soviet proclaimed the Estonians' declaration null and void. Moscow's intervention had destroyed the convictions of some that perestroika might be the avenue for realizing Baltic aspirations. All hope for an interactive approach of mutual benefit faded. Local communist parties would bear the brunt of the ensuing conflict. In December, the Soviet Congress of People's Deputies declared the Molotov-Ribbentrop Pact illegal, thus clearing a legal path to the Baltic republics' "renewal" of their drive toward independence. Gorbachev remained adamant in promoting his own plan for "renewing" the federation.

EVENTS OF 1989

In February 1989, Sąjūdis announced that the movement sought independence as its ultimate goal. The Estonian Popular Front and the Latvian Popular Front made comparable declarations in April and May, respectively. These three popular fronts took on an added revolutionary outlook in 1989 and advanced their positions with assistance from three developments: the increased visibility of more radical movements, such as the Estonian Independence Party, the Latvian National Independence Movement, and the Lithuanian Freedom League; the spread of nationalist mobilization from the Baltics to elsewhere in the Soviet Union (see "Soviet Ethnic Minorities Take Glasnost into the Streets"); the first more or less competitive elections in the Soviet Union in March.

On March 26, elections were held for the Soviet Union Congress of People's Deputies, an all-Union legislature comprised of 2,250 members. Sitting only briefly each year, it selected the smaller, central Supreme Soviet to function as a parliament and a head of state with broad powers. Candidates associated with the popular fronts performed exceptionally well in the balloting, winning 90 percent of the contests in Lithuania and up to three-fourths in Estonia and Latvia. Candidates from the Baltics ran as individuals because of growing disapproval of the Communist Party. Those seeking sovereignty, rather than autonomy, for the Baltic republics won the majority of ballots in all three Baltic elections. Later, evidence would come to light that the election results had persuaded at least one of Gorbachev's chief advisers that the departure of the Baltic republics had become "inevitable," a perspective that became progressively more prevalent within the Russian intelligentsia in subsequent months (see "Baltic Independence Fronts Plead to U.N.").

Victorious in the March balloting, the popular fronts' enhanced positions gave them self-assurance in dealing with the communist party. It became easier for reformers in the Estonian party to throw in their lot with the popular front, because it was clearly favored by the Estonian citizenry. The communist parties were separating along nationalist lines; native Baltic leaders who were not Russians increasingly responded positively to the emergence of groups expressing Baltic patriotism, as did most Estonians, Latvians, and Lithuanians.

The Estonian and Latvian popular fronts and Lithuanian Sąjūdis ratcheted up their efforts when they jointly met in Tallinn on May 13 and 14. The representatives resolved "[t]o coordinate joint policies of the biggest popular movements of the Soviet Baltic countries and to make the general public of the Soviet Union and the World at large aware of the democratic aspirations pursued by the Baltic popular movements." Without specifying political independence from Moscow at this point, they stressed instead economic independence. Some talked of a bloc of between eighty and ninety Baltic deputies who could act in unison in the all-Union Congress of People's Deputies. *The Times* on May 15 covers the joint assembly of "grass-roots political movements." They made a united approach to the United Nations and

> appealed for an international forum to decide their status, basing their claims on the illegality of the Stalin-Hitler pact. The assembly also passed a declaration spelling out the rights of "the people of the sovereign states of Estonia, Latvia and Lithuania" to choose their own form of economy. The statement said the current attempts at economic perestroika, or restructuring, had failed because they were inherently ineffective, mainly because they preserve a centralized economy.

The fronts identified themselves as "captive nations" (see "Baltic Independence Fronts Plead to U.N."). Soon after the joint assembly, the Latvian Popular Front, under pressure from the NIML, adopted independence as its purpose that same month. On May 18, Estonia issued a declaration condemning the Molotov-Ribbentrop Pact and reserved a right to ignore or limit Soviet laws if they infringed on Estonian sovereignty. On May 18, Lithuania asserted its sovereignty by stating that the only enforceable laws were those adopted by the Lithuanian Supreme Soviet or pursuant to a referendum. Latvia's mid-summer declaration would be more cautious.

Also by this time, the Baltic representatives and the others had united in pressing the question of the 1939 Soviet-German secret protocols. In June 1989 in Moscow, the Congress of People's Deputies appointed a twenty-six-person commission to investigate the secret clauses. Headed by Aleksandr Yakovlev, the inquiry resulted from the demands of the three popular fronts but was also influenced by glasnost. Until then, Soviet bureaucrats, including foreign secretaries, had denied the existence of any secret protocols. When visiting Poland in July 1988, Gorbachev had refused to recognize any such agreement between Hitler and Stalin.

The Baltic Way: A Human Chain

Massive demonstrations sped the pace of the independence process, with the scale of these events weakening the will of local communist parties. In summer 1989, demonstrations occurred across the Baltic republics. Most determinative was the calendar demonstration of August 23 on the fiftieth anniversary of the Molotov-Ribbentrop Pact, when a human chain of hundreds of thousands held hands in an almost unbroken connection of nearly 400 miles, from Estonia's coast to the southern border of Lithuania. As many as 2 million Balts—two-fifths of the total native regional population, or approximately the size of the able-bodied Baltic adult population—took part directly or indirectly in this act of nonviolent resistance. The symbolic verdict of the Baltic peoples was powerfully clear: the secret protocols were illegal, and the people did not want to be part of the Soviet Union. Those participating in the human chain not only demanded the right to restore the Baltics' independent statehoods, but were also protesting the suppression of history.

The human chain stung Gorbachev into making a hostile statement about the Baltic republics, his first since becoming general secretary in 1985. In a televised harangue against "nationalist excesses" on August 26, he warned party leaders in the Baltic republics against submitting to extremism, separatism, and nationalist hysteria, an apparent retreat of sorts from his own principle of perestroika. He asserted that "the state of the Baltic people is in serious danger." By implication, perestroika was to be directed by the party; Baltic reformism was acceptable, but only so long as it adhered to a unitary state. Gorbachev's position was not that of the liberator, as often seen in the West. He may have acknowledged the aspirations of Estonia, Latvia, and Lithuania, but to him the integrity of the Soviet Union took precedence over any nationality's interests.

Autumn 1989

Reconstruction of a normal civil society became for the Baltics a means of defense. Cultural, ecological, political, and social groups multiplied. Latvians reopened churches and synagogues long closed by the communists, issued a mass circulation religious newspaper called *Svetdienas Rits* (Sunday Morning), and held cultural activities. Branches of the Latvian Popular Front in cities and towns increased their local actions, often joining with the National Independence Movement and other groups. The council and board of the popular front mounted pressure on the Latvian Supreme Soviet.

Meanwhile, Gorbachev, in his report to the central committee plenum on the question of nationalities in September 1989, continued to maintain that the three Baltic republics had voluntarily joined the Soviet Union in 1940 and, therefore, "there is no reason to question the decision." He argued that being members of the Soviet Union gave the three republics a sense of "belonging to one of the mightiest states of today, with enormous natural resources, a developed economic complex, and an arsenal of scientific knowledge, technical possibilities, a rich culture and the ability to safeguard its security by all means" (Pontin, Gerner and Hedlund 1993, 63).

On September 13, Gorbachev met with the Baltic governments and insisted on a federal solution to the so-called nationality conflicts. Moscow's adamant stance, however, only served to strengthen the hand of the proponents of absolute independence. Autumn 1989 saw the Baltic regimes and popular fronts unambiguously define their claims to full independence. The Lithuanian communist party had 200,000 members, so identification between the party of Lithuania and Moscow was closer than that in Estonia and Latvia. Even so, the Soviet party remained displeased by the viewpoint of the Lithuanian Supreme Soviet in October 1989 that the Soviet Union had been illegally occupying the country since 1940.

Prior to autumn 1989, the Baltic way to independence had been self-generating and was also motivating other, comparable movements elsewhere in the Soviet Union. In the final months of 1989, the revolutions of Eastern Europe provided Baltic nationalists with additional impetus. Radio Free Europe, the BBC, Voice of America, and other media had been jammed by Soviet authorities until 1988, when Moscow ceased interference with broadcast signals and transmissions began coming through from them as well as those of Finnish and West German television; information also flowed through Baltic samizdat. If the Eastern bloc states could jettison communism and leave the Warsaw Pact, what was stopping the Baltic peoples from following suit? Gorbachev, visiting Finland, added fuel to the fire. *The Times* on October 26, 1989, reports:

> President Mikhail S. Gorbachev declared today that the Soviet Union has no moral or political right to interfere in the affairs of its East European neighbors, and held up neutral Finland as a model of stability in stormy Europe. His spokesman embroidered the theme jokingly, saying that Moscow had adopted "the Sinatra doctrine" in Eastern Europe. "You know the Frank Sinatra song, 'I Did It My Way?' " said Gennadi I. Gerasimov to reporters. "Hungary and Poland are doing it their way." "I think the Brezhnev doctrine is dead," he added, using the Western term for the previous Soviet policy of armed intervention to prevent changes in the communist governments of the Warsaw Pact. ("Gorbachev, in Finland, Disavows Any Right of Regional Intervention")

By the end of 1989, all three republics had declared a goal of full independence and restored their national flags as legitimate emblems. On December 6, the Lithuanian parliament brought to an end the communist monopoly on power by establishing the first multiparty system in the Soviet Union. Two weeks later, during December 19–20, the Lithuanian communist party seceded from the Communist Party of the Soviet Union. The secession constituted a basic challenge to the imperial nature of the Soviet Union. Furthermore, Nadia Diuk and Adrian Karatnycky (1993) point out, "many Party members [had] developed a double allegiance, belonging to both the popular front and the Party. In Lithuania at the end of 1989, this process had advanced so far that the [Lithuanian] Communist Party determined that the only way it could regain the loss of prestige and influence was to break away entirely from the CPSU" (p. 114).

In Moscow, on December 23, Yakovlev's commission presented its findings to the Soviet Union Congress of People's Deputies. On December 24, Yakovlev informed the congress that an historian, Lev Besymenskii, had found a copy of the Molotov-Ribbentrop secret protocols among the papers of Vyacheslav Mikhailovich Molotov. They had been erroneously filed under 1946. The duplicate corresponded with facsimiles already in publication and could no longer be rebuffed. The congress released a declaration conceding the existence of the protocols and condemned them as illegal and invalid. The voting was 1,432 in support of the resolution with 252 against.

When the Congress of People's Deputies proclaimed the Soviet-Nazi pact illegal, the question thus shifted to *when* the Baltic lands would regain their sovereignty, not whether. Ironically, the liberal communists and moderate reformers in the Baltic republics had gained in standing; they had been unquestioning about the validity of the state, instead using the rubric of perestroika for their independence quests. "By establishing the illegality of the treaty under international law, they were . . . establishing a fact that was already widely known and accepted abroad," Diuk and Karatnycky (1993) note. "The insistence on establishing a legal basis for challenging their annexation showed their commitment to a peaceful, nonviolent disengagement from the Union" (p. 115).

Events of 1990

Following the Lithuanian communist party's secession from the Communist Party of the Soviet Union of late 1989 and the Estonian communist party's split from the Soviet party in early 1990, most Latvian members of their country's communist party departed to establish an alternative organization. In March 1990 elections, the popular fronts and nationalists in all three Baltic republics did well and formed non-communist governments. Gorbachev condemned the Lithuanian communist party's decision to form an independent party. In Estonia following the first partially free balloting for the Supreme Council, the elected council declared Estonia to be an occupied country, proclaiming that it had entered a period of transition leading to restoration of the Estonian Republic.

Attempting to prevent economic weakening from leading to dissolution of the Soviet Union, Gorbachev moved to implement political reforms. By February 1990, he had persuaded the Congress of People's Deputies to remove from the Soviet constitution language guaranteeing a "leading role" to the Communist Party, before elections in the Baltic republics. This meant that the Politburo could no longer act as the government of the Soviet Union. In March, Gorbachev allowed himself to be "elected" to a new position as the president of the Soviet Union; he assumed the office on March 12. On March 11, Lithuania had become the first republic of the Soviet Union to announce its independence, fearing that once Gorbachev became president, on March 12, he would exert executive powers over it. The newly elected parliamentary Lithuanian Supreme Soviet, now under direct control of Sąjūdis, voted unanimously to restore the country's prewar independence.

In Moscow, the Extraordinary Congress of Peoples' Deputies determined Lithuania's declaration to be illegal and called for restoration of "order and legitimacy" there. The Lithuanian announcement can be treated alternatively as an act of civil disobedience. The Lithuanians saw it, according to Miniotaitė (2004), as "defense and consolidation of statehood" (p. 230). Notes Miniotaitė, "The essential difference was that the Lithuanian government had the prevailing support of the Lithuanian people, whereas the government of the Soviet Union could rely mainly on its repressive machinery" (ibid.). For Anatol Lieven (1993), the declaration "only increased the determination and morale of ordinary Lithuanians. Those who, immediately after the declaration, had been critical of Landsbergis and Sąjūdis, became increasingly supportive, and popular demonstrations returned to their pre-independence dimensions" (p. 239).

Gorbachev sought to force Lithuania's new president, Vytautas Landsbergis, to rescind the declaration of independence. Landsbergis refused, but would later be obliged to accept a temporary moratorium following a campaign of threats by Moscow. The Soviet Union imposed an economic embargo, sanctions, and an oil blockade. Landsbergis would later write, "Clearly I recognized that they had the power to crush us at any time, but . . . we were convinced that the present government of the Soviet Union would neither wish nor dare to adopt Stalin's methods" (Landsbergis 2000, 175, 178). It would not be long before the republics of Armenia, Estonia, Georgia, Latvia, and Moldova would declare their planned eventual secessions from the Soviet Union.

On May 4 in a carefully worded resolution, a newly elected Latvian Supreme Soviet declared its intention to restore independent statehood to Latvia and proclaimed the illegality of its 1940 annexation by the Soviet Union. It marked the start of a transition to full independence—rather than immediate restoration, as in Lithuania—and a newly empowered Supreme Council and council of ministers were recognized by Latvian citizens as their own, rather than a foreign encumbrance. The historical Republic of Latvia was reinstated. Estonia announced the beginning of its transition to independence in two segments, on March 30 and May 8. In early summer, Estonia dropped the status of being a Soviet socialist republic.

The Soviet sanctions and oil blockade of Lithuania had generated a display of solidarity in March between the three popular fronts, evident in the revival of the Council of Baltic States, a coordinating body that called on the Soviet Union to end its threats of military intervention. Despite initial concerns about the prudence of Lithuania's declaration of independence, Estonia and Latvia were soon facilitating the entry of supplies into Lithuania. On May 12, the presidents of Estonia, Latvia, and Lithuania met in Tallinn for their first presidential summit in half a century. A joint declaration was signed renewing the Baltic entente of 1934. Estonia's president, Arnold Rüütel, argued for Baltic problems to be treated as a process, rather than issues to be pursued separately. On June 13, the three presidents held a second summit and sent a telegram to Gorbachev asking to meet to negotiate a schedule for redefining their relations with the Soviet Union.

In Estonia and Latvia, the nationalist movements took control of the government, while leaving the party chairmanship in communist hands for the purpose of compromise; in Lithuania, the nationalist movement held the chairmanship and the majority in government. The new governing institutions were initially frail, but most of the Baltic populations, including Russians, obeyed the newly passed decisions, decrees, and laws of the three emerging democracies.

Gorbachev announced on May 14 that Latvia's independence declaration was null and void. With no means of defense—lacking armed forces and even police—the new authorities found themselves vulnerable. Large numbers of Soviet troops remained stationed in Latvia. Tensions rose in the debate concerning independence between ethnic Latvians and non-Latvians, mainly Russians, who comprised nearly half the republic's population, as *The Times* reports on May 15, 1990:

> Even without direct sanctions organized by Moscow, economic pressures on Latvia have increased since the independence movement began to pick up strength. The Soviets' partial blockade of Lithuania, imposed after the government in Vilnius declared independence on March 11, has caused a sharp drop in gasoline supplies here, because much of Latvia's gasoline arrives by way of a Lithuanian refinery. Few cars were on the streets today, and a private taxi driver complained of having to buy gasoline on the black market at six times the usual rate ("Gorbachev Bars Independence Bids of 2 Baltic Lands").

Times correspondent Celestine Bohlen also reports, "Scuffles broke out . . . in front of the Latvian Parliament when groups of Soviet Army officers and soldiers gathered to protest against laws they find threatening and insulting."

In summer 1990 in Latvia, the Citizens' Movement, a civic campaign established in 1989, reached fruition. Modeled on an Estonian example, it proposed to register all legal citizens of the republic who had held citizenship prior to the First Republics independence period and their descendants. Those who did not meet these criteria were invited to express their fidelity to Latvia's independence by registering as "candidates for citizenship." Those advocating registration considered it a necessary step for the recovery of national identity.

Another goal was the election of a representative body of Latvian citizens, or "citizens' congress," plus committees to protect local interests. Thousands of volunteers, many from the NIML and others from the popular front, managed the registration process. Their procedures were declared illegal by the Latvian Supreme Soviet and "counterproductive" by wary members of the popular front. Registration and elections took place under strict electoral rules, despite fear that Soviet authorities or troops might violently interrupt them. By August 1990—when the election of delegates to the "citizens' congress" took place—more than 800,000 citizens out of an estimated 1.6 million had registered. In the similar Estonian process, 850,000 had registered. The newly elected congress met on April 31 and May 1 to draft a blueprint for independence. It lost influence later, when the Supreme Soviet, renamed the Supreme Council, assumed a broader leadership role.

Extremist Reactions from Internal "International Fronts"

Political polarization had increased in the Baltic republics in late 1988 and early 1989, as extremist organizations with connections to hard-line communists in Moscow formed international fronts in an effort to counter the popular fronts and Baltic independence. These "intermovement" (*interdvizhenie*) groups, called "interfronts" (in Latvia and Estonia) and Unity (Yedinstvo, in Lithuania), enlisted minorities—Russian speakers in Latvia and Estonia, and Polish and Russian speakers in Lithuania—in their countermobilization efforts. On August 30, 1987, *The Times* cites Soviet demographers in recalling that "ethnic Russians now make up a little more than half of the population" of Latvia (in Lithuania, the corresponding figure was 9 percent.) Dominated by Slavs and Russians, the interfronts gained followers as laws established Estonian, Latvian, and Lithuanian as the official languages of their respective republics. The interfronts saw themselves as the vanguard for reestablishing the Soviet Union as a formidable, centralized world power. The organizing of such internal resistance groups—which stood in opposition to the majoritarian, rapidly growing nationalist mobilizations—were a last gasp of Russian alienation in the Baltics. Nonetheless, they complicated the situation.

In Riga, the interfront called on Moscow-loyal Russians to stage a general strike and rally on May 15. Only a few workplaces closed, but army officers (without arms) and army cadets turned out at the Supreme Council building and demanded suspension of the declaration of independence, arousing fears of violence. Within hours, however, a larger multitude of Latvians, having heard radio reports and seen television accounts, formed a counterdemonstration to protect the council. The poise of the defenders won the day as police separated the two sides.

In Lithuania, talks got under way in August 1990 about revising the 1922 Union Treaty dating to the First Republics, but by this time conservative elements in Moscow had consolidated their position; within a week, the Soviet delegation walked out. Confederation might have placated the Baltic states in 1989, but by 1990 independence had become the goal. In December, Gorbachev placed a deadline of summer 1991 for a new treaty, but all three Baltic republics dissociated themselves from it. Baltic leaders were politically skillful, but they also benefited from internal conflict in Moscow. Reformist and conservative wings of the Communist Party there were engaged in their own struggle for supremacy, but agreed that further concessions would only increase the centrifugal forces at work throughout the union. Gorbachev dithered.

In autumn 1990, the special troops of the Otryad Militsii Osobovo Naznacheniya (OMON) from the Soviet Interior Ministry employed terror techniques. These so-called black berets bombed monuments that had been erected in memory of Latvian soldiers killed in World War II. Other explosives were detonated at party headquarters, Russian schools, the KGB building in Riga, and near residential apartments (possibly meant to provoke responses that would offer pretexts for crushing countermeasures). Loyalists of the Soviet Union incessantly demanded the return of "law and order."

With tensions running high, the Latvian Popular Front issued the Announcement of the Board of the Popular Front of Latvia to All the Supporters of Latvia's Independence. Known as the "Appeal for the Hour X," it outlined a program for how to behave in the event of a coup d'état or imposition of presidential rule (that is, unilateral action by Gorbachev). In short, it was a plan for civilian national defense. The front called upon Latvians to rely solely on nonviolent means. Extreme disparity and asymmetry between the Baltic republics and the Soviet superpower rendered violent resistance unrealistic and unfeasible.

Published Guidelines for Civilian Defense

The technique of nonviolent civil resistance played an essential role in the struggles for independence from 1988 to 1991 in Estonia, Latvia, and Lithuania. According to Miniotaitė (2004), the use of nonviolent methods against the *nomenklatura* in Vilnius and Moscow was typical for the first stage of Lithuania's struggle for independence. (The nomenklatura comprised a Communist Party ruling class in control of central and local officialdom, representing thousands of persons and their families; see **"Introduction: Strikes, Sinatra, and Nonviolent Revolution."**) In the second stage, Miniotaitė observes, "the fight was directed against the Soviet military and political *nomenklatura* in order to preserve and consolidate the declared independence" (p. 230). Miniotaitė says the use of civilian defense, a branch of the technique of nonviolent action, was laying the groundwork for Lithuania to become the first country in the world to incorporate into its national defense policy the concept of nonmilitary civilian defense.

Indeed, published guidelines for civilian defense were instrumental in the final stage of the Baltic independence struggles. In November 1989, Miniotaitė had gone to a Moscow conference also attended by Gene Sharp, a scholar of civil resistance based in Boston, at which he gave her page proofs for his forthcoming 1990 book, *Civilian-Based Defense: A Post-Military Weapons System*. She in turn gave them to Audrius Butkevicius, director-general of the Lithuanian Department of National Defense, who had translations made into the Baltic languages and sent to nationalists and reformers in Estonia, Latvia, Lithuania, and the rest of the Soviet Union. The translations were used in drafting nationally distributed guidelines for massive noncooperation in the event of a coup d'état or military occupation and were spread by the many civil society organizations that had developed since 1987 and 1988. Embryonic national defense ministries that were forming in Estonia, Latvia, and Lithuania also published and disseminated the guidelines.

The guidelines provided instruction on how to prevent an invader or occupying force from accomplishing its aims through a variety of unarmed noncooperation measures, or civilian defense. They advised compliance with national laws, dismissal of Soviet military orders or governors that might be forcibly interposed, refusal to participate in spurious balloting or referendums, and documentation of crimes committed by the occupiers. Plans were drafted in accordance with the guidelines by new transitional governmental authorities in Estonia, Latvia, and Lithuania for the protection of buildings in a crisis by nonviolent means.

The new governments did not empower armed units (although small networks of unofficial defense groups organized that were not involved in shooting incidents). The hard part, according to Miniotaitė, was the education of the Lithuanian public in the use of the "weapons" of civilian defense—one element in the technique of civil resistance. To enlighten the public, major Lithuanian newspapers carried articles on the history and methods of nonviolent resistance, and television broadcasts explained the principles in the guidelines. Asked in April 1991 about the import of the guidelines and Sharp's writings on nonviolent struggle and civilian defense, Butkevicius said, "If I had to choose between the atom bomb and Dr. Sharp's book, I would choose this book."

Events of 1991

In January 1991, events took a turn that involved the interfronts. In Estonia, Latvia, and Lithuania, authorities announced unpopular price hikes after Christmas celebrations, resulting in violent demonstrations primarily by ethnic Slavs. The pro-Soviet interfronts in Estonia and Latvia set up National Salvation Committees and denounced the Estonian and Latvian nationalists as "counterrevolutionaries." Such committees, pro-Soviet interfront groups seeking restoration of Soviet hegemony, were organized by Moscow loyalists as a device to allow the Soviet Union to claim that it was acting in response to local constituents.

On January 2 in Riga, ostensibly at the behest of the National Salvation Committee, the Soviet "black berets" took over the building where major Latvian newspapers and magazines had their offices. In response, 10,000 rallied in a demonstration at the headquarters of the central committee of the communist party. In another meeting, employees in the press building decided to abandon their workplaces, refusing to obey the central committee. Latvia's new government swiftly pledged new printing presses and paychecks. On January 7, Soviet authorities announced additional paratrooper divisions to be deployed in the Baltic republics, in theory to ensure young males' compliance with conscription orders. They appeared, however, to be supplementing the black berets' taking of key locations and repression of Latvian citizens.

On January 9, the National Independence Movement (NIML) issued a statement entitled "Appeal of the National Independence Movement of Latvia Board to Members of the NIML and Other Organizations, to All the Population of Latvia," asking Latvians "to nonviolently resist the actions of the Soviet Union military authorities and their supporters." The appeal listed ways to avoid cooperating with an occupying force: don't sleep at home; regard those detained as prisoners of war; pretend not to know the Russian language; say you know nothing about neighbors or colleagues; be uninformed about street locations if asked; remove numbers from houses, detach signposts, and eliminate place names; hide documents; establish mutual communications networks; use church bells to warn or summon people; do not distribute communist literature; do not offer food or water to the army; maintain records on those collaborating with communists or Soviet military; resist and disobey the demands of the black berets and Soviet troops, a legal practice under Latvian law (Eglitis 1993).

In succession to the January 2 blow against Latvia by the local Polish and Russian members of the interfront, Soviet authorities aimed a direct show of force against Lithuania, the first of the Baltics to declare its independence (see "Parliament in Lithuania, 124–0, Declares Nation Independent"). When the Soviets' economic embargo, sanctions, and oil blockade failed to crush Lithuanian determination, Moscow launched what would turn into an aborted coup d'état against the Lithuanians (and leave an enduring perception of Gorbachev as irresolute).

Soviet paratroopers arrived in Vilnius in early January, allegedly invited by the National Salvation Committee to detain men who disobeyed forced conscription into the Soviet army. On January 9 on national radio, President Landsbergis implored of Lithuanians, "Come and help your own government, otherwise a foreign one will overcome us." Television broadcast Richard Attenborough's film "Gandhi" that night. On January 11, Soviet paratroopers and armored vehicle and tank units occupied the press building radio and television facilities. The Soviets used live ammunition, wounding at least four persons. They also occupied the Vilnius railway station and halted train service. Landsbergis tried several times to reach Gorbachev by telephone, but could not.

On January 12, thousands of unarmed Lithuanian citizens converged in Vilnius at the parliament building, the television tower, and the intercity telephone station—as outlined by the civilian defense guidelines noted above—as the Lithuanian Supreme Council, the legislature installed after the previous year's declaration of independence, urged citizens to surround government buildings to defend them. On January 13, Bloody Sunday, Soviet troops killed fourteen civilians and wounded hundreds, stopping short of storming the parliament and detaining Landsbergis. Bloody Sunday precipitated a chain of events that would by December 1991 lead to the fall of the Soviet Union (see "Soviet Loyalists in Charge after Attack in Lithuania").

According to Miniotaitė (2004), black berets eventually injured 702 Lithuanians among the peaceful crowds that had gathered to protect the broadcast buildings. "The unarmed people stopped the tanks and rendered an abortive coup," Miniotaitė states (p. 230). *The Times* on January 13, 1991, reports, "A group of young Lithuanian men stood their ground before the column of a score of tanks and armored personnel carriers that nevertheless continued advancing, leaving three or four bloodied on the ground" ("Soviet Tanks Roll in Lithuania"). The final official count was fourteen civilians killed, according to *Lithuania 1991.01.13: Documents, Testimonies, Comments* (1992), issued by the State Publishing Center in Vilnius. *The Times'* reporting in the flush of the upheaval does not convey the extent of preparation for this show of planned civilian defense, with its refusal to cooperate with the occupiers. Keller writes that "thousands gathered outside the center who had been singing and dancing through the night in playful protection of the broadcast center." Rather, these Lithuanians were carrying out a strategy of civil resistance based on the assumption that they could not counter Moscow's aggression with the paltry arms in their possession.

Keller notes that the parliament building was "surrounded around the clock by thousands of Lithuanians bused in from across the republic, who vowed they would form a human barrier if troops are sent." Widespread circulation of civilian defense guidelines on the level of state institutions began after Bloody Sunday, accompanied by television broadcasts and articles in major Lithuanian newspapers and magazines. The deliberate employment of civilian defense—a calculated, strategic response—was not recognized at the time.

Meanwhile, *The Times* editorial board was obviously stunned by the events in Vilnius. Gorbachev had become the darling of Western hopes for reform of the Soviet Union. *The Times* on January 14, 1991, editorializes,

> Since coming to power in 1985, Mikhail Gorbachev's daring, realism and flexibility have captured America's imagination and approval. When he uses tanks to crush singing students, and freedom, he instead ignites America's anger and disgust. Thousands of demonstrators in Vilnius chant "Freedom!" and sing "Tautos Giesme," the Lithuanian national anthem. It's a haunting hymn about home, about

a Lithuanian homeland. Today, people around the world mourn and sing with them ("The New Old Face of Tyranny").

In another editorial, on January 17, *The Times* further comments, "Glasnost was Mikhail Gorbachev's way to criticize the past in order to reform the present. But glasnost opened newspapers and airwaves to many voices he could not control, and apparently cannot abide. Now glasnost is the first casualty of Soviet repression. Perestroika, or reform, could be next. It is no accident that unarmed Lithuanians died defending Vilnius's broadcast center. The objective of the Soviet tank assault on [Bloody] Sunday was to seize and silence the independent voice of Lithuania" ("Broken Glasnost").

A week later saw bloodshed in Riga, when six civilians lost their lives as black berets seized the Interior Ministry. "The black beret force, which numbers more than 100 men, has free reign at night in this normally peaceful city," *The Times* reports on January 22 ("Latvia to Create Self-Defense Unit"). Soviet troops were trying to restore Soviet sovereignty by using forcible tactics against unarmed Latvian demonstrators in Riga. On February 28, the Supreme Council of Lithuania issued the following statement: "In the event a regime of active occupation is introduced, citizens of the Republic of Lithuania are asked to adhere to principles of disobedience, nonviolent resistance, and political and social noncooperation as the primary means of struggle for independence."

In March, the Soviet army conducted unscheduled military maneuvers, making clearer the necessity for civilian defense planning that made no use of military weapons systems. As Soviet forces continued to roll into Vilnius, *The Times* on March 23, 1990, reports that Gorbachev has "demanded that the Lithuanians drop any plans for a self-defense system and ordered the K.G.B. to reinforce Soviet border posts." It continues, "The Lithuanian Prime Minister, Kazimira Prunskiene, responded today to the Kremlin's moves by saying, 'There is a concerted effort from Moscow to provoke trouble in Lithuania.' She [Prunskiene] vowed that the republic would not be frightened into retracting its declaration of independence." Conducting dozens of interviews on the streets of Vilnius, *Times* correspondent Esther B. Fein found people "indignant at the sight of an armored convoy rumbling through the streets" ("Upheaval in the East; Lithuania Assails Moscow's Tactics as Convoy Arrives").

Lines of authority became confused. Fein quotes Gen. Ginutis Taurinskas, the head of Lithuania's civil defense agency and chief of the Voluntary Society for Cooperation with the Army and Navy, as telling enraged lawmakers in Lithuania's parliament that he had been summoned by the commander of Soviet ground forces and informed that their "weapons would be taken by force if they were not handed over voluntarily." The general told parliamentarians that he issued the order for the transfer and that "all organizations handed over all weapons to military units" as of March 23. Taurinskas said that as a military officer, he was "obliged to obey orders." Fein reports legislators hissing at Taurinskas, rebuking him for failing to consult the Lithuanian government first. According to Fein's dispatch, the general admitted turning over some 16,000 vehicles requested by the still Soviet-controlled military. Meanwhile, "Moscow continued its war of nerves this afternoon, dispatching a convoy of 13 armored personnel carriers, five trucks carrying military hardware, and a jeep. . . . It has refused to inform the Lithuanian leadership of its intentions despite repeated requests." She reports the Lithuanian parliament's appeal to the world's governments to oppose the possible use of violence against the republic.

Nonviolent Civil Resistance in the Heart of the Soviet Union

Gorbachev, after two weeks of equivocation and vacillation, finally stated publicly that the National Salvation Committees had acted unconstitutionally. Regardless, in Baltic eyes, the onslaught of black berets had resulted in Moscow losing whatever legitimacy it might have had.

Bloody Sunday in Vilnius resulted in repercussions against the government in Moscow throughout the Soviet Union and played an important role in the events leading to its final collapse. Referendums conducted in the Baltic republics in February and March on the question of independence revealed widespread support there, with an overwhelming majority in favor. The minority ethnic populations, such as Russians, had begun to support secession, fearing that economic and political calamities lay ahead for the Soviet Union.

The Baltic movements for independence and transitions from communism in east-central Europe had reduced Gorbachev's latitude in employing violent repression and also spelled the beginning of the end of the Soviet Union. By March, an all-Union referendum on preserving the Soviet state drew a turnout so low that in the Baltic republics the results were declared invalid. Civil resistance spread among the Soviet republics.

Boris N. Yeltsin had availed himself of the opportunity afforded by Gorbachev's introduction of competitive elections to the Soviet Union's Congress of People's Deputies, the new Soviet parliament, to gain a seat in March 1989 and won by a landslide in a Moscow constituency. The following year, on May 29, 1990, the parliament of the Russian Soviet Federative Socialist Republic (RSFSR) elected him president of the republic despite Gorbachev's opposition. (The RSFSR, the largest in population and size of the fifteen Soviet republics, would become the Russian Federation after the collapse of the Soviet Union.) Yeltsin had pledged to build Russian statehood. In this role, he began publicly to support the rights of the Soviet republics to greater autonomy within the Soviet Union, among other reforms. As chair of the Russian parliament, he had issued a joint statement with the three presidents of the Baltic States disapproving "armed acts damaging each other's state sovereignty," following the deployment of the black berets and other forces.

On June 12, 1991, Yeltsin was elected president of the Russian republic in the first direct, open elections for the presidency, winning 57 percent of the vote. Having allied himself with the Baltic states in their plans for independence, in July Yeltsin entered into a treaty recognizing Lithuanian sovereignty. Meanwhile, the remaining twelve Soviet republics that continued in negotiations on a new union treaty reached concurrence for a radical devolution of powers from Moscow to the republics. On August 19, the eve of the planned signing of a new treaty among the republics, hardliners in Moscow staged an attempted coup d'état, ultimately bringing an end to the Communist Party and hastening the momentum for disbanding the Soviet Union. They included party, KGB, and military authorities trying to avert a new liberalized union treaty and seeking a return to old-line party values. The decision to overthrow Gorbachev and seize power was overwhelmingly shaped by Moscow's poor management of the nationalist upheavals across the Soviet Union, not solely in the Baltic republics.

Yeltsin disregarded the coup leaders and bade resistance in Moscow while calling for Gorbachev's return. When the coup disintegrated a few days after it had begun, Yeltsin emerged as the country's most powerful political figure. As president of the Russian republic, Yeltsin read a statement standing atop a tank in Moscow on August 19, 1991, in which he urged the citizenry to resist nonviolently the attempted coup d'état. According to political scientist Mark Kramer, "One of the main organizers of the coup, KGB chairman Vladimir Kryuchkov, planned to send an elite KGB Alfa unit to storm the White House, the headquarters of the Russian government headed by Boris Yeltsin. Soldiers under the command of another coup organizer, defence minister Dmitrii Yazov, were to assist in the crackdown. But when faced with the prospect of using repressive violence against a peaceful crowd that had gathered at the White House, the coup plotters backed down" (Kramer 2009, 109).

The coup collapsed on August 21 following extensive nonviolent civil resistance, especially in Moscow. Gorbachev had been detained in a dacha by the Black Sea, while Yeltsin remained free. As Yeltsin and the Russian parliament resisted, impeding the coup with their own brand of civil resistance, word of the putsch reached Lithuania, where Vytautas Landsbergis went on national television to reiterate that "the main resistance of Lithuania in case of occupation is unarmed nonviolent resistance."

The international community, which had never recognized Stalin's annexation of the Baltic lands, now avoided triumphalism in its response. An editorial in *The Times* on August 23, 1991, cites U.S. president George H. W. Bush as speaking for much of the world, when he said, "[T]he faster that independence is granted, the better." Referring back to the January seizures of strategic locations and deaths, the newspaper reminds that "with or without Mr. Gorbachev's assent, Moscow struck clumsily, even murderously at the Baltics, closing frontiers and using despised 'black beret' irregulars to cow rebellious but unarmed civilians." It continued, "The peoples of Lithuania, Estonia and Latvia have earned the freedom their parliaments have proclaimed." *The Times* further remarks:

> A shaken Mikhail Gorbachev spoke generously yesterday about his hopes for democratic reforms, nonviolent change and the regeneration of Soviet society. A splendid way to start would be to deal reasonably, fairly and promptly with the special claims of Moscow's unwilling subjects in the three states.
>
> As Mr. Bush re-emphasized, the United States has never recognized the forcible annexation of the Baltic States by Stalin, the dirty booty in a secret protocol of the 1939 Nazi-Soviet pact ("Baltic Freedom in a New Light").

Observing the dramatic events in Moscow, in part sparked by their own popular mobilizations, the Baltic states calmly proceeded along the paths on which they had set out. On August 20–21, during the uncertainty surrounding the coup in Moscow, the Estonian and Latvian supreme councils declared their de facto independence. Lithuania reinforced its earlier declaration of March 11, 1990.

The Nordic countries were the first to recognize the Baltic republics' secession. On August 26, *The Times* reports that the Scandinavians had cleared the way for the rest of Europe to accept Estonia, Latvia, and Lithuania as "sovereign equals." Statues of Lenin across the Baltics fell. *The Times* on August 22 reports on Gorbachev's return to Moscow to reassert control after the collapse of the ill-conceived coup and the withdrawal of the tens of thousands of Red Army troops stationed in the Baltic republics during the Soviet Union's collapse ("Gorbachev Back as Coup Fails, but Yeltsin Gains New Power").

Within days of the failed August coup, the Russian republic recognized Baltic independence. Amid an upsurge of popular anger against the central Soviet government and its bureaucracies dominated by communists, a majority of the Soviet Union's republics intensified their own campaigns for independence. On September 6, 1991, the State Council, the interim executive body of the Soviet Union, recognized the independence of the Baltic States. Estonia, Latvia, and Lithuania were admitted to the United Nations on September 17, 1991. In December, Russia assumed the assets and liabilities of the Soviet Union, which had formally ceased to exist.

Lithuania became the first country ever to incorporate into its national defense policy the concept of civilian-based defense. According to Miniotaitė (2004),

> Just after the recognition of Lithuania's independence, with the country's first steps of setting up its national security system, many theoreticians and enthusiasts of civilian defense cherished the hope that Lithuania would become the first country in the world having its security system based on the ideas and methods of nonmilitary civilian resistance. One cannot say that Lithuania has totally failed to live up to their expectations, for elements of civilian-based defense have indeed been included in its security and defense policies. It is to be noted that even though all Eastern and Central European countries have experienced the efficiency of nonviolent struggle, Lithuania alone has officially recognized its viability. The role accorded to civilian resistance in documents representing Lithuania's security and defense policies is unique in defense conceptualizations currently predominant in the world (pp. 236–237).

All three Baltic states held parliamentary elections and created democratic constitutions. The Western powers insisted that Russian troops withdraw completely and that Moscow recognize and treat them as fully independent, sovereign nation-states. The last Russian troops left Lithuania at the end of August 1993. Russian combat troops had departed from Estonia and Latvia by late August 1994. Estonia, Latvia, and Lithuania joined the North Atlantic Treaty Organization's Partnership for Peace initiative soon after its launch in January 1994.

Conclusion

The Baltic states' independence process rested on a platform of history. Their citizenry had over time chafed under czarist administrations and German and Polish landlords. The divvying up of their independent nations by Hitler and Stalin in 1939 remained a burning grievance, buttressing their argument that the annexation of their nations by the Soviet Union had been illegal. Compounding this wrong was the Soviets' suppression of the "dirty booty" resulting from the secret protocols to the August 1939 nonaggression treaty between the Soviet Union and Germany.

The drive for independence in the Baltics was not created by perestroika nor nationalism. Rather, the Baltic peoples cherished their past—their folklore, their singing, their cultures—and glasnost made it easier for authors, academicians, activist intellectuals, artists, musicologists, scientists, and poets to commemorate historical events and anniversaries through calendar events. Communists in Tallinn, Riga, and Vilnius understood earlier than in Moscow that successful economic liberalization required loosening communist party rigidity and control. Gorbachev contributed mightily to "new thinking" in the Soviet Union, but his adamantine insistence that the Baltics had voluntarily joined the Soviet Union in 1940 made the transition difficult. Anatol Lieven (1993), a journalist-historian of Latvian descent, explains:

> The Baltic experience demonstrates the central dilemma of Gorbachev's entire effort. . . . Glasnost was inevitably going to bring a new honesty about the past; but since the entire communist claim to legitimacy and to positive achievements was based on lies, this honesty would sooner or later bring down the whole system. The key role in undermining the communist will to power was the Soviet Union's manifest economic failure in comparison with the West, and a keen awareness among younger communist officials that they would have better lives under a capitalist economy. However, the discrediting of the communist past was also a crucial, if secondary, factor (p. 222).

Many Western observers, and probably Gorbachev himself, mistakenly perceived the Baltic independence movements as springing from nowhere. The first autonomous political activity, neither officially condoned nor prohibited, had been the protests against environmental policies, which were tolerated within a year of Gorbachev's rise to power in 1985. For the Baltics, environmental threats represented more than adverse pressure on pristine forests, springs, and dunes, important though they were. More alarming was the prospect of the continuing degradation of Baltic lands through deadly and life-threatening chemicals industries and phosphate mining, and the thousands of migrant Russians that followed in their wake. The Chernobyl nuclear disaster of April 1986 exemplified the catastrophic consequences of doing nothing. Balts were forcibly dispatched to rescue efforts in Ukraine without protection against the failed plant's lethal radiation.

Building upon ecological organizing that had taken root during 1986–1987 in all three republics, Baltic independence advocates had shifted the emphasis toward culture and the preservation of monuments, including the restitution of such national symbols as flags and anthems. Three popular fronts came into existence in 1988, calling their republics "captive nations" and creating a path that encouraged members of local communist parties to join what would eventually become pragmatic independence movements led by resourceful politicians and determined activist intellectuals.

Gorbachev's principle of glasnost created openings for venting ideas and debating topics previously banned. Perestroika provided the cover for organizing new entities, despite the rigidities of a coercive system that abhorred innovation. Of great importance, any opposition to independence within local communist parties had the potential to be won over or at least split; such adversaries were not particularly effective. As *The Times* observes on October 25, 1988, "Paradoxically, the communist party, which prides itself on its skill with the masses, appears unfamiliar with the power of grass-roots public activity" ("How Patient Is Moscow?").

Circumstances of brute annexation, authoritarianism, isolation of the Baltic republics one from another, and remoteness from the world beyond the Soviet Union dictated that the Baltic mobilizations be self-generating. Any fight—initially for autonomy and then for independence—would have to be made without depending on external allies or sources. The intentional entangling of Baltic economies with those of the Soviet Union that followed upon annexation meant that any free-standing independence groups must work with meager resources and rely only on themselves.

The Baltic peoples share an identity affected by history and geography, yet they also possess unique identities arising from ethnic and other differentiations between the three nations. Leaders of the Estonian, Latvian, and Lithuanian popular fronts were politically astute in coordinating "fronts," which by their very name meant they could absorb broad cross-sections of society (and later play a transitional role as post-communist political parties and institutions developed). They benefited also from internal conflicts in Moscow.

International allies and Baltic émigré communities in Europe and North America shared information with would-be sympathizers concerning the nationalist opposition building in the region and the calendar events, thus sustaining the memory of 1939–1940. Once the Soviet Union stopped jamming broadcasts in 1988, Radio Free Europe and Voice of America were able to broadcast into Baltic lands. Beyond these measures, however, the role of international third parties was minimal in the Baltics' independence struggle. Although the United States had been pressing for observance of human rights in the Soviet Union since the Carter administration in the late 1970s, Washington generally adopted a guarded approach toward the Baltic quest for independence. In December 1990, for example, Lithuanian prime minister Kazimira Prunskienė was asked to enter the White House through a rear entrance, so as not to agitate Moscow. Nevertheless, refusal by the United States to recognize the 1940 Baltic annexation by the Soviet Union remained a constant.

The Baltics' most significant external allies were within the Soviet Union and Eastern bloc. The three popular fronts could not have flourished without some protection from Moscow, which refused to repress them in their early stages and sometimes eased their ascent. As *The Times* reports on October 25, 1988, Moscow had evidently "told the party leadership in each republic to allow the movements to develop so as to build support for Mr. Gorbachev's policies by appearing responsive to local movements" ("How Patient Is Moscow?"). Independence was not, however, without cost in human lives:

> Compared with national liberation struggles elsewhere, the number of victims associated with the Baltic independence struggles was minimal: from January 1987 through August 1991, 25 people were killed and 935 people injured in the Baltic independence campaigns—with all of the deaths occurring in 1991. Moreover, the Baltic popular fronts inspired numerous attempts at emulation throughout the former Soviet Union, acting as a catalyst that transformed the political landscape and helped to trigger the break-up of the Soviet state (Beissinger 2009, 232).

In their struggles to achieve independence from a Soviet Union that they never sought to join, the Balts helped to bring down the Soviet Union and the Communist Party that had given rise to it. Even so, the Soviet government could have smashed all three Baltic independence movements in 1988 or 1989 had it been determined to do so. Soon after the Baltic popular fronts had formed in 1988, similar popular movements emerged among Azerbaijanis, Belarusians, Georgians, Moldavians, Tajiks, Turkmenians, and Ukrainians, with a comparable national group active in Armenia. By mid-1989 and 1990, as nationalist affirmation advanced and several independence movements simultaneously confronted the Soviet Union, Moscow's ability to manage the situation in the Soviet Union as a whole fell into disarray. It is possible that the Baltic popular fronts might not have been successful in their independence struggle had it not been for reverberations from other nationalist movements contesting the Soviet Union and the massive waves of unrest in the satellite nations of Eastern and Central Europe.

Demonstrations against Soviet Rule Tolerated

History provided the catalyst for the Baltic nonviolent movements that got under way in 1986. After 1918, when Estonia, Latvia, and Lithuania achieved independence, their national identities came under assault. The Soviet Union and Germany signed a nonaggression and friendship agreement, the Molotov-Ribbentrop Pact, on August 23 and September 28, 1939. In secret protocols, the Baltic states were allocated to the Soviet sphere of interest, allowing Stalin to annex Estonia, Latvia, and Lithuania, ending what the Balts referred to as their First Republics era (see **Baltic States, Introduction,** and "Text of Secret Protocols to 1939 Hitler-Stalin Pact"). *The Times* reporter Esther B. Fein, on August 27, 1989, provides details involving the pact.

> Poland was divided between the two nations, and the Baltics, then independent states, were assigned to the Soviet Union. The Soviet Army took up positions in the three republics during the war, held elections under the pressure of the military and forced the puppet parliaments to seek admission to the Soviet Union ("Moscow Condemns Nationalist 'Virus' in 3 Baltic Lands").

With the Baltic states forcibly incorporated into the Soviet Union, for the next fifty years they experienced under Stalinism and successive Soviet policies not only military occupation, but massive deportations to Siberia, economic exploitation, and environmental ruination. National flags, songs, and symbols were banned along with independent political activity. By the 1980s, however, ideas about how to transform their situation would begin to alter the approach of the republics' citizenry. The Balts began holding so-called calendar events, or calendar demonstrations, to protest the secret protocols and mark other historical benchmarks on an annual basis. The rise of nationalism—expressed in language, song, flags, and history—reinforced the Balts' conception of themselves and their identities as peoples independent of the Soviet Union.

A Lithuanian group that sought to monitor adherence to the Helsinki Final Act was established in 1976. Its first manifesto stressed that its goal was restoration of the independent Lithuanian state; the group was decimated by arrests in 1981. Another harbinger of mass movements for the independence of Estonia, Latvia, and Lithuania surfaced in Latvia in 1986. A group calling itself Helsinki '86 emerged in the port city of Liepāja, led by Martins Bariss, Raimonds Bitenieks, and Linards Grantins. Making a point of operating openly, the first public statement by these three young laborers established their purpose as "to monitor how the economic, cultural, and individual rights of our people are respected," a reference to the Helsinki Final Act of 1975, signed by the Soviet Union (see **"Introduction: Strikes, Sinatra, and Nonviolent Revolution"**).

A year later, on June 14, 1987, in the Latvian capital of Riga, Helsinki '86 rallied the first unofficial assemblage of the postwar period at the Liberty Monument, a column honoring Latvia's independence between the wars. Topped with a Lady of Liberty statue holding three stars outstretched toward the sky, it was erected in 1935, five years before the Soviet Union annexed Estonia, Latvia, and Lithuania. The purpose of the demonstration was to memorialize the Stalinist mass deportation in 1941 of 14,000 Latvians to Siberia. Some 1,000 persons marched to the monument, readied for any police action by the law officers scrutinizing them.

Between 2,000 and 3,000 others, too afraid to join the demonstration, observed near the monument. To everyone's surprise, the march, an early show of Latvian national identity and self-confidence, proved to be a success. Estonian and Lithuanian activists in attendance vowed to organize similar efforts in their respective capitals.

The Times did not cover the rally, the significance of which became apparent in retrospect. This was the first of many calendar demonstrations that would over the next three years commemorate the critical historical events of the Baltic republics' early independence period and the betrayals of the 1940s. Although the KGB's surveillance of Helsinki '86 led to arrests and harassment, the situation by 1987 was unlike those in the past, when such a rally would have been smothered by fear. The new policy direction of Soviet leader Mikhail S. Gorbachev was part of the difference in addition to another element: this political demonstration opposed Stalinist crimes, instead of Soviet dominion. This approach confounded Soviet authorities, who had themselves denounced Stalin. In subsequent days, Latvians visited the monument to leave flowers, a certain route to prison if done a few years earlier.

In August in one of the first signs of emerging popular dissent in Lithuania, protest groups met in the capital of Vilnius on the anniversary of the Molotov-Ribbentrop Pact. *The Times* correspondent Bill Keller, on August 24, 1987, observes the singing of anthems and speeches to honor those who suffered under Stalin. He notes that the event was the first permitted by Lithuanian authorities involving displays of resentment toward Soviet rule. Though the official press denounced the event, police standing by did not interrupt it. Parallel demonstrations took place in Riga and the Estonian capital of Tallinn. In his article, Keller quotes Janis Barkans, a member of Helsinki '86 who had been arrested three times for his activities.

AUGUST 24, 1987
LITHUANIANS RALLY FOR STALIN VICTIMS
Demonstrations in Latvia and Estonia Are Also Allowed
By BILL KELLER
Special to the New York Times

Vilnius, U.S.S.R., Aug. 23 – More than 500 Lithuanians gathered in the old quarter of this Baltic capital today to sing anthems of independence and to hear defiant speeches honoring "the victims of Stalin."

It was the first time the authorities in Lithuania had permitted such an open demonstration of popular resentment against Soviet rule. The gathering was sharply denounced in the official press and closely watched by the police, but it was not interrupted.

Similar demonstrations were reported in the Latvian capital of Riga and in Tallinn, the capital of Estonia, to mark the 48th anniversary today of the secret pact between Hitler and Stalin that ceded the three Baltic states to the Soviet Union.

Crowds Put at Thousands

Dissidents reached by telephone said the crowds in those two cities had numbered in the thousands, but the estimates could not be independently confirmed.

The Baltic states were annexed by Stalin during World War II, in a move that is still not recognized as legitimate by the United States. Lithuanians, Latvians and Estonians independent from the Soviet Government still maintain small diplomatic missions in the United States.

Many Baltic residents date their loss of independence to Aug. 23, 1939, when the Soviet Government signed a nonaggression treaty with Nazi Germany. The secret protocol, describing the Baltics as a Soviet sphere of influence, later became Stalin's justification for sending in troops.

Participants in the demonstration in Vilnius said they were disappointed by the size of the crowd. They said people stayed away because of fear of the authorities and the distraction of special entertainment events staged by the local government today to divert attention from the demonstration.

But they said the fact that the demonstration went on unmolested was itself extraordinary.

"It's the first signal of freedom," said one woman in the crowd clustered about the monument to the Polish poet Adam Mickiewiez, a local hero who attended the university here. "For the first time you can come here and nobody will put you in prison."

While the crowd was evidently united in its outpouring of patriotic emotion, only a handful of dozens interviewed said they saw the gathering as part of a real struggle for independence from Soviet rule.

Most said such a desire was impractical and called for more modest concessions to Lithuanian pride. They demanded publication of the secret agreement on the Baltics, which has still not been published here. They also called for a memorial to honor Lithuanians who were deported to Stalin's labor camps after the war, and for greater freedom for the Roman Catholic Church, which still claims a large percentage of the population.

"If there should be a referendum on independence, of course it would pass," said one woman who identified herself as a "Lithuanian patriot," Communist Party member and staunch supporter of Mikhail S. Gorbachev, the Soviet leader. But it is more realistic to push for "greater democracy and political rights" within the existing system, she said.

Other Nationalist Displays

The demonstrations today were the latest in a series of nationalist displays that have caused deep concern among Soviet officials. They have included an anti-Russian riot in Alma Ata in December, a large demonstration in Latvia two months ago and protests last month in Red Square by Crimean Tatars who were deported from their homeland after the war.

The official concern was evident in a remarkable crescendo of articles and polemics in the national press in the last week, including two lengthy reports by Baltic commentators on prime-time national television.

The reports defended the 1939 pact as necessary to save the Baltics from being overrun by the Nazis, hailed economic advances under Soviet rule and portrayed the coming demonstration as an event incited by Western radio stations at the behest of foreign intelligence agencies.

Broadcasts Called Meddling

"If this is not an interference in the domestic affairs of another state, then what is it?" the Government daily newspaper Izvestia said Friday of broadcasts on the Voice of America, the BBC World Service and other Western radio services about the planned demonstrations.

Some reports by the official press agency Tass drew a parallel with the unrest in Hungary in 1956 and Czechoslovakia in 1968, both of which ended with the introduction of Soviet troops.

. . . [F]or example, a Tass dispatch said: "Provocation is the Western voices' specialty. They played their mean role in Hungary in 1956, in Czechoslovakia in 1968 and in Poland not so long ago. Now it is the Soviet Baltic region that appears to have been targeted by them."

Ironically, while a few participants today said they had learned of the demonstration from Voice of America or the Vatican radio broadcasts popular in this mostly Catholic republic, most said they first heard of it from the hostile reports in the Soviet press.

Today's demonstrations were organized by members of longstanding human rights groups, some of whom have spent time in labor camps or psychiatric hospitals for their activities.

Some Wore Black Ribbons

The crowd also included young people and families with children, who gathered shortly before noon in the sunny square next to St. Anne's Church in the Vilnius Old Town. Some wore black ribbons pinned to their chests in remembrance of relatives deported to labor camps under Stalin.

Nijole Sadunaite, who served six years in prison for underground publishing, led off the meeting with a call for "freedom for Lithuania, Latvia and Estonia," which brought a lusty cheer from the crowd. The gathering sang a Catholic hymn and the patriotic anthem that was Lithuania's national song during the 22 years of independence before the war.

A few hundred people crowded the monument and listened for about two hours to impassioned accounts of parents who disappeared into labor camps, of priests imprisoned for violating limits on religious practice or of a woman's experiences in a psychiatric hospital.

Uniformed policemen monitored all of the roads leading to the square, and plainclothesmen filmed the event from a nearby window. "There is no trouble now, but we don't know what the K.G.B. will do with our photographs," one young man remarked.

A Tass report read tonight on national television condemned the Vilnius event as a "hate rally," and said it consisted of "a paltry group of aggressive extremists" and 250 to 300 "casual passers-by."

Big Riga March Reported

Janis Barkans, a Latvian who has been arrested three times for his work with the Helsinki Group [Helsinki '86], a human rights organization, said in a telephone interview from Riga that more than 5,000 Latvians had streamed through the city on their way to the city's monument to war victims.

He said the police had broken into the apartment of several organizers afterward. An unknown number were reported to have been arrested.

Tass did not report any arrests, but it implied that some sort of action had been taken against the crowd. The report gave no estimate of the crowd, but said that "Latvian workers, students and intellectuals" had cried out, "Clear the streets of the provocateurs!"

Jaak Juriado, an Estonian activist who lives in Sweden, said his contacts in Tallinn had estimated that 2,000 demonstrators took to the streets in a peaceful protest at Hirve Park in the city center. Tass put the number at "several hundred curious onlookers."

CALLS FOR GLASNOST RAISE EXPECTATIONS

Latvia's nonviolent quest for independence materialized in 1987 with commemorative calendar demonstrations. Estonians and Lithuanians soon followed with their own, similar calendar events. Estonia would take the lead in the Baltic republics' independence drive during 1988–1989 with economic reforms, though not straightforwardly until autumn 1989. By March 1990, Lithuania would be leading the Baltic democratic transitions. Environmental issues sparked some actions, in part because the first autonomous political activity tolerated in the Soviet Union was that in support of ecological preservation.

An April 1986 deadly explosion at the Chernobyl nuclear power station in Soviet Ukraine focused attention on the nuclear reactor in Ignalina, Lithuania, that was the same type as Chernobyl's. To Baltic nationals, Chernobyl came to symbolize the Soviet Union's scorn for their environmental resources. More than four decades of hurried overdevelopment of heavy industry, excessive reliance on pesticides, subpar sewage and purification technologies, and heedlessness toward environmental consequences had severely damaged the environment. Half a century of Soviet recklessness had resulted in constant flows of agricultural, human, and industrial waste into lakes and rivers, and thence to the Baltic Sea, the most polluted in Europe. The Soviet military presence also defiled large portions of Baltic landscape and coastline.

Moreover, after the Chernobyl meltdown, thousands of Estonians and other Balts had been involuntarily dispatched to take part in the rescue efforts in Ukraine, despite being insufficiently protected from the lethal radiation. In Lithuania, the authorities suppressed for two years any discussion of danger from the Ignalina reactor. Had the planned reactor gone forward, it would have been the most powerful in the world. By the time of an announcement that it would become operational in March 1988, political consent in Lithuania and the other Baltic states had changed, largely because of popular disapproval.

The free hand given to Soviet leader Josef Stalin in 1939 meant that the exploitation of natural resources had proceeded for decades, with no accountability, no price paid for human loss, and no cleanup. In Estonia, 61.5 percent of the population consisted of Estonians, while by the late 1980s 30.3 percent of the 39 percent of non-Estonians were Russians. The prospect of 10,000 more Russian workers emigrating into Estonia to work on phosphorite ore mining and extraction of oil shale, accompanied by families—altogether 40,000 new Russian immigrants—meant that Estonians could become a minority in their republic (Pontin, Gerner and Hedlund 1993, 73).

In April 1987, at the university in Tartu, Estonia's second largest city and intellectual hub, a meeting about destructive Soviet policies instead became a demonstration. The poet Hando Runnel called for a referendum, and the university's board joined the protests. At a May 1 parade, participants carried placards condemning the expansion of phosphorite mining. On May 2, youths marched in Tallinn. The demonstrations in Estonia resulted in the postponement of the environmentally degrading mining and stimulated more nationalist organizing.

In February 1987, two years after Mikhail S. Gorbachev had taken the helm of the Communist Party and laid out his visions for *perestroika* (restructuring) and *glasnost* (openness), the Soviet leader had visited the Baltics (just before the announcement on plans for new phosphorite mining). In Riga, on February 17, Gorbachev attacked "Baltic émigré circles and their Western supporters" for "their hate-filled lies" and commended Russian soldiers as defenders against foreign invaders and liberators. In Tallinn, on February 19, he spoke of strengthening "internationalist" education, code for Russification, and called for eliminating "extreme nationalist tendencies in some parts of the Soviet Union" (Pontin, Gerner, and Hedlund 1993, 76–77). Gorbachev described Estonia as an economic burden to the Soviet Union, annually receiving 3 billion rubles, but contributing only 2.5 billion. Estonians, however, viewed this picture from the perspective of prices for Estonian "exports" to the Soviet Union as being set below those of world markets, while Estonian "imports" were fixed above market prices.

Gorbachev's visit to the Baltic republics was reported by *The Times,* on February 26, 1987, in "Gorbachev Candid about Opposition." Philip Taubman describes his speeches concerning economic initiatives, workers' incentives, and reductions of centralized management. Gorbachev said new goals had resulted in a "revolution of expectations," in commenting on public impatience for results. "Many want a speedy social and material return," he said. "I can judge this from recent meetings with the working people of Latvia and Estonia."

Despite Gorbachev's acknowledgments, Estonian academicians and activist intellectuals feared setbacks to their hopes for political rebirth, reversing ecological degradation, and halting Russian immigration. Criticism of Russian influence and numbers continued, however, to be voiced. A novelist, Teet Kallas, questioned the writing of official programs and documents in Russian first and Estonian second. Mati Hint, a writer, explained in a series of publications the link between language and democracy. The seriousness of the language question gained ground with a decision to change street names from Russian to Estonian, a time-honored nonviolent action method. A special commission in Tallinn was set up to handle the matter, and on July 2 local authorities released a list of the first twenty street names to be revised to traditional Estonian designations.

Summer 1987 featured painstaking discussions in the three republics. On August 15 in Estonia, a small committee began work on publishing the 1939 Molotov-Ribbentrop Pact, including the secret protocols that had divided Eastern Europe into German and Soviet spheres of influence (see **Baltic States, Introduction**, and "Text of Secret Protocols to 1939 Hitler-Stalin Pact"). Although the Soviet Union continued to deny the existence of any secret clauses, the committee examining them was able to secure official permission for a demonstration. Hopes for attendance were slim, but between 5,000 and 7,000 persons turned out.

The spread of civil resistance became evident on August 23, the anniversary of the Molotov-Ribbentrop Pact, as major demonstrations occurred in all three Baltic capitals. In Latvia, Helsinki '86 arranged Black Ribbon Day. In Estonia, open public dissent called for publication of the pact's secret protocols. Among the coordinators was Tiit Madisson, who became the first "dissident" expelled from Estonia during Gorbachev's tenure. Several dozen others were soon exiled. Official media denounced the planners as "national extremists" and diminished the meaning of the demonstrations, reporting that only a few hundred attended.

AUGUST 30, 1987
SOVIET ETHNIC MINORITIES TAKE GLASNOST INTO THE STREETS
By BILL KELLER

Vilnius, U.S.S.R – When Mikhail S. Gorbachev called [in] February [1987] for "a revolution of expectations" in the Soviet Union, he probably did not have in mind the crowd that gathered here in Lithuania . . . to chant "Freedom! Freedom! Freedom!" and sing nostalgic songs of pre-Soviet independence.

Small and peaceful, more sentimental than menacing, the gathering was nonetheless an unsettling reminder that calls for "glasnost" and democratization, and Mr. Gorbachev's anti-Stalinist campaign, are raising some expectations that Soviet authorities cannot easily satisfy. The Lithuanian demonstrators, like other ethnic minority activists in the country, have been emboldened by the more liberal atmosphere to dredge up their resentment of Soviet power.

In June, Latvians streamed through the streets of Riga in a peaceful protest with strong nationalist overtones. In July, the Crimean Tatars, embittered since Stalin deported them from their Crimean homeland in 1944 for alleged collaboration with the Nazis, converged on Moscow by the hundreds for their share of glasnost, chanting slogans near the Kremlin.

. . . [O]n the anniversary of the secret 1939 Stalin-Hitler protocol that cleared the way for Soviet annexation of the three Baltic states—Lithuania, Latvia and Estonia—more than 500 Lithuanians gathered here to hear speeches honoring "the victims of Stalinism," while even larger gatherings were reported in Latvia and Estonia.

There have been nationalist stirrings in the heavily Moslem Central Asian republics, including an anti-Russian riot last December in Kazakhstan. Soviet officials worry that a reported resurgence of Islam in the Central Asian republics may someday be susceptible to fundamentalist influence from neighboring Iran. In the Ukraine and Byelorussia, demands have increased for more teaching and literature in the local languages. Against these impulses stands a formidable police and security apparatus that seems to be seeking a new place to draw the line between openness and public disorder. The Tatars were allowed to demonstrate, then were put on trains back home.

Latvians Arrested

Sunday's demonstrations in Vilnius and Tallinn, the Estonian capital, were watched and photographed by the K.G.B., but were unimpeded. But in Riga, Latvia, where the police seemed to be less tolerant after a demonstration two months earlier, witnesses said organizers were kept under house arrest; the press reported that 86 protesters were detained.

Ethnic dissenters who demonstrate face not only the police, but also the resentment of the Russian majority, whose sense of being surrounded by alien forces grows with each census report. Soviet demographers say ethnic Russians now make up a little more than half of the population, but will be a minority themselves by the year 2000 because of lopsided birth rates in the Asiatic regions of the country.

A Soviet official sighed heavily the other day during a discussion of the Crimean Tatars. The foreigner must understand, he said, the Russian people endured 300 years of subjugation to the Tatars' forebears, the Mongols, and then spent the recent decades pulling the Asian republics up from primitive standards of living. It is because of this sacrifice, the official insisted, that the Russian Republic lags economically behind the Baltics, the Ukraine, Georgia and other Soviet republics. This white-man's-burden attitude, common among Russians, is a dubious explanation for the economic stagnation in the Russian heartland; but it helps explain the condescending tone officials and the press sometimes take toward minority complaints. The Baltic republics are an especially ticklish case for the authorities. Anti-Russian sentiment lies close to the surface. An Estonian, accepting a compliment on the European charm of Tallinn not long ago, said, "You should have seen it before the Russians."

The United States considers the Baltic states "captive nations," and recognizes the small diplomatic missions for the three "independent" states, which were taken over in 1940 when Stalin sent in troops and staged rigged elections, ending about two decades of independence for each of the states. Washington underwrites radio broadcasts that help keep dissent alive in the region. But there is little sense here of a serious separatist movement. The prospect of the Soviet Union's dismantling of postwar borders is remote, and many Baltic citizens have no desire to upset a relatively comfortable status quo.

But others in the demonstration here said they had less ambitious goals: an open discussion of how the Baltics came under Soviet rule, honors for the many Baltic residents who were deported to Stalin's camps, more freedom for the Roman Catholic Church, a halt to efforts to "Russify" the culture.

The nationalities question, then, is less a threat to stability than a test of Mr. Gorbachev's political poise and his concept of democracy. To what extent will he allow divisive historical grievances to be aired? What will the Government do to redress them?...

Georgians and Armenians, have been kept relatively content by being given a little freer rein, especially to run their own economic affairs. Even in the Baltics, a senior Western diplomat said, "they could certainly defuse a lot of the resentment if they allowed much greater cultural autonomy and if they slowed down the process of Russification."

ESTONIA: NATIONALIST ACTIVITY GOES MAINSTREAM

The principles of *perestroika* (restructuring of the economy), *glasnost* (openness), and democratization advocated by Soviet leader Mikhail S. Gorbachev provided the rubric under which the popular fronts could organize themselves in the Baltic republics.

In spring 1988, Latvian artists and intellectuals began for the first time to criticize Soviet policies overtly. On March 3, Latvia's creative unions met to consider the responsibility of intellectuals and academicians to interpret what had transpired as a result of oppressive Soviet policies. The first officially approved demonstration, protesting the Soviets' suppression of history, took place in Riga on March 25, 1988. On April 19, thousands marched in a funeral procession in honor of Gunars Astra, a Latvian "dissident" consigned to years in Soviet labor camps. Protestors unfurled a Latvian flag to honor him and publicly sang the national anthem gustily for the first time since World War II. On April 27, some 10,000 people, mostly students and schoolchildren, marched against a proposed Riga subway project.

On June 14, various environmental groups joined with Helsinki '86 in re-creating the pioneering calendar demonstration of the previous year, which commemorated the 1941 Stalinist mass deportation of 14,000 Latvians to Siberia. They even succeeded in securing official permission from the authorities to do so. Bearing aloft the red and white flag from the days of Latvian independence, marchers proceeded to the Monument of Liberty, calling for far-reaching reforms.

The popular fronts that emerged in 1988 in Estonia, Latvia, and Lithuania were alternative political entities in fledgling civil societies, but not political parties. These civic associations consisted of a broad spectrum of coalitions of reformist, nationalist, and popular dissent groups, including communists from inside and outside the governing Baltic regimes. The fronts grew at an astonishing rate, benefiting from family ties, friendships, and associations at places of work.

In April 1988, the Estonian National Heritage Society formed, nominally dedicated to the restoration of architectural and artistic monuments. During April 14–17, in Tartu—Estonia's second largest city and intellectual center—the society hosted a celebration of Estonian cultural history. Between 20,000 and 30,000 people attended lectures on culture and the arts, exhibition openings, and large demonstrations. Also in April, the society became the first openly to parade the blue, black, and white Estonian national flag, banned since the country's fleeting period of independence after World War I.

Across the Soviet Union, anticipations were high for a June 1988 party congress in Moscow. In the Baltic republics, the delegations would be selected in multicandidate elections by local communist party central committees. The Balts hoped that such a vote would represent an advance toward eventual free elections. In Estonia, 600 candidates were nominated for the thirty-two slots. In a surprise move, the Estonian communist party chief, Karl Vaino, presented a separate list of thirty-two for the secret ballot, which was accepted, although protested, and later came to be regarded as the last gasp from the old system. The Moscow congress approved Gorbachev's plan for political reforms, including democratization, and inaugurated secret balloting to elect party officials from a range of candidates. In its relationships with the Baltic republics, Moscow now said it wanted association based on law, common interests, and reciprocal consent.

In early June, Estonians held a song festival in Tallinn patterned on the 1869 Tartu choral fête that had celebrated the fiftieth anniversary of the eradication of serfdom, an event that had been among the first national awakenings of the nineteenth century (see **Baltic States, Introduction**). Approximately 100,000 assembled at Lauluväljak, Song Square, also called Singers' Field. The artist Heinz Valk referred to the event as the Singing Revolution and the name stuck.

On June 13, a parliamentary committee called an emergency meeting, in response to the cumulative effects of these events. Arnold Rüütel, who chaired the Estonian Supreme Soviet, the legislature for the local communist party, convened the committee. By June 14, proposals had begun circulating for Estonian to be restored as the republic's official language and reinstatement of the original national flag. Vaino's response was to ask Moscow for military assistance, notwithstanding its inconsistency with directions espoused by Gorbachev.

Hereafter, in all three republics calendar events on June 14 would mark Stalin's 1941 deportations, activities on August 23 would memorialize the Molotov-Ribbentrop Pact and its secret protocols, and gatherings on November 18 would commemorate the independence pronouncements of the Estonian, Latvian, and Lithuanian First Republics in the pre-Soviet era. Such calendar demonstrations built momentum along the road to independence.

On June 16, the Estonian communist party central committee appointed a new first secretary, Vaino Väljas, to replace Karl Vaino, who disappeared in the bureaucracy in Moscow. On June 17, some 150,000 Estonians congregated in singers' field to convey a message to the thirty-two delegates selected to attend the Moscow party congress. The Estonian flag was flying everywhere.

In Moscow, an initially hostile reception yielded to approval for the Estonians to experiment with a proposal for economic autonomy, reflecting their leading role in economic reforms in the Baltics. On September 26, 1987, four mid-level Estonian party members, two of them economists, had drafted principles for an new Estonian economic order—though within the Soviet Union—terming it the IME project, from Ise Majandav Eesti, or Self-Managing Estonia. The nine-point program called for Estonian control of the economy, promotion of market principles, convertible currency, a budget separate from the Soviet Union's, economic self-determination, competition, independent enterprises, and abolition of controlling bureaucracies (see "Soviet Ethnic Minorities Take Glasnost into the Streets"). IME ultimately would not be implemented, but the party congress in Moscow gave a partial go-ahead on the IME proposal, noting that "the notion of transferring the republics to economic self-management deserves attention."

The Estonian mobilization continued to gather steam. "Within six weeks of its founding the Estonian Popular Front [would claim] a membership of over 40,000 in 800 localities" (Beissinger 2009, 234). The Estonian Popular Front emerged as a free-standing group that could speak to Moscow for Estonians. The sociologist and social psychologist Aleksei Semjonov describes the front as "the first national liberation movement in the Soviet Union" (Semjonov 2002, 108). Despite some voices calling for secession, the fronts did not consider independence as their proffered goal. Instead, they built their appeals on Gorbachev's reform processes and began by calling for autonomy within the Soviet system and fulfillment of their national aspirations within the framework of perestroika.

JULY 21, 1988
ESTONIA NATIONALISTS BEGIN TO CHALLENGE MOSCOW DOMINANCE
By PHILIP TAUBMAN
Special to The New York Times

Tallinn, U.S.S.R. – Last fall, the Premier of the Soviet republic of Estonia, Bruno E. Saul, ridiculed a proposal for sharply curtailing economic ties with Moscow.

This spring, he endorsed the suggestion after thousands of citizens demonstrated in favor of the idea.

In June the republic's K.G.B. chief, Karl Y. Kortelainen, challenged the appearance in public of the blue, white and black flag that was the emblem of Estonia in two decades of independence between the world wars.

Moments later, a senior Communist Party leader told him, within earshot of Estonian journalists, that the ban against use of the flag, which went into effect when the Soviet Union annexed Estonia in 1940, was being lifted.

Mr. Saul and Mr. Kortelainen are just two of hundreds of officials suddenly feeling the effect of a grass-roots political movement that is challenging the established order in Estonia, including the primacy of the Communist Party and the supremacy of Moscow.

The movement, called the People's Front of Estonia, is the leading edge of a resurgence of nationalist activity in Estonia, and the nearby Soviet republics of Latvia and Lithuania, that in recent weeks has brought demands for political, economic and cultural autonomy from the fringe to the mainstream of political action.

The activity in the Baltic states is taking place at a time of high stress in another part of the Soviet Union, the southern Caucasus region, where the republics of Armenia and Azerbaijan have been at odds over the Nagorno-Karabakh Autonomous Region. Armenians are the largest ethnic group in that autonomous region, which is part of Azerbaijan. On Monday, the Soviet Government rejected calls from the region and from Armenia that it be transferred to Armenian control.

The Baltics and the Armenian-Azerbaijan tensions represent different strains of the Soviet nationalities problem. But both are serious for Mikhail S. Gorbachev, the Soviet leader, because both involve forces pulling apart the union, the Baltics tugging directly against the center, Armenia and Azerbaijan against one another.

Acting in the name of Mr. Gorbachev's campaign to reshape the country, the Estonian front has forged an imperfect but powerful form of participatory democracy that has thrown officials on the defensive.

"Gorbachev is our angel," said Andres Raid, an Estonian television producer. "We can do many things in his name that we could not hope to do before."

Entire System Is the Target

Unlike previous nationalist agitation, which was usually quickly subdued by the authorities, the new activity is not limited to a small band of dissidents or a blatantly separatist agenda. The target is the entire authoritarian system, including the rule Moscow has exercised since annexing the three republics in 1940.

"We've come to the moment when it is impossible to continue on in the old ways," said Tiit Made, an economist, who established an environmental-protection lobby similar to the front.

Mr. Made, whose proposals for economic autonomy helped launch the front, said: "We are pushing for democracy, for the right to manage our own affairs, to make our leaders responsive to the people, to preserve our national culture and environment. I think we've started something major in Estonia."

A similar front has been formed in Lithuania, and one is being established in Latvia.

The Estonian front's popularity and influence were evident during a recent visit to Tallinn, the Estonian capital, which has been an active Baltic seaport since the 13th century, when it was a member of the Hanseatic League.

Party Leader Replaced

Since its birth in mid-May, the front has successfully pressed for the replacement of the republic's party leader, gained the endorsement of local officials for proposals to increase Estonian independence from Moscow, and abolished the 48-year ban on the blue, white and black flag.

The new party leader, Vaino Valas, who was appointed last month, approved many of the front's positions when they were incorporated into proposals carried to the Communist Party conference in Moscow in late June.

Mr. Valas, who roomed with Mr. Gorbachev years ago when the two men were enrolled in a leadership course organized by Komsomol, the Communist youth group, gave the front another lift when he ordered that meetings of the party leadership here be conducted in Estonian instead of Russian.

The front claims support groups in more than 800 schools, factories, hospitals, institutes and other enterprises and reports it has more than 100,000 members.

150,000 Demonstrated

On June 17, more than 150,000 Estonians gathered in a Tallinn park to demonstrate their support for the front and hear from Estonian delegates who were headed to the party conference.

Among dozens of banners displayed at the rally was one that mocked Mr. Saul's change of heart about economic autonomy. The banner, which quoted his different opinions on the issue, was greeted with loud applause.

Blue and white posters bearing the front's name in Estonian, Rahvarinne, hang in many of the shops tucked away in Tallinn's Old Town, a warren of narrow, cobblestone streets that dates to the Middle Ages.

Neatly arranged bulletin boards with the latest announcements from the front and usually a copy of its newsletter were prominently displayed in workplaces and government offices.

Own Currency Suggested

On a warm July evening, a crowd of 400 Estonians gathered in the main auditorium of the Institute of Marxism-Leninism to hear speakers from the front discuss proposed economic changes that could hardly delight the heirs of Marx and Lenin in Moscow, including a suggestion that Estonia develop its own currency.

The burst of political action has come naturally to a people that have long chafed under Soviet control and waited impatiently for any sign of change in Moscow.

Estonia has a population of 1.5 million, including more than 900,000 native Estonians.

Almost an Opposition Party

While the front's goals are consistent with Mr. Gorbachev's efforts to limit the role of the party and foster citizens' involvement in the political process, the front comes close to being an alternative party.

Mr. Gorbachev has made clear that alternative, or opposition, parties will not be tolerated.

"The front is an opposition party in all but name," an Estonian scholar said.

In a letter published recently in Estonia's main Russian-language newspaper, Sovetskaya Estoniya, a Tallinn resident said, "True, the People's Front operates in close contact with the party, but the new movement must never be allowed to lose its autonomy."

Slate of Candidates Urged

Many of the support groups have recommended that the front nominate and support candidates for elective office, including local legislative bodies, or soviets, that are expected to gain greater power under Mr. Gorbachev's government reorganization plan.

There has also been discussion of backing candidates in party elections, a move that might be seen by the party as unacceptable interference in its internal affairs.

For some Estonians the next step—openly making the front an opposition party—seems clear and inevitable.

The Estonian youth newspaper said last month that "48 years of a one-party system in Estonia have provided much evidence that such a system, in addition to being unethical, is inefficient."

LITHUANIA: SHUNNING SOVIET RULE

A Lithuanian restructuring movement had taken shape on June 3, 1988, and by August was confidently under way. It formally constituted itself in Vilnius during October 23–24. This Lithuanian popular front—Lietuvos Persitvarkymo Sąjūdis, or Sąjūdis, meaning "co-movement" or "joint movement"—was sometimes translated as the Lithuanian Perestroika Movement or the Lithuanian Movement for the Support of Perestroika. The front worked under the protective masthead of the new policy of *perestroika* (restructuring), yet Sąjūdis more correctly suggests consensus. No politicians or prominent dissidents were involved in Sąjūdis, which acted as a galvanizing group within the larger, all-embracing nationalist movement. A different individual was chosen to chair each of the group's meetings, but the music historian Vytautas Landsbergis would eventually be elected to chair the umbrella organization.

Although some members of Sąjūdis advocated immediate steps toward full Lithuanian independence, as *The New York Times* reports on October 24, 1988, resolutions approved by the group would not go that far, but still sought wide latitude for the local government in managing the Lithuanian economy, diplomatic relations, use of the Lithuanian language, and exposure of the details of the 1939 Molotov-Ribbentrop Pact (see **Baltic States, Introduction,** and "Text of Secret Protocols to 1939 Hitler-Stalin Pact").

After adjournment of Sąjūdis's inaugural congress, *Times* correspondent Philip Taubman ponders in the October 25, 1988, edition the new developments, specifically "a sense that the harmony of the moment between party and independence groups may be a veneer," and whether a clash will inevitably come in which hopes for more independence will be crushingly disappointed ("How Patient Is Moscow?"). Taubman shares his analysis:

> Moscow has apparently told the party leadership in each republic to allow the movements to develop so as to build support for Mr. Gorbachev's policies by appearing responsive to local movements. The party seems to believe that it will gain

credibility with the groups and some influence over their decisions. Paradoxically, the communist party, which prides itself on its skill with the masses, appears unfamiliar with the power of grass-roots public activity. The party may well have underestimated the strength of the Baltic movements and their ability, almost overnight, to build and manage large-scale independent political organizations (Ibid.).

On October 21, two days before the Sąjūdis convocation began, under a new communist party first secretary, Algirdas Brazauskas, who had replaced Rimgaudas Songaila, Vilnius Cathedral had been returned to the Roman Catholic community. The regime had for decades used the cathedral as a museum of fine arts, but in the 1960s, as underground nationalist organizations began to grow, the church became central to the emerging national awareness. As in Latvia and Estonia, Lithuania's revolution was empowered by civic symbols, among which retrieval of the cathedral was important. Brazauskas's administration offered the conciliatory gesture. During October, calls had been issued for Songaila to resign. Having become leader of the party in late 1987, he was one of the conservative apparatchiks who dismissed "alien philosophies" of "nationalist extremists." Moscow decided to remove him and in his place appoint a Sąjūdis supporter whose government had declared Lithuanian the official language.

OCTOBER 24, 1988
LITHUANIANS MOVE TO LIMIT MOSCOW TIES
By PHILIP TAUBMAN
Special to The New York Times

Vilnius, U.S.S.R., Oct. 23 – The inaugural congress of a grass-roots political movement in the Soviet republic of Lithuania today approved a founding platform dedicated to curtailing, but not totally eliminating, Soviet rule in Lithuania.

With emotions and hopes running high, more than 1,000 delegates representing the new group, the Lithuanian Movement for the Support of Perestroika, voted at the end of their two-day meeting to endorse resolutions that would all but sever the political and economic links with Moscow that have existed since the Soviet Union annexed Lithuania in 1940.

A Rally by 200,000

After a last-minute appeal today for caution and patience from Lithuania's newly appointed communist party leader, Algirdas Brazauskas, the congress stopped short of calling for full independence, dropping from its platform a resolution calling for the right of the republic to secede from the Soviet Union.

Cheered by thousands of supporters who attended the meeting at the indoor sports arena in Vilnius, the Lithuanian capital, and a crowd of more than 200,000 that gathered Saturday evening for a torchlight rally downtown, the delegates seemed, in a single weekend, to vent decades of Lithuanian anger and frustration.

"After 50 years of repression, our nation is seeking to regain its liberty," Jurgis Oksas, a historian, told the congress on Saturday. He was one of dozens of delegates to address the often-raucous gathering from a lectern placed before a huge red, green and yellow banner—the Lithuanian national colors that until recently were illegal to display.

Resolution Details

Another delegate, Antanas Terleckas, advocating immediate steps toward full independence, brought the delegates to their feet when he declared, "The Soviet Government must withdraw its occupational military forces from Lithuania."

The resolutions approved by the congress, while not going quite that far, would give Lithuania wide latitude in managing its own economy, establish a separate Lithuanian currency, permit the republic to maintain diplomatic missions abroad, make the Lithuanian language the official tongue, and expose details of the 1939 Soviet-Nazi nonaggression pact that sanctioned the annexation of Lithuania.

The meeting, which was broadcast live on Lithuanian television day and night, attracting hundreds of thousands of viewers, was the latest in a series of remarkable political gatherings in recent weeks in the Baltic republics of Estonia, Latvia and Lithuania.

Estonia and Latvia, like Lithuania, were independent nations between the world wars and were forcibly incorporated into the Soviet Union in 1940.

Emboldened by Mikhail S. Gorbachev's call for increased democracy, tens of thousands of citizens in the three republics have established independent political movements that are challenging the Communist Party's monopoly on power.

Rewriting the book on permissible political activity in the Soviet Union, the movements have made demands for political, economic and cultural autonomy acceptable that only a few months ago were considered tantamount to treason. The movements, rooted in long-suppressed nationalist sentiment, have thrown local party organizations on the defensive.

Mr. Brazauskas, the new Lithuanian party leader, was appointed . . . two days before the congress opened, in an apparent effort to defuse antiparty hostility in the reform movement. The new group, known formally as the Movement for the Support of Perestroika, is widely called Sajudis, or Movement.

Mr. Brazauskas, like his counterparts in Latvia and Estonia, quickly offered sympathy and cautious support to the new political force in his backyard, leaving the impression that the party is prepared to tolerate considerable change, but not outright independence, of the Baltic region.

A Model for Change?

Mr. Gorbachev seems to hope that the Baltic republics, more Westernized and industrious than other regions of the country, can serve as a model for economic and political change while avoiding the kind of nationalist tensions that have shaken the republics of Armenia and Azerbaijan this year.

Mr. Brazauskas, conceding party errors in the handling of Sajudis, including initial efforts to discourage its formation, told the congress in a speech on Saturday, "The goals of Sajudis reflect the interests of all people residing in Lithuania."

He added, "We should not be frightened by the fact that activities and views of Sajudis differ to some extent from those of the party."

Sajudis has made clear that it intends to nominate its own candidates for government and party posts in elections.

Mr. Brazauskas, who was greeted warmly by the delegates, told them that Mr. Gorbachev wished to extend greetings to the gathering and had told him last week that he saw in Sajudis "the driving force of reform capable of strengthening the authority of Lithuania."

Other Lithuanian party leaders sat grimly through the congress in the grandstands. Every time a speaker thundered against the established order, the party leaders, most of them older men in dark suits, seemed to flinch, then applauded weakly as hundreds of delegates turned to observe their reaction.

In a news conference Friday, Mr. Brazauskas said he was eager to improve relations between the party and the Roman Catholic Church.

Of Lithuania's population of 3.6 million, 80 percent are Lithuanian. The Catholic Church claims 2.5 million believers in the republic.

A number of delegates took pains to note that Sajudis does not advocate discrimination against nationalities that are minorities in Lithuania, including Russians and Poles. But the congress, like the initial meetings of independent political movements in Estonia and Latvia, endorsed a proposal to limit immigration into the republic.

Out of the 1,021 delegates to the conference, 980 were Lithuanians and 8 Russians. Sajudis says it has a membership of 180,000.

Becoming Independent

Moscow's ongoing insistence on a narrative that the Baltics had been voluntarily incorporated into the Soviet Union only strengthened Baltic proponents for absolute independence, rather than autonomy, within the communist system. On November 16, 1988, the Estonian Supreme Council had issued a Declaration of Sovereignty, granting precedence to Estonian laws and giving itself authorization to veto the application of all-Union legislation to Estonia. The presidium of the Moscow Supreme Council, formerly the Supreme Soviet, declared Estonia's declaration unconstitutional, but the Estonians went on to write laws establishing Estonian as the official language. Hundreds of thousands of Estonia's 1.5 million inhabitants signed petitions opposing counterproposals by Soviet leader Mikhail S. Gorbachev.

On November 18, the anniversary of the independence declarations of the First Republics, the national anthem and flag of Lithuania were legalized by local authorities. The colors of the Lithuanian Soviet Socialist Republic were retired and its anthem shelved. As 1988 came to a close, Lithuanians openly celebrated the Christmas holiday for the first time since World War II. On Christmas Eve, they turned off their houselights for half an hour and placed candles in windows as a symbolic referendum on independence. In darkened cities and towns across the land, hundreds of thousands of candles twinkled and sputtered.

In February 1989, Sąjūdis declared independence as its final goal. Similar declarations would be made by the Estonian Popular Front in April and the Latvian Popular Front in May. The popular fronts markedly advanced in 1989, eased by the increased assertiveness of pro-independence movements—such as the Estonian Independence Party, the Latvian National Independence Movement, and the Lithuanian Freedom League—that outflanked them, making them appear to be moderate; nationalist mobilization spreading from the Baltics to elsewhere in the Soviet Union, including Armenia, Azerbaijan, Byelorussia, the Central Asian republics, Georgia, Moldova, and Ukraine; and the first, more-or-less competitive elections in the Soviet Union that spring.

On March 26, the Soviet Union held elections for the Congress of People's Deputies, an all-Union legislature comprising 2,250 members. Sitting only briefly each year, the congress was charged with selecting the smaller, central Supreme Soviet to function as a parliament and electing a head of state with broad powers. In 1989, multicandidate choices were allowed for the first time. Most voters chose from among three to twelve candidates, although in 385 constituencies only one name appeared on the ballot. Baltic candidates ran as individuals, because of mounting disapproval of the communist party.

The candidates associated with the popular fronts, which referred to themselves as "captive nations," performed well, winning 90 percent of the contests in Lithuania and up to three-quarters in Estonia and Latvia. Those advocating complete sovereignty for the Baltic republics won the majority of ballots in all three elections. In Estonia, the front won 27 out of 36 seats, 29 of which went to ethnic Estonians. Sąjūdis candidates took 36 out of 42 Lithuanian districts. Many communist party candidates suffered defeat. Newly elected candidates from nationalist groups took control of numerous town and city councils.

Evidence later came to light that the election results had persuaded at least one of Gorbachev's advisers that the secession of the Baltic republics from the Soviet Union was "inevitable"—a perspective that became progressively more prevalent within Moscow's elites in subsequent months. On May 15, 1989, the Estonian and Latvian Popular Fronts and Lithuania's Sąjūdis jointly approached the United Nations in an effort to garner international support for their effort.

KEY PLAYER IN THE BALTICS
Gražina Miniotaitė (1948–)

Gražina Miniotaitė was born in 1948 in Raseiniai, Lithuania; she was an only child. Her fellow students nicknamed her "the Philosopher" in secondary school, and at age eighteen she moved from a small Lithuanian town, Birzai, to the philosophy department at Moscow State University. After eight years of study in Moscow, she earned her doctorate in philosophy in 1977. Her doctoral dissertation concerned the theory of justice propounded by the American philosopher John Rawls, and was the first thesis in the Soviet Union to be written on Rawls, considered by many to be the most significant political philosopher of the twentieth century; his noteworthy essay on civil disobedience published in 1958 brought obedience and disobedience into the mainstream of political theory. Thus, while still relatively young, Miniotaitė had established a specific interest in philosophical liberalism and the justifications for civil disobedience. She was subsequently inspired by changes occurring in the Soviet Union in the 1980s, such as *perestroika* (restructuring), and by the Polish and Czechoslovak nonviolent struggles in Central and Eastern Europe that she observed through the lens of her professional interest in political philosophy.

Returning to Lithuania, Miniotaitė embarked on her academic career in the philosophy department of the Lithuanian Academy of Sciences, in Vilnius. Stimulated by inquiries from doctoral students about her research activities, she concentrated on issues pertaining to the connections between morality and politics. Her passion for reading and a flare for table tennis, swimming, and cycling proved to be helpful to her in developing rapport with the students, and through these informal interactions, she had an influence on those who shared her interest in political liberalism and nonviolent action.

When the Lithuanian liberation movement Sąjūdis, meaning "co-movement" or joint movement, was established in 1988, Miniotaitė was an active participant and became a member of the Sąjūdis Council of the Lithuanian Academy of Sciences. In November 1989 in Moscow, she participated in an international conference on the "ethics of nonviolence," which brought together leading theoreticians and practitioners of nonviolent action. There she met the scholar Gene Sharp and Robert Holmes of the Fellowship of Reconciliation, among others, and made a presentation on the Lithuanian independence movement and its popular front, Sąjūdis. Sharp and Holmes gave her their writings, which she subsequently studied and shared with others. Soon after, in March 1990, Lithuania would declare its independence, and in April establish the Department of National Defense whose building was "destroyed by the Soviets many times," according to Miniotaitė.

Her essay "Civil Disobedience: Justice against Legality," published in 1990, places the Sąjūdis movement and its goals for a liberated Lithuania in a broad historical and political context.

Both practitioner and scholar, during 1991–1992 Miniotaitė headed the Commission for Psychological Defense and Civil Resistance in the Department of National Defense in Lithuania. The commission

(Continued)

(Continued)

contributed to national educational efforts on civil resistance and justifications for nonviolent strategies. She was a research fellow in 1995 at Princeton University's Center of International Studies and subsequently worked as a research fellow in 1996 at the Copenhagen Peace Research Institute. From 1991 to 1995, she served as a founder and president of the Lithuanian Center for Nonviolent Action. She was a NATO research fellow from 1997 to 1999, working from Vilnius.

Miniotaitė is a professor in the political science department of the Lithuanian Military Academy and a senior research fellow at the Lithuanian Institute of Culture, Philosophy and Arts, both in Vilnius. Her research interests include moral and political philosophy, paradigm shifts in international relations theories, political identity, and security issues. Miniotaitė is currently a member of the editorial boards of *Cooperation and Conflict*, a Nordic journal of international affairs, and *Logos*, a journal of religion and philosophy. She served on the International Board of Advisors for the Gandhi Institute for the Study of Nonviolence from 1996 to 2007.

Miniotaitė has published widely. The research and writing for *Nonviolent Resistance in Lithuania: A Story of Peaceful Liberation* (2002) was supported by a grant from the Albert Einstein Institution in Boston. Her other works include *Lithuania's Evolving Security and Defence Policy: "Not Only Consumer, also Contributor?"* (2008) and *Justice against Legality: Theory of Civil Disobedience and Liberal Political thought* (2009, in Lithuanian). Other recent publications include *Search for Identity in Modern Foreign Policy of Lithuania: Between the Northern and Eastern Dimensions* (2005) and *"Normative Power Europe" and Lithuania's Foreign Policy* (2006). Miniotaitė also penned the essay "Civilian Resistance in the Security and Defence System of Lithuania: History and Prospects" (2004). She plans to write a book on the prospects for nonviolent civilian defense in the post–cold war era.

MAY 15, 1989
BALTIC INDEPENDENCE FRONTS PLEAD TO U.N.
By ESTHER B. FEIN
Special to The New York Times

Tallinn, U.S.S.R, May 14 – Leaders of popular political movements from the Soviet Union's three Baltic republics appealed today to the United Nations to help them become independent nations.

Saying they wanted their status resolved "on the international level," representatives of the Popular Fronts of Estonia and Latvia and the Lithuanian movement Sajudis adopted a joint document that called on the United Nations and the Conference on Security and Cooperation in Europe "to heed the aspiration of our nations for self-determination and independence in a neutral and demilitarized zone of Europe."

After an interval of independence between the world wars, Estonia, Latvia and Lithuania were forcibly incorporated into the Soviet Union in 1940, after Hitler and Stalin signed a nonaggression treaty and a secret protocol in 1939 carving up Europe into spheres of influence.

The Soviet annexation is still not recognized as legitimate by the United States, and Lithuanians, Estonians and Latvians maintain small independent diplomatic missions in the United States.

Voiding of Protocol Asked

Members of the three popular movements said in their statement that they believed the Soviet Government should—and within the year would—"renounce and declare null and void" the treaty and the secret protocol, thus dissolving any Soviet legal claims to the Baltic republics.

Under Mikhail S. Gorbachev's leadership, the Soviet authorities have begun to present a more honest version of a history long distorted, but they still deny that there ever was a secret protocol. Excerpts from the pact have been printed in Baltic newspapers.

The Soviet Government had no immediate comment on the Baltic statement today, but Mr. Gorbachev has stressed recently that he is "resolutely against" the calls for secession being issued by various nationalist groups.

Grass-roots political movements were officially founded in Estonia, Latvia and Lithuania less than a year ago, but already they have gained wide support from both their ethnic populations and local Communist party leaders.

The groups grew out of a fear that nationalist concerns were being subordinated by Moscow and a feeling that the current political changes in the Soviet Union presented an opportunity to win greater economic and political autonomy.

The action today, taken at the first assembly of all three Baltic popular movements, marks the first time that these groups have appealed for an international forum to decide their status, basing their claims on the illegality of the Stalin-Hitler pact.

The assembly also passed a declaration spelling out the rights of "the people of the sovereign states of Estonia, Latvia and Lithuania" to choose their own form of economy. The statement said the current attempts at economic perestroika, or restructuring, had failed because they were inherently ineffective, mainly because they preserve a centralized economy.

While many of those concepts have been put forth before by the popular fronts individually, the joint demands and strategy were more radical than previous ones.

Local Party Chiefs Absent

Apparently expecting that this conference would adopt more extreme positions, none of the Communist party leaders from the three republics were in attendance this weekend.

"I think our leaders were a little bit afraid to attend," said Kazimieras Antanavicius, a leader of the Lithuanian Sajudis and a deputy-elect to the new Soviet Congress of People's Deputies. "But this does not represent a confrontation between the party leaderships and the popular fronts."

At a rally Saturday night in the medieval town square here, thousands of Tallinn residents and visitors from the other Baltic republics watched the lighting of a symbolic torch of Baltic unity as similar flames were being ignited in Riga, the Latvian capital, and Vilnius, the Lithuanian capital.

Underneath the flags of all three republics, the long-banned national anthems of the republics' independent period were played.

"The last time I sang this song freely was the 18th of July 1940," said Janis Blum, a 64-year-old engineer from Riga, who cried as he sang "God Bless Latvia" under his homeland's flag. "My dream is to once again sing it as a completely free man."

HUMAN CHAIN ACROSS THE BALTICS

In Eastern Europe in the 1980s, the Poles chose the nonviolent method of strikes in seeking economic and political rights and reforms. The East Germans selected massive candlelit demonstrations and protest emigration. The Czechs mounted successive days of huge demonstrations. The Balts sang.

By summer 1989, demonstrations were taking place across the three Baltic republics. The singing of traditional songs, deeply rooted in the Baltic cultures, was a feature in all these mass protests. Latvians have five synonyms for the verb "to sing" that they use in everyday communications, and musicologists have identified more than 1 million Latvian folk songs. Lithuanian folk songs are known to have inspired great European composers, including Chopin, Schumann, and Schubert. Most decisive of countless public rallies was the August 23 calendar demonstration, called the Baltic Way—the formation of a human chain stretching from Estonia's coast to the southern border of Lithuania. It commemorated the fiftieth anniversary of the Molotov-Ribbentrop Pact and the secret German-Soviet protocols that led to annexation of the Baltic states by the Soviet Union (see **Baltic States, Introduction,** and "Text of Secret Protocols to 1939 Hitler-Stalin Pact"). Hundreds of thousands of people held hands in an almost unbroken connection across the three republics. Some two-fifths of the native populations in the three republics may have taken part directly or indirectly. Those forming links in the chain sang national songs to call for independence, making memorable the apex of the 1987–1991 years of nonviolent collective action. The powerful, symbolic judgment was unmistakable: the secret protocols were illegal, and the Baltic peoples did not want to be part of the Soviet Union.

From Riga northward to the Estonian capital of Tallinn, an almost uninterrupted line of women and men, boys and girls, of every age stood, holding hands and singing. Southward to the Lithuanian capital of Vilnius, hands of all ages clasped. Overhead in Lithuania, helicopters dropped thousands of red and yellow flowers. Church bells pealed. Candles were lit in memory of those who had been executed or deported during the Soviet era. The two popular fronts and Sąjūdis issued "The Baltic Way," a joint statement highlighting the nonviolent and parliamentary methods chosen to regain Baltic independent nationhood. The specific aim of the chain and statement was to remind the world of the Molotov-Ribbentrop Pact and its devastating consequences.

Given the scale of the human chain—by several contemporary accounts, 2 million persons were involved directly or in a support function—it could not have occurred without the tacit support from the three increasingly nationalist regimes. *The New York Times* correspondent Esther B. Fein conservatively estimates that more than one million persons took part in the 400-mile human chain linking Estonia, Latvia, and Lithuania. (Journalists often underestimate the size of crowds as a precaution against exaggeration.) In Moscow on August 26, the Central Committee of the Communist Party issued a statement entitled "About the Situation in the Baltic Soviet Republics." It read, "if [Baltic leaders succeed] in achieving their goals, the consequences could be catastrophic for the peoples. Their viability itself could be questioned." In a televised statement on August 26, Soviet leader Mikhail S. Gorbachev referred to "nationalist excesses" and warned party leaders in the Baltics against submitting to nationalist impulses. He warned that "the state of the Baltic people is in serious danger." By implication, *perestroika* (restructuring) was to be directed by the party; Baltic reformism would be acceptable so long as it adhered to a unitary state. Gorbachev's words suggested that no exceptions could be allowed for any union republics, because the integrity of the Soviet Union took precedence.

Moscow's displeasure was partly attributable to a view held by communist reformers in the Latvian Popular Front, who saw the front as an organization working for change within the Soviet system, and thus acting within the bounds of perestroika and *glasnost* (openness) to bring about limited reforms. On August 27, 1989, in *The Times,* Fein reports denunciations of the human chain by the Soviet central committee ("Moscow Condemns Nationalist 'Virus' in 3 Baltic Lands"). In a statement that Fein says "marked the first time the party leadership had directly denounced the Baltic states for the stepped-up independence campaign," the Central Committee "accused people in the Baltics of abusing these policies for 'extremist' goals. 'They step by step steered the course of affairs toward an alienation of the Baltic republics from the rest of the country.'" Further,

The Soviet Constitution guarantees the right of any republic to secede from the Soviet Union, but this has long been considered a symbolic right and one that would be vehemently resisted by Moscow. The statement said that leaders of the republics were to blame for failing "to contain the process" and that some communist party leaders "lost heart" and "began to play up to nationalist sentiments." Communist party and government officials in all three republics have been enthusiastic supporters of grass-roots political movements that have become ever bolder in their calls for complete independence from the Soviet Union, and many attended and spoke at [the human chain] demonstrations.

Fein's dispatch reveals a significant development: while the central committee in Moscow was condemnatory, Baltic communist officials, who were often native Estonians, Latvians, and Lithuanians, were shifting their allegiances and adopting the nationalism of their citizens.

Older residents of Tallinn, the capital of Estonia, join hands on August 24, 1989, in a human chain that stretched across Estonia, Latvia, and Lithuania. Singing nationalist songs, the demonstrators, by some estimates numbering 2 million directly or in some way involved, demanded the right to restore the Baltics' independent statehood. Called the Baltic Way, the mega-demonstration commemorated the fiftieth anniversary of the Molotov-Ribbentrop Pact—with its secret Soviet-German protocols that led to the military occupation and annexation of the Baltic states by the Soviet Union—while also contesting the Soviets' suppression of Baltic history. The secret clauses acted as a trigger for Nazi Germany's attack on Poland of September 1, 1939, which launched World War II. Estonia's singing in huge choral festivals was a leading method through which ideas of resistance and independence spread, hence the name Singing Revolution.

Source: AP Images/cbg/str/Robert Tonsing

AUGUST 24, 1989
BALTIC CITIZENS LINK HANDS TO DEMAND INDEPENDENCE
By ESTHER B. FEIN
Special to The New York Times

Tallinn, U.S.S.R., Aug. 23 – Hundreds of thousands of Estonians, Latvians and Lithuanians were reported today to have linked hands across their Baltic homelands and demanded the right to "restore their independent statehood."

Some government officials and Communist Party figures joined popular movement leaders in a sharply worded declaration issued to mark the 50th anniversary of the Soviet-Nazi nonaggression treaty, which had secret protocols that opened the way to Soviet absorption of the three Baltic states.

The statement said the Soviet Union "infringed on the historical right of the Baltic nations to self-determination, presented ruthless ultimatums to the Baltic republics, occupied them with overwhelming military force, and under conditions of military occupation and heavy political terror carried out their violent annexations."

A Joint Statement

The statement advocating the right of the Baltics to determine their own political futures was drawn up jointly by representatives of popular political movements from Estonia, Latvia and Lithuania.

"Self-determination is the natural desire of all nations," said the Estonian President, Arnold Ruutel, speaking from atop the medieval Tall Hermann tower here to a vast crowd of people gathered below to begin a human chain across the three republics.

Organizers estimated that nearly a million people stood side-by-side in the evening chill, hands clasped, from the cobbled streets here in the capital of Estonia, more than 400 miles across Latvia to the Lithuanian capital of Vilnius.

The crowd estimate could not be confirmed, but film taken from the air and broadcast on Estonian television showed a nearly continuous line of people stretching across the Baltic countryside.

A secret protocol attached to the Soviet-German nonaggression pact of Aug. 23, 1939, and subsequent secret agreements, divided Europe into German and Soviet spheres of influence and cleared the way for Soviet occupation and annexation of the Baltics in 1940.

The Soviet authorities have only recently admitted the existence of the secret protocols, but insist they did not directly result in absorption of Estonia, Lithuania and Latvia, and thus have no bearing on the current boundaries.

The day was marked by defiant but measured declarations of independence, reflecting the growing passion for freedom and the uncertainty about what Moscow will stand for.

Call From Lithuania

In Vilnius, the 220-member [Seimas, or parliament] of the Lithuanian popular front, or Sajudis, called for "the creation of an independent, democratic Lithuanian republic, without political, cultural or administrative subordination to the Soviet Union."

There was strong sentiment in the group for stronger language specifying that Lithuania should be outside the Soviet Union, but Sajudis leaders pleaded for compromise wording to avoid antagonizing Moscow.

Leaders of Sajudis, which holds most of Lithuania's seats in the national Congress of People's Deputies, came under sharp attack in this morning's Pravda, which accused them of hiding the real purpose of their desire to break with Moscow.

An editorial in the Soviet Communist Party newspaper attempted to discredit Sajudis leaders and some sympathizers in the Lithuanian Communist Party by associating them with people accused of being former Nazi collaborators.

First Official Challenge

On Tuesday, a commission of the Lithuanian parliament became the first official body to challenge the legitimacy of Soviet rule by declaring that the annexation of the republic in 1940 was illegal.

Lithuanians said the statement, expected to win approval of the full Lithuanian legislature early next month, could eventually provide the legal basis for a secession attempt.

For citizens impatient with the approach of the popular front groups, smaller independence parties mounted protests that drew thousands in Vilnius and Tallinn,

Estonia, calling for immediate separation from the Soviet Union.

In Moscow today, a small demonstration by Baltic supporters was broken up by legions of special riot policemen using clubs. The Soviet press agency Tass said 75 people were detained at the rally, which was timed to catch movie crowds pouring from a nearby cinema and snarled traffic in the city center.

On Soviet Television

Soviet television showed film of the human chain tonight and said it should not be regarded as "a manifestation of a separatist mood." But in the streets of the Baltics, there was much talk of complete independence.

Rita Urbanovich brought her 7-year-old twin sons from Tallinn to a spot along the Viljandi Highway several miles outside the city.

"This is something I feel in my heart," she said. "We suffered. Our whole country suffered—every person. And I brought my children because this is my way to explain to them why independence is important for their future."

More Assertive and Radical

Popular political movements in the three Baltic republics held their founding congresses less than a year ago, raising aloud the long-whispered call for greater political and economic autonomy.

Since those beginnings, however, some leaders of these groups have been elected to the new Soviet congress and been made ministers in the governments of their republics, adding more authority and confidence to their demands.

In that short time, too, people throughout the Baltics have become more assertive and radical in their positions. Where once they called for more freedom from Moscow, they are now insisting on complete independence.

"During this past year we have come even closer to the ideals that our people have carried in their hearts for 50 years," said Marju Lauristen, a leader of the Estonian popular front and a deputy to the new Soviet congress. "Why this shift? Why are we talking more openly about these things? Because all of us want to have freedom, and freedom without independence is impossible."

LITHUANIA: INDEPENDENT STATEHOOD RESTORED

On March 11, 1990, Lithuania became the first Soviet socialist republic to declare its independence. As part of the process, it changed its name to the Republic of Lithuania and renamed the Supreme Soviet, or parliament, the Supreme Council. The first stage of Lithuania's independence process had begun with the establishment of the independent Sąjūdis (translated as "co-movement" or joint movement) in 1988 and ended with the de facto declaration of independence in March 1990. The second stage lasted until Lithuania's acceptance into the United Nations, on September 17, 1991 (see "Lithuanians Move to Limit Moscow Ties" and "Gorbachev Says Coup Will Hasten Reform").

Attempting to lessen the destructive effects of a weakening economic situation, Soviet leader Mikhail S. Gorbachev instituted political reforms in the late 1980s. In 1989, he introduced the Congress of People's Deputies and a new Supreme Soviet, both under communist domination. By February 1990, the Congress of People's Deputies had agreed to remove from the Soviet constitution its language guaranteeing a "leading role" for the Communist Party, prior to scheduled elections in the Baltic republics. In March 1990, Gorbachev gained emergency presidential powers and allowed himself to be "elected" by the Supreme Soviet to the newly created position of president of the Soviet Union, with his installation planned for March 12. Lithuanians decided to announce their declaration of independence the day before, on March 11, fearing the potential exertion of power by a president Gorbachev. Less than two years had passed since the group Helsinki '86 had organized the first openly conducted demonstration without official approval in the postwar period, on June 14, 1987 (see "Lithuanians Rally for Stalin Victims").

Elections during 1990 institutionalized the power base of the three popular fronts in the Baltic republics. In February, Sąjūdis ran on a platform of complete Lithuanian independence and won. It was generally assumed that independence would proceed in stages, beginning with a declaration of separation from the Soviet Union. On February 3, Vytautas Landsbergis, the musicologist leading Sąjūdis, offered two routes to independence: a decolonization model, beginning with the reestablishment of equal, state-to-state relations with the Soviet Union, or unilateral political action "to regain sovereignty ourselves" prior to negotiations. Landsbergis preferred the first approach, as was undertaken by Estonia and Latvia. In Lithuania, members of the nationalist movement headed Sąjūdis while also taking control of the government. In Estonia and Latvia, control of the government had for the moment remained in local, communist hands.

Baltic nationalists had since 1939–1940 regarded the Soviet Union as a foreign and despotic interloper. The Baltics' popular fronts of the 1980s saw themselves as decolonization movements, in addition to pro-democracy mobilizations. They had swiftly activated hundreds of thousands of supporters who turned out repeatedly for calendar events, exerted sufficient popular pressure to put like-minded politicians into power, systematically pressured their local communist parties to adopt the cause of independence, and, starting with Lithuania, took control of government. The fronts routinely used the term *decolonization* to characterize their struggle and the vocabulary of empire to depict the Soviet Union (although the union was not technically a colonial state).

The cry of empire became a rallying call for non-Russian Baltic nationalists seeking independence and was also used by Eastern Europeans to define and undermine Soviet jurisdiction over their satellite states. Furthermore, Balts had experienced two decades of independence during the First Republics in the early twentieth-century that had enhanced their self-image; they therefore attached their cause to international norms opposing conquest and colonization, as enshrined in the UN Charter and subsequent conventions and resolutions. By 1989, the popular fronts had begun appealing directly to the United Nations to generate international support for their cause (see "Baltic Independence Fronts Plead to U.N."). The impediments to independence lay in the Kremlin's refusal to tolerate secession by the Baltic republics, but also in the passivity of the international community in not standing up for the majority expressions of the Baltic peoples.

As events proceeded in Lithuania, the internal dynamic became such that a vote against independence due to procedural questions would have been regarded as opposition to sovereignty. *The New York Times* correspondent Bill Keller on March 12, 1990, reports on the March 11 vote. An updated account reveals that out of 124 parliamentarians, only 6 abstained; according to Miniotaitė, no votes were cast against the measure. On March 12, 1990, *The Times* editorializes,

> Mikhail Gorbachev thinks Lithuanians are wrong to secede but accepts their right to be wrong. That's a mark of his liberation as well as theirs. Lithuania only declared itself independent yesterday. Now it must negotiate terms and timing. But Mr. Gorbachev

has already said yes to the principle of a free Lithuania by agreeing to talks and by refusing to use force. What a welcome transformation in a land that Americans have known for half a century as a captive nation ("Two Liberations in Lithuania").

To the contrary, Soviet troops were already on a state of alert as tanks rolled into Vilnius following the March 11 declaration of independence. Within days, the Extraordinary Congress of People's Deputies in Moscow pronounced Lithuania's declaration illegal and called for restoration of "order and legitimacy" in Vilnius. Gorbachev demanded cancellation of the independence proclamation. Soviet agents from the Interior Ministry began seizing Vilnius buildings previously owned by the Communist Party. Soviet paratroopers apprehended Lithuanian deserters from the army on the streets. Fears of bloodshed and armed incidents intensified, particularly because Lithuanian police loyal to the republican government were lightly armed. The Lithuanian parliament pleaded with the international community to protest any use of violence, while the Lithuanian government asked Lithuanians "to behave peacefully at all times."

Gorbachev sought the devolution of certain powers to the republics, while retaining a central Soviet role in economic affairs, foreign policy, and defense. Yet Soviet military measures, according to Anatol Lieven, a journalist-historian of Latvian descent, "only increased the determination and morale of ordinary Lithuanians. Those who, immediately after the declaration, had been critical of Landsbergis and Sąjūdis, became increasingly supportive, and popular demonstrations returned to their pre-independence dimensions. . . . The declaration of Lithuanian independence became a national talisman" (Lieven 1993, 239, 240).

KEY PLAYER IN THE BALTICS
Arnold Rüütel (1928–)

• •

Born in Saareema, Estonia, Arnold Rüütel, a lifetime pro-reform communist leader, helped create the conditions for political transition to democracy and would become the freely elected president of a democratic Estonia.

Rüütel began his career in agriculture. After graduating from the Janeda Agricultural College in 1950, he entered government as a senior agronomist in the Department of Agriculture. He spent his early career teaching at the Tartu School of Mechanization of Agriculture and serving as the head livestock expert for the Estonian Institute for Livestock Breeding and Veterinary Science. He became rector of the Estonian Agricultural Academy in 1969.

His position at the academy introduced him to politics. Throughout the 1970s, he became increasingly involved in the Estonian government, rising to deputy prime minister in 1978. He held that position until 1983, when he was elected chairman of the presidium of Estonia's Supreme Council. He was one of fifteen deputy chairs of the Supreme Soviet of the Union of Soviet Socialist Republics.

Rüütel was initially Estonia's most emphatic champion of sovereignty within the political machinery of the Soviet Union. As a pro-reform communist, Rüütel subsequently played a role in composing Estonia's

(Continued)

(Continued)

declaration of sovereignty. In 1988, Rüütel was involved in the Estonian Supreme Soviet's adoption of the declaration, issued on November 16 of that year. The Supreme Soviet, similar to a legislature for the local communist party, was renamed the Supreme Council when Estonians declared their government functionally independent and held free elections. In 1990, Estonians elected Rüütel to the Supreme Council, which voted him in as chairperson. In those two years, from March 1990 to October 1992, Rüütel led the council to further distance itself from Moscow, declaring Soviet authority illegal. He also led in establishing the Council of the Baltic States to unite Estonia with Latvia and Lithuania in their mutual quest for independence.

As a member of the Constitutional Assembly in 1991 and 1992, Rüütel helped draft Estonia's new constitution. He served as chairman until 1992, when Estonia held its first elections for its parliament, or Riigikogu, as an independent nation. Rüütel ran for president, but lost.

In 1995, he was elected to the Riigikogu and became its vice chairman. He spent 1994 to 2000 serving as chairman of the Estonian Rural People's Party, which was renamed the Estonian People's Union in 1999. He lost another bid for the presidency in 1996.

Rüütel was finally successful in his quest for the presidency when in 2001, at age seventy-three, he received 186 of 366 electoral college votes. He served as the second president of the Republic of Estonia until 2006. After a hotly contested election, he lost his bid for another term.

He is married to Ingrid Rüütel, an internationally renowned scholar of Estonian folklore and song and the president of the folklore association Baltica. He has two daughters with Ingrid, and they have six grandchildren.

MARCH 12, 1990
PARLIAMENT IN LITHUANIA, 124–0, DECLARES NATION INDEPENDENT
No Soviet Reaction
New Leaders Are Named to Negotiate Future Ties With Moscow
By BILL KELLER
Special to The New York Times

Vilnius, Lithuania, March 11 – Lithuania tonight proclaimed itself a sovereign state, legally free of the Soviet Union, and named the leaders of a non-Communist government to negotiate their future relations with Moscow.

The Lithuanian parliament voted 124 to 0, with [6] abstentions [and no opposition], to restore the independent statehood ended by Soviet annexation 50 years ago. The Lithuanian Communist Party, which won only a minority of seats in parliamentary elections last month, joined the non-Communist majority in the vote, and in an outburst of songs and embraces that followed.

"Expressing the will of the people, the Supreme Soviet of the Lithuanian Republic declares and solemnly proclaims the restoration of the exercise of sovereign powers of the Lithuanian state, which were annulled by an alien power in 1940," said a resolution passed late tonight. "From now on, Lithuania is once again an independent state."

Full Implications Unclear

It was not immediately clear what the full implications of the Lithuanian action were. According to Lithuanian leaders, Mikhail S. Gorbachev, the Soviet President, has indicated a willingness to negotiate the conditions of independence. But there was no immediate reaction to the declaration of independence either from Mr. Gorbachev or the Soviet Government.

Tass, the Soviet press agency, issued a factual report of the Lithuanian action without comment. Reports on national television were similar.

[The Bush Administration urged the Soviet Union to respect the Lithuanian move, but stopped short of an explicit statement of recognition of the newly declared government. Noting instead that the United States never recognized Soviet authority over the Baltic republics, officials urged nonviolence and said that only through talks with Moscow, not unilateral action, would Lithuanians achieve what they want.]

Hundreds of Lithuanians gathered outside the parliament building, singing national hymns and chanting independence slogans, as the legislators changed the name of the Lithuanian Soviet Socialist Republic to simply the Lithuanian Republic and ordered the hammer and sickle replaced by the old Lithuanian coat of arms.

At one point, people in the crowd outside used screwdrivers to pry the copper Soviet insignia from the front of the building, to a roar of approval.

But behind the united front, many legislators and ordinary citizens voiced deep worry about how Moscow would respond to this precedent-setting breach in the union. The most common fear was a wave of economic reprisals that could produce fuel shortages and unemployment, threatening the state with chaos.

Other legislators worried that such a dramatic act of defiance, especially on the eve of an important Soviet congressional gathering, would weaken President Gorbachev, who has so far generally acquiesced to Lithuania's drive for freedom.

Before approving the law completing the political break with Moscow, the parliament elected as Lithuania's new president Vytautas Landsbergis, a soft-spoken music professor who led the pro-independence movement called Sajudis from an eclectic band of dissidents to a legislative majority.

By a vote of 91 to 38, the Sajudis-dominated legislature elected Mr. Landsbergis over Algirdas Brazauskas, the Lithuanian Communist Party leader, whose personal popularity has soared since his party broke with the Soviet Communist Party in December, but not enough to overcome the Communists' association with decades of occupation.

New Leader Urges Calm

Mr. Landsbergis urged the 3.7 million citizens of the republic to be calm and united as they enter a period of tense negotiations aimed at persuading Moscow to treat them as a friendly neighbor.... [T]he parliament is to consider an appeal to Mr. Gorbachev asking for withdrawal of the more than 30,000 Soviet troops based in Lithuania and the speedy repatriation of Lithuanian men serving in the Soviet Army.

"We cannot ignore the interests of our neighbors, particularly our neighbors to the east," the new Lithuanian president said. "But we will not be asking for permission to take this or that step."

Mr. Brazauskas is an economist by training, and supporters said the Communist leader would be a more reassuring presence at the bargaining table where details of the disengagement are to be worked out. But Mr. Landsbergis represented a clean break with the 50-year period that Lithuanians regard as an armed occupation.

The neighboring Baltic republics, Latvia and Estonia, are also moving toward secession.

"It will be contagious for other republics," said Mr. Brazauskas, who voted for today's decision but had earlier argued for a more gradual separation. "Perhaps some will follow our example. But a great state like the Soviet Union will not collapse easily."

Although the Communists here voted for the declaration of independence, Mr. Brazauskas declined an offer to be vice president, and other party members said they were not interested in prominent positions in the new government.

Other Officials Named

Mr. Landsbergis appointed three deputies, one a Communist and two who have quit the party, and named as prime minister a market-oriented economist, [Kazimira] Prunskiene, who has announced her plans to leave the party.

Justas Paleckis, the Communist party ideology chief, said that the Communists were persuaded that Sajudis did not want to share power on a more equal basis and that some party officials had decided they would remain aloof from the government and let Sajudis take responsibility for the consequences.

In the corridors outside the parliamentary chamber, Mr. Brazauskas's Communists—about one third of the 133 legislators—and some non-Communists wondered aloud about the wisdom of moving so quickly to declare independence.

"Probably a third of the deputies think it is crazy to rush into this," said a local journalist sympathetic to Sajudis. "But anyone who speaks against it is sure to be branded a traitor."

No representatives of Moscow were evident in the hall.

Rights Advocate Applauds

Though there was no official reaction from the Kremlin, members of the parliamentary opposition in Moscow sent a message of congratulations, and Sergei Kovalyov, a human rights advocate and former political prisoner recently elected to the Russian republic's parliament, came here to applaud Lithuania's move.

"A lot of Russians will say, 'We liberated you from the Germans, we helped you industrialize,' " Mr. Kovalyov said in a brief address to the parliament. "None of them will say that we deported half of the Lithuanian people to Siberia."

In recent days Mr. Gorbachev and other Soviet officials served notice that Moscow would make billions of rubles in financial claims on Lithuania if it secedes, and challenged Lithuania's boundaries, including its right to the Baltic seaport of Klaipeda, [formerly] called Memel. Mr. Gorbachev has also repeatedly cited security risks for Moscow in the loss of the republic, and promised to defend the rights of the republic's non-Lithuanian minority, 20 percent of the population.

There have already been some signs of stepped-up pressure, including a freeze by the Soviet Government-controlled banks on the assets of Lithuanian savings banks, that have led leaders of the republic to speculate about a possible economic blockade.

What Moscow Could Do

Annual trade between Lithuania and other Soviet republics is estimated at $24 billion at the official rate of exchange, including almost all of Lithuania's subsidized oil supplies.

Another fear is that Moscow could shut down centrally run industrial enterprises, throwing half a million Russian blue-collar workers out of jobs and raising ethnic tensions.

"My fear is that if we do not understand the progressive forces in Moscow, we can bring them a lot of danger," Mr. Paleckis added. "And it will be danger for us as well. If Mr. Gorbachev loses, our declaration of independence will make moral sense, but . . . ."

Mr. Landsbergis replied that "the people of Lithuania are not naive. Even after listening to frequent warnings about how difficult it was going to be, they voted all the same for the Sajudis platform. We consider that a kind of referendum." Mr. Landsbergis said he hoped for prompt recognition from foreign countries, including the United States, which has never formally acknowledged the annexation of the three Baltic republics but has been wary of undermining Mr. Gorbachev.

The vote was the climax of a campaign that began gathering momentum less than two years ago, with the creation of the Sajudis initiative group in June, 1988.

A year ago, the alliance proved its strength by capturing most of the republic's seats in a new Soviet Parliament.

Mr. Landsbergis and several other lawmakers said they would no longer participate as voting members of the Soviet Parliament, although they might come to Moscow as observers or as members of a bargaining team to work out the details of secession.

- - -

LATVIA: PARLIAMENTARY APPROVAL FOR INDEPENDENCE

The final phase of the Baltic independence process took on the character of a struggle between governments, as Moscow gradually fell under the domination of hardliners intent on using brute force to preserve the Soviet Union, and the Baltic republics mobilized to secede and reassert their historic sovereignty. Both claimed authority over the same lands. Soviet repression intensified, as the Kremlin not only refused to accept the secession of elected Baltic governments, but sought also to bring about their downfall and replace them with puppets. Western powers remained mute.

Lithuania's March 11, 1990, unilateral declaration of de facto independence from the Soviet Union placed Latvia and Estonia in an awkward position. It was expected that they would follow immediately with comparable independence proclamations. Indeed, the two countries had such plans under way. Yet, Moscow not only condemned Lithuania's action, it also began troop maneuvers and threatened increased economic sanctions along with an oil blockade. (Moscow had made similar official threats against tentative comparable moves by Estonia.) *The Times* on March 18, 1990, notes that "Mr. Gorbachev, no longer even a member of the Congress, personally led the docile legislators in drafting a resolution condemning Lithuania's declaration of independence" ("Mr. Prezident; Democracy, Gorbachev's Way").

Both Latvia and Estonia had more cause for fear from economic sanctions, fuel blockades, army maneuvers, unemployment, KGB-controlled troops, and hard-core communist bureaucrats in Moscow than did Lithuania. Soviet mass deportations to Siberia earlier in the century and heavy systematic migration of Russians during the previous five decades had resulted in their two small nations having nearly half-Russian populations. In Lithuania, only 20 percent were minorities. Some worried that neither the Latvian nor the Estonian popular fronts could win the two-thirds majority required for making constitutional changes to their Soviet-inspired laws and statutes. Moreover, thousands of Soviet troops remained stationed on Baltic lands. On February 2, an assembly of Estonian leaders had declared limited independence, while Latvian parliamentarians had petitioned Gorbachev to open talks with them about their independence.

On March 18, 1990, the first more-or-less democratic elections for Latvia's Supreme Council, or parliament, were conducted. Candidates from the Latvian Popular Front and the National Independence Movement of Latvia, both nationalists and pro-independence, swept the balloting. The front won 68.2 percent of the votes; only 21.5 percent cast ballots in opposition. Estonia's first partially free elections for the parliamentary Supreme Council were held simultaneously; its new Supreme Council chose the most circumspect and careful route to independence of the three republics: on March 30, the council proclaimed Estonia an illegally occupied and annexed country, declaring that it had entered a period of transition aimed toward restoration of the pre-1940 Estonian republic. Equally momentous was its formation of a popular front government led by Edgar Savisaar and a cabinet comprised mainly of pro-independence former communists.

In the Latvian capital of Riga on May 4, 1990, the new Supreme Council—aware of the Kremlin's oil blockade against Lithuania—carefully worded a resolution restoring de jure independent statehood while proclaiming the illegality of its 1940 annexation by the Soviet Union and its intent to restore the interwar Latvian republic, with its 1922 First Republic Constitution. It renamed the country the Republic of Latvia, supplanting the Latvian Soviet Socialist Republic. With this action, perceptions shifted. The newly empowered Supreme Council and council of ministers were recognized by Latvian citizens as their own, legitimate non-communist government, rather than a foreign encumbrance.

The Latvian Supreme Council proclaimed agreement with UN human rights conventions and the Conference on Security and Cooperation in Europe, which emerged from the Helsinki Accords (see **"Introduction: Strikes, Sinatra, and Nonviolent Revolution"**). On May 5, defying Soviet rebukes against the popular fronts, Latvia's Supreme Council announced the start of its transition to reestablishing the republic's independence. Immediately after the declaration, the leadership walked to the Daugava River embankment, where environmental protests against a hydroelectric power station had helped to launch the independence process and where tens of thousands now celebrated. Dainis Īvāns, who chaired the Popular Front and helped lead

Videz Aizsardzibas Klubs, which led the mobilization against the power station, was nearly smothered with flowers. On May 14, Gorbachev declared Latvia's transition to independence null and void.

On May 8, Estonia announced the commencement of its transition to independence, dropping its status as a Soviet socialist republic. The Supreme Soviet renamed itself the Supreme Council. A month later, the council passed laws providing for the right to own private property. By August, Estonia simply had announced that it had ceased to be part of the Soviet Union. Gorbachev soon thereafter denounced the move.

The concept of citizenship in Estonia and Latvia in the 1980s and 1990s was new and linked to the restoration of independence. (Lithuania had been administered by Lithuanians starting in the Middle Ages, but this was not true for Estonia and Latvia; [see **Baltic States, Introduction**.]) Stalinism had destroyed Baltic citizenship, but by the late 1980s the idea had begun to resurface, reinforcing the independence struggle and the revival to nationhood. Estonia and Latvia advocated the principle that citizenship in the First Republics had remained uninterrupted and should be officially restored. The Baltic states strove to internationalize their predicament. Tangible support was not forthcoming from the Western powers, but sympathy intensified, leading to Gorbachev being viewed with increasing skepticism.

MAY 5, 1990
LATVIA LAWMAKERS MOVE TO DISSOLVE LINKS TO MOSCOW
Complete Break Avoided
Parliament, Mindful of Need for Russian Talks, Votes 138–0 for a Transition
By ESTHER B. FEIN
Special to The New York Times

Riga, Latvia, May 4 – Defying Moscow's warning to curb separatist movements, the Latvian Parliament today declared the beginning of a transition period leading to establishment of the republic's independence.

The action was taken despite the Kremlin's continuing economic sanctions against Lithuania, the neighboring Baltic republic, which declared itself fully independent of Moscow eight weeks ago, and despite growing official criticism of similar moves by Estonia, the third of the three Baltic states.

Lithuanian Example

But the Latvian legislators seemed mindful of the consequences suffered by Lithuania, now in its third week of a partial fuel blockade by Moscow, and eager to maintain the talks that they have begun with the Kremlin over Latvia's future relationship with the Soviet Union. Estonia's Parliament pledged on March 30 to restore full independence gradually; since then, President Mikhail S. Gorbachev has offered Estonia a special status in what he has described as a new kind of Soviet confederation if it drops its plan for independence.

The Latvian document stops short of declaring a complete break between Latvia and the Soviet Union and explicitly states that for the most part the Soviet Constitution and laws continue to be valid here during the transition period.

Faces Serious Opposition

While the Latvian approach was cautious, the declaration still faced serious opposition in the Parliament, though not enough to prevent the two-thirds majority needed for it to pass. In protest, 57 deputies refused to take part in a vote that they called premature and dangerous. The declaration was adopted by a vote of 138 in favor, none opposed and 1 abstention.

It is not clear how Moscow will react to the Latvian declaration. The Kremlin could regard the move as a conciliatory gesture or a sign of confrontation and defiance.

"I think there will be some kind of conflict with Moscow," said Anatolijs Gorbunovs, who was re-elected this week as chairman, or president, of the Latvian Parliament.

"We didn't fulfill certain things that Moscow asked of us—for example, we specified that we are re-establishing the independent state of Latvia and we formally declared a transition period," he said. "But the way we did it is very important. We think we left the door open and that our dialogue with Moscow will still continue."

Moscow has said that any republic is free to leave the Soviet Union if it follows the law on secession recently established by the Soviet Parliament, which includes the support of two-thirds of the voters in a public referendum, a negotiation period of up to five years with Moscow and other republics on territorial, financial and other matters, and final approval by the full Soviet Congress.

The Baltic republics, Latvia, Estonia and Lithuania, assert that they are not bound by the new Soviet law because they were illegally incorporated into the Soviet Union. All three were independent nations when they were occupied by the Soviet Army in 1940 as a result of a secret treaty between Stalin and Hitler and then annexed.

Lithuania and Estonia have already rejected outright the possibility of using the secession law as a means of breaking with the Soviet Union. Latvia said as much today. The declaration states the republic's application to join the Soviet Union was "invalid from the moment of adoption," and the document further describes Latvia's desire not to secede, but rather to "restore de facto the free, democratic and independent republic of Latvia."

Conciliatory Tone Explained

But one of the main actions taken by Lithuania and Estonia that angered the Kremlin was the suspension of the Soviet Constitution in those republics. In its declaration, the Latvian Parliament re-establishes the constitution of the former independent Latvian republic. But the declaration immediately suspends that constitution until it can be revised and adopted, except for articles "expressing the constitutional and legal foundation of the Latvian state."

Those articles do not challenge outright the authority of the Soviet Constitution, and the declaration leaves standing Soviet laws that do not contradict Latvian sovereignty.

The declaration further guarantees new rights to all Soviet citizens who choose to continue living in the republic.

Latvian legislators said today that any conciliatory tone in their declaration was not a response to the Kremlin's tough stance toward Lithuania. Caution, they said, was dictated by the fact that independent-minded deputies won two-thirds of the seats in the Parliament only narrowly. People of Latvian descent make up barely half the population of their own republic, and many non-Latvians oppose independence.

"The situation in Latvia itself objectively dictated what I would call not caution but our realism," said Dainis Ivans, leader of the Popular Front, one of the first grassroots organizations to call for Latvian independence, and first deputy chairman of the Parliament. "But there should be no question about what we have done. We have taken the first step on the road to independence."

Many deputies at the session today said that that road was chosen hastily and without sufficient consideration, prompting dozens of them to refuse to take part in the vote.

"The fate of a nation shouldn't be decided in three hours," said Anatoly Alekseyev, leader of Interfront, an organization composed mainly of non-Latvians opposed to Latvian independence. Mr. Alekseyev was the lone deputy to walk out of the parliamentary chamber in protest during the vote.

"I sat and ate soup for lunch while I read through their documents," he said. "This is not right. They should have given the deputies several days to read them, they should have published them in the paper and allowed people to express their opinion."

At Rally, Flowers and Tears

Alfreds Rubiks, head of the Latvian Communist Party faction loyal to Moscow, said the declaration could bring strikes and possibly violence within the republic and possible economic sanctions from Moscow.

A small group of people opposed to independence stood with Soviet flags outside Parliament today as several dozen held a small demonstration.

Hundreds of supporters of independence waited anxiously alongside them. After the vote, the deputies left, passing through a crowd in the Old City's cobbled streets. The people embraced the legislators and many wept as they pressed flowers into the deputies' arms as they walked to a rally of several thousand people gathered at sunset on the banks of the Daugava River.

LITHUANIA'S BLOODY SUNDAY

Among the forces at work restraining Soviet repression against the Baltic independence drives was the so-called Gorbachev factor, that is, the personal reluctance of President Mikhail S. Gorbachev to use violence against nationalist movements. Notwithstanding what may have been a personal aversion to ordering bloodshed, Gorbachev agreed to a campaign of intimidation against the Baltic republics to frighten them into giving up their pursuit of independence or to stimulate reactions that would provoke pretexts justifying severe reprisals and crackdowns.

In summer 1988, extremist organizations connected to hard-line communists in Moscow formed international fronts, or "interfronts" (in Latvia and Estonia) and Unity, or Edinstvo (in Lithuania). Dominated by Slavs and Russians, these pro-Moscow "intermovement" (*interdvizhenie*) groups opposed independence for the Baltic states. In all three republics, such groups fought against the popular fronts and sought restoration of Soviet hegemony (see **Baltic States, Introduction**). Organized by Moscow loyalists, often members of Polish or Russian minorities, they served as a device to allow the Soviet Union to claim that it was acting in response to local constituents. In early 1991, Soviet officials precipitated an artificial crisis by encouraging protests by these local groups against price rises in an attempt to foment violence. The interfronts established National Salvation Committees and denounced the nationalists as "counter-revolutionaries."

In Estonia, Latvia, and Lithuania, unpopular price hikes were announced after the Christmas 1990 holiday season. When the Lithuanian government raised food prices by 320 percent on January 7, 1991, citing inflation, the interfronts and Unity claimed that the republics had slipped into chaos. The next day, Unity members and the communist party assembled a protest rally at the Lithuanian Supreme Council. The price hikes were revoked, and Prime Minister Kazimira Prunskienė, Lithuania's first premier subsequent to the republic's March 11, 1990, declaration of independence, and her cabinet resigned, but not before paratroopers were ordered into the capital of Vilnius, ostensibly to ensure compliance by young males with Soviet conscription orders. Balts, however, regarded the use of paratroopers as a provocation and pretext whose actual purpose appeared to be to supplement members of the "black berets" in taking control of key locations and instituting repression.

The National Salvation Committee claimed it was taking "responsibility for the fate of the republic." With this alleged call for help as a pretext, on January 10 Gorbachev threatened imposition of direct presidential control and demanded that the Lithuanian Supreme Council take action. In response, the council coolly requested negotiations while exhorting the population not to participate in any referendums or political rallies held by occupying authorities in the event of military occupation. Gorbachev called the Lithuanian independence declaration illegal and tried to force the country's new president, Vytautas Landsbergis, into rescinding it. Landsbergis refused. Gorbachev tightened the economic embargo, economic sanctions, and oil blockade imposed in April 1990 (see "Latvia Lawmakers Move to Dissolve Links to Moscow").

When such measures failed to crush Lithuanian determination, Gorbachev launched a coup d'état of sorts. Soviet troops invaded the Lithuanian Department of National Defense in Vilnius and two other cities at midnight on January 11. Soviet KGB troops and paratroopers used live ammunition on unarmed, peaceful Lithuanian citizens in Vilnius, as the soldiers occupied the press house, radio and television building, and television transmission tower, surrounding them with armored vehicles and tanks. Yet they may not have accomplished their intended goals or instructions.

In one of the most dramatic moments of the democratic transitions of the former Soviet states, unarmed Lithuanian citizens sought to halt the Soviet tanks and end the coup. The populace had been preparing to act in accord with civilian defense guidelines that had been circulating since 1990 (see **Baltic States, Introduction**). On January 9, President Landsbergis had addressed Lithuanian citizens on national radio, imploring them, "Come and help your own government, otherwise a foreign one will overcome us." Richard Attenborough's film "Gandhi" was broadcast nationally.

According to Gražina Miniotaitė (2004), a Lithuanian political scientist and former Sąjūdis member, between 7,000 and 9,000 unarmed Lithuanians surrounded the parliament building and the main television broadcasting tower. Singing national folk songs and playing music, they formed a human barrier around the tower and, without weaponry, attempted to defend it and the parliament building from Soviet soldiers. A priest conferred absolution.

Miniotaitė emphasizes (2004) that "numerous resolutions" of the Lithuanian Supreme Council and Sąjūdis had "stressed nonviolent discipline in the pursuit of independence" (on Sąjūdis, see "Lithuanians Move to Limit Moscow Ties"). (Landsbergis later wrote that Lithuanian border guards loyal to the Sąjūdis government were trained that their weaponry should not be used in self-defense against attack because their return fire could be used as a pretext for the dispatch of Soviet troops.) Miniotaitė witnessed large numbers of Lithuanians who had traveled to Vilnius to respond to Landsbergis's call acting "in an orderly manner." Sąjūdis instituted a permanent watch of the buildings involved in communications. "The unarmed policemen and undergraduates of the Academy of the Police joined the watch," Miniotaitė writes, "with the task of preventing armed confrontations" (p. 231). The police remained loyal to the republic. To Miniotaitė, the government of Lithuania "viewed civilian defense as a matter of calculated organization, not merely [a] spontaneous outburst of people power" (ibid.). According to her, if the citizenry could not immobilize the Soviet troops, they were at least able to thwart their ambitions:

> Although the Press Centre, Radio and Television building, [and] Television Transmission Tower were brutally occupied, the goal that [had] been written down in Gorbachev's telegram to [the] Lithuanian [Supreme Council], "immediately and completely re-establish the validity of the constitutions of the USSR and the Lithuanian SSR, and revoke the anti-constitutional acts which have been adopted," was not achieved. On the night of January 13, 1991, the unarmed people stopped the tanks and rendered an abortive coup (Miniotaitė 2004, 230).

According to a subsequent official record published in 1992, on January 13 during what became known as Bloody Sunday, fourteen civilians and a KGB officer were killed, and 702 wounded (*Lithuania 1991.01.13*, p. 36). Some of the casualties had resulted from being crushed by tanks as KGB elite Alfa units stormed the broadcasting tower. The troops stopped short of attacking the parliament and removing Landsbergis from leadership. Yet Bloody Sunday ultimately precipitated a chain of events that by December 1991 would lead to the end of the Soviet Union (see "Gorbachev Says Coup Will Hasten Reform").

The journalist-historian Anatol Lieven (1993), of Latvian descent, notes, "The solidarity and the courage of the peaceful, unarmed crowds outside the parliaments at Riga and Vilnius, convinced that they were about to be attacked, but standing their ground, is indeed one of the most moving political images of modern times, not only for Balts but for Europe" (p. 254).

While the Soviet troops held the television tower and radio stations, improvised transmissions continued from the city of Kaunas. The Supreme Council eventually returned to the air, beaming appeals to Soviet units: "Do not shoot at peaceful people!" At an emergency session, the council passed a resolution authorizing formation of a provisional authority, in case the council became unable to make decisions freely.

Soviet interior minister Boris K. Pugo defended the military action and, as reported by *The New York Times* correspondent Bill Keller on January 14, 1991, blamed the Lithuanians for the violence. Pugo claimed that the National Salvation Committee—correctly identified by Keller as "a front for the communist party"—had appealed to the military to intervene, because the elected Lithuanian parliament had "lost control" in the Baltic republic. To Keller, Pugo's "statement eerily echoed the Soviet pretext for suppressing democratic movements in Hungary in 1956 and Czechoslovakia in 1968" (see **Hungary, Introduction; Czechoslovakia, Introduction**). Keller notes Gorbachev's support of the military's actions.

The Lithuanian Supreme Council would not surrender, Keller observes, and remained working in its barricaded building, expecting to become the Soviets' next target. As parliamentarians labored, ambulances loaded with the dead and wounded rushed across Vilnius. The encircled Lithuanian government led by Landsbergis had, according to Keller, strong moral support from crowds outside the parliament—as many as 20,000—irrespective of Landsbergis's requests that they now go home to safety. Gorbachev ended the operation after the first bloodshed and proceeded to deny responsibility for the carnage. The Moscow government found itself beset with repercussions from throughout the Soviet Union. These negative judgments would be critical to the events leading to the final collapse of the Soviet Union.

JANUARY 14, 1991
SOVIET LOYALISTS IN CHARGE AFTER ATTACK IN LITHUANIA; 13 DEAD; CURFEW IS IMPOSED
2 Sides Open Talks
Crowds, in a Deal With Military, Agree to End a Day of Protests
By BILL KELLER
Special to The New York Times

Vilnius, Lithuania, Jan.13 – The National Salvation Committee, a faceless group of Communist Party loyalists, imposed a series of repressive measures on Lithuania today after the Soviet Army, with tanks and machine guns, had seized power for the committee overnight.

The committee ruled today in force but not in spirit, after a night of violence that left 13 people dead and more than 100 wounded by bullets or tank treads, according to official reports.

The Salvation Committee announced on the radio at 8 A.M. that a major general of the Soviet Army had been named commandant of Vilnius, the Lithuanian capital.

Curfew Declared

Using the Lithuanian state broadcast studios and transmitter captured early this morning, the committee installed by Moscow declared a curfew, banned public gatherings, outlawed the possession of television cameras or tape recorders and imposed a "social regime" of personal searches and random document checks.

The events here, in addition to repressing the nationalist movement that intensified when Lithuania declared its independence in March, also menace the many other Soviet republics—including the largest, Russia—that have, to one degree or another, flouted the authority of President Mikhail S. Gorbachev.

In Red Square today, thousands of people marched in a protest rally and shook fists at the walls of the Kremlin. Speakers denounced the use of military force and accused Mr. Gorbachev of making a mockery of his 1990 Nobel Peace Prize.

Tension Eases Some

Late tonight, there was some easing of the tense situation. The military commandant of the city met with a Lithuanian delegation led by Vice President Kazimieras Motieka and arranged an agreement that a huge crowd of civilians standing vigil outside the Parliament would finally leave. In return, the army was to return to its base and not attempt to attack the Parliament.

In talks that were brokered by a four-man delegation dispatched by President Gorbachev from Moscow, they also agreed to continue negotiations on Monday aimed at the withdrawal of Soviet Army troops who have occupied the city's broadcasting and publishing facilities.

The Gorbachev delegation assured the Lithuanians that it recognizes the legal authority of the Lithuanian government.

President Gorbachev's Interior Minister, Boris K. Pugo, tonight defended the military's behavior, saying in a national television interview that the violence was started by the Lithuanians.

Mr. Pugo asserted that the National Salvation Committee, by all indications a front for the Communist Party, had appealed to the military to intervene after the elected Lithuanian Parliament "lost control" of the situation in the republic. His statement eerily echoed the Soviet pretext for suppressing democratic movements in Hungary in 1956 and Czechoslovakia in 1968.

"The step taken was not the best step, but that's the way it is," Mr. Pugo said. "The situation is controllable."

Parliament Refuses to Quit

The earlier violent action and the ensuing takeover appeared to have the full support of President Gorbachev, who had warned of reprisals if Lithuania failed to back down from its independence claims and who has not commented publicly on the army's attack.

The democratically elected Lithuanian Parliament, which dared Moscow's wrath last March by declaring independence, refused to surrender, working in its barricaded building in constant expectation that its members would be the next and final target.

As the Parliament worked, ambulances filled with the dead and wounded raced across the city.

At Hospital No. 1 in the city center, two bodies lay contorted on a floor in a spreading puddle of blood, one of them a boy who appeared to be about 10 years old. An ambulance pulled up with three more corpses, including a woman and an elderly man with a bullet hole above his right eye.

Doctors said that most of the casualties came from bullet wounds, although there were also numerous mangled limbs run over by armored vehicles.

Based on a survey of Vilnius hospitals, the Parliament information office today reported 13 people known dead, including one soldier shot in the head, and 164 wounded.

The besieged government led by President Vytautas Landsbergis drew moral support from a crowd outside the legislature that swelled this morning to more than 20,000 people, in defiance of the new commandant's ban and despite appeals from their leaders to go home to safety.

Throughout the day they burst into musical chants of "Lithuania" "Shame" and especially "Freedom," as thunderous as the tank cannon that had rocked the city during the night.

Many of them professed their willingness to die in the square to prove their devotion to independence.

Call for General Strike

The Parliament was fortified by a cordon of buses and trucks and barriers of iron grillwork. Several hundred pro-independence militia inside prepared to resist and attack with about 100 hunting rifles, firebombs, sticks and fire hoses.

The Sajudis independence movement, where most of those in the Lithuanian government began their political lives, called a general strike to begin on Monday.

The violence inflicted on crowds during the night seemed almost certain to mark the end of President Gorbachev as the hero of Soviet reform. The Soviet leader had publicly acquiesced in the demands of hardliners for a restoration of discipline in the country. Even if it should emerge that the military exceeded whatever license Mr. Gorbachev gave them, he made no apparent move to stop the bloodshed.

The new commandant of Vilnius, Maj. Gen. Vladimir N. [Uskhopchik], had told reporters at a press conference hours before this morning's violence that he derived his authority from Mr. Gorbachev.

Delegation From the Kremlin

A Kremlin delegation including the presidents of Armenia and Byelorussia shuttled between the Parliament and the National Salvation Committee today without disclosing any resolution to the crisis.

"Our first purpose is not to have any more victims in Vilnius," said Boris Oleinik, a Soviet parliamentary leader and a member of the delegation.

After being shown film footage of the tank raid, he said, "It was impossible to imagine something like this. This is an archive of bloody events."

The capture of Lithuania began just hours after Mr. Gorbachev had named the delegation to seek a political settlement to the Kremlin's dispute with the republic and had reportedly pledged not to use additional force against the Lithuanians.

A Reprieve, Perhaps

The diplomatic initiative seemed to promise a reprieve from five days of coordinated tension, including strikes and anti-independence protests sponsored by the Communist party and army raids on a printing plant, a police training center, a railroad dispatch office and other facilities.

Outside Parliament today Lithuanians likened Mr. Gorbachev to the Iraqi President, Saddam Hussein, and the former Romanian dictator, Nicolae Ceausescu.

'Is It True Bush Sold Us?'

They had little good to say about President Bush.

President Landsbergis, spotting an American reporter in a Parliament corridor early this morning, stopped and asked in halting English: "Is it true Bush sold us? We have heard by radio that he said he is ignoring events in Lithuania because he is concerned on gulf."

The military takeover was preceded by five days of protests and strikes involving primarily Russian and Polish workers at Vilnius manufacturing plants, angered by what they consider ethnic discrimination and by the Lithuanian government's move to increase prices on . . . goods.

The Soviet Defense Ministry announced last week that it was sending special paratroop units to the Baltics and four other republics to force compliance with the military draft in areas of dramatically low registration.

Committee Not Identified

None of the members of the National Salvation Committee have been publicly identified, purportedly for fear of reprisals. The spokesman for the group has been Juozas Jarmalavicius, a professor of Marxism-Leninism and ideology secretary for the hard-line Lithuanian Communist party.

At 1:35 this morning, the first percussion of tank artillery crashed through the city. A convoy of T-72 combat tanks and armored personnel carriers roared up a hillside to take over the republic's television and radio transmitter.

The tanks hesitated briefly at a barricade of parked trucks and cars, then growled ahead over the barrier and through a pack of young men who stood in the way.

The 1,100-foot tower was surrounded by hundreds of men, women and teen-agers summoned by the Landsbergis government to defend the facility with their presence.

Much of the gunfire was into the air, but soldiers perched atop their vehicles sometimes fired into the crowd.

Punctuated by the blast of cannon blanks and the rattle of machine gun ammunition, loudspeakers repeated over and over the following message in Lithuanian and Russian, the first and so far only statement of what the new rulers stand for:

"Brother Lithuanians, in the name of the National Salvation Committee, I report to you that all power in the republic has transferred into the hands of our committee. This is the power of simple working people, workers, peasants and servicemen. The power of people like you.

"True, some of you have come under the influence of deceits, lies, demagoguery and intimidation. These are the weapons that official powers have used up to now, playing games in the Parliament and the government of Lithuania. They expressed the interests of rich people, fraudulent people, corrupt elements.

"That is not our course. Our interests are connected with hopes for a better life based on our common labor. Therefore there is no sense in becoming hostile. There is no reason to remain in confrontation. There is no reason to unleash fratricide.

"I ask you not to resist. I ask you to go home, where your parents, your mothers and fathers, are waiting for you, your brothers and sisters, your grandfathers and grandmothers. Go home. Confrontation is senseless. Our ideal is humaneness. A war of brother against brother is inconsistent with this."

Many Lithuanians refused to retreat under the attacks. At the television tower, sporadic gunfire was heard for at least 90 minutes.

Parliament Has Planning Session

Throughout the night Parliament met to demonstrate its legitimate claim to power and to lay the groundwork for what comes next.

The Lithuanian Foreign Minister, Algirdas Saudargas, who was in Warsaw, was authorized to form a government in exile if the Parliament was taken.

Deputies huddled over shortwave radios broadcasting the American Radio Liberty and pirate programs from the . . . Lithuanian city, Kaunas. The army also captured the broadcasting center in that city, but radio staff members continued to broadcast from a clandestine site.

During the night the crowd in front of the Parliament building dwindled to a few thousand who braved the drizzle while sharing tea and sandwiches. They seemed subdued but determined.

At about 3 A.M., a government official called over the public address system for the crowd to leave.

Coup Transforms Gorbachev, Elevates Yeltsin

Soviet violence persisted against the three Baltic republics during spring and summer 1991. The Soviet Interior Ministry had in autumn 1990 introduced to Latvia special forces from the Otryad Militsii Osobovo Naznacheniya (Militia Unit for Special Assignments, OMON, or the "black berets"), which carried out terror operations, attacking civilians and municipal officials. The Latvian Popular Front issued "Appeal for the Hour X," which outlined a program on how to behave in the event of a coup d'état or imposition of presidential rule (see **Baltic States, Introduction**). For months the black berets bombed monuments, communist party headquarters, schools, Riga's KGB building, and residential apartments, in addition to assaults and killings at customs posts and installations newly established by the Baltic governments along their borders. As in Lithuania, a shadowy pro-Moscow National Salvation Committee sought to prevent "bourgeois dictatorship" in Latvia; in tandem, black berets carried out incendiary actions. These assaults were intended to provoke reactions, which would in turn provide pretexts for more countermeasures. *The New York Times* reporter Bill Keller on January 18, 1991, notes the use of this same tactic elsewhere in the Baltics, observing that the "chronology of events and witnesses' accounts point to an orchestrated campaign directed from Moscow to create the impression of civil conflict as a pretext for military intervention so the republic's move to independence could be halted" ("Soviets Insist They Won't Use Force to Unseat Lithuanians").

On February 9, Lithuanians voted 9 to 1 in favor of independence and assumed they were next in line to bear the brunt of Moscow's wrath. On January 13, 500,000 Latvians had converged in Old Riga to protest the killings by Soviet troops on Bloody Sunday in Vilnius and signify their determination to fend off any assault on Riga. They blocked roadways leading to the capital with trucks, tractors, buses, and heavy equipment. The awaited offensive against Latvia never occurred. On February 28, the Lithuanian Supreme Council, or parliament, issued a resolution: "In the event a regime of active occupation is introduced, citizens of the Republic of Lithuania are asked to adhere to principles of disobedience, nonviolent resistance, and political and social noncooperation as the primary means of struggle for independence." A March

3 referendum in Latvia produced a large majority for independence. An Estonian countrywide referendum of the same day produced similarly overwhelming results.

On June 20, as rumors swirled of an imminent coup d'état in Moscow, or further Soviet onslaughts against the Baltic republics, the Latvian Supreme Council announced a Nonviolent Defense Center. Its basic document, "Guard Your State: What Should Latvian Patriots Do in Case of a Coup d'État?" states that all Soviet violence would be met with noncooperation from Latvians, to make it difficult if not impossible for the Soviets to accomplish their goals.

Pledging to advance Russian statehood, Boris N. Yeltsin had been elected president of the large Russian republic by the parliament on May 29, 1990, despite efforts by Soviet leader Mikhail S. Gorbachev to prevent such an outcome. On June 12, 1991, he was elected president of the Russian Soviet Federative Socialist Republic with 57 percent of the vote, becoming the first popularly elected president of the Russian republic. Chairing the Russian Supreme Soviet, in early 1991 Yeltsin had contributed to halting Soviet aggression in the Baltics when he allied himself with the republics in their plans for independence, and joined leaders of Estonia, Latvia, and Lithuania on January 13 in contesting Moscow's employment of violence and incursions there. Locked in a power struggle with Gorbachev over the pace and extent of reform, Yeltsin released an "Appeal to Russian Soldiers," calling upon them to avoid acting "against legally constituted state bodies" in the three Baltic republics. Some Russian officers and soldiers refused to be stationed in the Baltics or said they would not follow future orders to use violence against civilians. In July, Yeltsin entered the Russian republic into a treaty recognizing Lithuanian sovereignty. Meanwhile, twelve Soviet republics in negotiations on a new union treaty reached concurrence on a radical devolution of power from Moscow to the republics.

On August 19, 1991, a day before the new treaty was to be signed, an unsuccessful coup d'état in Moscow altered the landscape. As Latvians learned of the coup under way, the Nonviolent Defense Center in Riga secretly sent 2,000 copies of its booklets on self-defense into Latvian towns and villages. With Riga militarily occupied by the Soviet army, citizens were asked to "make every village, town, and home a center of resistance" (Eglitis 1993, 39). Serious nonviolent civil resistance began, although full implementation of the civilian defense plans would ultimately be unnecessary. The putsch in Moscow was compromised two days after it started.

Leaders of the coup had formed a body called the State Committee for the State of Emergency, seized power, and claimed to be acting to preserve the Soviet Union. Key figures in the communist party, KGB, and military, the hardline coup leaders may have been unaware of public sentiments sweeping the Soviet Union after years of operating in secrecy and isolation. It is unlikely that they recognized the power being generated around them by the idea of reclaiming former national independence, national identities, yearnings for sovereignty, desires for openly elected representation, or even the concept of citizenship. As Philip Taubman notes in *The Times* on October 25, 1988, "the communist party, which prides itself on its skill with the masses, appears unfamiliar with the power of grass-roots public activity" ("How Patient Is Moscow?") Did the coup leaders fail to grasp that at least in the Baltic republics well-organized civic associations had strengthened civil society, that democratically elected governments had taken power as representatives of the populace, that pursuit of independence had been framed as a challenge to the legality of annexation, and that parliamentary procedures had been maintained even while capital cities were being stormed by Soviet troops? Aspects of the attempted overthrow of Gorbachev await clarification by historians, yet it seems indisputable that the breadth and speed of nationalist mobilizations in the Baltics will be revealed as playing a part in the explanation.

Reporting on August 22, 1991, *The Times* correspondent Serge Schmemann notes President Mikhail S. Gorbachev's return from his Crimean summer retreat, where he had been put under house arrest at the beginning of the putsch:

> The coup crumbled . . . as abruptly as it began, without any formal announcement from its leaders, who sent tanks into Moscow . . . and declared themselves in command. It seemed simply to fizzle under the disdain of masses rallying to the summons of Mr. Yeltsin, who rose to condemn the coup almost from the moment it became known, and the irresolution of plotters who failed to garner support or even to maintain the loyalty of their forces. . . . Yeltsin declared that the communist party had been 'the organizing and inspiring force' behind the coup, and the implication was that with its last, desperate rear-guard action the once-formidable force that had controlled the Soviet Union for more than 70 years might finally be exhausted. . . .
>
> Even as Moscow waited for Mr. Gorbachev to reappear, it was evident that the balance of power and the course of the Soviet Union's history had shifted, that the communists who had fought a rearguard action against change had suffered a potentially fatal blow, that Mr. Gorbachev himself was now beholden to the anti-Communist forces that had rescued him, and above all to Mr. Yeltsin. . . . the indisputable man of the hour, and the advocates of economic and political reform were clearly ascendant. . . .
>
> It was Mr. Yeltsin's dramatic condemnation of the coup virtually at the same time as the rebellion first became known . . . that roused resistance across the Soviet Union and made his headquarters on the Moscow River into a rallying point of the opposition. The image of Mr. Yeltsin addressing supporters from atop one of the tanks that had come over to his side became the icon of resistance ("Gorbachev Back as Coup Fails, but Yeltsin Gains New Power").

Collective nonviolent action unfolded on Moscow streets to halt the coup, as Schmemann notes:

> Thousands of Muscovites heeded [Yeltsin's] call and formed a cordon around the . . . [building where Yeltsin was based], sealing approaches with makeshift barricades of buses, trucks and building materials. All across the nation, liberal politicians and supporters of Mr. Yeltsin organized demonstrations and mass meetings. He issued decrees declaring the actions of the junta unconstitutional and assuming temporary control over all government and security forces on Russian territory.
>
> Addressing the Russian parliament . . . , Mr. Yeltsin declared that it was the defection to his side of several military units that had prevented the junta from interning the Russian government. . . .
>
> The awareness that the coup had failed came with the first gray light of dawn, when it became evident that army tanks had not moved against the headquarters of the Russian republic's government in the capital. Relief spread among the thousands of Muscovites who had spent two drizzly nights at makeshift barricades around the building, called the "White House," a wedding-cake-like building on the banks of the

Moscow River, from which Mr. Yeltsin marshaled the anti-coup forces ("Gorbachev Back as Coup Fails, but Yeltsin Gains New Power").

Thus the leaders of the coup proved to be incapable of withstanding nonviolent civil resistance in Moscow itself, as well as in the Baltic states. Estonia and Latvia seized the moment and took advantage of the disorder, as their parliamentary Supreme Councils declared de facto full independence during August 20–21. *The Times* on August 21, 1991, reports that in the Estonian capital of Tallinn, "lawmakers voted unanimously for the declaration." Among the parliamentarians was Heinz Valk, who had coined the phrase "Singing Revolution." He told parliament, "The proclamation of independence is a challenge to the enemies of perestroika and the enemies of world peace and democracy" ("Reports from the Republics Vary From Relative Calm to Threats of Military Action"). The Estonian parliament called for parliamentary elections to be held the following year in accord with a new constitution.

Lithuania reinforced its earlier declaration of March 11, 1990 (see "Parliament in Lithuania, 124–0, Declares Nation Independent"). Almost immediately, the international community acknowledged Lithuanian independence. Approximately 100 Soviet tanks that had in the previous two days moved into Vilnius began to withdraw, according to the *Times* on August 22, 1991 ("Lithuanians Clash with Soviet Force"). A parliamentary spokesperson said Soviet soldiers had departed the Lithuanian television center occupied by them since January 13, and telephone links had been restored (see "Soviet Loyalists in Charge after Attack in Lithuania").

The Times reports reveal internal upheaval in the Soviet machinery. Even before the coup had collapsed in Moscow, Soviet troops were seizing television stations and transmitters in the Baltics as assets in the propaganda war seeking to deny their secession from the Soviet Union. As late as August 22, Soviet troops had taken Estonia's television station and primary transmitting antenna. Broadcasts from Tallinn stopped. In what *The Times* on February 9, 1991, calls "intensifying propaganda barrages over state television," Moscow had portrayed the bloody confrontation in Lithuania as pitting "nationalist totalitarianism" against ethnic minorities ("Shadow of Moscow Darkens Lithuania Independence Vote"). Media broadcasts had another effect: Political scientist Mark R. Beissinger quotes Soviet general Yevgenii Shaposhnikov, an actor in foiling the coup to overthrow Gorbachev, as later recalling, "After Vilnius and the television scenes that I saw of our soldiers beating civilians with the butts of their automatic rifles, I understood that a decisive and final end had to be put to this" (Beissinger 2009, 237). In following weeks, the OMON black berets were withdrawn from the Baltics (see "Latvia Lawmakers Move to Dissolve Links to Moscow"). Across the Baltics, statues of Lenin were dragged down and destroyed.

The Nordic countries became first to recognize the Baltic republics' independence. Argentina, Iceland, Japan, Germany, and the United States followed. *The Times* reports on August 26, "The flurry of diplomatic welcomes followed by a day the issuance of two decrees by Boris N. Yeltsin, declaring that his Russian federated republic recognized the independence of Estonia and Latvia. Russia had earlier endorsed Lithuania's claim. . . . Although most Western nations, including the United States, never extended recognition to the Soviet [1940] annexation, their reluctance until now to do more than give verbal and moral support have disappointed Estonians, Lithuanians and Latvians" ("Soviets' Rush toward Disunion Spreads").

In the final act, the Soviet State Council and Gorbachev, who had been restored temporarily to lessened power in Moscow, recognized the Baltic states' independence. By December 25, the Soviet Union had been dissolved. As the three Baltic states embarked on their long-anticipated journey to independence and statehood, they were admitted to the United Nations on September 17, 1991, and subsequently welcomed to the Conference on Security and Cooperation in Europe, which had grown out of the Helsinki Accords.

AUGUST 23, 1991
GORBACHEV SAYS COUP WILL HASTEN REFORM; YELTSIN LEADS THE CELEBRATION IN MOSCOW

Party Purge Seen

Soviet Leader Says That Ousting Reactionaries Will Lead to Unity

By BILL KELLER

Special to The New York Times

Moscow, Aug. 22 – President Mikhail S. Gorbachev, chastened and isolated by his betrayal at the hands of men he trusted, said today that his rescue from the failed coup had taught him that he must join more closely with "democratic forces" and speed the pace of reform.

While elated Muscovites streamed through the streets in celebration of their triumph over the conspiracy, one of the putsch leaders, Interior Minister Boris K. Pugo, killed himself. And the circle of high-level Gorbachev confidants implicated in the plot widened to include the leader of the Soviet Parliament, Anatoly I. Lukyanov, who was accused by a high Soviet official of being the coup's mastermind.

But at a news conference tonight, the weary but steely Soviet President refused to join President Boris N. Yeltsin of the Russian federated republic and hold the Communist Party responsible for the rebellion. He reasserted his determination to remain as party leader, declaring that the party could still be purged of "reactionary forces" and made into a vehicle of national unity and reform.

Anti-Communists Bolstered

Mr. Gorbachev left little doubt, however, that his 72-hour ordeal had transformed the chemistry of Soviet politics, establishing the anti-Communists who rallied against the coup as the predominant engine of political and economic change.

The Soviet leader spoke with emotion of his strengthened partnership with Mr. Yeltsin, who by galvanizing the resistance to the conspiracy carried out by Communist hard-liners became the ascendant power in the new Soviet politics.

Mr. Gorbachev credited Mr. Yeltsin with the leading role in rebuffing the coup, saying the conspirators finally panicked because of the "implacable position" of the Russian leaders and their followers, including defections in the army.

Mopping Up by Russians

Today Mr. Yeltsin led the capital in a day of explicitly anti-Communist rejoicing, and mapped a mopping up campaign against the vestiges of Communist power in his own republic.

Mr. Yeltsin, who had been Mr. Gorbachev's bitter rival since the Soviet leader threw him out of the Communist Party Politburo four years ago, has by standing up to the conspirators made himself the most indispensable ally in the Soviet leader's campaign to remake the country.

"So many lies are being told about these two individuals, that it's probably difficult to understand, but we have been bound together by the situation," Mr. Gorbachev said. "We know what the situation is. We know who is who."

He Suddenly Seems Isolated

One of the most striking impressions during the Soviet leader's 90-minute news conference was a sense of his sudden isolation.

While many of Mr. Gorbachev's original collaborators in reform have quit the Communist Party and remain estranged by his devotion to it, the hard-liners upon whom he relied to run his government, military and police agencies have proven treacherous.

Today the Premier of the Russian Republic, Ivan Silayev, charged that Mr. Lukyanov, Mr. Gorbachev's friend since they attended law school together in the 1950's and one of his most trusted aides, was "the chief ideologist of this junta."

Mr. Lukyanov was suspended today as Chairman of the Soviet Parliament pending an investigation.

Mr. Gorbachev said he had met with Mr. Lukyanov, who insisted he had done his best to negotiate an end to the coup, but the Soviet leader sounded as though he needed to be convinced.

Parliament to Meet Monday

The governing presidium of the Soviet Parliament announced that Mr. Lukyanov would not preside over an emergency session of the legislature on Monday, which is to include an assessment of his role in the crisis.

Mr. Pugo, named Interior Minister by Mr. Gorbachev last year, fired two bullets into his wife and then shot himself in the head while the authorities were en route to arrest him, the Russian television news program "Vesti" reported.

The Interior Minister, one of eight members of the State Committee for the State of Emergency that ousted Mr. Gorbachev on Sunday, died in a hospital. His wife survived but was in grave condition.

All but one of the remaining committee leaders, including Mr. Gorbachev's Prime Minister, Defense Minister and K.G.B. chief, were reported under arrest tonight. Among the other prominent figures arrested for complicity were Gen. Valentin I. Varennikov, the Deputy Defense Minister and commander of Soviet ground forces, and Valery Boldin, the chief of Mr. Gorbachev's administrative apparatus at the Communist Party.

'I Believed in Them'

Mr. Gorbachev admitted that he had badly misjudged some of the men he appointed, especially Defense Minister Dmitri T. Yazov and the K.G.B. chief, Vladimir A. Kryuchkov, whom the Soviet leader said had held his special trust.

"I see now that it was a mistake, and I'll tell you perfectly straightforwardly because I do not have any problem with speaking the truth, I believed particularly Yazov and Kryuchkov," he said. "I believed in them."

The aftermath of the coup leaves Mr. Gorbachev with a formidable task in organizing a new government that commands public trust.

One day after he named Gen. Mikhail A. Moiseyev to take over as acting Defense Minister, the newspaper Izvestia published evidence that the general, the armed forces Chief of Staff, had at least acquiesced in the takeover. The Chief of Staff of the Moscow military district, Lieut. Gen. Leonid Zolotov, told Izvestia that General Moiseyev had issued written orders for the deployment of troops securing parts of the city for the Emergency Committee.

"We must not organize a witch hunt," Mr. Gorbachev warned tonight. "After defeating reaction, we must not follow the same road."

The Soviet leader said he believed that the coup had been timed to prevent the signing of a new union treaty, which would surrender vast authority to the republics.

"There are just a few months to go and we will have a totally new way of life here," he said, indicating that he remained committed to the treaty. "So that is why everybody was in such a hurry—both those for and those against."

In a televised address to the public tonight, Mr. Gorbachev said the takeover failed because the conspirators "underestimated the main thing—that the people, in these very difficult years, have been transformed."

"They have breathed the air of freedom, and nobody can any longer take that away from them," he said.

'An Enormous Opportunity'

"We should not only see the disaster which occurred, but also we have to see this as an enormous opportunity, namely, an opportunity in the sense that our people's true position has been made clear."

Although the Soviet leader spoke with calm resolve of the steps he is taking to set his reform program back in motion, he paused at times to compose himself as he recounted details of his 72-hour ordeal under house arrest at his vacation home in the Crimea.

He said his wife, Raisa, had been badly shaken by the experience.

"She is not feeling well at all, but we think this will pass," he said. "Yesterday we thought, well—anyway, it was hard, and you can understand why."

Told Aide: 'To Hell With You'

Mr. Gorbachev said that when his longtime aide, Mr. Boldin, arrived as the emissary from the conspirators with a demand to turn over power voluntarily, he said "to hell with you" and told him that the plot was doomed.

In an earlier interview, upon his arrival back in Moscow early this morning, the Soviet leader said he would have killed himself rather than go along.

While Mr. Gorbachev fielded calls from world leaders and began replacing the arrested members of his Government, Mr. Yeltsin basked in the cheers of a roaring throng outside his government building, then sent them on a triumphal march through the city to Red Square.

Tonight thousands gathered outside the K.G.B. headquarters and chanted anti-Communist slogans as a crane sent by Moscow's liberal Mayor, Gavriil K. Popov, toppled the statue of the founder of the secret police, Feliks Dzerzhinsky.

The Russian Parliament voted today to abandon the flag of Soviet Russia, with its Communist hammer and sickle, and restore the white, blue and red tricolor of pre-revolutionary Russia.

Mr. Yeltsin also announced that he had used special powers granted by his Parliament to dismiss the leaders of four Russian provinces who had professed allegiance to the Emergency Committee. All four are hard-line Communists who had battled Mr. Yeltsin's efforts to loosen the party's grip.

The response to the coup has become an instant litmus test for politicians, with the main loser being the Communist Party. The conspirators were all members of the party's governing Central Committee, whose leaders remained mute throughout.

"All the anti-constitutional actions by the State of Emergency Committee were tacitly authorized by the neo-Stalinist leadership of the Soviet Communist Party," Mr. Yeltsin charged.

Yeltsin Moves Against Party

Mr. Yeltsin's allies said measures were in the works to nationalize the party's Moscow headquarters and party papers, including the Communist flagship Pravda, that served as mouthpieces for the Emergency Committee.

Mr. Gorbachev, however, said many party leaders, including his second-in-command, Vladimir Ivashko, had pressed the conspirators for access to Mr. Gorbachev.

During the coup, the Russian President extended his republic's claim of sovereignty by asserting jurisdiction over all industrial enterprises and other property on Russian territory and creating a new Russian national guard.

Asked about these measures, Mr. Gorbachev, who in the past has challenged Mr. Yeltsin in a war of conflicting decrees, said they were justified, but left the impression that he considered them temporary.

"I think that in the situation, the Russians have acted in the best interests of us all," he said. "And what they have adopted was dictated by the situation."

Advance for Baltics

The failure of the coup also appeared to advance the cause of independence for the three Baltic republics, after months of sporadic violence against secessionist leaders by the Soviet military, K.G.B., and Interior Ministry troops. The army today withdrew from places it had occupied, including the Lithuanian broadcasting center seized in a bloody assault in January.

Latvia and Estonia declared their full independence from the Soviet Union after the takeover was announced, joining Lithuania, which proclaimed its freedom last year. Mr. Gorbachev has repeatedly declared Lithuania's independence claim illegal, while Mr. Yeltsin has endorsed full freedom for the Baltics.

The collapse of the coup left many organizations scrambling to dissociate themselves from charges of complicity.

The K.G.B. today issued a statement insisting that its agents "have nothing in common with the illegal actions by the group of adventurists" and were embarrassed that the agency's head was among the conspirators. The Communist Party's Secretariat announced plans to "discuss the responsibility" of party members who took part.

The official Tass news agency denied reports by independent Soviet journalists that the state news service had advance knowledge of the coup. Tass described as "a lie from beginning to end" the charge published in the non-government newspaper Nezavisimaya Gazeta, which said the news agency had received texts of the coup leaders' statements 24 hours in advance.

Secret Pact Challenges Soviet Legitimacy

The Soviet and Nazi governments ended Estonia, Latvia, and Lithuania's brief two-decade period of independent statehood when they authorized the signing of the Molotov–Ribbentrop Pact of nonaggression and friendship on August 23 and September 28, 1939. Ulrich Friedrich Wilhelm Joachim Von Ribbentrop, Germany's foreign minister (later hanged for war crimes after the Nuremberg trials), signed for the German Reich, and Vyacheslav Mikhailovich Molotov, foreign affairs commissar of the Soviet Union, signed "with full power of the government of the U.S.S.R." Although the treaty is referred to as the Molotov-Ribbentrop Pact, Molotov and Ribbentrop acted on behalf of their bosses, Soviet leader Josef Stalin and German führer Adolf Hitler. Most significant in the August 23 agreement was the secret protocol that provided for the partition of Poland, Finland, and the Baltic states between their two countries. After the signing of the protocol, Germany attacked Poland on September 1 and launched World War II.

Under the Soviet-German pact signed in September, Lithuania was transferred from the German sphere to the Soviet realm (after Germany had wrapped up its operation against Poland and Soviet forces had maneuvered to occupy eastern portions of Poland on September 17). On September 28, 1939—the day of the signing of the second Soviet-German agreement—the Soviets compelled the Baltic republics, under threat of military incursion, to agree to confidential defense and mutual assistance protocols between Moscow and themselves. The Soviets obtained rights to establish bases, naval facilities, and airfields in the Baltics and to station troops there. Estonia signed the mutual assistance pact on September 28, and Latvia and Lithuania followed suit on October 5 and October 10, respectively. Stalin was granted free rein in dealing with the three Baltic States. A *New York Times* editorial on August 23, 1991, recalls that "the United States has never recognized the forcible annexation of the Baltic States by Stalin, the dirty booty in a secret protocol of the 1939" ("Baltic Freedom in a New Light").

On June 16, 1940, the Soviet Union accused the Baltic states of violating the mutual assistance pacts and plotting against the Soviet Union. Moscow demanded unlimited entry of its armed forces and the formation of pro-Soviet governments. Bullying, menacing, and interposing Soviet troops, Stalin forced out the independent Baltic governments. Under Moscow's bidding, communists and fellow-travelers rigged parliamentary balloting, as Fein describes for *The Times* on March 16, 1990: "Puppet parliaments dubiously elected under the pressure of the Soviet Army later requested that the three republics be admitted to the Soviet Union" ("Soviet Congress Rejects Lithuanian Secession Move"). Not surprisingly, the Baltic applications to join the Soviet Union were approved; admission was granted during August 3–6, 1940. New governments were installed, and the former presidents of Estonia and Latvia were detained and then sent to Russia, where they died. The president of Lithuania, Antanas Smetona, escaped to Germany on June 15, 1940, and died in the United States in 1944.

The Baltic states forcibly remained part of the Soviet Union for half a century. Under Stalinism, they experienced not only military occupation, but severe repression, massive deportations, economic exploitation, and environmental ruination (see **Baltic States, Introduction**). On August 24, 1989, *The Times* published the secret Soviet-German protocols, fifty years after their signing, based on texts translated by the U.S. government from microfilm copies of the original German Foreign Ministry documents obtained by the Allies at the end of World War II. One phrase stands out: "This protocol will be treated by both parties as strictly secret." For five decades Soviet leaders, including Mikhail S. Gorbachev, refused to acknowledge that the agreements existed (see "Baltic Independence Fronts Plead to U.N.").

At the close of 1989, a twenty-six-person commission set up in Moscow by the Congress of People's Deputies presented its findings about the protocols. Headed by Aleksandr N. Yakovlev, a U.S.-educated Politburo member and collaborator with Gorbachev, the investigation had been the result of demands by Baltic popular fronts aided by the new Soviet policy of *glasnost* (openness). Despite ongoing Soviet denials, by August 1989 the German Bundesarchiv had produced facsimiles of the secret agreements, which had been published in Soviet news media. Yakovlev told the congress on December 24 that the historian Lev Besymenskii had found a copy of the secret protocols among Molotov's papers, erroneously filed under 1946, which precisely corresponded with the Bonn facsimiles. The congress conceded the existence of the secret protocols and condemned the pact as illegal and invalid, by a vote of 1,432 supporting the resolution, and 252 opposing. When Soviet authorities were unable to dodge the issue any longer, the legal path was cleared for the Baltic republics' "renewal" of their independence.

AUGUST 24, 1989
TEXT OF SECRET PROTOCOLS TO 1939 HITLER-STALIN PACT
Special to The New York Times

Washington, Aug. 23 – The secret protocols to the August 1939 nonaggression treaty between the Soviet Union and Germany are cited by residents of the Soviet Union's Baltic republics in support of their argument that the Soviet annexation of the area was illegal. Here are the texts of the protocols, as translated by the United States Government from microfilm copies of the original German Foreign Ministry documents, which were turned over to the Allies at the end of World War II.

Secret Additional Protocol

On the occasion of the signature of the nonaggression treaty between the German Reich and the Union of Soviet Socialist Republics, the undersigned plenipotentiaries of the two parties discussed in strictly confidential conversations the question of the delimitation of their respective spheres of interest in Eastern Europe. These conversations led to the following result:

1. In the event of a territorial and political transformation in the territories belonging to the Baltic States (Finland, Estonia, Latvia, Lithuania), the northern frontier of Lithuania shall represent the frontier of the spheres of interest both of Germany and the U.S.S.R. In this connection the interest of Lithuania in the Vilna territory is recognized by both parties.

2. In the event of a territorial and political transformation of the territories belonging to the Polish state, the spheres of interest of both Germany and the U.S.S.R. shall be bounded approximately by the line of the rivers Narev, Vistula and San.

The question whether the interests of both parties make the maintenance of an independent Polish state appear desirable and how the frontiers of this state should be drawn can be definitely determined only in the course of further political developments.

In any case both governments will resolve this question by means of a friendly understanding.

3. With regard to southeastern Europe, the Soviet side emphasizes its interest in Bessarabia. The German side declares complete political disinterest in these territories.

4. This protocol will be treated by both parties as strictly secret.

Moscow, Aug. 23, 1939.

FOR THE GOVERNMENT OF THE GERMAN REICH:

VON RIBBENTROP

WITH FULL POWER OF THE GOVERNMENT OF THE U.S.S.R.:

V. MOLOTOV

Secret Supplementary Protocol

The undersigned delegates establish agreement between the Government of the German Reich and the Government of the U.S.S.R. concerning the following matters:

The secret supplementary protocol signed on Aug. 23, 1939 is amended at No. 1 in that the territory of Lithuania comes under the U.S.S.R. sphere of interest, because on the other side the administrative district "Woywodschaft" of Lubin and parts of the administrative district of Warsaw come under the German sphere of influence (map accompanying the boundary and friendship treaties ratified today). As soon as the Government of the U.S.S.R. takes special measures to safeguard its interests on Lithuanian territory, the present Germany-Lithuanian border will be rectified in the interests of simple and natural delimitation, so that the territory of Lithuania lying southwest of the line drawn on the accompanying map will fall to Germany.

It is further established that the economic arrangements in force at the present time between Germany and Lithuania will be in no way damaged by the aforementioned measures being taken by the Soviet Union.

Moscow, Sept. 28, 1939.

VON RIBBENTROP

FOR THE GOVERNMENT OF THE GERMAN REICH.

V. MOLOTOV

ON THE AUTHORITY OF THE GOVERNMENT OF THE U.S.S.R.

Secret Protocol

Graf von Schulenburg, the German Ambassador, acting for the Government of the German Reich, and the Chairman of the Council of People's Commissars of the U.S.S.R., V. M. Molotov, acting for the Government of the U.S.S.R., have agreed upon the following points:

1. The Government of the German Reich renounces its claims to the portion of the territory of Lithuania mentioned in the Sept. 28, 1939 Secret Protocol and shown on the included map.

2. The Government of the Union of Soviet Socialist Republics is prepared to compensate the Government of the German Reich for the territory mentioned in Point 1 of this protocol by payment of the sum of 7,500,000 gold dollars, or 31,500,000 reichsmarks to Germany.

Payment of the sum of 31.5 million reichsmarks will be accomplished by the U.S.S.R. in the following way: one-eighth, i.e., 3,937,500 reichsmarks, in shipments of nonferrous metal within three months of ratification of this treaty, and the remaining seven-eighths, 27,562,500 reichsmarks, in gold by a deduction from the German payments in gold which the German side was to bring up by Feb. 11, 1941. On the basis of the correspondence concerning the Feb. 11, 1940 economic agreement between the German Reich and the Union of Soviet Socialist Republics in the second section of the agreement between the chairman of the German economic delegation, Herr Schnurre and the people's commissar for U.S.S.R. foreign trade, Herr A. I. Mikoyan.

3. This protocol has been prepared in both German and Russian (two originals) and goes into effect upon being ratified.

Moscow, Jan. 10, 1941.

(Illegible [signature], presumably von Schulenburg)

FOR THE GOVERNMENT OF THE GERMAN REICH

V. MOLOTOV

ACTING FOR THE GOVERNMENT OF THE U.S.S.R.

Bibliography

Beissinger, Mark R. 2009. "The Intersection of Ethnic Nationalism and People Power Tactics in the Baltic States, 1987–91." In *Civil Resistance and Power Politics: The Experience of Non-Violent Action from Gandhi to the Present*, ed. Adam Roberts and Timothy Garton Ash, 231–246. Oxford: Oxford University Press.

Bleiere, Daina, et al. 2006. *History of Latvia in the 20th Century*. Riga: Jumava.

Dembkowski, Harry E. 1982. *The Union of Lublin Polish Federalism in the Golden Age*. New York and Boulder: Eastern European Monographs; Distributed by Columbia University Press.

Duik, Nadia, and Adrian Karatnycky. 1993. *New Nations Rising: The Fall of the Soviets and the Challenge of Independence*. New York: John Wiley.

Eglitis, Olgerts. 1993. *Nonviolent Action in the Liberation of Latvia*, Monograph Series no. 5. Cambridge, Mass.: Albert Einstein Institution.

Gerner, Kristian, and Stefan Hedlund. 1993. *The Baltic States and the End of the Soviet Empire*. London and New York: Routledge.

Hiden, John, and Patrick Salmon. 1994. *The Baltic Nations and Europe: Estonia, Latvia and Lithuania in the Twentieth Century*, 147–194. London and New York: Longman.

Kramer, Mark. 2009. "The Dialectics of Empire: Soviet Leaders and the Challenge of Civil Resistance in East-Central Europe, 1968–91." In *Civil Resistance and Power Politics: The Experience of Non-Violent Action from Gandhi to the Present*, ed. Adam Roberts and Timothy Garton Ash, 91–109. Oxford: Oxford University Press.

Landsbergis, Vytautas. 2000. *Lithuania: Independent Again*. Seattle: University of Washington Press.

Lieven, Anatol. 1993. *The Baltic Revolution: Estonia, Latvia, and Lithuania and the Path to Independence*. 2d ed. New Haven: Yale University Press.

Lithuania 1991.01.13: Documents, Testimonies, Comments. 1992. Vilnius: State Publishing Center.

Miniotaitė, Gražina. 2004. "Civilian Resistance in the Security and Defence System of Lithuania: History and Prospects." In *Lithuanian Annual Strategic Review 2003*. Vilnius: General Jonas Zemaitis Lithuanian Military Academy, 223–38. www.lka.lt/EasyAdmin/sys/files/strategic_review2003.pdf.

———. 2002. *Nonviolent Resistance in Lithuania: A Story of Peaceful Liberation*, Monograph Series no. 8. Cambridge, Mass.: Albert Einstein Institution.

Plakans, Andrejs. 1995. *The Latvians: A Short History*. Stanford, Calif.: Hoover Institution Press.

Pontin, Jolyon, Kristian Gerner, and Stefan Hedlund. 1993. *The Baltic States and the End of the Soviet Empire*. London: Routledge.

Roberts, Adam. 1999. *Civil Resistance in the East European and Soviet Revolutions*, Monograph Series no. 4. Cambridge, Mass.: Albert Einstein Institute.

Semjonov, Aleksei. 2002. "Estonia: Nation-Building and Integration: Political and Legal Aspects." In *National Integration and Violent Conflict in Post-Soviet Societies: The Cases of Estonia and Moldova*, ed. Pål Kolstø, 105–157. Lanham, Md.: Rowman and Littlefield.

Senn, Alfred Erich. 1995. *Gorbachev's Failure in Lithuania*. New York: St. Martin's Press.

———. 1990. *Lithuania Awakening*. Berkeley: University of California Press.

Sharp, Gene, assisted by Bruce Jenkins. 1990. *Civilian-Based Defense: A Post-Military Weapons System*. Princeton: Princeton University Press.

Thomson, Clare. 1992. *The Singing Revolution: A Political Journey through the Baltic States*. London: Michael Joseph.

Tusty, Maureen, and James Tusty. 2007. "The Singing Revolution." Film by Mountain View Productions, www.singingrevolution.com/cgi-local/content.cgi.

From *The New York Times*

Bohlen, Celestine. 1990. "Gorbachev Bars Independence Bids of 2 Baltic Lands." May 15.

Clines, Francis X. 1991. "Latvia to Create Self-Defense Unit." January 22.

Fein, Esther B. 1990. "Soviet Congress Rejects Lithuanian Secession Move." March 16.

———. 1990. "Upheaval in the East; Lithuania Assails Moscow's Tactics as Convoy Arrives." March 23.

———. 1989. "Moscow Condemns Nationalist 'Virus' in 3 Baltic Lands." August 27.

———. 1988. "Latvians Establish a Movement to Seek Sovereignty." October 10.

———. 1988. "Moscow Calls for Talks with Estonians." November 18.

Keller, Bill. 1991. "Soviet Tanks Roll in Lithuania; 11 Dead." January 13.

———. 1991. "Soviets Insist They Won't Use Force to Unseat Lithuanians." January 18.

———. 1991. "Soviets' Rush toward Disunion Spreads; Europe Embracing Baltic Independence; 3 Nordic Lands Act." August 26.

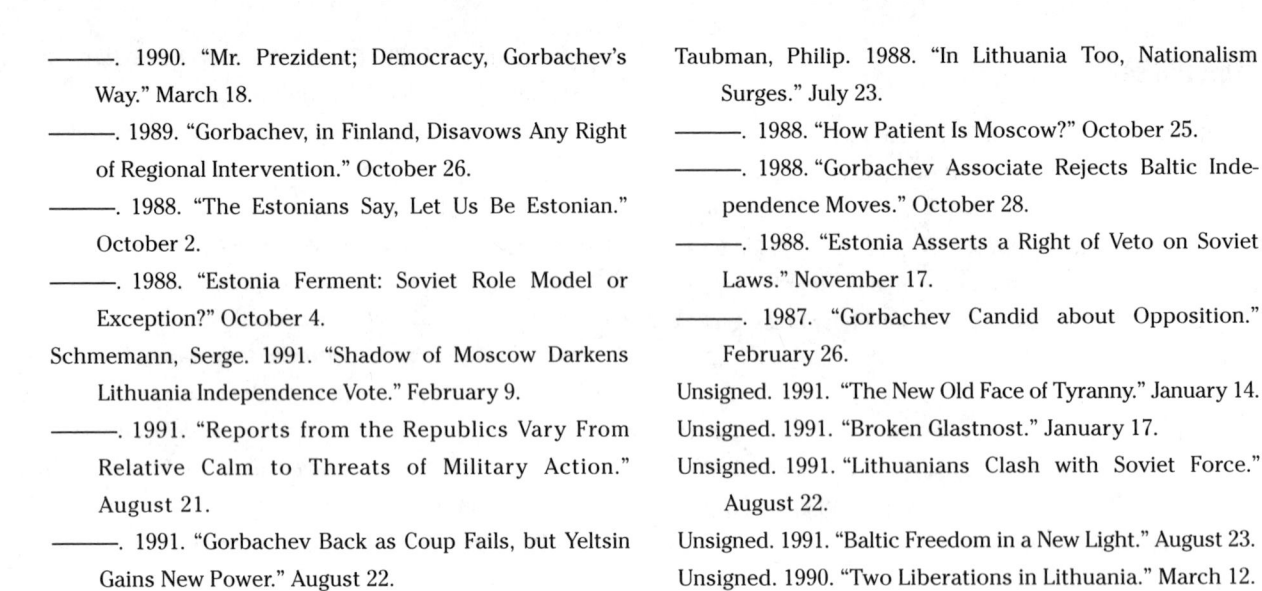

———. 1990. "Mr. Prezident; Democracy, Gorbachev's Way." March 18.

———. 1989. "Gorbachev, in Finland, Disavows Any Right of Regional Intervention." October 26.

———. 1988. "The Estonians Say, Let Us Be Estonian." October 2.

———. 1988. "Estonia Ferment: Soviet Role Model or Exception?" October 4.

Schmemann, Serge. 1991. "Shadow of Moscow Darkens Lithuania Independence Vote." February 9.

———. 1991. "Reports from the Republics Vary From Relative Calm to Threats of Military Action." August 21.

———. 1991. "Gorbachev Back as Coup Fails, but Yeltsin Gains New Power." August 22.

Taubman, Philip. 1988. "In Lithuania Too, Nationalism Surges." July 23.

———. 1988. "How Patient Is Moscow?" October 25.

———. 1988. "Gorbachev Associate Rejects Baltic Independence Moves." October 28.

———. 1988. "Estonia Asserts a Right of Veto on Soviet Laws." November 17.

———. 1987. "Gorbachev Candid about Opposition." February 26.

Unsigned. 1991. "The New Old Face of Tyranny." January 14.

Unsigned. 1991. "Broken Glastnost." January 17.

Unsigned. 1991. "Lithuanians Clash with Soviet Force." August 22.

Unsigned. 1991. "Baltic Freedom in a New Light." August 23.

Unsigned. 1990. "Two Liberations in Lithuania." March 12.

SERBIA: FROM DICTATORSHIP TO DEMOCRACY

Nestled in the Balkans, between Europe and Asia, Serbia has long been a flashpoint for conflict. Serbs have a strong national and cultural identity and an even more fervent desire for self-determination. A small, landlocked state—slightly smaller than South Carolina—Serbia has experienced turbulence between ethnic and religious factions, especially in the twentieth century. According to the 2002 Census, the vast majority of Serbia is ethnically Serb (82.9 percent), and 85 percent of Serbs are practicing Serbian Orthodox. The country additionally has numerous minorities, including ethnic Albanians, who are united by language and religion to Muslims in Kosovo, southern Serbia, and Albania; Bosnian Muslims; Catholic Croats; the Roma people; Vlachs (Romanians); Gorani (Mountain People Highlanders), believed to be a pre-Slavic people, also called Illyrians; and Hungarians. Bosniaks and Croats both speak Serbo-Croat. The Gorani are Muslims who live in the mountains in southern Kosovo and speak a Slavonic language closely related to Macedonian. Sitting astride one of the major land routes from Turkey to Europe, Serbia has continuously been at the center of international land trade and commerce in the Balkans.

The Balkans include Albania, Bosnia and Herzegovina, Croatia, Bulgaria, Macedonia, Moldova, Montenegro, Romania, Serbia, and Slovenia. *Balkan* is Turkish for mountain, and the Balkan Peninsula is mountainous, particularly in the west. The term "Balkanization" refers to fragmentation by multiple ethnic groups and partly derives from compartmentalization resulting from mountainous peaks and contours. The Balkans are bordered by Italy to the northwest, Austria and Hungary to the north, and Ukraine on the north and northeast. The Mediterranean Sea lies to the south, the Adriatic Sea is on the west, the Ionian Sea to the southwest, and the Black Sea is in the east.

The medieval Serbian Empire was one of the largest in the region, but from the sixteenth to the nineteenth centuries, a series of wars between the Habsburg dynasty of the Austro-Hungarian Empire and the Ottoman Empire battled for different parts of Serbia. Most of Serbia was under Turkish administration for hundreds of years, isolating it from Europe and bequeathing a culturally mixed and polyglot society where intolerance was acceptable. In a series of national revolutions during the nineteenth century, for the first time in the history of the Ottoman Empire a Christian population attempted to seek independence from the sultan (Glenny 1999). Serbia lasted throughout that century as the Principality of Serbia, independent from the Ottoman Empire, and in 1882 was elevated to become the Kingdom of Serbia.

Indeed, conflicting claims in the Balkans were rooted in the Ottoman invasion of more than a half millennium ago, and some disputing assertions went back a thousand years. Most European populations had generally ceased migration by approximately the tenth century, but movement into and out of the Balkans continued into the twentieth. The formation of independent nation-states sometimes exacerbated ethnic problems. The in and out migration of ethnic groups into the Balkans often made it impossible to define state boundaries that corresponded with ethnic classifications. Boundaries often broke established patterns of cultural, economic, and social traditions, generating predicaments for minorities that would curse politicians for generations. New state borders separated villages from their summer grazing pastures or severed their connections with churches or monasteries; religious orders were estranged from properties that provided their income. Although Serbia had adopted a liberal constitution in 1835 and had a functioning parliamentary democracy by the end of the century, such dilemmas arose from the creation of supposedly modern states in areas where social and economic conditions varied, and where there was little history of liberal representative democracy.

In the early twentieth century, the people of Serbia established their independence as the "Kingdom of Servia" and sustained a relatively strong state. Concerning the nineteenth century, historian David Fromkin notes in *The New York Times* on March 9, 2003, "European leaders were astonished when indigenous European empires . . . including Serbia . . . won independence for themselves" ("A World Still Haunted by

QUICK FACTS ABOUT SERBIA

- On June 28, 1914, Archduke Francis Ferdinand, heir to the Austro-Hungarian throne, was assassinated by Gavrilo Princip, a Bosnian Serb anarchist; the deed eventually led to World War I.
- During World War II, a brutal Ustashe regime of Nazi collaborators in Croatia killed more than 600,000 Serbs.
- After World War II, Marshal Josip Broz Tito (1892–1980) united the territories of the Balkan Peninsula.
- In 1948, Tito asserted his independence from Stalin in an exchange of letters with Moscow.
- On April 7, 1963, the Federal People's Republic of Yugoslavia changed its official name to Socialist Federal Republic of Yugoslavia, and in 1974 Tito was named president for life.
- Until 1991, the Socialist Federal Republic of Yugoslavia would be made up of six republics: Bosnia-Herzegovina, Croatia, Macedonia, Montenegro, Serbia, and Slovenia.
- On May 8, 1989, Slobodan Milošević (1941–2006) became president of Serbia.
- In 1989, Milošević annulled the 1974 constitution, which had guaranteed a measure of autonomy for Kosovo.
- Following a referendum, on June 26, 1991, Croatia declared its independence.
- In 1991, ethnic Albanian leaders declared Kosovo's independence and intensified a massive province-wide program of noncooperation with Serbia.
- On September 24, 1992, Milošević was reelected to the Serbian presidency.
- Signed in Paris on December 14, 1995, the Dayton peace accord ended the war between Serbia and Bosnia.
- In March 1999, NATO began airstrikes against Serbian military and government targets to drive Serbian forces out of Kosovo.
- The November 1996 municipal elections, won by the Zajedno ("Together") coalition of political parties, were annulled by Milošević.
- On December 17, 1998, a nonviolent student organization (Otpor!) launched its first action, a march from Belgrade to Novi Sad, Serbia's second largest city, to protest Serbian laws that would restrict free speech and academic freedom. Otpor took a leading role in the campaign to unseat Milošević.
- On September 24, 2000, Vojislav Koštunica won the presidential election, but Milošević refused to accept the results, triggering nationwide peaceful protests.
- In Serbia's "Bulldozer Revolution," on October 5, 2000, Milošević's control collapsed in the way that Otpor had planned: hundreds of thousands inundated Belgrade, steering bulldozers and tractors, jamming roads with loaded buses, flooding government buildings, as police and state security forces looked the other way.
- On October 6, 2000, Milošević resigned the presidency and went into hiding.
- On March 31, 2001, Milošević surrendered and was arrested, the first head of state ever asked to account for war crimes.
- On March 11, 2006, Milošević died in his cell while on trial at The Hague.

Ottoman Ghosts"). This history of seeking independence in the midst of conflict forged strong nationalist sentiment and ethnic identity among Serbs.

In 1914, Serbia found itself at the center of a conflict among the Great Powers. On August 2 of that year, Albert Bushnell Hart chronicles for *The Times* the event of June 28 that triggered World War I ("Austrian Fear of Serb Empire is Real War Cause"). A Bosnian Serb anarchist, Gavrilo Princip, assassinated the Archduke Francis Ferdinand, and the dual monarchy of Austria-Hungary declared war on what had become the Kingdom of Serbia. In response, Russia, a Serbian ally, began to ramp up attacks, leading Germany to declare war on Russia. Within a month, World War I had broken out. The hostilities were devastating to the Serbian population. When the war ended, the Kingdom of Serbia joined with the State of the Slovenes, Croats, and Serbs to become the Unitary State of Slovenes, Croats, and Serbs, governed by Peter I of Serbia. The conflict, however, was far from over.

Emerging from five centuries of a slumbering Ottoman Empire, Muslims had migrated into Albania, Bulgaria, Bosnia, Kosovo, and Macedonia. Some were migrants from Turkey, others were prisoners of war or freed slaves, still others converts. By contrast, ethnic Serbians, who think of themselves as indigenous Europeans, are in the majority Serbian Orthodox Christians. A tempest of cultures, civilizations, and religions has long meant uproar within Serbia's boundaries. Indeed, persistent, brutal ethnic warfare has often characterized the Balkans, and these conflicts have claimed hundreds of thousands of lives and created millions of refugees and displaced persons. Within its own borders, Serbia has known acrid and sometimes murderous ethnic tensions. Serbia included the southernmost province of Kosovo until 2008, when the former province declared its independence. Within Kosovo, 92 percent are ethnic Albanian, with a majority of Sunni Muslims, reflecting their heritage of Ottoman rule.

At the outset of World War II, the Kingdom of Yugoslavia signed the Tripartite Pact with the Axis powers. Pledging loyalty to the Axis, Yugoslavia received a promise that no troops from Germany or Italy would cross its national borders, according to *The Times* on March 26, 1941 ("Belgrade in Axis"). The population revolted again. The government was overthrown, and the new government withdrew its support for the Axis powers. In response, on April 6 Nazi Germany invaded the Kingdom of Yugoslavia, which unconditionally surrendered on April 17. Serbia came under the control of a joint military-German regime. The war period was marked by significant violence and bloodshed, including a brutal Ustashe regime of Nazi collaborators in Croatia that killed more than 600,000 Serbs. The wounds from that genocide run deep and permeate Croat-Serb relations to this day. *The Times* on November 13, 1993, reports that as many former Ustashe supporters took power in government in the newly established Croatia, "Ustashes were among Himmler's most enthusiastic helpers in slaughtering tens of thousands of Serbs and Jews" ("Nationalism Turns Sour in Croatia").

After World War II, the Balkan territories were united in the Socialist Federal Republic of Yugoslavia, under the dictatorship of Marshal Josip Broz Tito. Tito had been an antifascist leader of the Resistance during the war, and after the fall of the Axis, he became the leader of a new totalitarian, federalist, communist state. Serbia was one of six federal territories under the regime. Tito discouraged any notion of ethnic identity within the federal structure—he wanted to encourage a pan-Slavic movement under the banner of "Greater Yugoslavia." To tighten controls by the unitary state and lessen postwar tensions, Tito discouraged regionalism and promoted measures such as a national flag. Serbian influence in the central government was seriously weakened.

Unlike other leaders in Eastern Europe, Marshal Tito did not fall under the influence of Josef Stalin, and Yugoslavia was largely outside the orbit of the Soviet Union. The communists owed their triumph to their numbers within the various resistance movements against the Nazis and to the general disengagement by the Western powers from the Balkans. Tito declared his independence from Stalin shortly after the end of World War II in a letter written to the Soviet leader and Vyacheslav Mikhailovich Molotov, foreign affairs commissar of the USSR (on Molotov, also see **Baltic States, Introduction;** "Lithuanians Rally for Stalin Victims"). In the April 13, 1948, communication, Tito says, "We study and take as an example the Soviet system, but we are developing socialism in our country in somewhat different forms. . . . No matter how much each of us loves the land of socialism, the USSR, he can in no case love his own country less." By 1947, Stalin had concluded that Tito held too much influence, and Moscow vetoed a Balkan federation. In 1948, Yugoslavia was excluded from the communist empire.

In Tito's Yugoslavia, nationalist confrontations were prohibited, in favor of "brotherhood and unity," as the dictator balanced contending interests. Since the Serbs were the nation's largest group, and their capital, Belgrade, was also Yugoslavia's capital, the prospect of Serb domination—which had afflicted prewar Yugoslavia—threatened to become troublesome. In 1961, Tito made Yugoslavia a founding member of the Non-Aligned Movement, which Philip Shenon would describe some thirty years later in *The Times* as an organization "that would represent underdeveloped nations seeking to preserve their independence in the midst of a cold-war rivalry that threatened to swallow them up" ("Non-Aligned Bloc Seeks a New Reason for Being"). Yugoslavia developed by focused internal concentration, unbothered by the cold war and reach of the Soviet Union. No noteworthy Serb nationalism surfaced until the 1980s, when acute economic decline followed Tito's death. A weak, central, revolving presidency replaced Tito, but it was unable to manage reforms.

In 1986, in the midst of economic despair and political pessimism, a group of Serbs issued a manifesto holding Tito responsible for denying Serbia's legitimate claims to greatness and its aspirations regarding the province of Kosovo. The manifesto corresponded with the emergence of Slobodan Milošević, a ruthless politician who anticipated the impending collapse of communism.

Milošević Takes Power

Slobodan Milošević rose to power pledging to protect Serbs wherever they were. He seized control of the Serbian communist party, and by 1989, he had risen to authority among the League of Communists of Serbia, one of a number of regional governing bodies within Yugoslavia. Rising swiftly within his own League of Communists, he gained significant control over the league in the Yugoslavia Central Committee, the national governing body. He engineered constitutional changes that gave him three of the eight votes in the federal committee.

Promoting Serbian patriotism, he reduced the influence of other autonomous regions of Yugoslavia. The demographic makeup of Serbia meant that internal ethnic strife had always been high. Given the history of the Ottoman Empire and the more recent Ustashe regime of Croatian Nazi collaborators, those who were ethnically Serb had always distrusted the other ethnic groups in the Balkans. Milošević capitalized on this suspicion and solidified his rule in Serbia by mercilessly manipulating the fears of rural peasants and industrial urban populations alike, easily winning the first multiparty elections of the republic. The five other republics of the Yugoslav Federation were soon challenging what they termed "Serboslavia." Slovenia, the wealthiest republic in the federation, wanted to secede, but Milošević promoted ideas of a "Greater Serbia," composed of ethnic, Serb-speaking, Serbian Orthodox Europeans, and he sought control over lands conceded to Serbia by the international community (Banac 2006). This idea, never realized, would have meant redrawing the borders by force.

Milošević's aims for a Yugoslavia controlled by Serbs made easier the arousal of independence movements in Croatia, Bosnia and Herzegovina, Slovenia, and Macedonia. His intentions for the future of Serbia—exploiting its national identities and histories—not only caused a breakdown in Tito's pan-Slavic Balkan state and destroyed Yugoslavia, but also set in train a drive toward warfare in Bosnia, Croatia, and Kosovo. The independence mobilizations led to the creation of a new Yugoslav government involving Serbia and Montenegro, called the Federal Republic of Yugoslavia. Milošević remained the leader of the latest government, although the political opposition claimed that his influence was that of a dictator who craved enemies and needed to fight some ethnic group or another to stay in power. Letting loose a nationalist frenzy, his autocratic regime repeatedly asserted its power in illegitimate if not criminal means that led to wars, secession, and various forms of resistance.

Conflict in the Balkans

From 1992 to 1995, ethnic tensions led to war between Bosnia and Herzegovina and Croatia. Although Serbia was not directly involved, Milošević's government gave considerable financial and military resources to the Serbian forces in the conflict. This involvement resulted in biting international economic sanctions against Serbia, which created financial hardships. The country went into serious economic decline, and the population began to rebel against its leadership. In response, the government grew more heavy-handed. The international community may have been attuned to the victims of violent strife, particularly in Bosnia and Kosovo, but the population of Serbia suffered as well.

The turning point came in July 1995 with the massacre of 8,000 Muslim men and boys by Serbian forces in the small Bosnian town of Srebrenica, as well as killings in the town's safe zone. These atrocities led to indictments against military and government leaders of the Bosnian Serbs by the International Criminal Tribunal for the former Yugoslavia. Ambassador Richard Holbrooke, a senior U.S. State Department official, brought together the Balkan leaders for twenty-one days in November 1995. The Dayton Agreement, or General Framework Agreement for Peace in Bosnia and Herzegovina, was reached at Wright-Patterson airbase near Dayton, Ohio, as a result of the negotiations.

Formally signed in Paris on December 14, 1995, the accords ended more than three years of war in Bosnia, one of several armed conflicts in the former Socialist Federal Republic of Yugoslavia. The talks followed unsuccessful peace bids and bombardment of the Bosnian Serb military. The United States and Russia in particular exerted strong pressures on the leaders of the three sides to attend the negotiations in Dayton, a site chosen to minimize exploitation by the various sides in the news media. In meetings from November

1 to November 21, participants from the region included Milošević. (Milošević represented Bosnian Serb interests in the absence of Radovan Karadžić, the president of Republika Srpska, the Serbian Republic of Bosnia and Herzegovina, a self-proclaimed state within the internationally recognized territory of the Republic of Bosnia and Herzegovina. Karadžić was later detained at The Hague by the UN for war crimes committed against persons of Muslim faith.) Also participating was Croatian president Franjo Tuđman, Bosnian president Alija Izetbegović, and Bosnian foreign minister Muhamed Sacirbey. The peace conference was led by U.S. Secretary of State Warren Christopher and Ambassador Holbrooke, with assistance from European Union (EU) and Russian representatives. The Dayton Agreement authorized Croatian and Bosnian Muslim independence from Yugoslavia and agreed upon the existing political demarcations and boundaries of Bosnia and Herzegovina and its government structure. Milošević gave up Serb areas of Sarajevo, and some formerly Serb lands in western Bosnia were returned to Serbia. In theory, Bosnia remained one state, but was divided into the Federation, including Croatian and Muslim regions, and the Republika Srpska. The agreement mandated international monitoring, oversight, and implementation. A NATO-led force of approximately 60,000 was made responsible for implementing military aspects of the agreement and deployed in December 1995.

The peoples of the former Yugoslavia had experienced none of the fruits of popular mobilization resulting from the nonviolent revolutions led by the peoples of former Soviet satellites in Eastern Europe and several former states of the Soviet Union. The national civil resistance movements in Eastern Europe had brought about major political change, combined with dispirited communist parties and reforms instituted by Communist Party general secretary Mikhail S. Gorbachev. By August 1989, Poland had formed its first non-communist government of the postwar era (see "To His Volatile Young Allies, Walesa Preaches Conciliation"). Hungarian communist officials on May 2, 1989, removed the barbed wire fence that comprised the Iron Curtain, and the communist party dissolved itself on October 7 (see "In Hungary, the Political Changes Are Tempered by Economic Fears; New Hungary Marks '56 Uprising: 'Gorby!' and 'Russians Out!' Mix"). East Germany's communist party on November 9 decided to open the Berlin wall (see "East Germany Opens Frontier to the West for Migration or Travel; Thousands Cross"). Czechoslovakia's hard-line communist regime collapsed in December 1989 in favor of a parliamentary democracy led by a former political prisoner (see "Havel Tells Festive Czechoslovaks That Honesty Is Key to Recovery").

THE ZAJEDNO ("TOGETHER") COALITION: A HARBINGER

The mood in Serbia's capital, Belgrade, and Kosovo's capital, Pristina, was depressed, fearful, and fatigued. Nevertheless, Serbia was widely seen as holding the key to stability in the Balkans. Citizens had begun to organize in opposition to Milošević in 1991, before the war, but the effort was crushed. In 1996, after the war ended, they began to mobilize again. In Serbia's November 1996 municipal elections, the Zajedno ("Together") coalition's common slate of candidates won in fourteen of the nineteen largest cities. Milošević annulled the elections. In response, Zajedno—diverse and heterogeneous in makeup with three political parties ranging from social democrats to nationalists—organized daily demonstrations of tens of thousands of people in the streets of Belgrade and other cities throughout December. In Washington, the White House spokesperson, Michael D. McCurry, warned Milošević, as Steven Erlanger reports in *The Times*, that crackdowns on the demonstrators "could doom the country's hopes to be freed of economic and political sanctions" ("U.S. Warns Serbia Against Crushing Protests"). It would be a setback for Serbia, McCurry said, "if there was to be any violent repression of the dissent now taking place in Belgrade and elsewhere in Serbia." As some 100,000 demonstrators turned out each day, *The Times* correspondent Chris Hedges reports that Milošević closed the country's last independent news station, jammed student radio in Belgrade, blocked busloads of demonstrators heading for the daily rallies, and arrested thirty-two student activists for "brutal attacks on people's property" ("Screws Tightened on Serbian Opposition"). Hedges describes Milošević 's denunciations on national television of the demonstrators as "rampaging hordes." Hedges says opposition leaders in speeches explicitly invited the country's police and army to participate in the daily protests. Discerning that Milošević stood to lose support from some of his police officers, Hedges notes police did not intervene when dozens of students sprayed the parliament building with detergent—a symbol of the necessity to cleanse the government.

Students led an entirely separate mobilization, which attracted 25,000 participants into demonstrations at noon each day. The students told *The Times* that their movement was outside politics and they refused to meet with the Zajedno coalition. On December 10, however, Hedges notes an openly political tone to student opposition, yet reports the students' attacks on Milošević were not for starting the war in Croatia and Bosnia, but for his failure to win it ("Fierce Serb Nationalism Pervades Student Foes of Belgrade Leader").

By early January 1997, demonstrators were shutting Belgrade down with street demonstrations. Hedges writes on January 6 that the influential Serbian Orthodox Church supported the protests by publicly denouncing the behavior of the government (see "Literally Filling the Streets, Serbian Demonstrators Give New Meaning to Political Gridlock"). After the large demonstrations began, Milošević invited the Organization for Security and Cooperation in Europe (OSCE, a security organization of more than fifty nation-states that grew out of the Helsinki Accords) to examine the election results (see "**Introduction: Strikes, Sinatra, and Nonviolent Revolution**"). The OSCE verified the results of the November municipal balloting.

A nationwide mobilization primarily based on noncooperation was developing in Serbia against Milošević. The significance of a strategy of noncooperation at the heart of the mobilization is manifested in the words of the opposition leader, Zoran Djindjic, who told 100,000 supporters gathered in the Square of the Republic, "We are the ones who will now impose sanctions on the regime. . . . We will drive them out. Let them get used to a Serbia that is shut down."

After seventy-seven days of huge daily rallies in the streets of Belgrade and elsewhere, and with intense pressure from foreign diplomats, Milošević reversed his nullification of the elections. Reporting for *The Times* on February 5, Hedges explains: "After Mr. Milošević annulled the election results, citing unspecified 'irregularities,' he found himself increasingly embattled and isolated, even within his own circle. Police and army commanders refused calls by hard-liners in the governing Socialist Party to crush the protests. Top officials, in statements that would have been unthinkable three months ago, called for the election results to be respected" ("Serbian President Accepts Victories by his Opponents"). The same day, *The Times* reports, 20,000 students marched to police headquarters calling for release of twenty political prisoners and were joined by 1,000 lawyers who had gone on strike and were offering free legal services. Actors and singers also went on strike, and movie theaters closed for two days.

After riot police had carried out sporadic beatings for three nights running, according to Hedges, on February 5 students tossed bones at the feet of police officers and taunted them by barking, while the crowd chanted "Ustashe," referring to the Croatian fascist puppet regime established by Nazi occupiers during World War II. A subtext of Serbian nationalism is perceptible in the same article, as Hedges portrays Zoran Djindjic, a main opposition leader in the Zajedno coalition, as having close ties with the Bosnian Serbs and opposing the NATO bombing in autumn 1995 that got the Bosnian Serb army to the negotiating table. During the Bosnian elections, he campaigned for the governing party, led by Radovan Karadžić. All three members of the coalition, according to Hedges, articulated reservations about the Dayton Agreement that ended the war in Bosnia.

By February 9, *The Times* reports that power is slipping from Milošević. Hedges says radio and television stations had started to defy the regime's tight control, disclosing "several devastating defections from the President's hermetic inner circle" ("Now TV Interrupts Milosevic's Programming"). Many in Belgrade, Hedges writes, believed that Milošević's inability to control the news media is what finally made him recommend to the Serbian parliament in early February the recognition of the opposition electoral victories. In response to Radio Free Europe's offer to broadcast reports from one radio station, the government let the station back on air. By mid-February, the combination of large demonstrations with staying power, defections from Milošević's inner sanctum, criticism by the Serbian Orthodox patriarch, and opposition from business executives and politicians led Milošević to agree to the seating of the elected coalition representatives in Serbian municipalities.

The street demonstrations continued, however, and after eighty-eight days, on February 22, *Times* reporter Jane Perlez was present as Zoran Djindjic took control of Belgrade ("Belgrade Opposition Takes Control of the City Council"). Perlez notes that Djindjic was a philosopher who became a politician. He became the first democratically elected mayor since World War II.

Meanwhile, international third-party sanctions, also called tertiary sanctions—meaning nonviolent actions of disapproval by third parties that are not disputants in the conflict—were severely affecting the Serbian economy. Industry was operating at 25 percent of capacity; unemployment was high. Many Serbs blamed Milošević for their troubles and wanted to recast Serbia's institutions so that they would be democratic, to include an independent judiciary, free press, and opportunities for private markets. Although local news media access improved as Zajedno's representatives took office, most families still watched national television, as yet under government control. Sanctions imposed by the United States were multipronged. Erlanger writes on December 4, 1996, that the sanctions denied Serbia "full diplomatic relations with the United States, most-favored-nation trading status, and credit through American government trading agencies. They also mean an effective American veto on Serbian participation in the United Nations, International Monetary Fund, World Bank and the Organization for Security and Cooperation in Europe" ("U.S. Warns Serbia Against Crushing Protests").

Legislation passed in May 1996 had tightened the Serbian regime's controls over universities and academicians. Hedges notes on December 10 that the destruction of the country's educational system did not start under Milošević; rather, it had begun under Tito, who purged professors who refused to incorporate Marxism into their courses. The rise of Serbian nationalism further compromised academic freedom. By the mid-1980s, some departments were using Byzantine culture to undermine Western ideas, Hedges writes, as Serbian philosophers who "espoused theories of racial superiority, including the idea that the Serbs were the oldest human race, dominated university classrooms." War intensified the decline. More than 400,000 Serbs, including the young and talented, had departed the country in the early 1980s. Hedges writes, "Academic standards fell as Mr. Milosevic put party hacks in charge of schools and departments and sliced government spending for education" ("Fierce Serb Nationalism Pervades Student Foes of Belgrade Leader").

The Zajedno nonviolent demonstrations were a harbinger of the larger mobilization to come. Citizens began organizing en masse. In an article in *The New York Times* Sunday magazine, on November 26, 2000, Roger Cohen reports that on October 10, 1998, half a dozen "survivors" from the student movement of 1996 founded Otpor! (Resistance!). The student organization, based at the University of Belgrade, was set up in response to restrictive Serbian laws newly passed to circumscribe free speech and academic freedom at universities and in the media. Attempting to turn Milošević's favorite image of a red fist of communism against him, Cohen explains, Otpor adopted a clenched white fist set upon a black background, or vice versa, as its symbol in a revival of 1930s communist poster art ("Who Really Brought Down Milosevic?"). Otpor gathered steam quickly, in part because a new coalition made up of a wide range of political parties, Alliance for Change, was viewed with cynicism by the young, university-based grassroots activists. On December 17, Otpor launched its first action—a march from Belgrade to Novi Sad, Serbia's second largest city.

Kosovo

Kosovo borders Albania, Macedonia, Montenegro, and "inner Serbia." Kosovo was often referred to as "old Serbia" because of its position in the medieval Kingdom of Serbia. After five centuries of Ottoman rule, the territory was annexed into Serbia by force in 1912 and, at the end of World War I, became part of the Kingdom of the Serbs, Croats, and Slovenes, or the first Yugoslavia. In World War II, the Axis powers reunited much of Kosovo with Albania. With the defeat of the Axis powers, Kosovo again became part of Yugoslavia, once more in Serbia. In 1974, the central government of Yugoslavia under Marshal Tito granted Kosovo regional autonomy, and it became an autonomous province of Serbia, with equal representation to Serbia in the federal presidency. By then it possessed a distinct Balkan identity independent of Greater Albania, the separate nation-state to the west, while retaining major ethnic and religious cleavages with Serbia.

Although religion is the obvious divide between Orthodox Serbs and Catholic Croats, the Albanians are one people; they are mostly Muslim, but also Orthodox and Roman Catholic. This complex state of affairs is embedded from the Ottoman past, when the Sublime Porte, the Ottoman government, did not recognize the reality of national groupings. Rather, it admitted religious communities, which were given protection by the sultan and allowed an extent of self-administration through the millet system. (*Millet* is the Ottoman Turkish term for an autonomous self-governing religious community, organized under its own laws.) When Milošević took control in 1989, he stripped Kosovo of its regional autonomy and placed it under the governance of Belgrade. Kosovo's population was then approximately 2 million, of whom 90 percent were Muslim ethnic Albanians in the province they called "Kosova."

The province's industries, such as the mining of gold, lead, lignite, silver, and zinc; chemical production; and electric power plants gave important assistance to Yugoslavia's economy. Kosovo was also significant militarily, because it had landing facilities and acted as a strategic buffer against threats to the south. Its greatest importance to Serbia is emblematic, as Kosovo is the seat of the Serbian Orthodox Church and the location of religious shrines and historical sites. The Kosovo Albanians consider themselves descendants of the ancient Illyrians and therefore the original or aboriginal people, in contrast to the Slavs, who arrived in the sixth and seventh centuries. Serbs reject this interpretation of history. They have often treated Kosovo Albanians as "immigrants" and twice in the twentieth century tried to repatriate them to Turkey. Despite these differences, Albanians and Serbs have lived together in Kosovo for longer than the United States of America has existed.

Milošević used Kosovo as a major front in his pursuit of his plan for "Greater Serbia." In 1987, he addressed a Serbian crowd in Kosovo, claiming Serbian supremacy in the region and assuring supporters that "no one will be allowed to beat you again." He rejected reports of Serbian persecution of the ethnic Albanians or any efforts to strip Kosovo of its representational votes in the Yugoslav assembly. Yet, when he became president of Yugoslavia in 1989, he annulled constitutional guarantees and proceeded to strip Kosovo of the regional autonomy it had possessed since 1974. The 1974 Tito constitution had disappointed the Kosovo Albanians because it did not grant independence, while Serbs in Belgrade were disgruntled because it gave Kosovo autonomy. The 1989 amending of the constitution by Milošević to end Kosovo's autonomy was accompanied by a policy of "Serbianization," which included human rights abuses and the ratcheting up of repression. Some 127,000 Kosovo Albanians were made jobless. Secret police dossiers were opened to gather information on 120,000 Kosovo Albanian men.

From 1974 to 1989, the Kosovo Albanians not only enjoyed relative autonomy, but also had the opportunity to develop a way to organize unified social action. A nonviolent struggle must either locate or create the political space for collective action. Drawing inspiration from the East European nonviolent revolutions of 1989, the Kosovo Albanians judged that civil resistance would be the best way to fight for independence and gain international support. During the decade from 1988 to 1998, one of the most wide-ranging examples of the use of nonviolent civil resistance in the contemporary era occurred in Kosovo.

Ibrahim Rugova, an Albanian literary historian, semiologist (a student of signs and symbols), and a pragmatist in his thinking, was persuaded that the independence of Kosovo could best be achieved by an advanced method of nonviolent intervention known as alternative, or parallel, institutions. He encouraged a policy modeled on a program that Mohandas K. Gandhi called "constructive work," or the "constructive program," in which parallel structures are set up as a method for accomplishing institutional change while still living under the old order. In this case it meant transferring the formerly autonomous instruments of governance to a new self-declared Republic of Kosovo or in some instances developing new systems. Rugova led training programs for this form of civil resistance, which involved establishing and maintaining free-standing Albanian community entities and systems, particularly in education.

The Kosovo Albanians carried out their plans for parallel structures with remarkable precision, rejecting the Serbian regime's monopolistic state structures and organizing their own institutions. Virtually the entire society in Kosovo was engaged in alternative institutions by the early 1990s. In 1991, when ethnic Albanian leaders declared Kosovo's independence, Serbian authorities stopped paying Kosovo Albanian schoolteachers. By August, Serbian officials had fired 6,000 secondary schoolteachers and principals of 115 elementary schools. Across Kosovo, parents, children, and teachers arrived at schools only to find armed police standing in doorways. The sacked teachers set up 441 primary schools, which, although interrupted and harassed, were able to function. Between 1990 and 1997, Kosovo Albanians brought out 156 new textbooks for schools and the university. More than half the medical personnel of Kosovo were dismissed after August 1990. Fired physicians and nurses organized ninety-one "Mother Teresa" clinics, named for the Albanian humanitarian. Meanwhile, the tax collectors thrown out of their jobs set up an alternative system of revenue collection. Voluntary taxation was soon financing these unprecedented systems of health care, education, and political referendum. For the better part of a decade, the Kosovo Albanians engaged in a massive program of noncooperation with Belgrade, creating and sustaining their own de facto institutions of governance and self-rule (Clark 2000).

Miners held five days of demonstrations, and 1,200 miners later went on hunger strikes for nine days pursuing their promised reinstatement, a promise not kept. Eleven fractious political parties put aside their chronic disagreements and formed the Democratic League of Kosovo (DLK). Operating by consensus, within months 700,000—nearly the entire voting-age population of Kosovo Albanians—had joined the DLK.

In May 1992, as a result of political noncooperation and a boycott of Yugoslav and Serbian elections, separate elections were held in Kosovo. Rugova was overwhelmingly elected as the first president of Kosovo and of the DLK. Even so, the Kosovo Albanians faced serious problems, among them the failure of the international community to comprehend the implications of a largely unified population's strict adherence to nonviolent resistance. Observers often do not recognize the extent of discipline needed for average people to work for change in this way. Scholars have shown that most successful civil resistance campaigns have been organized by populations without a philosophical commitment to the principles of nonviolence; rather, they choose the technique as the most effective for their circumstances. Certainly this was the situation in Kosovo.

The second and major blow was that the Kosovo Albanians were not invited to Dayton for the 1995 talks that ended the Bosnian War and led to Croatian and Bosnian Muslim independence from Yugoslavia. The exclusion of the Kosovo Albanians from the peace table irreparably weakened Rugova's position. The agreement did not mention Kosovo, and the international community turned its back on resolving the province's dilemma.

David Hartsough of Peaceworkers, a San Francisco nongovernmental organization, traveled to Kosovo four times between 1996 and 1998, taking U.S. university students to practice "accompaniment," in which a person trained in working nonviolently accompanies organizers of nonviolent movements to offer some protection from repressive governments. Hartsough carried with him *Protest, Power, and Change: An Encyclopedia of Nonviolent Action* and *From Dictatorship to Democracy*, a manual for planning nonviolent civil resistance, by the scholar Gene Sharp. Hartsough gave the manual to Albin Kurti and the Albanian Student Union in Kosovo's capital, Pristina. Nedime Belegu of the Center for the Defense of Human Rights translated it into Albanian. These materials aided the massive nonviolent mobilization in Kosovo.

Ultimately, however, the meticulous program of nonviolent action by the Kosovo Albanians failed against the repression of the regime. From outside came diasporan Kosovo Albanians, who formed the Kosovo Liberation Army (KLA), a rebel cadre. In April 1996 the KLA began violent offensives against Serbian targets in the Kosovo region. These guerrilla fighters had not been part of the rigorous preparations for nonviolent action. Having prepared themselves outside Kosovo, they flooded into the province to "help" through the hastily set up KLA. This pattern is not unfamiliar in nonviolent mobilizations; those who have neither been involved in the decision to fight without violence, nor participated in the exacting processes of study, planning, and preparation necessary for successful civil resistance, decide to "assist" with guns. Such "assistance" usually triggers harsh repression and can provide their adversary with an excuse for crushing reprisals. In a December 23, 1996, editorial *The Times* writes:

> Mr. Milosevic began his ascent from Communist functionary to President of Serbia with an emotional speech in Kosovo commemorating a Serbian defeat there in 1389, tapping into the Serbian sentiment that Albanians are outsiders on Serbian sacred ground. Upon taking power in 1989, Mr. Milosevic began an ethnic cleansing of the Albanians, who had autonomy under Communism. The Communist officials who controlled the government, schools and police were local Albanians.
>
> The Milosevic regime fired them, and most Albanians employed in government and industry. Albanian schools are now outlawed. According to a new report by Human Rights Watch, police detain or beat up dozens of Albanians every day. Security forces have killed 21 Albanians in the last two years. Ethnic Serbs, especially war refugees, are encouraged to go to Kosovo and take jobs from Albanians. Nearly 350,000 Albanians have emigrated.
>
> An Albanian terrorist group began attacks this year, but the vast majority of the Albanians have chosen nonviolence ("Serbia's Apartheid Victims").

The Kosovo Albanians had no army or security apparatus under their control and were greatly outnumbered by the Serbs. In other words, the conflict was asymmetrical. The Kosovo Albanians were unarmed against the military superiority of Serbian security systems provisioned with ballistic weaponry, but such a situation could have been beneficial for the nonviolent protagonists. The KLA'S introduction of military strikes changed the conflict to a symmetrical affray in which both sides appeared to utilize violent weaponry, but gave the advantage to the attackers with superior military weaponry. When the balance of power is lopsided and both sides use violent weapons, the better-equipped attackers have the advantage.

The KLA's introduction of armed struggle on the Kosovo Albanian side, five months after the Dayton Agreement ratified Croatian and Bosnian Muslim independence from Yugoslavia, destroyed the benefits of the Kosovo Albanians' extensive nonviolent resistance and gave a pretext for retaliation to the Serbian forces. Many ethnic Albanians in Kosovo concluded that violence had paid off for the Croatians and Bosnians. They embarked on an effort to get NATO and the EU similarly to rescue them from Serbian supremacy. In a sense they succeeded. Yet massive repression of the nonviolent movement followed, and the gains of the alternative-institution policy were soon eroded, as the KLA's armed struggle negated a decade of disciplined nonviolent resistance.

As Serb repression hardened in response to the KLA's violent strikes in Kosovo, the armed conflict intensified. The KLA triggered retaliation of an enormity not seen before, as radicals argued that armed uprising was the "only thing that would work." Their supposition was that guerrilla warfare would force outside powers to intervene, while blaming the policy of nonviolent struggle for Kosovo's inability to secure independence. Milošević and the Serbian forces initiated a campaign to "cleanse" ethnic Albanians, a euphemism for ethnically instigated murder. Investigators later found mass graves from massacres, including as many as 2,000 slaughtered Albanians in one place. Military conflict in the region displaced Serbs and Kosovo Albanians alike, with "the thunderous crescendo of butchery that filled Muslim mass graves in Bosnia and similar pits of death in Kosovo," in the words of Misha Glenny. Within two years, NATO unenthusiastically concluded that it must act. The KLA's militants demanded independence, but NATO and the EU did not agree to it. Pressure from Western powers and U.S. assurances of support brought the KLA to accept instead "autonomy" for Kosovo, with a NATO presence there and in Serbia. The Serbs would not accept such deployment. In the war that followed, NATO for all intents and purposes was allied with KLA forces inside Kosovo.

In response to the Federal Republic of Yugoslavia's actions in Kosovo, seventy-eight days of NATO airstrikes began in March 1999, hitting Serbian military and government targets. As international opinion condemned Milošević and backed the military actions, President Bill Clinton, upholding the military engagement, commented on the lessons the international community had realized from World War II: "We learned that if you don't stand up to brutality and the killing of innocent people, you invite the people who do it to do more of it."

The Serbian population at home had mixed reactions. Tight government controls over the media and the airwaves prevented news coverage of the military action from reaching the populace. The Serbians still had deep memories of the brutal ethnic cleansing waged against them by the Ustashe regime. No one knew the degree to which Milošević had acted against the ethnic Albanians in Kosovo, so it was difficult to discern whether the NATO actions were justified. On March 25, 1999, *Times* reporter Blaine Harden writes that the Milošević government, which had always appealed to nationalist sentiment, argued that the bombings were another Western attack on Serbian unity ("Conflict in the Balkans, The Serbs; Honor Compels Opposition to Rally around Belgrade"). The Milošević government argued that the bombings in Kosovo were a "strong but measured response to Albanian terror." In fact, the NATO bombings helped Milošević orchestrate a crackdown on independent media and the opposition.

The NATO bombings also eviscerated the nonviolent movement in Kosovo. Once the bombardments began, the activities of the nonviolent campaign with its extensive alternative institutions basically came to a halt. Although the Kosovo Albanian citizens were informed of the time and location of anticipated bombings, the demands for physical and psychological security superseded everything else.

Indeed, NATO's bombs exacted devastating costs from the people of Serbia. Although casualties were minimal, the attacks were debilitating in their economic and psychological effects on the Serbs. *The Times* estimates that the NATO bombing campaign halved the economic output of the country and put 100,000 people out of work. Damages projected by independent economists range from $40 billion to $100 billion, writes Steven Erlanger on April 30, 1999 ("Bombing Unites Serb Army as It Debilitates Economy—Production Cut in Half, Experts Say"). Nearly 600,000 persons were displaced from their homes, with 150,000 leaving the country entirely, according to *The Times* ("The Kosovo Refugee Emergency"). After the bombings stopped, however, the exorbitant economic, social, and psychological costs of the war became yet another rallying point for the Serbs to depose Milošević.

THE OUSTER OF MILOŠEVIĆ

On June 11, 1999, Serbian forces withdrew from Kosovo, and the military operations ended. Domestic opposition to Milošević began to grow. Otpor launched a continuation of its efforts to rid Serbia of Milošević, which had been stopped because of the government's crackdown in March 1999. Afraid that Milošević's authoritarian regime would swiftly shut it down, Otpor established a decentralized leadership structure. Roger Cohen explains the approach, quoting Jovan Ratkovic, an initial member: "The idea was, cut off one Otpor head, and another 15 heads would instantly appear" ("Who Really Brought Down Milosevic?"). Otpor based its mobilization on three demands: free and fair elections in Serbia, academic freedom, and a free news media. Civic associations across Serbia began to mobilize political opposition.

Peaceworkers' David Hartsough took Sharp's *From Dictatorship to Democracy* to Women in Black, an independent peace group. Marek Zelazkiewicz, a Polish American sociologist on the Peaceworkers board of directors, smuggled the book into Belgrade and gave it to the Center for Civic Initiatives (Grazdanska Initiativa), a Serbian nongovernmental organization directed by Milenko Dereta. Nevena Pantović translated it into Serbian, and the center published and distributed 5,500 copies at no charge.

Starting in 1998, Otpor developed a "user manual" with six different training programs for sharing knowledge about the technique of nonviolent civil resistance, which was printed in late 1999. Otpor trained more than 400 organizers in nonviolent methods with the user manual, which relied upon Gene Sharp's three-volume work, *The Politics of Nonviolent Action*. Otpor trained another 1,000 activists in forty-two cities of Serbia in nonviolent action, in mass weekend training programs in December 1999 and January 2000. In addition, "Otpor developed a comprehensive plan of action in case an Otpor member was arrested. In this way, civic activists had a sense of confidence that they would not be left behind" (Nikolayenko 2009, 14). Erlanger reports in *The Times* on August 21, 1999, that Otpor staged a mock birthday party for Milošević in Belgrade in conjunction with a rally calling for elections and the regime's ouster. The regime termed the rally a "failure," maintaining that it had attracted only 25,000 participants; other witnesses said that 100,000 gathered. The mock birthday party in *The Times* account turned Milošević propaganda into a call for his removal. Otpor lit candles on an enormous cardboard cake, flamboyantly making a wish that Milošević resign (see "Rally against Milosevic Fails to Bind Opposition Parties").

In early 2000, as the call for elections grew stronger, the Milošević regime began to crack down on the opposition. After organizing informally across the country, on February 17, 2000, Otpor held its formal founding congress, having grown to eighty chapters within Serbia. From seventy cities across Serbia, 1,000 representatives came to participate in the congress.

From March 31 to April 3, 2000, the International Republican Institute, a foreign policy arm of the U.S. Republican political party, conducted a workshop on the technique of nonviolent strategic action in Budapest, Hungary, for thirty Otpor organizers. The sessions were led by Robert L. Helvey, a retired U.S. Army colonel who was deeply familiar with the Burmese prodemocracy nonviolent movement of a decade earlier. Helvey emphasized theories of political power, their sources, bulwarks of institutions and organizations that support political power, how to analyze a regime's origins of power, and strategic planning for the nonviolent civil resistance to which Otpor was already committed. Helvey also supplied to the participating activists Sharp's three volumes of *The Politics of Nonviolent Action*. Cohen's *Times* magazine article notes, "The Otpor activists listened as Helvey dissected what he called the 'pillars of support' of the regime. These naturally included the police, the army and the news media, but also the more intangible force of Milosevic's 'authority.' That is, his capacity to give orders and be obeyed."

In mid-May, the government accused Otpor of planting bombs across the country, and the group's leaders were nearly forced underground. The government took control of the main opposition television station, shut two independent radio stations, and began to detain prominent opposition leaders and activists. Nevertheless, the call for elections continued. Otpor, now bigger and more popular than any political party, was adamant in appealing for unity in its public statements. By May 2000, Otpor had a presence in more than 100 towns across Serbia and approximately 20,000 members, of whom only 60 percent were students. Toward year's end, Otpor had 70,000 members in 130 branches, according to Cohen. He writes:

> Through marches and mockery, physical courage and mental agility, Otpor grew into the mass underground movement that stood at the disciplined core of the hidden revolution that really changed Serbia. No other opposition force was as unsettling to the regime or as critical to its overthrow. . . . Under cover of night, [its activists] were out spray-painting Otpor fists and election slogans—"Gotov Je" ("He's Finished") and "Vreme Je" ("It's Time") ("Who Really Brought Down Milosevic?").

Hoping to take the opposition by surprise, at the beginning of September, Milošević called an election earlier than expected. Foreign aid flowed in to support the eighteen opposition political parties, and Otpor took a leading role in the presidential campaign. Vojislav Koštunica, a constitutional lawyer, emerged as the main opposition leader. The campaign run by the Milošević forces expressed loud support for the dream of a Greater Serbia and a posture against the West. The motto of Milošević's political party, the Socialist Party of Serbia, was "Serbia does not kneel." Still, Milošević trailed in public opinion polling across the country.

Fear remained that the elections would be rigged. While groups such as Otpor were leading collective efforts to vote Milošević out, the Center for Free Elections and Democracy (CeSID) spearheaded an effort to prevent election fraud. CeSID developed a sound statistical methodology and led a research effort that included hundreds of interviews; it created a storehouse of collected data to expose systematic election fraud. CeSID published its results nationwide in order to encourage further nonviolent action. In one of the most glaring public relations debacles for Milošević, as Steven Erlanger reports on September 23, 2000, the director of CeSID, Slobodanka Nedovic, was handed a ballot already filled in for Milošević when she went to vote ("Fears Deepen Milosevic Will Rig Vote").

On September 24, Milošević was defeated. "Dawn is coming to Serbia," Koštunica declared. Voter turnout was high. After his loss, by approximately 2 percent, Milošević announced that he would not resign until the expiration of his term in summer 2001. On September 29, Erlanger reports on the opposition's announced intentions to boycott any second round of voting. The opposition political parties prepared to ask the citizens of Serbia at a planned rally to carry out "any act of civil disobedience they have at their disposal" until Milošević leaves office. Erlanger quotes Zarko Korac, a party leader, "[t]alking of rolling strikes, the closing of roads, cinemas, theaters, shops and schools," and saying: "We know it's a high-risk game. . . . Through the rigging of votes, Milosevic is clearly challenging us, and since we are being pushed into the street, we must accept it. It is Milosevic who has declared war." Erlanger also reports that the opposition party leaders met to decide strategy and chose two tracks: first, a legal challenge in the courts upon which Koštunica insisted; second, "people power—pressure through a mixture of rallies, strikes and other demonstrations." According to Erlanger, the opposition claimed "clear evidence of fraud, including the sudden disappearance from the rolls of 600,000 voters, the inclusion of invalid ballots to lower Mr. Kostunica's percentages and the counting of ballots from polling stations in Kosovo that apparently never opened" ("Civil Disobedience Is Planned to Try to Force Milosevic Out").

On October 1, Erlanger reports that Milošević was calling for an October 8 runoff, saying that the opposition had not cracked the 50 percent barrier (see "Yugoslav Opposition Preparing for a Risky Showdown"). Koštunica refused to participate in a runoff, as suspicious vote counts led many to believe that the votes had been manipulated. With the opposition coalition refusing to participate in an additional election, citizens took nonparticipation a step further: activists urged general strikes to shut down the country. As one strike leader argues in *The Times:* "We don't want to drag everything out as we've done in the past, with endless rallies. This time we want to finish it in a blitzkrieg and shut the country down." General strikes had been used elsewhere in East European democratic transitions, dating to that of the Solidarity union in Poland led by Lech Walesa (see "Polish Union Opens Convention").

A general strike, which aims to bring all economic activity to a standstill, is one of the most potent noncooperation methods in the inventory of nonviolent civil resistance, but it cannot be used repeatedly without losing its impact. Given the extensive training of Otpor organizers and a decade-long struggle that had been under way, the Serbs unquestionably understood the potency of such an economic shutdown. In Erlanger's words "Unwilling to accept the alleged vote fraud, Mr. Kostunica and the opposition have announced a series of rolling rallies and a general strike, . . . to convince Mr. Milosevic to concede a first-round defeat. It is a risky strategy, despite the confusion in the ruling coalition and divisions between its two partners, Mr. Milosevic's Socialists and the Yugoslav United Left headed by [Milošević's] wife, Mirjana Markovic." In Vojvodina, Erlanger reports, Miodrag Isakov, a local opposition leader, thought the handwriting was on the wall: "The people around Mr. Milosevic and Mrs. Markovic have had problems telling them that he lost the election . . . first, we need his admission of our victory." To do that, opposition leaders said, the citizens of Serbia had to organize. Erlanger explains the beginnings: 150 employees of the local Novi Sad television station protested the resignation of the state channel's chief after he did not give equal time to the opposition, and six news editors lost their jobs when they pledged equal time to the opposition. Petar Petrovic, sacked as chief news editor of Novi Sad television, told Erlanger that the concept of a general strike was insufficient, yet if the roads and cities were blocked, Milošević would receive a clear message.

Protests erupted across Serbia. A countrywide strike began in the Kolubara mines, in a sense the electrical engine of the country, forty miles south of Belgrade. The mine produced the coal for possibly half of Serbia's electricity. Koštunica visited the mines and was greeted as "President." Erlanger, on October 4, 2000, reports from what he calls "the coal-black heart of Serbia's revolt against Slobodan Milosevic," where "miners in overalls milled nervously around their idle machinery," and where they showed "solidarity, anxiety and contempt for Mr. Milosevic's effort to cling to power." The 4,500 workers of the Kolubara coal mines went on a spontaneous strike, Erlanger notes. He reports one miner saying to his fellow workers, " 'No one can make us work. . . . I'm calling on you to stay here no matter what the pressure. The army and police can make us leave if they dare, but they can't force people to go to work for them." Another said, "We either stay here four more days or four more years," the term of the Yugoslav president; "It's really a very simple choice." Erlanger's account quotes Ranko Radasinovic, an electrical engineer, explaining that everyone at Kolubara recognized the importance of the strike: "Everything starts from here, and here it should be finished. If Milosevic wins there is no future for anyone but to leave the country." According to Erlanger, the workers said they had removed important parts from essential machines to prevent officials from bringing in Serbian strikebreakers from Kosovo to run the mine. "It would take us three days to get working again," one miner said, but "It would take them 15 days" ("Striking Serbian Coal Miners Maintain Solidarity").

Inspired by the Kolubara miners, a range of civil-society groups organized a nationwide strike for October 2. Otpor, along with labor organizations, newly elected opposition government leaders, and various nongovernmental organizations shut down facilities, from industrial plants to garbage pick-ups. Students left classrooms in school boycotts, actors and artists went on strike, rolling strikes were organized, demonstrations took place at dispersed locations, roads were blockaded, and in Belgrade the newly elected mayor called a citywide general strike. Actions were organized by groups whose work ranged from the environment, human rights, and economic development to women's activism.

The Times' coverage of Serbia's nonviolent transition from dictatorship to democracy reveals glimpses of an important development: the police and security forces began to side with the nonviolent challengers. As early as December 4, 1996, Chris Hedges reports that the Zajedno (Together) coalition's leaders explicitly invited the country's police and army to participate in the daily protests ("Screws Tightened on Serbian Opposition"). Hedges writes that the police did not intervene as students sprayed the parliament building with detergent—symbolizing the need to cleanse the government. Erlanger writes on October 6, 2000, that "the Belgrade police did not take serious action against the protesters and many joined them" ("Showdown in Yugoslavia: The Overview; Yugoslavs Claim Belgrade for New Leader"). And in Tim Judah's article of September 26: "The riot police deployed in the center of Belgrade to head off potential clashes between supporters and opponents of Mr. Milosevic ended up chatting with the people who were chanting" (see "The Crumbling of the Milosevic Fortress"). Judah's reporting corroborates a property of collective nonviolent action: the technique has the ability to sow dissent within the camp of the target group and sometimes to split its ranks. This capacity is not shared by the introduction of violence or military measures, which instead tend to unite the supporters of the adversary or consolidate the target group.

"October 5 Overthrow," or "Bulldozer Revolution"

After twelve years of dictatorship, the Milošević regime fell in a mere twenty-four hours. On October 5, 2000, the protests reached their climax, as several hundred thousand demonstrators from across the country arrived in Belgrade. The national media broadcasting center (RTS) was taken over and renamed Novi RTS (New RTS). Milošević was again called upon to resign. Throngs marched on the parliament building, as neither fires nor tear gas could hold back the crowds. Koštunica restrained the multitude from storming Milošević's residence by urging the assembled people, "Answer their violence with nonviolence. Answer their lies with the truth." According to Erlanger on October 6, "the Belgrade police did not take serious action against the protesters and many joined them" ("Showdown in Yugoslavia: The Overview; Yugoslavs Claim Belgrade for New Leader"). News accounts noted that police units stood by and observed as demonstrators blocked roadways, a Belgrade police battalion that reportedly turned in its riot gear, and some local police who flatly disobeyed orders to remove the opposition's roadblocks. Two days later, Milošević announced his resignation.

As Erlanger summarizes for *The Times* on April 2, 2001, "Milosevic is widely considered to be the main protagonist behind the wars that broke apart Yugoslavia in the 1990's infighting between Serbs, Croats and Muslims that left some 200,000 people dead" (see "After the Arrest: Wider Debate about the Role of Milosevic, and of Serbia").

Vojislav Koštunica became president on October 7, 2000, and Milošević was arrested in April 2001. In the words of *The Times,* "It was a strange end to the former president's long rule, nearly six months after his defeat at the polls and his resignation as a result of a popular uprising in October. He had continued to live in the official presidential residence and to carry on as leader of the Socialist Party." Steven Erlanger and Carlotta Gall write, "The main charges against Mr. Milosevic concerned financial misdealings, causing damage to the Serbian economy and bringing instability to the country during the period of hyperinflation in the early 1990's" ("The Milosevic Surrender: The Overview; Milosevic Arrest Came with Pledge for a Fair Trial"). Milošević's arrest came "only after protracted and sometimes dangerous negotiations at his residence during which he was assured that he would get a fair trial and that his arrest was not a pretext for transfer to The Hague." Yet his trial for war crimes began there on February 12, 2002. Milošević insisted upon defending himself. The trial was never resolved, however, because Milošević died of a heart attack in his cell in early 2006.

Milošević's fall began the future of Serbia as a democratic republic. From 2003 to 2006, the State Union of Serbia and Montenegro held sway as the legal successor to the Federal Republic of Yugoslavia. The secession of Montenegro in 2006 led to the formation of the new Republic of Serbia. In early 2008, Kosovo declared independence, continuing the tradition of the Balkans' peoples to assert their self-governance and self-reliance.

Conclusion

The impetus for the Serbian people to jettison their dictatorial regime was not war, economic crises, or international factors, but ballot-box fraud in a national election. Voters mobilized in record numbers in late 2000 to bring, in the words of Vojislav Koštunica, "dawn to Serbia." When the ballot box was not enough, Otpor and other groups led a nationwide mobilization to force the government of Slobodan Milošević to step down. A conflict-ridden country, historically at the boiling point, overcame disunity and created an avenue for self-determination through nonviolent means, without destroying its basic constitutional system.

In May 1999, during the Kosovo War, Milošević was indicted by the UN's International Criminal Tribunal for the

Former Yugoslavia, for crimes against humanity in Kosovo. He died in prison at The Hague (see "After the Arrest: Wider Debate about the Role of Milošević, and of Serbia").

Kosovo affirmed independent statehood in February 2008, along the lines of a plan put forward by Martti Ahtisaari, a former president of Finland, UN official, and Nobel laureate.

The world community, particularly the United States, had disregarded a decade of exemplary and widespread nonviolent civil resistance by the Kosovo Albanians. This included the organizing of hundreds of alternative institutions (schools and clinics) in response to Milošević's policy of "Serbianization" of Kosovo. *The Times* acknowledged the saliency of this endeavor in a December 23, 1996, editorial: "An Albanian terrorist group began attacks . . . , but the vast majority of the Albanians have chosen nonviolence" ("Serbia's Apartheid Victims"). As the guerrilla fighters of the rebel force referred to by *The Times*, the KLA, in April 1996 began violent assaults against Serbian targets in Kosovo, Milošević's Serbian security forces cracked down on Kosovo's ethnic Albanian majority, some of whom had decided to support the diasporan KLA.

For seventy-eight days, NATO bombed Serbia and Montenegro to drive the Serbian armed units out of Kosovo. UN Security Council Resolution 1244 was passed as the Serbian army withdrew from Kosovo, establishing the United Nations mission in Kosovo as the sole government authority in the province. Some experts believe that the bombing campaign prolonged Milošević's stay in power, as the Serbs, who had grown disenchanted with his leadership, rallied sympathetically to his side. The bombing penalized Serbs collectively, lessening the possibilities for cordial coexistence in Kosovo.

In the end, Kosovo's leadership pledged to execute the Ahtisaari plan in full, which includes accepting international supervision and providing decentralized authority and rights and privileges to the Serb and other minority communities. The plan assumes concurrence by all parties. Serbia, backed by Russia at the United Nations, has nevertheless refused to allow the loss of what it deems to be its possession. The United States and most European countries have recognized Kosovo's independence, although a few EU members remain reluctant, either because of ties with Serbia or fear of separatist movements within their own nation-states. With a need for consensual decision making in the context of the United Nations, field missions are obliged to act neutrally on status issues, thereby fettering their own usefulness and exasperating Kosovo Albanians who seek respect for Kosovo's independence.

Protests Follow Government's Refusal to Honor Election Results

Serbian political leader Slobodan Milošević rose to power in the Socialist Federal Republic of Yugoslavia in 1989 by promoting a plan for a "Greater Serbia." Milošević exploited the strong pride that Serbians feel for their heritage and history to assert his claim. Within Yugoslavia, Milošević quickly engineered greater power and influence for the Serbian coalitions. His political maneuverings led, in part, to the breakup of the Balkans, as Bosnia, Croatia, Macedonia, and Slovenia all sought independence. In 1992, Milošević united the provinces of Serbia and Montenegro under the new government of the Federal Republic of Yugoslavia.

Milošević harbored regional ambitions for his hoped-for Greater Serbia. Seeking territory historically occupied by Serbia, he involved himself in the Croatian-Bosnian war from 1992 to 1995 and promoted the cause of the Serbs at home, to the detriment of the ethnic Albanians in Kosovo. Yet Serbia was crumbling. International sanctions imposed in the mid-1990s had led to a degenerating economy, while heavy state control of the news media and printing presses kept a restless public in the dark. Milošević's plan for a prosperous Greater Serbia never came to pass. Although the Federal Republic of Yugoslavia was nominally a democracy, Milošević and his governing Socialist Party controlled most of the media, the national government, and almost all cities and municipalities.

In November 1996, coherent signs of popular resistance to Milošević began to show. In local elections, the opposition Zajedno coalition won victories in fourteen of the nineteen largest cities in Serbia. Milošević annulled the election results.

Various sectors around the country and worldwide responded sharply. As *The New York Times* reporter Chris Hedges writes in the article below, the Serbian Orthodox Church, in which 85 percent of the country's population was active, issued strong denouncements of the government (see **Serbia, Introduction**). A commission from the Organization for Security and Cooperation in Europe called upon Milošević to accept his party's electoral defeats. Five Supreme Court justices in Serbia lodged their disapproval.

Since November 19, protestors had been demonstrating daily in cities across Serbia. Student groups were the first to organize, but civic groups such as Women in Black gathered countrywide opposition. The protests were disciplined and nonviolent. "Both policemen and demonstrators were peaceful," said Bojan Aleksov, an organizer for Women in Black, as "people tried to make friends with policemen" (Balkan Peace Team 1997).

After Milošević nullified the election results, he found himself isolated, even within his own ranks. Daily street rallies in Belgrade and elsewhere, along with pressure from foreign diplomats, exerted sufficient pressure that Milošević reversed the voided elections and honored the results. Over a period of three months in winter 1996–1997, with daily demonstrations persisting in Serbian cities, student leaders also began working through institutionalized political channels and meeting with government officials. Avenues outside the established political institutions were wedged open, as Zajedno set up an alternative opposition government in January 1997. When the regime eventually accepted the results of the local elections, it permitted the opposition movement to gain footholds in more than a dozen regional parliaments. Although Milošević still held substantial power, after a cumulative eighty-eight days of demonstrations, the government conceded further ground to Zajedno, as the democratic opposition to the Milošević regime continued to make strides.

JANUARY 6, 1997
LITERALLY FILLING THE STREETS, SERBIAN DEMONSTRATORS GIVE NEW MEANING TO POLITICAL GRIDLOCK
By Chris Hedges

Belgrade, Serbia, Jan. 5 – Tens of thousands of anti-Government demonstrators defied a police ban on street marches by paralyzing the capital with snaking parades of cars and throngs of gleeful supporters who crowded between vehicles.

The ear-splitting din of horns, whistles, bells, firecrackers, clanking pots and pans and pulsating car alarms resounded through the streets. Traffic police, helpless against the onslaught, watched passively. And the thousands of riot police deployed in the city, who on Dec. 24 used force to stop the protests, remained out of sight.

"It's a great day," said Vladimir Marjanovic, a 27-year-old student who had piled into a small Fiat with three friends and was stalled in the snarl of traffic. "We have taken back the streets."

The opposition's decision to defy the ban, however, has only increased the tension in the seven-week battle with the Socialist Government of President Slobodan Milosevic. And the daily protests, organized after the Government annulled election victories by the opposition Zajedno coalition in 14 of Serbia's 19 largest cities, seem set to broaden, as opposition leaders began talking of other forms of resistance.

"We are the ones who will now impose sanctions on the regime," an opposition leader, Zoran Djindjic, told some 100,000 supporters gathered in the Square of the Republic. "We will drive them out. Let them get used to a Serbia that is shut down. Our next move will be to refuse to pay our electricity bills and our television bills. Let them cut off our electricity."

Opposition leaders urged supporters to block roads throughout the country in three or four days if the Government did not honor the results of the Nov. 17 elections.

"All roads will be jammed, for a few days, until we liberate Serbia," said another opposition leader, Vuk Draskovic, to roars of approval.

Many motorists had decorated their cars with bunches of dried leaves and balloons for the Orthodox Christmas on Tuesday. In the center of the city, where traffic was at a standstill, many drivers had lifted their cars' hoods and stood smoking and chatting. Several cars were cranked up on jacks, and when a bus bumped into the back of a small Yugo the raucous crowd began to taunt two uniformed police for failing to file an accident report.

"Investigate! Investigate! Investigate!" the demonstrators chanted in good humor.

Ana Marjanovic, 25, a political science student, leaned out the window of her motionless car to watch five men in front of her slowly push a vehicle through the traffic as if it had broken down. A light, cold rain had matted down the hair of the men and left large drops on her black leather jacket.

"The regime has to realize that we just won't stop," she said. "People want change too badly. Everything, from the economy to the repression, stinks."

The Zajedno coalition, which says that President Milosevic still hopes he can use force to get the protesters off the streets, called again today on the security police not to suppress the protests.

The appeal followed public denouncements of the Government's handling of the election by leaders of the Serbian Orthodox Church and reports of splits within Mr. Milosevic's governing Socialist party.

Late last month, the Organization for Security and Cooperation in Europe issued a report concluding that the opposition had won control of 14 key cities, including Belgrade. Western governments, including Washington, have called on Mr. Milosevic to accept the report's recommendations.

The Government, in a response to the report on Friday, conceded that Zajedno had won a few of the smaller cities, but insisted that the Government either had control, or there was no clear majority, in most of the disputed cities.

Use of Force Against Serbia Imminent

Serbia often had been a flashpoint of conflict, and within Serbia the province of Kosovo became the heart of struggle between Serbians and ethnic Albanians. Kosovo in 1999 had only 10 percent ethnic Serbs, but Serbians considered this southernmost province of the Yugoslav federation an integral part of their culture and identity.

The 1974 Yugoslav constitution under Marshal Tito had declared Kosovo an autonomous province within Yugoslavia, a decision that pleased neither the Kosovo Albanians, because it did not grant independence, nor the Serbs, because it offered Kosovo autonomy. When he became president of Yugoslavia in 1989, Milošević stripped Kosovo of its regional autonomy and sought to use the province to pursue his dream of Greater Serbia. By annulling Kosovo's constitutional guarantees, Milošević enflamed Serb-Albanian tensions. Along with Milošević's policy of "Serbianization" came serious human rights abuses; 127,000 Kosovo Albanians lost their jobs. From the late 1980s, reports were heard of Serbian violence against ethnic Albanians, and Serbs often talked about Albanian persecution of the ethnic Serbian minority.

Throughout the 1980s, as Yugoslavia began to fracture, Kosovo Albanians had been calling for their own independence. Kosovo's population was then approximately 2 million, of whom 90 percent were Muslim ethnic Albanians in the province they called "Kosova." Led by an Albanian pragmatist, Ibrahim Rugova, they rejected the regime's monopolistic state structures and planned to organize their own institutions to parallel the state structures. Virtually the entire society in Kosovo was engaged in alternative institutions by the early 1990s, and in 1991, ethnic Albanian leaders declared Kosovo's independence. When Serbia retaliated by cutting off funds to pay public employees, consistent with the "Serbianization" policy, Kosovo Albanians were ready to set up their own schools and clinics.

Milošević insisted that Kosovo was integral to Serbia. Acute conflict continued in the province, although it did not compare to the deadly strife in the nearby Bosnian war. In May 1992, separate elections were held in Kosovo, as eleven fractious political parties put aside their chronic disagreements and formed the Democratic League of Kosovo (DLK). Operating by consensus, within months, 700,000—nearly the entire voting-age population of Kosovo Albanians—had joined the DLK. Rugova was overwhelmingly elected as the first president of Kosovo and of the DLK.

In the aftermath of the 1995 Dayton Agreement, violence escalated in Kosovo. The Kosovo Albanians, who were determined to bring about change through nonviolent action, had not been invited to participate in the 1995 Dayton talks that settled the conflict between Bosnia and Croatia. In April 1996, the Kosovo Liberation Army (KLA), an ethnic Albanian rebel military group made up of volunteers from the Albanian diaspora elsewhere in the world, returned and began to attack Serb targets in Kosovo. Milošević sent army reinforcements in response (see **Serbia, Introduction**).

The benefits of Kosovo's nonviolent civil resistance movement dissipated as the KLA provided a pretext for retaliation by the Serbian forces. The meticulous program of nonviolent action and parallel institutions by the Kosovo Albanians failed against the repression of the regime, even as Croatia and Bosnia won their independence. In addition, many ethnic Albanians in Kosovo believed that provoking Serbian violence against them was the way to get NATO and the European Union to rescue them from Serbian supremacy. In a sense they succeeded. As the KLA negated a decade of one of the most disciplined examples of massive nonviolent resistance in the contemporary era, massive repression of the nonviolent movement followed.

Part of Milošević's retaliation was therefore justified—the KLA was attacking specifically Serb targets within the province of Kosovo. Yet, as the international community began to recognize that Milošević's actions there constituted ethnic cleansing, bordering on genocide, it responded. Jane Perlez reports for *The Times* on March 24, 1999, that Serbian military police were setting fire to homes of Albanians indiscriminately and killing Albanian civilians. In October, before NATO began the bombing Perlez describes, U.S. ambassador and diplomatic envoy Richard Holbrooke negotiated a ceasefire agreement. The Kosovo Albanians accepted; Milošević refused the terms of the agreement.

NATO involvement in the region came about primarily because of the reports of genocide and ethnic cleansing. As *The Times* correspondent reports, President Clinton said in defense of the attacks, "If President Milošević is not willing to make peace, we are willing to limit his ability to make war on the Kosovo Albanians." Limiting "his ability to make war" consisted of attacking strategic targets in the south of Serbia.

In the end, Milošević's actions in Kosovo, according to a report of the United Nations quoted in *The Times* article, resulted in more than 450,000 Albanian refugees being displaced from their homes. Other *Times* reports put the figure higher. An article dated April 1, 1999, says nearly 600,000 persons were displaced from their homes, with 150,000 leaving the country entirely ("The Kosovo Refugee Emergency"). After eleven weeks of NATO bombing, however, most of the Albanian refugees came home, and more than 100,000 Serbs—half the province's Serb population—fled. Another casualty of the NATO bombings was the nonviolent movement in Kosovo.

NATO's seventy-eight-day bombing campaign to drive Serbian forces out of Kosovo stepped up the domestic and international pressures on Milošević. The gathering of intelligence associated with the military action showed that Serbian troops in the region had committed serious atrocities and human rights abuses—murder, mutilation, and rape—against the Albanians. Javier Solana, NATO secretary-general, is quoted in *The Times*, "We must stop an authoritarian regime from repressing its people in Europe at the end of the 20th century. We have a moral duty to do so. The responsibility is on our shoulders and we will fulfill it." The military action and economic sanctions also hurt Milošević domestically: the damage resulting from war and the economic downturn caused by the sanctions increased unrest across the population. On June 11, 1999, Serbian forces withdrew from Kosovo. As the military operations ended, domestic opposition to Milošević ratcheted up.

MARCH 24, 1999
CONFLICT IN THE BALKANS: THE OVERVIEW; NATO AUTHORIZES BOMB STRIKES; PRIMAKOV IN AIR, SKIPS U.S. VISIT
Forces at Ready
Officials Say the Raids on Targets in Serbia May Start Tonight
By JANE PERLEZ

Washington, March 23 – NATO today authorized air strikes against Serbia as President Clinton declared that force was necessary to halt the aggression by Serbs against ethnic Albanians in Kosovo.

The air campaign, using primarily American aircraft and cruise missiles, is poised to begin over southern Serbia and targets in Kosovo under cover of night Wednesday, NATO officials said.

It would come almost a year after the conflict in Kosovo began and more than six months after NATO, backed by the Clinton Administration, first threatened the use of force.

In his first full explanation of why the Administration had decided NATO should strike, Mr. Clinton said in a speech to a union group here today, "If President Milosevic is not willing to make peace, we are willing to limit his ability to make war on the Kosovars."

Echoing concerns in the Pentagon about the possible loss of pilots as they attack the air-defense systems of the Yugoslav Army, Mr. Clinton said: "I want to level with you. This is like any other military action. There are risks in it."

But Mr. Clinton said that not acting against Slobodan Milosevic, the Yugoslav President, would "discredit" NATO by showing that "we didn't keep our word."

Because of the near certainty of air strikes, the Russian Prime Minister, Yevgeny M. Primakov, ordered his aircraft turned around over the Atlantic Ocean as it was heading for Washington and postponed a planned three-day visit to the United States.

Russia, which adamantly opposes NATO air strikes, had made clear that Mr. Primakov would take it as a slap in the face if Serbia, a traditional (if frayed) ally of Russia, was attacked during the Prime Minister's visit. Russia also said it would ask for a Security Council meeting if NATO attacks.

But President Clinton recalled this century's world wars to argue for military action. "What if someone had listened to Winston Churchill and stood up to Adolf Hitler earlier?" he asked. "How many people's lives might have been saved? And how many American lives might have been saved?"

The President also referred to the four-year war in Bosnia. "We learned that if you don't stand up to brutality and the killing of innocent people, you invite the people who do it to do more of it," he said.

As the allies' plans accelerated, Mr. Milosevic's forces in Kosovo continued to set fire to homes, sending ethnic Albanians fleeing into the countryside. Serbian artillery took aim at villages in the central Drenica region, the heartland of the guerrillas of the Kosovo Liberation Army.

More than 40 members of Congress met with President Clinton at the White House this morning, and after hearing his arguments for intervention, rallied around him. The Senate voted tonight 58 to 41 in support of a one-sentence resolution authorizing President Clinton to carry out bombing and missile attacks.

"History will judge us harshly if we do not take action to stop this rolling genocide," said Senator Chuck Hagel, Republican of Nebraska.

The authorization of the air strikes by the NATO Secretary General, Javier Solana, occurred at his headquarters in Brussels tonight after Mr. Clinton's envoy, Richard C. Holbrooke, failed to persuade Mr. Milosevic to agree to a cease-fire in Kosovo that would pave the way for talks on a peace settlement that the Albanians have already agreed to.

Mr. Holbrooke, who has negotiated many times with Mr. Milosevic, talked with the Yugoslav leader for about six hours in Belgrade. An American officer, Lieut. Gen. Edward G. Anderson 3d, who accompanied Mr. Holbrooke, spelled out to Mr. Milosevic that NATO was planning a heavy air campaign that would crush his forces.

But while Mr. Holbrooke was trying to induce Mr. Milosevic to take a path of peace, the Serbian parliament, apparently under orders from the authoritarian leader, railed today against foreign forces in Kosovo.

After the collapse of what Clinton Administration officials called a "last chance" for Mr. Milosevic, a subdued Mr. Holbrooke flew to Brussels, where he briefed Mr. Solana. Afterward, Mr. Solana gave the order to NATO's Supreme Commander, Gen. Wesley K. Clark, to proceed with an air campaign. The Secretary General called Mr. Holbrooke a "great diplomat" but said his organization was taking over.

"We must stop an authoritarian regime from repressing its people in Europe at the end of the 20th century," Mr. Solana said. "We have a moral duty to do so. The responsibility is on our shoulders and we will fulfill it."

The planned air attacks would come after a series of diplomatic efforts by the Clinton Administration in the last six months.

The previous October, after the massacre of more than 20 ethnic Albanian civilians by Serbian forces, Mr. Holbrooke persuaded Mr. Milosevic to agree to a cease-fire in Kosovo, accept more than 1,000 unarmed monitors on Serbian soil and reduce the number of Yugoslav Army troops and special police units in the province, which has a 90 percent ethnic Albanian majority. But within two months Mr. Milosevic violated the agreement by increasing the number of troops and unleashing them against Albanian civilians and guerrillas.

After more than 40 civilians were killed in January at Racak, Secretary of State Madeleine K. Albright orchestrated a diplomatic effort that culminated in peace talks near Paris. But while the Albanians, including the Kosovo Liberation Army, signed an agreement that gave Kosovo autonomy rather than the independence they were seeking, Mr. Milosevic treated the talks with contempt. The talks, which resumed March 15, collapsed on Friday.

When Mr. Holbrooke presented the settlement to Mr. Milosevic on Monday and argued that it would benefit Yugoslavia because it called for the disarming of the guerrillas, Mr. Milosevic was equally dismissive.

As the last diplomatic efforts gave way to preparations for military action, Mr. Milosevic's forces in Kosovo showed no sign of letting up in their effort to wipe out the guerrillas.

The Serbian offensive, which intensified on Saturday as the international monitors pulled out, rolled on today, said relief agency officials in Kosovo.

The United Nations High Commissioner for Refugees said that 25,000 ethnic Albanians had been forced to flee their homes since Friday and that another 85,000 had become refugees since the peace talks opened last month in Rambouillet, near Paris. In all, there are a total of 460,000 ethnic Albanian refugees, the United Nations agency said.

For the first time since NATO has threatened force, the State Department said that it was suspending all activities at the American Embassy in Belgrade and that the remaining core staff, including the charge d'affaires, Richard Miles, would leave on Wednesday morning. Other Western embassies, concerned about being targets of Serbian anger, said they were also closing down.

As NATO geared up for the final showdown on Wednesday night, Administration officials and diplomats in Brussels said they saw only a remote chance that

Mr. Milosevic would back down. "For Milosevic to change his mind—I'd say that's very remote," an official said in Brussels.

Both NATO and Pentagon planners said the air campaign would be directed at Yugoslav military bases, lines of communication, fuel supplies and ammunition storage areas. The idea is to crimp the ability of the Serbian police units and Yugoslav soldiers to wage war in Kosovo.

After a briefing by the Pentagon today, Senator Joseph I. Lieberman, Democrat of Connecticut, said, "Unfortunately it's going to be a devastating series of attacks."

Describing how the air attack would unfold, an official in Brussels said that once the air defense systems had been destroyed and supply sites and radar attacked, mobile missiles would be tracked down. "If they concentrate in one place, we smash them; if they move, we find them," said the official. In this way, Mr. Milosevic's ground force would be "left without protection."

The risks to everyone—civilians on the ground and the pilots in the air—are much higher than in the desert warfare that the Pentagon has waged against Iraq, planners said.

Attacking the fairly sophisticated air-defense systems of the Yugoslav Army was also less inviting in another respect. "There won't be the impressive hits of a desert war and there may not only be misses but also collateral damage," a NATO official said, referring to unintended damage and casualties.

There was also some nervousness about whether air power would be enough to persuade Mr. Milosevic to give up. "What do we do then?" asked a Pentagon official, repeating a concern expressed last week at a congressional hearing by Gen. Charles C. Krulak, Commandant of the Marine Corps.

European diplomats said today that there is mounting concern about the need for prolonged attacks against Mr. Milosevic's forces. This could provoke further killings of ethnic Albanians by Serbian forces and retaliation by ethnic Albanians against Serbs, said a European diplomat about to leave Belgrade.

"If pictures emerge from Kosovo of a slaughter, then there will be a lot of pressure for the intervention of ground troops," the diplomat said.

But NATO officials said there were no plans for intervening with roughly 10,000 NATO soldiers who have been stationed in neighboring Macedonia for possible use as a peacekeeping force. "Nobody is putting together an invasion force, it has never been part of the discussion," said an Administration official.

For some diplomats and officials at NATO headquarters in Brussels, where General Clark has made no secret of his judgment that an air campaign against Mr. Milosevic was justified long ago, the mood this evening was almost jubilant.

"It's accelerating and exhilarating," said one.

Opposition Groups Disagree on Milošević Ouster

The disputed municipal elections of autumn 1996, which were followed by almost three months of massive street demonstrations, showed that opposition to Milošević was possible and that he could be forced to bend to the popular will (see "Literally Filling the Streets, Serbian Demonstrators Give New Meaning to Political Gridlock"). After the bombings that began in Kosovo in March 1999, with NATO occupying forces deployed in Serbia, and the economic downturn resulting from international third-party sanctions, the domestic ire and discontent with the Milošević regime grew dramatically. Yet, as *Times* reporter Steven Erlanger writes on August 21, 1999, the groups working in opposition to Milošević had a difficult time coming together to mount a successful national campaign of civil resistance (see "Rally Against Milosevic Fails to Bind Opposition Parties").

After the NATO occupation of Serbia, Milošević called for new national elections. Erlanger's dispatch illustrates the principal political cleavages in the opposition parties. Vuk Draskovic of the Alliance Party agreed with Milošević's call for new elections and urged a fair contest with international observers present. In response, Zoran Djindijic, the democratically elected mayor of Belgrade under the Zajedno (Together) Party, protested.

The opposition parties may have been fragmented and riven by personality clashes, but they were united in their condemnation of the Milošević regime. They were able to convene tens of thousands of people at a rally where Djindijic, according to *The Times,* made the terms clear: "There are two sides in Serbia today—the regime and the people . . . everyone will soon have to take a side." Still, the internal dissensions were made clear at the rally: Draskovic was booed lustily by the crowd when he endorsed the call for early elections.

The election debate was merely one element of a full-throated Serbian dialogue on ridding themselves of Milošević. Within the fractious opposition, arguments raged about both strategy and tactics. Should the people attempt to oust Milošević with massive street protests? With elections? With armed force? As *The Times* reports, one Alliance leader, a former general, was skeptical: "Only with a well-organized, even military-style action can we remove this regime."

The Zajedno demonstrations in winter 1996–1997 served as a harbinger of the larger mobilization to come. Citizens began organizing en masse, including the student organization Otpor! (Resistance!). Based at the University of Belgrade, Otpor was set up in 1996 to protest restrictive Serbian laws that limited free speech and academic freedom at universities and in the news media. On December 17, 1998, Otpor launched its first action—a march from Belgrade to Novi Sad, Serbia's second largest city. One of Otpor's founders, Srdja Popovic (see **Key Player in Serbia**), said that their ambition was "to change the political consciousness of the Serbian populace." Of Otpor, Roger Cohen writes:

> . . . [A]fter NATO's 1999 bombing, . . . it was not the capital that toppled Milosevic, for all the stirring images of the federal Parliament in flames on October 5 [2000]. Rather, his overthrow came through a provincial uprising stirred in large measure by Serbian youth acting through a grass-roots movement called Otpor ("Resistance"). The provinces and the young turned on Milosevic with a venom that the dithering, protest-by-news-conference political dilettantes of the capital could never muster ("Who Really Brought Down Milosevic?").

Political scientist Anika Locke Binnendjik and international relations analyst Ivan Marovic note that Serbian organizers consciously

> reflected on the failed anti-Milosevic protests in 1996–1997, which had ended with a whimper and impressed upon them the difficulty of sustaining a long-term popular presence in the streets. . . . In light of these [and other] failures, Serbian Otpor strategists concluded that two objectives would need to guide their future planning. The first was to rapidly draw at least one million protesters to Belgrade in order to confront Milosevic. The second was to ensure that [an] order to shoot would not be followed by Serbian security forces. As they pursued these goals, Otpor decided, they would place a priority on the maintenance of nonviolence discipline within their ranks (Binnendjik and Marovic 2006, 412–413).

Otpor mounted its organized national resistance based on three demands: "free and fair elections in Serbia, a free university, and guarantees for independent media." Afraid that the authoritarian government would quickly shut it down, Otpor established a decentralized leadership structure. Cohen, in the same article, explains the approach, quoting an early member, Jovan Ratkovic: "The idea was, cut off one Otpor head, and another 15 heads would instantly appear." Civic associations across Serbia began to mobilize political opposition.

In addition, Otpor shared knowledge from writings of nonviolent practitioners and distributed literature across the country. Starting in 1998, Otpor developed a "user manual" with six different training programs about the technique of nonviolent civil resistance, which was printed in late 1999. Otpor trained more than 400 organizers in nonviolent methods with the user manual, which relied upon *The Politics of Nonviolent Action* (Sharp 1973). Otpor also trained more than 1,000 activists in forty-two cities of Serbia in nonviolent action, through mass weekend training programs in December 1999 and January 2000.

After the NATO bombings began in Kosovo in March 1999, Otpor publicly stated that Milošević had to go. As Erlanger's report in *The Times* shows, the student activists urged passers-by not to "give a dinar" for reconstruction efforts, as the government was urging, but to give it for further protests to urge Milošević's resignation. Otpor staged a mock birthday party for Milošević in conjunction with a rally calling for elections and the regime's ouster in Belgrade. Officials termed the rally a "failure," alleging that it had only attracted 25,000 participants, although other witnesses reported 100,000. Otpor's "party" turned Milošević propaganda into a call for his removal, as demonstrators lit candles on an enormous cardboard cake and ostentatiously made a wish that he resign. Otpor eventually grew into a broad civic association across the country, becoming a national force for uniting the splintered opposition, whose fragmentation is disclosed by this article.

KEY PLAYER IN SERBIA
Zoran Djindjic (1952–2003)

Zoran Djindjic was the first democratically elected mayor of Belgrade since World War II and later was elected prime minister of Serbia. He was a founder of the Serbian Democratic Party and worked to unify the splintered democratic opposition into an effective coalition.

Djindjic was born in Bosanski Samac, Bosnia, Yugoslavia. He was graduated from Belgrade University with a degree in philosophy in 1974. As a student he became a well-regarded opponent of the communist government and was even imprisoned for forming an independent student organization. He went to Germany to study and received his doctorate in philosophy from the University of Konstanz, in Baden-Württemberg in 1979. His academic supervisor was the philosopher and sociologist Jürgen Habermas.

In 1989, he became one of the founders of the moderate nationalist Serbian Democratic Party with Vojislav Koštunica. He served as president of the executive board in 1990, and became president of the party in 1994.

In 1996, Djindjic became the first democratically elected mayor of Belgrade since the middle of the twentieth century. When Slobodan Milošević ignored opposition victories in local elections, Djindjic and others organized three months of daily protest rallies in Belgrade and elsewhere. After eighty-eight days of major street protests, they succeeded and Milošević relented, confirming their wins. Djindjic's coalition collapsed, and he was voted out of the mayoral office in September 1997.

After a brutal war in Kosovo was ended with NATO airstrikes in 1999, Milošević lost his bid for reelection but refused to step down. Djindjic and Koštunica were among the politicians who joined in organizing huge demonstrations to drive Milošević from power. With Milošević gone, however, they were left with a flagging economy and organized crime resultant from Milošević's security system. Members of the deposed dictator's secret police were sufficiently disillusioned with their leader to ally themselves with Djindjic to bring down Milošević, but they were not entirely aligned with the new government. Milošević's arrest led to a rift between Djindjic and Koštunica, who had become president, and it deepened when Djindjic helped to orchestrate Milošević's trial at The Hague for war crimes.

Djindjic was elected prime minister of Serbia in 2001, in Serbia's first fully democratic election. He faced a divided government with representatives from eighteen political parties.

In 2002, he received the Polak Award in Prague, given for contributions to democratic and economic reforms in Central and Eastern Europe.

In 2003, while in office as prime minister, he survived an assassination attempt when his car was run down by another vehicle, only to be shot and killed outside his office less than a month later. He was fifty years old and left behind his wife, Ruzica, and two young children.

Twelve men were convicted for the assassination; the mastermind was the ringleader of an organized crime group in Serbia.

AUGUST 21, 1999
RALLY AGAINST MILOSEVIC FAILS TO BIND OPPOSITION PARTIES
By STEVEN ERLANGER

Belgrade, Serbia, Aug. 20 – While opposition politicians spoke with pleasure today about the size and passion of Thursday night's rally against President Slobodan Milosevic, they continued to disagree on how best to harness that energy effectively.

But all seemed to agree that a period of reflection was in order, and that they needed more time to agree on the best way to oust Mr. Milosevic, who showed no signs of volunteering to resign.

Vuk Draskovic, the leader of the largest opposition party, the Serbian Renewal Movement, insisted that the only way forward would be to schedule early elections in November under fair conditions and with international observers, conditions that would have to be negotiated with Mr. Milosevic.

But the leaders of the Alliance for Change, in particular Zoran Djindjic of the Democracy Party, were explicit in calling for more street protests to force Mr. Milosevic's resignation, and were ambiguous at best about early elections, saying the only way a fair election could be held was if Mr. Milosevic resigned first.

"There are two sides in Serbia today—the regime and the people," Mr. Djindjic said at a news conference today. "Everybody will soon have to take a side." But Mr. Djindjic also seemed to pull back from the 15-day deadline he announced at the rally Thursday night for Mr. Milosevic to resign or face such protests.

Vladan Batic, the coordinator of the Alliance, said, "The citizens of Serbia want the removal of Slobodan Milosevic, and they do not want compromise or any deal with the Government." Mr. Batic said the group will wait for another rally in Belgrade on Sept. 21 before organizing street protests and a general strike.

But at the same news conference, another member of the Alliance, Vuk Obradovic of the Social Democracy Party, a former general, warned that street protests could prove to be a dangerous route. "Only with a well-organized, even military-style action can we remove this regime," he said.

Leaders of the Serbian Orthodox Church will try next week to get all the opposition leaders to agree on a single platform, but that will be a difficult task.

A key Draskovic aide said that after the rally, the divisions between his party and the Alliance are "worse than before." He said he was surprised by the crowd's desire to force Mr. Milosevic to leave office without elections or a transitional government, but he said he doubted, based on polling information, that the rally was representative of Serbia as a whole.

The crowd booed Mr. Draskovic when he urged early elections, and some called him a traitor. Mr. Draskovic had harmed himself by first refusing to speak at the rally, and then crashing it to speak anyway.

"Djindjic says that Milosevic must go in 15 days, but after 15 days he will still be there, and Djindjic can't force him to go," said the Draskovic aide. "We agree he should go. But how, no one knows. Not him, and not us."

The only answer, Mr. Draskovic insists, lies in early elections, much as Mr. Milosevic's aides have been suggesting. But Alliance officials, with less support among the voters, say Mr. Milosevic is only buying time with the idea of fresh elections, which he will manipulate through state propaganda and fraud. They say Mr. Draskovic is simply playing Mr. Milosevic's game, seduced or pressured by power.

"I don't know what Draskovic is thinking," a key Alliance official said. "He must know that Milosevic is close to the end."

But aides to Mr. Draskovic say that is not self-evident, and that the exodus of Serbs from Kosovo under NATO rule allows Mr. Milosevic to claim that he was right to try to fight for Kosovo and that the opposition is only furthering NATO's efforts to finish the war by ousting him.

The state-run news media called the rally a failure and a disappointment to its organizers, claiming that only 25,000 people attended. Other estimates had ranged from 50,000 to more than 100,000.

Mr. Djindjic was conciliatory about Mr. Draskovic's sudden decision to speak at the rally. But he said: "We are hoping that after this rally all those who thought they could make a deal with Milosevic have realized they were wrong. The people understand that."

But in Nis today, a monument to the icon of Mr. Draskovic's party, Draza Mihajlovic, the monarchist World War II guerrilla leader, was destroyed. Mr. Draskovic told Reuters that the Democratic Party was responsible for the incident, but that he would not retaliate.

"There will be no conflicts with the Democratic Party," he said. "They have made us give up on having any relations with them."

Today was Mr. Milosevic's 58th birthday, and student members of the Otpor, or Resistance movement, staged a mock party for him in Belgrade. They sang to him, lit candles on a huge cardboard cake and made a wish that he resign.

In a spoof of a Government plea to "give a dinar" to reconstruction efforts after the war, the students asked passers-by on a main pedestrian shopping area to "give a dinar for resignation." They said those dinars—not foreign funds—would pay for future protests.

The cake was sliced into nine pieces, representing parts of the former Yugoslavia lost by Mr. Milosevic in his 10 years in power.

• •

OTPOR ASSERTS ITSELF AS LEAD OPPOSITION GROUP

In the year following the 1999 NATO bombings and occupation, organized resistance to Milošević ramped up, and the regime crackdown escalated in response. On May 22, 2000, Steven Erlanger traces Otpor's development from a small student resistance group to one of the largest organizations in opposition to Milošević (see "Student Group Emerges as Major Milosevic Foe"). The student movement had arisen alongside the Zajedno coalition of political parties' elections in autumn 1996. The staying power of the massive demonstrations by tens of thousands of people had shown that opposition to Milošević was possible. It had applied sufficient pressure to force him to yield, but not ousted him (see "Literally Filling the Streets, Serbian Demonstrators Give New Meaning to Political Gridlock").

Otpor emerged from the remnants of the Zajedno student mobilization. It was founded on October 10, 1998, by half a dozen "survivors" at the University of Belgrade, as documented by Roger Cohen ("Who Really Brought Down Milosevic?"). It set its sights on what Anika Locke Binnendjik and Ivan Marovic, a founding member of Otpor, call "blatant election fraud," which would provide a "high-profile rallying point around which . . . to mobilize large numbers of citizens." At the core of its strategy would be exposure and the "challenging [of] fraudulent election results" (Binnendjik and Marovic 2006, 413).

Otpor was one of the principal organizations disseminating translated materials on nonviolent resistance, and it provided a coherent voice to opposition groups by training activists in numerous cities of Serbia in nonviolent action (see "Rally against Milosevic Fails to Bind Opposition Parties"). Most significant, Otpor established a policy of nonviolent struggle as the primary means for achieving Serbia's transition. The Zajedno demonstrations, although attention-grabbing, were short-lived. Otpor's goal was to create civic networks of sustained, nonviolent civil resistance across the country that would endure for more than one set of protests.

On February 17, 2000, Otpor, now eighty chapters strong, held its formal founding congress. From seventy cities across Serbia, 1,000 representatives participated in the congress (Paulson 2005). The study of nonviolent strategic action continued into the spring with instruction from Robert L. Helvey, a retired U.S. Army colonel, who dissected for Otpor the Milošević regime's "pillars of support," the police, the army, the news media, and the leader's capacity to give orders and be obeyed. The nonviolent revolutions that brought about democratic transitions in former Soviet states, including Poland's Solidarity movement (see "Strikers in Poland Defy Gierek Appeal") and movements elsewhere in the Eastern bloc and Baltic States (see "Estonia Nationalists Begin to Challenge Moscow Dominance"), had been self-generating and dependent on their own resources (see **Baltics, Introduction**). By the late 1990s, as *The Times* reports, however, aid had started to flow from a number of Western pro-democracy organizations. U.S. and European funds greatly expanded Otpor's reach and facilitated the training of its members.

The scale of Otpor could not be ignored. From its original status as a student movement, Otpor quickly gained the attention of established political leaders. Dobrica Cosic, formerly Yugoslavia's president, according to Erlanger's article in *The Times,* walked into an Otpor office and filled out a membership form. Cohen notes Otpor's advantages:

> Its flat organization would frustrate the regime's attempts to pick a target to hit or compromise; its commitment to enduring arrests and even police violence tended to shame the long-squabbling Serbian opposition parties into uniting; it looked more effective in breaking fear than any other group; it had a clear agenda of ousting Milosevic and making Serbia a "normal" European state; and it had the means to sway parents while getting out the critical vote of young people ("Who Really Brought Down Milosevic?").

In contrast to the KLA's guerrilla military tactics, which unleashed the murderous ethnic cleansing and near genocidal reprisals of the Milošević regime in Kosovo (see **Serbia, Introduction**), Otpor's collective nonviolent action distinguished it. "We're kind of like a marketing agency," one Otpor leader said, "promoting one idea, the idea of resistance as a habit of mind, a way of standing up in dignity. To me, dignity is very similar to resistance." As Erlanger's dispatch to *The Times* shows, Otpor provoked and mocked the regime's authorities with regular "happenings" and witty slogans, such as "Bite the system." In only three months, the network was producing almost daily demonstrations, had put up 400,000 posters, and distributed 2 million pamphlets, fliers, and badges throughout Serbia.

One of Otpor's organizer founders, Srdja Popovic (see **Key Player in Serbia**), comments on the often hip and goofy veneer to Otpor's methods:

> The nonviolent strategy implemented during the first summer days under conditions of virtually complete repression was three-pronged. First, *fear control* training started.... Activists had no doubts that the police would arrest them, and, accordingly, they received detailed instructions about what to do when arrested. Second, *humor* increasingly became a feature in actions. On a strategic level, this emphasis on humor in otherwise moribund, kitsch and propaganda-saturated public space proved farsighted. Actions became silly and benign. Their lighthearted content made the inevitable arrests of activists all the more senseless—arresting neighborhood kids for clowning around on the streets because of their "subversive, terrorist actions" simply made no sense to any normal parent or grandparent. Lastly, a renewed emphasis was placed on *unity and solidarity*. Arrests, beatings, and confiscation made this an absolute necessity: in more that 500 instances, persistent and massive protests occurred in front of police stations while they interned activists inside. The activists saw that not only their movement support[ed] them, more importantly, they saw—as did their captors—that their community support[ed] them (Popovic 2001a).

Erlanger's account for *The Times* appeared just as the Milošević regime began to crack down on Otpor. Realizing that they were losing the war of public opinion, in mid-May the government accused Otpor of planting bombs across the country. The Milošević establishment attempted to paint Otpor as a terrorist organization, detaining, as *The Times* reports, more than 200 members of the group in the week leading up to this article. The regime sensed the danger to its power in Otpor's ideas, but with Otpor organizers maintaining scrupulously nonviolent discipline, the authorities found it difficult to fight the group. The government took control of the main opposition television station, shut two independent radio stations, and began to detain prominent opposition leaders and activists. Nevertheless, the call for elections continued. Otpor, now bigger and more popular than any political party, was adamant in appealing for unity in its public statements (Paulson 2005). By the end of 2000, Otpor was believed to have 70,000 members in 130 branches.

Otpor served as a staging group for many different ideas of the opposition's eighteen political parties. Several opposition leaders who had fought amongst themselves would be united at Otpor rallies, yet Otpor also remained critical of those in the opposition who remained outside the fray, such as Vuk Draskovic, whom the students criticized for remaining in Montenegro during major political actions.

Some cite the economic downturn in Serbia as the reason for the establishment of Otpor and the rise in civic participation among youth. As Erlanger notes, "These students feel they have no future, no employment. They can't travel and work. So they are fighting for their own future, which is also the future of the country." Recalling that Milošević's repressive actions and murderous policies had provoked the international third-party economic sanctions and the restrictions on travel and employment, Otpor and the rest of the opposition unambiguously judged that Milošević had to go.

Erlanger's article anticipates the crackdown of the regime on the demonstrators. Shortly after the article was published, hundreds more demonstrators were arrested, and the government continued labeling the organization a violent extremist group. By late May 2000, Otpor was nearly forced underground.

KEY PLAYER IN SERBIA
Srdja Popovic (1973–)

Srdja Popovic is a founding member of a student organization dedicated to bringing about social and political change through nonviolent collective action.

Popovic was born in Belgrade and studied biology at the University of Belgrade. His family included famous Serbian journalists. His father was the first war correspondent from the former Yugoslavia to be wounded on the battlefield, in Beirut in 1978.

Popovic was a founding member of Otpor! (Resistance!), the nonviolent youth movement that led the successful effort to oust President Slobodan Milošević. The average age of Otpor members was twenty-one years, Popovic said in an interview on "Fresh Air" (National Public Radio) in 2002. Popovic was in charge of campaigns, human resources, and ideology, and served as the national director of the "He's finished" campaign. He specialized in the targeted communications that are essential in nonviolent struggles. Additionally, Popovic founded "Greenfist," the environmental branch of Otpor. He was arrested by the Milošević regime on December 15, 1999, soon after the NATO bombings began, and suffered beatings while in detention. He was released following public protests and interventions by Amnesty International and the UN Commission for Human Rights.

He subsequently became a member of the Democratic Party of Zoran Djindjic and sought to unite partisan political sectors with Serbian civil society organizations.

According to Popovic, the ambition of the national student movement epitomized by Otpor was "to change the political consciousness of the Serbian populace." Roger Cohen, writing in *The New York Times* Sunday magazine on November 26, 2000, describes Popovic: "Lean and trenchant, Srdja calls himself—half jokingly—the 'ideological commissar' of Otpor. He combines a Leninist intensity with the skills of a Washington lobbyist. (His favorite word is 'networking.') It was he who coordinated the training of Otpor's 70,000 members in 130 branches ("Who Really Brought Down Milosevic?")." Popovic and Otpor are featured in the 2002 York/Zimmerman documentary film *Bringing Down a Dictator* that aired on the U.S. Public Broadcasting Service.

Since 1992, Popovic has been a member of Serbia's Democratic Party, led by Prime Minister Zoran Djindjic. (Djindjic was assassinated in 2003.) Popovic served as the executive secretary of the Democratic Youth (1993), party president (1994/1995), and as a member of the DP National Committee from 1993 to 2000. From 2001 to 2003, he served as a special adviser to Prime Minister Djindjic on environmental issues.

In 1996, Popovic became the youngest elected member of the Belgrade City Assembly and member of the Municipal Assembly of Vracar. He was reelected to these two positions in September 2000 and served in office until 2004.

In late 2000, he was elected to the Serb Republic's parliament, the Serbian National Assembly, and served in that body until 2004.

In 2004, Popovic co-founded the Centre for Applied Nonviolent Action and Strategies (CANVAS), based in Belgrade, a network of trainers and consultants that include technical advisers from countries such as Serbia, Georgia, Ukraine, and South Africa where civil resistance helped to produce effective political transformations. CANVAS consultants gained experience in developing successful action strategies for building democracy in their own countries. The network is currently at work with more than two dozen independent groups in different parts of the world. It has helped to prepare activists who were

(Continued)

(Continued)

involved in developing nonviolent strategies in Africa, Georgia, the Maldives, and Iran (see www.canvasopedia.org/).

In recent years, Popovic has been a leader in Serbia's environmental movement. He acts as a national focal point for sustainable development with the UN Division for Sustainable Development, which provides leadership within the United Nations system on sustainable development, in connection with the UN Commission on Sustainable Development. He is president of the first Serbian environmental fund, ECOTOPIA (see www.ecotopia.rs).

MAY 22, 2000
STUDENT GROUP EMERGES AS MAJOR MILOSEVIC FOE
By STEVEN ERLANGER

Belgrade, Serbia, May 21 – A student movement demanding sweeping political change is surging in popularity and is now a significant target for attack by the government of the Yugoslav president, Slobodan Milosevic.

The movement, called Otpor, or Resistance, has given fresh energy, insouciance and an arrogant innocence to Mr. Milosevic's political opposition. Otpor has not been shy about criticizing opposition leaders for their lack of unity and credibility.

Loosely organized and without a clear leadership structure that could be subject to arrest, Otpor is intended to be difficult to repress. But it shows few signs of becoming a serious revolutionary organization.

Still, government officials are attacking the group as "fascist hooligans" and "terrorists." The officials are giving strong signals that Otpor will be a prime target of—or at least the pretext for—a sweeping new law on terrorism that could be introduced as early as Monday.

The law, said to be largely based on the emergency measures in force here during NATO's bombing war last year, could provide for detention without charges or limitations, restricting the rights of the accused.

At the moment, people can be detained for questioning for 72 hours without being charged, a measure the police have been using liberally against young Otpor activists all over Serbia.

During the war, the police could detain people on national security grounds for up to 60 days without trial, and the police were given the right to search people or property without warrants. The law under consideration would also authorize the police to confiscate all firearms, registered or not.

If passed in such a form, the law would create an informal state of emergency. It could be used against opposition politicians and also against independent journalists, whom the government accuses of working for NATO and the "enemies of the state."

Otpor spokesmen say more than 200 of their members have been detained in the last week throughout Serbia. They are often arrested at home in the early hours, questioned by the police for up to a day or more, threatened and sometimes beaten.

On Saturday another 34 Otpor people and eight opposition politicians were detained, questioned and later released.

"The regime senses the danger, that we don't care a lot about anything else other than taking them down," said Milan Samardzic, 23, a law student with Otpor. "We're not in it for power or money, unlike many of the opposition politicians. We just want change. The idea of resistance itself is very powerful."

Vukasin Petrovic, 23, a political science student and one of Otpor's steadily changing spokesmen, says that about 25,000 people have signed up to become members, and that the organization may be able to call on as many as 50,000 people.

More ask to join every day, Mr. Petrovic says, "and we're getting a little overwhelmed. Things are moving at a very quick pace."

Otpor started as a student response to a restrictive law on universities in October 1998. While many regard it as a movement of arrogant rich youths from nice families, its surge in popularity is a direct result of disappointment with this generation of political leaders, who have failed during the last decade to bring down Mr. Milosevic.

Otpor activists say they want to inspire the population and "guide" the political opposition, as a kind of monitor, to keep them unified.

"The opposition leaders have shown that they are very vain, and that their petty interests are more important to them than our larger interests as a country," Mr. Samardzic said. "We say we've seen through the regime and we're disappointed in the opposition. The opposition leaders don't seem to have a solution, and people don't trust them. But we do deserve the people's trust, at least so far."

During the last large opposition rally in Belgrade, on April 14, an Otpor member was on stage with leaders of political parties and said, "Our task is to secure your victory." He then warned them in vulgar terms: "Gentlemen, this time there will be no betrayal, because whoever betrays now is scum."

At a later rally, on May 15, many leaders including the Democratic Party head, Zoran Djindjic, wore Otpor T-shirts, bearing a fist, though in Mr. Djindjic's case he wore a stylish black sport jacket over it. It was also a gesture of solidarity with two young Otpor activists and a lawyer who had been beaten badly in Mr. Milosevic's hometown, Pozarevac, by bodyguards working for his son, Marko.

The case was important because two local judges and a prosecutor resigned, apparently over pressure from the government to bring charges of attempted murder against the young men, who asserted that they had not begun the fight. One judge who released them quit after they were rearrested.

The government has tried its best to impugn the organization. When Bosko Perosevic, a senior official of Mr. Milosevic's party, was slain in Novi Sad on May 13, the government announced that the 50-year-old killer was an Otpor activist and a supporter of the opposition figure Vuk Draskovic's party, suggesting that both were in the pay of Western intelligence agencies.

Both charges were denied, but the police said they had found Otpor leaflets in the killer's apartment.

"We're kind of like a marketing agency," Mr. Petrovic said, "promoting one idea, the idea of resistance as a habit of mind, a way of standing up in dignity. To me, dignity is very similar to resistance."

Otpor tries to provoke and mock the authorities with sometimes daily happenings and with slogans like "Bite the system." In the last three months, Mr. Samardzic said, Otpor has put up 400,000 posters and handed out two million leaflets and badges throughout Serbia.

Otpor insists that this is paid for solely with donated materials, labor and money from Serbs abroad. But the organization is also getting money and advice from the West through programs to "promote democratization" in Serbia.

After the seizure of the main opposition television station Studio B last week, Mr. Samardzic said he was appalled by the confused reactions of the opposition, especially Mr. Draskovic, the leader of the Serbian Renewal Movement, who remained in Serbia's sister republic, Montenegro, for two days before returning to Belgrade.

"The silence of the opposition has not just been strange, it's been a disaster," Mr. Samardzic said. "People assume Vuk is afraid. Well, so are we all. But he's not selling popcorn"—he is a political leader.

Otpor is proposing a program of civil disobedience, of the kind Gandhi used against the British in India. When he is reminded that the Serbian authorities are not British and behave by different rules, Mr. Samardzic only shrugs.

Milan Milosevic, an analyst for the independent weekly Vreme, who is no relation to the president, said: "Otpor is important because they are a litmus test for popular feeling against the authorities. It is true that they are a judgment on the opposition, but no one sees them as a political alternative. They show no leadership or management. People make the Otpor fist to show the political leaders that they're not serious enough."

One opposition leader, Zarko Korac, a psychologist and university professor who heads the Social Democratic Union, says teachers are accustomed to being criticized by students.

Otpor matters, he says. "They have the energy and the innocence of youth, and they are uncompromising and unyielding," he said, noting that the government of President Suharto in Indonesia had been toppled by student demonstrations.

"These students feel they have no future, no employment," Mr. Korac said. "They can't travel and work. So they are fighting for their own future, which is also the future of the country."

Otpor's symbol, the fist, "is a clear, clean message," he said.

So clean that one of Serbia's most influential writers and briefly Yugoslavia's president, Dobrica Cosic, walked into an Otpor office this month and filled out a membership form. Mr. Cosic, a nationalist picked by Mr. Milosevic and then discarded by him, is blamed by some for helping to create the myth of Serbian sacrifices in Kosovo. A drawing by a noted cartoonist, Corax, showed Mr. Cosic scrubbing himself clean in a bathtub using the skeletal fist of Otpor.

Still, with signs pointing toward an attempted crackdown and even a ban on Otpor, the organization will need whatever help it can get.

Mr. Korac says such a crackdown on Serbia's children, like the seizure of Studio B, has cumulative consequences with the public. "It's like insults in a marriage," he said. "It adds up. It may not show right away on the streets, but it's building. People are very angry."

Opposition Fatalistic about Election Outcomes

In January 2000, as Serbian democrats of all stripes agreed to build a united opposition, the Milošević regime finally gave Serbs the opportunity they sought. *The Times* had been reporting that notable opposition leaders such as Zoran Djindijic and international observers were afraid that Milošević, if he were able to call an election himself, would also be able to control the rules and process to retain his personal power. It appears he did just that. In 2000, Milošević changed the constitution to make his own office directly electable, and in September called an election nine months ahead of the anticipated timeframe in order to throw off his opponents.

Erlanger, on September 10, outlines the electoral choices facing Serbia's voters in terms of game theory (see "Out in Front, Serbia's Opposition Prepares to Lose"). He presents the voting as interplay between election results and the actions of the Milošević regime. As Erlanger notes, the electorate has a choice, but if they throw Milošević out, he "also gets to make a choice: whether to accept the choice of the people if it goes against him, or to manipulate the totals and declare victory regardless." Should Milošević do *that,* Erlanger continues, the people of Serbia "will have another chance to choose, but not in the voting booths": will they "accept Mr. Milošević's choice, or will they come out onto the streets to defend their own choices."

As Vojislav Zanetic—a marketing consultant, playwright, and newspaper columnist—put it: "This is a pseudo-democracy, in which the opposition is complicit. It's a kind of society that must fall apart slowly—it can't be ripped apart in one day, in one election. We don't have a political crisis here or even an economic one—we have a systemic crisis, a crisis of society and political will." Observers within and outside of Serbia prepared for the possibility that Milošević, even if he lost the elections, would declare himself the winner. Erlanger recognized that a rigged landslide was a distinct possibility, grasping that replacing the Milošević regime would be a combination of ballot-box participation and civil engagement outside the institutionalized elections.

Groups rallied to the cause of fighting electoral fraud with creative protests, noncooperation, and civil disobedience. Otpor took a leading role in the presidential campaign, shouting in response to Milošević: "Gotov Je!" (He's finished!). Otpor distributed sixty tons of literature and began strategies focused both on persuasion and get-out-the-vote, particularly among under-mobilized young people.

Although the opposition in Serbia had been split in the past, when it came time for the election members of the opposition aligned themselves behind Vojislav Koštunica as their presidential candidate (see "Rally Against Milosevic Fails to Bind Opposition Parties"). Koštunica had been the leader of the small Democratic Party of Serbia and enjoyed nominal name recognition. Public opinion polling showed that his freshness and restrained nationalism made him a model opposition candidate, and support solidified behind him. The eighteen challenging political parties found a way to unite. Even so, Koštunica admits in *The Times* that the democratic opposition was discouraged. According to the opposition leader, "people are fatalistic about the way they see these elections." Many of his own supporters in the polls, Koštunica said, "believe that Milošević will win."

SEPTEMBER 10, 2000
OUT IN FRONT, SERBIA'S OPPOSITION PREPARES TO LOSE
By STEVEN ERLANGER

Belgrade, Serbia – Democracy is about choice, but in the Yugoslav version, which is now playing itself out with Slobodan Milosevic's future at stake, there are likely to be more choices than usual.

Mr. Milosevic, Yugoslavia's president, changed the Constitution to make his office subject to direct election, and he has now called a vote nine months earlier than he had to. So on Sept. 24, Yugoslavs will vote for a federal president, Parliament and municipal officials in an election that will appear like most others, with voters getting to choose between the incumbent and his party, and an array of challengers.

But as election day approaches, a strong opposition candidate is doing better than Mr. Milosevic in the opinion polls, and this points up the piquancy of Yugoslavia's system. Mr. Milosevic also gets to make a choice: whether to accept the choice of the people if it goes against him, or to manipulate the totals and declare victory regardless.

And then the people will have another chance to choose, but not in the voting booths: will they accept Mr. Milosevic's choice, or will they come out onto the streets to defend their own choices, possibly against the arrayed power of the police and even the army.

This is a political netherworld, in which the forms and substance of both democracy and authoritarianism are clearly visible. In an instructive way, they live side by side here, and both have their limits, depending on the stakes. But with Mr. Milosevic's own hat in the ring the hopes of long-divided opposition leaders are coming up hard against their cynicism. This is, after all, a system that Mr. Milosevic, a master technician, has manipulated when necessary for the last 12 years.

"This is a kind of authoritarianism that needs a form of democratic legitimation from time to time," said Vojislav Zanetic, a marketing consultant, playwright and columnist.

"This is a pseudo-democracy, in which the opposition is complicit," he said. "It's a kind of society that must fall apart slowly—it can't be ripped apart in one day, in one election. We don't have a political crisis here or even an economic one—we have a systemic crisis, a crisis of society and political will."

It is a form of parallel political universe. There is a campaign, with speeches and tours and open meetings. There are billboards and opinion polls and marketing experts. There are monitors ready to examine the voting and counting procedures, and Web sites devoted to the election and the campaign.

And even though the state media, especially television, are thoroughly and aggressively in the hands of Mr. Milosevic, there is a lively independent press, including local television and radio, that is both outspoken and combative in the face of government pressure and derision. In general it has lined up dutifully in support of Mr. Milosevic's main rival, Vojislav Kostunica.

Yet among these opponents there is also a resigned conviction that Mr. Milosevic will steal as many votes as he needs to ensure victory in the first round—since he needs an unquestionable victory to achieve his aims of re-legitimation.

And that adds a new quality of edge and risk. "For Milosevic, this election has turned into Russian roulette," one opposition leader said. "But for him to allow a second round would be suicide."

But what of the people of Serbia? Will they defy the regime and defend the opposition or their own choice? Among the opposition, there are deep concerns that the Serbs, atomized and impoverished, will not.

"Frankly I'm not so optimistic," said Vuk Draskovic, the head of the Serbian Renewal Movement, who is living in Montenegro after two attacks on his life. "All of us together are fighting a battle we cannot win. I'm quite sure Milosevic has right now in his pocket the result of the elections. What will happen after 24 September, when the opposition people will face the crackdown on their hopes?"

Even Mr. Kostunica says that "people are fatalistic about the way they see these elections." Many of his own supporters in the polls, he said, "believe that Milosevic will win."

Mr. Kostunica plans to declare victory the night of the election, as his aides presume Mr. Milosevic will. In the case of massive election fraud, he hopes people will come out into the streets the way they did for months after Mr. Milosevic refused to acknowledge opposition victories in the 1996 local elections.

But even Mr. Kostunica is not sure they will.

Natasa Kandic, director of the Humanitarian Law Foundation here and a critic of Mr. Milosevic and Serb actions in Kosovo, said that Mr. Milosevic won't freely cede power even if everyone voted against him.

"What will happen, I don't know," she said. "It is, however, important that we do not sit at home on Sept. 24, but go outside and defend our votes."

But Ms. Kandic is facing troubles of her own; the Yugoslav Army is threatening to bring her to court over articles she wrote criticizing the behavior of Serbian forces in Kosovo. (She has also criticized Albanian attacks on Serbs after the war ended.) The army's threats are part of a skillful effort by the government to intimidate opposition leaders and their supporters, including the student movement, Otpor, or Resistance. The message is clear: the government will react with force, if necessary, against any revolution in the streets.

There are, in addition, mysterious events that create a chill, like the kidnapping two weeks ago of the former Serbian president Ivan Stambolic, who was Mr. Milosevic's mentor.

In a swift party coup, Mr. Milosevic ousted him in 1987. Although there have been rumors—which his wife denies—that Mr. Stambolic was considering a run for the presidency, Mr. Milosevic and the government forcefully deny any role in the disappearance.

These events create an undercurrent of tension quite apart from Mr. Milosevic's political campaign against the opposition, in which he stresses its support for and ties to the United States and the NATO countries who bombed Yugoslavia last year. The other night, for example, a news program on the state television cut from a meeting between Secretary of State Madeleine K. Albright and opposition leaders to a close-up of Mr. Kostunica, who had not attended, then back to the meeting, giving the false impression that he, too, had been at the feet of Dr. Albright.

Mr. Zanetic, the marketing expert, thinks the government is better than the opposition at propaganda and political marketing, understanding that most Serbs get their information from television.

"In politics here, it doesn't matter if you tell the truth or lie—you must be clear," he said.

Which is why, if Mr. Milosevic claims victory, he is also likely to declare a landslide. And then one may better see where the new balance lies between democracy and authoritarianism.

Milosevic Campaigns Against NATO

Milošević's calls for a united "Greater Serbia," which had brought him to power and kept him there for over a decade, peaked in the autumn 2000 election. *Times* reporter Steven Erlanger explains that Milošević, in his first contested election as the leader of Serbia, was running "against NATO and the United States, not against his democratic opposition" (see "Milosevic, Trailing in Polls, Rails Against NATO"). The Serbian dictator was not entirely wrong. Although the people of Serbia had in Vajislav Koštunica a major opposition figure to Milošević, Western governments and NATO also lent a hand to the organized opposition efforts across the country.

Outside forces gave moral support and financial assistance to the opposition. The leaders of the challenging political parties, having unified themselves to fight the regime by nonviolent methods, turned for philosophical inspiration and guidance beyond Serbia. Otpor and the rest of the democratic opposition wanted to ensure two things. First, they wanted the ability to undermine the loyalty of the police and state security forces that were engaged in repression (Binnendjik and Marovic 2006). In reality, this meant that the entire machinery of the nation-state, which seemed so difficult to topple, would be dislodged and unseated one piece at a time. *The Times* had been reporting that in the earlier rallies, citizens and police officers were on friendly terms (see "Rally against Milosevic Fails to Bind

Opposition Parties"). As early as December 4, 1996, *Times* correspondent Chris Hedges reports that police did not intervene when dozens of students sprayed the parliament building with detergent to symbolize the need to cleanse the government ("Screws Tightened on Serbian Opposition"). Second, Otpor wanted to ensure that should state police or security agents ever fire upon the citizens or engage in violent behavior, the opposition had a planned nonviolent response. Having a strong but nonretaliatory rejoinder would leach legitimacy away from the regime and earn sympathy for the challengers (Binnendjik and Marovic 2006). Both of these ideas, according to Binnendjik and Marovic, were derived by the Otpor organizers from study of the writings of Gene Sharp and other theoreticians of nonviolent civil resistance.

Ideas spread, as Western groups and governments provided the lubrication of funding to media outlets, civic associations, and political parties. *The Times* article reports that even before the Kosovo war, "the United States was spending up to $10 million a year to back opposition parties, independent news media and other institutions opposed to Mr. Milosevic." In this campaign, external money funded polling, advertising, and campaign costs for much of the opposition, as Erlanger reports.

The regime-run newspaper, *Politika,* and Milošević attempted to use Western influence as a reason to vote against the opposition. *The Times* reports that Milošević charged organizations such as the Center for Free Democracy, which sought independently to audit the elections, with being a tool of U.S. propaganda, and *Politika* accused the U.S. Central Intelligence Agency of wanting to "colonize and control" Serbia. In the dozen years of his dictatorship, Milošević had used his aspirations for an ethnically pure Greater Serbia to justify his leadership; castigating Western influence in seeking election outcomes was a way for him to make a compelling case once again.

Some of Milošević's accusations were true: the Clinton administration, as Erlanger reports, requested from Congress more than $40 million for "democratization" efforts in Serbia. Moreover, because of the regime's tight controls on television, radio, and newspapers, without external assistance, the Serbian opposition political parties and groups like Otpor would never have been able to present their case to the voters. They needed printing capability for tons of flyers, paint for graffiti, and supplies for distribution of information. The opposition organizers and leaders were themselves wary: Koštunica, in *The Times* article, expresses doubts as to whether U.S. interventions were made with Serbian well-being at heart.

As Zarko Korac, an opposition leader, put it, "These elections are crucial . . . because for the first time Mr. Milosevic will be delegitimized in the eyes of his own people. He was an elected dictator, with popular and legal legitimacy. But from now on he's a true dictator, and he will only be able to rule by force."

With the September 24, 2000, election, the public would make its choice.

Supporters of Serbian opposition leader Zoran Djindjic participate in a protest march in Belgrade on October 17, 1999. Djindjic, who helped bring about the trial of Slobodan Milošević in The Hague, served as Serbia's prime minister from 2001 to 2003, when he was assassinated.

Source: AP Images/Darko Vojinovic

SEPTEMBER 20, 2000
MILOSEVIC, TRAILING IN POLLS, RAILS AGAINST NATO
By STEVEN ERLANGER

Belgrade, Serbia, Sept. 19 – In his race for re-election, President Slobodan Milosevic of Yugoslavia is running against NATO and the United States, not against his democratic opposition.

He is not entirely mistaken to do so. The United States and its European allies have made it clear that they want Mr. Milosevic ousted, and they have spent tens of millions of dollars trying to get it done.

Portraying himself as the defender of Yugoslavia's sovereignty against a hostile, hegemonic West led by Washington, Mr. Milosevic and his government argue that opposition leaders are merely the paid, traitorous tools of enemies who are continuing their war against him by other means. In March 1999, NATO began a 78-day bombing campaign to drive Serbian forces out of Kosovo.

The Yugoslav elections are on Sunday, but there has hardly been a day since the bombing began that state television news has not railed against "NATO aggressors."

With the campaign at its height, the government has spread its attacks to include all opposition political parties, independent newspapers, magazines and electronic media, the student organization known as Otpor—or Resistance—and any nongovernmental organization working to promote democracy, human rights or even economic reforms.

While Mr. Milosevic is trailing the main opposition leader, Vojislav Kostunica, in opinion polls, the anti-Western campaign is having an impact. The money from the West is going to most of the institutions that the government attacks for receiving it—sometimes in direct aid, sometimes in indirect aid like computers and broadcasting equipment, and sometimes in suitcases of cash carried across the border between Yugoslavia and Hungary or Serbia and Montenegro. Most of those organizations and news media could not exist without foreign aid in this society, which is poor and repressive and whose market is distorted by foreign economic sanctions.

Even with foreign aid, government restrictions on newsprint supplies and high and repeated fines after suspiciously quick court cases make it hard for the independent news media to reach their natural market.

As for the opinion polls that show Mr. Kostunica in the lead, the information minister, Goran Matic, charges that the polls are orchestrated and manipulated by the Americans and the Central Intelligence Agency, who help pay for them. According to Mr. Matic, Mr. Milosevic is actually far ahead of Mr. Kostunica, and the polls simply serve as a vehicle for the opposition to claim that the government stole the election once Mr. Milosevic wins.

Mr. Matic asserts that the Atlantic alliance has come up with various scenarios, such as infiltrating soldiers wearing Yugoslav Army and police uniforms, to make it possible for the opposition to start civil unrest in the streets after the election while claiming that the police and the army are actually on their side.

Mr. Matic has attacked various nongovernmental organizations, including the Center for Free Elections and Democracy, which is trying to monitor the fairness of the election, as paid instruments of American and alliance policy. Many such organizations have been raided by the police, who confiscate computer files and also appear to be gathering evidence about foreign payments.

"President Milosevic will win this election," said Ljubisa Ristic, the president of the Yugoslav United Left party, founded by Mr. Milosevic's wife, Mirjana Markovic. "This is not Hollywood." Washington and the West, she said, "are like little kids, wanting something to happen so much they're fooling themselves."

Ms. Ristic said the alliance's war produced a new solidarity among Yugoslavs and "killed many illusions people had about the West and about their own opposition leaders, who went to the countries that were bombing us to seek their support."

The issues, Ms. Ristic said, are clear now. "It's a decisive time," she said. "This is not an election so much as a referendum, a decision on being an independent country or a colony. People see what's happened in Kosovo, what happens when NATO troops enter the country, and they are not going to allow the alliance's hand-picked candidates to win."

Even before the Kosovo war, the United States was spending up to $10 million a year to back opposition parties, independent news media and other institutions opposed to Mr. Milosevic. The war itself cost billions of dollars. This fiscal year, through September, the administration is spending $25 million to support Serbian "democratization," with an unknown amount of money spent covertly to help the failed rallies of last year, which did not bring down Mr. Milosevic, or to influence the current election. For next year, the administration is requesting $41.5 million in open aid to Serbian democratization, though Congress is likely to cut that request.

Independent journalists and broadcasters here have been told by American aid officials "not to worry about how much they're spending now," that plenty more is in the pipeline, said one knowledgeable aid worker. Others in the opposition complain that the Americans are clumsy, sending e-mails from "state.gov"—the State Department's address—summoning people to impolitic meetings with American officials in Budapest, Montenegro or Dubrovnik, Croatia.

But there is little effort to disguise the fact that Western money pays for much of the polling, advertising, printing and other costs of the opposition political campaign—one way, to be sure, to give opposition leaders a better chance to get their message across in a quasi-authoritarian system where television in particular is in the firm hands of the government.

While that spending allows the opposition to be heard more broadly, deepening the opposition to Mr. Milosevic, it also allows the government here to argue that it has real enemies, and that the Serbian opposition is in league with them.

Just today, in the state-run newspaper Politika, a long article used public information from the United States—including Congressional testimony and Web site material—to show that the United States is financing the opposition.

" 'Independent,' 'nongovernmental' and 'democratic' are the standard phrases the C.I.A. uses to describe organizations established all over the world to destroy the governments and the societies that the U.S. government wants to colonize and control," the paper wrote.

The Congressional testimony, from July 29, 1999, cited American officials then involved with Yugoslav policy, like Robert Gelbard and James Pardew, telling Senator Joseph Biden of Delaware about their projects. They describe the creation of a "ring around Serbia" of radio stations broadcasting into Serbia from Bosnia and Montenegro, the spending of $16.5 million in the previous two years to support "democratization in Serbia," and another $20 million to support Montenegro's president, Milo Djukanovic, who broke away from Mr. Milosevic in 1998.

The testimony listed some of the recipients of American aid here, including various newspapers, magazines, news agencies and broadcasters opposed to Mr. Milosevic, as well as various nongovernmental organizations engaged in legal defense and human rights and projects to bring promising Yugoslav journalists to the United States for professional training.

All such projects are portrayed by Politika and state television as a way to undermine the legal government, and the recipients are labeled traitors to their country.

Opposition leaders like Mr. Kostunica regard such tactics by the government as crass propaganda, but even he is skeptical of American intentions in paying for nongovernmental organizations, some of whom, he believes, are even unconsciously working for American imperial goals and not necessarily Serbian values.

Other democratic leaders, like Zoran Djindjic and Zarko Korac, regard such attacks as an indication of Mr. Milosevic's desperation and anxiety on the eve of the first election he is likely to lose in his entire political career. Given the stakes for Mr. Milosevic, they believe that he will do all he can, including the wholesale stealing of votes, to ensure a victory in the first round of voting.

"The stakes are fundamental for Milosevic," Mr. Korac said. "These elections are crucial, not necessarily for the immediate handover of power, but because for the first time Mr. Milosevic will be delegitimized in the eyes of his own people. He was an elected dictator, with popular and legal legitimacy. But from now on he's a true dictator, and he will only be able to rule by force—that's a big step for Serbia."

OPPOSITION BOYCOTTS ELECTION RUNOFF

In the September 24, 2000, election, whether or not Slobodan Milošević stayed in power depended both on his actions and that of the people. If his party lost at the polls and Milošević refused to accept defeat, could he count on the complacency of the people of Serbia to allow him to remain in power?

Fear that the elections would be rigged was widespread. While action groups such as Otpor were leading collective efforts to vote Milošević out, nongovernmental civic organizations such as the Center for Free Elections and Democracy (CeSID) spearheaded efforts to prevent election fraud. CeSID developed a sound statistical methodology and led a research effort that included hundreds of interviews and created a repository of collected data that could unmask systematic election fraud. According to political scientist Michael McFaul:

> Exit polls were illegal in 2000, so CeSID conducted a parallel vote tabulation, a technique now used in many transitional democracies. . . . They posted their representatives at 7,000 polling sites, which allowed them to produce a remarkably sophisticated estimation of the actual vote. On election night, [democratic opposition] officials announced the results of their own parallel vote tabulation, but did so knowing that their results corresponded with CeSID results. CeSID, in other words, provided the legitimacy for the claim of falsification. CeSID's figures also supported Koštunica's claim that he had won more than 50 percent in the first round and therefore did not need to stand in a second round" ("Transitions from Postcommunism" 2005, 10).

CeSID published the results nationwide to encourage further nonviolent action. In one of the most glaring public relations debacles for Milošević, Steven Erlanger reports in *The Times*,

CeSID's director, Slobodanka Nedovic, was handed a ballot already filled in for Milošević. She was not the only one. Erlanger writes: "Some state workers have reported that they expect to be handed such filled-out ballots, with instructions to return the blank ones that they receive at the polling stations to their supervisors on Monday morning" ("Fears Deepen Milosevic Will Rig Vote").

With a high voter turnout in Serbia—perhaps more than 80 percent, including a stunning youth turnout—Milošević was defeated. The people of Serbia chose Vojislav Koštunica, the opposition leader. The outcome was a blow to Milošević, but he was not yet finished.

As Erlanger reports on September 29, Milošević refused to accept the election results, and the opposition announced its intentions to boycott a second round of voting sought by the regime ("Civil Disobedience Is Planned to Try to Force Milosevic Out"). Moreover, the opposition coalition prepared to ask the citizens of Serbia to carry out "any act of civil disobedience they have at their disposal" until Milošević leaves office.

On October 1, Erlanger reports that Milošević called for an October 8 runoff, saying that the opposition had not cracked the 50 percent barrier (see "Yugoslav Opposition Preparing for a Risky Showdown"). Koštunica refused to participate in a runoff, because suspicious vote counts had led many to believe that the first election results had been manipulated. The opposition coalition called for Milošević to resign immediately, as Erlanger writes, to "spare the country." Milošević continued to press for a runoff election and declined to step down, and the opposition coalition persisted in its refusal. The people of Serbia were weary, and simply by refusing to accept the runoff, the opposition hoped, the nightmare would be over. Even so, they were prepared to take the next step and organize a general strike.

The Times article traces the origins of the general strike in Vojvodina, one of the many cities across the country that were organizing to preserve acceptance of the true election results. In Vojvodina, Erlanger reports, Miodrag Isakov, a local opposition leader, saw an omen: "The people around Mr. Milosevic and Mrs. Markovic have had problems telling them that he lost the election . . . first, we need his admission of our victory." In order to do that, the citizens of Serbia, opposition leaders said, had to organize. If the strike held, and the roads were blocked and cities clogged, Milošević would receive an unmistakable message. It was obvious a few days after Milošević's defeat that he would not accept the results, but this time the people of Serbia were not going to be complicit.

OCTOBER 1, 2000
YUGOSLAV OPPOSITION PREPARING FOR A RISKY SHOWDOWN
Rallies, Strike and Boycott of Runoff Are Called in an Effort to Force Milosevic's Hand
By STEVEN ERLANGER

Novi Sad, Serbia, Sept. 30 – Aleksandar Djurkovic's mother, 65, has been tending the flowers on her balcony for nearly two years. On Friday, when high school students marched past her window to a rally against the Yugoslav president, Slobodan Milosevic, she ripped off the blooms and tossed them down, on to their heads.

But Mr. Djurkovic, 36, says he is anxious, unable to sleep. "My girlfriend wept with joy after she heard that Milosevic lost" the presidential election on Sunday to the challenger, Vojislav Kostunica, he said. "But I'm so nervous it will all collapse, that Milosevic, that Bolshevik, will succeed again at buying time and exhausting everyone."

Mr. Kostunica and the 18-party coalition that backs him have vowed not to run in a runoff against Mr. Milosevic on Oct. 8, saying that Mr. Kostunica was elected outright last Sunday, winning more than 50 percent of the vote. He and the opposition say the government manipulated the vote with major fraud to push Mr. Kostunica below the 50 percent margin, although only just.

A boycott of the second round is awkward here in Vojvodina, where voters must vote in a second round for a regional assembly that the opposition has a strong chance to control for the first time since Mr. Milosevic stripped this region of autonomy when he stripped it from Kosovo, too, in 1989. Leaders here need to tell people to vote Oct. 8, but not for the presidency, a mixed message that is likely to be misunderstood.

Unwilling to accept the alleged vote fraud, Mr. Kostunica and the opposition have announced a series of rolling rallies and a general strike, to begin Monday, to convince Mr. Milosevic to concede a first-round defeat. It is a risky strategy, despite the confusion in the ruling coalition and divisions between its two partners, Mr. Milosevic's Socialists and the Yugoslav United Left headed by his wife, Mirjana Markovic.

The opposition's call for people power seems particularly risky this weekend, when Serbs are tending to their own affairs. Mr. Milosevic used the occasion to make his first public appearance since the elections, at a graduation at a military academy. The rallies on Friday in Belgrade and here in Vojvodina were relatively small, feeding Mr. Djurkovic's anxiety.

But Monday will be different, insists Miodrag Isakov, president of the Reformists of Vojvodina, one of the two main opposition parties here. "It's D-Day," he said. "We don't want to drag everything out as we've done in the past, with endless rallies. This time we want to finish it in a blitzkrieg and shut the country down."

The ruling Socialists are anxious, Mr. Isakov said. "I think they're ready to give up, but they're testing us, to see if we're strong enough and if the people are ready to defend their votes and their rights. And I think the people are ready."

The people around Mr. Milosevic and Mrs. Markovic have had problems telling them that he lost the election, Mr. Isakov said. "Now he needs a couple days and some real pressure to get used to it. Of course, he wants to buy himself some time, but his options are very narrow."

What matters to the opposition, Mr. Isakov said, is not that Mr. Milosevic leave the country. "First we need his admission of our victory," he said. "That will change everything." But to secure that, he added, Serbia simply must rise up on Monday.

And if Mr. Milosevic is still sitting firm by Thursday, say? Mr. Isakov laughed nervously. "It's like the joke during the NATO bombing," he said. " 'Clinton: give up now or we're all going to die.' Well, if Milosevic doesn't kill himself by then, then we will all have to kill ourselves."

In Novi Sad, there is real resentment of NATO and its destruction of the only three bridges across the Danube River. The main bridge, the Varadinski Duga, is nearly repaired now, waiting only to be asphalted, and Mr. Milosevic is likely to come here to open it before Oct. 8.

But Vladimir Horowic, a leading member of the Vojvodina Bar Association, says people are offended at the notion that somehow the ruling parties reconstructed the bridges, "and not the people themselves." Mr. Horowic says the street protests on Monday will have to escalate quickly into a blockage of roads and railway traffic, and become a confrontation with Mr. Milosevic's police.

"Really, it has to be over in a few days," he said. "People must move from the squares to the president's palace and install a new one. They can't just sit around the squares and have a rock concert. It can be done with good humor, but the police and the army must see the people in front of them claiming their victory."

But Mr. Horowic's wife, Sanja, also a lawyer, is skeptical. "The opposition doesn't look strong enough in itself and eager to take anything other than Gandhi-like attitudes," she said. "And that's not enough."

Her husband laughed, then said: "I'm absolutely optimistic and any pessimism I have I'm repressing. That's the way every person has to think. People now realize for the first time in this country that a majority of them think the same way."

Petar Petrovic, fired as chief news editor of TV Novi Sad, the state channel here, in 1990, has just been elected as a member of the Novi Sad city government, running on the opposition ticket. "Monday must be D-Day and it must go fast," he said. "Milosevic has been exhausting us for 10 years now, and we can't let him do it again."

The idea of a prolonged general strike is not enough, he said. "The idea of telling people to stop work and drink coffee is funny here. That's all anyone has been doing for 10 years!" But if the roads and cities are blocked, he said, Mr. Milosevic will get the right message.

Mr. Milosevic, though, is less the problem than the system that depends on him, Mr. Petrovic said. "Even if he wants to go, many of them don't want to let him. They need him to survive, especially JUL, his wife's party. Without the couple, they disappear. They're not a political party, but just a business association, a kind of mafia. Without him and her, they lose everything."

On Friday, 150 workers at TV Novi Sad signed a protest letter asking for the resignation of the chief editor, and six news editors were fired when they refused to run the state television news and promised equal time to the opposition. They came to the opposition rally last night here, but they were not allowed to speak.

"We need to welcome those who leave the power now, to encourage others to shift, but not make too much of them, and offend those who were fired 10 years ago," Mr. Isakov said. "It's a delicate balance—until yesterday, these people were busy cheating us."

In America, he was told, the phrase is: the train's leaving the station. "We welcome them on board," he said. "But not in first class."

Slavko Caric, a businessman, says there is a revolution under way. "But the crucial point is that the high-ranking people from the police and the army have to be convinced that the population has reached a critical mass, that all Serbia wants him out and wants him out fast. They know he's lost support, but they must see it."

Striking Miners Defy Police

On October 5, 2000, *Times* reporter Steven Erlanger provides a compelling snapshot of how the massive general strike began in response to Milošević's actions and quickly spread across the country (see "Serbian Strikers, Joined by 20,000, Face Down Police"). For Milošević to fall, the people of Serbia had to demand it. The nationwide strike movement in the first week of October was a mass action of noncooperation that hastened the end of the regime. After the electoral results of September 24, the opposition coalition's candidate, Vojislav Koštunica, toured Serbia, hailing the electoral defeat of Milošević and decrying the regime's call for a runoff.

Erlanger describes a confrontation between striking workers at the Kolubara coal mine, which produced half of Serbia's electricity, and state police urging the workers to go back to their jobs. Workers had been striking since soon after the election. Koštunica himself visited the strike and was greeted with cries of "President!" No matter what Milošević did, Koštunica had already won the election in the minds of the Kolubara coal workers.

As a campaign reverberating with nationalism and symbolism, the Kolubara strike was particularly outstanding. Kolubara was famous in national folklore, *The Times* reports, as the place where the Serbs turned back the Austro-Hungarian army in 1914. The Kolubara workers had been hailed, one worker said, as "heroes" by the Milošević government just months before. "During the NATO war, we worked four shifts, including Sundays. . . . I saw the missiles flying over my head." Now, the government was calling the striking workers traitors for subverting the national interest.

The strategies of nonviolent resistance pursued by the opposition had since 1996 sought to win over police and security services—among the bulwarks of support for Milošević. As early as December 4, 1996, *Times* correspondent Chris Hedges reports that police did not intervene when dozens of students attempted to "cleanse" the government by spraying the parliament building with detergent (see **Serbia, Introduction**; "Screws Tightened on Serbian Opposition").

The Kolubara coal miners' strike had an electrifying effect similar to that evoked by the strike of workers in the Lenin shipyard in Gdańsk, Poland. The strike, which began on August 14, 1980, was the spark that touched off the democratic transitions in the Eastern bloc and former Soviet states (see "Polish Labor Crisis Deepens as Workers List Their Demands"). One miner said, "This is the heart of protest, the heart of Serbia, and we're not leaving until Milošević leaves." The strategic and symbolic importance of Kolubara expressed the national spirit; the strike began the collapse of Milošević.

OCTOBER 5, 2000
SERBIAN STRIKERS, JOINED BY 20,000, FACE DOWN POLICE
Encounter at Coal Mine
Opposition Leader, in a Visit, Says Miners Are Defending the Will of the People
By STEVEN ERLANGER

Kolubara, Serbia, Oct. 4 – If the regime of Slobodan Milosevic breaks and Vojislav Kostunica takes office as Yugoslavia's president, it could be because of what happened at this gritty coal mine here today.

Hundreds of Interior Ministry policemen swooped in to break a protest strike at the Kolubara mine, which produces the coal for half of Serbia's electricity. The police ordered the workers, who have been on strike . . . demanding Mr. Kostunica's inauguration as president, to leave.

But the strikers refused, calling for help. Confronted with up to 20,000 people pouring into the mine to defend the workers, some from as far away as the city of Cacak in central Serbia and Belgrade, the capital, 40 miles to the northeast, the police broke and stood aside.

One police commander said: "I'm fed up with this. After this, I'm throwing my hat away and going home. The police in Serbia are more democratic than you think."

The police watched as Mr. Kostunica himself arrived this evening, pushing through the crowd of miners and their families, to cheers and shouts of "President," coming closer to claiming the prize he says he won with an outright majority in elections on Sept. 24.

"I will be with you until we defend what we won on Sept. 24," Mr. Kostunica said. "Is there anything more honest than the miners of Kolubara rising to defend their votes?"

Some miners began to chant, some to cry. "I'm telling you, what you are doing here is not subversion," Mr. Kostunica shouted, his voice breaking up over the primitive sound system set up beside him on the steps of a single-story wooden office building. "You are defending the people's will, and those who step on the people's will and try to steal their votes are the ones committing subversion."

Mr. Kostunica has accused the government of stealing votes and faking the election results. He is appealing to Mr. Milosevic to recognize his defeat and step down to spare the country. The opposition is planning a huge rally in Belgrade . . . , which it hopes will be decisive and push Mr. Milosevic out.

. . . [T]he Serbian government issued a stern warning to the organizers of this spreading strike, saying that they would be arrested for action that "threatens citizens' lives, disrupts normal functioning of traffic, prevents normal work of industry, schools, institutions and health facilities."

The government has accused the strikers here of subverting the national interest, and early Tuesday morning sent the country's top general, Gen. Nebojsa Pavkovic, to tell the workers to go back to work or face punishment. Blaming the miners, the government began power cuts all over Serbia on Tuesday, a reminder of last year's NATO bombing war over Kosovo. And a judge issued a warrant for the arrest of 11 strike leaders, plus two opposition politicians.

But the police failed to make the arrests today. Miners asserted they had behaved correctly and, said Dragan Micandinovic, an electrical engineer, with "a sense of shame." Mr. Micandinovic has remained here for three days except for two brief visits home to see his children.

"During the NATO war, we worked four shifts, including Sundays, and the government called us heroes," he said bitterly. "I was here and saw the missiles flying over my head. Now the government calls us enemies."

"But we are victims," he said. "Their victims."

Slavoljub Sajic, a mechanical engineer, said, "This is the heart of the protest, the heart of Serbia, and we're not leaving until Milosevic leaves."

The police hung back while Mr. Kostunica spoke, but did not immediately withdraw from the office buildings and other facilities they had occupied earlier in the day. Tonight, workers were negotiating with them about whether they would withdraw altogether, but expressed confidence that the police could not get the mine going again.

The police, in camouflage uniforms and riot gear, with helmets and batons, arrived about 11 a.m. when only about 100 workers were gathered.

"They came from all directions," Mr. Micandinovic said. "They threatened us and told us to leave or they would drag us out. It was very risky."

"There are a lot of people here now," he said. "But it was pretty risky this morning."

The police set up a cordon around the mine with roadblocks and moved into offices, talking with a strike committee and the management, who are supporting the workers.

But Mr. Micandinovic and others began to telephone opposition politicians in nearby Lazarevac, 30 miles south of Belgrade, and independent Radio Lazarevac spread the news. Relatives, workers and ordinary people began to come toward the mine, some dodging the police roadblocks by crossing fields and streams.

By early afternoon about 1,000 people were trapped behind a police roadblock on a bridge just outside the mine itself. Two opposition politicians, Vuk Obradovic, a former general, and Dragoljub Micunovic, negotiated with the police, to no avail.

"This shows the weakness of the regime," Mr. Micunovic said as he stood at the bridge. "They are faking this campaign of an electricity shortage to frighten people and make them suffer and blame it on the opposition."

The Kolubara coal mine is critical, he said. "Copper mines are on strike, too, but people can live without copper, not without electricity."

But the police were clearly unhappy with their orders, Mr. Micunovic said, adding, "Both sides are being very patient."

One young policeman, accepting some water, said quietly, "This is a mess." He stopped, then said, "Don't worry, everything will be all right."

A bus full of protesters moved slowly through the crowd and, almost gently, shoved aside a police van blocking the bridge. The crowd surged forward; the police moved aside, looking sheepish. Some protesters gave them apples and clapped them on their shoulders.

The mood on the long walk from the bridge to the strike headquarters was that of exhilaration, even as opposition leaders sped by in cars and buses. Then more cars moved by, with license plates from Cacak and other towns, full of people who had come to defend the mine. People shouted, "Cacak! Cacak!" and the slogan of the student resistance movement, "Otpor" ("He's finished"). . . .

In 1914, Kolubara was the site of one of the most famous Serbian victories, when the Serbs turned back the Austro-Hungarian Army. The "Kolubarska bitka," or "Kolubara battle," became part of nationalist folklore, and the famous writer and later, briefly, Yugoslav president, Dobrica Cosic, featured it in his novel, "Time of Death."

That part of the novel became a stage play in Belgrade in 1986, as Serbian nationalism was growing. At one point, the Serbs wait for ammunition from the French, but when it arrives it turns out to be the wrong caliber. As the soldiers start to wail and weep, the commander turns to the audience and says, "Don't cry, no one can do anything to us."

On the Kolubara coal field this evening, those words were echoed, unwittingly, by Milanko Bulatovic, a miner here for 26 years, who has been here every day of the strike from 6:30 in the morning until the evening.

"This is the end of him," he said. "This is the beginning of the new Serbia. Milosevic cannot do anything to us now."

● ●

Milošević Regime Falls

In what is now known as the "Bulldozer Revolution," Milošević's reign of a dozen years ended in a single day. *The Times* editorialized on October 6, 2000, that Milošević's control collapsed in ways that Otpor had hoped and planned from the beginning: hundreds of thousands descended upon Belgrade, driving bulldozers and tractors, blocking roads with crammed buses, taking over government buildings, as the police and state security forces "melted away" (see "Liberating Yugoslavia"). The election fallout had been a contest between public defiance and government repression, and the regime backed down first.

In planning for the final overthrow of Milošević, Otpor and the others in the democratic opposition knew that numbers were important. In the first week of October, as general strikes spread across the country, they planned the nationwide march on Belgrade. Otpor sought to paralyze the regime by literally clogging the streets, making any movement impossible, and their regional networks were able to mobilize crowds big enough to gain their objective.

Critical to Otpor's success was maintaining internal discipline. Vigilantly maintaining a strategy of nonviolent resistance, Otpor instructed its more than 70,000 members in 130 branches internally not to fight back against any intended repression (see "Student Group Emerges as Major Milosevic Foe"). *The Times* editorial hails the result: "important elements of the security forces stood aside as the protesters converged on Belgrade yesterday, indicating that their loyalty is to the Serbian people, not Mr. Milošević."

The challengers moved swiftly. They took over government buildings and declared a sea change. They took control of the national media broadcast center (RTS) and renamed it Novi RTS. They called upon Milošević to resign. On October 6, 2000, Erlanger describes how Koštunica addressed the nation by way of the newly "free" station: " 'Good evening, dear liberated Serbia!' " The crowds shouted his name, and he called back: "Big, beautiful Serbia has risen up just so one man, Slobodan Milošević, will leave."

Some in the multitudes set the old parliament building on fire and overwhelmed Milošević's palace. Milošević and his family fled, and by the time the new leader addressed the nation, the old dictator's whereabouts were unknown ("Showdown in Yugoslavia: The Overview; Yugoslavs Claim Belgrade for New Leader").

As *The Times* editorializes, "it is appropriate that Mr. Milošević's downfall is being engineered by his own people, not his many foreign foes." Although the resistance had support and financial assistance from other countries, in the end, it was the self-organized people of Serbia who brought down the regime.

OCTOBER 6, 2000
LIBERATING YUGOSLAVIA

The long tyranny of Slobodan Milosevic was crumbling in Belgrade yesterday. In a tumultuous day reminiscent of the anti-Communist revolutions of 1989, the leading symbols of Yugoslav government power, like the Parliament and the state television station, fell to opposition demonstrators as police resistance melted away. Hundreds of thousands of people took to the streets and, refusing to be intimidated, demanded that the recent election of Vojislav Kostunica as president be respected. Their courage and determination impressed a watching world.

As the day ended, it seemed likely that Mr. Milosevic's tenure as Yugoslavia's leader would soon expire, perhaps in a matter of hours. Unless he can somehow assert command of the army and security forces for a desperate and doubtless bloody defense of his regime, his options will be few, including accepting an orderly transfer of authority to Mr. Kostunica or attempting to flee the country. After yesterday's decisive events, he can no longer count on support from the three main props of his 13-year rule: the security forces, the state-controlled media and the political and business cronies who have profited from his administration. Mr. Milosevic, who was indicted for war crimes by an international tribunal last year, should eventually be brought to trial.

It is appropriate that Mr. Milosevic's downfall is being engineered by his own people, not his many foreign foes. The Clinton administration and other Western governments are right to offer verbal encouragement but otherwise stand aside. President Clinton's promise to lift economic sanctions against Yugoslavia is a tangible incentive for change.

Russia has much to gain, and little to lose, by using its influence in Belgrade to speed Mr. Milosevic from power. President Vladimir Putin should abandon Moscow's neutrality on the outcome of the Yugoslav election and affirm Mr. Kostunica's victory.

Once they firmly gain power, Mr. Kostunica and his allies will confront the challenge of creating a democratic government and free society on the ruins of a collapsed tyranny. In some ways, they will have a simpler task than Belgrade's Central and East European neighbors faced in 1989. Yugoslavia already has a legitimately elected president and Parliament that can now assume legal authority. While a majority of the legislators elected last month ran as Milosevic allies, many may now transfer their loyalties to democratic government.

A crucial step will be to depoliticize the army and police, which have been agents of repression under Mr. Milosevic. Many commanders will have to be removed, and some should be brought to trial for their role in enforcing Mr. Milosevic's brutal policies. Encouragingly, important elements of the security forces stood aside as the protesters converged on Belgrade yesterday, indicating that their loyalty is to the Serbian people, not Mr. Milosevic.

The victory of democracy in Yugoslavia will have significance for all Europe. For nearly a decade, Mr. Milosevic's policies of military aggrandizement and ethnic persecution have blighted the Balkans and embroiled the United Nations and NATO. He brought war and suffering to Croatia, Bosnia and Kosovo, driving hundreds of thousands of people from their homes—including many Serbs after these wars went badly for Belgrade and its allies. Once he has left office, Europe will at last be democratic and whole from the Atlantic to the borders of the former Soviet Union and beyond.

• •

Milošević Arrested

After the throng stormed Belgrade and Vojislav Koštunica assumed power, Slobodan Milošević went into hiding. Serbia had moved on with its newly elected leader and its fledgling government, but the arrest and detainment of Milošević stirred one final national battle about his legacy. The former dictator did not go quietly: as *Times* reporter Steven Erlanger notes in news analysis on April 2, 2001, Milošević threatened suicide before succumbing to authorities on March 31, 2001 (see "After the Arrest: Wider Debate about the Role of Milošević, and of Serbia"). He was initially incarcerated and called before a judge who was investigating a series of financial crimes, but Erlanger notes that Milošević probably would face more serious charges such as conspiracy to murder political opponents. "And, in time," writes Erlanger, "at the end of any vista is Mr. Milosevic's likely transfer to the international war crimes tribunal in The Hague."

Most Serbs, however, appeared merely glad to move on. The well-organized resistance that led to Milošević's downfall did not muster the same energy for his capture and detention. Erlanger writes: "The Serbs who once followed him to battle and who voted against him . . . reacted to his arrest with pleasure, indifference or disgust—but the rallies of supporters that the new government feared did not materialize." Predrag Simic, one of Koštunica's advisers, told *The Times,* with regard to Milošević's arrest, that another task awaited: "an important part of our political process from now on will be how to explain to our own people what happened over the Milosevic years."

Among the main leaders in the opposition was Zoran Djindjic, who had been part of the Zajedno coalition's demonstrations in 1996 and 1997 against the annulment of municipal elections that launched the process that would culminate in Milošević's collapse (see "Literally Filling the Streets, Serbian Demonstrators Give New Meaning to Political Gridlock"). Djindjic had become prime minister, and, as the charges on lesser crimes of corruption, economic misdealing, embezzlement, and promoting instability failed for want of evidence, it fell to Djindjic to arrange for Milošević to be taken to The Hague, Netherlands.

At the International Criminal Tribunal for the former Yugoslavia, Milošević was charged with crimes against humanity, violating the laws or customs of war, breaches of the Geneva Conventions, and genocide for his role in the wars in Croatia, Bosnia, and Kosovo. Milošević died in his cell, apparently of a heart attack, on March 11, 2006, as Marlise Simons and Alison Smale report for *The Times*.

Milošević was the first head of state ever asked to answer for charges of war crimes. During his trial, his former ally, Milan Babic, a leader of the minority Serbs in Croatia and himself accused of war crimes, summed up his legacy, as *The Times* obituary quotes: "You brought shame upon the Serbian people. You brought misfortune on the Croatian people, on the Muslim people" and, Babic argued, "orchestrated the Balkan conflict" ("Slobodan Milosevic, 64, Former Yugoslav Leader Accused of War Crimes, Dies"). Milošević's trial lasted almost four years, but was halted when he died. Although Milošević left Serbia a war-torn, bankrupt country, its self-reliant people reinforced by their own struggle removed him without still more violence or injustice.

APRIL 2, 2001
AFTER THE ARREST: WIDER DEBATE ABOUT THE ROLE OF MILOSEVIC, AND OF SERBIA
By STEVEN ERLANGER

Belgrade, Serbia, April 1 – The arrest of Slobodan Milosevic early today closes one cycle of Balkan history and opens, only now, the possibility of a considered debate in Serbia about his role in the wars that devastated the former Yugoslavia and horrified the world.

Having threatened to kill himself and his family rather than go to prison, Mr. Milosevic went comparatively quietly in the end, his surrender broken only by a few gunshots fired wildly by his anguished daughter, Marija.

For Mr. Milosevic, who is just 59, the future stretches out as a series of courtrooms and jail cells.

Today the man who once called himself "the Ayatollah Khomeini of Serbia" found himself jailed and called up before a judge investigating a series of crimes, initially financial, that will very likely include more serious charges like conspiracy to murder political opponents.

And, in time, at the end of any vista is Mr. Milosevic's likely transfer to the international war crimes tribunal in The Hague, to face charges over his role in the 1999 Kosovo war, with further indictments on Bosnia and Croatia expected to follow.

When and if that happens may depend on constitutional changes in Yugoslavia as well as continued pressure from the United States and other nations, but many here are already considering his transfer an inevitability despite the opposition of Mr. Milosevic's successor, Vojislav Kostunica.

Mr. Milosevic is widely considered to be the main protagonist behind the wars that broke apart Yugoslavia in the 1990's infighting between Serbs, Croats and Muslims that left some 200,000 people dead.

The Serbs who once followed him to battle and who voted against him . . . [on September 24] reacted to his arrest with pleasure, indifference or disgust—but the rallies of supporters that the new government feared did not materialize.

Even Mr. Milosevic's Serbian Socialist Party worked to persuade him to surrender after armed guards at his residence thwarted two arrest attempts at the start of the weekend, the party understanding that it has a future only with Mr. Milosevic gone.

His political career is over. But "the great debate about Milosevic in Serbia, among Serbs, is only about to begin," said Aleksa Djilas, a historian who has studied his career. "This debate will go on for a very long time." He added that "those who think of him as just an obstacle to the future have too rosy an idea of the future," especially in the economy.

"People won't simply blame him for everything," Mr. Djilas said. "I think chances are that in a year people will blame him less than now." Foreign aid will come slowly, he said, the economy will continue to falter in the midst of a global slowdown, and anti-Western sentiment may increase.

Predrag Simic, an adviser to President Kostunica, who defeated Mr. Milosevic in an election last fall, said: "I forsee witch hunts to come, and Milosevic will be loudest in asking for a witch hunt. But that's normal. This country is undergoing a painful transformation. With his arrest, an important part of our political process from now on will be how to explain to our own people what happened over the Milosevic years."

Mr. Milosevic, who is known for long periods of depression and indecision, pleaded innocent to all charges against him today and is expected by those who know him to bounce back and conduct a vigorous defense of himself, his policies and his government. He is expected to argue that he stole nothing for himself and did what he could to keep the country together and running in the face of international sanctions and hostility that were aimed not merely at him but at all Serbs.

His main theme came out in his last published interview, . . . when he said, "I always considered myself to be an ordinary person, whom, at one point in life, historical circumstances placed in a position to devote his whole life to the nation that had everything in jeopardy."

Mr. Milosevic is seen as a fighter with good tactical skills who will try to demolish what is so far a largely circumstantial case against him. "The people putting him on trial," Mr. Djilas said, "are themselves not above reproach, and those who respect the rule of law may not come out the winners."

A public trial even on domestic charges is likely to provide considerable room for embarrassment to many senior officials and politicians, including a number of new democrats who supported or flirted with Mr. Milosevic and Serbian nationalism in the past, like Vuk Draskovic of the Serbian Renewal Movement and Zoran Djindjic, the current Serbian prime minister.

Mr. Kostunica also supported the right of the Bosnian Serbs to independence, but kept his distance from Mr. Milosevic or any paramilitary organization.

A trial in The Hague would most likely implicate or severely embarrass senior and former Yugoslav police and army commanders, like Momcilo Perisic, Mr. Milosevic's former chief of staff and now a Serbian deputy prime minister.

Mr. Milosevic could also have much to say, his aides have suggested, about key figures in the military of other states of the former Yugoslavia—let alone current allies of the West like Milo Djukanovic, the president of Montenegro, and Agim Ceku, a former Croatian general who runs the Kosovo Protection Corps, the civilian face of the supposedly dismantled Kosovo Liberation Army.

The key roles of prominent Serbian intellectuals, journalists and institutions, like the Serbian Academy of Sciences and the Serbian Orthodox Church, in fanning Serbian nationalism may come under new scrutiny. Mr. Milosevic, with longstanding contacts with senior Western politicians and diplomats, is thought likely to be able to embarrass them, too.

"We had both liberal and nationalist options, and to explain why the nationalist, crypto-fascist one prevailed is complicated," Mr. Simic said. "Milosevic took advantage of upheaval and our state of mind, like a rider on a wave. But what happened in Yugoslavia was made possible by the West's reaction to the crisis."

Mr. Milosevic's career is over, Mr. Simic said. "But the failure to deliver on their promises could put the reformers in a precarious situation, and help those who would cry that Milosevic was right, that reforms bring nothing, that he defended Serbian interests." After the arrest, he said, "we now need strong, sensible support in Washington."

Slobodan Spremo, a 33-year-old physics professor buying juice at Belgrade's flea market today, said Mr. Milosevic was never a nationalist, but simply manipulated public opinion to hold on to power. "He and his wife are egomaniacs, and they used people's national feelings," he said. "Yugoslavia would have collapsed without Milosevic, but differently, and we wouldn't have been satanized in the same way."

Ivan Radovanovic, a Serbian journalist and author, said the arrest of Mr. Milosevic, like the death of the Romanian dictator Nicolae Ceausescu, left him with a sense of nausea. "Whenever a dictator gets his punishment, you feel a little sick, because for years and years he was on top and we have some responsibility for that, too," he said.

"For years we were in a kind of war with the world and with ourselves," Mr. Radovanovic said. "And now something is over, we don't know exactly what, but it may allow us a certain peace, I think. And it will help define a path to our future, because the West is where we belong."

Mr. Djilas, who is critical of the Hague tribunal as an essentially political court, also sees important lessons for international behavior that could come out of a war-crimes trial of Mr. Milosevic.

"Some kind of new international order is being constructed, intentionally or not," Mr. Djilas said. "And there will be a blessing in disguise through his trial. Something will crystallize: what kinds of nationalism are justified or not, what kinds of intervention are justified or not, how much are great powers entitled to respond, and how. It will not be a sterile exercise."

• •

MILOŠEVIĆ GAMBLES AND LOSES

"The Serbs went to war," according to journalist Tim Judah, writing elsewhere, "because they were led into it by their leaders. But these leaders drew on the malign threads of their people's history to bind them and pull them into war. . . . [T]he conjunction of historical circumstances, personalities, arrogance and misjudgments . . . led to the war[s], and it is important to keep in mind that the Serbs, as a people, are no different from anyone else in Europe. . . . The Serbs . . . were misled but they were not sheep. Supremely confident of victory, too many were happy to be misled" (Judah 1997, xiii).

In an article written for *The Times* before the final outcome of the Serbian elections of September 24, 2000, was known, Judah asks, "How did Slobodan Milosevic, the arch-tactician who, until now, had gambled and lost everything except his own hold on power, make such a fatal mistake?" (see "The Crumbling of the Milosevic Fortress"). Judah answers his own question and explains how the turnabout occurred, giving Otpor the credit for mobilizing people against the dictator.

Throughout the coverage by *The Times* of Serbia's transition from dictatorship to democracy are occasional glimpses of a critical development: the police and security forces began to side with the nonviolent challengers. On October 6, 2000, Steven Erlanger reports, "the Belgrade police did not take serious action against the protesters and many joined them" ("Showdown in Yugoslavia: The Overview; Yugoslavs Claim Belgrade for New Leader"). Judah's article records "the riot police . . . ended up chatting with the people who were chanting." *The Times*' reports reveal and validate a property of collective nonviolent action—the ability to sow dissent within the camp of the target group and sometimes split its ranks, while the introduction of violence or military measures tends to unite or consolidate the supporters of the adversary or opposition.

SEPTEMBER 26, 2000
THE CRUMBLING OF THE MILOSEVIC FORTRESS
Opinion
By TIM JUDAH

London – As Yugoslavia voted on Sunday, one friend's e-mail message from Belgrade summed it all up: "We're all in election fever, hope and horror at the same time. Wish us luck!" No amount of analysis and informed guesswork could have caught the mood better.

At dawn yesterday, less than 12 hours after the polls had closed, Zarko Korac, my friend and the leader of one of Serbia's opposition parties, sent this: "It is a cold and cloudy morning in Belgrade, but I see some strange light. Whatever happened, Serbia changed."

Of course, it's not over yet. As I write, both the opposition and the forces of Slobodan Milosevic, the Yugoslav president, are claiming victory, though no official results have been announced. But whatever happens next, Serbia is highly unlikely ever to be the same. Mr. Milosevic has suffered a tremendous blow. He may not be out, but he is certainly down.

This was clear already on Sunday night, when the riot police deployed in the center of Belgrade to head off potential clashes between supporters and opponents of Mr. Milosevic ended up chatting with the people who were chanting: "Slobo, kill yourself! Save Serbia!" Only a couple of hundred Milosevic supporters showed up, and, dejected, they went home.

With the opposition saying it has won a landslide in both presidential and local elections, it would seem very hard now for Mr. Milosevic to recapture the genie of democracy that he unwittingly released. Of course his own camp is also declaring victory, but in a muted sort of way. And that is important. With credibility oozing away, the bonds of loyalty loosen.

It is not too late, of course, for Mr. Milosevic to clamp down and send Serbia squarely back on the road to becoming Europe's own pocket Cuba. But with every hour that passes, it becomes more difficult.

How did Slobodan Milosevic, the arch-tactician who, until now, had gambled and lost everything except his own hold on power, make such a fatal mistake? He set the terms of the election. He said: "It's me or NATO!" But the opposition finally managed to unite, and it shrewdly chose a candidate, Vojislav Kostunica, who could not be tarred as a tool of NATO. . . . This turned the tables. The question became: Mr. Milosevic or someone else? And more people than ever before have chosen someone else.

In part this is thanks to the students from the Otpor (Resistance) movement who trudged the highways and byways of Serbia, quietly mobilizing people against their president. Many political commentators in the West dismissed this sort of challenge to Mr. Milosevic, saying dictators are not removed through the ballot box. But that is to misunderstand the nature of Mr. Milosevic and to fall prey to our own Western rhetoric of Serbian tyranny and dictatorship. For Serbs, Mr. Milosevic is an authoritarian ruler, but not a tyrant.

Shooting Albanians or Muslims may be one thing, but Mr. Milosevic has not been shooting young Serbs, at least as of yesterday. Thousands have been detained, beaten and intimidated. Newspapers have been shut down, and one brave journalist, Miroslav Filipovic, is in prison. But there is no Serbian gulag, and there are no mass graves of young Serbs who have raised their voices against Mr. Milosevic. Whatever he does now, and unless he does start shooting people, it is equally unlikely that Otpor and the opposition will give up the struggle until he is gone.

So, what if Mr. Milosevic is indeed on the way out?

First, the issue of independence for Montenegro would fade away, since most Montenegrins are not anti-Yugoslav as much as anti-Milosevic. The question of Kosovo would not, but with Mr. Kostunica at its head, a new Serbia would argue with words, not bullets, that Kosovo belonged to Serbia. That would be bad news for Kosovo's Albanians, who want independence and for whom Mr. Milosevic, an indicted war criminal with whom no one could be expected to talk, has therefore been an asset.

And for Serbia itself, for the heartland? It is now a disaster zone economically and socially, not helped by 78 days of NATO bombing, of course, but a catastrophe primarily of Mr. Milosevic's making. The last 10 years of war, sanctions and isolation have knocked Serbia back to an extraordinary degree. Huge problems remain to be solved, both among the Serbs and between Serbs and their neighbors. But it seems clear that there is reason for hope and that Zarko Korac is right: Something has changed.

Bibliography

Albert Einstein Institution. 2004. "Report on Activities," 15. Available at http://aeinstein.org/organizations/org/2004-04rpt.pdf.

Balkan Peace Team. 1997. "Thousands Take to the Streets." *Nonviolent Activist*. January-February. See http://www.warresisters.org/nva/nva197-1.htm.

Banac, Ivo. 2006. "The Politics of National Homogeneity." In *War and Change in the Balkans*, ed. Brad Blitz. Cambridge: Cambridge University Press.

Binnendijk, Anika Locke, and Ivan Marovic. 2006. "Power and persuasion: Nonviolent strategies to influence state security forces in Serbia (2000) and Ukraine (2004)." *Communist and Post-Communist Studies*, 411–429. September.

Cevallos, Albert. 2001. *Whither the Bulldozer? Nonviolent Revolution and the Transition to Democracy in Serbia*. Special Report No. 72. August 6. United States Institute of Peace. See http://www.usip.org/pubs/specialreports/sr72.html.

Carothers, Thomas. 2001. "Ousting Foreign Strongmen: Lessons from Serbia." Policy Brief no. 5. Washington, D.C.: Carnegie Endowment for International Peace. See http://www.carnegieendowment.org/publications/index.cfm?fa=view&id=705.

Clark, Howard. 2000. *Civil Resistance in Kosovo*, 95–121. London: Pluto Press.

Glenny, Misha. 1999. *The Balkans*. New York: Viking.

Judah, Tim. 1997. *The Serbs: History, Myth and the Destruction of Yugoslavia*. New Haven and London: Yale University Press.

McFaul, Michael. 2005. "Transitions from Postcommunism." *Journal of Democracy* 16 (3): 5–19.

Nenadić, Danijela, and Nenad Belčević. 2009. "Serbia—Nonviolent Struggle for Democracy: The Role of Otpor." In *People Power: Unarmed Resistance and Global Solidarity*, ed. Howard Clark, 26–38. London and New York: Pluto Press.

Nikolayenko, Olena. June 2009. *Youth Movements in Post-Communist Societies: A Model of Nonviolent Resistance*. CDDRL Working Papers, vol. 114. Stanford University, Center on Democracy, Development, and the Rule of Law; Freeman Spogli Institute for International Studies. See http://cddrl.stanford.edu/publications/youth_movements_in_postcommunist_societies_a_model_of_nonviolent_resistance/.

Otpor. See www.otpor.com for documents and articles.

Paulson, Joshua. 2005. "Removing the Dictator in Serbia—1996–2000." In *Waging Nonviolent Struggle: 20th Century Practice and 21st Century Potential*, ed. Gene Sharp, 315–339. Boston: Porter Sargent Publishers.

Popovic, Srdja. 2001a. "An Analytical Overview of the Application of Gene Sharp's Theory of Nonviolent Action in Milosevic's Serbia." Serbian Arena for Nonviolent Conflict, CANVAS Total Index. January 31. See http://comminit.com/en/node/274331.

———. 2001b. "The Theory and Practice of Strategic Nonviolence." See www.canvasopedia.org.

Powers, Roger S., et al., eds. 1997. *Protest, Power, and Change: An Encyclopedia of Nonviolent Action*. New York and London: Garland.

Sharp, Gene. 2002. *From Dictatorship to Democracy: A Conceptual Framework for Liberation*. Third edition. Boston: Albert Einstein Institution. Available at www.aeinstein.org.

———. 1973. *The Politics of Nonviolent Action*. Three volumes. Boston: Porter Sargent.

York, Steve. 2002. Film: *Bringing Down a Dictator*, www.aforcemorepowerful,org.

From *The New York Times*

Cohen, Roger. 2000. "Who Really Brought Down Milosevic?" November 26 (magazine).

Erlanger, Steven. 2000. "Fears Deepen Milosevic Will Rig Vote." September 23.

———. 2000. "Civil Disobedience Is Planned to Try to Force Milosevic Out." September 29.

———. 2000. "Striking Serbian Coal Miners Maintain Solidarity." October 4.

———. 2000. "Showdown in Yugoslavia: The Overview; Yugoslavs Claim Belgrade for New Leader." October 6.

———. 1999. "Bombing Unites Serb Army as It Debilitates Economy—Production Cut in Half, Experts Say." April 30.

———. 1996. "U.S. Warns Serbia against Crushing Protests." December 4.

Erlanger, Steven, and Carlotta Gall. 2001. "The Milosevic Surrender: The Overview; Milosevic Arrest Came with Pledge for a Fair Trial." April 2.

Fromkin, David. 2003. "A World Still Haunted by Ottoman Ghosts." March 9.

Harden, Blaine. 1999. "Conflict in the Balkans, The Serbs; Honor Compels Opposition to Rally around Belgrade." March 25.

Hart, Albert Bushnell. 1914. "Austrian Fear of Serb Empire is Real War Cause." August 2.

Hedges, Chris. 1997. "Now TV Interrupts Milosevic's Programming." February 9.

———. 1997. "Serbian President Accepts Victories by his Opponents." February 5.

———. 1996. "Screws Tightened on Serbian Opposition." December 4.

———. 1996. "Fierce Serb Nationalism Pervades Student Foes of Belgrade Leader." December 10.

Perlez, Jane. 1999. "Conflict in the Balkans: The Overview; NATO Authorizes Bomb Strikes; Primakov in Air, Skips U.S. Visit." March 24.

———. 1997. "Belgrade Opposition Takes Control of the City Council." February 22.

Peters, C. Brooks. 1941. "Belgrade in Axis." March 26.

Shenon, Philip. 1992. "Non-Aligned Bloc Seeks a New Reason for Being." September 2.

Simons, Marlise, and Alison Smale. 2006. "Slobodan Milosevic, 64, Former Yugoslav Leader Accused of War Crimes, Dies." March 12.

Unsigned. 1999. "The Kosovo Refugee Emergency." April 1.

Unsigned. 1996. "Serbia's Apartheid Victims." December 23.

Unsigned. 1993. "Nationalism Turns Sour in Croatia." November 13.

GEORGIA'S ROSE REVOLUTION

Although the roots of Georgia as an independent state trace back to the fourth century B.C.E., by the beginning of the nineteenth century, Georgia had become part of the Russian Empire. A small territory in southwestern Asia between the Caucasus Mountains and the Black Sea, Georgia has long had a largely homogeneous population. According to its 2002 Census, 83.8 percent of Georgia is ethnically Georgian. Religious orientation runs deep—the people of Georgia converted to Christianity in the fourth century, and today, 83 percent of the population is Georgian Orthodox. Despite this strong homogeneity, Georgia has had internal ethnic tensions, and the northwest territory of Abkhazia has always been semi-autonomous. Georgia is considered economically important, as the country is strategically located east of the Black Sea, and controls much of the land and shipping traffic through the Caucasus. As Georgia lies along the historic Silk Road routes, it has often been a flashpoint between rival powers and empires.

Throughout the Middle Ages, as with many Eastern European countries, Georgia was under imperial dominance. The largely Christian Georgians faced a stiff battle for independence, with the Ottoman Empire and Savafid Persia at odds and continually fighting over their territory. As a Christian nation, Georgia did not want to acknowledge the sovereignty of these largely Muslim empires, yet the Georgians lacked the resources and manpower for fending off invasions. The rise of the Christian Russian Empire in the late eighteenth century made for a more appealing protective alliance. In 1783, Georgia signed the Treaty of Georgievsk with Russia to guarantee its protection, and on September 12, 1801, Tsar Alexander I decreed the Georgian incorporation into the Russian Empire.

UNDER RUSSIAN RULE

For much of the nineteenth and twentieth centuries, Georgia was under Russian domination, sharing its similar agricultural tradition and common religious rituals in their Orthodox Christianity. In the early twentieth century, however, a Georgian patriotic movement began to rise. Russia had subjugated Georgian culture in several ways, including attempting to make Russia the official language of the region, rather than the indigenous Georgian language, and by diminishing the autonomy of the Georgian Orthodox Church.

In October 1917, the Russian Revolution resulted in civil war, creating confusion throughout the empire. In the midst of political uncertainty, the territory of Georgia declared its independence as the Democratic Republic of Georgia. On May 8, 1989, *The New York Times* reporter Bill Keller succinctly explains:

> Liberated from Russian rule by the 1917 Bolshevik Revolution, Georgia spent three years as an independent state. That status ended when the Red Army overthrew the Menshevik Social Democrats in 1921. The ensuing decades of Soviet power paradoxically laid the groundwork for a rebirth of Georgian patriotism. Moscow brought industry, expanded educational opportunities, groomed a native party and government apparatus, and tolerated a flourishing of Georgian culture, all of which raised aspirations of Georgian autonomy (see "In Soviet Georgia, a Longing for Freedom but Little Sense of How to Get It").

The Mensheviks (Russian for minority) Keller refers to were a faction of Russian revolutionaries that developed in 1903 following disagreements between Vladimir Lenin and Julius Martov, both members of the Russian Social-Democratic Labor Party. Their main conflict concerned minor questions of party organization. Martov's supporters, ultimately in the minority, came to be called "Mensheviks," while Lenin's supporters were called "Bolsheviks," meaning majority. As the split deepened over pragmatic matters of historical interest, the Mensheviks tended toward moderation; the Bolsheviks sought collaboration with those of more radical tendencies and the peasantry. After the Russian Revolution, the Bolsheviks took power, leaving the Mensheviks in an ambiguous position. They were divided in their support for the Red and White nationalist sides in the ensuing civil war, which lasted for several years, with the Bolsheviks finally victorious. The revolution prepared the way for the Soviet Union. The Menshevik Social-Democratic Party was outlawed by the Soviets in 1921.

The new Soviet regime recognized the sovereignty of the Democratic Republic of Georgia in the 1920 Treaty of

QUICK FACTS ABOUT GEORGIA

- Georgia is situated between the Caucasus Mountains and the Black Sea and shares borders with Armenia, Azerbaijan, Russia, and Turkey.

- According to its 2002 Census, 83.8 percent of Georgia is ethnically Georgian. The people of Georgia were among the earliest to convert to Christianity, in the fourth century C.E. Today, 83 percent of the country is Georgian Orthodox.

- In 1783, Georgia signed the Treaty of Georgievsk with Catherine the Great of Russia to guarantee its protection; on September 12, 1801, Tsar Alexander I decreed Georgian incorporation into the Russian Empire.

- For much of the nineteenth and twentieth centuries, Georgia was under Russian domination, sharing a similar agricultural tradition and common religious rituals in their Orthodox Christianity. The Georgian patriotic movement began to rise in the early twentieth century.

- In October 1917, during the Russian Revolution, Georgia declared its independence as the Democratic Republic of Georgia. The new Soviet regime recognized its sovereignty in the 1920 Treaty of Moscow, and an independent Georgian state existed from 1918 to 1921. In 1921, however, Josef Stalin sent the Red Army into the Caucasus, in an invasion that essentially seized full military control of Georgia.

- In 1956, Soviet leader Nikita S. Khrushchev announced a policy of "de-Stalinization" and instituted steps for the Soviet Union to divest itself of the cult of personality around Stalin. Stalin was Georgian by birth, and many Georgians interpreted Khrushchev's plan as an attack on their culture. Protests erupted. In March 1956 in Tbilisi, the Soviet military opened fire on demonstrators killing approximately 100, mostly students.

- In 1978, a Soviet plan to drop the Georgian language as the official tongue was met by as many as 20,000 demonstrators, according to *The New York Times* ("Soviet Georgians Take to the Streets to Save Their State Language"). As thousands rallied in protest, sixteen demonstrators were killed when military troops moved to disperse the crowd. The event increased a sense of urgency for Georgia to gain its independence from the Soviet Union.

- Among the more independence-minded Soviet republics, Georgia declared its sovereignty on November 19, 1989, and its independence on April 9, 1991, when a referendum approved independence with 98.9 percent of the vote.

- On April 9,1989, Soviet troops attacked demonstrators—Abkhaz nationalists demanding secession from Georgia—in Tbilisi, killing twenty and injuring hundreds. This episode, and the earlier bloodshed in retaliation against unarmed demonstrators in 1956 and 1978, contributed to Georgian resolve not to use firearms in pursuit of political goals.

- In May 1991, Zviad K. Gamsakhurdia was elected president with 87 percent of the vote. Before long, Gamsakhurdia was jailing political opponents and suppressing free speech.

(continued)

(continued)

- In late 1991, Gamsakhurdia's policies led to the outbreak of civil war. Gamsakhurdia's failed bloody revolution of 1991–1993 was another factor in the Georgian popular repudiation of violence and extreme militancy.

- Gamsakhurdia's overthrow made possible the eventual assumption of the presidency in 1995 by Eduard A. Shevardnadze, whereupon Georgia experienced several years of political instability and economic struggle. When Shevardnadze was reelected in 2000 by a wide margin, international observers criticized the results as fraudulent.

- In 2003, Mikhail Saakashvili, a thirty-six-year-old lawyer and opposition leader, challenged the legitimacy of the November parliamentary elections. Tens of thousands of Georgians took to the streets in nonviolent demonstrations that became known as the Rose Revolution.

- Many of the nonviolent protagonists who stood their ground in Tbilisi in autumn 2003 were from the student-founded, youth-run nonviolent civil resistance group Kmara, which means "Enough."

- In November 2003, shortly after meeting with Kmara, Shevardnadze announced his resignation. He had little choice as the military forces and policymakers switched their allegiance and began to support the demonstrations. Marchers placed roses in the soldiers' gun-barrels, and not one shot was fired.

- On January 4, 2004, Mikhail Saakashvili was elected president of Georgia with the highest voter turnout in the country's history. Bouquets of red roses were visible at polling sites throughout the country.

Moscow. In 1921, however, Josef Stalin sent the Red Army into the Caucasus, an invasion that essentially seized full military control of Georgia. The highly patriotic and newly independent Georgians were hostile to the Stalinist regime and proposed semi-independence as part of a Russian federation. In what is known as the "Georgian Affair," the central committee in Moscow debated how to handle Georgia and the rest of the trans-Caucasus countries that had been captured by the military. Finally, with Stalin urging the Soviets to "crush the hydra of nationalism" across the Soviet Union, along with other trans-Caucasus republics, such as Armenia and Azerbaijan, Georgia entered the newly formed union as one federative republic. The central appeal for Russian unity trumped Georgia's latent patriotism and brief independence.

The Times reporter Esther B. Fein on April 10, 1989, concisely reviews the Soviet-Georgian relationship

> Georgians have had a mixed relationship with the Soviet authorities ever since their land, which lies on the Black Sea coast and reaches into the foothills and mountains of the Caucasus, was incorporated into the Soviet Union in 1921.
>
> The Georgian people have survived centuries of conquest and rule by Mongols, Turks, Persians and Czarist Russians, and despite the domination, they have managed to keep alive their ancient language and their rich heritage, expressed in literature, dance and religion. The experience of history seems to have helped them do this under Soviet rule, although Georgians say they have often felt threatened by Moscow's attempt to unify the country under a homogenized Soviet culture. . . . Georgians frequently came into conflict with the Soviet authorities because of their bent for individual enterprise.
>
> Over the years, their fears and resentments of the Kremlin have flared in demonstrations and demands that their language and their way of life be left intact ("At Least 16 Killed as Protestors Battle the Police in Soviet Georgia").

Dan Bilefsky, writing for *The Times* on September 30, 2008, points out that contemporary Georgian history texts still laud Stalin for defeating Hitler's fascism and building the Soviet Union into an industrial power, "even as they criticized him for engineering the Red Army invasion that ended Georgia's short-lived independence in 1921" ("In Georgia, A Reverence for Stalin").

UNDER SOVIET CONTROL

During the Soviet era, Georgia remained firmly under the rule of the Soviet Union, despite the fact that Georgians are often regarded as exemplifying greater nationalism and independent thinking than other Soviet republics. In World War II, a group of ethnic Georgians seceded from their nation and fought under Nazi Germany. Known as the "Georgian Legion," they banded together and sided with the Axis powers in hopes of freeing Georgia from Soviet domination, as reported in *The Times* on August 28, 1993, by Stephen Engelberg ("General's Father Fought for Nazi Unit"). The Georgian Legion was not successful in its aims, and those Georgians who returned were convicted as traitors. Regardless, a pro-Georgian spirit remained.

For the duration of the Soviet Union, the Georgians built a history of nationalism and separatist movements; they also pioneered in the nonviolent opposition to Soviet control. Although Stalin had engineered the Soviet takeover of Georgia, the mere fact that Stalin was himself a Georgian created tremendous Georgian national pride (and in some cases, ambivalence), as *The Times* notes ("In Georgia, A Reverence for Stalin"). In 1956, Nikita Sergeyevich Khrushchev, general secretary of the Soviet Communist Party, announced a policy of "de-Stalinization" and instituted steps for the Soviet Union to cleanse itself of the cult of personality around Stalin. Many Georgians took Khrushchev's move as an attack on Georgian culture, and protests erupted. University students went on strike to contest the government's efforts to "desanctify" and "defame" Stalin, according to *The Times* reporter Harry Schwarz on March 24, 1956. Such actions appear, according to Schwarz, "unprecedented in modern Soviet history." *The Times* notes, "It is generally believed that these are expressions of Georgia nationalism." To find other examples of "open student resistance to the Soviet government," Schwarz asserts, observers must go back to the 1920s, "when many university students supported Leon Trotsky against Stalin" ("Soviet Students Strike in Tiflis, University Shut"). In Tbilisi, the capital of Georgia, in March of that year, the Soviet military opened fire and killed approximately 100. Most of the dead were demonstrating students.

Two decades later, Craig Whitney reports in *The Times* on April 15, 1978, on a defiant outpouring of demonstrators who publicly contested a government proposal: "A Soviet plan to drop Georgian as the official language of the proudly nationalistic Caucasian republic of Georgia sparked demonstrations today in the street of the capital city of Tbilisi" ("Soviet Georgians Take to the Streets to Save Their State Language"). As many as 20,000 demonstrators, according to one source, rallied in protest, while the Georgian Supreme Soviet (in effect, the legislature) met to consider a draft constitution that dropped the clause limiting Georgian as the state language. Instead, a new clause substituted the phrase "the possibility of using the native language." The earlier 1937 constitution, promulgated under Stalin, had provided for Georgian as the official language. Whitney points out that the upheaval was not reported in the Soviet news media. April 14 was declared the "Day of the Georgian Language," he notes for *The Times*. His dispatch retroactively reflects Georgian thinking of the time:

> The Georgian region has been under Russian dominance only since the early 19th century, when its Eastern Orthodox rulers sought protection against Moslem degradation. Since the Bolshevik Revolution, the independent spirit of the Georgians has often brought them into conflict with the central authority in Moscow. After Stalin died and fell into disgrace, there were riots in Tbilisi in March 1956 in which at least 100 people were reportedly killed protesting the desanctification of a native son [Stalin]. . . . Although Georgia national and cultural pride is strong, such overt manifestations as today's reported demonstration are rare. But beneath the surface, resentment of Russian domination runs deep.

Whitney indicates that the demonstrators demanding their "native tongue" in Tbilisi were mostly university students. The massive nonviolent protests led the Soviets to bow to pressure and scuttle the proposal. In a dispatch to *The Times* three days later, April 18, Whitney writes, "In an extraordinary concession to local patriotic feeling, authorities in the Soviet Union's Georgian Republic have reinstated Georgian as the official state language after a protest in the capital city of Tbilisi." The huge rallies of April 14 successful, the clause specifying Georgian as the state language was reinserted in the constitution. "Such a concession to a demonstration of popular displeasure is unusual in this country," Whitney says, "but ethnic feeling among Georgians, who outnumber ethnic Russians by nearly eight to one, is considered stronger than among most of the other major ethnic groups that form the basis for the Soviet Union's 15 constituent republics." The Communist Party chief, Eduard A. Shevardnadze, came out to address the demonstrating students, Whitney reports, assuring them that their native language would be preserved. According to Whitney, in the 1970 census of the Georgia population of 3.1 million, only 13,000 reported Russian as their first language ("Soviet Georgians Win on Language").

The years of Soviet administration of Georgia were marked by corruption and wrongdoing, but Shevardnadze, who had become party leader in September 1972, earned a reputation as a fighter of corruption within the Politburo.

Whitney's article mentions that Shevardnadze had been "cleaning house," meaning that he had been "periodically dismissing ministers [of government] and party officials for taking bribes, profiteering and laxity." Shevardnadze gained in popularity among Georgians for his role in the language dispute. In 1985, Shevardnadze was appointed foreign minister of the Soviet Union. A Georgian once again played a prominent role in Soviet policy.

Moves toward Independence

As the Soviet Union began to break up, a major push for Georgian independence developed among its population of nearly 5 million. The rise of Mikhail S. Gorbachev to power as general secretary of the Communist Party of the Soviet Union (and therefore the political leader of the country) in 1985 had led to "new thinking" in Moscow's foreign policy. In a 1987 book, Gorbachev spelled out his principles for reform. Although interconnected, they fell into four main categories: *perestroika,* Russian for restructuring the economy; *glasnost,* meaning openness or publicity; democratization; and new thinking in foreign policy (see **Introduction: Strikes, Sinatra, and Nonviolent Revolution**). Following the death in 1982 of Leonid Ilyich Brezhnev, general secretary of the Communist Party since 1964, the crises in the Soviet system became undeniable. Gorbachev's propositions were meant to revitalize the stagnating Soviet economy, which had been growing at only 2 percent annually for a decade. Gorbachev hoped that through managed change he could retain the Communist Party's monopoly of power, while improving the image of the Soviet Union through glasnost. In the mid-1980s, Gorbachev's perestroika principle for restructuring Soviet society came to include major reorganization of the outlying regions of the Caucasus. As Moscow debated what a new Georgia would look like under a reorganized Soviet Union, the Georgians began to ponder their own independence. By 1989, *The Times* suggests that Georgians, no matter the diversity of their political perspectives, were roughly in agreement that their prospects must include "a future of independence, free of Moscow, free of Communist rule, with a Western-style parliament and many political parties." So writes Keller on May 8 (see "In Soviet Georgia, a Longing for Freedom but Little Sense of How to Get It").

On April 9, 1989, Soviet troops, as they had done in 1956, again moved on hundreds of unarmed protestors in Tbilisi. Continuing a Georgian pioneering tradition of civil resistance, hunger strikers and other demonstrators gathered in the city square to press for Georgian independence. Military troops moved to disperse the crowds, and sixteen Georgians were killed, with hundreds more injured, as Fein reports for *The Times* on April 10 ("At Least 16 Killed as Protestors Battle the Police in Soviet Georgia").

Although fewer were killed in this attack than in 1956, the bloody events that occurred just before dawn came to be known as the Tbilisi massacre. The words still echo in Georgian ears. The Tbilisi massacre electrified the Georgian public and increased the sense of urgency for achieving independence from the Soviet Union.

Georgian sentiments were first put to the test in October 1990, when the Round Table–Free Georgia coalition won 70 percent of the vote compared to 30 percent received by the communists. For the first time in a nationwide Georgian election, noncommunists had won. The coalition's leader, Zviad K. Gamsakhurdia, was a well-known anti-Soviet, pro-independence activist. The die was cast.

On April 9, 1991, the people of Georgia held a referendum on independence, organized by Gamsakhurdia, and it was approved with 98.9 percent of the votes, according to *The Times.* Francis X. Clines reports on April 10, that the referendum was timed to coincide with the two-year anniversary of the Tbilisi massacre ("Secession Decreed in Soviet Georgia"). In the period between the election of Gamsakhurdia's coalition and the referendum, the Soviet Union had attempted to negotiate a reconciliation with Georgia, but the Georgian populace strongly urged independence as the sole option.

The Soviet Union ignored the referendum, but the Georgians continued to work on their own toward establishing an independent republic. Gorbachev offered a new union arrangement to Georgia and other Soviet territories. Intent on keeping Georgia in the union, Gorbachev made a tour in 1991 to promote a semi-autonomous arrangement. Yet the people of Georgia, particularly after the election of Gamsakhurdia, sent a strong statement as to their preferences. Gamsakhurdia campaigned on Georgian independence and control of the regions of South Ossetia and Abkhazia. In May 1991, he was elected president with 87 percent of the vote, as Serge Schmemann reports for *The Times* on May 28 ("Separatist Wins Soviet Georgia Vote").

An Independent Georgia

The referendum and Gamsakhurdia's election in early 1991 were the impetus for Georgian independence. Georgia was neither stable nor self-sustaining, however, and Gamsakhurdia's actions were hardly those of a democratic leader once he assumed the presidency. He proceeded to jail political opponents and suppress free speech. The wave of nationalism turned instead into vociferous and violent opposition against the new leadership, as riots broke out in the streets. Gamsakhurdia was forced into seclusion. Cities across Georgia were destroyed, and industrial production declined 21 percent. To stabilize the coup, Shevardnadze returned to Georgia to lead a substitute government called the "State Council," reports Celestine Bohlen for *The Times* on April 20, 1992 (see "Re-enter Shevardnadze, the Phoenix of Georgia").

Shevardnadze was in many ways an unlikely leader. Around the time of the independence referendum, his popularity rating was at 30 percent, but by early 1992 it had jumped to 70 percent, as Bohlen points out. Whereas many Georgians had once seen him as emblematic of the old Soviet regime, according to Bohlen other Georgians realized that under Gamsakhurdia they had, in the words of one citizen, gone "from unrestricted Communism to unrestricted Nationalism." If Shevardnadze was emblematic of the old regime, he was also decidedly Georgian. He and the State Council set about to quell the fighting, stabilize the state, and restore citizens' liberties. He allowed relatively free new media and supported the television station Rustavi-2. Yet Shevardnadze did not understand what was needed. According to Stephen Jones, an expert on Georgia history and politics, "[B]etween 1992 and 1995, Shevardnadze's government failed to establish its authority or democratic credentials. It was constructed from the roof downwards and although democratic scaffolding was in place, its core was a tradition-based patrimonial authority which ruled by custom, threat, private dispensations, and privileges. . . . The state was effectively privatized, in part by Shevardnadze's family" (Jones 2009, 320). Through the State Council, Shevardnadze became the unofficial ruler of Georgia until 1995, when he was formally elected president. The country still faced serious economic hardships and inflation, and the government even introduced a new currency during this period. Violence periodically flared. Indeed, Shevardnadze survived an assassination attempt in 1995, when he was nearly killed by a car bomb on the way to a signing ceremony for the new Georgian constitution. He still had broad international support, and after the car bombing, Germany offered him an armor-plated Mercedes. Shevardnadze managed somewhat to stabilize the country's economy—by the time of his election, inflation had decreased to 2 percent—according to Michael Specter in *The Times* October 19, 1995 ("Tragic Georgian or Fixer of a Broken Nation?"). Still, Shevardnadze would face major criticism for his old-school, Soviet-style autocratic tendencies. By 2001, he had attempted to close down the inde-pendent television station, an action that spurred reformers in his own government to create opposition political parties.

During Shevardnadze's presidency, Georgia experienced several years of political instability, internal dissent, marginal economic growth, and extreme poverty. Shevardnadze's policies often looked to the West, and he attempted to integrate Georgia into NATO and other multilateral organizations. By the time of Specter's article, Shevardnadze had been able to persuade fifty-five countries to recognize Georgia as an independent state, but he was criticized for suppressing civil rights at home. In 2000, Shevardnadze was reelected president, with more than 80 percent of the vote, but the election results were criticized by international observers, as *The Times* notes on April 11 ("Foreign Observers Criticize Lopsided Shevardnadze Vote").

THE REVOLUTION OF THE ROSES

The parliamentary elections of November 2, 2003, were largely seen as a referendum on Shevardnadze's coalition, For a New Georgia, and as a bellwether as to who would succeed Shevardnadze as president in the next election, to be held in 2005. *The Times* reports on November 6 that according to official results, For a New Georgia led the elections by a narrow margin. The United States and other foreign observers quickly declared that the elections were rigged in favor of Shevardnadze ("U.S. Cites Fraud in Vote"). The 2003 parliamentary elections were the tinder for what would soon blaze.

On November 3, the incumbent leadership of the Georgian government and For a New Georgia announced that the pro-Shevardnadze bloc had won the previous day's parliamentary balloting and declared the election results legitimate. In late November they attempted to seat the new parliament, with Shevardnadze's party at the head of the governing coalition. Instead, Mikhail Saakashvili, a thirty-six-year-old lawyer and the most prominent opposition leader, whose party had finished third in the election results, refused to enter the parliament with his political allies. Saakashvili, together with Zurab Zhvania, head of the United Democrats party, and parliament speaker Nino Burdzhanadze, called for demonstrations in Tbilisi and other cities against falsification of the vote and asked Shevardnadze to resign. Saakashvili's United National Movement party had sought to widen popular participation and was especially effective in increasing political involvement of the more isolated and provincial parts of the country. As Saakashvili urged nonviolent protests across the country, *Times* reporter Seth Mydans quotes him on November 21, as saying, "This Parliament is illegitimate." "We won't join the new Parliament," Saakashvili asserted, "and we will try to prevent it from holding its session" (see "Officials in Georgia Declare Shevardnadze Ballot Winner";

"Georgians Vote for Lawmakers in Preview of a Presidential Race").

Saakashvili tapped into accumulating popular dissent. "After the collapse of the Soviet Union, Georgian politics was an intoxicating mix of civic protests, boycotts, occupations, sit-ins, mass rallies, and vigils," Stephen Jones observes. "Although . . . overshadowed in the Western media by reports of violence, parliamentary fistfights, and attacks on religious minorities, these civic strategies were successful weapons against state arbitrariness. They [had] brought Gamsakhurdia's government to power, and they helped bring it down. In November 2000, non-violent rallies led to the resignation of the government and in October 2001, to the resignation of a number of powerful ministers." Now in 2003, Jones notes, "There was a strong and fruitful tradition of direct action and civil resistance to draw upon in Georgia" (Jones 2009, 327). Saakashvili's leadership of the anti-Shevardnadze coalition was a sign that Georgia was also heeding influences from beyond its borders in seeking greater individual liberties and democracy. Saakashvili was married to a Dutch citizen, and he had studied law at Columbia University before beginning a career in Georgia politics in the mid-1990s. He had served as a member of Shevardnadze's cabinet as minister of justice, where he pursued a vigorous anticorruption platform, until he resigned in 2001, saying, "I consider it immoral for me to remain a member of Shevardnadze's cabinet."

Georgia's comparatively free news media, led by the Rustavi-2 independent television station, encouraged the protests by offering forums for the various opposition political parties and nongovernmental organizations that had sprung into action. Rustavi-2 also broadcast exit polling that challenged the official election results.

Twenty days of massive nonviolent demonstrations, from November 3 to November 23, 2003, started in the capital city of Tbilisi and soon erupted in almost all the major cities and towns in Georgia. On November 17, more than 50,000 congregated in central Tbilisi's Freedom Square, where 3,000 demonstrators held hands and formed a human chain encircling the state chancellery. A brief, intensive series of mass nonviolent demonstrations occurred November 21–23, opening the way for Saakashvili eventually to win 96.2 percent of the vote and occupy the presidential office unopposed. This culmination of intensive direct action is known as the Revolution of the Roses (so called because the nonviolent protestors carried red roses and placed them in the barrels of soldiers' guns).

On November 21, the first day of the Rose Revolution, Mydans reports the decision of the election commission, which the day before in a volatile atmosphere had falsified results and certified that Shevardnadze's coalition had won a majority in the election (see "Officials in Georgia Declare Shevardnadze Ballot Winner"). On November 20, thousands of people arrived in Tbilisi in caravans of cars that stretched for miles, driving from western Georgia. The same day, the U.S. State Department issued a statement to the news media firmly saying that the results "do not accurately reflect the will of the Georgian people, but instead reflect massive fraud." A Radio Free Europe/Radio Liberty analyst commented that this is "the first time ever that the [United States] has openly accused the leadership of a former Soviet republic of rigging an election." Opposition leaders immediately questioned the validity of the election results and refused to take their seats in the parliament. On November 21, more than 100,000 assembled in Freedom Square to exert pressure on the opposition political parties not to enter the parliament building. When their effort failed, the demonstrators sought to disrupt the seating of the parliamentarians by blocking roads with vehicles and buses. The police and army troops stood by observing and took no action.

Prior to the 2003 parliamentary elections, the various opposition groups were merely hoping to build momentum for the 2005 presidential elections. The combination of electoral fraud, Shevardnadze's refusal to accept compromise, and the unity and discipline of the nonviolent civil resistance groups hastened his departure.

Kmara (Enough)

Many of the tens of thousands of nonviolent protagonists who stood their ground in Tbilisi in autumn 2003 were from Kmara (Enough), a student-founded, youth-run nonviolent civil resistance group modeled on the Serbian student organization Otpor! (Resistance!) (on Otpor, see "Rally Against Milosevic Fails to Bind Opposition Parties"; "Student Group Emerges as Major Milosevic Foe"; "Out in Front, Serbia's Opposition Prepares to Lose"). Kmara, founded in 2003 by reform-minded students at Tbilisi State University, originally contested corruption in higher education and sought greater employment opportunities for young Georgians at a time when only 4 percent of university graduates could find employment in the Georgian workforce. Kmara was helped into being by the Liberty Institute, Georgia's most prominent civil rights nongovernmental organization, which promoted human rights, freedom of the press, and religious tolerance. As internal dissension against Shevardnadze grew, many young Georgians began to take action, aided by the Liberty Institute and the United National Movement party. These groups and Kmara received significant funding and support from the West (see "Officials in Georgia Declare Shevardnadze Ballot Winner").

Starting in midsummer 2003, Kmara began to channel the opposition to Shevardnadze into youth activism, and the group's founders looked to nearby countries for examples. Kmara's primary inspiration and advice came from Otpor. The Kmara movement adopted Otpor's clenched fist as its logo, and Otpor activists came to Georgia to train Kmara's first leaders in the technique of nonviolent action and to help in the dissemination of leaflets and explanatory literature across the country. Some 5,000 members of Kmara attended summer workshops led by Otpor, funded by the Serbian Center for Applied Non-Violent Action and Strategies. Kmara also followed Otpor's model of nonhierarchal leadership, in which all were equal, making it easier for each person to find an outlet for action and harder for authorities to derail the group's direction (see **Serbia, Introduction**). The lessons from Otpor's experience in Serbia were plain, as Jones summarizes: "renounce armed struggle which had proved too costly in Georgia in the early 1990s; mobilize crowds onto the streets to prevent retaliation; ensure international media coverage; fraternize with the police and army; maintain a unified political opposition and establish an alternative source of authority" (Jones 2009, 324–325).

Kmara was well aware of where it fit into Georgia's historical narrative. The organization scheduled its first action, a 500-student march from Tbilisi State University to the state chancellery, for April 14, 2003. The date conspicuously commemorated the successful demonstrations of April 14, 1978 (see "In Soviet Georgia, a Longing for Freedom but Little Sense of How to Get It"). It was also chosen because that was the occasion when Shevardnadze had sided with students in their adamant efforts to retain Georgian as the official language of the Georgian republic.

Throughout 2003, Kmara organized simultaneous demonstrations across the country, so as to manifest well-organized civil resistance, holding its first nationwide action on May 12. The Shevardnadze regime pursued three avenues to weaken Kmara and other opposition groups: it sought to discredit the movement, ignore it, and suppress it, especially in areas beyond Tbilisi. In a graffiti campaign, twenty Kmara founders divided themselves into teams of three or four and painted "Kmara" in tens of thousands of places on Tbilisi's streets and roads. In the following weeks, Kmara's ubiquitous graffiti became visible in nine of Georgia's major metropolitan areas and became the top story in the news.

According to Valerie Bunce and Sharon Wolchik, Kmara had neither the influence nor the stakes held by Otpor. Kmara members were supporters of the popular resistance, but not the organizers, as was Otpor. Moreover, Kmara had greater institutional endorsement—partisan political leaders such as Mikhail Saakashvili benefited from, recruited from, and gave publicity to Kmara, while Kmara aided the opposition political parties in disseminating information, monitoring elections, and tabulating votes. Yet, Kmara was not the primary organizer and leader in the same way that Otpor had been in Serbia. *The Times* had given ample coverage over a protracted period to Otpor's activities in bringing about the fall of Slobodan Milošević (see "Out in Front, Serbia's Opposition Prepares to Lose"; "Milosevic, Trailing in Polls, Rails Against NATO"; "Liberating Yugoslavia"). Kmara does not receive the same kind of analysis from *The Times,* even though those affiliated or trained by Kmara made up the ranks of the demonstrators, and Kmara was a catalyst in puncturing widespread post-Soviet apathy and passivity. At several universities "committees of civil disobedience" formed, and through concentrated application of civil disobedience, some 10,000 previously sedentary university students became engaged. The strategy of Artcom, a committee of artists, was one of "disruption [including] sit-down demonstrations at regional administrative offices, occupations of universities, chains of people around the State Chancellery, strikes (some teachers responded), and synchronous horn blowing by Tbilisi's cars," according to Jones (2009, 325).

Kmara enlisted thousands of Georgian youth throughout the country and succeeded in giving a national face to the substantial desire of the people of Georgia to end Shevardnadze's regime. In theory, Shevardnadze's fate was not in danger in the parliamentary elections in 2003; his term was not due to expire until 2005, giving him two more years in office. Yet his party's narrow victory, combined with a cover-up, sparked widespread mobilization, for which Kmara was the kindling. Aslan Abashidze, an opposition figure who contested Shevardnadze and was based in Abkhazia, sent thousands of supporters to Tbilisi to engage in counter-demonstrations supporting the incumbent government.

Carrying Roses, a New Parliament Takes Office

On November 22, 2003, the new parliament was seated. Opposition supporters, led by Saakashvili, virtually all of whom were bearing roses in their hands, took possession, by virtue of their numbers, of the parliament building. As Thomas Vinciguerra would write for *The Times* on March 13, 2005, the emblematic use of roses gave the major nonviolent campaign the name "Revolution of the Roses." Vinciguerra notes: "Given the rise of satellite dishes, camera phones and other means of instantaneous visual communication, it was perhaps inevitable that mass movements would embrace eye-catching colors that transcend language barriers and make messages recognizable around the world" ("The Revolution Will Be Colorized").

To bring about this monumental change, the nonviolent challengers had swarmed the parliament building around the clock, blocking the entrances so that lawmakers could not gain access. They also surrounded Shevardnadze's quarters. Shevardnadze, in turn, declared a state of emergency in order to mobilize military troops against the demonstrators. Instead, the troops under arms joined the action, as the civil resisters distributed red roses to the soldiers. The soldiers began demonstrating *with* the multitudes outside the parliament, as the army officers in charge pledged to follow the orders coming from the rose-laden opposition. Seth Mydans reports on November 23, 2003, "Troops and the police, mostly armed with truncheons, blocked roads around Parliament and the nearby presidential offices but made no effort to prevent the storming of the building" (see "Foes of Georgian Leader Storm into Parliament Building"). When troops armed with military weaponry turned their firearms on the demonstrators, the protestors stuck roses down the gun-barrels, giving the upheaval its name, recounts *Times* reporter Ilan Greenberg on May 30, 2004 (see "The Not-So-Velvet Revolution"). Although thousands of protestors stormed the building in the presence of thousands of police and military, not a single shot was fired, according to Charles J. Fairbanks, professor of international relations and election observer, who was an eye-witness. Stephen Jones records that one window was smashed.

A co-founder of Kmara, Giorgi Kandelaki, explains the behavior of the police and soldiers:

> As for the police and military, the fact that their leaders agreed to negotiate [with the opposition] showed their realization that with virtually the entire country involved in the protest movement, any use of force would result sooner or later in self-destruction. By November 22 [2003], opposition leaders knew that some security units would not intervene, although the risk of violence was still great with no word from a number of special forces units loyal to the president. The significant factor for the police was that "critical mass" had been achieved. This was the number of protesters (120,000) necessary to give the revolution legitimacy and overwhelm the police at key moments, such as the takeover of government buildings.

On November 23, known as St. George's Day in Georgia, Shevardnadze met with Kmara and other opposition leaders. Recognizing that his support had disintegrated, shortly after the meeting he announced his resignation. "I'm going home now." With that short sentence to the news media, as *Times* correspondent Seth Mydans reports, Shevardnadze ended more than a decade of leadership in Georgia, the announcement coming less than twenty-four hours after he stated his intention to remain as the president of the country through the end of 2005. Mydans adds that Mikhail Saakashvili cited the military's change of allegiance as the most important contributing factor to the downfall of the Shevardnadze government (see "Georgian Leader Agrees to Resign, Ending Standoff").

AFTERMATH: THE SAAKASHVILI PRESIDENCY

Eduard Amvrosiyevich Shevardnadze was born and reared in a country dominated and controlled by communist ideologies, strategies, and tactics. Shevardnadze's leadership, from 1972 to 1985 as first secretary of the Soviet Communist Party, and from 1992 to 2003 as president, is viewed by Georgians as a period of extensive corruption. In the end, he was unable to lead a society seeking greater democratic freedoms. A week after he stepped down, the deposed leader gave the reason for his downfall, as Mydans reports in *The Times* on November 30: "It is not good to have too much democracy. I think this was a mistake" (see "The Giant Who Shrank").

Even with Shevardnadze gone, Georgians still had problems of national unity. Saakashvili formed an interim cabinet to address internal turmoil, asked Nino Burdzhanadze if she would remain as speaker of the parliament, and created a post equivalent to prime minister for the other chief opposition leader, Zurab Zhanavia. Yet Saakashvili would lead the nation. The Georgians held a special election for president, and on January 4, 2004, Saakashvili was elected with the highest voter turnout in the country's history. Bouquets of red roses were emblematically in view at polling sites everywhere. Saakashvili garnered 86 percent of the vote (some accounts give higher figures), and he claimed a mandate for governance moving forward, as Mydans notes for *The Times* on January 5 (see "With the Vote in Georgia, a Dynamic Young Leader and a New Era").

Georgia, however, was not entirely united. Aslan Abashidze, who opposed Shevardnadze from Abkhazia, had ruled the Autonomous Republic of Adzharia in what *The Times* describes as a "virtual fiefdom" for fourteen years. Abashidze had used methods similar to Shevardnadze's to suppress speech and his political opponents, and the region had not had free elections during Abashidze's reign. In Saakashvili's inauguration speech, he singled out Adzharia as a region that needed to be liberated from Abashidze the way Tbilisi had been freed from Shevardnadze ("With Powell on Hand, Georgians Install New Leader").

In what is termed the "Second Rose Revolution," groups such as Kmara worked to support the organizing of civil resistance to Abashidze. Rhetorical opposition throughout March 2006 increased the pressure on him, and on May 2 he heightened the conflict by blowing up bridges that connected Adzharia to mainland Georgia. On May 6, after protestors had led sustained demonstrations in the capital of Adzharia, Prime Minister Zurab Zhvania led negotiations to bring the Georgian Special Forces into the region. Abashidze resigned. The following day, Saakashvili entered Adzharia and declared a united Georgia to what *The Times* on May 7, 2004, calls "a chorus of cheers" ("Georgia Regains Region that Sought to Secede").

Conclusion

"The important thing was that the military switched sides," the opposition leader, Mikhail Saakashvili, told CNN, as Seth Mydans reports on November 24, 2003. Guns were pointed at demonstrating Georgians, but the civil resisters placed roses down the barrels, and not a single shot was fired (see "Foes of Georgian Leader Storm into Parliament Building"). As the Revolution of the Roses proceeded in autumn 2003, it had become clear to Shevardnadze that as Mydans quotes him saying, "I see that this could not have ended bloodlessly, and I would have had to exercise my power" (see "Georgian Leader Agrees to Resign, Ending Standoff"). The formal mechanisms of the state had already turned on Shevardnadze. Scholars who have studied the events believe that Shevardnadze did attempt to use force to turn back the crowds, but his subordinates—internally split, facing pressure from the United States, and, most important, remembering the significant popular backlash to the Tbilisi massacre of 1989—did not act. The evidence available to date suggests that they disobeyed orders. Mydans concludes that in the final days the military effectively switched sides, with their commanders pledging loyalty to the opposition. Saakashvili told CNN, as reported in *The Times*, that the effective exchange in loyalties in the bulwarks of coercive state power was the "turning point" in the Georgian fight to bring down Shevardnadze. When Shevardnadze realized that his government was no longer at his disposal, no longer obeying him, he had no choice but to resign.

The Times coverage of Georgia and the other countries considered in this volume suggests that a post-Soviet state with aspirations for democracy is beholden to the cooperation of its citizens, including the armed forces. When they cease to obey, governments are forced to bend to their will. The Rose Revolution brought down Shevardnadze in part because of what *The Times* as early as 1978 describes as the "national and cultural pride" of the Georgians, which proved more powerful and resilient than the machinery of coercion.

A number of factors contributed to the success of the Rose Revolution: the incumbent government had been weakened by institutionalized corruption; Shevardnadze's semi-liberal regime had allowed some strengthening of democratic-leaning institutions; a new mobilization of a fledgling civil society by civic associations had grown in recent years; a comparatively free news media had been allowed to flourish; and the nonpartisan, nonviolent youth group Kmara had learned how to be effective. The Rose Revolution inspired hopes for what Saakashvili called "a new wave of democratization." Western countries rallied to the support of the rose-bearing opposition. As Stephen Jones writes, "This revolution was about moral regeneration, clean government, joining the world, and sticking to the rules, not about creative destruction or the building of a new society. Yet the non-violent struggle was passionate. It resulted in the complete and sudden removal of the old political elites" (2009, 319).

Political turmoil is no novelty to Georgia and its population of nearly 5 million in an area somewhat smaller than South Carolina. Since Georgia gained independence in 1991, its first two leaders, Zviad K. Gamsakhurdia and Eduard A. Shevardnadze, were forced from office, the former in a bloody coup d'état and the latter after invalid elections had spawned the Revolution of the Roses.

In the final tallies, Mikhail Saakashvili received approximately 97 percent of the vote in the January 2004 presidential elections, with voter turnout close to 90 percent. He was reelected January 5, 2008. Yet Georgia still was not unified. Abkhazia and South Ossetia, long-disputed territories that also sought independence, remained equally set on self-determination. In July 2008, a conflict erupted in South Ossetia between Georgian forces and South Ossetian separatists. The Georgian military fired on the separatists, leading to the brink of war. The conflict intensified in early August when Russian troops moved soldiers into South Ossetia and Abkhazia. A settlement in mid-August led to the cessation of military force between Russia and Georgia, but Russia recognized the regions as independent states, while Georgia still claimed them as part of a union, according to *Times* reporters

Ellen Barry and Dan Bilefsky on September 8 ("Russia Agrees to Limited Pullout From Georgia").

By 1989, *The Times* reports, Georgians of whatever political perspective had generally agreed that they wanted "a future of independence, free of Moscow, free of Communist rule, with a Western-style parliament and many political parties" (see "In Soviet Georgia, a Longing for Freedom but Little Sense of How to Get It"). In some ways, the Georgians have achieved all of these aspirations, yet questions of nationalism, boundaries, and control will continue to plague Georgian hopes for stability and independence for years to come.

• •

Rival Georgian Factions Disagree on Goals

As the Soviet Union began to collapse, Georgians, at the southern edge of the territory under the Soviet Union's suzerainty, pressed for independence. The rise of Mikhail S. Gorbachev to power as general secretary of the Communist Party of the Soviet Union in 1985 had brought "new thinking" to Moscow's foreign policy (see **Introduction: Strikes, Sinatra, and Nonviolent Revolution**). By the mid-1980s, Gorbachev's principle of perestroika, or restructuring, included major reorganization of the outlying regions of the Caucasus. At the same time, the Georgians began to conceptualize their own vision of independence. By 1989, according to Bill Keller in *The New York Times,* the Georgians had decided on "a future of independence, free of Moscow, free of Communist rule, with a Western-style parliament and many political parties." Yet politically negotiating the actual arrangements for that independence would prove difficult in Georgia. While other former Soviet republics such as Estonia, Latvia, and Lithuania in the Baltics were able to channel anti-Moscow sentiment into eventual independent states (see **Baltics, Introduction**), Georgia was struggling with her destiny.

Georgia's history with Russia was long and complicated. As early as the beginning of the nineteenth century, Georgia had looked to the Russian Empire for protection and help in developing her statecraft. When the Persian kingdom and the Ottoman Empire threatened Georgian security in 1802, Georgia agreed to be annexed to Russia and looked to her for security and guidance for the greater part of a century. Yet a strong nationalist spirit remained. Under the Russian Empire, Georgia had been a semi-autonomous territory. With the exception of a brief period after World War I, when Georgia was an independent republic, Georgia was under Soviet control.

Despite their strong desire for autonomy, Georgians lacked the leadership that proposed a clear path forward. As Keller points out, "Ask a Georgian on the streets . . . what the Georgians really want and the answer is likely to be 'freedom' or 'independence.' But those who see separation from the Soviet Union as a desirable and realistic goal seem to be a small minority. Some define independence as having Moscow keep its hands off Georgia's marketeering economy. Others define it more generally as 'being left in peace.'"

In equally pointed words, Keller reports impediments in the consolidation of a coherent movement:

> An attempt by more moderate elements to harness the popular impulses under a broad popular front has so far made little headway against the schismatic tendencies of political independents here. "How many parties are there in Georgia?" mused

Mr. Abashidze, the editor of Moloyozh Gruzii. "About as many as there are Georgians. Perhaps it is something in our character" (see "In Soviet Georgia, a Longing for Freedom but Little Sense of How to Get It").

The top Georgian political figure in 1989, Eduard A. Shevardnadze, had become the foreign minister of the Soviet Union and was still strongly in favor of unification with the union. Moscow did not favor Georgian independence. While Gorbachev was open to the possibility of independence movements in the Eastern bloc satellite countries (see introductions for East Germany, Czechoslovakia, and Hungary), part of the restructuring inherent in Gorbachev's *perestroika* involved Georgia remaining a part of the Soviet Union. In 1989, Gorbachev was pressing proposals for the trans-Caucasian nations, like Georgia, to participate in a governance plan that would keep them under Soviet rule. One political leader in Georgia told Keller, "If we cooperate with perestroika, we only strengthen the people who are in power now."

Although, as *The Times* points out, Georgia failed to turn anti-Moscow sentiment into political cohesion, in 1989 early signs of organized resistance began to appear. Leaders across Georgia initiated a series of nonviolent actions such as hunger strikes, which are among the most advanced and impactful of nonviolent methods. On April 10, 1989, Esther B. Fein, a journalist for *The Times,* reports that organizers told her that they had intended to maintain their work stoppages, hunger strikes, and rallies until April 14, the anniversary of the successful 1978 campaign to retain Georgian as the official language of the republic. Fein reports that Soviet troops and tanks were dispatched to Tbilisi, following a demonstration that started with 158 hunger strikers, who demanded independence from Moscow. Their numbers swelled into work stoppages and demonstrations involving several thousand persons. After four days of round-the-clock demonstrations in Tbilisi, Georgian television officially reported 16 killed and more than 200 hurt when, before dawn on April 10, Fein reports, "thousands of demonstrators in Tbilisi refused to disperse and troops with riot sticks moved into the crowds." Fein, however, indicates that Tbilisi residents told her of lists of the dead and injured that were circulating, and the number killed was greater than the official count, with as many as 40 slain. (Numbers vary in differing reports.) By Fein's account,

> People who have been taking part in the protests said in telephone interviews that demonstrators were upset by the presence of troops, tanks and armored vehicles on the city streets, but that until the early morning hours . . . , the soldiers had been calm.
>
> Around 4 A.M., they said, with the streets lit by the moon, troops began urging the crowds outside the main government building to break up and go home. After their repeated requests were defiantly ignored, the soldiers became agitated and began exchanging shouts and insults with the demonstrators. The soldiers then tried to disband the crowd forcibly, but as they pushed at the people, the protesters pushed back, and suddenly, witnesses said, the troops were randomly flailing clubs at the demonstrators.
>
> "It was all very tense between the troops and the people," said a student who was there when the violence began and who said he was afraid to identify himself. "But just so suddenly, the troops starting beating people—anybody who was in front of them—and there was simply chaos. People started falling" ("At Least 16 Killed as Protestors Battle the Police in Soviet Georgia").

Once again—as in 1956—Soviet soldiers had killed Georgians and injured hundreds. In the aftermath, leaders of the still fledgling pro-independence movement suddenly found Georgian popular defiance seething. It would become easier to organize for the incipient independence struggle.

MAY 8, 1989
IN SOVIET GEORGIA, A LONGING FOR FREEDOM BUT LITTLE SENSE OF HOW TO GET IT

By BILL KELLER
Special to The New York Times

Tbilisi, U.S.S.R., May 7 – Speaking in the smoke-filled kitchen of an apartment in Tbilisi's west side, four dissidents shared their vision of Georgia's future.

It must be, they all agreed, a future of independence, free of Moscow, free of Communist rule, with a Western-style parliament and many political parties.

Almost anywhere else the conversation would have sounded like the beginning of an opposition political party.

But this being Soviet Georgia, the four articulate radicals are, in fact, leaders of four separate political parties. The rival factions are resolutely resisting merger because they cannot agree on the details of their dream: whether Georgia should break free of the Soviet Union at once or after a short transition period; whether to invite United Nations peacekeeping forces to police the divorce; whether their dream state should be nonaligned or a member of the North Atlantic Treaty Organization.

Awakening Old Resentments

Nearly a month after troops wielding shovels and firing toxic gas waded into a crowd of Georgian protesters, leaving 20 dead and hundreds injured, the clash is now recalled as "the tragedy" or "bloody Sunday" and has awakened old resentments, a sense of unity and a vague longing for independence.

But in contrast to Estonia, Lithuania and other Soviet republics tugging at their reins, Georgia has not seen nationalist grievances translated into a cohesive political movement.

For the authorities in Moscow, it is probably a relief not to face another organized popular front challenging the Communist Party in the streets and at the polls, as those in the Baltic republics have done.

But a number of Tbilisi intellectuals worry that unless it finds a political outlet, the brooding in Georgia will be a recurring source of danger for Moscow, expressed in violent conflict or general disenchantment.

"What worries me is that people will simply lose hope in perestroika," said Vakhtang I. Abashidze, editor of Moloyozh Gruzii, a youth newspaper with a distinctive independent streak. "There are already signs of this."

What Georgians Want

Ask a Georgian on the streets of this entrancing, Mediterranean-style capital what the Georgians really want and the answer is likely to be "freedom" or "independence."

But those who see separation from the Soviet Union as a desirable and realistic goal seem to be a small minority. Some define independence as having Moscow keep its hands off Georgia's marketeering economy. Others define it more generally as "being left in peace."

"Of course there are maximalists, especially among the young," said Tomas V. Gamkrelidze, director of the Oriental Studies Institute of Georgia and a newly elected member of the Soviet Congress. "But for the mass of people, it is a sort of euphoria in the face of abstract principles, freedom and independence."

A History of Setbacks

It is a yearning with a long history.

Liberated from Russian rule by the 1917 Bolshevik Revolution, Georgia spent three years as an independent state. That status ended when the Red Army overthrew the Menshevik Social Democrats in 1921.

The ensuing decades of Soviet power paradoxically laid the groundwork for a rebirth of Georgian patriotism. Moscow brought industry, expanded educational opportunities, groomed a native party and government apparatus, and tolerated a flourishing of Georgian culture, all of which raised aspirations of Georgian autonomy.

The growing intelligentsia often chafed under Moscow's rule, and this tension has burst into the open whenever Georgians felt their national pride under attack.

In 1956, after Khrushchev's secret speech to party leaders condemning Georgia's most famous native son, Stalin, the police and the army fired on Georgians marching in Stalin's honor, killing dozens of students and sparking a period of severe unrest.

Stalin is not so widely revered in Georgia now, but many Georgians seem to see the official attacks on Stalin—now, under Mikhail S. Gorbachev, far more intense than they were under Khrushchev—as implicit attacks on the Georgians themselves.

Fierce Nationalist Spirit

When Moscow tried in 1978 to remove a clause from the new Georgian Constitution proclaiming Georgian the official language, thousands of demonstrators poured into the streets, forcing the authorities to back down.

The nationalist demonstration last month in Tbilisi began as a response to demands by the republic's Abkhazian minority that their tiny region in the northwest of the republic be given its independence.

During four days of round-the-clock protests in front of the Georgian Government building, the crowds were joined by a number of independent political groups demanding that Georgia be given greater freedom from Moscow, with some calling for outright secession. The separatist slogans apparently alarmed authorities, who called in tanks and troops.

Although the tanks were withdrawn, a curfew lifted, the Georgian Communist leader replaced and solemn regrets uttered, passions have continued to run high.

No Trust in Moscow

When the physicist and human rights advocate Andrei D. Sakharov passed through a Tbilisi hospital on Friday, dispensing calm, he encountered a group of students who politely but firmly rejected his assurances. "We don't trust Moscow, and we don't trust Gorbachev," one student said.

"The very fact that the Government allowed such methods to be used against us—such a Government gives us no guarantees that it cannot happen again," said Georgi Antelava, the head of a department at the Institute of Oriental Studies.

A wide range of Georgians interviewed here say the resentment has not produced a political movement comparable to those in the Baltics because democracy here was stunted by Communist rule before the Georgians had a chance to try it.

Mikhail Yeligulashvili, a deputy editor at Molodyozh Gruzii, said the low level of "political culture" was demonstrated by Georgia's comparative indifference during the recent elections for a new Congress of Deputies.

While independent candidates were toppling Communist Party officials in many Soviet cities, in Georgia most of the party leaders won comfortably.

Moreover, most of the more radical political groups shunned the elections altogether, saying they would not take part until the Government legalizes the creation of alternative political parties.

A Flair for Hunger Strikes

"If we cooperate with perestroika, we only strengthen the people who are in power now," said Irinia Sarashvili, a 23-year-old history student and a leader of the National Democratic Party of Georgia, which advocates swift secession from the Soviet Union.

At least half a dozen groups, most claiming membership of a few hundred—and many calling themselves political parties in defiance of the Communist Party's legal monopoly—now call for a fully independent Georgia.

Their principal tactic has been small hunger strikes, hoping that the public will flock to their support.

Two days after the April clash, four small self-styled political parties that took part in the fatal demonstration formed an alliance to protest the jailing of their leaders—four dissidents remain in custody, charged with disrupting public order—and calling for independence.

But such alliances here have always proved short-lived.

An attempt by more moderate elements to harness the popular impulses under a broad popular front has so far made little headway against the schismatic tendencies of political independents here.

"How many parties are there in Georgia?" mused Mr. Abashidze, the editor of Moloyozh Gruzii. "About as many as there are Georgians. Perhaps it is something in our character."

Shevardnadze Heads Home to Lead Georgia

In 1992, Eduard Shevardnadze, former foreign minister of the Soviet Union, assumed the leadership of the State Council, the caretaker government of the Republic of Georgia, and began steering Georgia's recognition as an independent state through foreign governments and building an economy at home. The transition was an unlikely one for Shevardnadze, whom Celestine Bohlen describes for *The Times* on April 20, 1992, as "resilient," a "paradox," and "a lapsed Communist in what once had been a stronghold of Communism" (see "Re-enter Shevardnadze, the Phoenix of Georgia"). A former Soviet minister who, as recently as five months earlier, had been arguing for Georgia to remain a part of the Soviet Union had become the leading figure in Georgian independence.

How was such an evolution possible? In 1990, Shevardnadze's approval rating in Georgia, according to Bohlen, was 30 percent, because he was seen as a Soviet insider who was standing in the way of independence. By April 1992, however, he had more than 70 percent approval. Shevardnadze himself gives an answer: Why can't a politician evolve the way artists do? The events between the Tbilisi massacre in 1989 and Shevardnadze's assumption of power in 1992 may provide some clues. Two things were clear: Georgia wanted independence, and Georgia needed stability and recognition.

After the violence in 1989, Georgian pro-independence activism had not subsided (see "In Soviet Georgia, a Longing for Freedom but Little Sense of How to Get It"). Although Gorbachev sought to keep the Soviet Union intact, with its inclusion and incorporation of East European and Central Asian territories, the people of Georgia had made a firm commitment to self-determination. In 1991, Zviad K. Gamsakhurdia, an unapologetic nationalist opposition leader, won sweeping victories against the communists in plenary elections. The following year, on the anniversary of the Tbilisi massacre, he introduced a resolution for independence. More than 98 percent of Georgians voted for it (see **Georgia, Introduction**). Gamsakhurdia was elected president of Georgia in a landslide.

Gamsakhurdia's leadership of the republic, however, was erratic, and under him Georgia was not stable. As Bohlen notes, "Riding the wave of national liberation, [Gamsakhurdia] began to assemble a new authoritarian state, jailing political opponents, closing independent newspapers and taunting his rivals into a series of deadly street battles." The Georgian economy was a shambles, and the internal leadership was in a near–civil war. In December 1991, Bohlen writes, Gamsakhurdia's policies led to the eruption of a "ferocious war," where he, his family, and 4,000 supporters hid in a bunker for nearly two weeks, before fleeing. Bohlen concludes that Gamsakhurdia's overthrow made Shevardnadze's return possible. The country that sought stability as much as freedom was in fact open to leadership from powerful former defenders of the Soviet empire.

Shevardnadze returned to lead the State Council, an interim government established to restore order after the fall of Gamsakhurdia's government. Following Gamsakhurdia's suicide on December 31, 1993, *The Times* writes on January 6, 1994, that he was a "philologist and a political prisoner in the Soviet era," who "led Georgia's struggle for independence and became its first elected president in a landslide vote in May 1991.

But his popularity quickly ebbed amid protests against government human rights violations and his dictatorial style. He was overthrown after six months in office in fierce battles in Tbilisi." In a bloodless coup, Gamsakhurdia was driven from Tbilisi in January 1992, and subsequently based his insurgency in Grozny, in Chechenya ("Suicide by Caucasus Rebel Is Reported)."

Shevardnadze, whether seeking personal authority and credibility or the greater good of Georgia, changed from being a communist to becoming a Georgian nationalist. According to Bohlen, Georgia's experience with Gamsakhurdia "may have helped speed its transition to the kind of rational democratic system that still eludes so much of the former Soviet Union." She quotes Shevardnadze as saying, "We have had a very severe lesson. . . . The Georgian people have rejected both a totalitarian and an authoritarian regime. Our society realized this lesson very quickly." Lobbying foreign governments to recognize Georgia, and using his former position as the Soviet foreign minister, Shevardnadze was able to persuade fifty-five countries to recognize Georgia by the time Bohlen's article appeared. He initiated elections, in contrast to the Soviet posture of only a few months earlier, apparently recognizing the inevitability of some form of Georgia's self-determination.

APRIL 20, 1992
RE-ENTER SHEVARDNADZE, THE PHOENIX OF GEORGIA
By CELESTINE BOHLEN

Tbilisi, Georgia, April 17 – This week, Eduard A. Shevardnadze moved into yet another office, this one in the former Institute of Marxism-Leninism on Rustaveli Prospekt, the main boulevard that bears the scars of the civil war that raged here four months ago.

The former Soviet Foreign Minister's new domain has a provisional look about it, like the national government he now presides over. Phones and desks are still being installed, the walls of the waiting room are bare, and in the stairwell outside, a young man stands in the midst of a milling crowd, guarding the door with a machine gun.

This is the latest stop in a resilient career that in seven years has taken Mr. Shevardnadze from leader of the Georgian Communist Party, to Foreign Minister of the Soviet Union, and now back home again. In the meantime Georgia, an ancient land of five and a half million rooted in the Caucasus mountains, has changed from a small Soviet republic into a country proud of its successful revolt against Communism and of its independence.

Mr. Shevardnadze, unfazed by the paradox he presents in his new position—a lapsed Communist in what had been a stronghold of Communism—describes his return to Georgia a month ago as "the most difficult step in my life."

'Taking a Risk'

"It is difficult to pull the country out of chaos and crisis," he said in an interview. "I know that I am taking a risk making this step, but I can say that I am morally satisfied."

At 64 years old, Mr. Shevardnadze has proved capable of remarkable adaptation. Five months after he answered his old friend Mikhail S. Gorbachev's call to rejoin the crumbling Soviet Government, he is helping Georgia steer a totally independent course, staying away from the clumsy maneuverings of the Commonwealth of Independent States.

In his new role, he heads a State Council of about 60 people, many of them fierce opponents of the Communist Government he once represented, some of whom served time in prison at his orders.

Mr. Shevardnadze, whose mild demeanor and wan smile belies a reputation for toughness, considers his latest incarnation the logical progression of a man who treasures his right to change.

Why, he asked, can't a politician evolve, as artists do? "Picasso had his different periods, and other artists too," he said. "I made mistakes, I was sometimes unfair, but what is one supposed to do—to stick to one position to the end, to the death? We have all changed."

Gamsakhurdia's Brief Era

This spirit is shared by other members of the State Council. "There are many people sitting at the table who used to be opponents," said Eldar Shengelaya, a member of the State Council and one of Georgia's most noted film makers. "It is a reflection of the extraordinary changes that have taken place in the society, and in people themselves. This has not been a simple historical development. We have gone from one world to another."

A year ago, Mr. Shevardnadze's name was virtually taboo in Georgia, where a then-popular nationalist, Zviad K. Gamsakhurdia, had just been elected president with 87 percent of the votes. Mr. Gamsakhurdia, imprisoned by Mr. Shevardnadze for his outspoken anti-Communism, repeatedly denounced his old foe as an agent of the Kremlin, of the K.G.B. and of Russian imperialism.

But Mr. Gamsakhurdia's rule was short-lived. Riding the wave of national liberation, he began to assemble a new authoritarian state, jailing political opponents, closing independent newspapers and taunting his rivals into a series of deadly street battles.

In December, these clashes erupted into a ferocious war, fought up and down Rustaveli Prospekt around the giant Government building, where Mr. Gamsakhurdia, with his family and 4,000 supporters, holed up in a bunker for almost two weeks.

He escaped with a small entourage, retreating to the Chechenya region, formerly the Chechen-Ingush region, inside Russia, where he still convenes a rump parliament, and issues orders to die-hard supporters in western Georgia, who for two months have continued to fight Government troops.

Wary of His Popularity

Mr. Gamsakhurdia's overthrow made Mr. Shevardnadze's return possible. But Mr. Shevardnadze, whose popularity rating has jumped from 30 percent to more than 70 percent, is mindful of the pitfalls of setting himself as Georgia's latest savior.

He is likely to run in Parliament elections scheduled in the fall, but he, like many Georgians, is against the kind of strong presidential rule that has proved popular among Russians and that was abused by Mr. Gamsakhurdia. "I feel the people are apprehensive, that a new situation may arise with a new person having appeared on the scene," he said. "Therefore, I am very cautious."

In a curious way, Georgia's recent experience may have helped speed its transition to the kind of rational democratic system that still eludes so much of the former Soviet Union.

"We have had a very severe lesson," said Mr. Shevardnadze, who makes a point of withholding his personal views on Mr. Gamsakhurdia. "The Georgian people have rejected both a totalitarian and an authoritarian regime. Our society realized this lesson very quickly. For other nations, it will take a very long time."

According to Tengiz Kitovani, commander of Georgia's national guard, the fighting in western Georgia is all but over, leaving the Government troops with a mop-up operation and a continuing battle with small groups he labels criminal gangs.

Most of the political opposition is still concentrated in western Georgia, where Mr. Gamsakhurdia's family has its roots. Here in the capital, there are still occasional outbursts. For instance, a group of Gamsakhurdia supporters recently set a bonfire of books written by those they consider "enemies of Georgia."

But the fanaticism fed by Mr. Gamsakhurdia is beginning to ebb. Georgia's rich cultural life is returning to normal, under a Government that according to Deputy Prime Minister Irakly Surguladze, is committed to allowing its critics their chance to speak. At a recent charity function, Mr. Shevardnadze's wife joined in the laughter as a stand-up comic did a mocking imitation of her husband.

"Everyone says how unlucky we were," said Mr. Shengelaya. "I think God gave us a gift. We had our experience with Gamsakhurdia, but the roots of this were much deeper. The fight was with ourselves—from unrestricted Communism to unrestricted nationalism. Now we have gone through this cycle."

Still, evidence of Georgia's recent trauma is visible everywhere. An 11 P.M. curfew is still in effect in Tbilisi. The lower half of Rustaveli Prospekt is in ruins, as is the Georgian economy, battered by Mr. Gamsakhurdia's nationalist nostrums. Industrial production has dropped 21 percent, while inflation continues to soar. Because of a fuel shortage, city residents have been without hot water since last summer.

The Government is laying the groundwork for elections, while gingerly undertaking economic reform. But most important, Georgia—which three months ago was an outcast among the former Soviet republics—is now gaining the international recognition denied it during Mr. Gamsakhurdia's tenure.

International Voice

For this, Mr. Shevardnadze gets credit, a testament to the respect he earned as Soviet Foreign Minister. . . .

Asked about Mr. Shevardnadze's performance so far, ordinary people point to his success in bringing Georgia into the world of nations, giving it a chance to compete for the international aid and investment it so desperately needs.

"This is a man who could have retired to Acapulco," said the writer Chabua Amiredzhibi, a member of the State Council, who had been high on Mr. Gamsakhurdia's enemies list. "Instead, he came to Georgia, and as a result we have now been recognized by 55 countries."

Popular opinion in Georgia has been strongly against membership in the Commonwealth of Independent States, a view that Mr. Shevardnadze says he now shares. "I don't believe the commonwealth can survive, and believe me, you will see that it won't," he said. "It is not possible to give birth to such an enormous formation in 24 hours."

Comments on Gorbachev

Mr. Shevardnadze traces the collapse of the Soviet Union to the "revolution" that he and Mr. Gorbachev began in the mid-1980's. His most celebrated act of dissent was his dramatic resignation speech in December 1990, when he warned of a coup. In November, he briefly returned to his post of Foreign Minister, as the Soviet Union was about to collapse.

"Just as the countries of Eastern Europe took advantage of this principle of free elections," he said, "so we realized—I personally realized—that sooner or later, the issue of self-determination and freedom of choice would be raised inside the Soviet Union in the same acute and urgent manner.

"Of course, it should have been recognized two or three or even four years earlier. But Gorbachev, my friend, was late."

Parliamentary Elections Off to a Bumpy Start

After three years of running the country through the temporary State Council, Shevardnadze was elected president in 1995 and reelected in 2000. Yet many doubted that Georgia was the republic of "self-determination," marked by "free elections," that Shevardnadze had predicted and hoped for when taking office in 1992. As *The Times* points out on November 3, 2003, Shevardnadze's tenure was marked by corruption, a lagging economy, and internal strife (see "Georgians Vote for Lawmakers in Preview of a Presidential Race)."

The years of Soviet administration of Georgia had also been characterized by corruption and wrongdoing, but Shevardnadze, who became party leader in September 1972, had earned a reputation as a fighter of corruption within the Politburo. As the Communist Party chief, he was even known for "cleaning house," "periodically dismissing ministers [of government] and party officials for taking bribes, profiteering and laxity," as Craig Whitney reports for *The Times* on April 18, 1978 ("Soviet Georgians Win on Language").

Shevardnadze's election as president in 1995 and formal assumption of power in Georgia was not without significant conflict. In 1993, the deposed leader, Zviad Gamsakhurdia, returned to Georgia and led a 10,000 troop army against the central government, but was soundly defeated (see "Re-enter Shevardnadze, The Phoenix of Georgia").

Throughout the rest of Shevardnadze's leadership, political opposition was manifested in both violent attacks, including an assassination attempt against him with a car bomb, and collective nonviolent action. The nonviolent civil resisters were unable to build the unity that had characterized Serbia's transition from dictatorship to democracy (see **Serbia, Introduction**). Shevardnadze's government was often criticized for tactics that were reminiscent of authoritarianism, such as wiretapping and threats of political suppression, as reported by Michael Specter for *The Times* on October 19, 1995 ("Tragic Georgian, or Fixer of a Broken Nation?"). Even so, Shevardnadze easily won the presidency in 1995 and led Georgia through much of the next decade.

Widely respected by the world at large for his role in the fall of communism, Shevardnadze successfully lobbied for greater influence in and aid from the United Nations, the World Bank, the International Monetary Fund, and other multilateral organizations. At the same time, he used his former Soviet ties to gain great influence with Russia. Specter notes that as president of Georgia, Shevardnadze once said, "The Sun rises not in the East, but in the North," a phrase that his critics would often cite as examples of his shortcomings. Georgians began to see in Shevardnadze the attributes of communist totalitarianism: too Russian, too repressive, and too authoritarian in his policies and tactics.

Tangible domestic and international criticism arose in 2000, when Shevardnadze ran for reelection. Although the official results were announced with an overwhelming victory for Shevardnadze—said to have won with more than 80 percent of the vote—many Georgians, as well as election observers, doubted the fairness of the election, as Specter reports for *The Times* on April 11, 2000 ("Foreign Observers Criticize Lopsided Shevardnadze Vote"). Independent observers cited similar abuses countrywide. The United States had contributed $2.4 million to help Georgia prepare for the November balloting. Five thousand electoral observers had come from the National Democratic Institute for International Affairs and the International Republican Institute, both in Washington, D.C., as well as the Organization for Security and Cooperation in Europe, to join with nongovernmental organizations in Georgia (Jones 2009, 322). Electoral commissions that had been in the palm of the ruling parties had been overhauled to provide the opposition with representation. Charles J. Fairbanks, professor of international relations, was an eyewitness to voting fraud. He writes of "the same people voting again and again, voters and even members of the precinct-level electoral commissions arbitrarily thrown out of polling places, officials marking ballots for voters and refusing to carry out legally prescribed procedures to ensure fairness, instances of 'family voting' in which patriarchs voted for their households, a needless and clearly intimidating police presence inside polling stations; and much more."

The Times account of November 3, 2003, sets the stage for the turbulent parliamentary elections that resulted in upheaval in Georgia (see "Georgians Vote for Lawmakers in Preview of a Presidential Race"). For the first time, Georgians had a genuine choice of parties for the 235 seats in their parliament, an improvement over past taints, bartering, or hidden alliances with the government. Shevardnadze had become "deeply unpopular over unkept promises to eliminate corruption and improve living standards," *The Times* notes, and he had "failed to quell separatism that sprang from a civil war." He had divided political ranks at the upper reaches, while tolerating some expressions of political dissent from the grassroots, thereby offering a semblance of pluralism and openness. Although not a tyrant, he was also not a democrat. His party, For a New Georgia, entered the parliamentary elections, widely seen as a sign for the future direction of Georgia. Yet, according to The Times, twelve years of independence in Georgia, led since 1992 by Shevardnadze, had brought about neither stability nor a vigorous democratic culture.

NOVEMBER 3, 2003
GEORGIANS VOTE FOR LAWMAKERS IN PREVIEW OF A PRESIDENTIAL RACE

Tbilisi, Georgia, Nov. 2 – Georgian parliamentary elections, seen as a guide to who will succeed Eduard A. Shevardnadze, the veteran president, in 2005, got off to a bumpy start . . . with some polling stations failing to open and voter lists incomplete.

But the initial confusion in Georgia, a volatile former Soviet state, eased as the day went on. By afternoon, voting was proceeding smoothly at most polling stations. . . .

Western governments and businesses are closely watching the voting in Georgia, where a pipeline is under construction to carry Caspian oil across the Caucasus through Georgia and Turkey to Western markets in 2005.

Twelve years of independence in Georgia, led since 1992 by Mr. Shevardnadze, has not brought stability or a robust democratic culture.

Mr. Shevardnadze, 76, is still remembered in the West for his leading role, as Moscow's foreign minister, in ending the cold war and unifying Germany.

But at home he has become deeply unpopular over unkept promises to eliminate corruption and improve living standards. He also has failed to quell separatism that sprang from a civil war.

The Black Sea region of Abkhazia is defying Tbilisi's rule and looking more to Moscow, a source of great strains with Russia. South Ossetia also lies beyond central control, and fighting across the border in Chechnya casts its own shadow.

Mr. Shevardnadze's party, known as For a New Georgia, is one of five likely to clear the 7 percent barrier needed to enter the 235-seat assembly.

Despite procedural flaws, Mr. Shevardnadze told reporters as he cast his ballot, "I am sure it will be fair."

Many citizens were initially unable to vote. One polling station in the capital, Tbilisi, and another in Khobi in western Georgia were closed on procedural grounds. In Kutaisi, Georgia's second city, two-thirds of polling stations were closed throughout the morning, but most were operating after lunch.

"The elections are proceeding in normal fashion despite some violations of rules," said Nana Devdariani, Georgia's chief electoral official. "These were not unexpected."

Two of four opposition parties likely to win seats on party lists are led by the president's former allies. The Parliament speaker, Nino Burdzhanadze, heads one bloc, while a second is led by a former justice minister, Mikhail Saakashvili. Others in the running include the leftist Labor Party and the Revival Party.

Mr. Shevardnadze, who has survived many assassination attempts since returning to Georgia from Moscow, is barred from running for a new term in 2005. The United States, Russia and Turkey, among others, view the situation with concern, hoping for a smooth transfer of power.

SHEVARDNADZE RESISTS CALLS FOR HIS RESIGNATION

"As long as I am president, a legally elected president, I won't allow the nation to split and civil war to break out, although the real danger of this exists," Eduard Shevardnadze stated, as Seth Mydans reports in The Times on November 15, 2003 (see "President of Georgia Pleads for Calm as Protests Grow"). The Georgian leader's pronouncement may have come too late. Mydans cites an editorial in an English-language daily, The Messenger: "Despite the fact that he is adored in the West as an 'architect of democracy' and credited with ending the cold war, Georgians cannot bear their president." In the government-reported results of the parliamentary elections in November 2003, For a New Georgia led by a narrow margin, but

Georgian and international observers alike did not trust the results. The U.S. ambassador to Georgia released a statement saying, "The mismanagement and fraud" of the election "denied many Georgian citizens their constitutional right to vote," reports The Times on November 6 ("U.S. Cites Fraud in Vote").

The high expectations of change and the unsophisticated falsification of the voting led to indignation on a huge scale, and the Georgians began collective nonviolent action. Demonstrations started as a condemnation of "a manipulated parliamentary election on November 2," Seth Mydans explains, quoting one diplomat who said the vote was "a mess from start to finish." Mydans discerns three distinct currents that had been coursing toward the fall of the Shevardnadze government. The first was the rise of a viable opposition leader in Mikhail Saakashvili, who called for civil disobedience, tax resistance, and picketing. The other forces at work were the mounting recognition, both inside and outside of Russia, that Shevardnadze was a fraud, and the collapse of the institutions of formal state support.

NOVEMBER 15, 2003
PRESIDENT OF GEORGIA PLEADS FOR CALM AS PROTESTS GROW
Shevardnadze Resists Call to Step Down
By SETH MYDANS

Moscow, Nov., 14 – A postelection standoff erupted into turmoil in Georgia on Friday as thousands of antigovernment protesters filled the streets, surrounding the presidential compound as truckloads of soldiers stood by.

President Eduard A. Shevardnadze addressed the nation on television, pleading for calm and warning that the protests could spark a civil war. He rebuffed calls for his resignation but said he was ready to talk with opposition leaders in this former Soviet republic.

"As long as I am president, a legally elected president, I won't allow the nation to split and civil war to break out, although the real danger of this exists," said Mr. Shevardnadze, 75, waving his hands and looking pale.

"I still appeal to everyone to calm down and act peacefully for the sake of your motherland, of our motherland," he said. "From civil confrontation to civil war is a short step."

As many as 20,000 chanting protesters, shown on Russian television, danced and chanted slogans as evening fell, by far the largest crowd in more than a week of daily protests outside the Parliament building in Tbilisi, Georgia's capital.

A row of helmeted soldiers wearing black ski masks faced the crowd from behind their shields in front of the presidential office. Reporters on the scene said armored personnel carriers and truckloads of soldiers were parked nearby.

"The military is ready today to do everything to defend their motherland," Mr. Shevardnadze said.

The demonstrations began as a protest against a manipulated parliamentary election on Nov. 2, which one diplomat called "a mess from start to finish."

The protests have swelled into a cry of anger over a decade of mismanagement during which Mr. Shevardnadze has let this small nation in the Caucasus slide into poverty, joblessness, corruption and a breakdown in services. Few of the former Soviet republics have plummeted farther and faster since the collapse of the Soviet Union in 1991 than this ancient mountain land.

Mr. Shevardnadze, who as Soviet foreign minister watched the Berlin Wall fall, has led Georgia for 12 years. Under the Constitution he must step aside in a presidential vote in 2005, but calls for his immediate resignation have swelled in the last week.

"I am ready to continue dialogue with the opposition leaders," he said on television. "I am even ready to talk with their 'commander in chief,' Saakashvili."

Mikhail Saakashvili, a former protégé of Mr. Shevardnadze, is the most fiery of three major opposition leaders. . . . [H]e called for a campaign of civil disobedience and urged the demonstrators to remain peaceful, saying, "Let's not give grounds for a provocation."

"Starting from tomorrow, I ask everybody to stop paying taxes and fees to this repressive regime," he said, "and

I ask everybody who works for the state to stay away from work.

"To everyone else, I appeal to you to form pickets outside government buildings to prevent officials from getting to work."

When it became independent, Georgia seemed to have one of the brightest futures among the former Soviet republics, with its vineyards, orchards, tourism and hustling entrepreneurs.

But the collapse of its Russian markets, the corrupt culture inherited from Soviet times and the separatist conflicts and tensions that have threatened to tear it apart have turned it into a beggar nation.

For its size, this nation of 4.4 million people holds disproportionate interest for Russia, its northern neighbor, and for the United States, which has poured in $1 billion in aid in the last decade. That puts Georgia in the same league, per capita, as America's biggest aid recipients, Israel and Egypt.

The United States is also spending about $64 million over four years to train 2,000 Georgian soldiers, primarily as a counterterrorism force, a military involvement that has made Moscow unhappy.

Geographic location is one reason for America's interest, at a strategic crossroads between Russia, the Black Sea and Turkey. Oil is another, with the planned opening in 2005 of a pivotal $3 billion pipeline from the Caspian fields of Azerbaijan across to the Mediterranean coast of Turkey.

Affection for the man who helped Mikhail S. Gorbachev bring the ruined Soviet Union to a soft landing has also contributed to Washington's generosity. . . .

Georgians have a different perspective.

As the English-language daily The Messenger put it this week: "Despite the fact that he is adored in the West as an 'architect of democracy' and credited with ending the cold war, Georgians cannot bear their president."

He has been the dominant personality here for a quarter-century, serving as Communist Party chief from 1972 until he became foreign minister under Mr. Gorbachev in 1986. Mr. Shevardnadze took power in Georgia in what his opponents call a coup after a brief but ruinous civil war from 1991 to 1992.

His rule has not been easy. Over the years he has faced rebellions in four provinces, lost control of the breakaway region of Abkhazia and survived two assassination attempts. He was quoted the other day as saying he had been much happier when he was foreign minister.

Nino Burdzhanadze, the parliamentary speaker, who is a leader of the opposition, said Mr. Shevardnadze had squandered his moment in history.

"I was really proud to have a president who was friends with some of the most important people of the 20th century," she said the other day. "I'm truly sorry things have come to this point. The president had the chance to have his name written in gold letters in the history of Georgia."

- - -

Shevardnadze's Party Declared Winner in Disputed Election

The election on November 2, 2003, was immediately followed by twenty days of massive nonviolent demonstrations. Lasting from November 3 to November 23, the turmoil forced President Shevardnadze to step down. On the last day of the demonstrations, Shevardnadze met with the student group Kmara (Enough) and other opposition leaders. Recognizing that his support had disintegrated, he announced his resignation soon after.

Born into circumstances dominated and controlled by Soviet-trained former apparatchiks, and drenched in communist ideologies, systems, and tactics, Shevardnadze was ill-equipped to lead a society with aspirations for freedom and democracy. The social order in which he was reared would have found the events following the election unthinkable. On November 17, more than 50,000 people congregated in central Tbilisi's Freedom Square; 3,000 demonstrators held hands and formed a human chain encircling the chancellery. An intensive series of mass nonviolent demonstrations occurred in Georgia from November 21 to 23. This culmination of this intensive direct action is known as the Revolution of the Roses.

On November 21, Mydans reports the decision of the election commission, which the day before in a volatile atmosphere had falsified results and certified that Shevardnadze's coalition had won a majority in the election (see "Officials in Georgia Declare Shevardnadze Ballot Winner"). On November 20, thousands of people had arrived in Tbilisi in caravans of cars that stretched for miles, driving from western Georgia. The same day, the U.S. State Department issued a statement to the news media firmly saying that the results "do not accurately reflect the will of the Georgian people, but instead reflect massive fraud." A Radio Free Europe/Radio Liberty analyst contended that this "was the first time ever that the [United States] has openly accused the leadership of a former Soviet republic of rigging an election." Opposition leaders immediately questioned the validity of the election results and refused to be seated in the parliament. On November 21, more than 100,000 assembled in Tbilisi's Freedom Square to prevent officials from entering the parliament building. The effort failed, and the demonstrators instead sought to disrupt the seating of the parliamentarians by blocking roads with vehicles and buses. Police and army troops stood by observing, taking no action.

From Mydans's account, in seems clear that a Georgian transition to democracy in a practical sense would require the public to reject the validity of the elections. By questioning the election results, the internal and external observers had undermined Shevardnadze's legitimacy. Throughout the 1990s, Shevardnadze had maintained his power in the name of stability, and now *The Times* notes that he warned of civil war if the parliament could not be seated. Meanwhile, new Georgian leadership was arising in a multiparty political opposition, through the unifying figure of Mikhail Saakashvili, not a paramilitary figure such as Gamsakhurdia (see "Re-enter Shevardnadze, the Phoenix of Georgia"). Saakashvili had called for taking nonviolent action through civil resistance.

The Times suggests that in response to Shevardnadze's demand for the parliament to be seated, one of the regime's major instruments of control—media and public opinion—collapsed. The chief administrator of a government-run television station resigned, saying he could no longer present a "biased view."

Many of the tens of thousands of nonviolent protagonists who stood their ground in Tbilisi were from Kmara, the nonviolent civil resistance group. Throughout 2003, Kmara had organized simultaneous demonstrations across the country, so as to manifest organized civil resistance. It held the first nationwide action on May 12. As the Shevardnadze regime attempted to weaken Kmara and other opposition groups, especially beyond Tbilisi, the student group carried out a graffiti campaign, writing "Kmara" in tens of thousands of places on Tbilisi streets and roads.

Even though Kmara did not receive the kind of international coverage that Otpor! did in Serbia, Kmara was able to organize thousands of young Georgians to push for an end to Shevardnadze's rule (on Otpor, see "Rally Against Milosevic Fails to Bind Opposition Parties"; "Student Group Emerges as Major Milosevic Foe"; **Serbia, Introduction**). The widespread corruption in the parliamentary elections in 2003 was the spark that ignited the population's resistance.

A Georgian girl holds a leaf as she walks along a line of troops surrounding the government headquarters in downtown Tbilisi, Georgia, on November 18, 2003. Political tensions simmered in the country after Georgians and international observers concluded that the November 2 presidential election was rife with fraud. The troops put up no resistance to the Rose Revolution.
Source: AP Images/Shakh Aivazov

NOVEMBER 21, 2003
OFFICIALS IN GEORGIA DECLARE SHEVARDNADZE BALLOT WINNER
By SETH MYDANS

Moscow, Nov. 20 – The Central Election Commission of Georgia announced Thursday that supporters of President Eduard A. Shevardnadze had won a disputed parliamentary election held on Nov. 2, heightening tensions in the capital, Tbilisi.

The formal announcement confirmed a result that had already sent many thousands of protesters into the streets, and opposition leaders renewed their call on Thursday for the unpopular Mr. Shevardnadze, 75, to step down immediately.

"This Parliament is illegitimate," said Mikhail Saakashvili, the most prominent opposition leader, whose bloc placed third. "We won't join the new Parliament, and we will try to prevent it from holding its session."

In the final count, two blocs backing the president came in first and second. Mr. Shevardnadze's party, For a New Georgia, was awarded 21.32 percent of the vote. The Revival party, which threw its vote behind Mr. Shevardnadze at the last moment, finished with 18.84 percent.

Five opposition representatives walked out of the commission meeting, saying the count was fraudulent. International election observers had issued strongly worded criticisms of fraud and ballot manipulation.

Protests over the balloting have sharpened into calls for Mr. Shevardnadze's resignation, with demonstrators and their leaders blaming him for corruption, misrule and an economic collapse in the former Soviet republic.

Mr. Shevardnadze has said he will remain in office until his term ends and a new presidential election is held in 2005....

Mr. Shevardnadze has dismissed his opponents' criticisms and warned that continued demonstrations could lead to civil war as similar protests did in 1991.

He appeared to be heading toward a confrontation when he organized counter demonstrations made up mostly of young men and announced that he would immediately call into session the disputed Parliament.

For his part, Mr. Saakashvili said he would call for a march to demand that the president step down.

In a sign that Mr. Shevardnadze's support was slipping further, the chairman of a government-run television channel resigned Thursday, saying he could no longer present what he called a biased view.

Opponents Protest Seating of Another Shevardnadze Government

"The velvet revolution has taken place in Georgia," declared Mikhail Saakashvili, the leader of the opposition to the Shevardnadze government, when protestors shut down the Georgian parliament on November 22, 2003, as Seth Mydans reports in *The Times* the next day (see "Foes of Georgian Leader Storm into Parliament Building"). Saakashvili's citation of the "velvet revolution" alluded to the paralysis of the Czechoslovakian communist regime in the "Ten Days" of 1989 that led to the former political prisoner and playwright Václav Havel being elected as the leader of a newly democratic Czechoslovakia (see "Václav Havel and Truth"; "200,000 March in Prague as Calls for Change Mount"; "250,000 Czechs, Hailing Dubcek, Urge Ouster of Hard-Line Leaders"; "Prague Rivals Vie for Favor on Eve of Party Meeting"). Within Czechoslovakia, the term "velvet revolution" was used internally to describe the deliberately nonviolent character of the revolution (see **Czechoslovakia, Introduction**).

Saakashvili unequivocally stated, "We are against violence," Mydans reports. In retrospect it can be seen that on November 22 Georgia was moving toward the climax of its Rose Revolution, as thousands of citizens, under the leadership of political activists like Saakashvili, stormed Freedom Square and the parliament building to protest the seating of another Shevardnadze government. The Revolution of the Roses would force Shevardnadze to step down and clear the path for Saakashvili, a thirty-six-year-old U.S.-educated lawyer, to win 96.2 percent of the vote in a January 4, 2004, presidential election and take office unopposed.

The nonviolent challengers swarmed the parliament around the clock, blocking the entrances so that the legislators could not gain access. The demonstrators also surrounded Shevardnadze's quarters. Shevardnadze declared a state of emergency in order to mobilize military troops against the demonstrators. Instead, the troops under arms joined the action. The civil resisters distributed red roses to the soldiers, who began demonstrating *with* the multitudes. The army officers in charge pledged to follow the orders coming from the opposition. According to Mydans on November 24, 2003, Saakashvili later cited the military's change of allegiance as the most important contributing factor to the downfall of the regime (see "Georgian Leader Agrees to Resign, Ending Standoff").

Saakashvili alludes to Czech influence on the strategy and inspiration for the Rose Revolution, because, as *The Times* illustrates, foreign influences were having an effect on Georgia and its leaders. Saakashvili is a prime example. The opposition leader was both shaped and supported by forces beyond his Black Sea nation. Born in Tbilisi in 1967, Saakashvili went abroad for his education and received a law degree from Columbia University in New York in 1994. He married a Dutch citizen, Sandra Elisabeth Roelofs, a student of human rights, before returning to Georgia in the mid-1990s. Considered a rising star in Georgian politics, he had served in Shevardnadze's cabinet as minister of justice, where he pursued anticorruption reforms. In 2001, however, he resigned his position, saying, "I consider it immoral for me to remain a member of Shevardnadze's cabinet." That year, he formed the United National Movement (UNM), the party he led to a third-place finish in the elections of early November 2003.

The UNM and associated civic associations such as the Liberty Institute, the most prominent Georgian nongovernmental organization devoted to civil rights, and the youth organization Kmara, received significant funding and support from the West (see "Georgians Vote for Lawmakers in Preview of a Presidential Race"; "Officials in Georgia Declare Shevardnadze Ballot Winner"). The U.S. Open Society Institute (OSI), founded by philanthropist George Soros, a Hungarian émigré, had provided funding for Saakashvili and a number of prodemocracy student activists to visit Serbia and confer with young Otpor activists. Otpor and civil society groups were instrumental in toppling Slobodan Milošević after his government falsified election results in autumn 2000. OSI's funding made possible the establishment of Kmara (Enough), which modeled itself on Otpor and adopted the same symbol, a clenched fist. Kmara activists received training from Otpor in nonviolent strategic action. As a result, these independent organizations were able to facilitate the flow of literature that had been developed and utilized by Otpor and other civic associations in countries where similar movements of nonviolent civil resistance were mobilizing (see "Rally Against Milosevic Fails to Bind Opposition Parties"; "Student Group Emerges as Major Milosevic Foe"). Georgia benefited from the experience of movements elsewhere, not only for inspiration, but also for guidance, knowledge, and planning.

Shevardnadze also had gained influence because of his foreign allegiances. Backed by both the United States and Russia, Shevardnadze saw his long-standing foreign support erode in late 2003. Mydans reports that the United States and Russia became skeptical of the November 2 parliamentary election results, but in different ways. The United States openly disparaged the results of the election, accusing the Shevardnadze government of "massive vote fraud." Russian officials did not discount the election results, but alluded to "mistakes" in the election that had to be rectified, or else, they claimed, as Mydans reports, "the alternative is chaos" (see "Foes of Georgian Leader Storm into Parliament Building").

The November 2003 election was considered a vanguard for presidential balloting in 2005. Shevardnadze would be required by the Constitution to step down, but he wanted to see his party remain in power. The people of Georgia rejected the results. Protests following the election rapidly turned into demands for Shevardnadze to resign immediately. Saakashvili and other elected parliamentarians in the opposition led scores of protestors, roses in hand, into the parliament building on November 22, while Shevardnadze was officially opening the new term. Shevardnadze's bodyguards rushed him off the podium and outside, still holding the text of his uncompleted speech. Police were on hand, yet not one shot was fired. As Shevardnadze hurried out, Mydans notes, he stated his refusal to resign and his intention to serve out the remainder of his term through 2005.

KEY PLAYER IN GEORGIA
Giorgi Kandelaki (1982–)

Giorgi Kandelaki attended Tbilisi State University, where in 2001 he was elected to the university's first student government. The student government drew national attention as the members mounted a campaign to end corruption in state universities, reform higher education, and launch similar groups at other universities.

Dissatisfied with the presidency of Eduard Shevardnadze, young Georgians looked for ways to take meaningful action. In April 2003, Kandelaki and his contemporaries founded the youth nonviolent action organization Kmara (Enough). They were inspired by what the Serbian student nonviolent organization Otpor! (Resistance!) had done to help bring down the dictator Slobodan Milošević. Kmara members studied materials about Otpor, and Otpor activists came to Georgia to train Kmara's leaders in the techniques of nonviolent action. Kmara even adopted Otpor's clenched fist logo as its own insignia. Five thousand participated in Kmara summer workshops led by Otpor, funded by the Serbian Center for Applied Non-Violent Action and Strategies, most of whose staff had cut their teeth in the mobilization against Milošević. Kmara at its peak numbered 3,000 (Kandelaki 2006: 7–8).

As Kmara members worked to shift public opinion and build sympathy for their fight against corruption, they sought to involve people of all ranks and ages. To protest the rigged 2003 election, Kmara organized simultaneous street demonstrations across the country, communicating with its members by e-mail and cell phone provided by the Liberty Institute, a research and advocacy organization. Kmara's graffiti campaign resulted in the appearance of "Kmara" on walls in tens of thousands of spots on Tbilisi streets and gave the impression of ubiquity. In the following weeks, Kmara graffiti was seen in nine of Georgia's major urban centers, and the news media gave it top billing ("Georgia's Rose Revolution: A Participant's Perspective"; "Youth and Electoral Revolutions in Slovakia, Serbia, and Georgia").

Kmara adopted Otpor's approach of diffused and nonhierarchal leadership. All members were equal. The structure made it more difficult for authorities to interrupt and intrude on the group's direction.

Shevardnadze denounced Kmara, accusing the group of accepting Russian financing.

In the years since the fall of Shevardnadze, Kandelaki has trained young activists in organizing for nonviolent change in Belarus, Kazakhstan, Moldova, and Ukraine. While working in Belarus in 2005, he and his colleague, Luka Tsuladze, were detained by the authorities for eleven days. They were charged with "petty hooliganism"; Amnesty International, however, believes that the two men were being held as punishment for their political activities. After a court appearance, both men were released.

From 2005 to 2008, Kandelaki served as a senior adviser to President Mikhail Saakashvili. He is currently a member of the Georgia Parliament and serves as deputy chair of the foreign relations committee.

NOVEMBER 23, 2003
FOES OF GEORGIAN LEADER STORM INTO PARLIAMENT BUILDING
Shevardnadze Calls State of Emergency
By SETH MYDANS

Moscow, Nov. 22 – Protesters in Georgia broke into Parliament on Saturday, forcing President Eduard A. Shevardnadze to flee the hall surrounded by bodyguards, according to reports from the capital, Tbilisi.

Mr. Shevardnadze immediately declared a 30-day state of emergency and said he would not resign. He had been in the midst of opening a new session after a parliamentary election three weeks ago that was widely condemned as unfair.

"Order will be restored and the criminals will be punished," Mr. Shevardnadze said in a televised address. Standing beside him, Interior Minister Koba Narchemashvili, who commands the police, said he would obey all the president's orders.

Nino Burdzhanadze, an opposition leader who heads the Parliament, said that she would act as president in accordance with the constitution and that a presidential election would be held within 45 days.

She added, "Those who try to steal our victory will be punished."

As huge crowds celebrated in the streets, waving flags and honking horns late into the evening, a group of protesters also took over the presidential chancery, although Ms. Burdzhanadze said they would not enter any offices.

Local television stations reported variously that Mr. Shevardnadze was at a government residence in Krtsanisi on the outskirts of the capital, Tbilisi, or that he was at a military special forces training center.

The presidential office announced that Mr. Shevardnadze had talked on the telephone with Secretary of State Colin L. Powell and with President Vladimir V. Putin of Russia.

In Washington, which has a strategic interest in the former Soviet republic on the Black Sea, the State Department spokesman, Richard A. Boucher, called on both sides to refrain from violence and to initiate a dialogue.

The Kremlin said mistakes in the election must be corrected, or "the alternative is chaos." . . .

Troops and the police, mostly armed with truncheons, blocked roads around Parliament and the nearby presidential offices but made no effort to prevent the storming of the building.

Both sides have insisted that they want to avoid violence, recalling the civil war that erupted after the last demonstrations of this size, in 1991.

"If a confrontation starts, it will be all inclusive and much more dangerous than it was 10 years ago," the chief of Georgia's National Security Council, Tedo Dzhaparidze, said Friday.

Mr. Shevardnadze had just begun to speak when scores of protesters pushed their way into the Parliament building, shoving aside guards and scuffling with some lawmakers.

Local television showed the president being hustled out a rear exit as protesters overturned desks and chairs and leapt onto the podium.

"The velvet revolution has taken place in Georgia," said the leading opposition figure, Mikhail Saakashvili, standing in the spot Mr. Shevardnadze had fled. He added, "We are against violence."

The confrontation on Saturday followed a parliamentary vote Nov. 2 that was widely seen as a prelude to a presidential election in 2005, when Mr. Shevardnadze will be required by the Constitution to step aside.

Protests after the election quickly intensified into demands for Mr. Shevardnadze's immediate resignation. During his 12-year tenure as Georgia's leader, this former Soviet republic has sunk deeper into economic collapse, a breakdown in government services and all-pervasive corruption.

On Thursday, the State Department condemned the vote in a statement that said: "The results do not accurately reflect the will of the Georgian people, but instead reflect massive vote fraud. We are deeply disappointed in these results and in Georgia's leadership."

The open criticism from the United States, a strong supporter of Mr. Shevardnadze, reinforced the swelling complaints of the opposition, which has now spread to include some members of the government.

SHEVARDNADZE STEPS DOWN

"I'm going home now." With that short sentence to the news media, as *Times* correspondent Seth Mydans reports on November 24, 2003, Eduard Shevardnadze ended more than a decade of leadership in Georgia, fewer than 24 hours after he stated his intention to remain as the president of the country through the end of 2005 (see "Georgian Leader Agrees to Resign, Ending Standoff"). What caused Shevardnadze to change his mind in such a short time?

According to opposition leader Mikhail Saakashvili, "The important thing was that the military switched sides," after a brief series of nonviolent demonstrations. The number of protestors clearly counted. In Tbilisi, the crowd in Freedom Square that surrounded and filled the parliament building may have exceeded 100,000.

Shevardnadze was able to control Georgia as a unifying figure in a supposedly democratic society—until tens of thousands began to withdraw their cooperation and disobey, and as knowledge of how to fight for human rights and democracy without violence began to spread. As the army also refused to accept his orders, he had become powerless.

NOVEMBER 24, 2003
GEORGIAN LEADER AGREES TO RESIGN, ENDING STANDOFF
Economic Collapse Cited
Shevardnadze Faced Huge Mobs and Accusations of Election Fraud
By SETH MYDANS

Tbilisi, Georgia, Nov. 23 – President Eduard A. Shevardnadze of Georgia, once acclaimed for his role in helping to end the cold war, resigned in the face of huge public protests over the corruption and economic collapse that have marked his nearly 12-year rule.

"I'm going home now," Mr. Shevardnadze told reporters on live television after a final meeting with opposition leaders, and the streets of the capital erupted in celebration.

Fireworks exploded overhead and the air was filled with cheers, whistling and the mad honking of car horns. People hugged, kissed and shouted into their cellphones. They waved flags and held small children over their heads.

"I see that this could not have ended bloodlessly, and I would have had to exercise my power," said Mr. Shevardnadze, 75, referring to his futile declaration of a state of emergency after he was forced by protesters to flee the Parliament building in this former Soviet republic on [November 22].

"I have never betrayed my country, and so it is better that the president resigns," said Mr. Shevardnadze, who was born to a rural family in the village of Mamati, on Georgia's Black Sea coast.

He gave a small, tight smile and a wave to reporters as he turned away, ending a career that reached its high point when, as the Soviet foreign minister, he watched the Berlin Wall come down.

Mr. Shevardnadze was a major figure on the world stage. As foreign minister under Mikhail S. Gorbachev, he helped improve relations with the West and bring the superpower confrontation to an end. . . .

Mikhail Saakashvili, the main opposition leader, said new parliamentary and presidential elections would be held and that there should be no retribution against Mr. Shevardnadze.

The parliamentary speaker, Nino Burdzhanadze, who is also an opposition leader, stepped in as acting president, as mandated by the Constitution. She said elections would be held within a statutory period of 45 days.

Like the other opposition leaders, she spoke with respect for Mr. Shevardnadze and said history might be a gentler judge than the ferocious crowds in the streets.

The third major opposition figure, Zhurab Zhvania, said, "Shevardnadze said firmly and categorically that he is not going to leave Tbilisi, and is prepared to offer his assistance to future Georgian authorities."

Mr. Saakashvili told reporters it would be a point of honor for the country to provide Mr. Shevardnadze and his family with "guarantees of absolute security."

"The important thing was that the military switched sides," Mr. Saakashvili told CNN, describing the turning point after a three-week standoff following parliamentary elections that have been widely condemned as fraudulent.

In the final days, some military units had joined the round-the-clock crowds that were massed in front of the Parliament building, and their commanders pledged their support to the opposition.

Mr. Shevardnadze was also put under pressure during the weekend in telephone calls—one from President Vladimir V. Putin of Russia and one, jointly, from Secretary of State Colin L. Powell and Kofi Annan, the United Nations secretary general.

Foreign Minister Igor S. Ivanov of Russia arrived here on [November 22] and played a central role as an informal intermediary. On [the] evening [of November 23], he brokered what turned out to be a decisive meeting between Mr. Shevardnadze and the three main opposition figures.

Mr. Zhvania said that Mr. Shevardnadze had rejected the urging of some of his advisers to order a military assault on the protesters.

He said that Mr. Ivanov had proposed a compromise that would have allowed Mr. Shevardnadze to stay in office, but that the opposition leaders had persuaded the president that the huge, emotional crowds would not accept such an outcome.

"He took his decision in front of our eyes and I was really touched, very much, by how responsibly he was acting," Mr. Zhvania said. "It wasn't the gesture of an angry person but it was the gesture of a president who realized that he had failed, failed very badly."

Commenting on Mr. Shevardnadze's resignation, Mr. Gorbachev told the Interfax news agency: "He is not a coward and probably understood that the moment had come to make this step so that Georgia would not break up. I think he was right." . . .

But fury over the conduct of the election, which international observers condemned as fraudulent and blatantly manipulated, quickly escalated into demands for Mr. Shevardnadze's immediate resignation.

Mr. Saakashvili led the charge, staking out an uncompromising position on Mr. Shevardnadze's resignation. When Mr. Shevardnadze tried to convene the new Parliament on [November 22], it was Mr. Saakashvili who led protesters into the chamber, forcing the president to flee.

He appropriated for his movement the phrase of Czechoslovakia's peaceful overthrow of its Communist government, repeatedly calling it a "velvet revolution." On [November 23], he said he wanted to make his party's flag the national flag of Georgia.

On the other hand, when Ms. Burdzhanadze was asked whether she now planned to run for president, she said she had not decided.

"You know, it's not a very good idea to be a president of Georgia," she said. "Georgia is a country that has very serious problems. Ethnic problems. . . . Economic difficulties. A lot of very serious problems. So a person who will run for president should be very brave."

A Postmortem on Shevardnadze's Fall

Times correspondent Seth Mydans on November 30, 2003, quotes Shevardnadze's postmortem on how he lost power: "It is not good to have too much democracy," Shevardnadze said. "I think this was a mistake" (see "The Giant Who Shrank: A Post-Communist Tale"). Among the factors critical to democracy that contributed to the change in political leadership in Georgia in November 2003 were free and independent media; fair, independently observed elections; and healthy civic associations.

How did "too much democracy" contribute to Shevardnadze's downfall? The news media industry in Georgia was one element. As Charles Fairbanks notes, "In 2003, Georgia was arguably the only ex-Soviet republic with genuinely independent television." While most of the authoritarian regimes of Eastern Europe, the Baltics, and the Balkans utilized television to maintain the status quo, in Georgia, leading media outlets regularly criticized the regime. One of the largest black marks on Shevardnadze's administration prior to 2003 was his government's raid on Rustavi-2, the most notable of the independent media outlets. The authorities claimed to be searching for evidence of financial misdeeds, but the raid backfired when media outlets across the country carried coverage of the government's attempt to stifle the press. Protestors flooded the capital, as *The Times* reporter, Michael Wines, reports on November 2, 2001 ("TV Station Raid in Georgia Leads to Protests and Cabinet's Ouster").

As protests broke out following the 2003 election, independent media vigorously covered the massive demonstrations and rallies, as well as the independent international condemnations of the vote and Saakashvili's opposition campaign. His party's red-and-white flags dominated the airwaves, allowing Saakashvili and his followers visually to dominate Shevardnadze across the country. To Stephen Jones, an expert on Georgia, the flag of five crosses that "fluttered in thousands at every rally represented a return to a lost past of Christian morality and a repossession of Georgia's 'special place within European civilization' " (Jones 2009, 328). The flag, projected by independent television, was so powerful an image that Saakashvili proposed making it the national flag of Georgia (see "Georgian Leader Agrees to Resign, Ending Standoff").

According to one Kmara leader, Shevardnadze's resignation was much more than the opposition had anticipated. Kmara activists had been hoping to break down Shevardnadze's aura of invincibility in an effort to influence the 2005 presidential elections. Both Saakashvili's party and Kmara chapters across the country staged protests similar to those in Tbilisi. Although Kmara was not as big as Serbia's Otpor, it engaged in tactics such as widespread graffiti to give the impression of ubiquity and that it was larger than it actually was. Sympathetic news media broadcast these images nationwide. As one Kmara activist testified, "With virtually the entire country engaged in the protest, any attempt to use force would result sooner or later in self-destruction."

Georgia had a relatively free society, independent news media, and external accountability for election results—three factors that made it nearly impossible for Shevardnadze to continue to hold on to power. In the end, perhaps "too much democracy" indeed led to Shevardnadze's resignation.

NOVEMBER 30, 2003
THE GIANT WHO SHRANK: A POST-COMMUNIST TALE
By SETH MYDANS

In the cold light of defeat, Eduard A. Shevardnadze knows what he did wrong as the failed president of Georgia, and he is prepared to acknowledge his mistake openly: too much democracy.

"Democracy needs steering," he told a German television station after he was driven from office last Sunday by huge, angry crowds of protesters. "It is not good to have too much democracy. I think this was a mistake."

Stunned, pale, battered by chants of, "Get out! Get out! Get out!" Mr. Shevardnadze, 75, almost tottered as he walked away from his office—a long, long fall from his shining moment in history when, as the Soviet foreign minister a generation ago, he helped his country shed its Communist burden.

He had seemed a champion of democracy then, standing side by side with the last Soviet leader, Mikhail S. Gorbachev, and their close partners in Washington as the Berlin wall came down.

"George" was his friend—George P. Shultz, the secretary of state under President Reagan. So was "Jim"—James A. Baker III, the secretary of state under President George H. W. Bush.

But when Mr. Baker came to Tbilisi four months ago to try to persuade his old friend to hold an honest parliamentary election and salvage his tattered reputation as a democrat, Mr. Shevardnadze treated him as just another obstacle, making promises he had no intention of keeping.

Then, as his own personal wall seemed about to fall and he hunkered down out of earshot of the shouting crowds, Mr. Baker telephoned him from Washington, but Mr. Shevardnadze refused to take his calls.

It is hard to find anyone with a good word for Mr. Shevardnadze in Tbilisi today. His people are too bitter over years of corruption, cronyism, economic ruin, political manipulation and electoral fraud to spare a kind thought for him.

"We are talking about the transformation of a former democrat, former liberal, once darling-of-the-west President Shevardnadze into a trivial, post-Soviet dictator who ignored the will of his people," said his fiery young protégé, Mikhail Saakashvili, 35, who led an Oedipal assault on him and now appears poised to succeed him as president.

In fact his career had even more twists and paradoxes than that, and none of the labels quite apply. One of the unanswered questions about Mr. Shevardnadze is whether, at heart, he really did change.

He entered public life as an aggressive young member of the Communist Party and rose while still in his 30's to head the internal security agencies in Soviet Georgia—a job only a tough character could handle.

In 1972, at age 44, he became chief of Georgia's Communist Party, a position he held until Mr. Gorbachev picked him in 1985 to be his foreign minister and he reinvented himself as a statesman.

Among Soviet apparatchiks, he was conspicuous for his openness and even introspection. His American counterparts found in him something rare in those perilous cold-war negotiations: good will.

In an interview later with The New York Times, just after he returned to lead Georgia in 1992, he indulged himself in an un-Soviet flight of fancy. "Picasso had his different periods, and other artists too," he said. "I made mistakes, I was sometimes unfair, but what is one supposed to do- stick with one position to the end? To the death? We have all changed."

In the eyes of many of his countrymen, though, he remained the man he had always been, whether he was dealing with local warlords or secretaries of state.

"He was never a true democrat because he was a person shaped and molded in the Communist system," said George Khutsishvili, a political analyst at the International Center on Conflict and Negotiation here. "He was a bearer of the spirit of the system." He was a pragmatist, politically agile, a man who knew how to tailor his suit to fit the occasion, Mr. Khutsishvili said. But he never really understood the ideas that underlie civil society. "He was tolerant, but he was not a liberal."

Perhaps so, but he seemed something more than an opportunist or a cynical manipulator. Tolerance was a rare quality among post-Soviet leaders.

"It is difficult to pull the country out of chaos and crisis," he said when he stepped in to try to rescue Georgia from a civil war in 1992. "I know that I am taking a risk."

He succeeded at first, instituting democratic reforms and, with help from the World Bank and the International Monetary Fund, putting the economy back on its feet.

It was an accomplishment just to hold his country together. There was war in two breakaway provinces, abetted by his former comrades in Moscow. Criminal gangs terrorized the rest of the country. People repeatedly tried to kill him. He barely survived a bombing of his car. Another time, grenades were fired at his motorcade.

He took on all comers and stayed on top.

"He was Babe Ruth playing in the Babe Ruth League," said Lincoln A. Mitchell, director in Georgia of the National Democratic Institute, an American group.

In 1998, though, Georgia lost its markets when the Russian economy collapsed. Taxes went uncollected, salaries went unpaid, public services broke down, unemployment soared. Corruption devoured the country as Mr. Shevardnadze bought off clans and criminal consortiums.

Indeed, one of Georgia's few bright spots was its openness. To an unusual degree among the former Soviet republics, it has had a free press, free association and a lively civil society filled with human rights and good governance groups of all stripes.

It may well be that Mr. Shevardnadze allowed too much democracy, at least for his own good. His country grew too vigorous and clamorous to be held in the grip of one man.

When he resigned under furious pressure a week ago, he insisted that he was making one last sacrifice for his countrymen.

"It was obvious that what was happening in the country would have triggered bloodshed," he said. "I have never betrayed my people. So I considered it necessary to resign to avoid bloodshed."

Nothing of the sort, said his young rival, Mr. Saakashvili, who all but pushed him out the door. Mr. Shevardnadze had ordered troops to crush the demonstrations, only to be defied, he said. He had tried to flee but found the airports blocked by the crowds.

"We should say that we had a very narrow escape from that situation," Mr. Saakashvili said. "It was at the last, ultimate moment when he said, 'Yes, I'll resign.' "

Saakashvili Sees Mandate to Clean Up Government

Three days after Eduard Shevardnadze resigned as president of Georgia, Mikhail Saakashvili, the leader of the opposition and favored to be the new president, said, "The era of government dominated by one individual is over," according to Seth Mydans on November 26, 2003 ("Interim Leaders in Georgia Back Presidential Candidate"). Between Shevardnadze's resignation and the new election, Saakashvili made several promises that signaled a significant shift from Shevardnadze's rule.

First, to decrease the influence of one leader, Saakashvili pledged to involve all of the opposition leaders in his new cabinet. This included keeping Nino Burdzhanadze as the speaker of the parliament and creating a post equivalent to prime minister for the third opposition leader, Zurab Zhvania. He pledged free and fair elections—the catalyst for the Revolution of the Roses. He promised to attempt to forge national unity by addressing the concerns of the separatist region of Adzharia, led by Aslan Abashidze. For much of the interregnum, Saakashvili acted like a head of state, negotiating with foreign leaders and setting legislative priorities, and preparing for a formal electoral win, according to Mydans.

Symbolism was strategically and historically important throughout Georgia's fight for independence. Kmara held its first public action, a 500-strong student march, on April 14, 2003. The date commemorated the successful demonstrations of April 14, 1978, which persuaded the Soviet Union to reverse its plans to ban Georgian as the republic's official language (see "In Soviet Georgia, a Longing for Freedom but Little Sense of How to Get It"; "Officials in Georgia Declare Shevardnadze Ballot Winner"). In another example, the militant Georgian nationalist Zviad Gamsakhurdia had won against the communists in the 1991 plenary elections and one year later, choosing the anniversary of the March 1956 Tbilisi massacre that had killed 100 or more, introduced a resolution for independence. He was elected president of Georgia in a landslide partly as a result of the emblematic linkage to the 1956 massacre. By the end of 1991, however, Gamsakhurdia had brought the country to what *The Times* calls an authoritarian state and "ferocious war" (see "Re-enter Shevardnadze, the Phoenix of Georgia"). It was therefore fitting, as Mydans notes on January 5, 2004, that Georgian voters placed bouquets of roses on ballot boxes—the omnipresent emblem of the Revolution of the Roses in the preceding November (see "With the Vote in Georgia, a Dynamic Young Leader and a New Era").

With a record turnout in the January 4, 2004, special election, Saakashvili won in a landslide. Moreover, the election was open and deemed fair by external international observers. The symbolism of the change continued through to Saakashvili's inauguration later that month. *The Times* reports that helicopters dropped rose petals on the stage immediately prior to Saakashvili's inaugural address. The legitimacy of the election was further underscored by the presence of international figures such as U.S. secretary of state Colin Powell, as Steven Weisman reports for *The Times* on January 26 ("With Powell on Hand, Georgians Install New Leader"). Despite the U.S. support and looming Russian influence, the remarkable feature of Saakashvili's election is that the Georgian people had primarily accomplished it on their own. "This was a Georgian revolution made by Georgians in Georgian conditions," according to Stephen Jones (2009, 331).

KEY PLAYER IN GEORGIA
Mikhail Saakashvili (1967–)

Born in the Georgian capital of Tbilisi, Mikhail Saakashvili became the most influential leader of post-communist Georgia. He received his undergraduate degree from Kiev University's Institute of International Relations and then studied law at Columbia and George Washington universities in the United States. His Western education influenced his politics. Returning to Georgia in 1995, he was elected to parliament and chaired the Parliamentary Committee on Constitutional, Legal Issues, and Legal Affairs. He first made his name in politics fighting corruption and attempting to improve human rights in Georgia through constitutional law and judicial reform.

Saakashvili was part of a small cohort of sophisticated young Georgians who were enthusiastic about integration into Europe. Many of them, like Saakashvili, were Western educated. As a member of President Eduard A. Shevardnadze's government, Saakashvili worked to free Georgia's courts from Russian influence and initiated a program of choosing judges based on merit. He gained respect in parliament, becoming majority leader in 1998 when the Citizen's Union Party elected him as leader of their delegation. He was chosen to head the Georgian delegation to the Parliamentary Assembly of the Council of Europe, which elected him its vice president in 2000.

That same year, Saakashvili was appointed minister of justice. According to a BBC News profile of Saakashvili on January 25, 2004, "Shevardnadze began grooming the young lawyer for power." Saakashvili, however, "found it hard to stomach what he saw as corruption and cronyism in Georgia's leadership. He caused uproar at a cabinet meeting by producing documents which he said showed fellow ministers had acquired expensive villas from the proceeds of crooked deals" ("Profile: Mikheil Saakashvili").

In 2001, popular opinion turned against Shevardnadze's government after the murder of journalist Giorgi Sanaia, a television anchor. Sanaia worked for the independent broadcasting company Rustavi 2, which was well known for investigations of public corruption. Amid nationwide protests over the murder, Saakashvili resigned from the government and the Citizens' Union Party, claiming that it was unethical for him to remain a member of Georgia's government. Soon after, he formed a new party that would change the country's political contours, the United National Movement.

A Georgian populist who glorified "the people" and paraded his patriotism, Saakashvili was elected to chair the Tbilisi City Council in 2002. For the next two years, he used that position to criticize the national government as authoritarian and corrupt. He attracted attention for attending to everyday concerns, such as the repair of leaking roofs and broken elevators.

In 2003, Saakashvili ran for parliament from the United National Movement party, in hopes that the reform party would take the major bloc of seats. In the November parliamentary elections, official results showed that Shevardnadze's party, For a New Georgia, had overtaken Saakashvili's party, despite overwhelming polling evidence to the contrary and condemnation from a corps of 5,000 electoral observers. The falsified election results sparked the Rose Revolution.

Saakashvili called for collective nonviolent action to protest the election results. Zurab Zhvania, another opposition leader, joined with Saakashvili and the speaker of parliament, Nino Burdzhanadze, to plan large peaceful demonstrations in Tbilisi and across the country. Throughout twenty days of disciplined nonviolent rallies in November 2003, Saakashvili toured the country gathering ever greater

(Continued)

(Continued)

numbers for the crowds in Tbilisi. The processions and marches culminated as tens of thousands surrounded or entered the parliament building to stop the opening-day session that would have approved fraudulent election results. Saakashvili stepped through the doors of the parliament holding a red rose. When Shevardnadze was thrown out, the crowd stormed in. The police stood by, observing the throngs; no violence occurred; and the army, despite an attempt by Shevardnadze to impose a state of emergency, refused to obey. Shevardnadze resigned shortly thereafter.

In January 2004, Saakashvili was elected president in a landslide. His first term was plagued by mixed economic performance and domestic disputes. He attempted to restore federal rule to Abkhazia, Ajaria, and South Ossetia, three regions of Georgia that had been self-governing since the collapse of the Soviet Union. The threat of violence was high, and Saakashvili pulled back in 2005, offering a compromise package to South Ossetia that was rejected.

In 2007, criticism of Saakashvili intensified, as between 50,000 and 100,000 people demonstrated before the parliament building. C. J. Chivers reports in *The New York Times* on November 3 that the organized opposition to Saakashvili accused his administration of authoritarianism and corruption. Yet the protestors were not seeking another Rose Revolution. Badri Patarkatsishvili, said to be Georgia's richest individual, said, "We must struggle by evolution, not by revolutionary means" ("Thousands Rally in Capital Against Georgia Government"). Saakashvili responded by ordering a new round of elections, which he won with 53.47 percent of the vote.

Regional tensions continued to mount in Georgia. In August 2008, Saakashvili ordered an attack on separatists in South Ossetia and Abkhazia, justifying his actions as a necessary countermeasure to what he termed a Russian invasion. His political opponents said he acted prematurely. Georgia and Russia accused each other of initiating the conflict, according to *Times* reporter Ellen Barry on December 20 ("Russia Aside, Georgia's Chief is Pressed at Home"). After Russian forces routed Georgia's military in battle, a cease-fire brokered by the European Union led to the withdrawal of the troops. Saakashvili vowed to pursue the goal of bringing Abkhazia and South Ossetia under a unified, federal Georgia, yet tensions show no signs of abating.

Saakashvili's current presidential term ends in 2013.

JANUARY 5, 2004
WITH THE VOTE IN GEORGIA, A DYNAMIC YOUNG LEADER AND A NEW ERA
By SETH MYDANS

Kutaisi, Georgia, Jan. 4 – A bouquet of red roses lay beside the clear plastic ballot box in polling station 66 here on [January 4], and nobody seemed to mind that the emblem of Georgia's energetic new president was already in place before the first vote had been cast.

Almost everybody in this troubled nation voted for Mikhail Saakashvili, the 36-year-old lawyer who six weeks ago led what he called the Rose Revolution—the peaceful ouster of Eduard A. Shevardnadze from the office he had held for 12 years.

At a news conference after a preliminary count had pronounced him the overwhelming winner, Mr. Saakashvili outlined the huge tasks he faced and warned, "You cannot do everything in one day. We will go step by step."

An independent survey of voters leaving the polls put his winning total at about 86 percent. The Central Election Commission said that in this nation of close to 5 million people, 1.7 million had voted, a number Mr. Saakashvili said was the highest in Georgia's history.

In a performance that showcased his charisma, the young new president answered questions in rapid-fire English, Russian and French, as well as Georgian—and then introduced his popular Dutch wife, who did the same.

"We have got a very important mandate from the people to clean up Georgia, to make it peaceful and prosperous, to make Georgia efficient, investor-friendly, to consolidate power," Mr. Saakashvili said.

He added, "I realize how big a burden I have taken on my shoulders and how big a burden all of us have taken on our shoulders."

Thirteen years after the Soviet Union collapsed and Georgia became independent, this mountainous nation rich in fruits, vineyards and Black Sea beaches has fallen further than any other former Soviet republic.

Its economy has stagnated from corruption, mismanagement and the loss of former Soviet markets. Joblessness and poverty have become the norm. A breakdown in government services has left many without heat or electricity this winter.

Two large regions have declared themselves independent and did not take part in the vote on [January 4]. A third, led by a regional chief who had supported Mr. Shevardnadze in the final days, set up border checkpoints and mostly boycotted the election.

Strategically situated on Russia's southern border and with a vital pipeline due to begin carrying oil from the Caspian Sea to Turkey across its territory next year, Georgia is a pawn in a big-power rivalry between Russia and the United States.

A seven-hour drive across Georgia's main east-west highway on Wednesday was a disheartening tour of vacant factories, barren countryside, abandoned gas stations and half-empty villages where residents hawk shanks of meat by the roadside, signals of a collapsed economy.

The second largest city in Georgia, Kutaisi, about 200 miles west of Tbilisi, has lost much of its industry and population as workers travel to Russia to find jobs.

The popular uprising last month that followed a parliamentary election tainted by fraud has brought a burst of hope to Georgia, symbolized by the red roses handed to Mr. Saakashvili when he meets the public.

"I'm sure he'll be successful as president," said Mikhail Kintsurashvili, 85, a retiree, as he went to vote. "He takes things very seriously, and he's very motivated."

But as he himself said, Mr. Saakashvili must now justify people's hopes by improving their lives.

"If he tries, he can do it," said Dato Bashidze, 40, who like many Georgians supports himself by doing one thing and another. "He'll have a little time. That's why we elected him, to get to work on our demands."

Initial reports from monitors were that the voting had been markedly free of the manipulation that characterized elections under Mr. Shevardnadze. Mr. Saakashvili said the results in a handful of precincts where procedural violations had been reported would be invalidated.

He attributed his overwhelming victory to the absence of serious challengers in the six-candidate field. He has formed a governing alliance with his two partners in leading the popular uprising, Zhurab Zvania and Nino Burdzhanadze.

Mr. Saakashvili asserted [January 4] that Mr. Shevardnadze could keep his armed guard and remain in his home. But he said he did not want to talk about the former president. "Mr. Shevardnadze stays in the past for Georgia with many mistakes, and I would also say with many crimes," he said.

Asked at a polling station whether he had voted for the man who had driven him from power, Mr. Shevardnadze smiled an enigmatic smile and said, "You guessed my choice."

"He is young, he has a lot of energy, and is well educated," Mr. Shevardnadze said, and then added: "He should talk less and work more. Enough of populism. There is a lot to be done."

• •

Saakashvili Confronts Rebel Leader

President Mikhail Saakashvili took office in January 2004, but his hopes for national consolidation did not come to fruition until May. After conflict broke out as a result of Georgia's independence in 1991, Aslan Abashidze, a local governor and relatively minor Soviet politician, secured a role on the State Council as minister of Adzharia. A small region in southwest Georgia, Adzharia was almost entirely ethnic Georgian, unlike the other semi-autonomous regions of Abkhazia and South Ossetia. Abashidze built strong popular support by steering a middle course between the radical and bloody independence of the Georgian nationalist, Zviad Gamsakhurdia, and the relative autonomy of Eduard Shevardnadze, and soon became unrivalled leader of the Adzharia region.

For thirteen years, however, Abashidze had ruled Adzharia as, in the words of one commentator, a "personal fiefdom." He was known as a strong ally of Russia. Adzharia had experienced significant economic growth, but suspicions ran high that it was largely due to narcotics and organized crime, often in conjunction with Russia. Throughout his presidency, Shevardnadze had maintained a hands-off approach with Abashidze, and the leader of Adzharia had reciprocated. Saakashvili, however, was committed to fighting for openness and against corruption. According to *The Times,* Saakashvili said that as soon as Shevardnadze was gone, the new Georgian government would engage directly with Adzharia ("Interim Leaders in Georgia Back Presidential Candidate"). Abashidze, who had encouraged the residents of the province not to participate in the elections, did not respond.

Once Saakashvili was elected, he declared that Abashidze would not enjoy the same kind of authoritarian autonomy as in the past. With Colin Powell standing by his side, Saakashvili singled out Adzharia as a focus for specific reform ("With Powell on Hand, Georgians Install New Leader"). Saakashvili believed that the Georgians in Adzharia would feel liberated from Abashidze, as had those in Tbilisi, post-Shevardnadze. The conflict continued into the spring. In March, Saakashvili enforced an economic blockade of the Adzharia region; under pressure from Russia, he soon lifted it. Nevertheless, the move had asserted Georgia's power and independence as a free state. Saakashvili told reporters that Abashidze's time, like Shevardnadze's, had come and he should step down. On March 18, *Times* correspondent Seth Mydans quotes Saakashvili as saying: "The whole idea of losing their position as a result of free polls and the will of the people makes them totally confused and they refuse to accept it" ("Georgia's President Risks Showing Warlords Who's Boss").

On May 2, Abashidze worsened the conflict by blowing up the bridges between Adzharia and the rest of Georgia, as Ilan Greenberg recounts in *The Times* on May 30 (see "The Not-So-Velvet Revolution"). By then, pressure from inside and outside the region was mounting on Abashidze. Thousands of demonstrators, organized by many of the same activists who had planned the Revolution of the Roses, including Kmara, called for Abashidze to step down. On May 6, Abashidze was escorted onto a Russian plane, effectively resigning.

The thousands of protestors turned into cheering throngs. On May 6, Mydans describes the end of Abashidze's reign and the end of post-Soviet totalitarianism in Georgia (see "Georgia's Leader Declares Victory after Rebel Flees"). In what is now known as the "Second Rose Revolution," Mydans notes, Saakashvili announced the end of Abashidze's regime to the crowd by cheering, "Georgians: Aslan has fled! Adzharia is free!" Mydans points out that the autonomy and independence of regions *within* Georgia had become as contentious an issue as the independence of Georgia itself. Conflicts in Abkhazia and South Ossetia in 2008 reaffirmed the fragility of the Georgian nation. Georgians were in 2004 united in free, fair elections and finally achieved a post-Soviet society.

MAY 6, 2004
GEORGIA'S LEADER DECLARES VICTORY AFTER REBEL FLEES

Tbilisi, Georgia, Thursday, May 6 (Reuters) – Celebrations erupted in the Adzharia region of Georgia early [on May 6] after its rebellious leader fled in what President Mikhail Saakashvili hailed as the first step to unifying the country.

Thousands had massed on the streets of the regional capital, Batumi, in anticipation of the departure of Aslan Abashidze, who had run his Black Sea region as a personal fief for more than a decade.

Unruly crowds converged on Mr. Abashidze's luxurious residence and briefly began seizing furniture before officials restored order.

The announcement of Mr. Abashidze's departure, after Russia's former foreign minister, Igor Ivanov, began mediation to prevent violence, came from Mr. Saakashvili in the Georgian capital, Tbilisi.

"Georgians: Aslan has fled! Adzharia is free!" a beaming Mr. Saakashvili said at a news briefing from his office. "Today a new era has started," he said. "I congratulate everyone on this victory, on the beginning of Georgia's unification. Georgia will be united. No one could oppose the will of the people today and no one will do so in future."

A parliamentary official in Batumi said the president would fly to Batumi to take part in celebrations. Supporters of Mr. Saakashvili swept through the town, shouting "Victory, victory!" Prime Minister Zurab Zhvania appealed for calm on television, urging residents to turn in weapons within a week.

Mr. Saakashvili, elected in January after leading a bloodless revolution to oust Georgia's veteran leader, Eduard A. Shevardnadze, last year, has vowed to bring Adzharia and other unruly regions of the former Soviet republic back under central control. But bringing back to the fold two other regions—Abkhazia and South Ossetia—is likely to prove much more difficult.

Adzharia, whose residents are ethnic Georgians, had sought only autonomy. The other areas have different ethnic compositions and declared full independence a decade or more ago after wars costing thousands of lives. Mr. Abashidze had in recent weeks ignored calls for his resignation and imposed a state of emergency. He spent Wednesday evening in talks with Mr. Ivanov, who undertook his mission after months of confrontation threatened to spill over into bloodshed.

Mr. Abashidze and Mr. Ivanov slipped quietly away from the Adzharian leader's residence in Batumi. Reporters who raced to the airport found Mr. Abashidze's aircraft gone and his guards' saying he had left.

The speaker of the Georgian Parliament, Nino Burdzhanadze, said Mr. Abashidze had apparently left for Russia, which has in the past given tacit support for Adzharia as well as South Ossetia and Abkhazia.

Mr. Saakashvili had set the stage for the 65-year-old leader's flight by offering him safe passage if he stepped down and left.

- - -

GEORGIA FACES UPHILL BATTLE

Political turmoil is no novelty in the Caucasus nation of Georgia. Mikhail Saakashvili's two predecessors, Zviad Gamsakhurdia and Eduard Shevardnadze, were forced out of office, the former in a bloody coup d'état, and the latter after invalid elections spawned the Revolution of the Roses. Saakashvili was elected in January 2004 by a huge majority of the vote, according to Ilan Greenberg in *The Times* on May 30, but the same article offers a sobering *tour d'horizon* of the ongoing problems confronting independent Georgia (see "The Not-So-Velvet Revolution").

As Greenberg phrases it, the Rose Revolution ended when "protesters stuck flowers in the barrels of soldiers' assault rifles." While considering the host of dilemmas and predicaments facing Georgia that Greenberg reviews, one cannot help but notice a theme that appears frequently in *The Times'* coverage: the forces of security, police authority, and armies have turned on dictators. Soldiers have refused to follow orders and joined protesting demonstrators, rather than suppressing them, a development both indicative of and instrumental in the breakdown of the authoritarian regimes of the former Soviet states. "In the final days," Seth Mydans of *The Times* reports on November 24, 2003, of the Rose Revolution, "some military units had joined the round-the-clock crowds that were massed in front of the Parliament building, and their commanders pledged their support to the opposition" (see "Georgian Leader Agrees to Resign, Ending Standoff"). Saakashvili told CNN, as *The Times* reports, that the army's switch in loyalty away from Shevardnadze was the turning point in the drive to overturn the regime.

Yet successful democracies need stable institutions. The years of systemic corruption, strongman rule, cronyism, flagging economic growth, and weak institutions of governance, plus the litany of Georgia's quandaries that Greenberg lays out for *The Times,* will continue to breed volatility. Abkhazia and South Ossetia remain set on self-determination, and hostilities erupted in July 2008. Russia has recognized South Ossetia and Abkhazia as sovereign nations despite objections from Georgia, Ellen Barry and Dan Bilefsky report for *The Times* on September 8, 2008 ("Russia Agrees to Limited Pullout from Georgia"). Georgian, European, and U.S. officials say that Russia remains in violation of a cease-fire brokered by French president Nicolas Sarkozy. Georgia still is not unified.

MAY 30, 2004
THE NOT-SO-VELVET REVOLUTION

Can a notoriously corrupt former Soviet republic be strong-armed into accountability and democracy? The new president of Georgia has his ways.

By ILAN GREENBERG

Georgia's president, Mikhail Saakashvili—called Misha by just about everyone in the country—took power on Nov. 22, 2003, by storming Parliament on live national television. Yelling from the back benches, he ordered Eduard Shevardnadze, who was widely seen as having stolen the recent parliamentary elections, to step aside. Shevardnadze, the former Soviet foreign minister and custodian of Georgia's descent into poverty and lawlessness, seemed frozen, then shaken by Saakashvili's rhetorical fire. As Shevardnadze was shuttled out the backdoor, Saakashvili, who had served a contentious term as justice minister under Shevardnadze, marched to the lectern, scanned the riotous scene, found the cameras and drank Shevardnadze's tall glass of tea.

Out in the streets, protesters stuck flowers in the barrels of soldiers' assault rifles, and the Rose Revolution, as it was called, was over. Saakashvili, a charismatic 36-year-old graduate of Columbia Law School, was elected president two months later, winning 97 percent of the vote. Georgia—a nation cracked open by three breakaway regions, racked by corruption and a tsunami of crime, reeling from two civil wars, pocked by constant electricity and water shortages and unable to collect taxes from its citizens—was his to govern.

Saakashvili promises the country will be ready for European Union consideration within three years, will have reconstituted borders within five years and will operate under the rule of law pretty much immediately. His popularity remains high, but critics have begun to take shots. Koba Davitashvili, a revolutionary ally who broke with Saakashvili when the president pushed through controversial changes in the constitution that increased executive power, recently said, "Misha makes a lot of promises, but pensioners aren't getting paid and liberal society isn't being nurtured."

When it was part of the Soviet Union, Georgia was a popular holiday destination and the wealthiest Soviet republic. By the late 1990's, even adventure tourists considered the country too dangerous to visit, and Georgia had managed to become one of the poorest of the former Soviet states. The International Monetary Fund cut off financing in September 2003, and the World Bank severely cut back on lending. In January, after the revolution, George Soros, the New York financier, helped to establish a special anticorruption fund to supplement the paltry salaries of most government employees, from the president (who gets $1,500 a month from the fund) down to border guards ($500 a month).

Corruption had become pandemic under Shevardnadze, almost as much a physical part of the country's topography as broken roads, crumbled buildings and snowcapped mountains. "It's a big dilemma," said Irakli Okruashvili, the new prosecutor general. "There is too much evidence for too many cases." When we spoke in his office in Tbilisi, Okruashvili compared his walled-in life with those of the Sicilian antimafia judges who must live under around-the-clock protection. Under Shevardnadze, few managed to stay clean. "We could arrest everyone," Okruashvili said. But now, nepotism, cronyism, bribery, paying for school grades, even showing up for work at 11 A.M.—all of these have been labeled by Saakashvili's government as enemies of the revolution.

Recent history would suggest that implementing reform in a failing state is nearly impossible. Yeltsin in Russia, the former Communist chieftains who continue ruling in Central Asia and Shevardnadze in Georgia: across the former Soviet Union presidents have come to power making many of the same promises as Saakashvili. What reason is there to think Misha is different? Saakashvili argues that the difference is in the historical moment—he has learned from the others' failures, he says—and in his electorate too. The people are on board with his program, he says; other leaders never really had a mandate for radical change. "There's a popular will to change things from the bottom up," Saakashvili said. Still, for Georgians to cheer the arrest of Shevardnadze's son-in-law—who was detained in February for tax evasion and later released after his wife paid a $15.5 million fine—is one thing; for Georgians to condone the arrest of their own corrupt sons-in-law is another. Fady O. Asly, who until recently was the chairman of the American Chamber of Commerce in Tbilisi, said that right now in Georgia, "it's business as usual. At the top level, people are cautious; they're scared. At the lower level, the game is still on."

In the constellation of states that emerged from the breakup of the former Soviet Union, Saakashvili is not just an anomaly but also a president from another solar system. His predecessor, Shevardnadze, traveled with more than a dozen well-armed, U.S.-trained bodyguards. When Saakashvili decided to take a ride in Tbilisi's dilapidated subway (a bit of a campaign stunt), he took a handful of security men who kept their revolvers in hidden holsters.

"To me, the difference when Shevardnadze came into power was that people's relief was essentially backward-looking," said Mark Mullen, chairman of the Georgian branch of Transparency International, a global corruption watchdog group. "The country was blown to pieces, and there was the sense that Shevy could bring back stability. And he did that, but he didn't do anything other than that. Saakashvili needs to dismantle corrupt systems, bring in capital and fix things. This is a tougher path."

I flew with the president on his French-built helicopter one afternoon from Gudauri, a Georgian mountain resort, to Tbilisi. Saakashvili spent most of the flight brooding, gazing out the window. But then he suddenly pulled me into his chest so I could see the landscape below. "Do you see how the colors of the fields are distinct from one another?" he asked. "In Soviet times, the colors blurred because the farms were collectivized." Surprised at being clutched by the president, I mumbled how pervasive the Soviet backdraft in Georgia is. "You have no idea," Saakashvili said.

A famous joke from the Soviet era holds that under that system, the people pretended to work and the government pretended to pay them. At some point during the past 10 years, both Georgians and their government stopped even pretending. In the decrepit Chancellery Building housing the offices of the president and his staff, open doors reveal administrators playing computer solitaire or simply watching television. "Getting anything done in this building is practically impossible," said Natalia Kancheli, executive assistant to the president. Like 80 percent of government ministers, and like Saakashvili himself, Kancheli is young, 31. She boasts an American college degree, and she comes to the job with a turn-everything-on-its-head approach and a near-maniacal energy level. (Saakashvili, for his part, schedules appointments until 2 A.M.)

"The current orthodoxy is that if you change the system, you can get rid of corruption because people are rational actors," said Christopher Waters, a legal scholar and Georgia specialist at the Center for Euro-Asian Studies at the University of Reading in England. "There's truth to this, but Georgia is what in the 1960's people used to call an honor-and-shame society. It has relied so heavily in the last few decades on social networks and kinship that this not only demands corruption but ultimately economic stasis." It is no longer "fashionable" in studies of corruption to consider a nation's culture, Waters said. But in Georgia, culture "is really what the president is up against."

An estimated 50 percent of the Georgian economy is underground, unmolested by government bureaucrats. Tbilisi collects practically no taxes; when the government managed to raise its tax collections by 30 percent in the first two months of 2004—an additional $22 million, or approximately $5 for every citizen—it was heralded as a major victory. Saakashvili's tax collectors have begun to make anticorruption raids, which are meant to turn the country's businesses into taxpayers. But the zeal with which prosecutors have been swooping into offices to review the books has turned the business community into Saakashvili's angriest constituency. "It's confusion and despair," said Esben Emborg, a manager with Nestlé in Tbilisi.

Saakashvili took me along with him to a meeting with a delegation of visiting Americans from a group called Business Executives for National Security, or Bens, where he endured a battery of Developing Nation 101 advice: "Make your government transparent"; "Engineer your tax system to encourage foreign investment"; and, simply, "End corruption." Saakashvili nodded his head throughout, but an American government official who works with Bens later told me its consensus was to stay clear of Georgia.

"If you run the numbers, Georgia is not a buy," said Giorgi Bedineishvili, the president's chief economic adviser. He said he is determined to change that: "We have to be nicer to investors than other countries are. We need to cut down the number of cases where investors were abused. And we have to be very careful not to create new disasters."

One hundred and eleven days after the revolution, Saakashvili ordered the arrest of a fugitive from the law: Vasily Mkalavishvili, an excommunicated Orthodox priest who before the revolution was allowed by authorities to repeatedly lead his congregants on violent rampages against religious minorities, like Baptists and Jehovah's Witnesses. In one reported attack, Mkalavishvili used a large metal cross to beat a Jehovah's Witness bloody. The arrest of Mkalavishvili was messy and violent. The police were heavily armed; several dozen people were injured by batons and tear gas.

The tactics of the police immediately provoked fierce criticism by many who might be called the Tbilisi revolutionary vanguard—intellectuals and leftists, as well as business interests upset at what they see as an inclination, on the part of Saakashvili and his advisers, toward intimidation. "The government would like to create a culture of fear in all of Georgia," said David Gamkrelidze, leader of New Rights, the main opposition party in Georgia. "The business community is really afraid. All civil servants are afraid. People are thinking what the government wants, rather than what the law demands."

Saakashvili's supporters argued that Mkalavishvili's arrest was necessary. "This was the single most brave step Misha took," said Nick Rurua, a Saakashvili ally in Parliament who once worked for the A.C.L.U. in Atlanta. "This is an authoritarian church that wants to create a fundamentalist state in this country. Enforcement of the law doesn't always look nice."

Despite Rurua's words, a growing number of Georgians, as well as foreign observers, have grown wary of Saakashvili. Sitting in a plane on the way back from a meeting of Eastern European presidents in Bratislava, Saakashvili looked a bit stunned when I reeled off the criticism, not because he was hearing it for the first time but because he considered it outrageous. "We have a problem in this country: the opposition represents tiny interest groups, not mature parties," he said. "And it's us, the government, who are introducing the rule of law. People are objecting to tactics—that's not the most substantial thing. Look at what we're doing: we're putting people in jail who have stolen millions. That's the rule of law. Nobody should be scared of that."

Saakashvili's reform measures have created unintended consequences. Okruashvili, the prosecutor general, gets field reports from outlying cities that judges and cops have responded to the new anticorruption regime with a spasm of bribe-taking. Okruashvili's theory is that everyone is trying to extort as much money as possible while they can still get away with it. But Sarah, an American working along Georgia's eastern border (she insisted that she not be identified by her last name), offers a different analysis: Saakashvili simply isn't a factor in the outer regions, where life, and corruption, continue much as they had before.

In February, Saakashvili shut down a powerful Georgian corporate conglomerate called Omega Group for, among other things, supposedly smuggling cigarettes across the border. Then prosecutors raided an Omega-owned television station. They were there ostensibly to scrutinize the books, but they left with boxes of electronic equipment, causing several programs dependent on the equipment to be canceled, according to a journalist at the station. In a country that maintained a high degree of free media throughout the darkest days of the Shevardnadze regime, Saakashvili's TV-station sting raised criticism over eroding media freedoms. "I cannot say all media is controlled by the government," Gamkrelidze said. "But step by step they'd like to do it."

The parliamentary elections at the end of March set up a confrontation between the Saakashvili government and the ruler of an autonomous area in the southwest corner of the country called Adzharia. Aslan Abashidze, the dictator of Adzharia—until recently he held the title of president of the region—barred Saakashvili at the point of his militia's guns from crossing the border into his province, claiming that Saakashvili intended to invade the region. A tense overnight standoff ensued, which Saakashvili told me later was humiliating: here he was, the elected president, and he was being blocked from entering part of his own country by a "man out of the Middle Ages" who derived power by terrorizing his province with a private militia. The crisis ended after Saakashvili ordered a blockade of the railway and the port of Batumi, the source of Abashidze's wealth and a major conduit for goods, mostly oil, transported between Central Asia and the Mediterranean. The four-day blockade worked—Russia, which has a military base in Adzharia and often voices support for Adzharia independence, for once played a neutral role—and international organizations brokered a compromise.

So Saakashvili won, but he also lost. Foreign investors in the Adzharia port were furious over the blockade. "We put our plans on hold—$10 million a year that would've gone to local Georgian business," said Hew Crooks, an American investor who is on the board of the Batumi Oil Terminal.

Then, on May 2, Abashidze reignited the crisis when he suddenly blew up bridges connecting his territory with the rest of Georgia. This time, the region's chess masters came out of the shadows: the United States and Russia, each posturing to appear as an architect of regional stability, worked in tandem to persuade Abashidze to give up power, and on May 6 a Russian government plane flew the renegade strongman to Moscow and into exile.

Saakashvili was jubilant after Abashidze's retreat: a 13-year-old thorn had been vanquished without a drop of spilled blood. Crooks sent me an e-mail message tempering his previous fury. He said he and his investment group were entering into "a much more constructive relationship" with Saakashvili's government.

The Americans and the Russians have long sparred for influence over Georgia. For the United States, Georgia's strategic value is in the black crude to be transported in a Caspian-to-Mediterranean pipeline now under construction, as well as the bragging rights in becoming big brother to a formerly Soviet state. NATO officials announced this month that Georgia is being considered for eventual admission into alliance membership.

But Georgia's most dangerous and fraught relationship is with neighboring Russia, which has over the past 10 years alternately indulged and punished—but mostly punished—its weaker neighbor. Russia's interest in Georgia is complex, said Alex Rondeli, president of the Georgian Foundation for Strategic and International Studies in Tbilisi, involving interwoven compacts with neighboring states, a postimperial impulse to control its backyard and an emotional relationship with a people Russians consider both historical vassal and a reflection of Russia's own cultural aspirations.

Since taking office, Saakashvili has hugged Russia close, as a boxer does to prevent an opponent from being able to throw a punch. Saakashvili has publicly praised [Vladimir] Putin's involvement in Georgia without giving Russia any real concessions over outstanding policy disagreements. The strategy has apparently kept Putin from intervening in Georgian affairs for now, but many experts say that Russia will in return make heavy demands on Saakashvili behind the scenes. As Rondeli said, "The question for Misha is not whether he can get what he wants from Russia but what very high price he's willing to pay."

One hundred and thirty-four days after the revolution, Saakashvili, at his desk, returned a phone call from his prosecutor general. A personal friend and financial supporter of his presidential campaign had damaged a government helicopter that he had leased for his personal use. The friend had taken the controls of the helicopter, put his young son on his lap and promptly crashed. Damages were estimated as high as $1 million. The prosecutor general told Saakashvili the man was refusing to pay, shouting that he was a friend of the president. What, the prosecutor wanted to know, should he do?

For the past 13 years, being a friend of the president was more than enough to let you walk away from any legal obligation. Saakashvili told me that he realizes that many of the country's most pressing problems, like territorial integrity and judicial reform, will have to be dealt with gradually, with careful compromises. But he also said that he is determined to puncture the culture of corruption, and that change, he said, needs to start at the top.

On the phone, Saakashvili hesitated for just a moment and then shouted, "To jail!" and slammed down the receiver.

Bibliography

BBC News. 2004. "Profile: Mikheil Saakashvili." January 25.

Bunce, Valerie, and Sharon Wolchik. 2006. "Youth and Electoral Revolutions in Slovakia, Serbia, and Georgia." *SAIS Review of International Affairs* 26: 55–65.

Corwin, Julie A. 2005. "Fledgling Youth Groups Worry Post-Soviet Authorities." Radio Free Europe/Radio Liberty, http://www.eurasianet.org/departments/civilsociety/articles/pp041105.shtml. April 22.

Fairbanks, Charles J. 2004. "Georgia's Rose Revolution." *Journal of Democracy* 15, no. 2 (April): 110–124.

Jones, Stephen. 2009. "Georgia's 'Rose Revolution' of 2003: Enforcing Peaceful Change." In *Civil Resistance and Power Politics: The Experience of Non-Violent Action from Gandhi to the Present*, ed. Adam Roberts and Timothy Garton Ash, 317–334. Oxford: Oxford University Press.

Kandelaki, Giorgi. 2006. "Georgia's Rose Revolution: A Participant's Perspective." Special Report 167. United States Institute of Peace, http://www.usip.org/resources/georgias-rose-revolution-participants-perspective.

King, Charles. 2004. "A Rose Among Thorns: Georgia Makes Good." *Foreign Affairs* (March/April): 1–6.

Lang, D. M. 1962. *A Modern History of Georgia.* London: Weidenfeld and Nicolson.

McFaul, Michael. 2005. "Transitions from Postcommunism." *Journal of Democracy* 16 (3): 5–19.

Nikolayenko, Olena. 2009. *Youth Movements in Post-Communist Societies: A Model of Nonviolent Resistance. CDDRL Working Papers* 114. Stanford, Calif.: Stanford University Center on Democracy, Development, and the Rule of Law, Freeman Spogli Institute for International Studies, http://cddrl.stanford.edu/publications/youth_movements_in_postcommunist_societies_a_model_of_nonviolent_resistance/.

Radio Free Europe/Radio Liberty. 2003. *Caucasus Report* 24 (November) 1. Cited in Fairbanks, "Georgia's Rose Revolution" 116.

Suny, Ronald Grigor. 1994. *The Making of the Georgian Nation.* Bloomington: Indiana University Press.

Tudoriou, Theodor. 2007. "The Orange, Rose, and Tulip Revolutions." *Communist and Post-Communist Studies* 40 (September): 315–342.

From *The New York Times*

Barry, Ellen. 2008. "Russia Aside, Georgia's Chief is Pressed at Home." December 20.

Barry, Ellen, and Dan Bilefsky. 2008. "Russia Agrees to Limited Pullout from Georgia." September 8.

Bilefsky, Dan. 2008. "In Georgia, A Reverence for Stalin." September 30.

Chivers, C. J. 2008. "Russia Pulls the Bulk of Its Forces Out of Georgia." August 22.

———. 2007. "Thousands Rally in Capital Against Georgia Government." November 3.

Chivers, C. J., and Michael Schwirtz. 2008. "Georgian President Vows to Rebuild Army." August 24.

Clines, Francis X. 1991. "Secession Decreed in Soviet Georgia." April 10.

Engelberg, Stephen. 1993. "General's Father Fought for Nazi Unit." August 28.

Fein, Esther B. 1989. "At Least 16 Killed as Protestors Battle the Police in Soviet Georgia." April 10.

Mydans, Seth. 2004. "Georgia's President Risks Showing Warlords Who's Boss." March 18.

___. 2003. "Interim Leaders in Georgia Back Presidential Candidate." November 26.

Schmemann, Serge. 1991. "Separatist Wins Soviet Georgia Vote." May 28.

Schwarz, Harry. 1956. "Soviet Students Strike in Tiflis, University Shut." March 24.

Specter, Michael. 2000. "Foreign Observers Criticize Lopsided Shevardnadze Vote." April 11.

———. 1995. "Tragic Georgian or Fixer of a Broken Nation?" October 19.

Vinciguerra, Thomas. 2005. "The Revolution Will Be Colorized." March 13.

Weisman, Steven. 2004. "With Powell on Hand, Georgians Install New Leader," January 26.

Whitney, Craig. 1978. "Soviet Georgians Win on Language." April 18.

———. 1978. "Soviet Georgians Take to the Streets to Save Their State Language." April 15.

Wines, Michael. 2001. "TV Station Raid in Georgia Leads to Protests and Cabinet's Ouster." November 2.

Unsigned. 2004. "Georgia Regains Region that Sought to Secede." May 7.

Unsigned. 2003. "U.S. Cites Fraud in Vote." November 6.

Unsigned. 1994. "Suicide by Caucasus Rebel Is Reported." January 6.

UKRAINE'S ORANGE REVOLUTION

The facts surrounding Ukraine's Orange Revolution of autumn 2004 reveal how a flow of knowledge from the countries of Eastern Europe, on the rim of the Soviet Union, in the Balkans, and in the Caucasus in the preceding years was instrumental in helping the Ukrainians realize that they could be effective in their own behalf. In a political progression catalyzed by developments that had occurred in neighboring countries—from the strategic use of symbols, such as colors that became linked to particular nonviolent movements, to the overwhelming role of youth who had received specific training in nonviolent civil resistance—elements of Ukraine's momentous election of the opposition leader, Viktor A. Yushchenko, as president are part of a much larger narrative. As in the other countries considered in this volume, the story of Ukraine's revolution is one of people seeking self-liberation while simultaneously struggling against the larger, more powerful, imperial Soviet Union.

The territory of what is now Ukraine has been continuously inhabited since 3000 B.C.E. Ukraine and Russia have been entwined since the era of Kievan Rus, a Slavic kingdom that built up around the Ukrainian city of Kiev in the ninth century and fell to the Mongols in the thirteenth century, as Celestine Bohlen recounts in *The New York Times* on December 1, 1991. Bohlen writes, "Literally, Ukraine means borderland, which is appropriate given its position straddling Europe's two halves, its split between two religions—Eastern Orthodox and Greek Catholic—and a history that has repeatedly put Ukrainians at the mercy of other peoples' territorial ambitions—Mongols, Lithuanians, Poles, Austro-Hungarians, but mostly Russians, first under the czars and then under the Communists" (see "A 'Borderland' Whose History Reflects That Troubled Role"). Throughout its history, Ukraine contended for self-determination against influences from the west and east, Bohlen says.

At 52 million persons and roughly the size of Texas, Ukraine is the fourth-largest country in Europe. The country covers ground from the Black Sea and Poland in the west all the way to Russia in the east. Of the former Soviet Union's total land mass of 8,649,496 square miles, Ukraine makes up 2.7 percent of the total, Russia 76.2 percent, and all others 21.1 percent.

Stephen Kotkin, writing in *The Times* on May 3, 1998, reflects:

> Far in the northeast of Europe, the extreme northwest of Asia, amid thick forests and bogs, lived sparse tribes of hunters, fishers and agriculturalists who spoke languages identified as Finno-Ugric and East Slavonic. Around the turn of the ninth century, via the formidable rivers between the Baltic and the Black Seas, vikings arrived in pursuit of furs and silver. Known as Rus in Arabic sources, Rhos in Byzantine ones, the Scandinavians [were] assimilated and helped establish a series of principalities ("Czars to Bolsheviks").

The people of what is now modern-day Ukraine began to assert themselves with the rise of Kievan Rus, the first Slavic state in Europe, in the tenth century C.E. Spanning lands from the Black Sea in the south, through modern-day Poland in the west, and eastward nearly to Moscow, Kievan Rus was the most powerful state in Europe by the eleventh century. Civil war broke up the power of the state, and the Mongols weakened it from the east. In 1240, the Mongols sacked Kiev, leaving the empire in shambles. Kievan Rus is considered a forebear to modern-day Russia—in the thirteenth century even the Ukrainian and Russian languages were identical, Bohlen's article notes—but after the Mongol invasion, Kotkin writes, the power center of Russia shifted to Moscow for good.

The country has a largely Ukrainian majority, 77 percent, according to Ukraine's 2001 Census, and a 17 percent ethnic Russian minority. More than 75 percent of Ukraine's population are Orthodox Christians, two-thirds of whom pledge their loyalty to the Kiev Patriarchate, and the others follow the Eastern Church in Moscow. This split in

QUICK FACTS ABOUT UKRAINE

- After World War II, the Soviet Union suppressed Ukrainian culture and forced assimilation upon the Ukrainians, whose language is related to but different from Russian. By 1987, more than 50 percent of all students in Ukraine were attending Russian language schools. In the capital city, Kiev, only 70,000 of 300,000 pupils were studying their native Ukrainian language.

- The worst nuclear power plant accident in history occurred at the Chernobyl nuclear power plant, near Pripyat in Ukraine, on April 26, 1986. Soviet attempts to cover up the health and mortality consequences provoked outrage and dissent.

- The scale of Ukraine, its sizable population, and its industrial capacity made its status and possible independence a determining factor in the survival or dissolution of the Soviet Union.

- On January 22, 1990, the organization Rukh (Movement) fought for Ukrainian independence and the rebirth of Ukrainian national identity by organizing a human chain of 400,000 participants who held hands. It stretched from Lviv in the western region to Kiev.

- On December 1, 1991, Leonid Kravchuk, a pro-independence leader, won a landslide victory and became the first president of Ukraine. On the same ballot more than 90 percent of Ukrainians endorsed a referendum for independence. The next day, Boris N. Yeltsin gave the country formal recognition on behalf of the Russian Federation. Ukrainians had achieved independence.

- At the time of its independence, Ukraine's population was 52 million, a fifth of whom were ethnic Russians.

- In autumn 2004, President Leonid D. Kuchma, who had succeeded Kravchuk in 1994, faced constitutional term limits. Running to replace him were Prime Minister Viktor F. Yanukovich, his tapped successor, and Viktor Yushchenko, former prime minister and central bank chairman, the leader of the Our Ukraine opposition faction in the Ukrainian parliament.

- In early September 2004, Yushchenko fell seriously ill. He was debilitated, and his face was deformed with blisters and cysts. Government officials and Yushchenko's political opponents attributed his illness to food poisoning, but Yuschenko's doctors discovered that he had been poisoned with dioxin, a deadly toxin. Despite his illness, Yushchenko continued his campaign for the presidency.

- After the October 31, 2004, election, the Central Election Commission reported that Yanukovich had won 50 percent of the vote and Yushchenko had 32 percent. These figures were disputed amid allegations of election fraud, voter intimidation, and corruption. When it appeared that neither candidate had won a plurality of votes, a runoff election was scheduled for November 21.

- Two weeks before the election, the only television network not under state control had its license to broadcast suspended.

- After the second round of voting, Yanukovich was declared the winner, 49.4 percent to 46.7 percent. Tens of thousands of protestors rapidly assembled in Kiev's Independence Square. By week's end, nearly 1 million Ukrainians had gathered in Kiev for Yushchenko rallies. Among the reports of voting irregularities were systematic multiple voting and extra ballots for Yanukovich after the polls closed. Exit polling showed Yushchenko ahead in western and central provinces, but the official results were announced as a 3 percent margin of victory for Yanukovich. The widespread allegations of electoral fraud drove Yushchenko and his campaign to reject the results.

- In what is called the Orange Revolution, approximately 1 million demonstrators in Kiev continued their protest for seventeen days, demanding a revote. Similar actions took place in other cities, along with civil disobedience. The state police did not move to restrain the ongoing protests.

- Volunteers appeared to pitch tents, deliver food, unroll blankets, and organize rallying chants in unison, yet the Orange Revolution resulted from months of planning for expected ballot-box fraud. A student-based opposition organization, Pora! (It's Time!), that advocated strictly nonviolent action, was the galvanizing force behind the civil resistance.

- On December 3, the Supreme Court overturned the election results and ordered a fresh runoff election on December 26.

- In the third round of voting, Yushchenko received 52 percent of the vote to Yanukovich's 44 percent and was elected president of Ukraine.

- The Orange Revolution concluded with a legitimate handover of power and Yushchenko's inauguration on January 23, 2005.

culture—and loyalty—was central to the affairs and discourse of the territory for the better part of a millennium and contributed to the turbulent political transition of modern-day Ukraine. The Ukrainian-Russian conflict has dominated the republic's history.

UKRAINE UNDER RUSSIAN CONTROL

After the fall of Kiev, Ukraine came under Lithuanian control. In 1509, the territory was annexed to the Polish Republic and remained so until the Great Ukrainian Revolution of 1648, when 300,000 men rose up against the Polish army and asserted independence. Shortly after, Ukraine struck a treaty with the Muscovites, asserting the Russian-Ukrainian link. On February 17, 1918, Professor Michaelo Hrushevsky, president of the Ukrainian Rada (parliament), writes in *The New York Times* magazine that Ukraine had remained nominally independent, but a "vassal" of Moscow, until the partitions of Poland ("Ukraine's Struggle for Self-Government"; see also **Poland, Introduction**). From 1772 to the 1790s, the far reaches of western Ukraine were subsumed into the Austro-Hungarian Empire, and the rest of Ukraine became a part of the Russian Empire, an arrangement that continued throughout the nineteenth century. Ukraine became so central to the Russian Empire that in the 1890s, Peter the Great considered moving the capital from St. Petersburg to Kiev, *The Times* relates on March 18, 1894 ("Kiev or St. Petersburg").

With the collapse of the Austro-Hungarian Empire following World War I and the Bolshevik Revolution in Russia, as Hrushevsky writes, "There arose a party in the Ukraine who wished to attempt once again the fight for the independence of the country." Hrushevsky charts one cruel disillusionment after another for the Ukrainians, who opposed the "centralizing policy of the Russian Government."

From 1917 to 1921, several independent groups within the Ukraine territory made divergent claims to independence. The Polish-Ukrainian war was fought over control of the western part of the territory, and the Polish-Soviet war determined who would control the eastern land. After the Ukrainians were defeated in both wars, the western half of the country, Galicia, was incorporated into Poland, and the eastern part was controlled by the Soviet Union. By 1924, when Ukraine had become one of the constituent republics of the Soviet Union, Bohlen notes for *The Times* that parts of Transcarpathia, on the southern slopes of the Eastern Carpathian Mountains, were divided between Czechoslovakia and Romania (see "A 'Borderland' Whose History Reflects That Troubled Role").

To govern the republic, the Soviet Union developed a policy now called "Ukrainization." The Soviet term for the policy, *korenizatsiya* (putting down roots) involved a from-the-top encouragement of the Ukrainian language, culture, and history. Rather than attempt linguistic and cultural administration, the Soviet Union believed that there would be less resistance to Moscow if Ukrainians were able to keep their linguistic and cultural autonomy. If, as cultural Ukrainians, citizens felt comfortable as indigenous Soviet citizens, the territory would be easier to control as part of the Soviet Union, or so the policy prescribed.

In the early 1930s, however, the Kremlin abruptly changed the policy. Fearing cultural elites across the republics, the Soviets began a policy of "Russification" throughout the Soviet Union. Ukrainian-language newspapers were shut down, and the language was suppressed. Many in the Ukrainian intellectual and cultural coteries and academia were killed, as Ukrainian culture came under attack. On June 27, 1931, *The Times* notes the effects of Russification, reporting on "the case of the national minorities in Soviet Russia, [which] . . . presents the same startling crowding of new and old which confronts us in nearly every other phase of the communist experiment." *The Times* cites "the famous rule of imperialist practice: that minorities shall be governed by officials from the outside, and incidentally that local garrisons shall always be recruited from distant regions" ("Russian Minorities").

In the 1930s, a famine swept through Ukraine. Millions died of starvation, and *The Times* estimates that hundreds of thousands more were murdered. In 1991 Bohlen reports: "Between the wars, the Ukraine bore the brunt of Stalin's brutal collectivization campaign since it, more than Russia, had developed a class of small farmers, or kulaks, the main targets of the Communists' fanaticism. During a devastating famine in the 1930's, treated by the Kremlin as a state secret, an estimated 5 million people died of hunger in the Ukraine. In addition, thousands of others were killed for political reasons" (see "A 'Borderland' Whose History Reflects That Troubled Role").

The Soviets consolidated their control over their neighbors in 1939, when the Molotov-Ribbentrop Pact, which separated Eastern Europe into German and Soviet spheres of influence, delivered Galicia to the Russians (on Stalin and Hitler's nonaggression and friendship pacts, signed on August 23 and September 28, 1939, see **Baltic States, Introduction**; "Lithuanians Rally for Stalin Victims"). Yet two years later, Ukraine acted as a "borderland" again, as nearly all of historic Ukraine came under the Nazi onslaught. Bohlen writes, "In the summer of 1941 virtually all of the Ukraine was overrun by Nazi troops. At first, many Ukrainians welcomed the Germans as allies against Stalin, but the Germans scorned Ukrainian aspirations and guerrilla bands formed to fight the German invaders. At the war's end, the Soviet Union again pushed its frontiers westward, this time taking back all ethnically Ukrainian lands, including the much-disputed Western Ukraine." Indeed, Ukrainians experienced much of the collateral damage of World War II. An estimated 7 million Ukrainians were killed, and two of the major battles on the Eastern Front took place in Kiev and Odessa.

Ukraine was subsumed back into the Soviet Union after World War II. Stalin and his successors continued the Russification of Ukraine and the suppression of Ukrainian intellectual culture, while accelerating the introduction of Russian cultural emblems. More Russian-language schools were established, and *The Times* estimates that by 1987, more than 50 percent of children in Ukraine were speaking Russian in school. Although Ukraine played a central role in Soviet politics—Soviet Premier Leonid I. Brezhnev was a native Ukrainian—the Ukrainian people and their culture were suppressed.

THE PUSH FOR INDEPENDENCE

On April 26, 1986, a reactor exploded at the Chernobyl nuclear power plant near Pripyat, Ukraine. The accident killed 31, injured 200, and exposed hundreds of thousands of others to radiation sickness. An inspection of the plant, located about 68 miles north of Kiev, found it to be in "blatant violation" of safety regulations, according to Milt Freudenheim, Katherine Roberts, and James F. Clarity in *The Times* on July 12, 1987 ("The Trial Begins at Chernobyl"). The incident infuriated the Ukrainians, but the Soviet government's cover-up aroused even stronger outrage and triggered widespread dissent. Five days after the explosion, with radioactive material still in the air, the Soviet government was promoting massive participation in its annual May Day celebrations as if nothing had happened, according to a letter to the editor of *The Times* by Yuriy Mishchenko and Anatoly Panov on April 26, 1991, the fifth anniversary of the disaster ("Chernobyl Makes Ukraine Want Independence"). They write that the government exhorted participation, including children, in the annual parade down Main Street while "a highly radioactive plume hung over" the city of Kiev, where "unseen radioactive dust and ash had spread over that city's streets and sidewalks." In their denunciation, they say that the same government officials had clandestinely "earlier evacuated columns of their own children to distant safety in secretly commandeered planes and trains." Such duplicity of Soviet-backed officials sparked a political response among citizens of Ukraine, the first substantive pro-independence movement of the contemporary era.

The rise to power of Mikhail S. Gorbachev as general secretary of the Communist Party of the Soviet Union in 1985 led to the introduction of "new thinking" in Moscow's foreign policy. In a 1987 book, Gorbachev laid out four main categories of reform: *perestroika* (restructuring the economy); *glasnost* (openness); democratization; and new thinking in foreign policy (see **"Introduction: Strikes, Sinatra, and Nonviolent Revolution"**). Glasnost originally alluded to greater transparency of government policy, but the aftermath of the horrific explosion at Chernobyl disclosed the limited nature of glasnost. The failure of the official news media to provide basic information to citizens of the Soviet Union aroused anger not only in Ukraine but also in the nearby Baltic republics of Estonia, Latvia, and Lithuania (see "Soviet Ethnic Minorities Take Glasnost into the Streets").

After the revelations about the double standard, one for the apparatchiks and another for innocent Ukrainians, combined with the media's failure to warn the populace, several civic associations began to organize Ukrainian citizens. Most prominent was the People's Movement of Ukraine, Rukh (Movement), founded in 1989, which describes its purpose as "to act as an instrument of the people in the drive for national independence and the rebirth of a Ukrainian national identity."

In *The Times* on March 9, 1989, reporter Bill Keller describes the "awakening" produced by Chernobyl, in which Ukrainian activist intellectuals founded Rukh as a main opposition group to disseminate information to the media, support candidates for office, and organize demonstrations and rallies:

> Ukrainians by the millions turned on their television sets the other night to witness a wondrous sight, a popular Ukrainian literary critic in fiery debate with a senior ideologist from the republic's Communist Party. The issue was a recent move by the Ukrainian Writers Union to organize an independent political movement similar to the popular fronts that have attracted mass support in the Baltic republics [see "Estonia Nationalists Begin to Challenge Moscow Dominance"; "Lithuanians Move to Limit Moscow Ties"].
>
> Viewers rendered a split decision on who prevailed in the televised confrontation, but the event signified an important awakening here in the Soviet Union's second-largest republic: after a period of deceptive quiet, the Ukraine's intellectual establishment has ventured into open conflict with the Communist Party, and Ukrainian nationalism—or patriotism, as its adherents prefer—is becoming respectable ("Ukraine Intellectuals Lead Challenge to Communists").

As Rukh and other organizations—with scholar activists in pivotal roles, as in the other nonviolent revolutions considered in this volume—began to rouse the people of Ukraine, they found that both the state's proximity to Russia and its lack of established civic organizations made the mobilization of Ukrainian independence movements difficult. As one Rukh activist said, "In Poland, when people were beaten they got angry and fought back. . . . Here, people have been beaten and beaten until they don't feel anything anymore." The Ukrainians would soon make up for a lack of strong civil society organizations by mobilizing for clean elections on a large scale.

"Nationalism in the Ukraine, which is the Soviet Union's breadbasket and industrial engine, is surely high on Mikhail S. Gorbachev's list of nightmares as Soviet leader," Keller writes concerning Gorbachev's five-day tour of Ukraine in February 1989. "Here we're not talking about 1.5 million people, as in Estonia, but 50 million, a nation the size of France or Italy," Bogdan N. Gorin, a leader of the Ukrainian Helsinki Association, told Keller. According to Gorin, "We think the question of the Soviet Union, whether it survives or not, will be resolved not in Estonia, but in the Ukraine." Keller observes that many of the people he encountered in Ukraine believed that the republic's preeminence was a foremost reason that the Soviet leader made his "hastily arranged" tour. Keller finds: "A trip through the Ukraine in Mr. Gorbachev's footsteps—from Kiev, the capital, to the cultural center of Lviv in the west, to the industrial city of Donetsk in the east—found that rivulets of discontent have begun running together into a rising stream."

On January 21–22, 1990, a human chain of 400,000 participants holding hands and organized by Rukh stretched from Lviv to Kiev, a distance of 300 miles. The date for the demonstration was chosen to coincide with the unification of the Ukrainian People's Republic and the West Ukrainian National Republic in 1919. (On Estonia's human chain of August 23, 1989, called the Baltic Way, see "Baltic Citizens Link Hands to Demand Independence.")

Within one year, the Ukrainian executive government began to print its own currency, declined to enter into new economic agreements with Soviet regions, and made plans for an independent central bank, and the parliament debated establishing the republic's own army. Ukraine was beginning to seek the same independence that the Baltic republics had achieved a year earlier.

Gorbachev, however, had never endorsed democracy for Ukraine, even though he had tolerated free elections and manifestations of popular will in other republics. In the words of one Ukrainian politician, "There is still a Russian psychology that holds that the Ukraine and Byelorussia can never have pretentions to independent statehood," Serge Schmemann reports on October 30, 1991, in *The Times* ("Ukraine is Now Getting Serious about its Drive for Independence").

On December 1, 1991, Leonid Kravchuk, a pro-independence leader, was elected president of Ukraine in a landslide, and on the same ballot more than 90 percent of Ukrainians endorsed an independence referendum. The next day, Boris N. Yeltsin gave the country formal recognition on behalf of the Russian Federation, and Ukrainians had achieved independence, *The Times* reporter Francis X. Clines relates on December 3 ("Ex-Communist Wins in Ukraine; Yeltsin Recognizes Independence"). (Yeltsin had been elected president of the Russian Soviet Federative Socialist Republic on June 12. The first popularly elected president of the Russian Federation, he soon allied himself with the Baltic republics in their plans for independence. See **Baltic States, Introduction**.)

Independence did not, however, solve Ukraine's domestic problems. A decade of hyperinflation and economic stagnation had caused many citizens to lose their optimism about the country's future. Moreover, the leaders, Kravchuk and his successor, Leonid D. Kuchma, remained closely tied to Russia, as Steven Erlanger reports in *The Times* on September 8, 1993 ("Ukraine Questions the Price Tag of Independence"). Some nine years later, on March 29, 2002, Patrick Tyler's account for *The Times* says that economic downturns, widespread and entrenched corruption, and the continuing perceived fealty to Moscow greatly affected the perceptions of the Ukrainian public and therefore the popularity of the Ukrainian government ("Ukraine's Leader Struggles to Go Quietly").

THE 2004 PRESIDENTIAL ELECTION

In 2004, President Kuchma was constitutionally unable to seek reelection. Two main candidates arose to succeed him: the incumbent prime minister, Viktor F. Yanukovich, who was heavily supported by Kuchma, and the former prime minister and opposition leader, Viktor A. Yushchenko, leader of the Our Ukraine faction in parliament. Yanukovich ran a government-backed, pro-Russia campaign, while Yushchenko pushed for pro-Western, Europe-facing policies.

Yushchenko, a former central bank chairman, was a young, vibrant leader. Since the state-controlled television stations seriously limited their coverage of his candidacy, he built his campaign on contact with voters. He ran a grassroots campaign, opening hundreds of offices in cities and towns across Ukraine and seeking to have as many face-to-face meetings and public rallies as possible. His campaign manager, Oleksandr Zinchenko, is quoted by Jan Maksymuik for Radio Free Europe on August 11: "The people's president will have a people's election campaign." Yushchenko gained early support, and it looked as if the race would be close.

But Yuschenko's face soon changed—literally. After a dinner in early September, Yushchenko fell ill with what he thought was food poisoning. As his condition persisted, he flew to Vienna, where physicians found that he had been poisoned with dioxin. The toxins seriously incapacitated him and disfigured his face with pockmarks and cysts. He had to leave the campaign trail for several weeks, according to Jason Shaplen in *The Times* on September 25 ("Poison Politics in Ukraine").

Although still seriously ill, Yushchenko returned to lead his coalition into the election. The accusations of poison had the effect of crystallizing the pervasive anticorruption, anti-establishment sentiments in Ukraine, and Yushchenko's supporters at his rallies began to wear orange—the candidate's choice of campaign color, evoking the autumn season. Almost immediately, Yushchenko's orange scarf became the emblem of the growing consciousness and feelings of large numbers of Ukrainians.

The election took place on October 31, 2004. Steven Lee Myers reports in *The Times* the next day that the Central Election Commission, based on 15 percent of the ballots counted, announced that Yanukovich had won a plurality with 50 percent of the vote, compared to Yushchenko's 32 percent (see "Rivals in Ukraine Report Violations in Presidential Vote"). Yet Yushchenko's internal polling showed that Yushchenko himself had won 50 percent of the vote, and Yanukovich 27 percent. In addition, the Yushchenko campaign reported voting irregularities across the country. Vadym S. Galaychuk, a manager of Yushchenko's campaign, told *The Times* that "thousands of names had mysteriously vanished from voting lists. . . . [I]n some areas as many as 30 percent of voters could not cast ballots." With no clear-cut majority, a run-off election was scheduled for November 21.

Although exit polls showed Yushchenko up by 11 percent on election eve, the official state results showed Yanukovich winning the runoff election by 3 percent. The public immediately questioned the results. International election observers, including representatives from the European Parliament and NATO, issued a report saying that the election did "not meet democratic standards." Yushchenko appealed for his supporters to gather in Kiev's Independence Square, called the Maidan ("square"); and hundreds of thousands assembled and began chanting, "Freedom cannot be stopped!" Combining a fight for honest elections and use of massive civil disobedience, the link with other such mobilizations in the region was unambiguous. C. J. Chivers reports in *The Times* on November 23, that in the midst of a sea of orange—banners, flags, and scarves—student protestors waved the flag of the Republic of Georgia, which served as an instant reminder of the previous year's Revolution of the Roses and the defeat of Eduard A. Shevardnadze by Mikhail Saakashvili, another young pro-reform democratic leader (see "Premier

Claims He's the Winner in Ukraine Vote"; "Georgian Leader Agrees to Resign, Ending Standoff").

THE REVOTE

In the next three days, Yushchenko gathered approximately a million demonstrators in Kiev's Independence Square. According to political scientist Anika Locke Binnendijk and international relations analyst Ivan Marovic, "The ultimate scope of the crowds in Kiev . . . exceeded the expectations of both the regime and the opposition leadership. On the first day after the opposition leader Victor Yushchenko's call to the Kiev streets, 100,000 protesters arrived on Independence Square. . . . Over the next 24 hours, the number had nearly doubled. By Wednesday, November 24, hundreds of thousands more had arrived from regions around the country, and by the end of the first week, according to most estimates, nearly a million Ukrainians had gathered in Kiev" (Binnendijk and Marovic 2006, 414). The youth-led organization Pora! (It's Time!), which had learned its nonviolent organizing techniques from Otpor and Kmara (see **Serbia, Introduction; Georgia, Introduction**), was immediately on hand to organize tents, food, and banners for the gathering throng. Tents had first been pitched in the Maidan in October 1990 to shelter prodemocracy hunger strikers, so organizers knew how to erect them swiftly.

Clothed in orange as far as the eye could see, the crowd was able to win over some in the formal government apparatus. As with other nonviolent civil resistance in Eastern Europe, the Baltics, the Balkans, and the Caucasus, the Orange Revolution was a strictly nonviolent movement. Binnendijk and Marovic note that in Serbia and Ukraine, "blatant election fraud provided a high-profile rallying point around which the movements would be able to mobilize large numbers of citizens. Both the Serbian and the Ukrainian oppositions thus explicitly built their strategies around exposing and challenging fraudulent election results" (Binnendijk and Marovic 2006, 413).

Chivers's report of November 24 describes the scene in Kiev: "Yushchenko's supporters swarmed through the capital, staging highly organized rallies at Independence Square and the Supreme Rada, Ukraine's 450-seat Parliament," and on the night of November 23 "marched through lightly falling snow to the presidential administration building, where they were met by lines of helmeted police officers standing 12 deep" (see "Protests Grow as Ukraine Vote Crisis Deepens"). According to historian Andrew Wilson, "The authorities knew that there would be mass resistance and bloodshed if they moved against the Maidan [Independence Square]. They were sufficiently uncertain about the demonstrators' 'reserve tactics': the demonstrators could blockade the steep access roads to the Maidan with cars, and could put in the front line the militia who had defected. Regime soft-liners like Kuchma clearly baulked at the amount of violence that would be necessary" (Wilson 2009, 345).

Noting a significant development when the state police did not make any move to suppress the ongoing protests, Chivers reports in *The Times* on November 24 that the crowd began to call out that the police were siding with the demonstrators. He writes, "The police and the protesters appeared for the moment to have found a balance. 'The police are with the people!' the crowd chanted outside Parliament. At night, Mr. Yushchenko's supporters tied orange ribbons—a symbol of the opposition—to officers' riot shields." Chivers quotes an unnamed senior Western diplomat in Kiev, who told *The Times* that deep divisions existed in the top ranks of the Ukrainian government. The diplomat told Chivers of plausible reports that police units, the army, and the SBU [Sluzhba Bezpeky Ukrayiny, Ukraine's version of the KGB] "might be unwilling to put down the demonstrators by force." He told *The Times*, however, that the Interior Ministry might be prepared to use force, stating, "You have a government which in my opinion does not know what to do." The diplomat told Chivers that "two red lines" had been conveyed by his country to Kuchma: "the government was to use no violence, and second, that it was to take no step to certify the election" (see "Protests Grow as Ukraine Vote Crisis Deepens").

When Chivers describes the emergence of divisions within the ranks of the ruling government, he touches on a dynamic possibility that the technique of nonviolent struggle can produce. Among the properties of civil resistance is its ability to split the ranks of the target group, in which some among a regime's police, soldiers, or security forces may become persuaded of the argument being made by the nonviolent protagonists. (In contrast, violent struggle tends to solidify the target group against any challenge.) Bulwarks of the regime, such as the police and military, although they are beholden to the regime, may begin to shift allegiances. Even though obedience within security organizations is assumed to be unquestioning, individuals within them may disregard orders, implement directives poorly, or change their loyalties. In this case, Kuchma, Yanukovich's chief patron, was issuing orders that would undermine Yushchenko, but, as Chivers shows, the sympathies of the "helmeted police officers standing 12 deep" had begun to move toward the nonviolent challengers. In retrospect, the record in *The Times* is clear: the police had decided not to stand in the way of the prodemocracy activists. Indeed, they may have been disobeying orders: letting demonstrators tie orange ribbons onto their shields was not part of the antiriot officers' instructions. Meanwhile, as long as the demonstrators in Kiev retained strictly nonviolent discipline, the prospects could increase for outside third parties, such as the diplomat quoted by *The Times,* to respond positively to the resisters, and in his case bring pressure from his government.

The young demonstrators tying orange ribbons to the shields of the police, and military troops watching in Independence Square, were reminiscent of the Georgian democracy advocates who placed roses down the barrels of police weapons during the Rose Revolution in Georgia (see "Georgian Leader Agrees to Resign, Ending Standoff"). The demonstrators were able to achieve a primary goal of the Ukraine nonviolent movement: to split the ranks of the target group, be it police, soldiers, security forces, or the many in the establishment and among society's elites who had become sympathetic to Yushchenko's cause.

The massive protest rallies continued to grow, aided in their staying power by rock stars and musical artists who performed around the clock. Music ranging from Okean Elzy, the most popular group in Ukraine, to GreenJolly, whose hit song "Razom Nas Bahato" (Together We Are Many) was downloaded by thousands of young people nationwide. Local councils across Ukraine passed referendums that refused to accept the election results. Yushchenko, addressing the crowds in Independence Square several times a day, began to organize a general strike. Lech Wałęsa, the leader of the 10-million strong Solidarity Union movement that brought democracy to Poland, urged nationwide coordinated resistance (see "Polish Labor Crisis Deepens as Workers List Their Demands"; "Polish Union Opens Convention"; "To His Volatile Young Allies, Walesa Preaches Conciliation"). Poland's struggle had been a *national* mobilization. Chivers reports in *The Times* on November 26 that Wałęsa said to the throngs, "You can rely on the support of Poland and Wałęsa, but we cannot do it for you. You have to do it yourselves." In the same article, Chivers reports that on November 25, the Supreme Court temporarily blocked Yanukovich's victory, citing the widespread allegations of election fraud ("Ukraine Court Delays Results in Vote Dispute").

Yanukovich, however, had the backing of other courts, the state-controlled media, and Russian president Vladimir Putin, who pushed for the courts of Ukraine to certify the elections with Yanukovich as winner. Reporters covering the events playing out in Independence Square testified to hearing resounding "boos" every time Putin appeared on the television screens erected there, as Nicholas Kristof reports for *The Times* on December 4 ("Let My People Go"). The major protest rallies continued to grow in fervor, as the popular determination to resist appeared to deepen.

Writing on November 29, *The Times* reporter Steven Lee Myers describes a visible act of civil disobedience. Natalia Dimitruk, who interpreted for the deaf on the official state-controlled UT-1 television, disregarded the broadcaster's report on Yanukovich's victory claim and, in her small corner on the screen, used sign language to report something altogether different. "The results announced by the Central Electoral Commission are rigged," she signed. "Do not believe them." She proceeded to use her hands to declare that Yushchenko had won the election. "I am very disappointed by the fact that I had to interpret lies," she signed; "I will not do it any more. I do not know if you will see me again." Myers writes:

More than 200 journalists at UT-1 went on strike [on November 25] to demand the right to present an objective account of the extraordinary events that have unfolded since the vote, forcing the channel to broadcast a feed from another network before capitulating. Ms. Dimitruk walked out of the studio and joined them, protesting coverage that was skewed almost entirely on behalf of Mr. Yanukovich's campaign before and after the runoff election.

Journalists at One Plus One—a private station, but one that hewed closely to Mr. Kuchma's point of view—also rebelled. After its news editor resigned, the channel's director, Oleksandr Rodnyansky, appeared on the air.

"We understand our responsibility for the biased news that the channel has so far been broadcasting under pressure and on orders from various political forces," he said, adding that the station would from that point on guarantee "full and impartial" coverage of the events roiling Ukraine.

Since then the two channels have begun to show what until last week seemed unthinkable: the enormous protests in Kiev that have paralyzed the capital, and reports on Mr. Yushchenko himself. More important, the images reach across the country, including the east, where Mr. Yanukovich's support is strongest, in large part because his is the only view given significant time on state-owned or controlled networks. Channel 5, an independent channel that has become, in effect, the opposition's champion, does not broadcast in most of the east.

"The most important thing is we can show what is happening in Kiev," said Maksim Drabok, a special correspondent on UT-1. He led the campaign against government-controlled coverage and the one-day strike by the station's journalists that prompted a pledge from the station's directors to allow coverage of both sides ("A Silent Act of Rebellion Raises a Din in Ukraine").

The Organization for Security and Cooperation in Europe (OSCE) was also monitoring abuses in Ukraine. The group, which resulted from the Helsinki Final Act of 1975, is associated with advocating recognition of and respect for human rights across the European states (see **"Introduction: Strikes, Sinatra, and Nonviolent Revolution"**). The OSCE noted both the slanted media coverage of the campaign and the fundamentally unfair terms of the runoff.

On December 1, the Ukrainian parliament overwhelmingly passed a vote of no confidence in the leadership, including Prime Minister Yanukovich. It was becoming clear that the election results would be overturned and the candidates would have to conduct a third round of voting, Myers reports on December 2 (see "A New Election for Ukrainians Appears Likely"). Also in question was whether Kuchma, the departing president, would keep power. Kuchma had introduced a reorganization of the government, with major authority delegated to the prime minister. Political observers speculated that Kuchma would ensure that a pro-Kuchma puppet was appointed to the spot. In an editorial on December 4, *The Times* lauds the Ukraine Supreme Court for its December 3 decision that defied Putin and ordered a second runoff election by December 26 ("Saying No to Vladimir Putin").

Yanukovich's support quickly evaporated. During the next round of the campaign, medical authorities released information definitively concluding that Yushchenko had suffered dioxin poisoning, according to Elizabeth Rosenthal in the *International Herald-Tribune* on December 12, 2004 ("Liberal Leader from Ukraine Was Poisoned"). "Do you like my face?" Yushchenko would ask the multitudes in the runoff campaign, drawing attention to his cysts and scars. "This is the face of today's Ukraine!" he said, according to Chivers on December 5 ("Ukraine's Face Is Mirrored in a Candidate"). The sea of orange continued in Independence Square throughout the month, as the country anxiously awaited the December 26 election.

Transition in Ukraine

With 52 percent of the vote, Viktor Yushchenko was swept to victory in the December 26 runoff, Chivers reports for *The Times* on December 28 (see "Yushchenko Wins 52% of the Vote, Rival Vows a Challenge"). International observers from the United States, the European Parliament, and the OSCE certified the election as free and fair. Yanukovich claimed fraud and intimidation against his supporters, but the international election monitors did not validate his allegations. Less than one month later, Yushchenko took office as the third president of Ukraine.

Even so, Ukraine remained a divided country. Although Yushchenko received overwhelming support in the western part of the country, he received very few votes from the eastern sections, and a full 44 percent of the country voted against him. Yanukovich refused to attend the inaugural ceremony. Nevertheless, as *The Times* reports, Yushchenko's inauguration was part of a larger movement—something that the people of Ukraine acknowledged. On January 24, 2005, Myers describes for *The Times* the public responses of the crowds: "the loudest applause erupted for the leaders of countries who had over the decades risen up against Soviet domination: President Aleksandr Kwasniewski of Poland; Václav Havel, the former Czech president; and [Nino] Burdzhanadze, the speaker of Georgia's Parliament" (see "Ukraine President Sworn In, Promising to Promote Unity"). Yushchenko called for unity in his inauguration speech, and he demonstrated his point by making his first state visit the next day to Russia, Chivers notes for *The Times* on January 25 ("Ukraine's President Mends Ties with Putin"). The president of the "Borderland," facing years of a difficult balancing acts ahead, nevertheless represented the culmination of the Ukrainian people's collective struggle for clean elections and self-determination.

Conclusion

Ukraine produced its Orange Revolution in seventeen days in autumn 2004, ending the authoritarian rule of President Leonid Kuchma, who had maintained Soviet-style suppression. CNN and BBC correspondents reporting live from Kiev kept saying, "So far there's been no violence." What these journalists failed to report is that an organization called Pora had been conducting intensive training programs and had adopted an adamantine position against the use of violence, no matter the provocation. According to Andrew Wilson, "The opposition knew that the first side to use violence risked losing the battle for public and international opinion, although the former was of primary importance" (Wilson 2009, 343).

Ukraine clearly benefited from the successes in Eastern Europe, the Baltics, the Balkans, and the Caucasus, and a major reason was that it had become easier for the main galvanizing groups to learn and share the basic theories and methods for the technique of nonviolent civil resistance. In Lithuania, Richard Attenborough's film *Gandhi* was nationally televised (see "Soviet Loyalists in Charge after Attack in Lithuania; 13 Dead; Curfew is Imposed"). In Serbia, Otpor! (Resistance!) distributed its manual with six different training programs and trained more than 400 organizers in nonviolent methods based upon it (see "Rally Against Milosevic Fails to Bind Opposition Parties"; "Student Group Emerges as Major Milosevic Foe"; "Out in Front, Serbia's Opposition Prepares to Lose"; "Milosevic, Trailing in Polls, Rails Against NATO"). In Georgia, some 5,000 attended Kmara (Enough) summer workshops led by Otpor. Kmara enlisted thousands of Georgian youth throughout the country, and gave a national face to the deep desire of the people of Georgia to end Eduard A. Shevardnadze's regime (see "Officials in Georgia Declare Shevardnadze Ballot Winner"; "Foes of Georgian Leader Storm into Parliament Building"). In Ukraine, Pora, like Otpor and Kmara, distributed translated literature on the theories and methods of civil resistance across the country; in addition to sharing knowledge, they performed the crucial function of an information network to spread leaflets, prodemocracy slogans, and antigovernment messages (on Pora, see "Youth Movement Underlies the Opposition in Ukraine"). Writings by scholars such as Gene Sharp were translated into Serbian, Georgian, and Ukrainian. Computers, fax machines, translation of materials, and film helped to spread the word.

In Ukraine, Steve York's film "Bringing Down a Dictator," was used to show how the Serbian movement toppled Slobodan Milošević.

Contrary to popular notions, the *behavior* of participants defines nonviolent action, not the participants' convictions or beliefs. None of the movements considered here that brought about momentous change was dedicated to nonviolence as a creed; rather, each adopted nonviolent action as a technique. What is most consequential in a popular mass mobilization is adherence to a policy of nonviolent and nonmilitary engagement. Anarchism, charisma, faith, idealism, pacifism, religious tenets, or spirituality are neither implied nor required. What distinguishes the technique is that its practitioners focus on undermining the power of the target group, not the lives or well-being of its members. Movements of collective nonviolent action involve strategic planning and practical use of specific forms of power. The Ukrainian opposition unified itself and consciously decided to choose "tents over tanks," as an article published after the Orange Revolution quips (Wilson 2009, 337). The rationale for pressing forward with nonviolent methods is what Lech Wałęsa said to nearly a million orange-clad demonstrators: "to use peaceful methods to lower the risks of a possible tragedy."

Ukraine's History Shapes its Revolution

The key to understanding why the Orange Revolution in Ukraine was so "revolutionary" may be found in the meaning of the name of the country itself. As Celestine Bohlen points out in *The New York Times* on December 1, 1991, "Ukraine" means "borderland" (see "A 'Borderland' Whose History Reflects That Troubled Role"). The history of the nation, as with most of the countries discussed in this volume, is the story of how the people of Ukraine responded to being "swallowed by its neighbors." Writing on the day that the Ukrainians voted for independence from the Soviet Union, Bohlen recounts how Ukraine has been a proxy for East-West conflict—a history that shaped the events of its deeply flawed initial 2004 presidential election.

The Ukrainian capital of Kiev was once the capital of Kievan Rus, one of the largest empires of the Middle Ages, Bohlen notes. The Russians and the Ukrainians trace many of their cultural roots back to the empire, and linguists conclude that both cultures shared a common language (see **Ukraine, Introduction**). Despite the Ukrainians' centuries-long struggle for self-determination, until the twentieth century the territory was split between Polish or European domination in the west and Russian control in the east. At the end of World War II, the Soviet Union pressured Ukraine in an attempt to make the region more Russian. Bohlen describes how the Russians viewed traditional songs and dress as subversive and tried to eradicate the Ukrainian language. As other Soviet republics, such as Estonia, Latvia, and Lithuania in the

Baltics, were asserting their own historical and cultural identities, the Ukrainians also began to seek independence. The Chernobyl nuclear meltdown in April 1986 accelerated the process.

By the time of the referendum described in Bohlen's dispatch, independence was a foregone conclusion (see **Ukraine, Introduction**). On December 1, 1991, more than 90 percent of Ukrainians voted for independence, and on the same ballot elected a pro-independence president. On December 3, Francis X. Clines writes for The Times that the day after the referendum, Boris N. Yeltsin, on behalf of Russia, acknowledged Ukraine's independence ("Ex-Communist Wins in Ukraine; Yeltsin Recognizes Independence"). Although Ukraine had become independent of Russia and totalitarian rule as a formality, the next decade would demonstrate that, in practice, little progress had been made. The Orange Revolution of 2004 was in many ways the culmination of the referendum described by Bohlen.

DECEMBER 1, 1991
A "BORDERLAND" WHOSE HISTORY REFLECTS THAT TROUBLED ROLE
By CELESTINE BOHLEN
Moscow

Like much of Central Europe, the Ukraine has had a history of being swallowed by its neighbors, usually not in one piece. But the Ukraine—larger in size than most European countries, with almost as many people as France—has had the added misfortune of having never experienced modern statehood, except for one brief chaotic period at the end of World War I, just before the Bolsheviks moved in to assert Soviet power.

Today, as they vote in a republic-wide referendum, Ukrainians for the first time in their history will have a direct say on the shape of their nation. The most likely outcome is a vote for independence—which could prove to be the last jolt to break up the already-crumbling Soviet Union.

Literally, Ukraine means borderland, which is appropriate given its position straddling Europe's two halves, its split between two religions—Eastern Orthodox and Greek Catholic—and a history that has repeatedly put Ukrainians at the mercy of other peoples' territorial ambitions—Mongols, Lithuanians, Poles, Austro-Hungarians, but mostly Russians, first under the czars and then under the Communists.

Ever since the golden age of Kievan Rus, a Slavic kingdom that sprang up around the Ukrainian city of Kiev in the 9th century and fell to the Mongols in the mid-13th century, the history of the Ukraine and Russia have been intertwined. Both nations trace their conversion to Christianity to the same date—988, when the ruler of Kievan Rus, Vladimir in Russian (Volodymyr in Ukrainian), ordered his people into a tributary of the Dnieper River for a mass baptism.

According to the Encyclopedia Britannica, even the languages were indistinguishable until the 12th or 13th century, after the fall of Kievan Rus. However, by the 19th century, the Ukrainian vernacular had come into its own, providing the engine for a great literary and cultural revival as symbolized by the national poet Taras Shevchenko.

But like two competing brothers, both nations are as apt to dwell on their differences as they are to celebrate their common parentage. Most Ukrainian historians, for instance, dispute Russia's claim to being the lineal descendant of ancient Rus. This, they argue, amounts to cultural usurpation, and a dilution of the uniqueness of the Ukrainian nation.

The problem is that the Ukrainian nation, unlike its Russian brother, has had to struggle to assert its version of history. Even its name—with the definite article—is considered offensive by many Ukrainians, who see the offending "the" as an insidious inference that their country is no more than somebody else's province.

For much of the modern era, the Ukraine itself was split in half. The lands west of the Dnieper were under Polish domination, while the eastern half came under Russian domination in 1654, when Zaporozhian Cossacks, rebelling against the Poles, had nowhere else to turn but Moscow.

By the end of the 18th century, after the partition of Poland, Russia acquired parts of the Western Ukraine, except Galicia, which went to the Austro-Hungarian Empire. There, the Ukrainian language and culture were allowed a certain amount of freedom—more than in Russia, where by the end of the 19th century Czar Alexander II had banned the import and publication of Ukrainian books or the use of the Ukrainian language in schools. According to one historian, Russian authorities saw even embroidered blouses and folk songs as subversive.

But even as Russian politics tried to cut off Ukrainian nationalism at its roots, the two peoples continued to share a common fate. Despite the fertile plains and rich black soil that gave the Ukraine its fame as the empire's breadbasket, Ukrainian peasants lived in poor and crowded conditions: At the turn of the century, the Ukraine had twice as many inhabitants per arable acre as England. So when the Trans-Siberian Railroad opened the way for settlers heading east, many Ukrainians took the opportunity to leave home. By 1914, two million Ukrainians had settled in Russia's eastern reaches, while millions of others headed west, to the United States and Canada.

Industrialization

Equally, industrialization brought millions of Russians to the Ukraine, particularly to the Donets Basin, which by the end of the 19th century was producing 70 percent of the empire's coal. In the coal fields, only 25 percent of the miners and only 30 percent of workers in the related metallurgical industry were Ukrainians; most Ukrainians stayed in the countryside. In 1917, one-third of city dwellers in the Ukraine were Ukrainians; most of the others were either Russians or Jews.

The Russian Revolution of 1917 and the collapse of the Austro-Hungarian Empire in 1918 opened the way for the first independent Ukrainian state, combining both its eastern and western halves. But buffeted by six different armies—Ukrainian, Bolshevik, White Army, the Entente forces, the Poles and anarchists—an independent Ukraine, headed by a succession of governments, was to be short-lived.

By 1924, when the Ukraine became one of the constituent republics of the Soviet Union, Ukrainian lands were even more divided than before, with Bukovina annexed by Romania, parts of Transcarpathia taken by Czechoslovakia and Galicia handed back to Poland.

Between the wars, the Ukraine bore the brunt of Stalin's brutal collectivization campaign since it, more than Russia, had developed a class of small farmers, or kulaks, the main targets of the Communists' fanaticism. During a devastating famine in the 1930's, treated by the Kremlin as a state secret, an estimated 5 million people died of hunger in the Ukraine. In addition, thousands of others were killed for political reasons.

Under the Molotov-Ribbentrop pact of 1939, eastern Galicia was delivered to the Soviet Union, but in the summer of 1941 virtually all of the Ukraine was overrun by Nazi troops. At first, many Ukrainians welcomed the Germans as allies against Stalin, but the Germans scorned Ukrainian aspirations and guerrilla bands formed to fight the German invaders. At the war's end, the Soviet Union again pushed its frontiers westward, this time taking back all ethnically Ukrainian lands, including the much-disputed Western Ukraine.

In the postwar period, Ukrainian nationalism was suppressed by Soviet power, and dissidents who advocated greater cultural autonomy were hounded and jailed. The greatest fear of Ukrainian nationalists was slow assimilation by Russia, meaning a slow death for their own culture and language. By 1987, more than 50 percent of all students in the Ukraine were attending Russian language schools; in Kiev, only 70,000 out of 300,000 pupils were studying the Ukrainian language.

The Effects of Chernobyl

After the nuclear accident at the Chernobyl atomic plant in 1986, Ukrainian politics was never the same again. The incident—which was initially played down by the republic's hard-line Communist Party bosses—was a harrowing and embittering experience for much of the population, who soon began to demand greater local control.

Ethnic Russians, estimated at one-fifth of the Ukraine's 52 million people, have been generally supportive of the drive for independence, and their presence has also served to moderate the Ukrainian nationalists, whose goal has been to unite, rather than divide, the republic's different ethnic groups.

But many fear that with independence will come pressure from other republics for a review of old and painful border questions. Already, the republic of Moldavia has asked to reopen the question of Bukovina, while Russia, which lost the Crimea to the Ukraine in the 1950's, may also consider pressing its claims, if the political situation in the former Soviet Union deteriorates further.

ELECTIONS MARRED BY CHARGES OF ABUSE

Writing for *The Times* on November 1, 2004, Steven Lee Myers calls the autumn 2004 elections in Ukraine a "watershed in the country's history" (see "Rivals in Ukraine Report Violations in Presidential Vote"). Although Ukraine had been formally independent since 1991, its leaders had maintained close ties with Russia and, most notably, had maintained Soviet-style suppression. Myers highlights three features of the 2004 campaign that illustrate the state of Ukrainian society: the repressive tactics used against political opponents, most notably the poisoning of opposition leader Viktor A. Yushchenko; limitations on freedom of speech and the news media; and major electoral fraud and corruption.

In autumn 2004, President Leonid D. Kuchma faced constitutional term limits. Running to replace him were his chosen successor, Prime Minister Viktor F. Yanukovich, and Yushchenko, the leader of the Our Ukraine faction in the Ukrainian Rada (parliament). Yushchenko seemed to get off to a promising start, gaining substantial nationwide support, but in early September he fell ill with what seemed to be food poisoning. At a hospital in Vienna, Yushchenko's physicians discovered that he had been poisoned with dioxin, which left him debilitated and his face scarred. He tried to continue his campaign, but as *The Times* reporter Jason Shaplen notes on September 25, Yushchenko "had difficulty reading his text and was salivating excessively" ("Poison Politics in Ukraine").

Yushchenko was sufficiently recovered to lead the party into the elections at the end of October. Myers surmises that being poisoned was not Yushchenko's greatest obstacle to victory. In contrast to Georgia, where the news media were comparatively free (see **Georgia, Introduction**), the print press and live media in Ukraine were notoriously restricted. Myers reports that the only television network not controlled by the state had its broadcast license suspended two weeks before the election. *The Times* notes that state networks consistently covered Yanukovich, his rallies, and his positions, while largely ignoring Yushchenko. Instead, Yushchenko had to rely on a heavy travel schedule and large numbers of grassroots rallies to get his message across. Radio Free Europe quotes his campaign manager, Oleksandr Zinchenko, as saying, "The people's president will have a people's election campaign" (Maksymuik 2004).

Despite these obstacles, Yushchenko performed remarkably well in the October 31 elections, according to his own polling. By night's end, his internal tally showed him winning 50 percent to Yanukovich's 27 percent. With 15 percent of the ballots counted, however, the Central Election Commission released preliminary results that showed Yanukovich with 50 percent to Yushchenko's 32 percent. *The Times* explains the disparity: election fraud, voter intimidation, and corruption had caused thousands of pro-Yushchenko voters to disappear from the voter rolls. In addition, OSCE, NATO, European, and U.S. observers cast doubt on the outcome. In the end, neither candidate won a plurality of votes, leading to a runoff election scheduled for November 21.

NOVEMBER 1, 2004
RIVALS IN UKRAINE REPORT VIOLATIONS IN PRESIDENTIAL VOTE
By STEVEN LEE MYERS

Kiev, Ukraine, Monday, Nov. 1 – Channel 5, this country's only television network not controlled by the government or President Leonid D. Kuchma's allies, had its license to broadcast here in the capital suspended two weeks ago. A day later, a court froze its bank accounts in a legal dispute that turned on whether a leading challenger in the presidential election on Sunday had been poisoned.

As voters cast ballots, a weekold hunger strike by a handful of employees was shown at the top of each hour's news, which the channel continues to broadcast in spite of what its director, Vladyslav Lyasovsky, called the government's "political terrorism."

"This sword of Damocles is still hanging over us," he said.

The government's legal challenges to Channel 5, which remain unresolved, are part of what Mr. Kuchma's opponents, along with international election observers, have called a pattern of harassment and electoral irregularities that calls into question the fairness of the vote to elect Mr. Kuchma's successor.

By the time polls closed [on October 31] at 8 P.M., there was no letup in the accusations that had swirled around the campaign from the start.

Officials for the top 2 candidates in the field of 24—Mr. Kuchma's choice, Prime Minister Viktor F. Yanukovich, and Viktor A. Yushchenko, a former prime minister and central bank chairman—denounced what they said were flagrant violations at polling stations across Ukraine. They cited numerous reports of harassment—and in at least one case a violent assault—against voters and election observers from both camps.

Vadym S. Galaychuk, a manager of Mr. Yushchenko's campaign, said thousands of names had mysteriously vanished from voting lists. He said in some areas as many as 30 percent of voters could not cast ballots. Many were told to appeal to courts, which remained open into the night, though in at least one case in Kiev, Mr. Galaychuk said, a court had closed by 5 P.M.

"We expected this problem," he said in an interview, "but this is on a far more serious scale."

Initial vote counts released early [on November 1] showed substantially different results. The Central Elections Commission said that with 15 percent of the votes counted, Mr. Yanukovich had 50 percent of the vote and Mr. Yushchenko had 32 percent. But Mr. Yushchenko, appearing at his campaign headquarters, said his campaign's own count showed that he had 50 percent and that Mr. Yanukovich had 27 percent. If neither candidate gets more than 50 percent they will face each other in a runoff, scheduled for Nov. 21.

Mr. Yushchenko stopped short of claiming victory, but early [on November 1] he told cheering supporters, perhaps prematurely, "The democratic forces have won in Ukraine."

The country's presidential campaign is a watershed in the country's history, and has already been marred by charges of government abuses, accusations of interference from Russia, Europe and the United States, and a controversy surrounding Mr. Yushchenko's mysterious illness, which he attributed to an attempted assassination by poisoning.

Mr. Kuchma's decision to step down after two five-year terms has opened a fierce fight over the country's future, with Mr. Yanukovich promising to follow Mr. Kuchma's course and Mr. Yushchenko promising to steer the country toward a more open and democratic path, more closely allied with Europe.

"I want to live in a proper country where people respect honest leaders and do not fear them," Mr. Yushchenko, still showing the effects of his illness, said after voting in downtown Kiev.

Voting unfolded with a visibly heightened presence of police and military forces in the capital and elsewhere. On Oct. 23, tens of thousands of Mr. Yushchenko's supporters demonstrated outside the elections commission in a rally that ended with violence. The headquarters of both the election commission and the state's main television channel were surrounded [October 31] by barricades and military vehicles. "This step is quite unusual for a country with some democratic traditions," said Stepan B. Gavrish, a member of Parliament and a manager of Mr. Yanukovich's campaign.

Voter turnout appeared high, as were tensions, though there were no reports of serious disruptions or large demonstrations. Mr. Yushchenko's campaign asked supporters to delay any demonstrations until [November 1], when a large rally was planned in Kiev's Independence Square. At the same time, they said they expected Mr. Kuchma's government to provoke or even stage violent demonstrations to discredit Mr. Yushchenko.

Mr. Yanukovich's campaign reported what it called evidence of fraud and intimidation against his supporters, including the beating of some observers in a village near Lvov in western Ukraine, a region that is Mr. Yushchenko's stronghold. Both sides stopped short of saying the results should be declared invalid based on the reported irregularities.

Mr. Yanukovich, who became prime minister in 2002, has benefited from high-profile support offered by a politician who has no vote in this campaign: Russia's president, Vladimir V. Putin. Mr. Putin has lavished attention on Mr. Yanukovich in recent weeks, including a three-day visit last week, in which they appeared together at a military parade to commemorate the 60th anniversary of the liberation of Ukraine from Nazi Germany.

Mr. Yanukovich has also enjoyed an overwhelming advantage in coverage on television, which is either state owned or controlled by allies of Mr. Kuchma's, and the news reports have been overwhelmingly positive. Many stations receive daily orders from Mr. Kuchma's administration about the coverage of political events, the government's critics say.

Many of Channel 5's problems may stem from the political sympathies of its major shareholder, Petro Poroshenko, a deputy in Parliament who supports Mr. Yushchenko. Mr. Lyasovsky, the Channel 5 director, insisted that the channel aimed for balanced coverage "where not only Yushchenko, but representatives of any of the opposition had a chance to say something."

He said, however, that the station's fate under Mr. Kuchma's government underscored the importance of the vote.

"We have two ways," he said, echoing the feelings of many here, "forward or backward."

ELECTION RESULTS WIDELY DISCREDITED

In the presidential runoff election of November 21, 2004, Viktor Yanukovich, the incumbent prime minister and the government's candidate, was declared the winner, by 49.4 percent to 46.7 percent. Immediately after the results were announced, tens of thousands of demonstrators assembled in Kiev's Independence Square, chanting, "Freedom cannot be stopped!" *The Times* reporter C. J. Chivers on November 23 writes that opposition leader Viktor Yushchenko, addressing the crowds, had embarked on an endeavor to block Yanukovich's claims on the highest office (see "Premier Claims He's the Winner in Ukraine Vote"). Chivers reports that Yushchenko's "campaign—deprived of equal media coverage and pressured by the resources of the Ukrainian state . . . has adopted the tactics of the underdog."

Practice rallies had started in July 2004 and spread to regional cities. According to historian Andrew Wilson, these preparations "were a show of strength, but were also designed to show that any protests in November 'would be peaceful, fun, and, above all, safe' " (Wilson 2009, 342). Yushchenko now called for his supporters to "remain united and in the streets." He asked for an urgent session of the Ukrainian parliament to review the allegations of election fraud, and for the judiciary to investigate the complaints that had been documented. Yulia Tymoshenko, a member of the parliament and one of Yushchenko's most conspicuous supporters, called for a general strike. Chivers writes, "Opposition organizers pushed for protest and mass action," while Yushchenko vowed not to move until the election results were overturned. The election results were highly questionable. Exit polls, as *The Times* notes, gave Yushchenko an 11-point lead, but he lost by a sizable margin on election night. The international observers discredited the results quickly with a long list of violations. Crowds of Yushchenko's supporters materialized overnight and were prepared for a long protest, bringing food, tents, and warm clothing, and signs meant for the police, reading "Don't shoot!"

The Orange Revolution fit the grander phenomenon of nonviolent revolutions in the eastern bloc. Chivers reports a telling detail substantiating the spread of knowledge from one struggle to another: "Throughout the rally, young men had been waving white-and-red Georgian flags among the sea of orange banners, a not-so-subtle reminder of the so-called rose revolution of a year ago, when Mikhail Saakashvili deposed President Eduard Shevardnadze of Georgia, another Soviet-era leader, in a bloodless coup" (see "Premier Claims He's the Winner in Ukraine Vote").

Comparisons to Georgia are appropriate. Both countries were constituent republics of the former Soviet Union. Mikhail Gorbachev, as general secretary of the Communist Party of the Soviet Union, had refused to crack down on certain movements for independence and self-determination in Eastern Europe (see "As Jaruzelski Leaves Office: A Traitor or a Patriot to Poles?"; "Gorbachev Lends Honecker a Hand"; "Gorbachev Said to Reject Soviet Right to Intervene"; "Havel Tells Festive Czechoslovaks that Honesty is Key to Recovery"). Both Ukraine and Georgia, however, were territories that Gorbachev and others in Moscow wanted to remain under Russian control. Gorbachev had openly expressed alarm in 1991 as he saw his plan to reconstruct some sort of union of republics in jeopardy, according to *The Times* reporter, Francis X. Clines on December 3 ("Ex-Communist Wins in Ukraine; Yeltsin Recognizes Independence"). Moreover, both the Rose Revolution and the Orange Revolution were highly coordinated responses in countries whose populations aspired to build liberal democracies, had experienced highly suspect elections, and where Russian allies used authoritarian tactics to suppress pro-liberalization candidates or parties.

Yushchenko denounced the official election results as soon as they were announced, and with impressive speed, civic activists prepared the ground for a national movement of nonviolent civil resistance in which hundreds of thousands of Ukrainians would participate.

NOVEMBER 23, 2004
PREMIER CLAIMS HE'S THE WINNER IN UKRAINE VOTE
But Observers See Fraud
Crowds Protest State Tally—Outcomes to Affect Ties With the West
By C. J. CHIVERS

Kiev, Ukraine, Nov. 22 – Ukraine approached a political stalemate on [November 22], as vote counts of the presidential runoff election indicated that Prime Minister Viktor F. Yanukovich had won but international observers alleged systemic voting abuses and the opposition candidate refused to accept defeat.

With more than 99 percent of ballots counted, the government tally gave Mr. Yanukovich 49.42 percent of the vote to 46.7 percent for Viktor A. Yushchenko, whose supporters turned out in the tens of thousands in Independence Square here, vowing not to move until results were reversed.

"To victory!" said Nina Kovalevskaya, 53, who stood in the cold [November 22] evening air. "To our victory!"

With the opposition filling the landmark square, an international election observer mission—from the Organization for Security and Cooperation in Europe, the European Parliament, the NATO Parliamentary Assembly and the Council of Europe—released a preliminary report that buoyed them, declaring that the election did not meet democratic standards.

The observers' findings were seconded by Senator Richard G. Lugar, chairman of the Senate Foreign Relations Committee, who had led an American mission to Ukraine to urge the departing president, Leonid D. Kuchma, to organize fair elections.

"A concerted and forceful program of election-day fraud and abuse was enacted with either the leadership or cooperation of governmental authorities," the senator said [on November 22] in Kiev.

At stake is not only the prize of the presidency of a nation of nearly 48 million, but also the direction of the overwhelmingly Slavic country during the next five-year presidential term. The outcome will decide whether Ukraine will draw closer to Russia, its historical and cultural partner, or move toward greater economic and military integration with the West.

Mr. Yanukovich is the personally selected successor of Mr. Kuchma, a former Soviet technocrat who ruled the country in a centralized fashion for 10 years, amid sometimes tense relations with Washington and allegations of corruption and abuse of power.

The prime minister has vowed to continue on Mr. Kuchma's course, and to steer the county closer to Moscow. The Russian president, Vladimir V. Putin, telephoned Mr. Yanukovich on Monday from an official visit to Brazil to congratulate him, according to Interfax.

Mr. Yushchenko, himself a former prime minister, has described the incumbent bloc of state power as crooked and hidebound, and pledged to maintain ties with Russia while encouraging business and expanding Ukraine's relationship westward into Europe.

His support in the capital, and among young voters, is palpably high. His campaign—deprived of equal media coverage and pressured by the resources of the Ukrainian state, according to the reports of international observers—has adopted the tactics of the underdog.

The victory for the prime minister, by a margin of nearly 3 percentage points, that was given in official results diverged sharply from a range of surveys of voters at polling places that gave the opposition as much as an 11-point lead. Opposition organizers pushed for protest and mass action.

Mr. Yushchenko, addressing the public, began a multipronged effort to block Mr. Yanukovich's claim on office. He urged his supporters to remain united and in the streets, and called for an urgent session of Parliament to review extensive allegations of state manipulation of the election, and for the judiciary to investigate documented complaints.

"We express no confidence in the Central Election Commission because of its being a passive, or maybe a too active, participant in falsifications," he said.

Yulia Tymoshenko, a member of Parliament and one of Mr. Yushchenko's most visible supporters, called for a general strike.

Still, even while Mr. Yushchenko's supporters tried to force a political confrontation, the state maintained a position of official calm. It appeared to have the upper hand through the crucial first day. The prime minister's once-crowded campaign headquarters declared victory and closed down before lunch.

"We won, and we are going to sleep," said Gennady P. Korz, a senior campaign spokesman.

And while the demonstration grew, the police presence in the capital remained light. State security agencies did release a joint statement saying they were on high alert.

The findings of the international election mission included abuse of state resources in favor of the prime minister; the addition of about 5 percent of new voters to the rolls on election day; pressure on students to vote for the state's choice; pressure on state workers to turn over absentee ballot forms for presumptive use by someone else; widespread abuse of absentee voters, including some who were bused from region to region; the blocking of poll workers; suspiciously, even fantastically, high turnouts in regions that supported the prime minister; inaccurate voter lists and overt bias of state-financed news media.

Marek Siwiec, head of the delegation from the European Parliament, said certain electoral abuses "cast a shadow over the genuineness of the election."

Other prominent Western observers were unsparing in their criticism of the state's conduct of the election.

"Fundamental flaws in Ukraine's presidential election process subverted its legitimacy," the National Democratic Institute for International Affairs, sponsored by the Democratic Party in the United States, declared in its preliminary report. The institute, which had an observer mission in Ukraine, cited "systematic intimidation, overt manipulation and blatant fraud" that were "designed to achieve a specific outcome irrespective of the will of the people."

Many of the same criticisms had been levied against that state during the first round of presidential elections three weeks ago. Mr. Yushchenko narrowly won that round among a field of 24, leading to the two-candidate runoff on Sunday. Because the result on [November 22] conforms to the state's wish, few expected a significant presidential review.

Even stronger criticism came from the Dutch foreign minister, Bernard Bot, whose country holds the European

Union presidency. "We don't accept these results. We think they are fraudulent," he said at a news briefing, Reuters reported. Mr. Bot said that each of the union's members would call in the Ukrainian ambassadors to their countries to express concern, and that the election would be discussed at a European Union-Russia summit meeting in The Hague on Thursday.

Dr. Charles Tannock, a British member of the European Parliament, said the conduct of the election was less what he expected from Ukraine than from Turkmenistan, an authoritarian state.

He then worried aloud that what seemed to be the election's illegitimacy might serve to split Ukraine into a north and west supporting Mr. Yushchenko, and a region in the east supporting the prime minister. There were hints of this by nightfall, as Mr. Yushchenko claimed the support of at least four Ukrainian cities, including the city council in Kiev, which rejected the election results.

As the anxious rally continued through Sunday night to Monday morning [November 21 to November 22], at times the crowd chanted, "Freedom cannot be stopped!"

There were signs of careful planning and organization, which suggested the protesters were prepared for a long standoff. Within minutes of the opposition leaders' speeches in the morning, for example, young men set up rows of new tents in the crowd.

Food quickly appeared, as did blankets, foam mattresses, hats and winter coats. As the work continued, posters were taped to the tents and to some of the protesters' winter coats. They were messages to the police. "Don't shoot!" they read.

One detail was meant to lift the protesters' spirits.

Throughout the rally, young men had been waving white-and-red Georgian flags among the sea of orange banners, a not-so-subtle reminder of the so-called rose revolution of a year ago, when Mikhail Saakashvili deposed President Eduard Shevardnadze of Georgia, another Soviet-era leader, in a bloodless coup.

Mr. Saakashvili was elected to the presidency by a landslide, and has made pushing his country westward and fighting corruption principal elements of his policy. Some in the crowd on Monday spoke openly of the Georgian model of shrugging off a tired state. But they discussed these hopes in a more difficult setting.

Mr. Kuchma and his supporters have pointedly said there will be no revolution here, and some differences were clear. The Ukrainian economy is stronger than Georgia's, as are its security agencies. Moreover, Ukraine is culturally far more closely bound to Moscow than Georgia had been.

Mr. Yanukovich's supporters predicted that they would weather the demonstrations, and said they planned to have an inauguration next month.

— — —

Yushchenko Declares Victory

Within two days after the announced election results for the preliminary outcome of Ukraine's presidential election, the throngs in Kiev supporting Yushchenko had swelled to hundreds of thousands. Andrew Wilson remarks: "The speed with which protestors poured onto the Maidan ["square," meaning Independence Square] on the day after the second round of the election surprised everybody—10,000 to 20,000 by breakfast time on Monday 22 November and 100,000 by the afternoon. Numbers held up over a cold night, and by midday the next day exceeded 200,000" (Wilson 2009, 341). The issue for the protestors, *The Times* notes on November 24, was not only the election fraud that denied Yushchenko his victory, but also that the government's candidate, Yanukovich, had "vowed to tighten further the nation's strong ties with Russia."

The nonviolent demonstrators described in *The Times* on November 24 were deliberately, intentionally, and self-consciously acting with awareness of the rudiments of civil resistance (see "Protests Grow as Ukraine Vote Crisis Deepens"). Lech Wałęsa, founder of Poland's Solidarity union, addressed the crowds and urged the opposition "to use peaceful methods to lower the risks of a possible tragedy" (see "Poland Restricts Civil and Union Rights, Solidarity Activists Urge General Strike"). Wałęsa's words reflect the fact that the choice of nonviolent action in most historical instances is not a matter of idealism, but a practical method often chosen because it is less likely to worsen already aggrieved circumstances. Wałęsa's mere presence is indicative of the sharing of knowledge from one Eastern European movement to another, until it reached Ukraine (see "Heeding the Roar of the Street"). Moreover, Wilson observes, "The carnival in the Maidan [square] helped contribute to the decline of the fear factor" (Wilson 2009, 345).

Reporter Steven Lee Myers writes of shifts taking place within Ukraine's state-controlled media, particularly television, which exerted immense influence over political debate (see "Rivals in Ukraine Report Violations in Presidential Vote"). The state's treatment of news coverage was cited by OSCE observers, who also called the November 21 runoff vote fundamentally unfair. The turbulent week since the runoff between Yanukovich and Yushchenko ended with accusations of fraud, and Kuchma's controls over television had shown "signs of cracking."

The snow-covered demonstrators in Independence Square continued to push for a revote. With a rebellion occurring inside the state-controlled media, public opinion turning toward the opposition, senior state officials being divided on what to do, and police looking on sympathetically, the aims of the assembled activists appeared likely to succeed.

NOVEMBER 24, 2004
PROTESTS GROW AS UKRAINE VOTE CRISIS DEEPENS
Rival Declares Victory in Election That Has Split the Country
By C. J. CHIVERS

Kiev, Ukraine, Nov. 23 – Mass demonstrations against the preliminary outcome of the presidential election expanded here in the capital [November 23], as the opposition candidate, Viktor A. Yushchenko, declared himself the winner and tried unsuccessfully to force Parliament to invalidate government tallies showing him the loser.

Mr. Yushchenko's supporters swarmed through the capital, staging highly organized rallies at Independence Square and the Supreme Rada, Ukraine's 450-seat Parliament. On [the] night [of November 23] they marched through lightly falling snow to the presidential administration building, where they were met by lines of helmeted police officers standing 12 deep.

The demonstrators' numbers were visibly larger than the day before, when tens of thousands chanted antigovernment slogans, claiming the runoff election on [November 21] had been stolen by fraud.

The preliminary count of the Central Election Commission shows the government's candidate, Prime Minister Viktor F. Yanukovich, took a three-point lead ahead of Mr. Yushchenko, but the government has not declared a president-elect.

With regions announcing allegiance to one candidate or the other, the country remained split, and the government came to a near standstill. At what was shaping up to become a historic moment of confrontation for the nation of 48 million, and with its leadership at a crossroads, the lights to the huge presidential building were dimmed.

Mr. Yanukovich kept a low profile during the day, as did Leonid D. Kuchma, the departing president and Mr. Yanukovich's chief patron.

Jan Peter Balkenende, the Dutch prime minister, whose country holds the rotating presidency of the European Union, telephoned Mr. Kuchma to express the presidency's "serious concerns" about the election.

Western election observers reported inflation of voting lists on election day, multiple voting and the use of state resources to Mr. Yanukovich's favor, among other abuses.

Mr. Kuchma's office released a statement confirming that he had spoken with Mr. Balkenende, and warned that "political issues must not be solved in the street." The country also awaited the possible arrival of Lech Walesa, the Nobel laureate and former leader of the Solidarity movement in Poland, who said he was willing to try to mediate. Mr. Walesa urged the opposition "to use peaceful methods to lower the risks of a possible tragedy," according to Agence France-Presse.

Later in the day, Mr. Yanukovich's campaign declared him the president-elect and called for Mr. Yushchenko to concede. The position, stronger than that taken by Mr. Kuchma, was an unusual instance of public incoherence between the prime minister's and the president's camps.

In Kiev, buses with police officers were parked near the city's center and, at night, officers in riot gear were posted at barricades in front of the president's office. The police and the protesters appeared for the moment to have found a balance.

"The police are with the people!" the crowd chanted outside Parliament. At night, Mr. Yushchenko's supporters tied orange ribbons—a symbol of the opposition—to officers' riot shields.

With the situation unstable and the outcome uncertain, the White House issued a statement saying the United States was "deeply disturbed by extensive and credible indications of fraud" in the election, and urged the Ukrainian authorities "not to certify results until investigations of organized fraud are resolved."

Also in the United States on [November 23], four Ukrainian diplomats in Washington issued a letter protesting their own government's conduct of the election. "Guided by our conscience, our professional pride and our oath of loyalty to serve the Ukrainian state we express our solidarity with the voice of the Ukrainian people," the letter read, according to The Associated Press.

A senior Western diplomat in Kiev, speaking on condition of anonymity because of the sensitivity of the political situation, portrayed the Ukrainian leadership as being at an impasse, stung by public and diplomatic reaction, and unsure of how to react to the growing protests.

The diplomat also said he had credible reports that police units, the army and even the S.B.U. [Sluzhba Bezpeky Ukrayiny, the principal government security agency], Ukraine's successor to the K.G.B., might be unwilling to put down the demonstrators by force. His assessment suggested deep divisions at senior ranks in the Ukrainian government.

"You have a government which in my opinion does not know what to do," the diplomat said.

He also cautioned, however, that one law enforcement agency, the Interior Ministry, might be willing to use force. The diplomat said "two red lines" had been communicated by his country to Mr. Kuchma. First, he said, that the government was to use no violence, and second, that it was to take no step to certify the election.

The pressure on Mr. Kuchma appeared extraordinary. At issue was not just the direction of his country—Mr. Yushchenko has pledged to steer it westward, while Mr. Yanukovich has vowed to tighten further the nation's strong ties with Russia—but also his legacy, already tarnished by allegations of corruption, illegal arms dealing and state support for political violence.

. . . Many of Mr. Yushchenko's supporters hope a new government will investigate allegations of presidential involvement in corruption and politically motivated violence. As the pressure increased, Mr. Yushchenko aimed for symbolic stature. In an unofficial session of Parliament, he placed his hand on a Bible and read the presidential oath of office, a gesture without legal standing but meaningful to supporters massed outside.

The session had been an attempt to have Parliament declare no confidence in the election commission, but was boycotted by members supporting Mr. Kuchma and Mr. Yanukovich. Only 191 members were present, short of a quorum.

Both sides worked to demonstrate popular backing. The government of Donetsk, an eastern region that is home to many officials in Mr. Kuchma's government, passed a resolution noting "the complete and irrevocable victory of Yanukovich."

Almost simultaneously, the western region of Lviv recognized Mr. Yushchenko as president, a gesture similar to those already made on his behalf by four cities, including Kiev.

· ·

Youth-Led Movements Galvanize Protest of Election Fraud

Times correspondent C. J. Chivers on November 28, 2004, describes the planning and organization that lay behind the nonviolent demonstrations in Independence Square (see "Youth Movement Underlies the Opposition in Ukraine"). The youth organization Pora! (It's Time!) was the galvanizing force behind the civil resistance. Chivers explains that Pora fits with the work of Otpor, Kmara, and the narrative of youth-fueled nonviolent resistance movements across Eastern Europe. (On Otpor, see "Rally against Milosevic Fails to Bind Opposition Parties"; "Student Group Emerges as Major Milosevic Foe"; "Milosevic, Trailing in Polls, Rails Against NATO"; on Kmara, see "Officials in Georgia Declare Shevardnadze Ballot Winner"; "Foes of Georgian Leader Storm into Parliament Building.") One of the most striking aspects of the Orange Revolution is how *quickly* throngs materialized after the fraudulent election results of the November 21 runoff were announced—and how well organized the crowds were (see "Premier Claims He's the Winner in Ukraine Vote").

Anika Locke Binnendjik and Ivan Marovic point out that in Serbia and Ukraine, "blatant election fraud" was the catalyst for mobilizing the citizenry (see "Student Group Emerges as Major Milosevic Foe"). They interviewed a senior coordinator for Our Ukraine, Yushchenko's parliamentary faction, who told them: "In 2002 and 2003 we carried out careful analysis of the reasons for failures of previous protests, and the major reasons were the small number of people and the aggressive nature of such events. So our conclusion was that we needed to get out as many people as possible and to make sure that the protests would not be aggressive. We realized that no military—no special units—would dare to take up arms against such a huge group of people" (Binnendjik and Marovic 2006, 413).

Volunteers almost immediately came out to erect tents, deliver food and blankets, and to organize rallying cries in unison. As early as October 1990, tents had been pitched in the square to protect democracy advocates who were on hunger strikes. As a result, they could be hastily set up, and, indeed, they came to characterize Ukraine's struggle. Chivers depicts the Orange Revolution as the result of planning for expected corruption of election results and suppression of the truth. Chivers writes: " 'We heard that Yanukovich would try to organize this fraud, and we were prepared for this kind of situation,' " according to Mariana Savytska, 19, a Pora spokeswoman. " 'We decided we also had to do something, to raise the people's will' " (see "Youth Movement Underlies the Opposition in Ukraine").

Pora was the name of two different organizations associated with the 2004 campaign. Yellow Pora had connections to political actors and was an openly partisan, get-out-the-vote organization closely associated with Yushchenko's campaign, and Black Pora was a nonviolent, student-run group that closely mirrored Otpor and Kmara in its strategy and nonhierarchical leadership style. Also like Otpor and Kmara, Black Pora drew heavily on the published writings of the scholar Gene Sharp and distributed translated literature on the theories and methods of nonviolent civil resistance. Andrew Wilson points out that Yellow Pora operated in the mainstream, while Black Pora worked on an underground basis (Wilson 2009, 338).

Black Pora's first activity was in early 2004, when the members distributed leaflets across the country urging the removal of "Kuchism" from Ukraine. They used Kuchma's personal forcefulness and power as an argument for political turnover. Given the state-controlled media and information suppression documented by *The Times,* Pora performed a critical function as an information network to help spread prodemocracy slogans and antigovernment messages (see "Rivals in Ukraine Report Violations in Presidential Vote"; "Protests Grow as Ukraine Vote

Crisis Deepens"). According to Ukrainian political scientist Taras Kuzio, a tape recording was leaked of Kuchma authorizing violence against an opposition journalist. As awareness of this recording grew, it hardened the opposition to the government. Information on what the tape contained was spread through networks like Pora.

Chivers describes skepticism on the government's part concerning Pora's youthful activists. Some government officials cited by *The Times* said that they believed that Pora was a "front" for U.S. influence.

Chivers verifies that Pora members were trained in nonviolent action by seasoned activists from similar movements in the Eastern bloc. Kuzio writes of Pora leaders meeting with young activists from the other countries in their early stages of formation, in particular, a meeting with Otpor activists in Novi Sad to construct a specific strategy to oppose Kuchma. Otpor's Aleksandar Marić made a number of trips to Ukraine before the elections and recalled: "We trained them in how to set up an organization, how to open local chapters, how to create a 'brand,' how to create a logo, symbols, and key messages. . . . We trained them in how to identify the key weaknesses in society and what people's most pressing problems were—what might be a motivating factor for people, and above all young people, to go to the ballot box and in this way shape their own destiny." Marić stresses that "any successful effort requires the will and energy of the local population, who cannot be coerced or bribed into taking to the streets for weeks at a time" (Bransten 2004). Danijela Nenadic of Otpor scoffed when asked about media reports hinting that Otpor was pulling the strings of Kiev demonstrators: "There is no universal concept to fight authoritarianism. You have to have your own strategy. All we can do is share our experience" (Simpson and Tanner 2004).

The Times even quotes Mikhail Pogrebinsky, a political scientist and adviser to President Kuchma, who discounts the importance of funding: "It is the moral support, the media support, the technical support that is more important." Indeed, the training was a key to Pora's success; it was able to learn from those who had successfully organized nonviolent revolutions in Serbia and Georgia.

"Pora says it has 3,000 formal members among students in Kiev, and support from other groups throughout the country whose precise size and structure are unknown," writes Chivers. He quotes Savytska as saying, "We organize people for actions, we have temporary members, we grow for an event and shrink." Chivers observes, "The group's discipline is evident in its details. It works in cells, with different groups assuming different tasks—media relations, security, organizing demonstrations, logistics. It has rules—no public drinking, no drugs, no response to provocation."

The youth of Ukraine consistently outperformed expectations. In the words of one mature Ukrainian, quoted by Agnès Gruda, " 'Kuchma never feared my generation. However, he forgot that we would have children, and my children never knew the KGB' " (Gruda 2004).

Pora used humor and viral marketing. On one weekend, Pora activists dressed up as prisoners and attended rallies, claiming that convicts had been let out for the weekend to campaign for one of their own. They mocked Yanukovich's intelligence, calling him "Proffessor" (to make fun of the misspelling on Yanukovich's own curriculum vitæ. The rock band Grandzioly (GreenJolly) recorded the official song of the Orange Revolution, "We are many, we cannot be defeated." In Ukraine alone, the song had 1.5 million online downloads. According to Andrew Wilson:

> The organizers of what came to be known simply as "the Maidan" skillfully exploited the world media's appetite for positive pictures and symbolic events. . . . Entertaining the crowd with so much music was also astute: it obviously advertised nonviolent intent, the programme itself was deliberately wide and inclusive, and it helped reassure the militia that the crowd would remain stationary. The Maidan also began and ended every day with a multi-denominational religious service, to emphasize inclusivity and peaceful intent (p. 342).

Dozens of Pora activists had been arrested in September 2004, but by the end of November, as Chivers notes, Pora's stance was "Until we win." With their sheer size and organization, Pora activists believed the words to their official song, "We cannot be defeated."

KEY PLAYER IN UKRAINE
Natalia Dimitruk (1969–)

Twenty-five years old in 2004, Natalia Dimitruk worked as a sign-language interpreter for the official state-run UT-1 television station. An important figure in the Ukrainian deaf community, she could regularly be seen in the corner of television screens, interpreting the news.

Dimitruk staged one of the most symbolically significant actions of the Orange Revolution, on the morning of Thursday, November 25, 2004. The television news anchor began reporting the run-off election results of the heated contest between the opposition leader, Viktor Yushchenko, and the incumbent prime minister, Viktor Yanukovich. As the UT-1 news broadcaster proclaimed Yanukovich the winner, Dimitruk, appearing in her usual inset on the screen, decided to break from the anchor's script. Instead, she said in sign language, "The results announced by the Central Electoral Commission are rigged. Do not believe them." Dimitruk then signed that Yushchenko was the true winner of the election and that she would no longer interpret lies. "I do not know if you will see me again," she said with her hands.

Dimitruk later said in an interview that she had struggled with the decision to report the truth despite her ethical obligation as an interpreter to adhere to what needed to be translated. She decided to present her viewpoint because she felt that it was important to give Ukrainian deaf television viewers a chance to understand what was really happening.

Dimitruk's act of refusal to cooperate with ballot-box fraud was one part of massive national civil disobedience efforts, as ordinary Ukrainian citizens fought for clean elections. Dimitruk in particular helped to hasten the end of Ukraine's tightly controlled state television. More than 200 journalists employed by UT-1 went on strike and demanded the right to report the news objectively. Journalists at another station that was considered ideologically conservative followed suit. The result was that the state-controlled media began to broadcast accounts of the approximately 1 million Ukrainian nonviolent demonstrators camped-out in Kiev's Independence Square, who were protesting rigged election results.

NOVEMBER 28, 2004
YOUTH MOVEMENT UNDERLIES THE OPPOSITION IN UKRAINE
Students Help Force Government's Hand
By C. J. CHIVERS

Kiev, Ukraine, Nov. 27 – It began with a call from the center of the opposition movement's stage in Independence Square—Ukraine's officially defeated presidential candidate said [on November 22] that demonstrators would build a tent city and protest until he prevailed—and within minutes the tents appeared.

It continued all week, and much of it was the work of teenagers and university students, who have helped force the government and population of Ukraine to face a stark choice.

Before the Ukrainian opposition here reached its eventual great mass and overwhelmed Kiev, swift and sophisticated signs appeared of organization to ensure that the prodemocracy rally formed and grew, and almost all of it was young.

The youth movement in Ukraine has had many models, and it has learned its lessons well. For more than two decades, unarmed street movements challenged entrenched state power in the Soviet Union and in the breakaway republics it became. The protests ranged from far more dangerous days when Lech Walesa organized peaceful resistance in Poland to the rambunctious crowds that helped depose Eduard Shevardnadze in Georgia last year.

As the government of President Leonid D. Kuchma moved toward passing power to his personally selected choice in recent days, young Ukrainians, working in part through a somewhat cellular group that calls itself Pora, meaning It's Time, immediately occupied Kreschatik Street, a central retail boulevard adjacent to Independence Square.

Within minutes they pitched tents, posted unarmed sentries and produced mounds of food and winter clothing. Within hours they set up field kitchens and medical aid stations, circulated broadsheets outlining details for civil disobedience and urging the police not to shoot, and passed out a seemingly endless supply of posters, banners, ribbons, flags, stickers and badges that turned the ever expanding crowd into a telegenic bright orange.

The planning behind the youth occupation could not be missed. "We heard that Yanukovich would try to organize this fraud, and we were prepared for this kind of situation," said Mariana Savytska, 19, a Pora spokeswoman. "We decided we also had to do something, to raise the people's will."

The people who have swarmed the capital defy ready characterization.

They are students and intelligentsia, and they are westward-leaning citizens of urban centers who aspire for more extensive integration into Europe. But they include pensioners and war veterans, working-class men and women from western and northern Ukraine, people from a wide variety of professions and trades, including members of the police, more of whom appeared on the side of opposition on Saturday, some of their faces aglow with the surprise of their choice.

But in the first days a visible nucleus of young people acted with noticeable skill to ensure that the lines held until broader Ukrainian society stood beside them.

Their role was far from the only factor driving the peaceful uprising that has halted the government here. A senior Western diplomat in Kiev noted [on November 27] that the opposition was organized not just by skill or a faith in a candidate, but by the belief that it had the moral high ground and power of truth on its side.

But the influence of organized young Ukrainians in giving time, legitimacy and bargaining power to Mr. Yushchenko when he has needed all three, has also been clear. And the role of young people in general and Pora in particular has been one of the points of contention between the campaigns, and between the nations behind each side.

Mr. Yanukovich's supporters, and Russophiles, have portrayed the youth as naïve tools of the West, or as agents of foreign power, saying they have been seeded by the United States and other interests to interfere with Ukrainian political life.

Pora denies this flatly and says accepting foreign aid would undermine the group's local credibility. The American government also says that while it has provided $13.6 million in aid in recent years to encourage fair elections here, Pora has not been sponsored. "We provide zero money, directly or indirectly, to Pora," said an American diplomat in Kiev.

Mr. Yanukovich's supporters are unconvinced, and say money moves through American-sponsored non-government organizations to Pora, and that larger outside forces also have aligned to organize the youth here in ways helpful to the West. The degree of its organization, they say, cannot be coincidence.

"The money is not most important; there is enough money in Ukraine," said Mikhail Pogrebinsky, a political scientist and adviser to President Kuchma. "It is the moral support, the media support, the technical support that is more important."

Mr. Pogrebinsky said Pora had been trained by veterans of revolution drives elsewhere. Pora says it has 3,000 formal members among students in Kiev, and support from other groups throughout the country whose precise size and structure are unknown. "We organize people for actions, we have temporary members, we grow for an event and shrink," Ms. Savytska said.

The group's discipline is evident in its details. It works in cells, with different groups assuming different tasks—media relations, security, organizing demonstrations, logistics. It has rules—no public drinking, no drugs, no response to provocation. It unequivocally speaks in terms of nonviolence, although in language reminiscent of Socialist times Ukraine's security services have sometimes referred to it as a terrorist group.

While its members have been buoyed by their success, that is leavened by a realization that they may yet fail. Among some there has been detectable worry, especially at midweek, when Mr. Kuchma's government seemed more bold. Some students speak of crackdowns should the opposition's effort to break the ruling clan's grip on power fail. "The reprisals will start, and people will be arrested," Ms. Savytska said.

But they also say that one fact has been proved. No matter how this crisis ends, the democracy movement has shown its maturity and skill in Ukraine, and will last. "If necessary, we will continue our struggle underground," said Olga, 18, a Pora member and resident of Tent No. 1012, who gave only her first name, citing concern about her safety.

The group's members said they expected that the political crisis would attract new people to demonstrate, and part of their task has been to keep them on the streets. One neophyte was Petr Pavlishin, 29, a road worker from Ternopil, who said he had never taken part in direct action before, but now lives on Kreschatik Street, Tent No. 93.

"I didn't get into politics before, but I just couldn't watch this," said Mr. Pavlishin, bundled against the cold. Beside him in the tent were cartons of juice, a grapefruit and sleeping bags that Pora had provided to help coax him to stay. Ms. Savytska said the demonstrators at the tents were eating as often as seven times a day.

As the Parliament met [on November 27] to begin discussing a solution to the crisis, more people were arriving in Kiev. They said they had hitchhiked or come by bus, and said more demonstrators were behind them, waiting for rides.

Asked how long they would stay in the cold, they said they would try their best to remain. "As long as we can stand it," said Tania Yucherain, 20, a student from Lviv.

Ruslan Yatechin, 22, a bus driver who had been part of convoy picking up people on the highway to Kiev, used the terms of struggle. "Until we win," he said.

Parliament Seeks Resolution to Election Standoff

With thousands of demonstrators camped in Kiev's Independence Square, the Ukrainian parliament attempted to reach a political resolution to the confrontation resulting from the presidential runoff election of November 21, 2004 (see "Premier Claims He's the Winner in Ukraine Vote"). Amidst widespread complaints of fraud, Viktor Yanukovich, the incumbent prime minister and the government's candidate, was declared the winner. In cities and towns across Western Ukraine, including Kiev, many considered the election results illegitimate and denounced them. In an effort to avoid a territorial split, the parliament attempted to broker a political agreement that would make a revote politically feasible.

Moreover, according to *Times* reporter Steven Lee Myers on December 2, Yanukovich, "the candidate who last week was declared the winner and president-elect, filed his own appeal citing fraudulent voting in Kiev. In effect, Mr. Yanukovich added ammunition to arguments by his challenger, Viktor A. Yushchenko, that the election was fraudulent" (see "A New Election for Ukrainians Appears Likely"). This predicament led to proposals for the political structuring of the government.

At issue was the retention of power by Kuchma, the departing president, who had proposed a reorganization of the government, with major authority delegated to the prime minister. The opposition leader, Yushchenko, vigorously opposed Kuchma's proposition, describing it as a "a ploy to allow Mr. Kuchma to retain political influence by appointing a more powerful—and loyal—prime minister before stepping down." The opposition party—and thousands of demonstrators—saw no difference between the Kuchma government and a Yanukovich administration. Moreover, Kuchma's wished-for changes in the constitution, if Yanukovich were to win, would perpetuate and strengthen Kuchma's influence.

The debate in the parliament, therefore, centered around three primary issues. First, the members needed to decide whether to call a new election. The crisis, said by Myers to have "rattled the economy and raised fears of a territorial split," had led to the perception that parliament was likely to do so.

The second issue was the performance and approval of the current government—and the shape that a reorganized government structure might take. As Myers reports, the parliament narrowly voted to approve a resolution of "no confidence" in the current government—including Prime Minister Yanukovich. Internal and external observers, including European Commission representative Javier Solana, one of the chosen mediators, noted that a new election would probably not take place until the government had agreed to a reorganization.

Finally, the question remained of who would be the new leader. Public sentiment was shifting. Myers quotes Viktor Pinchuk, a powerful Kuchma ally, as saying, " 'If we have a new election it is, frankly speaking, highly likely that Yushchenko will be the new president.' "

The vote of no confidence electrified the Orange movement. Thousands of civil resisters were gathered around the parliament building during the proceedings, and when the vote was announced, the cheering throngs marched to Independence Square to join thousands more demonstrators who had bivouacked there in the preceding ten days.

DECEMBER 2, 2004
A NEW ELECTION FOR UKRAINIANS APPEARS LIKELY
Reordering of Political Power Is Under Way
By STEVEN LEE MYERS

Kiev, Ukraine, Dec. 1 – Ukraine appears to be headed toward holding a new election under an agreement announced . . . [December 1] to adopt a sweeping reorganization of political power.

The agreement, brokered between President Leonid D. Kuchma and the two men aspiring to succeed him, seeks to defuse a crisis that has brought the country to a standstill after a runoff election on Nov. 21 that was marred by accusations of fraud. The three politicians, meeting with European mediators, agreed to begin drafting "appropriate proposals for the completion of the election" after the Supreme Court rules on the fraud accusations.

It appears increasingly likely that the court will rule to overturn the results.

In the latest indication, Prime Minister Viktor F. Yanukovich, the candidate who last week was declared the winner and president-elect, filed his own appeal citing fraudulent voting in Kiev. In effect, Mr. Yanukovich added ammunition to arguments by his challenger, Viktor A. Yushchenko, that the election was fraudulent.

The efforts at mediation contrasted with pointed political confrontations. By a bare majority, Parliament approved a resolution of no confidence in Mr. Yanukovich's government.

Normally the parliamentary vote would force Mr. Yanukovich to resign as prime minister, along with his ministers, but his supporters and Mr. Kuchma's aides called the vote illegal on procedural grounds and refused to recognize it.

Yelena A. Grimnitskaya, Mr. Kuchma's spokeswoman, called the notion of dismissing Mr. Yanukovich "stupidity."

On the 10th day of the crisis, which has rattled the economy and raised fears of a territorial split, Mr. Kuchma, Mr. Yanukovich and Mr. Yushchenko met for a second time and appeared to lay the groundwork for a compromise, though many details remain unresolved.

Their agreement on reforming the political system revived a proposal by Mr. Kuchma to amend the country's Constitution to transfer significant powers from the presidency to the legislative branch, led by a newly empowered prime minister.

Parliament narrowly rejected the proposal in March, in large part because the opposition bloc led by Mr. Yushchenko saw it as a ploy to allow Mr. Kuchma to retain political influence by appointing a more powerful—and loyal—prime minister before stepping down. The questions now are how power will be redistributed, how a new presidential election will be held and the timing for both.

"I do not see how the election cannot be canceled at this point," Hryhoriy M. Nemyria, director of the European Center for International Studies in Kiev, said in a telephone interview. "It is only about saving face, especially for Yanukovich."

There were still more signs that Mr. Yanukovich was losing support of powerful allies. Viktor M. Pinchuk, a powerful businessman, a member of Parliament and Mr. Kuchma's son-in-law, said that if a new election was held, Mr. Yanukovich's prospects for winning, assuming that he was a candidate, were not high.

"If we have a new election it is, frankly speaking, highly likely that Yushchenko will be the new president," Mr. Pinchuk said in an interview. Mr. Yushchenko insisted that a new election be essentially a rerun of the runoff, which Ukraine's Central Election Commission declared that Mr. Yanukovich won by roughly 800,000 votes, or 3 percentage points.

Speaking to reporters after more than three hours of talks mediated by President Aleksandr Kwasniewski of Poland and Javier Solana, the European Union's foreign policy chief, Mr. Yushchenko said the mass demonstrations clogging Kiev would continue "until it is decided that the revote is scheduled for a certain date."

Mr. Yushchenko later told supporters in Kiev's central square that he wanted a new election on Dec. 19. He also reiterated his demands that a new election take place only on condition that Mr. Yanukovich's government step down and that certain provisions be enacted to prevent fraudulent voting using absentee ballots.

"There is small progress regarding the item which resolves the problem of elections," he said, referring to . . . [the] negotiations [of December 1], which took place in the ornate Mariinsky Palace next to the Parliament building. "We gave lawyers 24 hours to work and find the legal reply to the procedure of finalizing the election. Neither the law nor the Constitution gives the answer what has to be done if the runoff did not give any result."

Outside Parliament, as the vote against Mr. Yanukovich's government was broadcast on speakers, the crowd roared with elation. Then the demonstrators marched to Independence Square, joining thousands of others who have remained at the square for the last 10 days. Later in the evening, after the talks ended, Mr. Yushchenko returned to the square and urged the crowds to remain until the new election was set. Shortly after he spoke, fireworks exploded.

After all the recriminations of the campaign, including Mr. Yushchenko's accusation that he was poisoned, Mr. Yushchenko and Mr. Yanukovich, briefly and awkwardly, met, smiled and shook hands after Mr. Kuchma read a statement outlining the results of the negotiations.

After the meeting, Mr. Solana indicated that new elections were likely, but only after the political reforms were debated and passed by Parliament. It is unclear when those changes might take effect. If before a new election, then Mr. Kuchma would have the opportunity he sought earlier this year to appoint a new prime minister. But officials said that remained one of the crucial points to be negotiated before the impasse could end.

Still, Mr. Pinchuk said constitutional reform was now at the center of the negotiations, leaving all the other issues, including a new election, dependent on it. "This is the framework," he said.

Mr. Kuchma said earlier that he opposed another election between Mr. Yushchenko and Mr. Yanukovich, calling it a "farce" that would be unconstitutional.

Everything now appears to depend on the Supreme Court, which continued its hearings even as protesters chanted and cheered outside and Parliament's opposition members denounced Mr. Yanukovich and the Central Election Commission.

C. J. Chivers contributed reporting for this article.

• •

ELECTION RESULTS OVERTURNED

On December 3, 2004, twelve days after the demonstrations in Kiev began, the Supreme Court of Ukraine broke the stalemate by overturning the results of the presidential election, judging the election fraudulent, and ruling that a new runoff must take place before December 26. Steven Lee Myers on December 4 highlights in *The Times* three points about the court's decision: first, that the reception of the ruling was somewhat unexpected; second, how this issue exacerbated tensions in Russia's relationships with the Western powers in ways, Myers writes, "not seen since NATO bombed Serbia in 1999, and perhaps since the cold war"; and third, how after this ruling a victory for Yushchenko seemed almost a certainty (see "Ukrainian Court Orders New Vote for Presidency").

Myers describes the court ruling as "surprising and decisive." Sending dispatches to *The Times* from a country with heavily suppressed news media and significant self-acknowledged fraud and corruption, Myers and other observers might not have expected a fair result. Myers quotes one diplomat as saying, " 'Historically the [Ukraine] Supreme Court is subject to bribery and intimidation. . . . No one has ever considered it an institution subject to independence and integrity.' " Yet exposure of the court to certain fluctuations accompanying the awakening of civil society may have influenced its decision. *The Times* notes that the court proceedings with its twenty-one judges—and its ruling—were openly televised across the country, even on a channel, One Plus One, that had previously followed government interpretations. Popular pressure may have helped to create transparency, baring its actions to greater public scrutiny. One pro-Yushchenko member of the parliament called the ruling "courageous."

The revote, which was supported by Europe and the United States, aggravated Western tensions with the Russian Federation. The Russians had already accused Western governments of subtly funding the youth movement Pora (see "Youth Movement Underlies the Opposition in Ukraine"). Russia's parliament had adopted a resolution prior to the court's ruling that accused the European Union and the OSCE of "fomenting unrest in Ukraine." Russian president Vladimir Putin, a close ally of Kuchma and Yanukovich, was quick to declare Ukraine's election results legitimate and demand that the nation move on. Even the incumbent government had by this time lost faith in Yanukovich's chances. As Myers notes, Kuchma and Putin were calling for a completely new election, not a revote, "having implicitly conceded that the previous one would never produce a legitimate victory for Mr. Yanukovich." In a December 3 article, Myers writes that Putin said, "A rerun of the second round may also produce nothing. What happens then? Will there have to be a third, a fourth, a 25th round until one of the sides obtains the necessary result?" ("Putin Backs Ukrainian Leader, Dismissing Calls for New Runoff").

Throughout the campaign, Yushchenko derided Kuchma as a puppet of Russia, stirring up the Ukrainian-Russian ethnic tensions that had underscored the country's history for centuries. Kuchma's pro-Russia stance and KGB-like tactics were among the primary reasons for the formation—and popular appeal—of Pora. With the high court's ruling, according to Myers, Yushchenko and his supporters began to act as if he had already won the presidency. *The Times* reports that the protestors, who had been standing or encamped around-the-clock for twelve days at that point, celebrated a "democratic triumph" underneath "exploding fireworks." With the revote scheduled and a fair election more likely, Yushchenko appeared to have one more chance to win support of the Ukrainian people.

DECEMBER 4, 2004
UKRAINIAN COURT ORDERS NEW VOTE FOR PRESIDENCY
Finds Widespread Fraud
Challenger Hails Decision as Dawn of New Era–Runoff This Month
By STEVEN LEE MYERS

Kiev, Ukraine, Dec. 3 – Ukraine's Supreme Court overturned the results of the country's disputed presidential election on . . . [December 3], saying they were marred by "systemic and massive violations," and ordered a new runoff between the main candidates by Dec. 26.

The court's ruling—announced just before 6 P.M. after a day of suspense that halted Parliament's deliberations as well as talks aimed at a resolution of the impasse—was a surprising and decisive victory for Viktor A. Yushchenko, the opposition leader who asserted that he had been denied his rightful victory.

It came 12 days after tens of thousands of Ukrainians poured into the streets of Kiev and other cities and began round-the-clock protests denouncing what they considered a violation of their right to choose a successor to Leonid D. Kuchma, the departing president.

The streets, which had remained electric despite the tumult of seesawing momentum, exploded in jubilation. Thousands more poured into Independence Square in Kiev, forming a crowd larger than any other since the Nov. 21 runoff election that Prime Minister Viktor F. Yanukovich was declared to have won.

Beneath exploding fireworks, they celebrated a democratic triumph in a country of 48 million that only 13 years ago emerged from the Soviet Union with no democratic experience or traditions.

"Today we may say that Ukrainians—not only those who are here, but also those who see us on television and listen to the radio—began turning to justice, law and freedom," Mr. Yushchenko said. Speaking as if he had already won the presidency, though he must face the voters again, he called on Mr. Kuchma and Mr. Yanukovich to resign.

The court's decision signaled a turning point in a political and diplomatic crisis that paralyzed the government, rattled the economy and raised the specter of a civil conflict between the country's starkly divided regions, dominated by ethnic Ukrainians in the west and ethnic Russians in the east. The election also exposed tensions between Russia and the West not seen since NATO bombed Serbia in 1999, and perhaps since the cold war.

The ruling abruptly ended Mr. Kuchma's efforts, endorsed by President Vladimir V. Putin of Russia on . . . [December 2], to hold a new election from scratch, having implicitly conceded that the previous one would never produce a legitimate victory for Mr. Yanukovich. A completely new election would allow a new field of candidates and possibly a new pro-government, pro-Moscow candidate replacing Mr. Yanukovich.

Mr. Kuchma and Mr. Putin, whose support for Mr. Yanukovich has provoked angry protests here and abroad, mocked the idea of another runoff as impractical, in a meeting outside Moscow on . . . [December 2]. Several European leaders, by contrast, called for a new runoff, saying they were not supporting Mr. Yushchenko as much as a free and fair electoral process.

Mr. Yushchenko, on Independence Square, derided Mr. Kuchma's visit to Russia. "On the most crucial day for Ukraine, Leonid Kuchma went for advice not to his own people, but abroad," he said, prompting chants of "Kuchma out!"

The ruling appeared to stun the two men who, for now, make up the core of Ukrainian state power. Mr. Kuchma, who has served as president for 10 years, surviving protests and scandals that tarnished much of his legacy, did not immediately address the court's decision. His spokeswoman, reached by telephone, declined to say anything.

Mr. Yanukovich, the prime minister since 2002, also did not respond, though a spokeswoman, Hanna German, remained defiant and confident. She said he would run again—and prevail. But as the crisis unfolded, Mr. Yanukovich appeared to lose the backing of Mr. Kuchma and other important supporters, including his campaign manager, Sergey Tyhypko.

"He is sure he will win anyway," Ms. German said. "They can run the election five times, 18 times and anyway he will be the winner."

The Supreme Court, which has 85 judges in four chambers and a military collegium, has in the past displayed some independence from Mr. Kuchma's centralized power. Parliament elects judges to life terms, a basic step toward independence. Like judiciaries across the former Soviet Union, though, the court has been considered susceptible to government influence and pressure.

Only six days ago, a senior Western diplomat discounted the possibility that it would rule objectively on Mr. Yushchenko's appeal.

"Historically the Supreme Court is subject to bribery and intimidation," the diplomat said, speaking on condition of anonymity because of diplomatic protocol and the sensitivities surrounding the crisis. "It is as simple as that. No one has ever considered it an institution subject to independence and integrity."

Twenty-one of the court's judges began hearings on . . . [December 29] and continued through the week in full view of the nation. The proceedings were viewed on television in virtually every public place in Kiev, even on one channel, One Plus One, that before the election had carefully hewed to the government's positions.

Lawyers for Mr. Yushchenko presented what they called voluminous evidence of violations of campaign and election laws, often in numbing detail. On [December 1], Mr. Yanukovich unexpectedly filed his own appeal, accusing Mr. Yushchenko's campaign of election violations. While his appeal appeared to be a tactic to counter accusations of ballot stuffing on Mr. Yanukovich's behalf, it bolstered arguments that the election, over all, had not been fair.

The judges accepted most of Mr. Yushchenko's accusations that the government's manipulations before and during the voting had prevented a free and fair election, something called for in the Constitution. Mr. Yushchenko's lawyers based most of their case on constitutional issues, not the specifics of the election law.

The judges began deliberating on . . . [the morning of December 3] after hearing final arguments and, after voting in chambers, announced the ruling. The judges' vote was not disclosed.

Roman M. Zvarich, a member of Parliament and a lawyer who represented Mr. Yushchenko in the court's crowded chambers, said the judges had displayed a democratic maturity by establishing for the first time a larger precedent based on the primacy of constitutional rights above the election or other laws.

"The court took the initiative to fill in gaps in the election laws," he said. "This is a milestone decision. The court took a very courageous stand." . . .

The court's ruling reverberated beyond the nation's borders. The United States and European countries, having denounced the election results, welcomed the decision.

Mr. Putin, traveling in India, did not immediately react. In Moscow, Russia's Parliament adopted a resolution before the court's ruling that accused the European Union and the Organization for Security and Cooperation in Europe of fomenting unrest in Ukraine. The speaker of Parliament, Boris V. Gryzlov, represented Russia at the negotiations overseen by those institutions.

Grigory A. Yavlinsky, the leader of the liberal party Yabloko, reflected the divisions in Russia prompted by Ukraine's electoral crisis. At least a few on the margins of official power in Russia have found hope in the events unfolding in their Slavic neighbor.

"For the first time in the territory of the former U.S.S.R., a top judicial body has rejected falsification, the use of administrative resources and mockery of the people's will," he told the Interfax news agency.

Ukraine Suffers Along with Poisoned Yushchenko

"Do you like my face? This is the face of today's Ukraine." That is what Viktor Yushchenko asked the multitudes of thousands in Independence Square, calling attention to the pockmarks and cysts covering his once-young and vibrant face. As *The Times* correspondent C. J. Chivers notes on December 5, 2004, "in the battle for public perception, Mr. Yushchenko's face is one of his weapons . . . the illness underscores Mr. Yushchenko's message that in Ukraine, things are so fundamentally ugly that they must change" (see "Ukrainian Turns Illness Into Symbol for Nation's Woes"). Chivers's article sets the stage for the third round of voting, and the second runoff, between Yushchenko and the government's candidate, Yanukovich, that would finally determine the presidency.

Between the Supreme Court's ruling that mandated a revote and the actual runoff election, tests from an Austrian hospital revealed that Yushchenko's ghastly transformation resulted from poison, according to reporter Elizabeth Rosenthal writing in the *International Herald-Tribune* on December 12 ("Liberal Leader from Ukraine Was Poisoned"). Chivers reports that the government attributed the illness to "bad sushi or too much drink"; but Rosenthal's story reveals that it was actually caused by blood dioxin levels of "more than 1,000 times" the upper limits of what is considered normal.

With little television exposure, Yushchenko had relied on civic associations such as Pora to organize numerous mass rallies and on the symbolism of orange scarves and banners to spread his message. Yushchenko's recognizable orange scarf helped to ignite the movement, and the orange hue became ubiquitous. He was aided by acts of brazen defiance—such as the television personality who, in sign language, reported the November 21 runoff election to be a fraud—and by the nationally televised Supreme Court proceedings that had made government suppression of information more difficult (see "Protests Grow as Ukraine Vote Crisis Deepens"; see **Ukraine, Introduction**). *The Times* article by Chivers shows Yushchenko, with growing popular support and greater national coverage, embarking on an election campaign one last time.

In addition to the calls by Yushchenko and Pora for a change from the Kuchma regime, *The Times* also reports substantively on Yushchenko's platform, and how he hopes to change the face—literally and figuratively—of Ukraine. His platform incorporated public disclosure of government affairs and anticorruption measures such as banning gifts to public employees. The article also notes a primary barrier to Yushchenko's building a broad coalition in an ethnically and culturally split state: "Aside from the unifying cause of ousting Mr. Kuchma, Mr. Yushchenko has few issues that can bind his various blocs of supporters." The mixture of eager and animated students, free-market business executives, and entrenched party politicians created what Chivers quotes Oleksandra Kuzhel as calling a "situational majority" against Kuchma, but with few if any common goals.

Nevertheless, with three more weeks of campaigning to go, the "situational majority" may have been enough. The loss of the government's credibility in general, and Yanukovich's in particular, led to sweeping displays of orange across the country leading up to the elections on December 26.

KEY PLAYER IN UKRAINE
Viktor Yushchenko (1954–)

Viktor Yushchenko was born in Khoruzhivka, in the Sumy region of northeastern Ukraine, on the border with Russia. His father was an English teacher in a local school, and his mother taught physics and mathematics.

In 1975, Yushchenko was graduated from the Ternopil Finance and Economics Institute. He chose a financial career and worked as an accountant on a small collective farm. He soon went into the Soviet army for a brief stint and served on the southern border near Turkey.

By 1976, he had become the chief of the Ulyanovsk department of the State Bank. In 1984, he earned a graduate degree in finance and credit from the Ukrainian Institute of Economics and Agricultural Management.

In 1985, Yushchenko became the deputy director of administration for the Ukrainian Republican Office of the Soviet Union's state bank. He joined the board of directors at the Ukrainian Agro-Industrial Bank in 1988 and became first deputy chairman of the board at the Republican Bank Ukraine in 1990. In 1993, he was named head of the newly independent National Bank of Ukraine, a position he held for six years. While there, he worked to develop monetary, fiscal, and credit policies. In 1996, with his guidance, Ukraine moved from high inflation and surrogate money to the hryvnya, the nation's fairly stable currency, which he oversaw. He earned Western admiration as he led efforts to reform President Leonid Kuchma's governments during the 1990s.

Having managed to reduce the effect of a Russian debt default in 1998, Yushchenko was appointed as Ukraine's prime minister by President Kuchma. He was confirmed the following year, and served until 2001, during which time he helped to implement economic reforms. He pushed for increased government openness and worked to regain the public's trust in the government.

Yushchenko's popularity contrasted with President Kuchma's low ratings, and by 2001 the president had dismissed him. Released from his ties to Kuchma, Yushchenko accepted the bid from the opposition bloc and worked to consolidate a number of democratic political parties into one solid coalition called Our Ukraine (Nasha Ukrayina). At the next election, the Our Ukraine bloc won 101 of the 450 seats in parliament, enough to wield clout.

The presidential election of 2004 was marked by accusations of voter fraud, corruption, an assassination attempt, and government interference in behalf of Yushchenko's rival. The seventeen days of massive street protests and civil disobedience that followed the initial vote and the runoff election became known as the Ukraine's Orange Revolution. On December 26, Yushchenko won the presidency with 52 percent of the vote after Ukraine's third attempt to run a legitimate election.

In September 2004, during the presidential campaign, Yushchenko fell ill and needed to be hospitalized. He was found to have high levels of dioxin in his blood, which caused his face to become pockmarked and disfigured. Yushchenko maintained that his poisoning was an act of political reprisal, but he continued his campaign, despite needing a spinal drip of painkillers.

He was sworn into office in January 2005 as president of Ukraine in an event attended by notable figures from the movements that had brought democracy across the former Soviet Union. The crowds attending the inauguration wore orange scarves and hats and waved orange banners—the color painstakingly selected for the autumnal season when Ukrainians staged protest demonstrations—in celebration of the success of the Orange Revolution.

Yushchenko's election brought with it high ideals of clean governance, but his tenure has been hampered by the realities of controversy and infighting among opposition leaders. In 2005, Yushchenko fired his cabinet, after resignations and internal dissension had gotten out of hand. Government officials accused him of corruption. In 2006, Yushchenko approved the nomination of his former rival, the pro-Moscow Viktor F. Yanukovich, to the elected position of prime minister, a move that was met with mixed criticism.

Yushchenko continues to be a visible and polarizing figure in Ukrainian and European politics, as his approval rates have plummeted. In March 2009, he announced a sweeping program of economic and government reform.

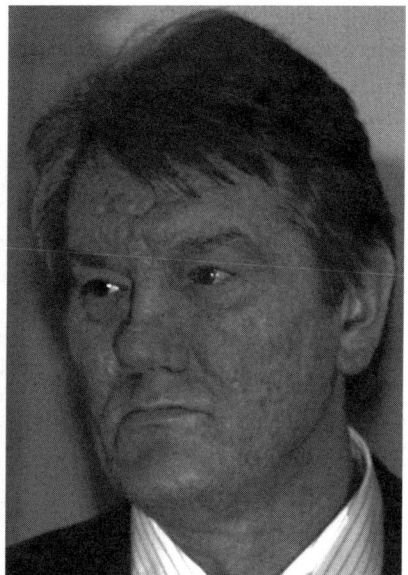

DECEMBER 5, 2004
UKRAINIAN TURNS ILLNESS INTO SYMBOL FOR NATION'S WOES
By C. J. CHIVERS

Kiev, Ukraine, Dec. 4 – Viktor A. Yushchenko, the opposition candidate who is trying to remake Ukraine through a sweeping change of power, stood on the stage in Independence Square here and surveyed the rapt crowd during one of his many appearances in two weeks of political crisis. His face, from chin to forehead, was a darkened mask of cysts. Its ugliness was unsettling.

"Do you like my face?" he asked, his voice passing through the huge speakers spread around the square. "This is the face of today's Ukraine."

Mr. Yushchenko is now surging, the leading candidate in a second presidential runoff that Ukraine's Supreme Court ordered because last month's was tainted by government fraud.

A former prime minister and head of Ukraine's central bank, he has seized the reform agenda in the battle against the incumbent government of the departing president, Leonid D. Kuchma.

Riding a wave of anti-Kuchma public sentiment, Mr. Yushchenko's message rests partly on the sustained exposure of what he calls the current government's ills. Many Ukrainians believe that Mr. Yushchenko is their best hope for changing the way the country has been ruled since Soviet times.

In this battle for public perception, Mr. Yushchenko's face is one of his weapons. Mr. Yushchenko said his recent disfigurement was a result of his being poisoned. Mr. Kuchma's camp says that he is afflicted by a mysterious disease, or that perhaps he ate bad sushi. But the illness underscores Mr. Yushchenko's message that in Ukraine, things are so fundamentally ugly that they must fundamentally change.

Mr. Kuchma's government, the opposition leader says, is shadowy, thuggish and corrupt, most recently expressed in its effort to force its choice for president, Prime Minister Viktor F. Yanukovich, into power. It remains rooted in a mix of post-Soviet centralization, economic banditry and an embarrassing subservience to Vladimir V. Putin, Russia's president. It is, as Mr. Yushchenko called it . . . [December 3], "a colossus on clay legs."

His administration, Mr. Yushchenko says, would be organized around ideas central to civil society: honesty, transparency, democracy and fairness. It would also nudge Ukraine toward the global world, expanding trade with Europe and urging the Ukrainian use of Western languages, all while seeking to unify a country that throughout the campaign has shown signs of an organic political split.

These are his positions. A question follows him. If he succeeds in toppling the current political clan, can he deliver on his promises?

Mr. Yushchenko's background is of a man who has lived in both the Soviet and Western worlds, and spent a great deal of his energy examining their economic models and links.

Mr. Yushchenko, 50, was born in a family of teachers in northeastern Ukraine, and began his career as an economist in a regional affiliate of the Soviet Union's state bank. He later held a series of bank management posts in Kiev, the Ukraine capital, in the Soviet Union's final years.

In 1993, two years after Ukraine broke from the Soviet Union, he was appointed head of the nation's central bank, a post he held until he became prime minister in 1999.

During his years at the bank, he was involved in steering Ukraine from Communism to a market economy, developing monetary and credit policies, and introducing the hryvnia, Ukraine's currency.

Ukraine is not a country known for its public integrity, and yet, in spite of his rival campaign's efforts to explore his past and smear him, Mr. Yushchenko has managed to navigate the intersection of Ukrainian government and business without a major or enduring scandal.

His reputation is clean enough that his opponents sometimes sneeringly refer to him as "the messiah."

His period as Mr. Kuchma's prime minister was short-lived and marred both by infighting in Parliament and what seemed his sense of powerlessness. Under the current Ukrainian Constitution, real power lies in the presidency.

In 2001, less than two years after Mr. Yushchenko assumed the post, as a potential protégé, Mr. Kuchma orchestrated a no-confidence vote against him, and those who had worked with him were forced to choose sides.

Mr. Yushchenko left office, vowing to return. It was a clear sign that he would try the opposition route, even though, not long before he lost his post he had said on Ukrainian television, referring to Mr. Kuchma, "I think that our relations are similar to those between a father and a son."

Some of the splits were bitter. Oleksandra Kuzhel, who worked for Mr. Yushchenko when he was prime minister and was one of the Yanukovich administration's liaisons to business, said Mr. Yushchenko had some of the worst characteristics of politicians, thinking more of his image and politics than of his government duties.

Some days, she said, he was more likely to go to political events than government meetings, and was chronically late.

"He is a good man, but he's not a manager," she said. "He does not plan his next day. He does not live up to his promises. He does not control the work he has set out before him. This is a death sentence for a business manager."

Such descriptions of him are of a type. Having assumed the role as foil to Mr. Kuchma, whose popularity in much of Ukraine has sunk, Mr. Yushchenko's own popularity has risen, as the government's efforts to demonize him have grown.

The state-run news media, or media owned by his rivals, have portrayed him as a radical and nationalist, and questioned whether his marriage to Kateryna Chumechenko, a Ukrainian-American who once worked in the State Department, has put him under the sway of the United States.

The bad press has not stopped him, and in a style of politicking reminiscent of campaigns in the West, he has reached out to almost all classes of voters, promising bold, instant change.

On . . . [December 2], addressing supporters in Independence Square, he appealed to Ukrainian history and his own roots in a small village on the border with Russia. He collects and restores rustic Ukrainian artifacts and relics from the country's ancient past. He keeps a house outside of Kiev, as his father and grandfather did.

For all his charisma on the stump, however, he can display stubbornness, a trait his opponents criticized again on . . . [December 4] as wrangling over the new election continued. He refused to follow the advice of doctors treating his mysterious ailment in Austria, and returned to campaigning in October with a catheter in his back to feed him painkillers.

He has campaigned partly by promising that as president he would immediately sign 11 decrees that would, among other things, fight public corruption, require local governments to make public reports of their activities, reduce the activities of the tax inspectors and accelerate withdrawal of Ukraine's soldiers in Iraq.

Those decrees could begin to nudge Ukrainian government away from its reputation as a gangster state. One includes a requirement for senior public officials to declare all income and expenditures and another would bar government employees from accepting gifts worth more than about $18.

His platform offers promises to almost every class of voter.

For young men, there is a pledge to cut the term of military conscription to 12 months from 18, and then, in 2010, to do away with it altogether. For young women there is a pledge to increase financial assistance at childbirth by a factor of 10. For those who lost savings during the runaway inflation of the 1990's, he included a promise to reimburse them, in part through trying to undo a privatization deal Mr. Kuchma made this year.

Those in the opposition camp say he may have one weakness: Aside from the unifying cause of ousting Mr. Kuchma, Mr. Yushchenko has few issues that can bind his various blocs of supporters.

His coalition is a mix of very different interests. They include students who seek revolutionary and absolute change; his own oligarchs, who are in part engaged in competition with the Mr. Kuchma's money clans, and who might seek protection or favors should Mr. Yushchenko become president; a raft of medium-size businesses that want law and agencies more favorable to their growth; and politicians in his camp who expect him to divide the president's powers with Parliament, and introduce a new degree of balance in Ukrainian political life.

As Mr. Yushchenko enters his next campaign, he will have to continue to navigate these sometimes conflicting pulls, which are, for now, largely quiet in the din of political battle against Mr. Kuchma.

Ms. Kuzhel, speaking before the momentum clearly shifted toward the opposition, called its base "a situational majority," which she defined as "a lot of people who use an image to get together to take power."

She also said no matter what his stature in Kiev and western Ukraine might be, Mr. Yushchenko's appeal had not been universal, and much of the country was against him, most notably the industrial interests in eastern Ukraine.

"I would like to remind you," she said, "that these people produce more than half of Ukraine's G.D.P."

A Clear Victory for Yushchenko

The results of Ukraine's presidential revote on December 26, 2004, would not have been predicted a year earlier. No one would have expected that Prime Minister Viktor Yanukovich, the candidate supported by the incumbent president, could be defeated or, if that did happen, that the government would acknowledge defeat. Yet after two internationally criticized elections, an assassination attempt, huge round-the-clock encamped demonstrations in Kiev, and what *The Times* calls a "surprising and decisive" Supreme Court ruling, the opposition leader Viktor Yushchenko was able to greet ecstatically cheering throngs as the president-elect of Ukraine (see "Ukrainian Court Orders New Vote for Presidency"). Unseen additional compromise had been required. The country's parliamentarians had on December 8 approved constitutional reforms that precluded the incoming president from enjoying full powers until January 1, 2006, in a swap for a free and fair December 26 revote.

The Times coverage suggests that the actual election of Yushchenko came as a collective exhalation. C. J. Chivers on December 28 notes, "Kiev was calm after weeks of demonstrations and civil disobedience" (see "Yushchenko Wins 52% of Vote; Rival Vows a Challenge"). A striking aspect of the postelection fallout, however, is that Yanukovich attempted the same strategy as Yushchenko: he decried the results as illegitimate. He asserted, *The Times* reports, that more than 4.8 million of his supporters could not vote, either through intimidation or procedural changes.

The fact that his argument did not gain any traction highlighted the impressiveness of Pora, Yushchenko's campaign organization, and in many ways the credibility of the larger cause behind the Orange Revolution. In disputing the initial election of October 31, Yushchenko was able to mobilize tens of thousands of nonviolent challengers almost overnight (see "Rivals in Ukraine Report Violations in Presidential Vote"). In contrast, Chivers describes Yanukovich's supporters: "On the corner outside the prime minister's headquarters, three young men had only one banner to wave, and they shared a single bottle of beer."

Chivers notes that "while Mr. Yanukovich appeared to be following the Yushchenko playbook in protesting the results, there were other unmistakable differences. Mr. Yushchenko's complaints last month were matched not just by Western leaders but by a huge outpouring of support in Ukraine. Parliament also took up his case." International observers noted a "substantial improvement" in election integrity, and Western leaders urged a quick certification of the results. Yushchenko's landslide reflected these perceptions.

Yet a full 44 percent of the country, even in light of government corruption and electioneering, voted against Yushchenko. The country remained divided. Yushchenko had organized an improbable victory against substantial odds, but Chivers quotes an observer who likens uniting Ukraine to "a Herculean task."

DECEMBER 28, 2004
YUSHCHENKO WINS 52% OF VOTE; RIVAL VOWS A CHALLENGE
By C. J. CHIVERS

Kiev, Ukraine, Dec. 27 – With virtually all votes counted, Viktor A. Yushchenko, the opposition leader, was Ukraine's presumptive president-elect on . . . [December 27]. But his opponent, Prime Minister Viktor F. Yanukovich, refused to accept the results and said he would challenge them in court.

Mr. Yushchenko led Mr. Yanukovich by 52.06 percent to 44.14 percent, a lead of more than 2.2 million votes, according to the Central Election Commission, which by late . . . [on December 27] had counted 99.89 percent of the ballots cast.

Kiev was calm after weeks of demonstrations and civil disobedience, and there were signs that the evident outcome of the election on . . . [December 26], the third round of voting for Ukraine's president within two months, was being recognized abroad.

Secretary of State Colin L. Powell said the election appeared free and fair. The Foreign Ministry of Belarus, Ukraine's neighbor and an authoritarian state that often echoes Moscow, told the Interfax news agency that it respected the decision of the Ukrainian people.

The European Union's foreign policy chief, Javier Solana, also signaled his satisfaction, saying Ukraine's leaders, after months of intrigue and scandal, had in the end "acted with a high degree of responsibility."

Importantly, the leaders of a prominent team of international election observers declared that the conduct of the voting on . . . [December 26] was a substantial improvement over previous rounds.

"The people of this great country can be truly proud that yesterday they took a great step toward free and democratic elections by electing the next president of Ukraine," said Bruce George, special coordinator of observers from the Organization for Security and Cooperation in Europe.

The organization's assessment was crucial to the election's legitimacy. In the previous round of voting, on Nov. 21, Western observers cited widespread fraud and abuse of state power on behalf of Prime Minister Yanukovich, who had claimed victory.

Their report lent credibility to Mr. Yushchenko's opposition movement and his supporters' mass demonstrations, provided a basis for an international outcry, and helped lead to a complaint to the Supreme Court, which nullified the voting.

This time, in a reversal of the Nov. 21 election, it was Mr. Yanukovich who was refusing to accept the outcome. Speaking . . . [December 27] evening at his headquarters, he asserted that a huge number of Ukrainians had been denied access to the polls, either by restrictive new voting rules or by intimidation by Mr. Yushchenko's supporters. He said he would file a challenge to the Supreme Court, seeking cancellation of the results.

"This is a crying fact: Millions of Ukrainian citizens did not have a chance to vote," he said. "They were thrown out. They were humiliated. There were more than 4,800,000 of such people."

Mr. Yanukovich's claim did not square with the reports of international observers or journalists, and although for a moment Kiev seemed bound for a continued standoff in this protracted race, the prime minister's challenge appeared destined to go forward without independent corroboration or European support.

Furthermore, while Mr. Yanukovich appeared to be following the Yushchenko playbook in protesting the results, there were other unmistakable differences. Mr. Yushchenko's complaints last month were matched not just by Western leaders but by a huge outpouring of support in Ukraine. Parliament also took up his case.

But Mr. Yanukovich was stepping into a much more lonely fight. He mustered few supporters in the capital on . . . [December 27], and Parliament ignored him, announcing plans through a spokesman to prepare for Mr. Yushchenko's inauguration.

Mr. George of the European organization, speaking generally about critics of the latest vote, also noted that anyone hoping to overturn the election would soon face a real test: providing evidence. "If you make an allegation about misconduct, then tell us where it took place, how it took place and who made that criminal act," he said. "If you cannot do that, withdraw the allegation."

It was easier to make allegations, he said, than to demonstrate them with facts.

Mr. George did say there were some problems with the election, including errors on voting lists and confusion over procedures for invalids voting at their homes. But without the independent corroboration of the sort of widespread fraud seen in the previous two rounds and given Mr. Yushchenko's strong margin of victory, the prospects for a challenge seemed poor.

The departing president, Leonid D. Kuchma, who had energetically backed Mr. Yanukovich in the previous two rounds of voting, made no public appearances or statements on . . . [December 27].

Mr. Yushchenko, who had claimed victory before his supporters in Independence Square early . . . [on December 27], remained out of public view as well through the rest of the day.

Political analysts noted that while the election challenge runs it course, Mr. Yushchenko, who has endured poisoning by dioxin and orchestrated fraud against his effort to gain the presidency, must now turn to the difficult tasks of governing.

His victory was clear, but it was not as overwhelming as voter surveys at the polls and early tallies had suggested. With the prime minister receiving more than 44 percent of the total, it was evident that a good part of the country opposed the presumptive future president.

Moreover, the results showed a deep geographic split, with the south and the east voting for Mr. Yanukovich by wide margins.

Mr. Yushchenko, facing a polarized electorate, must now select a cabinet and a prime minister and begin trying to forge a new, post-Kuchma identity for the country.

"Viktor Yushchenko is the new president of the new Ukraine," said Dr. Grigory Nemyria, director of the Center for European and International Studies here. "Yushchenko himself is important. But what is more important, long term, is the new Ukraine."

Dr. Nemyria said Mr. Yushchenko must try to modernize the economy in industrial regions in the east and south, an area he described as a rust belt reminiscent of Pittsburgh decades ago. He said that task would be especially difficult, because the region was where Mr. Yushchenko's support was weakest.

He also said the mass of people who turned out to support Mr. Yushchenko's challenge to the incumbent government, which is largely regarded as oppressive and corrupt, meant that there were high expectations that he would bring swift and clear change, in part by moving against corruption and creating open and independent civic institutions.

"One could call it a Herculean task," Dr. Nemyria said.

First he must wait to be declared the official winner, and for the court challenge to be examined by the Supreme Court. On one score, he seemed secure: the capital appeared to be with him.

A few of Prime Minister Yanukovich's supporters did show up on . . . [December 27] to wave his distinctive blue and white flags near his headquarters. But they numbered only a few dozen, and seemed more worried than inspired.

Mr. Yanukovich had previously said he planned to bring huge numbers of his supporters to Kiev in the event he lost the race, but his supporters on the streets on Monday said they were local people, and they showed little signs of organization or preparation.

On the corner outside the prime minister's headquarters, three young men had only one banner to wave, and they shared a single bottle of beer.

"There were falsifications on the Yushchenko side," said one of them, Doniyel Yashikov, 18, a student at the Interior Ministry's law enforcement academy. "I will never recognize him."

Asked how he would resist, Mr. Yashikov said he would go to rallies. There were no rallies in sight, just cars passing by with their drivers and passengers largely ignoring him. Many of their antennas bore the orange ribbons of the Yushchenko campaign.

YUSHCHENKO VOWS TO UNITE COUNTRY

The Times correspondent Steven Lee Myers on January 24, 2005, reports the remarks of the new Ukrainian president, Viktor Yushchenko ("Ukraine President Sworn In, Promising to Promote Unity"). Taking the oath of office with his arm draped over a 500-year-old Bible and a copy of Ukraine's constitution, Yushchenko declared: "Citizens of Ukraine have achieved a fair election. A legitimate handover of power has taken place."

The Orange Revolution, which culminated in Yushchenko's inauguration, was a "legitimate handover" in every sense of the term. Although a number of the transitions described in this volume were from authoritarian states to representative democracies, and even though Ukraine was nominally democratic before Yushchenko's election, a *handover,* in a functional definition, occurs when those who possess power willingly give it up. For a while, the departing president, Leonid Kuchma, and his chosen successor, Viktor Yanukovich, did not seem willing to release power. *The Times* quotes a retired miner at Yushchenko's inauguration: " 'To tell you the truth, to the last day I did not think it would happen. . . . When he showed up today, I cried.' "

Strenuous, sustained training by nonviolent activists, who studied translated materials and documentary films; stiff preparation by groups such as Pora; and strong image control and mass communications had forced the handover, leading to what *The Times* describes as "rivers of orange" in Ukraine's capital city, Kiev, on inauguration day. (On Pora, see "Youth Movement Underlies the Opposition in Ukraine.") Ukraine had made a choice, according to Hryhoriy M. Nemyria, head of the European Center for International Studies in Kiev, who was interviewed for *The Times:* "The choice was always between a consolidation of democracy or a consolidation of authoritarianism. The choice was made toward the consolidation of democracy, but it needs to be consolidated. The revolution is only the beginning."

The handover happened because a massive movement of political organizations pledged to nonviolent action had undermined the sources of power of the incumbent officials, forcing them to relinquish power. As the seven heads of state and countless representatives from other countries attending the inauguration testified, the Ukrainian people and the international community also viewed the surrender of command as "legitimate." Ukraine was self-consciously aware of its role as part of the democratic nonviolent transitions occurring across Eastern Europe and among former republics of the Soviet Union. Although the elated crowds applauded the foreign representatives who had traveled from across the world, Chivers reports, "The loudest applause erupted for the leaders of countries who had over the decades risen up against Soviet domination."

Yushchenko moved quickly to address international and domestic rifts. He urged his pro-Western, pro-liberalization supporters to recognize that "we are no longer on the edge of Europe. We are situated in the center of Europe."

Conscious that 44 percent of the country voted against him in the end, most of them pro-Russia eastern Ukrainians, Yushchenko visited Russian president Vladimir Putin the next day, as Chivers reports for *The Times* on January 25 ("Ukraine's President Mends Ties with Putin"). At once conciliatory and revolutionary, Yushchenko marked the peaceful transition of power with a forward-thinking focus on Ukraine's future.

JANUARY 24, 2005
UKRAINE PRESIDENT SWORN IN, PROMISING TO PROMOTE UNITY
Declares Victory of Freedom Over Fraud
By STEVEN LEE MYERS

Kiev, Ukraine, Jan. 23 – Viktor A. Yushchenko, his face disfigured by poison and his fate nearly undone by electoral fraud, took the oath of office as president of Ukraine on . . . [January 23], vowing to unite a poor and deeply divided country and lead it into the mainstream of Europe.

Speaking first in Parliament and then in Kiev's central square, Mr. Yushchenko declared Ukraine's freedom and independence in thinly veiled remarks aimed at the departing president, Leonid D. Kuchma, and at Russia and its president, Vladimir V. Putin, who openly supported Mr. Yushchenko's opponent.

"Armed only by their faith and beliefs, the people won a beautiful and peaceful victory," he told tens of thousands of Ukrainians waving flags and banners in Independence Square, the site of the demonstrations that helped usher him to office. "It is a victory of freedom over tyranny, of law over lawlessness, of future over past."

Mr. Yushchenko's inauguration punctuated an extraordinary period in Ukraine's history that included two rounds of voting last fall, followed by huge street protests and a legal challenge that ultimately overturned the declared victory of his opponent, Viktor F. Yanukovich, and led to the third round of voting on Dec. 26, in which he triumphed.

In his speeches, Mr. Yushchenko, 50, was alternately conciliatory and defiant. His, he said, was a victory for all Ukrainians, and he pledged to honor the people's right to worship in their own faith, to embrace their own politics and to speak in the language of their ancestors; the last was a reference to the divisive issue of the Russian language, which Mr. Yanukovich had promised to make equal in law to Ukrainian.

Mr. Yushchenko also vowed to fight the corruption and the shadowy economy that had become characteristic of the tumultuous decade under Mr. Kuchma, during which a few people closely allied with power accumulated vast fortunes. "We shall create a democratic power—honest, professional and patriotic," he said. "The wall that separates government from the people will be destroyed."

Mr. Yushchenko, a former central banker and prime minister under the man he ultimately replaced, became the third president of this country of 48 million people since it declared its independence from the Soviet Union in 1991.

He did so facing not only the usual challenges of a new leader, but also expectations intensified by the eruption of public discontent after efforts by Mr. Kuchma's government to install Mr. Yanukovich as his chosen successor.

"The expectations are too great," Yulia Tishchenko, of the Ukrainian Center for Independent Political Research in Kiev, said in an interview before the inauguration, warning that the public's jubilation over Mr. Yushchenko's victory would soon confront the harsh reality of governance. "Different segments of the population have different expectations. And he will not be able, in a short period of time, to live up to them."

The country has been strained by stark divisions of wealth, by poverty and by unemployment, which has forced millions to seek work abroad. Recent economic growth has slowed, while the federal budget has gone from a surplus to a deficit within months after a raft of campaign-related expenditures on pensions and other social benefits under Mr. Yanukovich, who until Dec. 31 was prime minister.

Mr. Yushchenko's aides and independent analysts also said that during the prolonged electoral dispute, the government continued to sell off state assets and provide long-term leases on commercial buildings in Kiev and entire enterprises in other parts of the country. "They are basically stealing stuff," said Roman M. Zvarich, a member of Mr. Yushchenko's coalition in Parliament.

Above all, Ukraine remains politically divided. In spite of Mr. Yushchenko's pleas for unity, Mr. Yanukovich did not attend the inauguration. Mr. Kuchma, who did, did not answer Mr. Yushchenko's subsequent call for all in Parliament to join him for his inaugural address on Independence Square.

Mr. Yushchenko also faces the difficulty of holding together the broad but fractious coalition that challenged the results of the first runoff. He has yet to announce his appointments for prime minister and other posts in the new cabinet, a delay that experts say has already slowed the momentum of his presidency in its infancy.

On . . . [January 23], the acting prime minister, Mykola Y. Azarov, who took over when Mr. Yanukovich stepped aside, announced his resignation, as required by law. But in Mr. Yushchenko's first act as president, he asked Mr. Azarov and the current government to continue working until he chose a new government.

"The choice was always between a consolidation of democracy or a consolidation of authoritarianism," Hryhoriy M. Nemyria, director of the European Center for International Studies in Kiev, said in an interview. "The choice was made toward the consolidation of democracy, but it needs to be consolidated. The revolution is only the beginning."

The inauguration was attended by the presidents of seven countries—Poland, Hungary, Romania, Slovakia, Estonia, Latvia and Molodova—as well as by political leaders from many others. For the United States, Secretary of State Colin L. Powell attended. Russia, by contrast, sent Sergei M. Mironov, the speaker of the upper house of Parliament.

As each of the leaders was announced in Parliament, the loudest applause erupted for the leaders of countries who had over the decades risen up against Soviet domination: President Aleksandr Kwasniewski of Poland; Vaclav Havel, the former Czech president; and [Nino] Burdzhanadze, the speaker of Georgia's Parliament.

Mr. Powell met with Mr. Yushchenko before the inauguration and, echoing a congratulatory telephone call from President Bush on . . . [January 22], said the United States was prepared to help in the country's transition. "The United States wants to do everything we can to help you meet the expectations of the Ukrainian people," Mr. Powell said. . . .

Mr. Yushchenko, after their meeting, responded with a list of requests, including recognition of Ukraine as a market economy, support for its membership in the World Trade Organization and a lifting of sanctions imposed under the Jackson-Vanik Amendment, a cold-war-era law that limits trade because of Soviet restrictions on emigration.

He later spoke of . . . [January 23] as a turning point in the country's history. "Today's event has proven once more that the Ukrainian nation and the Ukrainian state have arrived," he said in Parliament, after taking the oath of office with his arm draped over a 500-year-old Bible and a copy of the Constitution. "Citizens of Ukraine have achieved a fair election. A legitimate handover of power has taken place."

He later vowed that he would lead Ukraine into its proper place in Europe—and specifically in the European Union, which has only just absorbed many of Ukraine's Central and Eastern European neighbors and appears wary of inviting still another larger, developing nation.

"We are no longer on the edge of Europe," he said. "We are situated in the center of Europe."

Throughout Kiev, the mood was ebullient. Rivers of orange—flags, banners, scarves and hats in the color of Mr. Yushchenko's campaign—coursed through the streets. For many in Independence Square, it was enough to witness his inauguration and his address, which ended with confetti and balloons rising into a cold, leaden sky and a concert of the songs that provided the revolution its overture.

"To tell you the truth, to the last day I did not think it would happen," said Vitaly K. Samusevich, a retired miner who had joined the thousands who went to the streets to protest the initial results that made Mr. Yanukovich the winner. "When he showed up today, I cried."

Natalia D. Shafar, an economist and translator, came to the square with her daughter, Olya. She said the events of the last months had created a "national idea," something Ukraine lacked before.

"Of course, we do not expect that overnight we will have a better life," she said, "but at least now we have hope."

Collective Nonviolent Action Gains Momentum

Ukraine produced its Orange Revolution in autumn 2004 by forcing honest elections through round-the-clock demonstrations in the capital city that lasted for seventeen days and through civil disobedience that occurred in many parts of the country. It ended the authoritarian rule of President Kuchma, whose administration was marked by Soviet-style suppression. CNN and BBC correspondents reporting from Kiev kept saying, "so far there's been no violence." They seemed unaware of Pora and its efforts to coach Ukrainians in methods of nonviolent resistance. *The New York Times* did cover Pora and its activities appropriately, thereby making it clear that improvisation and spontaneity had little to do with the course of events, that credit was due to the planning and organization that brought together approximately 1 million nonviolent demonstrators in Independence Square (see "Youth Movement Underlies the Opposition in Ukraine").

The Times reporter Michael T. Kaufman on December 5, 2004, takes his readers from a birds-eye view of thousands camped out in Kiev to a glance around the world at the spread of the technique of collective nonviolent action (see "Heeding the Roar of the Street"). Kaufman finds that the "orange-draped Kiev crowds" evoke images of the nonviolent civil resisters "who, through peaceful free assembly, won union rights at the shipyards in Gdansk, or cheered a 'velvet revolution' in Prague, or rejoiced in Berlin as the wall came down." He finds it remarkable that nonviolent mass action has often worked in the contemporary era.

In the nonviolent revolutions covered by *The Times* in the 1970s, the covert distribution of the *samizdat* (Russian for self-published) that was so crucial to the Czechs' and Slovaks' Velvet Revolution had involved typing ten carbon copies on onion-skin paper (see "Czech Underground Literature Circulating from Hand to Hand"). The illegal printing presses, memorized manifestos, posters plastered on kiosks, journals that appeared from nowhere, and samizdat literature were crucial to the sharing of ideas, including ways to struggle against communist oppression without violence (see "Police in Prague Move to Break up Big Protest March"). The outpouring of underground publications continued to play a critical part in *The Times'* chronicle of democratic transitions in late 1980s Eastern Europe and the Baltic States.

Kaufman cites the Helsinki Accords as part of the explanation for the widening use of nonviolent action. On August 1, 1975, the Final Act was signed by the United States, Canada, and thirty-five European countries (Albania did not sign) and became known as the Helsinki Accords. The Final Act reflected the interests of both the West and the Soviet sphere. Its provisions for political freedoms and human rights soon supplanted the other specifications, and the Helsinki Accords became synonymous with human rights (see "**Introduction: Strikes, Sinatra,**

and Nonviolent Revolution"). Activist intellectuals saw the accords as a rubric under which they could organize Helsinki watch committees, even in societies where the mere act of meeting might have constituted a transgression or civil disobedience. Watch groups independently monitored implementation of the Helsinki Final Act in the Soviet Union, which helped to open up political space for reforms. Rather than challenging the legitimacy of the union initially, they insisted that Moscow obey the clauses in the Final Act that had been signed by the Kremlin. They persevered by pressing the Soviet Union to abide by its own agreements. Similar groups that appeared in the Baltics, Czechoslovakia, Poland, and elsewhere made the dissemination of information and knowledge easier—because the Soviet Union was a signatory.

If anything, the trend is toward greater use of the technique of civil resistance in the twenty-first century.

DECEMBER 5, 2004
HEEDING THE ROAR OF THE STREET
By MICHAEL T. KAUFMAN

It has been an evocative sight. The bird's-eye views of the crowds in Independence Square in Kiev over the last two weeks challenging the results of Ukraine's presidential election recalled many other spontaneous assemblages in recent years, most chillingly the prodemocracy protesters who filled Tiananmen Square in Beijing in 1989, only to be fired on by Chinese troops.

The tensions and risks remain high in Ukraine, but at times last week the prospect of violence seemed to recede, as a compromise emerged that would void the disputed election and allow for a new one. That would make the orange-draped Kiev crowds less reminiscent of Tiananmen and more suggestive of the protesters who, through peaceful free assembly, won union rights at the shipyards in Gdansk, or cheered a "velvet revolution" in Prague, or rejoiced in Berlin as the wall came down.

In fact, over the last 30 years, the stereotype of mass uprising has radically changed. Largely gone are the bricks and barricades and calls to arms. Much more common now are hordes of unarmed people, often young, filling the streets to voice their hopes and wishes to their countrymen, their leaders and, perhaps most importantly, to the world watching on television.

The remarkable thing about the "people power" tactics of nonviolent mass protest is how often they have worked. They are not foolproof, as the Chinese experience shows. But by the reckoning of Stephen Zunes, a professor of politics at the University of San Francisco, they have advanced democracy in Bolivia (1977 and 1982); Sudan and Haiti (1985); the Philippines (1986); South Korea (1987); Chile, Poland, East Germany and Czechoslovakia (1989); Mongolia and Nepal (1990); Mali (1992); Madagascar (1993); Bangladesh (1996); and Indonesia (1998). On top of that, he notes, spontaneous nonviolent action thwarted coups in Argentina (1987), Russia (1991), Thailand (1992) and Paraguay (1996 and 1999).

People power often prevails because national leaders fear the loss of international legitimacy and acceptance that would come from cracking down. Carol Bogart, the deputy director of Human Rights Watch, said that, in part, this tendency has grown out of the 1975 Helsinki Accords, when Moscow first agreed to accept that civil and human rights were legitimate issues of diplomatic discussion. "The idea that there are international standards in these areas has grown sharply over the last 20 years, and many leaders have realized that unless they comply, they can really lose ground in the world," Ms. Bogart said.

Ultimately, though, much depends on the particular character of the rulers being challenged in the streets, said Aryeh Neier, the president of George Soros's Open Society Institute and a prime mover in the Helsinki process. . . .

Before Helsinki, Mr. Neier said, the Soviet Union routinely dismissed any discussion of civil or human rights as "unacceptable interference in the internal affairs of a sovereign state," and other countries followed suit. Now the pendulum has swung so far that two foreign statesmen—President Aleksandr Kwasniewski of Poland and Javier Solana, the European Union's foreign policy chief—are mediating a dispute between rival Ukrainian political parties.

Factors that are unique to one country or one moment in time can make a big difference, Mr. Neier noted. For example, when South Korean students protested against the military government in 1987, the Olympic games scheduled for Seoul the following summer weighed heavily on the country's rulers. They ultimately agreed to step down rather than risk the national humiliation of a boycott of the games, as in Moscow in 1980 after the Soviet invasion of Afghanistan.

Mr. Neier said he wondered whether the course of the Ukrainian crisis would be different if the country's capital were an eastern city like Kharkiv, where most people support Viktor F. Yanukovich, the winner of the disputed election. As it is, the locus of government power and media attention is in Kiev, a western city where most people back the challenger, Viktor A. Yushchenko. . . .

While huge peaceful assemblies have sometimes brought about sudden and decisive changes at the top, as in Czechoslovakia or Lithuania, in other cases they have been dispelled by force, only to become the legendary platforms for future mobilizations and struggle. The Communist government of Poland sent troops to crush the independent Solidarity union and impose martial law in 1981; by 1989, the crowds were back, rallying around the union and, this time, forcing a change in government.

Bibliography

Aslund, Ånders, and Michael A. McFaul, eds. 2006. *Revolution in Orange: The Origins of Ukraine's Democratic Breakthrough.* Washington, D.C.: Carnegie Endowment for International Peace.

BBC News. 2008. "Profile: Viktor Yushchenko." October 9.

Binnendjik, Anika Locke, and Ivan Marovic. 2006. "Power and Persuasion: Nonviolent Strategies to Influence State Security Forces in Serbia (2000) and Ukraine (2004)." *Communist and Post-Communist Studies* 39, no. 3 (September-October): 411–429.

Bransten, Jeremy. 2004. "Ukraine: Part Homegrown Uprising, Part Imported Production?" Radio Free Europe/Radio Liberty, http://www.rferl.org/content/article/1056498.html. December 20.

Bunce, Valerie J., and Wolchik, Sharon L. 2006. "International Diffusion and Postcommunist Electoral Revolutions." *Communist and Post-Communist Studies,* 39, no. 3 (September-October): 283–304.

Gruda, Agnès. 2004. "Generation Orange." *La Presse.* December 5.

Kaskiv, Vladyslav, Iryna Chupryna, Anastasiya Bezverkha, and Yevhen Zolotariov. 2005. *A Case Study of the Civic Campaign Pora and the Orange Revolution in Ukraine.* See http://www.pora.org.ua.

Kuzio, Taras. 2006. "Civil Society, Youth, and Societal Mobilization in Democratic Revolutions." *Communist and Post-Communist Studies* 39, no. 3 (September-October): 365–386.

Liber, George O. 1992; 2002. *Soviet Nationality Policy, Urban Growth, and Identity Change in the Ukrainian SSR 1923–1934* (Cambridge Russian, Soviet, and Post-Soviet Studies). Cambridge: Cambridge University Press.

McFaul, Michael. 2005. "Transitions from Postcommunism." *Journal of Democracy* 16 (3): 5–19.

Maksymuik, Jan. 2004. "Yushchenko Vows 'People's Election Campaign' in Ukraine." Radio Free Europe, http://www.rferl.org/Content/Article/1054275.html.

Rosenthal, Elizabeth. 2004. "Liberal Leader From Ukraine Was Poisoned." *International Herald-Tribune.* December 12.

Rukh in Modern Ukrainian History. 2004.

Simpson, John, and Marcus Tanner. 2004. "Serb Activists Helped Inspire Ukraine Protests." *Balkan Crisis Report.* Institute for War and Peace Reporting. See http://www.iwpr.net/index.php?apc_state=hen&s=o&o=p=bcr&1=EN&s=f&o=155269. November 26.

Solohubenko, Olexiy. 2009. "How 1989 Fanned Flames in Ukraine." BBC News. See http://news.bbc.co.uk/go/pr/fr/-/1/hi/world/europe/8091737.stm. June 10.

Subtelny, Orest. 2000. *Ukraine: A History.* Toronto: University of Toronto Press.

Wanner, Catherine. 1996. "Nationalism on Stage: Music and Change in Soviet Ukraine." In *Returning Culture: Musical Changes in Central and Eastern Europe,* ed. Slobin. Durham, N.C.: Duke University Press.

Wilson, Andrew. 2009. "Ukraine's 'Orange Revolution' of 2004: The Paradoxes of Negotiation." In *Civil Resistance and Power Politics: The Experience of Nonviolent Action from Gandhi to the Present,* ed. Adam Roberts and Timothy Garton Ash, 336–353. Oxford: Oxford University Press.

———. 2005. *Ukraine's Orange Revolution.* New Haven: Yale University Press.

York, Steve. 2007. *Orange Revolution* (documentary feature film). See http://www.orangerevolutionmovie.com/.

———. 2002. *Bringing Down a Dictator* (documentary film). See www.aforcemorepowerful,org.

From *The New York Times*

Chivers, C. J. 2005. "Ukraine's President Mends Ties with Putin." January 25.

———. 2004. "Ukrainian Court Delays Results in Vote Dispute." November 26.

———. 2004. "Ukraine's Face Is Mirrored in a Candidate." December 5.

Clines, Francis X. 1991. "Ex-Communist Wins in Ukraine; Yeltsin Recognizes Independence." December 3.

Erlanger, Steven. 1993. "Ukraine Questions the Price Tag of Independence." September 8.

Freudenheim, Milt, Katherine Roberts, and James F. Clarity. 1987. "The Trial Begins at Chernobyl." July 12.

Hrushevsky, Michaelo. 1918. "Ukraine's Struggle for Self-Government." February 17 (magazine).

Keller, Bill. 1989. "Ukraine Intellectuals Lead Challenge to Communists." March 9.

Kotkin, Stephen. 1998. "Czars to Bolsheviks." May 3.

Kristof, Nicholas. 2004. "Let My People Go." December 4.

Mishchenko, Yuriy, and Anatoly Panov. 1991. "Chernobyl Makes Ukraine Want Independence." April 26.

Myers, Steven Lee. 2004. "A Silent Act of Rebellion Raises a Din in Ukraine." November 29.

———. 2004. "Putin Backs Ukrainian Leader, Dismissing Calls for New Runoff." December 3.

Schmemann, Serge. 1991. "Ukraine is Now Getting Serious about its Drive for Independence." October 30.

Shaplen, Jason. 2004. "Poison Politics in Ukraine." September 25.

Tyler, Patrick. 2002. "Ukraine's Leader Struggles to Go Quietly." March 29.

Unsigned. 2004. "Saying No to Vladimir Putin." December 4.

Unsigned. 1931. "Russian Minorities." June 27.

Unsigned. 1894. "Kiev or St. Petersburg." March 18.

INDEX

Note: page numbers in *italics* indicate photographs.

Abashidze, Aslan, 342–343, 366, 369–371, 375
Abkhazia, conflict with Georgia, 335, 338, 343–344, 368, 369, 370, 372
Action Program reforms, Czechoslovakia (1968), 154, 155
Activist intellectuals
  alliance in Poland with Catholic laity and workers, 21–24
  Charter 77 in Czechoslovakia and, 164–165
  collective nonviolent action and, 8
  in Czechoslovakia, Havel and, 200
  in Czechoslovakia, Prague Spring and, 154, 155–157
  in Czechoslovakia, Velvet Revolution and, 163–164, 207
  Czechoslovak industrial workers and, 188
  in Eastern Europe, cross-border communication among, 84, 85–86, 177–178
  in Eastern Europe and Soviet Union, 5–6
  in East Germany, 40th anniversary celebrations and, 120–122
  in East Germany, demonstrations and, 128
  in East Germany, writings of, 109
  Hungarian government restructuring and, 92
  in Hungary, 75
  in Hungary, on social contract with civil society, 76, 86
  in Latvia, Popular Front and, 223
  in Lithuania, Sąjūdis and, 224
  in Poland, 11–12
  Solidarity's semantics of change and, 66
  support for Czechoslovakia's Plastic People of the Universe by, 157–158
  in Ukraine, independence movement and, 381
Adamec, Ladislav
  Civic Forum meets with, 181, 186, 192, 194
  as Czechoslovak leader, 162, 199
  Havel and opposition request talks with, 175
  as potential replacement for Jakeš, 183, 188, 191
Adzharia region, Georgia, 342–343, 366. *See also* Abashidze, Aslan; Ajaria region, Georgia
Afghanistan, 4, 10, 67, 419
Ajaria region, Georgia, 368. *See also* Adzharia region, Georgia
Albania, 210, 287, 291
Albanians, 15, 291. *See also* Kosovo
Alexander I, Czar of Russia, 334, 335
Alexander II, Czar of Russia, 388
Alliance for Change, Serbia, 291, 304, 307, 308
Alliance of Democratic Youth (FIDESz), 76, 79, 99
Alliance of Free Democrats (Szabad Demokraták Szövetsége, SzDSz), 76, 79, 80, 89, 99, 101, 103, 173
Alternative (parallel) institutions. *See also* Kosovo
  across Eastern Europe, 5–6
  armed conflict and demise of, 293, 294
  in East Germany, 111, 113, 130
  in Kosovo during 1990s, 292, 298, 301
  in Serbia, 320–321
Amnesty, limited
  in Czechoslovakia, 152, 199, 205–206, 207
  in Poland, 20, 48, 52
Andelman, David A., 31, 32–36
Andropov, Yuri V., 56–57, 83
Antall, Jozsef, 80, 103, 210
Appeal for Hour X, Latvian Popular Front's, 6, 232, 273
Apple, R. W. "Johnny," Jr., 160–161, 181
Armenia, 230, 238, 245, 248, 251, 252, 272, 336
Association of Polish Youth, 36
Associations, Hungarian Law of, 87–88
Auseklis (Dawn) magazine, Latvia, 222
Ausreisewelle (wave of exits). *See* Protest emigration
Austria-Hungary, 11–12, 19, 285, 287. *See also* Hapsburg Empire

422 INDEX

Awakening, in Latvia, 222
Azerbaijan, 238, 248, 251, 252, 336

Balkanization, definition of, 285
Balkans, 285, 288–289. *See also* Serbia
Baltic Committee for Free and Independent Trade Unions, Poland, 23, 34, 39
Baltic Freedom Day (1985), 224
Baltic languages group, 212
Baltic model for economic reform, 226–227. *See also* IME economic proposal
Baltic states. *See also* Baltic Way human chain; Estonia; Latvia; Lithuania
  autumn 1989, 229–230
  autumn watershed (1988), 226–227
  communist party elections and, 227–228
  demonstrations against Soviet rule tolerated, 239–242
  Estonia's Popular Front, 220–222
  extremist reactions from interfronts, 231–232
  First Republics in, 214–215
  glasnost raises expectations in, 242–245
  Gorbachev's policies and, 217–218
  independence declarations (1990), 230–231
  independence of, 212, 214, 236–237
  key players in, 253–254, 261–262
  Latvia's Popular Front, 222–223
  Lithuania's popular front (Sąjūdis), 223–226
  nationalist opposition slowly builds in, 217
  nonviolent civil resistance in Soviet Union and, 235–236
  popular fronts in, 220–227
  published guidelines for civilian defense and, 232–233
  quick facts about, 213–214
  Russification and Sovietization in, 216–217
  Soviet annexation of, 215
  Soviet coup elevating Yeltsin and, 273–279
  transformation in, 14–15
Baltic Way human chain (1989), 15, 213, 228, 255–259, *257*
Bariss, Martins, 218, 239
Barker, Colin, 17
Barry, Ellen, 344, 372
Basic Treaty, between East and West Germany, 118
Bass, Eduard, 170
Batrla, Libor, 190
Batthyány Square, Budapest, Hungary, 88
Battle of the bridge, Budapest (1986), 82
BBC, 229, 241, 385, 417
Beissinger, Mark R., 220–222, 276
Belarus, popular front in, 238
Belegu, Nedime, 293
Benda, Václav, 158
Berecz, János, 82–83
Berghofer, Wolfgang, 127–128
Berklavs, Eduards, 217, 223
Berlin Wall. *See also* Iron curtain; Protest emigration
  Checkpoint Charlie barricades, 122
  chunks of, 148
  construction of, 133–134
  East Germans killed trying to get over, 107, 134
  fall of, as symbol for Eastern Europe, 11
  fall of, Poland's round-table talks and, 29, 30
  Honecker on shooting escapees over, 119, 126, 138, 139
  opening of, 13, 135–137, 142
Besymenskii, Lev, 229, 281
Beszélö (Speaker), Hungary, 75, 76, 86, 89
Bielecki, Czeslaw, 68
Bilefsky, Dan, 336, 344, 372
Binder, David, 128–129, 138–142, 143
Binnendjik, Anika Locke, 305, 308–309, 317, 383, 397
Bitenieks, Raimonds, 218, 239
Biuletyn Informacjny (Information bulletin), Poland, 23
Black berets, Soviet. *See* Otryad Militsii Osobovo Naznacheniya
Black Pora, 397
Black Ribbon Day, Latvia (1987), 219, 244
Bloody Sunday, Lithuania (1991), 15, 214, 233–234, 235, 268–273
Bohemia, as western Czechoslovakian region, 150, 151
Bohlen, Celestine
  on bilateral treaty between Budapest and Moscow, 104
  on Hungarian elections of 1990, 103
  on Shevardnadze's return to Georgia, 339, 348–351
  on Soviet pressures on Latvia, 231
  on Soviet pullout from Hungary, 104–105
  on Ukraine's history and revolution in, 386–388
  on Ukraine under Soviet control, 380
  on voter turnout in Hungary (1990), 80
Bolsheviks, 334. *See also* Russian Revolution
Bosnia. *See also* Serbia
  Dayton Agreement (1995) and, 289, 290, 301
  ethnic tensions and war in, 15–16, 288
  independence movement in, 298
  Milošević and, 327, 328
  radio broadcasts into Serbia from, 320
Bosnia-Herzegovina, 15, 285, 286
Bosnian Muslims, 15, 285, 289, 292, 293
Boycotts. *See also* Noncooperation
  in Czechoslovakia, 161, 175, 179, 180, 192, 199
  in East Germany of local elections, 109
  in Georgia, 340, 369
  in Serbia, of election runoff, 295, 320–323
  by Solidarity, 52
  of Yugoslav and Serbian elections, 292
Bratislava, Czechoslovakia. *See also* Public Against Violence
  demonstrations of 1989 in, 178, 183, 191, 192
  Dubček speaks at rally in, 184, 186, 187, 190
  strikes of 1989 in, 182
  Ten Days in Czechoslovakia (1989) and, 14
Brazauskas, Algirdas, 224, 226, 227, 250, 251, 263
Brezhnev, Leonid I.
  Carter and threats to Solidarity by, 27, 55, 67
  Gorbachev on managed change after, 217
  human rights provisions of Helsinki Accords and, 5
  pressure on Jaruzelski by, 69
  SALT I treaty and, 4
  Soviet rule under, 2
  Ukraine under, 380
Brezhnev Doctrine
  crushing of Prague Spring under, 14, 27, 76, 154, 155
  as doctrine of limited sovereignty, 3, 27
  East Germany under, 106
  Gorbachev's rejection of, 9–10, 30, 67–68, 109, 160, 163, 229
  reinterpretation of 1956 Hungarian uprising and demise of, 90–91
"Bringing Down a Dictator" (film), 386
Britain, 106, 143, 148, 150, 151
Brno, Czechoslovakia, demonstrations/strikes of 1989, 182, 183
Bronfman, Edgar M., 87
Browne, Malcolm W., 165, 166–167
Bruszt, László, 77, 78
Brzezinski, Zbigniew, 38, 69
Budapest School, 74–75. *See also* Kis, János
Bugajski, Janusz, 158
Bujak, Zbigniew, 22, 26, 29
Bulgaria
  as Balkan nation, 285, 287
  condemns its role in Warsaw Pact invasion of Czechoslovakia, 199
  ousting of communist chief in, 194
  Prague Spring and, 90, 151
  proclamation on 1956 Hungarian uprising and, 85
  Warsaw Pact dissolution and, 209–210
Bulldozer Revolution, Serbia (2000), 16, 286, 297, 325–327. *See also* Otpor!
Bunce, Valerie, 341
Burdzhanadze, Nino
  on Abashidze's resignation, 371
  Rose Revolution and, 339, 367
  Saakashvili on role for, 342, 366, 369
  on serving as Georgia's president, 363

on Shevardnadze as Georgia's president, 355, 361, 362
Yushchenko's inauguration and, 385
Bush, George H. W., 93, 119, 148, 189, 191, 236, 272
Butkevicius, Audrius, 232, 233
Butturini, Paula, 179
Byelorussia, 244, 252, 381

Calendar demonstrations (events)
Baltic Way human chain, 15, 213, 228, 255–259, *257*
dates in Baltic states for, 246
Freedom (Liberty) Monument demonstration (1987), 219, 239–240
Keller article on, 240–242
in Latvia (1988), 223, 245–246
in Lithuania, 225
Soviet press discounts effects of, 244
Čalfa, Marián, 163, 199
Calvin, John, 108
Capek, Karl, 170
Čarnogoursky, Ján, 181, 199
Carter, Jimmy, 10, 27, 38, 55, 67, 238
Casaroli, Agostino Cardinal, 171, 172
Center for Civic Initiatives (Serbian NGO), 16, 294
Center for Free Elections and Democracy (CeSID), 295, 320–321
Central Intelligence Agency (CIA), 27, 317, 319
Charter 77, in Czechoslovakia. *See also* Civic Forum
Budapest School support for, 75
development of, 157–158
government reprisals for, 158–159, 165–167
Helsinki Final Act and, 5, 14, 158, 165, 206
KSS-KOR representatives meet with, 159, 166, 170, 173
Movement for Civil Liberties and, 161
on nonviolent action, 9
proclamation praising 1956 Hungarian uprising and, 85
signatories and declaration of, 151, 164–165, 201–202
talks between government and, 175
Vaculík as signer of, 167, 168, 169–170

Charter 91, in Hungary, 81
Charter of Workers' Rights, Poland (1979), 23, 34, 39
Chernenko, Konstantin U., 57
Chernobyl disaster (1986), 9–10, 219, 237, 242, 378, 380, 387, 388
"Chinese solution," 112, 126, 137, 138, 139
Chirot, Daniel, 7
Chivers, C. J.
on opposition to Saakashvili, 368
on planning and organization for Ukrainian protests, 396–398, 400–401
on Ukrainian presidential election of 2004, 382, 383, 384, 391–394
on Yushchenko's candidacy, 409–411
on Yushchenko's inauguration, 415
on Yushchenko's poisoning, 407
on Yushchenko's victory, 411–414
Christian Democrats, in Hungary, 80, 103
Christopher, Warren, 289
Churchill, Winston D., 2, 11, 302
Church of Rome. *See* Roman Catholic Church
Citizens Committee of 100, Poland, 60
Citizens' Movement, Latvia, 231
City of Heroes, 108. *See also* Leipzig, East Germany
Civic Forum (Občanské Fórum), Czechoslovakia
coordination of nationwide collective nonviolent action by, 184
Dubček and, 186
East Germany's New Forum compared to, 195
general strike and, 192–194
government talks with, 189, 194
Havel and formation of, 203–204
on Husák's coalition government, 199
meets with Adamec, 192
Public Against Violence as partner with, 181
reaches out to military, 196
as speaker for Czechoslovak people, 180

Ten Days in Czechoslovakia (1989) and, 14, 162, 164
Civil disobedience. *See also* Noncooperation
electoral fraud in Georgia and, 17, 341, 354
Lithuanian independence declaration as, 230
against Milošević in Serbia, 16, 295–297, 313, 314, 321
Miniotaitė and, 253–254
in Poland, 19, 47
in Ukraine, 382, 384, 399, 400, 408, 417–418
Civilian defense, nonviolent, 232–233, 234, 236
Civilian militia, in Czechoslovakia, 191
Civil resistance, 8–9, 23, 121, 383. *See also* Nonviolent civil resistance
Clandestine publications. *See* Samizdat
Clines, Francis X., 338, 382, 387, 392
Clinton, Bill, 294, 301, 302–303, 327
Club for Socialist Restructuring, 174. *See also* Obroda
Club for the Defense of the Environment (Videz Aizsardzibas Klubs, VAK), Latvia, 218, 223
Coastal Worker (Polish magazine), 34, 36, 39
Cohen, Roger, 291, 295, 308, 309, 311
Collective nonviolent action. *See also* Nonviolent civil resistance; *Samizdat*
in Czechoslovakia, 184
in Eastern Europe, 8–9
in Poland, 11–12
Wałęsa on, 386
worldwide, Kaufman on widening use of, 417–419
Comecon, dissolution of, 210
Comenius, John Amos, 163, 206, 208
Committee for the Defense of the Unjustly Prosecuted (VONS), Czechoslovakia, 157, 166
Committee for the Workers' Defense. *See* Komitet Obrony Robotników
Commonwealth of Lithuania and Poland, 212

Communist party. *See also* Polish United Workers' Party; Socialist United Party of Germany
Baltic popular fronts and, 226–227
in Czechoslovakia, cedes control of newspapers, 189
in Czechoslovakia, conference on changing structure of, 205
in Czechoslovakia, factions emerge in, 153, 174, 183–184
in Czechoslovakia, hard-line on demonstrations by, 176–177, 183
in Czechoslovakia, hesitations on reforms by, 171
in Czechoslovakia against a general strike, 188
dissolution in Hungary, 73, 79, 81
East Germany ends role in government of, 143
in Estonia, Moscow party congress (1988) and, 221
governing Czechoslovakia, resignation of, 152
in Hungary, financing free elections, 99
in Hungary, reformers inside, 75, 78, 91–92
in Latvia, Moscow party congress (1988) and, 222
Moscow nineteenth conference (1988), 221, 222, 224, 225, 226, 246
in Poland, decline of, 20, 51
in Poland, economic crisis and, 64
in Poland, elections of 1989 and, 30
in Poland, round-table talks and, 65
in Poland, Solidarity on role of, 44
in Poland, Solidarity recognized by, 29
Prague Spring vs. Velvet Revolution and, 197–198
seizes control in Hungary, 72
in the Soviet Union, Gorbachev's perestroika and, 27–28
of Soviet Union, Lithuania's secession from, 229

takes power in Czechoslovakia (1948), 150, 151
waning of ideological commitment to, 7
Confederation of Independent Poland (KPN), 24
Conference on Security and Co-operation in Europe (CSCE), 4–5, 157, 210, 277
Confessing Church, Germany, 109
Corruption, in Georgia, 372–375
Cosic, Dobrica, 309, 313, 325
Council of Baltic States, 230
Council of Ministers, East Germany, 131, 132, 135, 141
Craxi, Bettino, 172
Creative unions
  in Estonia, 221
  in Latvia, 222, 245
Croatia
  as Balkan nation, 285
  Casaroli visit to, 172
  Dayton Agreement (1995) and, 301
  ethnic tensions and war in, 15–16
  independence movement in, 288, 298
  Milošević and, 327, 328
  Nazi collaborators kill Serbs in, 286, 287
Croats, Catholic, 15, 285, 287, 291, 297, 328
Czech Children, 173
Czechoslovakia. *See also* Brezhnev Doctrine; Prague Spring (1968)
  border closed to East Germans, 122
  Charter 77 development/ reprisals, 5, 157–159, 164–167
  crushing of Prague Spring, 2, 3, 154–156
  demonstrations for reforms in, 173–177
  East Germans emigrating through, 98, 131, 132, 178
  Gorbachev and perestroika effects on, 159–160
  Havel sworn in as president, 163
  Helsinki Final Act and, 157
  Hungarian territory ceded after World War I to, 72
  Hungary's opening of the iron curtain and, 78, 91
  "Just a Few Sentences" and, 161

key players in, 168–169, 185–186, 200–204
Munich conference (1938) on, 150
party leadership changes expected, 189–191
Polish samizdat publications and civil resistance in, 24
Prague Autumn (1989), 160–161
Prague Spring (1968), 153–154
President Havel delivers New Year address, 199, 205–208
protesters ask for moral reparations, 196–198
protesters call for communist leaders to step down, 184, 186–188
quick facts about, 151–152
samizdat publications and pro-democracy movements in, 84, 167, 169–170
6,000 strike committees ready general strike in, 192–195
under Stalinism, 150, 152–153
Ten Days of revolution in (1989), 13–14, 161–163, 177–184
"Ten Points Manifesto" and underground publications, 156–157
the Vatican vs. the communists in, 170–172
Warsaw Pact dissolution and, 209–210
Czech Republic, 204, 206

Darnton, John
  assigned to cover Polish strikes, 39
  on martial law in Poland, 26, 46, 49–51
  on Polish labor crisis (1980), 37, 40–41
  on riot police and Rural Solidarity, 25–26, 42–43
  on Solidarity's first convention (1981), 44, 45–46
Daugava River hydroelectric power project, Latvia, 218
Day of Shame, Czechoslovakia, 156
Dayton Agreement (1995), 286, 288, 289, 290, 292, 301

Declaration on the Rights of the Peoples of Russia (1917), 214
Decolonization, Baltic activists on, 10–11, 218, 260
Democracy Now! (Demokratie Jetzt), East Germany, 120
Democratic Awakening (Demokratischer Aufbruch), East Germany, 120, 121, 144
Democratic Initiative, Czechoslovakia, 157, 161, 184
Democratic League of Kosovo (DLK), 292, 301
Democratic Union of Scientific Workers, Hungary, 76
Democratic Youth, Hungary, 76
Democratization. *See also specific countries*
  Gorbachev on, 9, 75, 217, 226, 244, 245, 246, 338, 380
Demonstrations. *See also* Calendar demonstrations; Nikolai Church; Noncooperation; Nonviolent protest and persuasion; *specific countries*
  commemorating "victims of Stalinism," 143–144
  in Czechoslovakia, police break up, 176–177
  East German use of, 109
  in East Germany (1989), 107–108, 121–122, 123–124
  in East Germany, government acceptance of, 128, 135, 141
  in East Germany, violent police response to, 125, 126, 140
  in Estonia, Singing Revolution, 221
  in Georgia, Rose Revolution and, 340, 341
  largest in East Germany, 129–130
  in Latvia honoring deportees to Siberia, 222
  nonviolent, in Georgia, 16–17
  in Poland, 21, 25–26, 42–43
  for reform in Czechoslovakia, 173–175

on reunification of the two Germanys, 146
in Ukraine, Orange Revolution and, 393, 394, 403, 405
in Ukraine, Rukh activities and, 381
Dialog 89 (Czechoslovak journal), 174
Dienstbier, Jiři, 196, 198, 199
Dimitruk, Natalia, 384, 399, 407
Dionne, E. J., Jr., 171, 172
Diuk, Nadia, 229, 230
Djindjic, Zoran
  as key player in Serbia, 306–307
  Milošević's arrest and, 328, 329
  Otpor and, 313
  Serbian elections (1999) and, 304–305
  Serbian noncooperation and, 290
  supporters of, *318*
Draskovic, Vuk, 304–305, 307–308, 310, 313, 315, 329
Dubček, Alexander
  Action Program of reforms under, 154
  allowed interview with Western media, 173
  Bratislava rally and, 184, 187, 190
  calls for communist leader resignations, 186, 187
  debates over Stalinism and, 153
  as Federal Assembly Speaker, 163, 205
  Havel and, 189, 200
  as key player in Czechoslovakia, 185–186
  meets with Civic Forum, 162
  Prague Spring and, 14, 90, 151, 164, 177
  Soviet-forced resignation of, 155, 183
  students call for reinstatement of, 182
  as symbol of Prague Spring, 198
Dubček, Stefan, 185
Dubček's Sunday, 155

Eastern Europe. *See also specific countries*
  Brezhnev Doctrine and communist consolidation in, 3
  collective nonviolent action in, 8–9
  Communists take control of, 2–3
  definition of, 1
  Helsinki "watch" committees in, 5

holes in iron curtain around, 10–11
ideas and revolution in, 5–7
proclamation (1986) on cross-border awareness in, 76
Roman Catholic Church's moral and spiritual encouragement to, 171, 172
Schmemann on government changes in, 194–195
sharing samizdat publications in, 6, 24, 76, 156, 157, 167, 417
theories become reality in, 9–10
Western economic markets and, 7
East Germany. *See also* Berlin Wall
activist intellectuals in, 84
Berlin Wall collapse and reunification demands in, 142–145
Berlin Wall opening, 133–137
civil resistance in Czechoslovakia vs., 153
condemns its role in Warsaw Pact invasion of Czechoslovakia, 199
fears of free emigration from, 114–116
fortieth anniversary celebration demonstrations, 120–122, 125–126
Gorbachev on not interfering in affairs of, 117, 119
Havel on freedom fight in, 208, 209
Hungary's opening of iron curtain and, 9, 13, 73, 77–78, 91, 98–101
key players in, 112–113, 118–119
mass demonstrations across, 126–130
Pastors' Movement in, 13, 108–110, 122–124
peaceful revolution leads to party coup, 137–142
post–World War II creation of, 106, 108
quick facts about, 107–108
reunification with West Germany, 145–148
"revolution from below," 130–133

samizdat publications in, 24, 113, 120, 128
Soviet military in, 2, 210
staying to change things in, 111, 113–114
travel restrictions eased for, 6–7
Warsaw Pact and, 210
Economy/economic conditions. *See also* Strikes
centralized, in East Germany, 108
in Czechoslovakia, 152
in Czechoslovakia, civil society groups and, 175
in Czechoslovakia, general strike and, 188
in Czechoslovakia, Gorbachev's policies and, 159
in Czechoslovakia, Havel on honesty about, 204
in Czechoslovakia under Jakeš, 156, 173
in Georgia, 374
in Hungary, government reforms and, 92–94
in Hungary under Soviet control, 74
in Poland, Gierek's government and, 21–22
in Poland, round-table talks and, 65–66
in Poland, strikes of 1980s and, 28
in Poland during late 1970s, 24
in Poland under martial law, 26–27
in Serbia, opposition to Milošević and, 290
in Serbia, opposition to Milošević by, 302
Soviet encouragement of participation in Western markets and, 7
stagnation in communist-bloc countries, 3
stagnation in Soviet Union, 9
Edice Petlice (Padlocked Editions), Czechoslovakia, 156, 167, 168, 169–170, 201
Eglitis, Olgerts, 222
Emigration. *See* Protest emigration
Engelberg, Stephen, 67, 68–69, 337
Environmental activists
in Baltic states, 218–219, 224, 226, 237
in East Germany, 106, 108, 121
in Hungary, 77

Environmental Protection Club, Estonia, 218
Erlanger, Steven
on Belgrade police and protesters, 331
on crackdowns against Serbian opposition, 289
on economic effect of NATO bombing Serbia, 294
on independent Ukraine's ties to Moscow, 382
on Milošević's arrest, 297, 327, 328–330
on Milošević's campaign against NATO, 316–320
on opposition boycott of Serbian runoff election, 321–323
on opposition groups on ousting Milošević, 304, 307–308
on Otpor activities in Serbia, 294–295, 308–310, 312–314
on Serbian election of 2000, 295–296, 314–316
on striking miners defying Serbian police, 324–325
on third party sanctions against Serbia, 290
Esstimaa Rahvarinne (Estonian Popular Front), 220–222
Estonia. *See also* Baltic states
chaffing at Soviet authority over, 242–244
Declaration of Sovereignty by, 227, 252
declares independence (1990), 266
independence treaty with Russia (1920), 214
interfront group in, 231
Lithuania's declaration of independence and, 230
nationalist activity goes mainstream in, 245–249
Popular Front and Communist Party in, 226–227
Popular Front and independence for, 220–222, 247–249
public rallies and independence for, 14–15
Soviet phosphorite mining plans for, 218, 243
transition to Estonian Republic (1990), 230

Estonian Independence Party, 227
Estonian National Independence Party, 221
Estonian Supreme Soviet, 221, 222, 227
European Community, 104
European Parliament, 382, 385, 392, 393, 394
European Union
Czech Republic and Slovak Republic join, 209
Dayton Agreement and, 289
ethnic conflict in Kosovo and, 293–294, 301
Georgia and, 372
Hungary joins (2004), 81, 104
Ukraine and, 395, 403, 404, 406, 412, 416, 418
Evangelical Church, Estonia, 212
Evangelical Church, Germany, 108–109, 113–114. *See also* Nikolai Church
Exit. *See* Protest emigration

Fairbanks, Charles J., 342, 352, 363
Federal Assembly, Czechoslovakia, 14, 163, 196, 199, 205
Federal Republic of Germany (FDR). *See* West Germany
Fein, Esther B.
on Baltic popular fronts appeal to UN, 254–255
on Baltic Way human chain, 256–259
on Molotov-Ribbentrop Pact, 239
on popularly-based Baltic movements, 226
on Soviet-Georgian relationship, 336
on Soviets crushing Georgian resistors, 345
on Taurinskas and Soviet ground forces, 234–235
Feminists
in East Germany, 13, 107, 108, 120–121
Ferdinand, Archduke Francis, 286, 287
"Few Sentences, A," on democratization in Czechoslovakia, 152, 161, 169, 174, 175
Fiatal Demokraták Szövetsége (FIDESz), 76

Finland, 214, 215, 229, 280, 281
First Republics (Baltic states, 1918–1949), 214–215, 216, 223, 231, 239, 246, 252, 260, 265, 266
Flying University
    Hungary, 84
    Poland, 23, 39
Folk songs and folklore. *See also* Singing Revolution
    Baltic festivals of, 214, 220, 221, 226, 246, 257
    Baltic mass protests and, 255
    Baltic states' independence and, 213, 237
For a New Georgia (coalition), 339, 352–354, 357
Foreign policy. *See* Brezhnev Doctrine; Gorbachev, Mikhail S.
Forest Brotherhoods (Baltic states), 216
France, 106, 143, 148, 150, 151
Franco, Francisco, 65
Franz Joseph, emperor of Hapsburg Empire, 12, 72
Frederick III, 106
Free Democrats, Hungary. *See* Alliance of Free Democrats
Freedom League, Lithuania, 223, 226, 227
Freedom Monument demonstrations, Latvia (1987), 219
Free German Youth (Freie Deutsche Jugend, or FDJ), 118, 119
Friends of Czechoslovak-Polish Solidarity, 159, 166
Fromkin, David, 285, 287
Führer, Christian
    as key player in East Germany, 112–113
    on mass demonstrations, 123
    as Nikolaikirche activist pastor, 109
    Pastors' Movement and, 13, 124
    prayers for peace at Nikolai Church and, 123
    as scholarly activist, 5
    on staying to change East Germany, 111
Fusion, Gorbachev policy on, 217

Galaychuk, Vadym S., 382, 390
Gall, Carlotta
    on Milošević's arrest, 297
Gamsakhurdia, Zviad K., 335–336, 338–339, 343, 348, 350, 366, 370
Gandhi, Indira, 53
Gandhi, Mohandas K., 22–23, 44, 47
"Gandhi" (film), 233
Garton Ash, Timothy, 6
    on alterations in Poland vs. Hungary, 12
    on police force against East German demonstrations, 121
    on transformation in Czechoslovakia, 13–14, 161, 178, 184, 203
    on writers for Czechoslovak samizdat publications, 156–157, 167
Gazeta Wyborcza (Election gazette), Poland, 27, 47, 63
Gdańsk, Poland
    Jaruzelski and strikes in, 48
    labor strikes in, 24–25, 28, 30, 34–36, 37, 40–41, 58
    Solidarity formed in, 20
    worker demonstrations (1970) in, 21
Gdańsk accord (1980), 25, 58
Gediminas, Grand Duke of Lithuania, 224
General strike(s). *See also* Noncooperation
    called in Latvia by interfront group, 232
    calls in Ukraine for, 391, 393
    Czechoslovakia (1989), 152, 162, 179, 180, 182, 193–194, 204, 207
    Czechoslovak industrial workers and, 188, 195
    East Germany (1953), 108
    New Forum threatens East Germany with, 146
    in Poland (1981), 43, 50–51
    preparations in Czechoslovakia for, 192–193
    second threatened in Czechoslovakia, 199
    in Serbia (2000), 296, 321, 326
Genscher, Hans-Dietrich, 100, 146
Georgia
    calls for Shevardnadze's resignation, 353–355
    glasnost and nationalism in, 245
    independence of, 338–339
    key players in, 360, 367–368
    Kmara youth movement in, 336, 340–341, 342, 343, 355, 356, 359, 360, 364, 366, 370
    Lithuania's declaration of independence and, 230
    moves toward independence, 338
    nationalism in, 252
    new parliament takes office carrying roses, 341–342
    nonviolent demonstrations and independence for, 16–17
    opponents against seating of another Shevardnadze government, 358–359, 360–361
    parliamentary elections (2003), 351–353
    popular front in, 238
    postmortem on Shevardnadze's resignation, 363–365
    quick facts about, 335–336
    rival factions disagree on goals for, 344–347
    Rose Revolution in, 339–340
    before Russian rule, 334
    under Russian rule, 334, 336
    Saakashvili confronts rebel leader, 369–371
    Saakashvili presidency, 342–343
    Saakashvili's mandate to clean up government in, 366, 368–369
    Shevardnadze returns to lead, 348–351
    Shevardnadze's party declared 2003 winner in, 355–358
    under Soviet control, 336–338
    Ukrainian revolution compared to revolution in, 392
    uphill battle for, 371–375
Georgievsk, Treaty of (1783), 334, 335
Gerasimov, Gennadi I., 10, 229
Geremek, Bronislaw, 5, 22, 25, 35, 62
Gerlach, Manfred, 138, 141
German Democratic Republic (GDR). *See* East Germany
German Evangelischekirche, 108–109
Germans
    in Baltic states, 212, 214, 216
    in Czechoslovakia, 150, 151
Germany. *See also* East Germany; National Socialists; West Germany
    dismemberment of Czechoslovakia and, 150, 151
    dominance over Poland, 12
    Hungary's World War I alliance with, 72
    invades Yugoslavia (1941), 287
    on Poland's restoration, World War II and, 19
    post–World War II division of, 106
    withdrawal of Allied occupation forces from, 148
Gethsemane Church, East Berlin, 122, 125
Gierek, Edward
    interned by Jaruzelski under martial law, 49
    Kania replaces, 26, 45, 46
    Lenin shipyard strike (1980) and, 38
    meets with Pope John Paul II, 32–33
    permission for papal visit by, 31
    Polish labor crisis (1980) and, 37, 40, 41
    quasi-liberalization and modernization in Poland under, 21–22
Gimes, Miklos, 97
Glasnost
    in Czechoslovakia, 173, 174
    in East Germany, 114, 139
    Gorbachev on, 5, 9–10, 55, 75, 171, 217, 338, 380–381
    in Hungary, 85
    nationalism in Baltic states and, 15, 219, 220, 222, 224, 225, 227, 228, 237, 242–245, 256, 281
    The New York Times on Bloody Sunday and, 234
Glemp, Jozef Cardinal, 53–54
Glenny, Misha, 293
Goclowski, Tadeusz, 64
Gomulka, Wladyslaw, 21, 41
Goodwin, Jeff, 134–135
Gorani (Mountain People Highlanders), in Serbia, 285

Gorbachev, Mikhail S.
See also Brezhnev Doctrine; Glasnost; *Perestroika*; Sinatra doctrine
  Baltic states and, 217–218, 248, 251
  on Baltic states and Soviet Union, 229, 243
  Bloody Sunday (1991) and, 233, 268, 271, 272
  challenge by Eastern European activist intellectuals to, 85
  coming to power, *The Times* on, 56–58
  coup against, 235–236, 274–275
  on coup's effects on reform, 277–278
  on decisions about East German affairs, 117, 119, 148
  democratization in East Germany and, 109, 134–135
  democratization in Hungary and, 81, 87
  on East German upheaval effects for, 138
  40th anniversary of East German state and, 121–122, 125
  Georgia's independence and, 338, 344, 345
  Grósz talks on Soviet interventions with, 90–91
  Honecker loses ally of, 140
  Honecker's distrust of, 118
  Hungarian anniversary of 1956 uprising (1989) and, 102–103
  independence movement in Georgia and, 16
  Latvian petition on independence to, 213
  on Latvia's independence declaration, 231
  on Lithuanian independence, 264, 265
  on nationalist excesses in Baltic states, 228
  and new thinking, 9
  Polish elections of 1989 and, 30
  Polish transition to democracy and, 67, 68
  political liberalization in Czechoslovakia and, 173, 206
  political reforms (1990) by, 230
  Pozsgay on innovations of, 93
  Prague visit by, 171
  Radio Free Europe and, 6
  on recognition of Solidarity, 29
  rejects Brezhnev doctrine, 30, 67–68, 109, 160, 163, 229
  return to Moscow after coup attempt, 236
  sends Yakovlev to Lithuania, 225
  Shevardnadze and, 362
  Shevardnadze on, 351
  transition to democracy in Hungary and, 13
  turmoil in Czechoslovakia and Bush meeting with, 189, 191
  on Ukrainian independence, 380–381
  U.S. senators letters on Lithuanian independence to, 224
  Warsaw Pact dissolution and, 209–210
Gorbunovs, Anatolijs, 214, 267
Gorin, Bogdan N., 381
Gosizdat (official) publications, 5, 156, 167. See also *Samizdat*
Goulash Communism, in Hungary, 87
Grantins, Linards, 218, 239
Great Dukedom of Lithuania, 212
Greenberg, Ilan, 370, 371–375
Greenhouse, Steven, 193, 209–210
GreenJolly (Granzioly, Ukrainian rock band), 384, 398–399
Green Party, East Germany, 121
Gromyko, Andrei A., 57
Grósz, Károly
  commemorations of 1848 and 1956 and, 89
  Hungarian government restructuring and, 79, 91–92
  Németh distances self from, 78
  reform efforts in Hungary by, 75, 77, 93–94
  replaces Kádár as premier, 86, 87, 97
  talks with Gorbachev on Soviet interventions, 90–91, 160
Grudzien, Zladislaw, 49
Gysi, Gregor, 143

Hackenburg, Helmut, 127
Hager, Kurt, 130, 140, 141
Hájek, Jiři, 158
Hanisch, Gunter, 144, 145
Hankiss, Elemer, 72, 81
Hapsburg, Otto von, 95
Hapsburg Empire, 12, 19, 72, 152, 159, 173. See also Austria-Hungary
Harden, Blaine, 294
Hart, Albert Bushnell, 287
Hartsough, David, 292–293, 294
Havel, Václav. See also Edice Petlice
  addresses student demonstrators, 181, 182
  arrests and imprisonment of, 157, 159, 165, 166, 173, 176
  Charter 77 and, 158, 164, 201–202
  as Civic Forum leader, 162–163, 180
  on coal miners' support, 183
  Czechoslovak industrial workers and, 188
  and Dubček in Wenceslas Square, 186, 189
  elected president, 163, 205
  on end of Brezhnev Doctrine, 10
  on general strike, 193
  interviewed on Hungarian television, 178
  as key player in Czechoslovakia, 200–205
  New Year (1990) address to Czechoslovakia, 207–208, 209
  as nonorganizational initiator of Charter 77, 14
  on nonviolent action, 207
  offers limited amnesty as transition to democracy, 205–206
  publicly associates with popular cause, 161
  recognizing contributions of students, 186–187
  refuses passport to Sweden, 184
  as samizdat publisher, 175
  as scholarly activist, 6
  Soviet television requests interview with, 198
  speaking in Prague (1989), *201*
  Yushchenko's inauguration and, 385

Hedges, Chris, 289–290, 291, 297, 299–300, 317, 323
Hegenbart, Rudolf, 191
Heldenstadt (City of Heroes), 108, 109. See also Leipzig, East Germany
Helsinki '86 (human rights group), 213, 218, 219–220, 222, 239, 244
Helsinki Citizens Assembly, Hungary, 81
Helsinki Final Act/Accords (1975)
  Carter on Brezhnev's threats to Solidarity and, 67
  Carter's affirmation of human rights of, 10–11, 27, 55, 67
  Charter 77 inspired by, 14, 158, 165, 206
  Czechoslovakia and, 157
  Czechoslovaks' criticism of Prague regime on human rights and, 163
  Havel on disregard for, 157, 200–201
  human rights in Hungary and, 75
  mass deportations of Latvians to Siberia under, 15
  negotiation of, 4–5
  reprisals for Charter 77 in Czechoslovakia and, 159
  widening use of collective nonviolent action and, 417–419
Helsinki Watch Committees, 5, 26, 224
Helvey, Robert L., 295, 309
Hempel, Johannes, 127–128
Herger, Wolfgang, 139
Hermann, Joachim, 140, 141
Herzegovina. See Bosnia-Herzegovina
Hijra. See Protest emigration
Hint, Mati, 243
Historical Justice Committee, Hungary, 91, 94
Hitler, Adolf, 15, 109, 215, 280. See also Molotov-Ribbentrop Pact
Hlavsa, Milan, 157
Hofmann, Paul, 169–170
Holbrooke, Richard, 288, 289, 301, 303
Honecker, Erich. See also "Chinese solution"
  arrests of senior staff of, 143
  authorizes refugees' travel to the West, 131, 139–140
  East German emigrations and, 117, 119

East German press on abuses under, 135
40th anniversary demonstrations and, 125–126, 148
Gorbachev and, 121
as key player in East Germany, 118–119
Politburo meetings Oct. 1989 and, 140–141
resignation of, 128–129, 137, 141, 176
shoot-to-kill orders signed by, 119, 126, 138, 139
on Soviet deployment of short-range missiles, 123
on stopping demonstrations, 127
Horáček, Michal, 186
Horn, Gyula, 73, 78, 98, 100
Horthy, Nicholas, 72
Hrushevsky, Michaelo, 379
Human chain
across East Germany, 135, 160, 178
across Prague, 193
across Ukraine, 378, 381
in Baltic states (1988), 226
Baltic Way, from Estonia to Lithuania, 15, 213, 228, 255–259, 257
as collective nonviolent action, 8
Father Jerzy's memorial in Poland and, 53
in Georgia, 340, 355
in Ukraine, 378, 381
Human rights. *See also* Helsinki Final Act/ Accords
activists in Eastern Europe, connections among, 76
Carter on, 10–11, 27, 55, 67
KSS-KOR on egalitarian ideals and, 23
The Times on Gorbachev and, 57
Hungarian Democratic Forum (Magyar Demokrata Forum, MDF), 73, 76, 80, 103
Hungarians
in Czechoslovakia, 150, 151
in Serbia, 285
Hungarian Socialist Workers Party (Magyar Szocialista Munkáspárt, MSzMP), 72, 75, 82, 95
Hungarian Workers Party, 72
Hungary. *See also* Austria-Hungary
Brezhnev Doctrine demise and revisiting 1956, 90–91
commemorating 1848 in, 87–90
condemns its role in Warsaw Pact invasion of Czechoslovakia, 177, 199
Eastern Europeans on 1956 uprising in, 84–86
East German government fears of emigrations through, 114–116
economic and political changes in, 91–94
effects of Poland's round-table agreement in, 29
end of Brezhnev Doctrine and, 10
harbingers of change in, 76–77
Havel on freedom fight in, 208, 209
history of governmental structures of, 72
key players in, 89, 95
multipower politics in, 78–81
news in Czechoslovakia about events in, 163
opening of iron curtain by, 9, 13, 73, 77–78, 91, 98–101, 131, 138, 139
opposition leaders visiting Czechoslovak counterparts, 177–178
Polish samizdat publications and civil resistance in, 24
quick facts about, 73
reform-minded communists and, 75–76, 86–87
rehabilitation of Imre Nagy, 94–98
self-determination in, 12–13
"social contract" advocated in, 74–75
as Soviet satellite, 74
Soviet withdrawal from, 103–105
33rd anniversary of 1956 uprising, 101–103
uprising of 1956, 2, 73–74, 82–83
Warsaw Pact dissolution and, 209–210
Hunger strikes. *See also* Nonviolent intervention.
in Georgia, 338, 345, 347
Havel on living in Truth and, 167
in Hungary, 91
in Poland, 23, 68
in Serbia, 292
in Ukraine, 383, 390, 397
Hus, Jan, 152, 155, 173
Husák, Gustáv
calls for resignation of, 182, 187
campaigns of disinformation against Charter 77 signers, 165
Civic Forum's ousting of, 162, 180, 205
on independent organizations as criminal, 158
ousting of Dubček in 1968 by, 198
purges from Czechoslovak communist party by, 151, 157
resignation of, 199
re-Stalinization of Czechoslovakia under, 155, 206

Ignalina nuclear reactor, Lithuania, 219, 225, 226, 242
Illegal publications. *See Samizdat*
IME (Ise Majandav Eesti) economic proposal, four-man, 219, 221, 226–227, 247
Independent Peace Initiative (Nezávislé Mírové Sdružení, or NMS), Czechoslovakia, 159, 173
Independent Smallholders, Hungary, 80, 103–104
Independent Women's Association, East Germany, 120–121
Initiative for Peace and Human Rights (Initiative für Frieden und Menschenrechte), East Germany, 120
Intellectual activists. *See* Activist intellectuals
Intellectual centers, in Baltic states, 214
Inter-Factory Strike Committee (MKS), Poland, 25, 35, 37, 38, 42
Intermovement (interfronts, *interdvizhenie*) groups, 231–232, 233, 268
International Covenant on Civil and Political Rights, 5
International Covenant on Social and Cultural Rights, 5
International Institute of Strategic Studies, 103
International Monetary Fund, 290, 352, 365, 372
International Republican Institute, 352
International Students Day, Czechoslovakia, 178
International Tribunal for the former Yugoslavia, 288, 297–298, 328
Iron curtain. *See also* Berlin Wall
Carter's affirmation of human rights of Helsinki Accords and, 10–11
East Germans' escape through Hungary, 110
Hungary's opening of, 9, 13, 73, 77–78, 91, 98–101
Pan-European Picnic (1989) and, 95
Isakov, Miodrag, 296, 321, 322
Italy, 150, 151, 287
Ivanov, Igor S., 363, 371
Īvans, Dainis, 265–266
Izetbegović, Alija, 289
Izvestia (Soviet newspaper), 30, 62, 241, 278

Jakeš, Miloš
blamed for violent reprisals, 205
calls for resignation of, 187, 190
Civic Forum demands resignation of, 162, 180, 182
Czechoslovaks' lack of vindictiveness toward, 198
demonstrators' description of isolation of, 176
on demonstrators seeking chaos and anarchy, 183
normalization under, 173
purges from Czechoslovak communist party by, 151
resignation of, 192, 194
Stalinist dictatorship under, 156
Tagliabue on potential replacement of, 195
threatens that protests not permitted, 161
Jaruzelski, Wojciech
arrest of Kuroń by, 36
economic and political reform policies of, 56
elections of 1989 and, 30, 62
on Father Jerzy's killing, 27, 53
general strike of 1981 and, 43

as key player in Poland, 48
on martial law in Poland, 67, 69
martial law in Poland under, 26–27, 46, 49, 50–51, 63
partial lifting of martial law by, 52
round-table talks (1989) and, 65
Solidarity and, 20, 28, 29, 171
steps down as Poland's President, 68–69
Jews
in Baltic states, 212, 214
Confessing Church, Germany, and, 109
in Lithuania, 214
murdered in Baltic states during World War II, 216
Polish, World War II casualties among, 19–20
John Paul II, Pope. *See also* Wojtyla, Karol
on Catholic persecution in communist countries, 172
celebrates mass in Warsaw's Victory Square, 20, 24
Czechoslovaks petition inviting visit by, 170–171
Eastern European resistance to communism and, 151, 159
as first papal visitor to communist country, 31–32, *33*
Havel invites to Czechoslovakia, 207
second visit to Poland (1983) by, 26, 51
Jones, Stephen, 339, 340, 341, 342, 364, 366
Jøsten, Josef, 154
Judah, Tim, 297, 331–332
"Just a Few Sentences" (Několik vět), 152, 161, 169

Kádár, János
death of, 79, 94–95
decentralization of Hungarian economy, 74
forced to step aside as Hungarian premier, 86, 87, 93
Soviet installation as Hungarian leader, 82
uprising of 1956 and, 73, 82–83
Kahout, Pavel, 165
Kalanta, Roman, 223–224
Kallas, Teet, 243

Kamarek, Walter, 195
Kamm, Henry
on changing economics and political changes in Hungary, 91–94
on commemorating Hungary's 1848 revolution, 88–90
on communist party and democratic opposition, 78
on development of democracy in Hungary, 79
on effects of Poland's round-table agreement in Hungary, 29
on flexibility of Hungarian communist leaders, 86–87
on Kádár's funeral, 95
on lack of vindictiveness among victims of Czechoslovak communism, 196–198
on largest demonstration in East Germany, 129–130
on opposition demonstration participation in Hungary, 73
on parallel national celebration in Hungary (1989), 77
on reinterpretation of 1956 Hungarian uprising, 75
on state funerals for 1956 uprising dead, 94, 96–98
Kandelaki, Giorgi, 342, 360
Kania, Stanislaw, 26
Karadžić, Radovan, 289, 290
Karatnycky, Adrian, 229, 230
Kaufman, Michael T., 53–54, 83, 85–86, 417–419
Kazakhstan, 244, 360
Keine Gewalt (no violence), in East Germany, 112, 121, 125, 131, 133
Keller, Bill
on Bloody Sunday events, 234, 270–273
on glasnost and demonstrations in Baltic states, 244–245
on Gorbachev's declaration of end to Brezhnev Doctrine, 10
on Lithuanian independence, 260, 262–264
on Lithuanian rally for Stalin victims, 240–242
on rival opposition factions in Georgia, 344–345, 346–347

on Soviet leaders' reactions to coup, 277–279
Kennedy, John F., 134
KGB
in Baltic states, 265, 268–269
coup against Gorbachev and, 235–236, 274
Helsinki '86 surveillance by, 222, 240
Latvian Popular Front attacks on, 232, 273
reinforcing Soviet border posts and, 234
surveillance of Baltic protesters by, 242, 244
in Ukraine, 398
Khrushchev, Nikita S., 11, 21, 83, 153, 216–217, 335, 337, 347
Kievan Rus, 377, 386, 387
Kincl, František, 162, 182
King, Martin Luther, Jr., 23, 47
Kis, János
as activist intellectual in Hungary, 75
on democratic opposition and communist party, 78
on elections of 1990, 103
on Free Democrats as responsible opposition, 80
as key player in Hungary, 89
national commemorations of 1848 and 1956 and, 88, 89
proclamation praising 1956 Hungarian uprising and, 85
as scholarly activist, 6
Kiszczak, Czeslaw, 28, 29, 58, 60, 62
Klaus, Václav, 188, 198, 204
Klimova, Rita, 198
Kmara (Enough), Georgia
development of, 340–341, 359
Kandelaki and, 360
nonviolent demonstrations by, 16–17, 356
Shevardnadze meets with, 336, 355
on Shevardnadze's resignation, 364
symbolism used by, 366
Kocáb, Michael, 186
Kohl, Helmut, 143, 144, 146, 147–148, 195
Kohout, Pavel, 158, 165
Kolubara miners' strike, Serbia, 296, 323, 324–325

Komender, Zenon, 54
Komitet Obrony Robotników (Committee for the Workers' Defense, KOR), Poland, 22–23, 36, 37, 41, 63
Komitet Samoobrony Spolecznej (Social Self-Defense Committee, KSS-KOR), Poland
Charter 77 and, 158, 159, 166, 170
Czechoslovakia's VONS and, 157
disbanding of, 26, 44–45
formation of, 23
Lenin shipyard strike (1980) and, 38
as link in union activities, 25
papal visit and, 32
Kommunikat (Communiqué), Poland, 23
Konrád, György "George," 6, 81, 85
Korac, Zarko, 295, 313, 314, 317, 320, 332
Kosovo. *See also* Serbia
alternative (parallel) institutions, 292–293
civil resistance in, 292–293
declares independence, 286, 297, 298
ethnic Albanians in, 287
ethnic tensions and war in, 288, 293–294, 300–304
independence movement in, 15
Milošević and, 327, 328
NATO military strikes in, 16
repression in, 291–292
Kosovo Liberation Army (KLA), 293, 301, 303
Koštunica, Vojislav
Djindjic and, 306–307
opposition to runoff election by, 322–323
as presidential candidate, 314, 315, 318, 319, 320
as Serbian president, 297, 327
striking miners and, 324–325
wins Serbian election, Milošević refuses, 286, 295–296
Kramer, Mark, 235–236
Kravchuk, Leonid, 378, 381–382
Krenz, Egon
cancels Honecker's shoot-to-kill orders, 118, 138, 139
democratization orders by, 136

Gorbachev visit planned by, 130
government restructuring and, 133, 135, 141, 142, 195
halts crushing of Leipzig demonstration, 127
Politburo meetings Oct. 1989 and, 140
replaces Honecker in East Germany, 176
resignation of, 143
Kristof, Nicholas, 384
Kryuchkov, Vladimir, 235–236, 278
KSS-KOR. See Komitet Samoobrony Spolecznej
Kuchma, Leonid D.
presidential election of 2004 and, 383, 385, 389–391, 396, 402, 403, 404, 406
on revolution in Ukraine, 394
on street demonstrations, 395
ties to Moscow, 382
Yanukovich as handpicked successor to, 378, 393
Kundera, Milan, 153
Kuroń, Jacek
as activist intellectual in Poland, 6, 22, 36
arrested for speaking to media, 35
Charter 77 representatives and, 159, 173
elections of 1989 and, 62
on internal forces in overthrowing totalitarianism, 66–67
on KOR- and KSS-KOR-directed civil resistance, 23
as KOR spokesman, 37, 41
round-table talks (1989) and, 29, 61
as Solidarity adviser, 25
Kurti, Albin, 293
Kwaśniewski, Aleksander, 36, 385, 403, 416, 418

Landovsky, Pavel, 166
Landsbergis, Vytautas
Bloody Sunday and, 214, 233–234, 268, 269, 271
on Freedom League attack by police, 226
Gorbachev's pressure on, 230
on Lithuanian independence, 260
Lithuanian independence and, 263, 264
Sajūdis demonstration (1988) and, 224, 225
on unarmed nonviolent resistance, 236
Lange, Bernd-Luntz, 13, 124
Languages
in Baltic states, 212
in Baltic states, interfronts and, 231–232
in Baltic states, nationalism and, 243
in Ukraine, Soviets on, 386
Latvia. See also Baltic states; Latvian Popular Front
black beret attacks in, 232
black berets take over Riga press building, 233
independence treaty with Russia (1920), 214
interfront group in, 231, 232
Lithuania's declaration of independence and, 230
moves toward independence, 252–253
parliamentary approval for independence, 264–267
public rallies and independence for, 14–15
samizdat publications in, 6
Soviet repression in, 216–217
Latvian National Independence Movement (Latvijas Nacionalas Neatkaribas Kustiba, NIML), 222–223, 227, 229, 231, 233
Latvian Popular Front, 222–223, 226–227, 229, 232
Latvian Supreme Soviet, 229, 230
Lauder, Ronald S., 87
Lauluväljak (Song Square) Tallinn, Estonia, 221
League of Independent Trade Unions, Hungary, 76, 78, 79
League of Nations, 214–215
Leavers (Weggeher), from East Germany, 131
Lehmann, Karl, 143
Leipzig, East Germany, 107–108, 108, 129–130, 129, 144–145. See also Nikolai Church
Lenin, Vladimir I., 2, 143, 214, 334
Lenin shipyard. See Gdańsk, Poland
Lennon, John, 202
Letná Plain, Prague, 192
Letter of 100, from Hungarian activist intellectuals, 86
Liberty. See also John Paul II, Pope
history in Poland of, 19, 20
religious, in Poland, 24, 31
totalitarianism in Poland after World War II and, 21–22
Liberty Institute, Georgia, 340–341, 360
Liberty Monument demonstration, Latvia (1987), 239–240. See also Freedom Monument demonstrations, Latvia
Lietuvos Persitvarkymo Sajūdis, 224. See also Sajūdis
Lieven, Anatol, 230, 237, 261, 270
Ligachev, Yegor K., 57, 116
Limited sovereignty, doctrine of, 3, 27. See also Brezhnev Doctrine
Lis, Bogdan, 22, 29
Lithuania. See also Baltic states; Sajūdis
Bloody Sunday (1991) in, 214, 233–234, 268–273
civilian-based defense as national defense policy of, 236
declares independence (1990), 213, 230
independence restored, 259–261, 262–264
independence treaty with Russia (1920), 214
moves toward independence, 252–253
public rallies and independence for, 14–15
samizdat publications in, 6
shunning Soviet rule, 249–251
Soviet military in, 234–235
Unity (Yedinstvo) group in, 231
Lithuania 1991.01.13: Documents, Testimonies, Comments (1992), 234, 269
Lithuanian Church of Rome, 214
Lithuanian Movement for the Support of Perestroika. See Sajūdis
Lithuanian Supreme Soviet, 213, 227, 228, 229, 230
Living Stream, Czechoslovakia, 177
Lohmann, Susan, 113, 127
Lomakin, Viktor P., 189, 191
London Conference (1943), 106
Losonczy, Geza, 91, 97
Lublin Union (1565), 212
Lucan, Matej, 190
Lucas, Edward, 179
Lujans, Modris, 222
Lukács, György, 74–75
Lukasziewicz, Jerzy, 49
Luther, Martin, 106, 108
Lutheran Church, East Germany, 108–109, 111, 113–114. See also Evangelical Church, Germany; Nikolai Church
Lutheran Church, Estonia, 212, 214
Lutheran Church, Latvia, 214

Macedonia, 15, 285, 286, 287, 288, 291, 298, 304
Madisson, Tiit, 244
Magdalenka summit, Poland (1989), 29, 61. See also Round-table talks
Magic Lantern Theater, Prague, 14, 162, 180, 182, 192, 203
Magyars, of Hungary, 72
Maier, Charles A., 111, 120, 127
Major, Laszlo, 76, 90, 91
Maleter, Pal, 78, 94, 97
Malý, Vacláv, 181–182, 184, 191
Markovic, Mirjana, 296, 319, 322
Marovic, Ivan, 305, 308–309, 317, 383, 397
Martial Council for National Redemption, Poland, 49, 51
Masaryk, Tomas G., 152, 163, 206, 208
Masses for Poland, Father Jerzy's, 27, 52–53
Masur, Kurt, 127, 139, 144, 145, 147
Mazowiecki, Tadeusz, 22, 23, 25, 30, 35, 62, 67, 68
McCurry, Michael D., 289
MDF. See Hungarian Democratic Forum
Megyessy, Peter, 94, 96
Memorandum to the Central Committee of the Communist Party of Latvia, 222
Mensheviks, 334
Methods of Nonviolent Action. See Alternative institutions, Boycotts, Civil Disobedience, Demonstrations,

Human Chain, Protest emigration, Strikes, Vigils
Michnik, Adam
  as activist intellectual in Poland, 6, 22
  arrest of, 35
  Charter 77 representatives and, 159, 173
  on ethics of Solidarity's method of seeking social change, 27, 55
  as key player in Poland, 63
  Kuroń and, 36
  Nagy's state funeral/reburial in Hungary and, 78
  on nonviolent action, 12
  proclamation praising 1956 Hungarian uprising and, 86
  round-table talks (1989) and, 29, 65
  as Solidarity adviser, 25
  on Solidarity's consistent rejection of use of force, 47
  state funerals for 1956 uprising dead and, 94
Mickiewiez, Adam, 241
Middle classes, 3, 6–7, 103, 159
Mielke, Erich, 126, 140
Military
  in Czechoslovakia, concerns about coup by, 196
  in Georgia, Rose Revolution and, 341, 342, 343, 358, 362, 371–372
  Soviet, in East Germany, 106, 107
  Soviet, in Hungary, 73, 74
  Soviet, withdrawn from Czechoslovakia, 210
  Soviet, withdrawn from Hungary, 80, 102–105, 210
  in Ukraine, shifting allegiances of, 383–384, 396
  Warsaw Pact, Czechoslovak civil resistance to, 154
  Warsaw Pact, Prague Spring and, 2, 27, 74, 76
Militia Unit for Special Assignments, Soviet. *See* Otryad Militsii Osobovo Naznacheniya
Milošević, Slobodan
  arrest of, 327–330
  campaigns against NATO, 316–320
  ethnic cleansing of Albanians and, 293
  opposition groups on ousting, 304–306, 307–308
  opposition on election of 2000 and, 314–316
  overthrow of, 15–16, 294–297, 331–332
  refuses to honor election results, 298–300, 321
  repression in Kosovo by, 291–292
  Serbian history and, 286
  Serbianization policy of, 300–301
  takes power in Yugoslavia, 288
  violence/ethnic cleansing of Albanians and, 301–302
  Zajedno coalition's opposition to, 289–291
Miniotaitė, Gražina
  on Sąjūdis, 224
  on civilian-based defense as Lithuania's national defense policy, 236
  on civilian defense to Bloody Sunday, 234, 269
  as key player in the Baltic states, 253–254
  on Lithuanian declaration of independence, 230
  on nonviolent civilian resistance, 232
  on public education of civilian defense, 233
Mittag, Gunter, 140, 141, 142
Mkalavishvili, Vasily, 374
MKS (Inter-Factory Strike Committee), Poland, 25, 35
Mlynář, Zdeněk, 158, 165
Modrow, Hans, 141, 142, 143, 144, 146
Modzelewski, Karol, 36
Mohorita, Vasil, 199
Moldova, 230, 252, 285, 360
Molotov, Vyacheslav Mikhailovich, 215, 229, 280, 281, 287
Molotov-Ribbentrop Pact (1939)
  Baltic denunciation of (1979 and 1980), 217
  Baltic states on publishing, 213, 219
  Baltic states' partitioning under, 215, 280–281
  Baltic Way human chain (1989) on, 15, 228
  as grievance in Baltic states, 237
  as illegal, Soviet declaration on, 227, 229–230
  Keller article on, 240–241
  Latvian commemoration (1988) of, 223
  publishing of, 221, 223, 225, 243–244
  Soviet annexation of Baltic states and, 239
  text of, 281–282
  Ukraine and, 380, 388
Montenegro
  as Balkan nation, 285
  independence for, 331
  Kosovo and, 291
  NATO bombing of, 297
  radio broadcasts into Serbia from, 320
  as republic within Yugoslavia, 286, 288, 298
  State Union of Serbia and, 297
Moravia, 150, 151. *See also* Comenius, John Amos
Morawska, Anna, 22
Morawski, Kazimierz, 54
Moscow. *See* Soviet Union
Moscow, Treaty of (1920), 334, 335, 336
Moscow Protocols, on Czechoslovakia, 155, 157, 186
Movement for Civil Liberties (Hnutí za Občanskou Svobodu, or HOS), Czechoslovakia, 161
Movement for the Defense of Human and Civil Rights, Poland, 22
Movement for the Support of Perestroika. *See* Sąjūdis
Muller, Petr, 193
Munich agreement (1938), Czechoslovakia dismemberment and, 150, 151
Muskie, Edmund, 38
Mydans, Seth
  on calls for Shevardnadze's resignation, 353–355
  on Georgia's 2003 election results, 356, 357–358
  on nonviolent change in Georgia, 358
  postmortem on Shevardnadze's resignation, 363–365
  on protests against another Shevardnadze government, 358–359, 360–361
  on Rose Revolution, 339, 340, 342, 343, 372
  on Saakashvili and Abashidze, 370
  on Saakashvili as president, 368–369
  on Shevardnadze's resignation, 361–363
Myers, Steven Lee
  on Dimitruk's civil disobedience on state television, 384–385
  on revolution in Ukraine, 401–404
  on revote in Ukraine, 385, 404–406
  on shifts in Ukraine's state-controlled media, 395
  on Ukrainian presidential election of 2004, 382, 389–391
  on Yushchenko inauguration, 414–417

Nagy, Imre
  commemorating execution of, 93, 102
  execution (1956) of, 82
  Kádár and, 83
  popular Hungarian independence movement and, 12
  rehabilitation of, 94–95
  removed from power, 73
  state funeral and reburial of, 77, 78–79, 87, 91, 96–98, 96
Naimark, Norman M., 126
National Assembly, Hungary, 77, 79–80, 87–88, 103–104
National Democratic Alliance, Hungary, 95
National Democratic Institute for International Affairs, 352, 393
National festivals. *See also* Folk songs and folklore
  in Baltic states (1988), 226
Nationalism. *See also* Popular front(s)
  in Baltic states, expression of, 218–220, 239, 247–249
  in Baltic states, glasnost and, 15, 237
  in Hungary, 77
  in Hungary, 1848 revolution and, 72
  in Ukraine, Soviets on, 386
National Salvation Committee
  in Estonia and Latvia, interfronts and, 233
  in Lithuania, 268, 270, 272–273
National Socialists (Nazis), 19, 109, 150, 337, 380
NATO (North Atlantic Treaty Organization)

Baltic states join, 237
Czechoslovakia joins, 204, 209
Dayton Agreement and, 289
ethnic conflict in Kosovo and, 16, 293–294, 298, 301–302
Helsinki Accords (1975) and, 4–5
Hungary joins, 104
Milošević campaigns against, 316–320
Soviet/U.S. proxy war in Afghanistan and, 4
Warsaw Pact dissolution and, 210
Natural resources, Soviet exploitation in Baltic states of, 218–219, 242–243, 243
Natvijas Tautus Fronte (Latvian Popular Front), 223
Nedovic, Slobodanka, 295, 321
Németh, Miklós, 78, 79, 94, 96, *96*, 98, 102
Nemyria, Hryhoriy M., 403, 413, 414, 416
Neruda, Jan, 170
Network of Free Initiatives, Hungary, 76
Neues Deutschland (East German communist party), 116
Neumann, Vaclav, 177
New Forum (Neues Forum), East Germany
advocating socialist change, 122, 125, 131, 144
communist authorities on ceasing activities by, 124
Czechoslovakia's Civic Forum compared to, 195
demand for legalization of, 128
founding (1989) of, 120
on nonviolent demonstrations, 126
October 7 demonstration and, 140
threatens general strike, 146
New Rights (opposition party), Georgia, 374
News media. *See also* *The New York Times*; Radio; *Samizdat*; Television
in East Germany on Honecker regime abuses, 135
in Georgia, Rose Revolution and, 356, 363–364
Havel on importance of, 202

Kuroń and Michnik arrested for speaking to, 35
in Lithuania, Soviet troops and, 273
official Soviet, on Chernobyl disaster (1986), 9–10
restrictions in Ukraine on, 384, 389
in Serbia, government control of, 295, 310, 317
in Serbia, independent, 315, 325
in Serbia, Milošević and, 289, 290
in Ukraine, Rukh activities and, 381
Western, Dubček allowed interview with, 173
The New York Times. *See also specific reporters*
on civilian defense to Bloody Sunday, 234
on communist party and grass-roots activism, 237
correspondents in Prague for, 181
on East German visa applications (1989), 115
editorial on Gorbachev and Bloody Sunday, 234
editorial on Jaruzelski's declaration of martial law, 47
editorial on Milošević clashes with KLA, 293
editorial on Milošević regime falling, 326–327
editorial on stalemate in Poland (1986), 55
on Estonian Popular Front's first congress, 221
on Father Jerzy's funeral, 27
on Gdańsk striker demands (1980), 25
on Georgia's 2003 parliamentary elections, 353
on Havel as playwright in Czechoslovakia, 202
on independence for Baltic states, 236
on Latvian Popular Front formation, 223
on Lenin shipyard strike in Gdańsk, 38–39
on Lithuanian independence, 260–261
on martial law in Poland, 26

Molotov-Ribbentrop Pact text in, 281–282
publishes "A Cup of Coffee at the Interrogation," 168
on religious restrictions in Poland (1979), 24
on Soviet pressures on Latvia, 231
on U.S. on Soviet annexation of Baltic states, 215
viewing nonviolent transitions through, 17–18
Nicholas I, Czar, 72
Nikolai Church (Nikolaikirche). *See also* Leipzig, East Germany
call for moratorium on marches from, 144–145
demonstrations on reunification and free elections from, 146
large security forces deployed near, 126
as launching point for protests, 138
massive demonstrations (1989) from, 108, 109, 127
Monday candle marches from, 112–113
Pastors' Movement and, 13
the *Wende* begun in, 122–124
NIML. *See* Latvian National Independence Movement
Nixon, Richard M., 4
Nomenklatura, 2–3, 7, 20, 21, 62, 232
Non-Aligned Movement, Yugoslavia, 287–288
Noncooperation
in Baltic states, 216
economic, in Poland, 30
general strike as means for, 43, 108
as nonviolent action, 8, 9
in Poland, emigration as means for, 26, 47
protest emigration as, 107
"Ten Points Manifesto" in Czechoslovakia on, 156
Nonviolent civil resistance. *See also* Civil disobedience; Collective nonviolent action; Demonstrations; Human chain; Nonviolent direct action; Nonviolent struggle; Protest emigration; Strikes
advancing democracy with, 418
in Baltic states, 216
as class of nonviolent action, 8–9
in East Germany, 112, 121, 125, 131, 133
in Georgia, Rose Revolution and, 355–358
in Moscow, 275–276
as technique for change, 386
in Ukraine, Orange Revolution and, 392, 401, 417–419
violent reaction of East German police to, 124
to Warsaw Pact troops in Czechoslovakia, 154–155
Nonviolent collective action. *See* Collective nonviolent action
Nonviolent direct action, 17. *See also* Collective nonviolent action; Nonviolent civil resistance
Nonviolent intervention, 9, 292, 301. *See also* Hunger strikes
Nonviolent protest and persuasion. *See also* Demonstrations; *Samizdat*
in Baltic states, 216
as class of nonviolent action, 8–9
in East Germany, 112, 121, 125, 131, 133
in Georgia, Rose Revolution and, 355–358
in Moscow, 275–276
in Ukraine, Orange Revolution and, 392, 401, 417–419
violent reaction of East German police to, 124
to Warsaw Pact troops in Czechoslovakia, 154–155
Nonviolent revolutions, 1, 17–18. *See also specific countries*
Nonviolent struggle
about, 8
Chivers on, 383
in East Germany, 121
Kosovo Albanians and, 292, 293
Lithuania's civilian defense as, 236
Miniotaitė and, 253
in Poland, 30, 32, 59, 62

pragmatism of, 9, 23
protest emigration
 as, 107
in Serbia, 309, 311
Sharp on, 233
Wałęsa on, 52
Normalization, in
 Czechoslovakia
as Husák's term for
 re-Stalinization, 155,
 157, 161, 164, 167,
 198, 200
Jakeš's maintenance of,
 173, 179
Novotný, Antonin, 153, 183,
 185, 198
Nowa (Polish publishing
 house), 23
Nowina-Konopka, Piotr, 69
NSZZ "Solidarność"
 (Independent Self-
 Governing Union
 Solidarity). *See*
 Solidarity union
Nuclear proliferation,
 treaties on reducing,
 3–4, 10
Nyers, Rezso, 79, 195

Obroda (Rebirth, or
 Revival), 174, 175
October Springtime,
 Poland (1950s and
 1960s), 21
Olszowski, Stefan, 172
"Open Letter to Gustáv
 Husák" (Havel), 157,
 164, 200–201
"Open Letter to Members
 of the Polish United
 Workers' Party,
 An" (Kuroń and
 Modzelewski), 36
Open Society Institute, U.S.,
 359, 418–419
Opletal, Jan, 161, 178
Opposition Round Table
 (Ellenzéki Kerekasztal,
 EKA), Hungary, 78, 79,
 95, 98–99
Orange Revolution, Ukraine,
 17, 382, 385–386,
 398–399, 407, 408. *See
 also* Pora!
Orban, Viktor, 78, 90, 94, 97
Organization for Security
 and Cooperation in
 Europe (OSCE)
Georgia's 2003
 parliamentary
 elections and, 352
Serbian elections (1996)
 and, 290, 299, 300
on Ukrainian news media
 and elections, 395
Ukrainian presidential
 election of 2004 and,
 385, 392, 406, 412
Ostrava, Czechoslovakia,
 demonstrations/strikes
 in, 182, 183, 191

Otpor! (Resistance!), Serbia
influence on Kmara in
 Georgia, 341,
 359, 360
opposition to Milošević
 by, 305–306, 308–
 310, 312–314
overthrow of Milošević
 and, 16, 286,
 294–296, 325–326,
 331–332
rebirth of, 291
training of Pora leaders
 in Ukraine by, 397
Otryad Militsii Osobovo
 Naznacheniya (OMON),
 Soviet Union, 220, 232,
 233, 234, 273, 276
Ottoman Empire, 72, 285,
 334, 344. *See also*
 Serbia
Our Ukraine faction. *See*
 Yushchenko, Viktor A.

Padlocked Editions
 (Edice Petlice),
 Czechoslovakia, 156,
 167, 168, 169–170, 201
Palach, Jan, 155, 173–174
Pan-European Picnic (1989),
 95
Pantović, Nevena, 294
Parade of sovereignties,
 227. *See also* Baltic
 states
Parallel institutions.
 See Alternative
 institutions; Kosovo
Partnership for Peace,
 NATO's, 237
Party of Democratic
 Socialism, East
 Germany, 143
Pastors' Movement, East
 Germany, 8, 13, 109,
 121, 124. *See also*
 Nikolai Church;
 Protestant churches
Pavlicek, Frantisek, 166
Peace groups. *See also*
 Women in Black
in East Germany, 108,
 109, 123–124
Peasant Solidarity (Poland),
 42
People's Militia,
 Czechoslovakia,
 177, 199
People's Party,
 Czechoslovakia, 177
Perestroika. See also Sąjūdis
in Czechoslovakia, 159–
 160, 171, 173, 174,
 189, 206
disintegration of
 Brezhnev Doctrine
 and, 10
in East Germany, 114,
 117, 127, 139, 141
in Georgia, 344, 345,
 346, 347

Gorbachev on, 9, 27–28,
 54–55, 75, 217, 256,
 338, 380
in Hungary, 86
nationalism in Baltic
 states and, 219,
 220, 222, 223, 224,
 224–225, 227, 228,
 230, 234, 237, 243,
 245, 247, 276
use of term banned in
 East Germany, 139
*Perestroika: New Thinking
 for Our Country and the
 World* (Gorbachev), 9
Perlez, Jane, 290, 301,
 302–304
Peters, Janis, 222
Peter the Great, 214, 379
Petofi (Sandor) statue,
 Budapest, 12, 76, 77,
 82, 88
Phosphorite mining,
 Estonia, 218, 219, 243
Pieńkowska, Alina, 35
Pinchuk, Viktor, 402, 403
Plastic People of
 the Universe
 (Czechoslovak rock
 group), 157–158
Plot 301, Hungarian uprising
 for 1956 victims buried
 in, 91, 97–98
Pogrebinsky, Mikhail,
 398, 401
Polach, Martin, 179
Poland. *See also* Gdańsk;
 Solidarity union
alliance of activist
 intellectuals,
 Catholic laity, and
 workers in, 21–24
civil resistance in
 Czechoslovakia vs.,
 153
collective nonviolent
 action in, 11–12,
 419
communist regime in, 2
condemns its role
 in Warsaw Pact
 invasion of
 Czechoslovakia,
 177, 199
East Germans emigrating
 through, 98
election of non-
 communist govern-
 ment in, 28–30
Gorbachev's *perestroika*
 and *glasnost*, 54–58
Havel on freedom fight
 in, 208, 209
history of democracy
 in, 19
Hungarian activist
 intellectuals and
 activist intellectuals
 of, 75
Hungary's opening of the
 iron curtain and, 78

Jaruzelski exits
 government in,
 66–69
key players in, 39,
 48, 63
Kingdom of, Great
 Dukedom of
 Lithuania and, 212
march toward
 democracy in, 10
martial law in, 26–27
Molotov-Ribbentrop Pact
 and, 215
news in Czechoslovakia
 about events in, 163
opposition leaders
 visiting Czecho-
 slovak counterparts,
 177–178
Pope John Paul II's
 interventions on
 Solidarity trial in, 171
Pope John Paul II visits,
 31–33
quick facts about, 20
restored to European
 maps, 19–20
riot police break
 up Bydgoszcz
 demonstration,
 25–26
rites for Father Jerzy,
 51–54
samizdat publications
 in, 6
in the shadow of the
 Soviet Union, 27–28
Solidarity and Wałęsa
 rebound in, 60–62,
 64–66
Solidarity's inaugural
 convention, 42–46
Solidarity urges a strike,
 46–47, 49–51
Soviet military in, 210
strikers defy
 government, 38–39,
 40–41
30th anniversary of 1956
 Hungarian uprising
 marked in, 84–86
under totalitarianism,
 20–21
Warsaw Pact dissolution
 and, 209–210
workers halt strikes,
 58–60
workers unite and issue
 demands, 24–26,
 34–36, 37
Poles and Polish speakers
in Baltic states, 212, 214
in Czechoslovakia, 150,
 151
in Lithuania, 231
Police. *See also* Secret
 police
shifting allegiances
 during Orange
 Revolution, 384–385,
 395, 396

Polish United Workers'
    Party (PZRP), 20,
    21, 22, 27, 29, 30,
    48, 62
"Political Opposition in
    Poland" (Kuroń), 36
*Politics of Nonviolent Action,
    The* (Sharp), 293, 306
Popiełuzko, Father Jerzy, 27,
    52–54
Popovic, Srdja, 305, 310,
    311–312
Popular front(s)
    in Baltic states, 213,
        220–227, 228
    broad cross-sections of
        society in, 238
    communist system and,
        248
    elections of 1989 and,
        252
    in Estonia, 220–222
    extremist reactions
        from interfronts to,
        231–232
    glasnost and, 245–249
    in Latvia, 222–223
    in Lithuania, 223–226
    Soviet Union and,
        227, 238
Popular Front for the
    Support of Perestroika,
    Estonia, 220–222
Pora! (It's Time!), Ukraine
    international media
        awareness of, 417
    planning and organiza-
        tion by, 396–399,
        400–401, 412, 414
    presidential election of
        2004 and, 17, 379,
        383, 407
    training programs on
        nonviolence, 385
Potočka, Jan, 158, 165
Potsdam Conference (1945),
    106
Powell, Colin L., 361, 362,
    366, 370, 412, 416
"Power of the Powerless,
    The" (Havel), 203
Pozsgay, Imre
    Hungarian government
        restructuring and,
        79, 88, 90, 99
    on Hungarian uprising of
        1956, 91, 93
    as key player in Hungary,
        95
    MDF and, 76
    state funerals for 1956
        uprising dead and,
        94, 96, 96
Prague Spring (1968). *See
    also* Czechoslovakia
    arrests on 21st
        anniversary of
        crushing of, 177
    crushing of, 2, 27, 74, 76,
        154–156
    Dubček and, 185–186

events of, 153–154
    as inspiration to Poles, 21
Mohorita admits (1989)
    invasion was a
    mistake, 199
spirit of, in Velvet
    Revolution, 197–198
Pravda (Slovakia's
    communist party
    newspaper), 193
Pravda (Soviet communist
    party daily), 3, 27, 76,
    154, 258, 279
Prayers, public, 13, 14. *See
    also* Nikolai Church
Premyslid, Agnes, 192
Přestavba (Czech for
    perestroika), 189
Primakov, Yevgeny M., 302
Princip, Gavrilo, 286, 287
Protestant churches, East
    Germany, 108–109, 110,
    113–114, 145, 153. *See
    also* Nikolai Church;
    Pastors' Movement
Protestant Reformation, 72,
    106, 108
Protest emigration
    (hijra). *See also*
    Noncooperation
    from Baltic states, 216
    from Czechoslovakia,
        151, 156
    East German fear of,
        114–116
    from East Germany, 13,
        77–78, 107, 110, 130–
        131, 134, 138, 139
    history of, 9
    of Poles to the U.S., 19
    as Polish method of non-
        cooperation, 26, 47
    of Serbs due to educa-
        tion system decline,
        291
Prunskienė, Kazimira, 234,
    238, 263, 268
Prussia, 19
Public Against Violence
    (Verejnost' proti
    Nasiliu, or VPN),
    Slovak group
    as Civic Forum partner,
        14, 162, 164, 181, 184
    formation of, 204
    government talks with,
        194
    on Husák's coalition
        government, 199
Pugo, Boris K., 270, 271, 277
Putin, Vladimir
    Rose Revolution, Georgia,
        and, 361, 362
    Saakashvili and, 375
    Times on Yugoslavia
        policy of, 327
    Ukrainian presidential
        election of 2004 and,
        384, 391, 404, 405
    Yushchenko mends ties
        with, 415

Racz, Sandor, 85–86, 97
Radio. *See also* BBC;
    News media; Voice of
    America
    in Baltic states, U.S.
        and, 245
    in Budapest, 1956
        storming of building,
        76, 85
    in Czechoslovakia, Civic
        Forum on, 196
    in Czechoslovakia,
        on size of
        demonstrations, 183
    in Czechoslovakia,
        Soviet troops and,
        155
    in East Germany,
        awakening of,
        128, 130
    in East Germany,
        demonstration
        broadcast on, 132
    in Latvia,
        demonstrations and,
        232
    in Latvia, Soviet troops
        and, 270
    in Lithuania, demon-
        strations and, 232
    in Lithuania, Soviet
        troops and, 233,
        268–269, 272
    in Poland, regional
        broadcasts
        suspended, 50
    in Poland, Solidarity
        demands for airtime
        on, 29, 45, 61
    Polish state-owned,
        restrictions on,
        24, 31
    "ring around Serbia"
        broadcasts,
        319–320
    from West Germany to
        East Germany, 125
Radio 100/Radio Glasnost,
    113
Radio Free Europe/Radio
    Liberty
    airtime for opposition
        on, 6
    announcements of
        strikes in Czecho-
        slovakia on, 180
    broadcasts open to
        Baltic states, 229,
        238
    Czechoslovakia
        government stops
        jamming, 173
    Eastern European news
        for Czechoslovaks
        on, 178
    on Georgia's 2003
        presidential election,
        340, 356
    Helsinki '86 political
        documentation
        on, 222

Soviet press on
    broadcasts in Baltic
    states by, 241
on strike at Lenin
    shipyard (1980),
    Gdańsk, 25, 35
Ten Days in
    Czechoslovakia
    (1989) and, 14, 163
Rajk, Laszlo (father and
    son), 86, 97
Rákosi, Mátyás, 72, 73, 82, 83
Rakowski, Mieczyslaw, 62,
    65, 140, 195
Rapprochement, Gorbachev
    policy on, 217
Ratkovic, Jovan, 294–295,
    305
Reagan, Ronald R.
    Baltic Freedom Day and,
        224
    cautions against Soviet
        intervention in
        Poland (1981), 43
    on dismantling Berlin
        Wall, 119
    on Grósz as Hungarian
        leader, 87
    policies in opposition to
        Soviet Union under,
        27, 67
    SALT II treaty and, 4
    on tearing down the
        Berlin Wall, 134
Realistic Theatre, Prague,
    179, 180
Realpolitik (Leninist)
    canon, 9
Rebirth and Renewal
    (Atdzimsana un
    Atjaunosanas), Latvia,
    219
Reformed League, Germany,
    109
Refugee trains, from East
    Germany, 130–131, 132,
    139–140
Republic of Latvia, 230. *See
    also* Latvia
Republic of Lithuania, 213,
    234. *See also* Lithuania
Republika Srpska, 289.
    See also Bosnia-
    Herzegovina
Reuters, 38
Reverse strike, 155. *See also*
    Strikes
Revival party (Georgia), 357
Ribbentrop, Joachim von,
    215, 280. *See also*
    Molotov-Ribbentrop
    Pact
Riga, Latvia
    black berets in, 233, 234
    as capital city, 212, 214
    creative union meetings
        in, 222
    Freedom (Liberty)
        Monument demon-
        stration (1987), 219,
        239–240

Gorbachev visit to (1987), 218
underground Soviet prison in, 217
Roberts, Adam, 135
Rock-and-roll march, Lithuania, 225
Rock bands, 157–158, 384, 398–399
Rock 'n' Roll (Stoppard), 158
Roman Catholic Church
  alliance with Solidarność, 38
  in Baltic states, 212, 214, 241
  in Czechoslovakia, civil resistance and, 156
  in Czechoslovakia, petition for religious rights and liberties and, 159
  Czechoslovak labor camps and, 152–153
  Father Jerzy's Mass for Poland, 27, 52
  on human rights in Czechoslovakia, 170
  laity, alliance in Poland with activist intellectuals and workers, 21–24
  Lithuanian, intelligentsia and, 214
  Luther on abuses and corruption by, 106
  moral and spiritual encouragement to Eastern Europe by, 171, 172
  under party-state control in Czechoslovakia, 152–153
  persecution in Czechoslovakia, 151
  and Poles of Austria-Hungary and Germany, 19
  Pope John Paul II as head of, 24, 170
  return of Vilnius Cathedral, Lithuania, 250
  Solidarity's semantics of change and, 66
  support for Sąjūdis by, 224–225
  totalitarianism in Poland after World War II and, 21
  Wałęsa and, 64
Romania, 85, 106, 107, 209–210, 285, 379, 388
Romania revolution, 11
Roma people (Romani Gypsies), 15, 150, 285
Roosevelt, Franklin D., 2
"Roots, Branches and Blossoms of Solidarnosc, The" (Ziółkowski), 43, 53, 66

ROPCiO (Polish acronym for Defense for the Human and Civil Rights), 24
Rosenthal, Elizabeth, 385, 407
Rose Revolution, Georgia, 17, 366, 369. *See also* Kmara
  Orange Revolution, Ukraine and, 392
  Second, 343, 370
Round Table-Free Georgia coalition, 338
Round-table talks (Poland, 1989)
  as beginning of democracy, 12, 29, 61
  events leading to, 58–59
  Jaruzelski and, 69
  Kuroń and, 36
  labor unrest and, 28
  regional effect of, 11, 30
  Wałęsa campaigning for democracy during, 64–66
Rousova, Pavlina, 179
Rudé Právo (The Red Light, or Red Law), Czechoslovakia, 166, 169
Rugova, Ibrahim, 292, 301
Rukh (Movement), Ukraine, 378, 381
Rumania. *See* Romania
Rural Solidarity (Poland), 25–26, 42–43
Russia. *See also* Soviet Union
  Bolshevik Revolution (1917) in, 2, 214, 334
  czarist, Baltic states claimed by, 212
  Dayton Agreement and, 289
  dominance over Poland, 12
  Georgian separatist states and, 368, 372
  on Polish Constitution of 1791, 19
  on protests against another Shevardnadze government, 359, 361
  strategic value of Georgia to, 375
  tensions with West over Ukrainian elections, 404, 405
Russian Orthodox Church, 212
Russian Revolution (1917), 2, 214, 334
Russians
  in Baltic states, 231, 265
  in Georgia, 334
  in Ukraine, 377
Russian Soviet Federative Socialist Republic (RSFSR), 235, 236
Rüütel, Arnold, 214, 231, 246, 258, 261–262

Saakashvili, Mikhail
  confronts rebel leader, 369–371
  elected president of Georgia, 336, 366
  foreign influences on, 358–359
  as key player in Georgia, 17, 367–368
  presidency of, 342–343
  rise of, 354–355, 357–358
  Rose Revolution and, 339–340, 343
  on Shevardnadze's resignation, 365
  Ukraine's Orange Revolution and, 394
  uphill battle for, 371–375
  on velvet revolution in Georgia, 361, 363
Sacirbey, Muhamed, 289
Sąjūdis (Lithuania's popular front)
  Baltic Way human chain and, 258
  Bloody Sunday (1991) and, 271
  declares independence (1990), 229
  development of, 223–226
  Lithuanian elections and, 252, 260
  Lithuania's communist party and, 226–227, 229, 249–251
  Miniotaitė and, 253
Sakharov, Andrei, 5, 217
Salami tactics, of Hungary's communist party, 72
SALT I and II treaties, 4
Samizdat (clandestine publications)
  in Baltic states, 217
  collective nonviolent action and, 417
  connections across Eastern Europe among authors of, 76, 163
  in Czechoslovakia, 14, 84, 156–157, 159, 166, 167, 169–170, 175
  in Eastern Europe and Soviet Union, 6
  in East Germany, 120, 128
  in Germany, 113
  Havel's reliance on, 202–203
  in Hungary, 75
  in Hungary vs. Poland, 84
  in Lithuania, 223
  The New York Times reports on, 169–170
  in Poland, 24, 26–27, 51–52
  Soviet Union, 5
  Vaculík as publisher of, 168
Sarkozy, Nicolas, 372
Saul, Bruno E., 219, 226, 247

Savisaar, Edgar, 220
Saxony, Germany, 106
Schabowski, Günter, 135, 136, 142
Schmemann, Serge
  on Berlin Wall opening, 136–137
  on demonstrators and idea of reunification, 144–145
  on Dresden meeting of government officials and protesters, 127–128
  on East Berlin rally for change, 132–133
  on East German demonstrations (1989), 108, 127, 131–132
  on East German emigrations, 98, 100–101, 115–116, 135
  on East German turning point and coup, 138–142
  on 40th anniversary demonstrations in East Germany, 124, 125–126
  on Gamsakhurdia's election as Georgia's president, 338
  on general strike in Czechoslovakia, 194–195
  on Moscow not interfering in East German affairs, 117, 119
  on new Hungarian Republic celebrations, 80, 101, 102–103
  on police and protesters clash amid East Berlin festivities, 122
  on reunification of the two Germanys, 147–148
  on Soviet coup against Gorbachev, 275–276
  on Soviet hold on Ukraine and Byelorussia, 381
Scholar activists. *See* Activist intellectuals
Schwarz, Harry, 337
Schwarz, Michael, 179
Second Rose Revolution, Georgia, 343, 370
Secret police. *See also* Stasi
  across Eastern Europe, 2
  in Baltic states, 279
  in Czechoslovakia, 199
  in East Germany, 110, 124, 134, 138–139, 145
  in Hungary, 92
  in Poland, 27
  in Serbia, 292, 307

SED. *See* Socialist United Party of Germany
Sejm (lower chamber of Polish parliament), 29, 61, 62
Self-immolation, as protest, 155, 173–174, 223–224
Self-Managing Estonia (IME) proposal, 219. *See also* IME economic proposal
Semjonov, Aleksei, 247
Senate, Polish, 16, 20, 29, 30, 61, 62
Senn, Alfred Erich, 221, 225
Serbia
  Bulldozer Revolution in, 297
  conflict in the Balkans, 288–289
  demographics, geography, and history of, 285, 287–288
  key players in, 306–307, 311–312
  Kosovo's autonomy and, 291–294
  Milošević arrested, 327–330
  Milošević ousted from, 294–297, 325–327
  Milošević takes power in, 288
  opposition boycotts election runoff, 320–323
  opposition fatalistic about election outcomes, 314–316
  opposition groups on ousting Milošević, 304–305
  Otpor becomes lead opposition group, 308–310
  protests after refusal to honor election results, 298–300
  quick facts about, 286
  striking miners defy police in, 323–325
  use of force against, 300–304
  youth movement and Bulldozer Revolution in, 15–16
Serbian Center for Applied Non-Violent Action and Strategies, 341, 360
Serbian Orthodox Christians, 285, 287, 288, 290, 291, 300, 307, 329
Serbs, 287–288
Shaplen, Jason, 382, 389
Sharp, Gene
  resistance in Baltic states and, 232
  resistance in Poland and, 16, 47
  resistance in Serbia and, 16, 293, 294, 306, 317
  resistance in Ukraine and, 397
Shenon, Philip, 287–288
Shevardnadze, Eduard A.
  Abashidze and, 370
  calls for resignation of, 353–355
  foreign influences on, 359
  on Georgia's official language, 337
  as Georgia's president, 336, 338, 339, 352–353
  opponents against seating of another government under, 358–359, 360–361
  parliamentary elections (2003) and, 355–358
  political opposition to, 351–352
  postmortem on resignation of, 363–365
  resignation of, 342, 361–363
  Rose Revolution and, 343
  as totalitarian ruler in Georgia, 16–17, 348–351
Siberia. *See also* Stalin, Josef
  Balts deported to, 216
  demonstrations on Latvians deported to, 222, 223
  Latvians deported to, 15, 213
  Poles deported to, 19, 20, 69
Simmons, Michael, 201
Simons, Marlise, 328
Sinatra doctrine, 10, 30, 68, 229
Singing. *See also* Folk songs and folklore
  in the Baltic states by activists, 14–15, 241
Singing Revolution, for Estonian independence, 213, 221, 246
Skoda, Jan, 184, 190
Sladkevicius, Vincentas Cardinal, 224
Slovakia, 150, 151, 153. *See also* Bratislava, Czechoslovakia
Slovak Republic, 184, 204, 206. *See also* Bratislava, Czechoslovakia
Slovaks, 150, 151, 171, 205. *See also* Dubček, Alexander
Slovenia, 15, 285, 286, 288, 298
Smale, Alison, 328
Smetona, Antanas, 215
Socialist Party, Czechoslovakia, 162, 177
Socialist United Party of Germany (Sozialistische Einheitspartei Deutschlands, SED), 106
  Honecker and, 118
  name change for, 143
  national elections (1989) and, 123
  October 9 demonstrations and, 127
  Protestants on "the church in socialism" under, 109
  protest emigration, street demonstrations and coup within, 137–138
  purges within (1953), 108
  on refugee trains as expulsion, 130
  renounces Stalinist past, 109
  travel restrictions eased by, 135
  travel restrictions under, 131, 134
  West German television broadcasts and message of, 107, 128
Social Self Defense Committee. *See* Komitet Samoobrony Spolecznej
Solana, Javier, 302, 303, 403, 412, 418
Solidarity union (Poland). *See also* Round-table talks; Wałęsa, Lech
  East German contacts with, 128
  elections of 1989 and, 30
  Father Jerzy's funeral and, 53–54
  Father Jerzy's sermons supporting, 52–53
  first convention (1981), 44, 45–46
  formation of, 20, 25
  Jaruzelski declares martial law and arrests leaders of, 46–47, 49, 51
  Kuroń and, 36
  mass strikes by, 12, 30
  meetings with Polish government (1988), 58
  as model of nonviolent transition in Eastern Europe, 9, 66
  nonviolent resistance to martial law by, 26–27
  planning national referendum on Polish government, 49–50
  proclamation praising 1956 Hungarian uprising and, 85
  rebound from martial law, 60–62
  round-table negotiations (1989) and, 11
  semantics of change used by, 42, 55–56, 66
  strike in support of Rural Solidarity by, 25–26
  wildcat strikes to legalize, 58–60
Solidarność (Solidarity) strike information bulletin, 25, 38
Songaila, Rimgaudas, 225, 226
Song Square (Singers' Field), Tallinn, Estonia, 221
Soros, George, 87, 359, 373
South Korea, collective nonviolent action in, 418, 419
South Ossetia, 338, 343–344, 368, 369, 370, 372
Sovereignty. *See also* Brezhnev Doctrine
  declarations in Baltic states for, 227, 252
Soviet Union. *See also* Brezhnev Doctrine; Gorbachev, Mikhail S.; Warsaw Pact
  annexation of Baltic states by, 215
  attack by German Nazis (1941), 19
  awareness of Jaruzelski's intention to declare martial law, 46, 49
  Baltic popular fronts and disintegration of, 238
  Berlin Wall construction and, 133
  bilateral treaty with Hungary and, 104
  Brezhnev Doctrine and economic stagnation in, 3
  communication ban between its satellite states, 84
  condemns its role in Warsaw Pact invasion of Czechoslovakia, 199
  Congress of People's Deputies, 227–228, 229–230
  crushing Hungarian uprising (1956), 2, 12, 94, 96–97

disbanding of Warsaw Pact and troop removals by, 80, 81
East German emigrations and, 117
Extraordinary Congress of People's Deputies, 230
on German reunification, 108, 146
Havel on freedom fight in, 208, 209
Helsinki Accords (1975) and, 4–5, 417–418
international agreements and reforms in, 3–5
Lithuanian petition on ecological threats by, 224
nationalism in republics of, 244
nonviolent civil resistance in, 235–236
Polish elections of 1989 and, 62
Polish general strike of 1981 and, 43
Polish transition to democracy and, 67
post–World War II division of Germany and, 106
Prague Spring (1968) crushing by, 197–198
Russification and Sovietization under, 380
samizdat publications in, 6
sanctions and oil blockade of Lithuania, 230
on Solidarity's potency, 27
state funerals for 1956 Hungarian uprising dead and, 97
troops in East Germany, 106, 107
troops in Hungary, 73, 74
troops in Latvia, 270
troops in Lithuania, 233, 268–269, 272, 273
Ukraine under control of, 379–380, 386–387, 388
withdraws troops from Czechoslovakia, 210
withdraws troops from Hungary, 80, 102–105, 210
Spain, Poland's road to democracy vs., 65
Specter, Michael, 339, 352
Staatssicherheitsdienst (State Security Service), East Germany, 106. *See also* Stasi

Stalin, Josef. *See also* Molotov-Ribbentrop Pact
Baltic states' demonstrations honoring victims of, 241
banishes Poles to Siberia, 19, 20
control of Czechoslovakia by, 150, 152
on occupation of Poland after World War II, 20–21
seizes control of Georgia, 335, 336
Soviet rule under, 2
Tito and, 287
Stark, David, 77, 78
Stasi (State Security Service), East Germany, 13, 106, 107, 108, 131, 145, 146
State Property Agency, Hungary, 104
Stayers (*Dableiber*), in East Germany, 111, 113–114, 121, 122, 125, 131–132
Štěpán, Miroslav, 162, 182, 184, 190, 194, 205, 207
Stephen, Saint, 72
Stock exchange, in Hungary, 92
Stoph, Willi, 141
Stoppard, Thomas, 158
Strassenburg, Gerhard, 127
Strategic Arms Limitation Talks, 3, 4
Strategic Arms Reduction Talks, 3, 10
Street names
changes in Czechoslovakia to, 185
changes in Estonia to, 218, 243
Strikes. *See* General strike(s); Hunger strikes; *specific countries*
St. Thomas Church, Leipzig, 124
Students. *See also* Youth movement(s)
alliance with Polish workers during 1970s, 22
in Czechoslovakia, as new government is formed, 199
in Czechoslovakia, civil resistance to Warsaw Pact troops by, 154
in Czechoslovakia, Prague Spring and, 154
in Czechoslovakia, Velvet Revolution

and, 161–162, 178–180
Czechoslovak industrial workers and, 188
in Georgia, nationalism of, 337
Havel acknowledges contributions of, 204
Hungarian reform efforts of, 76
meet with Adamec, 181
in Serbia, opposition to Milošević by, 289, 290
unrest in Czechoslovakia (1967) by, 153
uprisings in Poland (1968) by, 21
Student Solidarity (Poland), 42
Sudetenland, annexed by Germany from Czechoslovakia, 150, 151
Suicide, as protest, 155, 173–174, 223–224
Svetdienas Rits (Sunday Morning, Latvian newspaper), 229
Symbols. *See also* Folk songs and folklore
Baltic Way human chain as, 228, 256
Berlin Wall as, 11, 107, 109, 110, 132, 134, 136
burning candles in East Germany as, 121
end of Warsaw Pact as, 210
Havel's election as, 163, 186, 204, 205, 208
Kolubara strike in Serbia as, 323–324
Nagy's reburial in Hungary as, 78, 88, 94, 98
of nationalism in Baltic states, 216, 220, 221, 223–224, 226, 237, 239, 250, 252, 255
Nikolai Church in East Germany as, 123
of Orange Revolution, Ukraine, 407, 408
Otpor's clenched fist as, 291, 313
for Poland, Pope John Paul II as, 31
Prague Spring (1968) as, 154, 156
of resistance, Wałęsa as, 64
of roses in Georgia, 17, 366, 369
Soviet nuclear reactors as, 242
used by Kmara in Georgia, 359, 366
used in Czechoslovakia, 189, 193

used in East Germany, 143–144
used in Serbia, 289, 297, 317
use in Hungary, 12
use in Ukraine, 377
Szczesniak, Andrezej, 59
Szilagyi, Jozsef, 97
Szürös, Mátyás, 73, 79, 80, 94, 96, 101, 102

Tageszeitung (West Berlin alternative paper), 113
Tagliabue, John
on conciliation as Wałęsa theme, 64–66
on demonstrators urging ouster of Czechoslovak hardline leaders, 187–188
on first free and fair vote in Poland since 1945, 56
on Havel speech in Wenceslas Square, 163
on Polish workers' agreement to end strikes, 59–60
on Prague march for change, 182–184
reporting from Prague, 181
on staying to change East Germany, 111, 113–114
on upheaval in Czechoslovakia, 175, 176–177
Tajikistan, popular front in, 238
Tallinn, Estonia, 212, 214, 218. *See also* Baltic states
Tartu, Estonia, 214, 220, 246. *See also* Baltic states
Tatars, Crimean, 241, 244, 245
Taubman, Philip, 224–225, 226, 247–249, 249, 250–251
Taurinskas, Ginutis, 234–235
Tbilisi massacre (Georgia, 1989), 338
Tehran Conference (1943), 106
Television
boycott in Czechoslovakia (1989), 175
in Czechoslovakia, general strike and, 193
in Czechoslovakia, government control of, 190
in Czechoslovakia on size of Nov. 19 demonstration, 180–181

demonstrations broadcast in Czechoslovakia by, 186
in East Germany, awakening of, 128, 130
in East Germany, demonstration broadcast on, 132
in Georgia, Rose Revolution and, 363–364, 367
in Georgia, Saakashvili's raid on, 374–375
in Poland, regional broadcasts suspended, 50
in Poland, Solidarity demands for airtime on, 29, 45, 61
restrictions in Ukraine on, 390–391, 404
in Ukraine, journalist strikes against, 384–385, 399
in Ukraine, shifts in, 395
from West Germany, East Germans and, 107, 138
Ten Days in Czechoslovakia (1989), 14. *See also* Velvet Revolution
"Ten Points Manifesto," Czechoslovakia, 156
Terleckas, Antanas, 223, 250
Thatcher, Margaret, 57, 87
Thoreau, Henry David, 22
Tiananmen Square massacre, Beijing (1989), 112, 126, 139, 160, 418. *See also* "Chinese solution"
Tito, Josip Broz, 286, 287, 291, 300
Tolstoy, Leo, 22
Tomášek, František Cardinal, 159, 171, 172, 173, 181, 182
Totalitarianism
in Baltic states, 216, 222, 276
Czechs and Slovaks on, 150
end of, in Poland, 61, 66–67
in Georgia, 352, 370
Havel on, 182, 200, 202, 203
Lutheran Church in East Germany against, 111, 132, 143–144
middle classes on, 7
in Poland, 11–12
in Poland after World War II, 21–22
proclamation on 1956 Hungarian uprising and, 76, 84

Wende in East Germany against, 109
Trade unions. *See also* Strikes
Travel restrictions, 6–7, 115–116, 130–131, 144. *See also* Iron curtain; Protest emigration
Truman-Reagan Medal of Freedom, 39
Truth, Havel on living in, 167, 200, 202–203, 206
Tuđman, Franjo, 289
Turkmenistan, popular front in, 238
Turner, Gerry, 169
"Two Thousand Words" (Czechoslovak manifesto, 1968), 154, 156, 167, 168, 169, 174–175
Tyler, Patrick, 382
Tymoshenko, Yulia, 391, 393

Uhl, Petr, 158, 165
Ukraine
clear victory for Yushchenko in, 411–414
collective nonviolent action in, 417–419
election results overturned, 404–406
election results widely discredited, 391–394
history shapes revolution in, 386–388
key players in, 399, 408–409
nationalism in, 244, 252
Orange Revolution in, 17, 385–386
parliament seeks resolution to election standoff, 401–404
popular front in, 238
presidential election of 2004 in, 382–383, 389–391
push for independence in, 380–382
quick facts about, 378–379
religion and conflict with Russia, 377, 379
revote in, 383–385
under Russian control, 379–380
transition in, 385
youth-led movements on election fraud in, 396–399, 400–401
Yushchenko declares victory, 394–396

Yushchenko's poisoned face as symbol for, 407, 409–411, *409*
Yushchenko vows to unite, 414–417
Ulbricht, Walter, 106, 108, 118
Underground publications. *See Samizdat*
Unitary State of Slovenes, Croats, and Serbs, 287
United Left, East Germany, 120
United National Movement, Georgia, 339, 340–341, 359, 367
United Nations
Baltic popular fronts appeal (1989) to, 218, 253, 254–255
Baltic states admitted to, 236
Charter 77 on Universal Declaration of Human Rights of, 14, 158, 165, 202
Churchill and Roosevelt on Soviet membership in, 2
East and West Germany as members of, 118
Lithuania's Freedom League petition to, 223
mission in Kosovo, 298
United Press International, 38
United States
Baltic Freedom Day (1985) and, 224
Baltic quest for independence and, 238
on Baltic states as captive states, 245
ethnic conflict in Kosovo and, 293–294, 303–304
foreign aid to Georgia, 355
on Georgia's elections of 2003, 340
Helsinki Accords (1975) and, 4–5
post–World War II division of Germany and, 106
on protests against another Shevardnadze government, 359, 361
SALT treaties and Afghanistan war and, 4
Serbian sanctions imposed by, 290
strategic value of Georgia to, 375

support for Poland's round-table agreement by, 12
support for Serbian opposition by, 317, 318–320
televised series alleging espionage activities in Czechoslovakia by, 166–167
Ukrainian presidential election of 2004 and, 392, 393, 404, 406, 416
on voting fraud in Georgia, 356
Unity (Yedinstvo) group, Lithuania, 231–232, 268
Urban, Jan
Charter 77 development and, 158
on Gorbachev and perestroika, 159
on KSS-KOR as inspiration for Charter 77, 166
on nonviolent protest, 163
on Prague Autumn, 209
on reform potential under Czechoslovak communist state, 154
on "Two Thousand Words," 168
Urban, Otto, 179
Urbánek, Karel, 192, 195
Urbanik, Zdenek, 166
Ustashe regime of Nazi collaborators, Croatia, 286, 287

Vacek, Miroslav, 205
Vaculík, Ludvík. *See also* Edice Petlice
arrests and imprisonment of, 165
Charter 77 and, 158
as key player in Czechoslovakia, 168–169
on samizdat publications, 156
as samizdat publisher, 167, 169–170, 174–175
as scholarly activist, 6
Vaino, Karl, 221, 246, 247
VAK, 223. *See also* Club for the Defense of the Environment
Väljas, Vaino, 221, 247, 248
Valk, Heinz, 221, 246, 276
Vatican, 12. *See also* John Paul II, Pope
Velvet Revolution. *See also* Czechoslovakia
elements for success of, 14

in Georgia, Saakashvili on, 358
government of national understanding and, 199
history leading to, 150
immediate events leading to, 177–178
samizdat publications and, 6, 156–157
spirit of Prague Spring in, 197–198
Ten Days of, 152, 161–163, 177–182
The Times reports on, 182–184
Versailles, Treaty of (1919), 19
Victims of Communism Memorial Foundation, 39
Vigils, 8. *See also* Nonviolent protest and persuasion
at Berlin Wall, 11, 135
in East Germany, 114, 121, 122, 125, 126, 144, 145
in Georgia, 340
in Lithuania, 271
Vilnius, Lithuania, 212, 214, 224. *See also* Bloody Sunday
Vinciguerra, Thomas, 341–342
Violent revolutions, 2–3
Vlachs (Romanians), in Serbia, 285
Voice of America, 222, 229, 238, 241
Von Ribbentrop, Joachim, 215, 280. *See also* Molotov-Ribbentrop Pact
VONS (Committee for the Defense of the Unjustly Prosecuted), Czechoslovakia, 157, 166
Von Weisacker, Richard, 145, 147
Vulfsons, Mavriks, 222
Vyskocil, Ivan, 200

Waldheim, Kurt, 223
Walentynowicz, Anna, 34, 36, 39
Wałęsa, Bogdan, 52
Wałęsa, Danuta, 52
Wałęsa, Lech
academicians and committee of experts, 25
alliance with theoreticians and religious elite, 12
arrested under martial law, 49
challenges to leadership as Solidarity leader, 50
elected Solidarity leader, 26
elections of 1989 and, 30, 62
end to wildcat strikes of 1988 and, 58–60
eulogy for Father Jerzy, 53
fasting during arrest under martial law by, 47
Gdańsk strikes (1980) and, 24–25, 34–35, 40, 41
general strike of 1981 and, 43
intermittent strikes of 1981 and, 43–44
meets with Pope John Paul II, 26
Michnik and, 63
on nonviolent action, 386
as president of Poland, 48
rebound from martial law, 60–62
rehired at Lenin shipyard, 36
release from prison (1982), 51
on solidarity among Poles, 23
Solidarity's first convention (1981) and, 45–46
student uprising of 1968 and, 21
swearing in as president, Jaruzelski and, 68
talks and debates with government officials, 28–29
Ukrainian demonstrations (2004) and, 384, 394–395
on Warsaw Pact dissolution, 210
Warsaw Fire-Fighting School, 52
Warsaw Pact
condemns its role in Czechoslovakia invasion, 199
construction of Berlin Wall and, 133
dissolution of, 209–210
Eastern bloc on disbanding, 80, 104
East Germany as core of, 106
Hungarian anniversary of 1956 uprising (1989) and, 102
Hungarian troops and Czechoslovakia invasion by, 74
Hungary's opening of the iron curtain and, 100, 139
invasion of Czechoslovakia (1968) by, 151, 154, 185
Nagy's negotiations for Hungary's withdrawal from, 94
Poland and, 21
Prague Spring (1968) crushing by, 197–198
Soviet Union and, 2
Weisman, Steven, 366
Wenceslas Square, Prague, 178–180
arrests of 1989 in, 175
demonstration of 1988 in, 159, 173
demonstrations of 1989 in, 190
Havel and Dubček in, 186, 189
new government celebrated in, 199
Palach's self-immolation suicide in, 155
police break up march (1989) in, 176–177
Ten Days in Czechoslovakia (1989) and, 14, 161–162
Wende (policy reversal), in East Germany, 109
The New York Times on, 138–142
Nikolai Church and, 122–124
West Berlin, surrounded by Berlin Wall, 134
West Germany. *See also* East Germany; Germany
constitutional right of citizenship for East Germans, 116
response to Berlin Wall in, 136, 137
reunification with East Germany, 108, 110, 146, 147–148
SED credibility in East Germany and television from, 107, 128
travel restrictions eased for, 6–7
Whitney, Craig R., 138–142, 163, 205, 206, 207–208, 337–338
Wilson, Andrew, 383, 385, 391, 394, 397, 399
Wines, Michael, 363
Without Violence (Polish group), 47
Wojtyla, Karol, 12, 31. *See also* John Paul II, Pope
Wolchik, Sharon, 341
Wolf, Markus, 139
Wolff, Christa, 131, 133
Women, 12, 30, 41, 66. *See also* Feminists
Women in Black, Serbia, 294
Workers' Defense Committee, Poland. *See* Komitet Obrony Robotników
Worker's movement, in Poland, 21–24
World Bank
Georgia and, 352, 365, 372–373
World War I
Hapsburg Empire and, 72
Serbia and, 287
Writers' Union, Czechoslovakia, 153, 168
Writers' Union, Hungary, 86
Writers' Union, Lithuania, 224
Wyszyński, Stefan Cardinal, 22, 43

Yakovlev, Aleksandr N., 225, 228, 229, 281
Yalta Conference (1945), 2, 106
Yanayev, Gennadi I., 209, 210
Yanukovich, Viktor F., 17
disdain for Pora's organizing, 400–401
election results widely discredited, 391–394
on revote announcement, 406
Ukrainian presidential election of 2004 and, 378–379, 382, 384, 385, 389–391
on voting fraud, 401–403, 411–412, 413
Yazov, Dmitrii, 236, 278
Yellow Pora, 397
Yeltsin, Boris N.
Baltic states' independence and, 15, 235–236, 274, 278–279
recognized Ukraine's independence, 378, 382, 387
Soviet coup and, 277
York, Steve, 386
Youth movement. *See also* Kmara; Otpor!; Pora!; Students
in East Germany, demonstrations and, 128
in Georgia, 16–17
Havel acknowledges contributions of, 204
in Hungary, 76, 79, 99
in Poland, 36

in Serbia, 15–16
in Ukraine, 17
Yugoslavia, 15, 210, 286.
    See also Serbia
Yushchenko, Viktor A., 17
    election of, 377, 385,
        412–414
    inauguration speech,
        414–417
    as key player in Ukraine,
        408–409
    on Kuchma as puppet of
        Russia, 405
    Orange Revolution and,
        391–394
    poisoning and orange
        scarf of, 407, *409*
    Ukrainian presidential
        election of 2004
        and, 378–379, 382,
        383–384, 389–391,
        409–411
    on voting fraud, 402, 403

Zajedno ("Together")
    coalition, Serbia, 286,
    289–291, 297, 299–300,
    304–305
Zappa, Frank, 157
Zelazkiewicz, Marek,
    294
Zhvania, Zurab
    on Abashidze's
        resignation, 371
    Adzharia demon-
        strations and,
        343
    Rose Revolution and,
        339, 367
    Saakashvili on role for,
        342, 366, 369
    on Shevardnadze's
        resignation,
        362, 363
Zinchenko, Oleksandr,
    382, 389
Ziółkowski, Janusz, 23, 30,
    43, 53, 66
Ziółkowski, Theodore, 2
Zvarich, Roman M.,
    406, 416
Zwingli, Ulrich, 108, 109